W9-BWU-300

LITERATURE FOR TODAY'S YOUNG ADULTS

Kenneth L. Donelson
Alleen Pace Nilsen

Arizona State University

Scott, Foresman and Company

Glenview, Illinois

Dallas, Tex.   Oakland, N.J.   Palo Alto, Cal.   Tucker, Ga.   London

To Annette, Betty, Sherri, Allen, and Jason from Ken
To Don, Kelvin, Sean, and Nicolette from Alleen

And to Bob Carlsen,
partly for what he has done
in a lifetime of service to young adult literature,
but mostly for what he has done for both of us

The authors and publishers would like to thank all sources for the use of their material. The credit lines for copyrighted materials appearing in this work appear in the Acknowledgments section beginning on page 472. This section is to be considered an extension of the copyright page.

Copyright © 1980 Scott, Foresman and Company.
All Rights Reserved.
Printed in the United States of America.

Library of Congress Cataloging in Publication Data

Donelson, Kenneth L.
    Literature for today's young adults.

    Includes bibliographies and index.
      1.   Children's literature—History and criticism.
I.   Nilsen, Alleen Pace, joint author.   II.   Title.
PN1009.A1D65   823'.009'9283   79-28253
ISBN 0-673-15165-4
  2 3 4 5 6-VHJ-84 83 82 81 80

Preface

We had many reasons for writing this book, but chief among them was our belief that it was needed and worth doing. When we surveyed teachers of young adult literature in Library Science, English, and Education departments in 1977, an overwhelming majority expressed a need for a scholarly and readable textbook to provide history and background of the field. One teacher wrote that her major problem "in establishing and promoting the work of the course was the sometimes skeptical view of colleagues about the worth of this literature," and added she would welcome a book to educate professionals in related fields about the growing body of good young adult books. Another worried about the isolation of young adult books from literature in general and suggested that "in an ideal world, we ought to change our course from 'Literature and the Adolescent' to 'Books and People.' " Others wanted help in integrating young adult literature and first-rate literature of all sorts into a sound English curriculum.

We hope our book will answer some of those needs, as well as the more general ones of providing a framework and background information for classes in young adult literature. We also hope it will serve librarians, teachers, counselors, and others working with young people between the ages of twelve and twenty.

Initially, we planned to limit our discussion to books distributed by the juvenile divisions of publishing houses, but we soon realized we would be telling only half the story. Young people read much more than just books published specifically for them. Besides, sometimes little more than chance determines whether a book will be released by the adult or the juvenile division of a publishing house. For our purposes, we mean "young adult literature" to include any book freely chosen for reading by a person between the ages of twelve and twenty. (We say "young adult" rather than "adolescent" because many people, particularly students, find the word "adolescent" condescending.) About eighty percent of the books read by younger teenagers will have been distributed as juvenile titles; books read by older teenagers will more likely have been intended for the general public. We refer to books shelved in libraries and bookstores under no specific age designation as "adult books."

We organized our book as we teach our courses: first, an introduction to young adult literature, then a history of the field, then a look at contemporary books, and finally a view of the professional's role in relation to books and young readers. There is, obviously, nothing sacred about the organization, and, depending on the background of the students in your class and their needs and interests, you may wish to rearrange chapters and to give more or less attention to particular sections.

At various points in Part Three, we present criteria for evaluating different kinds of books. Evaluation is complex and one sports novel, for example, is often so different from other sports novels that any list of definitive criteria would be foolish, if not impossible. These criteria, then, are not Mosaic Law and should be considered starting places only. Students should realize they will need to develop their own skills in evaluation. That comes only with practice and wide reading.

Because so many excellent new books are written each year, lists of suggested or recommended titles are doomed to be dated almost before they are printed. You can supplement the lists here with the help of current reviewing sources and annual lists of recommended titles compiled by *School Library Journal*, the Young Adult Services Division of the American Library Association, the *New York Times*, and the University of Iowa Books for Young Adults Program.

Although we realize that in most classes and in many libraries it is the paperback editions of books that are usually read by young adults, in our book lists we show the original hardback publishers where we were able to identify them. We did this for two reasons. First, we wanted to give credit to the companies who found the authors and did the editorial work and the initial promotion on each book. Second, by relying on the hardback editions we were able to achieve a greater degree of consistency and accuracy than if we relied on the paperback edition. The paperback publishing industry is relatively fluid and a title may be published and then go out of print within only a few months. To find whether there is a paperback edition of a book available, we suggest you refer to the most recent issue of *Paperbound Books in Print* published annually (with frequent supplements) by R. R. Bowker Company and purchased by practically every library in the country.

The subject of young adult literature is vast and we were not always able to mention books and authors that we might have liked, some of them our personal favorites. The historical chapters needed to cover so much so rapidly that the compression of material became breathless at times. We wanted to keep the book short enough that students could read it and still have time for the most important part of the course, the reading of young adult books. Charles Weingartner ended one of his talks at a National Council of Teachers of English convention by relating an argument he had had with a colleague over a book. They couldn't come to any agreement, not even on details, much less on the basic idea of the book. Finally, in exasperation, Weingartner asked, "Have you read the book?" "Certainly!" came the reply and then, almost as an afterthought, "Well, not personally."

We hope students will not let our words about books substitute for reading them "personally." It is the personal reading that will give students understanding of what young adult literature is all about and enable them to develop the skills for both evaluation and promotion of young adult books.

We want to acknowledge the assistance of the Arizona State University Department of English and Department of Educational Technology and Library Science who gave us more help than they may have realized. We thank all those people who have helped us in so many ways—colleagues Karen Beyard-Tyler (Arizona State University) and Christy Tyson (Mesa, Arizona Public Library); secretaries Liz Outcault, Terri Martin, Beth Bartlett, and Susan Dawson; and graduate research assistants Mary Bulduc, Marilyn DeSelms, and Dixie Hamilton. Over the years students have made us aware of books we might have missed. They have reacted to—and sometimes even changed—our ideas. Among those who helped with parts of this book, often without knowing it, are Susan Bardon, Kathy Bell, Joy Bernard, Mike Carlson, Margaret Ferry, Brian Flynn,

Susan Garvin, Mary Lou Goldstein, Karen Hess, Sue Hodge, Lynn Jett, Gerry McBroom, Iris McIntyre, S. T. Marinella, Sandy Sackman, Nadine Shimer, Yolanda Thomas, and Nel Ward.

We are grateful to our Scott, Foresman editors, JoAnn Johnson and Joanne Trestrail, whose experience, interest, expertise, and patience shaped much of the book. We thank the readers of the manuscript who saved us from making more errors than we might otherwise, Richard Abrahamson, Mary K. Chelton, Theodore Hipple, Zena Sutherland, and Richard Western.

Finally, we must thank all those erstwhile friends and colleagues who spurred us on by wondering what we were doing in young adult literature, a field they clearly thought pointless and worthless. As one former friend said, "Kids don't read uplifting, elevating, worthwhile books. All they read is trash." We do not believe that. We deeply believe in young adults, and we deeply believe the books they read, whether written for them or for adults, deserve thoughtful attention from teachers, librarians, and parents. We feel no sorrow, but rather joy, in spending our lives working in a world of literature that is always changing, exciting, and alive. We feel what Edward Salmon felt ninety years ago when he responded to people wondering about his work in children's literature:

> It is no uncommon thing to hear children's literature condemned as wholly bad, and some people are good enough to commiserate with me on having waded through so much ephemeral matter. It may be my fault or my misfortune not to be able to see my loss. I have spent many pleasant and I may say not unprofitable hours in company with the printed thoughts of Mr. Kingston, Mr. Ballantyne, Mr. Henty, Jules Verne, Miss Alcott, Miss Meade, Mrs. Molesworth, Miss Doudney, Miss Yonge, and a dozen others, and hope to spend as many more in the time to come as a busy life will permit.*

And that, really, is why we wrote the book.

Kenneth L. Donelson
Alleen Pace Nilsen
Tempe, Arizona

*"Should Children Have a Special Literature?" *The Parents' Review* 1 (June 1890): 339.

Contents

LITERATURE FOR TODAY'S YOUNG ADULTS

PART ONE

Understanding Young Adults and Books

1

Young Adults
and Their Reading

Young adult literature, teenage books, and *adolescent literature* would have been strange, even meaningless, terms one hundred years ago. At that time, young adults were reading the adult classics, *Pilgrim's Progress, Robinson Crusoe,* and *Gulliver's Travels.* But until Louisa May Alcott wrote *Little Women* in 1868 and her contemporary Oliver Optic published his endless series of books, there was almost nothing written specifically for adolescents. Shortly after Optic began writing, dime novels in the millions were to be found in the United States—to the joy of the young and the anguish of the old.

Nevertheless, it was not until fairly recently that literature for young adults developed as a distinct unit of book publishing and promotion. Because of the newness of the concept and practice, there are no long-standing traditions as in children's literature. No major prizes are given and opinions vary tremendously on whether or not there is even a need for a specialized approach to teenage books. An optimist might describe the whole field of adolescent literature as "dynamic," while a pessimist would say it was "unstable."

The development of such books coincides with the development of the concept of adolescence as a specific and unique period of life. It was not until the twentieth century that society began to regard young adults as a separate group with separate tastes and needs—in many ways a separate culture. Puberty is a universal experience, but adolescence is not. Even today, in nontechnological societies the transition from childhood to adulthood may be quite rapid, but in the United States it begins at about age twelve or thirteen and continues through the early 20s. This stretching out of the transition between childhood and adulthood came about after the Civil War. Until then, people were simply considered either children or adults. The turning point took place at about age fourteen or fifteen when children could go to work and become a valuable economic asset to the family and the community. But as the predominantly agricultural society in which children worked with their families gave way to a techno-logical society in which people worked in factories, offices, schools, and stores, there weren't enough jobs and those that were available required specialized training. As the society became more and more complex, children were expected to prepare for adult-hood by staying in school for longer and longer periods. The children became "young adults," a newly distinct segment of society.

Any change that affects this many people in such a major way demands adjust-ments and a reshuffling of priorities and roles. Such changes do not always come automatically. As Lou Willet Stanek has observed:

> The study of a segregated time in man's development between puberty and maturity is a concept young in the history of ideas. Paradoxically, the century that discovered adolescents appears to have the most difficulty in raising them.[1]

UNDERSTANDING YOUNG ADULTS

What are the special needs and expectations of these adolescents? What part does reading play in their lives? These are questions we must constantly ask ourselves if we are concerned in any way with bringing young people and books together.

Anyone who works professionally with teenagers should take a solid course and read widely in the psychology of adolescence. It is important to know about the phys-ical, psychological, and social changes that teenagers experience and to understand how these changes influence each other and, today, make adolescents different from both children and adults. Psychologists representing several schools of thought have explored this period of life, and their theories complement each other by focusing on different aspects of adolescence. We will not consider these theories in any depth, but we can mention those that are important since they all have something significant to say about the relation of the psychological development of teenagers to their reading.

Cognitive or intellectual development has a tremendous influence on reading interests at all stages from early childhood through adolescence. Jean Piaget has theo-rized that at about the age of twelve, the "formal operational" stage of thinking begins to develop. It is not until this stage is developed that a person can reason logically and consistently, handle abstract ideas, infer cause and effect, and make generalizations. Another way of saying this is that the teenager is able to consider variant possibilities and to imagine actions and their results even though there is no way to actually try them out. Boyd McCandless and Richard Coop describe this stage of thinking as an ability to "adopt several different viewpoints for considering a given act: a policeman's view, a parent's view, even the views of a dog, a Martian, society in general, or God. In short, [the young person has] gained possession of all the powers of *If*."[2] In relation to imaginative literature, there is probably no intellectual quality more important than possessing "the powers of *If.*" This is true not only of fantasy and science fiction, but of any literature dealing with subjects and viewpoints beyond the reader's actual experience. Even in realistic novels, for example, we are asked to enter into the being and viewpoint of other characters and must think "as if" we were another.

There is probably no intellectual quality more important than "the powers of *If.*"

The behaviorist school of thought as shown in the writings of B. F. Skinner and others acknowledges the difference between child and adolescent thought processes. However, it attributes the change not to a new developmental stage but to the influence on behavior of conditioning experiences consisting of a continuous flow of punishments and rewards. The behaviorists point to the development of verbal ability in economically secure, small families in which there are parental encouragement and individual attention, and in which books and other forms of cultural stimulation are provided.[3]

The aspect of adolescence of primary concern to the Freudian school of psychology is the sexual awakening that takes place during these years and the emotional conflict it brings. Other psychologists put less emphasis on the sexual awakening and consider it only one of the contributing factors that make it necessary for the teenager to form a new identity for himself or herself. Erik H. Erikson wrote:

> I have called the major crisis of adolescence the *identity crisis:* it occurs in that period of the life cycle when each youth must forge for himself some central perspective and direction, some working unity, out of the effective remnants of his childhood and the hopes of his anticipated adulthood; he must detect some meaningful resemblance between what he has come to see in himself and what his sharpened awareness tells him others judge and expect him to be.[4]

As part of this identity crisis, the opinions of others become tremendously important to teenagers. They try to leave behind the emotional dependence on their parents that was a natural part of childhood to gain an independence that will be tempered and balanced by the expectations of society. In making this adjustment, the peer group becomes increasingly important, and many teenagers become members of groups, cliques, or gangs. This group identification does two things. First, it allows teenagers to postpone for a bit making individual decisions about who and what they are. They can achieve a kind of independence by showing through their choice of group-approved clothing, language, music, entertainment, and various other social conventions that they are no longer under the domination of a parent or adult value system. The second benefit of a strong peer group is that it gives the teenager a chance to try out various roles ranging from conformist to nonconformist, from follower to leader. These roles can be acted out by individuals within the group or they can be acted out by the group as a whole, as, for example, when one gang challenges another gang. Individual members in this situation are caught up in a kind of emotional commitment that they would seldom feel as individuals.

The importance of the peer group is undoubtedly one of the reasons that teenagers show a strong preference for reading books about people of approximately their own age. Young adult literature actively extends the peer group. It gives teenagers a chance to participate vicariously in peer groups other than their own. Because the time of the identity crisis is limited to a few years and because teenagers are simultaneously engaged in other tasks such as going to school and preparing to earn a living, many young people get all of their real-life experience in a single group, or at least in a rather limited setting. Yet they are understandably curious about the decisions they are making, the values they are choosing, and the attitudes they are adopting. How will they be judged by other groups? By other individuals? What are the possible results of certain choices? What are attractive and reasonable alternatives? Reading is a likely and practical way for young people to be exposed to such alternatives and to explore realities beyond their own immediate situation.

Two more schools of thought have something important to say about young adults and the books they read. The developmental tasks outlined by R. J. Havighurst are briefly discussed in Chapters 5 and 6, and the theories of Lawrence Kohlberg and his associates on the development of moral reasoning are mentioned in Chapter 12.

WHAT IS YOUNG ADULT LITERATURE?

Even now, although most of us are quite sure we know what a teenager is, no hard and fast rules have developed for defining *teenage books, adolescent literature,* or *books for young adults.* The terms are vague and in professional literature are used interchangeably although some individuals do make distinctions. For our purposes in this text, we are using the term *children's literature* to include books written specifically for children from prekindergarten to about sixth grade. We mean *adolescent literature* or *teenage books* to include books published for young people from about grade seven through grades eleven or twelve. Technically, these books, along with the children's books, will be published by the juvenile division of a publishing house. When we talk about *adult books,* we mean literature written for the general public. These are the titles in bookstores *not* in some way labeled for the age of the reader. We use *young adult literature* as a broad term to include books freely chosen for reading by persons between the ages of twelve and twenty. They could be released from either the juvenile or the adult division of a publishing house and may be found in either the adult or young people's sections of public libraries. We should probably note that although the term *adolescent literature* is well established, especially in the titles of college courses, many young readers feel that it has a negative connotation and so some teachers and librarians avoid it.

Our other reason for preferring the term *young adult literature* is that we would be telling only half the story if we limited ourselves to what is technically defined as adolescent literature. Young people read much more than that. Not only are many of today's adult best sellers read by young people, but many of yesterday's adult titles are kept in print because of the young people who find and read such books as *Gone with the Wind, Mrs. Mike, Rebecca, A Tree Grows in Brooklyn,* and *The Catcher in the Rye.* Another reason that we have chosen to use the term *young adult* is that we want to stress the point that we are focusing not just on the books, but on young people as they read and interact with these books.

Where does this literature come from, these books for young adults? Many of the books we will be considering here were published by juvenile trade-book publishing houses. But like teenagers themselves, who may be treated as adults one day and as children the next, teenage books are almost as likely to be issued by publishers of books for adults. (It wasn't until the 1920s and 30s that most publishers divided their offerings into adult and juvenile categories.) Today, it is sometimes little more than chance whether an adult or juvenile editor happens to find a manuscript.

Robert Cormier had never thought of himself as a writer for young people, but when his agent submitted *The Chocolate War* to Pantheon, the editor of the juvenile division was the one who was the most enthusiastic about it. He convinced Cormier that, good as the book was, it would be simply one more in a catalog of adult books. On the other hand, if it were published for teenagers, it might sell well, and it certainly would not be one more in a long string of available adolescent novels. The editor's

---

Cormier's initial reaction to becoming a "young adult" author was one of shock followed by a month-long writer's block.

---

predictions came true, and Cormier later acknowledged that although his initial reaction to becoming a "young adult" author was one of shock followed by a month-long writer's block, he now feels grateful for what he considers to be stronger editorial help and more attention from reviewers at the juvenile level. Although he had already published several stories and three novels, it was *The Chocolate War* that brought him his first real financial gain.

Until very recently an author who had a choice of a book coming out as an adult title or a juvenile title probably would have automatically opted for the adult division in hopes of receiving greater respect, acclaim, and financial rewards. This is less true today because of several breakthroughs. Teenage books are now frequently made into successful movies and television specials. In our youth-oriented society, the general public likes to see young people on the screen, and many teenage books are of a length and complexity that makes them appropriate for one- or two-hour television specials.

In a similar way, people like to read about young adults, and it is fairly common for paperback publishers to pay large sums of money for popular teenage titles and to market them through their regular adult channels as well as through their school divisions.

The widespread selling of paperbacks in high schools has also increased the potential for financial success of young adult titles. Within recent years, the high-school market has grown tremendously because of several related factors. Reading has come into the high-school curriculum as a regular class taken for at least one semester by many students. In such classes, there has to be something for students to read, and, in many cases, this something is teenage fiction. Another factor is that during the late 1960s students and teachers turned away from the "classics" and the standard, required four years of English. English departments began offering electives, and courses in modern literature that included both adult and teenage fiction were popular with students. Many teachers who had previously scorned teenage books found themselves being forced to take a new look and to conclude that it was better to teach adolescent literature than no literature at all.

All of the interest has had a circular effect. The more important books for teenagers have become, the more respect the field has gained, and the better talent it has attracted. For example, on the basis of his Pulitzer Prize-winning play, *The Effect of Gamma Rays on Man-in-the-Moon Marigolds,* Paul Zindel was invited by Harper & Row to try writing teenage fiction. His first book was the very successful *The Pigman.* Both M. E. Kerr and Robert Cormier, who are two of the most respected writers for this age group, have acknowledged taking positive note of this book as they pondered the effect that writing books for teenagers might have on their own careers.

A BRIEF, UNSETTLED HERITAGE

The whole field of young adult literature is one some writers, teachers, and other interested parties have many questions about. It is, after all, a relatively new area. Teenage books have not always enjoyed the best reputation. An article in the *Louisville Courier-Journal* in 1951 indicates no great fondness for adolescent literature:

> The blame for the vulgarity, the dull conformity and the tastelessness of much in American life cannot be laid altogether at the doors of radio, television, and the movies as long as book publishers hawk these books for young people. Flabby in content, mediocre in style, narrowly directed at the most trivial of adolescent interests, they pander to a vast debilitation of tastes, to intolerance for the demanding, rewarding and ennobling exercise which serious reading can be. . . . Like a diet of cheap candies, they vitiate the appetite for sturdier food—for that bracing, ennobling and refining experience, immersion in the great stream of the English classics.[5]

Fourteen years later, J. Donald Adams, editor of the "Speaking of Books" page in *The New York Times Book Review* wrote:

> If I were asked for a list of symptoms pointing to what is wrong with
> American education and American culture, or to the causes for the
> prolongation of American adolescence, I should place high on the list the
> multiplication of books designed for readers in their teens. . . .
>   The teen-age book, it seems to me, is a phenomenon which belongs
> properly only to a society of morons. I have nothing but respect for the writers
> of good books for children; they perform one of the most admirable functions
> of which a writer is capable. One proof of their value is the fact that the
> greatest books which children can enjoy are read with equal delight by their
> elders. But what person of mature years and reasonably mature understanding
> (for there is often a wide disparity) can read without impatience a book
> written for adolescents?[6]

Those of us who have more positive attitudes toward teenage books can argue
that these critics were writing about books that are far different from the good adolescent literature being published today. We can also conjecture that they were making
observations based on a biased or inadequate sampling. Teenage books were never as
hopelessly bad as such statements imply. Criticism of any field, young adult literature
or ornithology or submarine designing, begins with first-hand experience of the subject. Critics who decide to do a cursory piece on young adult literature once a year or
so seldom have the reading background necessary to choose representative titles. People who make generalizations about an entire field of writing based on reading only
five or ten books are not merely unreliable sources, they are intellectual frauds. Wide
knowledge surely implies a background of at least several hundred books.

Although we have grounds for rejecting the kind of negative criticism quoted
above, we need to be aware that it still exists, though to a lesser extent than in years
previous. This pessimistic view of teenage books is an unfortunate literary heritage
that may very well be influencing the attitudes of school boards, library directors,
parents, teachers, and anyone else who has had no particular reason actually to read
and examine the best of the new teenage literature. Besides, so many new books
appear each year (approximately 2,500, with about one third of these aimed at teenagers) that people who have already made up their minds about adolescent literature can
probably find titles to support their beliefs no matter what they are. We can look at
much of the disagreement and at the conflicting views as inevitable in an area as new
as young adult literature. Controversies and differing viewpoints are signs of a lively
and interesting field.

SOME MYTHS ABOUT YOUNG ADULT LITERATURE

Many of the old—and a few new—beliefs about teenagers and books have taken on
the characteristics of myths. Some of the myths grew out of attempts to explain apparent contradictions; others are true in certain circumstances but have been overgeneral-
ized and exaggerated; others have been used in such a way that they have become self-

fulfilling prophecies. It seems appropriate at the beginning of a survey of young adult literature to examine some of these myths and to test them out against what we know about teenage reading and the best young adult literature. Your own wide and continued reading will help you form your own opinions.

We did some research to come up with a body of books that would be representative of what both young adults and professionals working in the field consider the best books. But we should caution you that books are selected as "the best" on the basis of many different criteria, and someone else's "best" will not necessarily be yours or that of the young people with whom you work. We hope that you will read many books so that you can recommend them, not because you saw them on a list, but because you personally enjoyed them and judge them to contain qualities that will appeal to a particular student.

In drawing up our list of "best books," we started with 1967 because in looking back this seemed to be a milestone year in which writers and publishers turned in new directions. We looked at the books published then and in the decade that followed. We thought these books were recent enough to portray the new trends, but old enough to have fairly well-established reputations. We went to several groups to see what titles they had considered to be the best books in each of these years. The groups included the Young Adult Services Division of the American Library Association, 160 professors of adolescent literature in American colleges who responded to a survey, the editors of *School Library Journal*, the editors of *The New York Times Book Review*, and the University of Iowa Book Poll printed in *English Journal* since 1972. Because this poll was not available before 1972, a special list of popular books put out by the A.L.A. Young Adult Services Division called "Still Alive in '75" was used for books published in the years 1967 through 1971. Any book that was named as an outstanding book by three or more of these five sources was put on a master list and studied in some detail. This master list, hereafter referred to as the "Honor Sampling," is reprinted in this chapter for your convenience. A table with more complete information appears in Appendix A.

1977

Hard Feelings. Don Bredes.
I Am the Cheese. Robert Cormier.
Ludell and Willie. Brenda Wilkinson.
Trial Valley. Vera and Bill Cleaver.

1976

Are You in the House Alone? Richard Peck.
Dear Bill, Remember Me? Norma Fox Mazer.
The Distant Summer. Sarah Patterson.
Home Before Dark. Sue Ellen Bridgers.
Never to Forget: The Jews of the Holocaust. Milton Meltzer.

Ordinary People. Judith Guest.
Singin' and Swingin' and Gettin' Merry Like Christmas. Maya Angelou.
Tunes for a Small Harmonica. Barbara Wersba.
Zero Makes Me Hungry: A Collection of Poems for Today. Edward Lueders, ed.

1975

Circus. Alistair Maclean.
El Bronx Remembered. Nicholasa Mohr.
How Democracy Failed. Ellen Switzer.
Is That You, Miss Blue? M. E. Kerr.
The Lion's Paw. D. R. Sherman.
The Massacre at Fall Creek. Jessamyn West.
Rumble Fish. S. E. Hinton.
Women of Wonder: Science Fiction by Women, About Women. P. Sargent, ed.
You Can Get There from Here. Shirley MacLaine.
Z for Zachariah. Robert C. O'Brien.

1974

Alive: The Story of the Andes Survivors. Piers Paul Read.
The Chocolate War. Robert Cormier.
Feral. Berton Roueche.
House of Stairs. William Sleator.
M. C. Higgins the Great. Virginia Hamilton.
Trying Hard to Hear You. Sandra Scoppettone.
Watership Down. Richard Adams.

1973

A Day No Pigs Would Die. Robert Newton Peck.
The Friends. Rosa Guy.
A Hero Ain't Nothin' But a Sandwich. Alice Childress.
If I Love You, Am I Trapped Forever? M. E. Kerr.
Nilda. Nicholasa Mohr.

1972

Deathwatch. Robb White.
Dinky Hocker Shoots Smack. M. E. Kerr.
Dove. Robin Graham.

Man Without a Face. Isabelle Holland.
My Name Is Asher Lev. Chaim Potok.
Sticks and Stones. Lynn Hall.
Teacup Full of Roses. Sharon Bell Mathis.
Woodstock Craftsman's Manual. Jean Young.

1971

The Autobiography of Miss Jane Pittman. Ernest Gaines.
Go Ask Alice. Anonymous.
His Own Where. June Jordan.
That Was Then, This Is Now. S. E. Hinton.
Wild in the World. John Donovan.

1970

Bless the Beasts and Children. Glendon Swarthout.
Daddy Was a Number Runner. Louise Meriwether.
I Know Why the Caged Bird Sings. Maya Angelou.

1969

The Andromeda Strain. Michael Crichton.
I'll Get There. It Better Be Worth the Trip. John Donovan.
Sounder. William Armstrong.
Where the Lilies Bloom. Vera and Bill Cleaver.

1968

The Pigman. Paul Zindel.
Red Sky at Morning. Richard Bradford.
Soul on Ice. Eldridge Cleaver.

1967

The Chosen. Chaim Potok.
House of Tomorrow. Jean Thompson.
Mr. and Mrs. Bo Jo Jones. Ann Head.
The Outsiders. S. E. Hinton.
Reflections on a Gift of Watermelon Pickle. Stephen Dunning, ed.

It was this list as much as anything else that convinced us that we would be telling only part of the story if we limited ourselves to books published as juvenile titles. Out of the sixty-three books on this list, twenty-four came from adult divisions and thirty-nine from juvenile divisions. The only reviewing source that did not include both adult and juvenile titles on its best-book lists was *The New York Times*. But, since it has both adult and juvenile reviewers, this was probably a matter of territorial division rather than a statement about the relative values and appeal to teenagers of adult and juvenile titles.

The strength and value of this list is that not only does it draw upon a widely read group of adults but that it also represents the actual reading tastes of young adults. The University of Iowa list is totally made up of books chosen by upper-division high-school students, and the lists drawn up by the American Library Association, as well as some of the other lists, have considerable input from young readers.

Many of these books will be described in more detail in Chapters 6–11. Here, they will simply be cited as the evidence we used to assess the following generalizations or myths as they relate to the best of modern young adult literature. By dispelling some of the myths, we will establish a clearer view of what young adult literature is and can be. But we should caution that we too are using a biased sampling. Whereas many critics use the worst books as examples, we have restricted ourselves to the best. You should, therefore, realize that some of the myths that we reject in relation to the Honor Sampling may very well be true of other books.

Myth No. 1: Teenagers Today Cannot Read

During the past few years, newspapers and magazines have trumpeted forth to a waiting world the news that "Teenagers Can't Read" and "Illiteracy Rate Rising" and "Tests Prove That Schools Not Doing Job." Ever since 1955, when Rudolf Flesch made such a stir with his book *Why Johnny Can't Read*, journalists, politicians, and general critics have found that as prophets of doom, they can easily gain a large and sympathetic audience. Of course parents want their youngsters to learn to read and are concerned about whether or not schools are succeeding. But few people look for the facts behind the stories of falling test scores and widespread illiteracy. There are seldom enough facts to support the claims.

Jaap Tuinman, Michael Rowls, and Roger Farr conducted an extensive study to measure the validity of such claims. The main finding of their study was that there simply isn't enough evidence to make comparisons between today and a few decades ago. They found that extensive performance data are not available for past years and that "the issue of adequacy of reading skills in terms of life-related performance has only recently been given attention. Little historical perspective is available."[7] The team examined census information and Armed Forces achievement data and found that the definitions of literacy were too broad to be useful. Reading achievement scores for individual schools were not useful because the populations of schools, especially in the large cities, which were the ones most likely to collect data on reading scores, have changed considerably as middle class people have moved to the suburbs. Also, the age at which children are in particular grades in school has continually moved down. The material that they found to be the most useful included: (1) extant research literature in which studies on changes in reading performance were reported, (2) records of reading achievement in large public school systems (rather than individual schools), and (3) records of statewide reading tests.

They found fifty studies that in some way measured reading achievement spanning 102 years. The clear indication of these studies was that education is improving, but it was less clear just what parts of education were improving. Thirteen studies focused specifically on reading and twelve of these showed that reading skill was

---

Thirteen studies focused specifically on reading and twelve of these showed that reading skill was improving.

---

improving. Four significant studies which in themselves were summaries showed the same trend. Records of test performance in schools also support the continued improvement except that in some cases there does appear to have been a slight rise in test performance of students in the years between 1960 and 1965. Tuinman, Rowls, and Farr concluded:

> We believe that, from the information we were able to gather, we would
> conclude first that there is no reason for *en masse* pessimism; second, that the
> gradual improvement in reading competency over the four decades prior to
> 1965 may have lessened or halted; and finally, over the last ten years there
> may have been a very slight decline in reading achievement. Of all our
> hesitant interpretations, we feel least certain about the last one. We are
> convinced that anyone who says that he *knows* that literacy is decreasing is
> ignoring the data. Such a person is at best unscholarly and at worst dishonest.[8]

While scholars have been making such careful studies as the one described above, teachers, librarians, and booksellers have been informally observing that the book business is as brisk as ever—in many cases, more brisk. Individualized reading classes are among the most popular of the elective offerings in high-school English and reading programs. Libraries are holding their own with the young adult college-bound readers they have traditionally served, and they are successfully using different approaches to attract a whole new clientele.

Myth No. 2: Young Adult Literature Is Simplified to Accommodate Low Reading Skills

This myth has more truth to it than some of the other myths, but it is still overgeneralizing to think, as some people do, that the reason for the rise in popularity of young adult literature over the last few years is that teenagers are incapable of reading regular adult books or "great literature." None of the books on the honor list is of the controlled vocabulary or the easy-to-read variety. However, one of the characteristics of juvenile books as compared to adult books is that they are shorter. The average length of the juvenile titles in the honor list is 184 pages while the average length of the adult titles is 265 pages. Not one of the juvenile titles has over 300 pages. Two of them, June Jordan's *His Own Where* and John Donovan's *Wild in the World*, have fewer than 100 pages and another six have fewer than 150 pages.

Young adults, teachers, librarians, and editors have come to accept this matter of length as a given. In 1964, when the British author, Leon Garfield, submitted his first novel to a publishing house it was turned down "after three or four agonizing months, when they said they couldn't quite decide whether it was adult or junior." He next submitted it to an editor who was just beginning to develop a juvenile line. Garfield said, "She suggested that, if I would be willing to cut it, then she'd publish it as a juvenile book. And of course, though I'd vowed I'd never alter a word, once the possibility of its being published became real, I cut it in about a week."[9]

It is worth pointing out that reading difficulty and level of literary sophistication do not always correlate with length. Furthermore, teenagers *will* read longer books, as is shown by the length of some of the adult titles on the list. For example, Chaim Potok's *My Name Is Asher Lev* has 369 pages. Jessamyn West's *The Massacre at Fall Creek* has 373 pages, Piers Paul Read's *Alive: The Story of the Andes Survivors* has 352 pages, Don Bredes' *Hard Feelings* has 377 pages, and Richard Adams' *Watership Down* has 429 pages. (Quite possibly, it was the length of *Watership Down* that influenced American publishers to release it as an adult book rather than as a juvenile title, as it was originally published in England.)

It has often been said that teenage books are stylistically simple and that the plot moves forward without subplots or deviations. Again, this is not so much a myth as it is an overgeneralization. It is true of the majority of books that teenagers read, but there are certainly exceptions. Robert Cormier's *I Am the Cheese*, for example, has a very complex plot, and June Jordan's *His Own Where* is far from being stylistically simple. In both Alice Childress' *A Hero Ain't Nothin' But a Sandwich* and Paul Zindel's *The Pigman*, readers must draw together and sort out the alternating viewpoints and chronology. And it is obvious from perusing some of the adult titles that are popular with teenagers, Judith Guest's *Ordinary People* and Chaim Potok's *My Name Is Asher Lev*, for example, that their appeal is based on something other than an easy reading level.

Myth No. 3: Teenage Books Are All the Same

The existence of this myth says more about the reading patterns of the people who believe it than about the state of young adult literature. There is a tremendous variety of types, subjects, and themes represented in the Honor Sampling. Forty-nine out of the sixty-three titles are fiction. Thirty-five of these, including two collections of short stories, are realistic; four, including one collection of short stories, are science fiction; five are historical; two are suspense; two are humorous; and one is fantasy. Two of the books are collections of poems and two are biographies. Seven are written in the form of the new journalism. They are based on true events, but the authors have used the techniques of fiction, such as character development, the building of suspense, and the creation of dialogue to make their stories more than purely informative accounts. Books of this type include Robin Graham's *Dove*, Piers Paul Read's *Alive: The Story of the Andes Survivors*, Shirley MacLaine's *You Can Get There from Here*, the anonymous *Go Ask Alice*, and Ellen Switzer's *How Democracy Failed*.

The Honor Sampling is relatively short on informative nonfiction. It contains only two books of this type: Milton Meltzer's *Never to Forget: The Jews of the Holocaust* and Jean Young's *Woodstock Craftsman's Manual*. The reason is that, although the various lists included several informative nonfiction books, they were not the same from one list to the next. Apparently critics and readers do not agree as easily on what is a good informative book, or else there is simply such a variety of informative books that particular ones are not as apt to come to popular attention.

In looking at the content of the realistic fiction, which makes up the largest part of the Honor Sampling, there is evidence of a wide variety of themes. The theme commonly thought to be at the center of teenage books is that of gaining maturity, i.e., going through the rites of passage from childhood to adulthood. Many of the books do have this theme, but the stories are more than repetitious case histories. They communicate a sense of time and change, a sense of becoming something and catching glimpses of possibilities, some that are fearful, others that are awesome, odd, funny, perplexing, or wondrous. They announce, "We're on our way to somewhere. We don't know where, but we're on our way, and off we go!"

But the theme of growth and change is not the only one to be found in teenage books. The quest theme which is common in fantasy and science fiction runs through much young adult material as well as much of the great literature of the Western world. In the Honor Sampling, it is seen in William Armstrong's *Sounder* and John Donovan's *I'll Get There. It Better Be Worth the Trip*. Themes such as alienation and loneliness are seen in John Donovan's *Wild in the World* and Eldridge Cleaver's *Soul on Ice*. The need for a hero is seen in Robert Newton Peck's *A Day No Pigs Would Die* and Glendon Swarthout's *Bless the Beasts and Children*. Threats to the social order are explored in William Sleator's *House of Stairs*, Robert C. O'Brien's *Z for Zachariah*, and Robert Cormier's *I Am the Cheese*. A search for values is shown in Richard Bradford's *Red Sky at Morning* and S. E. Hinton's *That Was Then, This Is Now*. What it means to care for others is examined in Isabelle Holland's *Man Without a Face*, Paul Zindel's *The Pigman*, and Ann Head's *Mr. and Mrs. Bo Jo Jones*. Our need for others and our eternal need for laughter are both shown in M. E. Kerr's *Dinky Hocker Shoots Smack* and *If I Love You, Am I Trapped Forever?* First love is explored in Brenda Wilkinson's *Ludell and Willie*, Barbara Wersba's *Tunes for a Small Harmonica*, Sarah Patterson's *The Distant Summer*, and June Jordan's *His Own Where*.

There is nothing terribly new or exciting about any of these themes. They have been explored in literature throughout the decades and literary critics have discussed them endlessly. But the themes are fresh to anyone young for the first (and last) time, and one of the values of young adult literature is that it presents these universal themes in contemporary settings featuring characters with whom young readers can identify.

Myth No. 4: Teenage Books Avoid Taboo Topics and Feature White, Middle-Class Protagonists

In 1959, when Stephen Dunning wrote his dissertation on the adolescent novel, he observed that "junior novels insistently avoid taboo concerns," and that "junior novels are typically concerned with socially and economically fortunate families."[10] Although this was undoubtedly true then, when the popular books were *Going on Sixteen, Practically Seventeen, Class Ring,* and *Prom Trouble,* the mid-1960s witnessed a striking change in attitudes. One by one, taboos on profanity, divorce, sexuality, drinking, racial unrest, abortion, pregnancy, and drugs have disappeared or been ignored so that today these remarks no longer apply to teenage novels.

Books have become painfully honest about the reality of young people and their frequently cold and cruel world. Some critics have suggested, in fact, that modern young adult literature is exclusively pessimistic or cynical. This is as much of an overgeneralization as the counterclaim that teenage books present a romanticized and frivolous view of life. What has happened in recent years is that restrictions have been lifted so that writers can explore a variety of topics and concerns. It is also worth noting that the number of these more frank books published by juvenile houses is growing.

The Honor Sampling shows a steady increase in the number of popular and respected books coming from the juvenile divisions of publishing houses. From 1967 through 1972, four juvenile titles are listed for every three adult titles. But from 1973 through 1977, six juvenile titles appear for every three adult titles. This would seem to contradict the trend that has been noticed in which teenagers seem to be maturing faster and reading sophisticated books at younger ages. Books that used to be read by college students are now being read by high-school students, and books formerly read by senior-high students are now being read by junior-high students. By looking a little closer at the statistics and the situation, we see that these two observations are not really contradictory. What has happened is that as publishers have been given more freedom to publish controversial material, books that formerly would have appeared as adult books are now being released as juvenile titles. Probably today both Ann Head's *Mr. and Mrs. Bo Jo Jones* and Jean Thompson's *House of Tomorrow,* which are about the pregnancies of unwed teenage girls, would be published as teenage rather than as adult books, which they were in 1967.

But even though restrictions have been lifted, juvenile publishers have not cast them aside completely, especially in regard to sexually explicit material. Note that in 1977, Don Bredes' *Hard Feelings,* which graphically describes the sexual awakening of a sixteen-year-old boy, came out as an adult rather than a juvenile title. And when Bradbury Press decided to publish Judy Blume's *Forever* (which is not on the honor listing), they created an adult division, which they had never had before, probably hoping to forestall adverse criticism for presenting to teenagers a warm and positive story about premarital sex.

The Honor Sampling strongly refutes the idea that the protagonists in young adult literature are mainly white and middle class. Probably because there was such a void in good books about non-middle-class protagonists and also because this is where some very interesting things were happening, many writers during the 1970s focused their attention in this direction. On the honor list there are more books with ethnic group settings than there are members of these minority groups in the general culture. Twenty-six, or approximately 40 percent of the books have main characters who are not white middle-class Americans. Twelve of the books feature black protagonists. Authenticity is especially valued: all of the books about blacks except for *Sounder* are

---

Books that formerly would have appeared as adult books are now being released as juvenile titles.

---

by black authors, and many of the ethnic books include biographical elements. Nicholasa Mohr writes about Puerto Ricans in New York; Chaim Potok and Milton Meltzer treat Jewish experiences; Vera and Bill Cleaver and John Donovan write about isolated, rural families; and Sue Ellen Bridgers writes about a family of southern migrant farm workers. There are no Mexican American or Native American protagonists, but these two groups play important roles, respectively, in *Red Sky at Morning* and *The Massacre at Fall Creek*. Only one fiction title is set outside the United States and this is D. R. Sherman's *The Lion's Paw*, which has a young bushman as its protagonist.

Myth No. 5: Teenage Books Are Didactic or Preachy

In this list of myths, this is the one that comes closest to being true. Of course adults want to teach young people what they have learned about life, so when they set out to write a book they probably want to share with their readers some kind of an insight, an understanding, or a lesson. This might be said of everyone who writes for readers of any age, but writers for young people have often had more confidence in doing this because of the greater distance between the experience of writer and reader. The major difference between the books on the Honor Sampling and those published in earlier years is the subtlety with which the messages are presented. In earlier books there was a direct hard sell, but today's writers tell stories that point the reader in specific directions and then leave it to the reader to arrive at a final conclusion.

Writing in 1977 about British young adult literature and a smattering of American young adult novels, Sheila Ray observed that "despite their outspoken coverage of a wide range of controversial topics, the majority of teenage novels tend to reinforce conventional and establishment attitudes."[11] Books on the Honor Sampling support her observation. They are clearly on the side of the angels. Even when the subject is sexuality, alcoholism, divorce, or drugs, the books support conventional middle-class standards. This is to be expected because many writers came from the middle class or aspired to it when young. Also it is the middle-class value system that supports schools and libraries. And, for that matter, most adult novels reinforce the same attitudes.

Myth No. 6: Teenage Books Are Anti-Adult, Especially Anti-Parent

Another common belief is that as part of their desire to achieve independence from their parents, teenagers are resentful of adults and, at least in fiction, could as easily do without them. But such books as Sandra Scoppettone's *Trying Hard to Hear You*, Robert Cormier's *I Am the Cheese*, D. R. Sherman's *The Lion's Paw*, Jessamyn West's *The Massacre at Fall Creek*, Virginia Hamilton's *M. C. Higgins the Great*, Alice Childress' *A Hero Ain't Nothin' But a Sandwich*, Chaim Potok's *The Chosen*, the anonymous *Go Ask Alice*, William Armstrong's *Sounder*, Judith Guest's *Ordinary People*, and Sue Ellen Bridgers' *Home Before Dark* do not support this view. In each of these books at least one parent is presented as a strong, positive character who plays an important role in the teenage protagonist's development. In *A Day No Pigs Would Die*, the boy has a great love for his father, and a main point in *Dinky Hocker Shoots Smack* is that Dinky wants attention from her mother.

However, it is true that young adult readers want the protagonists in their stories to be young. In trying to discover why, of the hundreds of popular adult books appearing in recent years, these particular twenty-four titles on the Honor Sampling rose to the top as favorites of teenagers, we found that one common denominator was the age of the protagonists. Even counting the few suspense pieces that feature adults, the average age of the protagonists in the adult books is twenty-two and a half. This is not much older than the average age of the protagonists in the juvenile titles, which is seventeen years.

But chronological age does not seem to be as important as life-style in determining the kinds of protagonists with whom young adults can identify. Apparently in the eyes of teenagers, the big dividing line—the final rite of passage—between youth and adulthood is having children of one's own, becoming a parent. Young adults easily identify with adults and think of them as just slightly older than themselves as long as little or no mention is made of family responsibilities as in Berton Roueche's *Feral*, Alistair Maclean's *Circus*, Eldridge Cleaver's *Soul on Ice*, and Michael Crichton's *The Andromeda Strain*. None of the fictional protagonists, except for Miss Jane Pittman whose story is made to read like an autobiography, were parents although *House of Tomorrow* and *Mr. and Mrs. Bo Jo Jones* are both about pregnancy.

Myth No. 7: Girls Read About Girls and Boys; Boys Read Only About Boys

Of all the myths, this is the one that has the most potential of becoming a self-fulfilling prophecy. Studies done in the early 1950s indicated that starting with fourth or fifth grade, boys showed a slight preference for reading stories about males. This kind of information was widely publicized especially in the education explosion that followed the launching of Russia's Sputnik. During this period, there was great emphasis on teaching boys to read and encouraging them in academic endeavors in the hope that they would grow up and become the engineers and the scientists who would help Americans compete successfully with the Russians. Teachers, librarians, publishers, and authors often heard or read statements to the effect that whereas girls will read books about both boys and girls, boys will read only those books that feature males.

This led authors and publishers to concentrate on stories about males because they naturally wanted the largest possible market for their books. For example, Scott O'Dell tells how he was asked to change Karana, the heroine in *Island of the Blue Dolphins*, to a boy so that it would be read by more people. He refused since it was a true story and much of its value rested on the fact that Karana was a female who in order to survive had to break her tribal male/female restrictions.

O'Dell's experience was typical of a publishing world that considered males to be the reading audience to be wooed. Then, as now, young girls read more than did boys, so there was always a market for so-called girls' books. But the kind of books produced with females as the intended audience were the kind of lopsided romances that tended not to be read by boys.

However, the books on the Honor Sampling do not support the idea that boys will not read books about girls. The juvenile titles are almost evenly divided between nineteen male and sixteen female protagonists. Boys are reading such books as *Go Ask Alice*, M. E. Kerr's *Dinky Hocker Shoots Smack*, Louise Meriwether's *Daddy Was a Number Runner*, the Cleavers' *Where the Lilies Bloom*, and Robert C. O'Brien's *Z for Zachariah*. And if other more romantic titles such as Ann Head's *Mr. and Mrs. Bo Jo Jones*, Sandra Scoppettone's *Trying Hard to Hear You*, Barbara Wersba's *Tunes for a Small Harmonica*, Jean Thompson's *House of Tomorrow*, Rosa Guy's *The Friends*, Brenda Wilkinson's *Ludell and Willie*, and Norma Fox Mazer's *Dear Bill, Remember Me?* are read more by girls than by boys, then teenage girls must be more avid readers, at least of fiction, than are boys and therefore have a bigger say in what becomes a popular and/or respected book. There is not an equivalent set of books from this list that would be read mostly by boys.

Perhaps the literary level at which these books are written has something to do with their contradiction of this myth about "sex appeal." After all, they were chosen as the "best" books by many knowledgeable people. The segregation of books by sex may occur only with exaggerated romances, adventure stories, and pornography. Apparently honest literature comes across as a representation of real life and can be appreciated by readers of either sex regardless of the sex of the protagonist.

This brings up an interesting relationship between the sex of the author and the sex of the protagonist. Apparently men do not feel as comfortable in writing about females as women do in writing about males. With the adult books, the only male to write a book centered on a female was Ernest J. Gaines with *The Autobiography of Miss Jane Pittman*. And with the juvenile titles there was only Robert C. O'Brien with *Z for Zachariah* and Richard Peck with *Are You in the House Alone?* Two other titles give almost equal treatment to a male and a female: *The Pigman* by Paul Zindel and *House of Stairs* by William Sleator. In comparison, male authors wrote twenty books featuring male protagonists.

On the other hand, with the juvenile titles on this list, female authors wrote almost as many books featuring males, ten, as they did featuring females, thirteen. S. E. Hinton says that she feels more comfortable writing "from the male perspective" and she therefore goes by her initials instead of her given name (Susan Elizabeth) so that readers will think of her as male. But other women authors are not at all shy about being female while writing about males in such books as Isabelle Holland's *Man*

Without a Face, June Jordan's *His Own Where,* Sharon Bell Mathis' *Teacup Full of Roses,* Alice Childress' *A Hero Ain't Nothin' But a Sandwich,* Virginia Hamilton's *M. C. Higgins the Great,* and M. E. Kerr's *If I Love You, Am I Trapped Forever?* It is interesting that of the four books on this honor list that treat the subject of male homosexuality (*Man Without a Face, Sticks and Stones, I'll Get There. It Better Be Worth the Trip,* and *Trying Hard to Hear You*), three were written by women. However, with the adult titles, women apparently do not feel as free to write about men. Only Judith Guest's *Ordinary People* and Jessamyn West's *The Massacre at Fall Creek* feature males as compared to seven featuring females.

Myth No. 8: If Teenagers See the Movie, They Won't Read the Book

This is a myth that over time has proved unfounded. Although people used to worry about it, today the idea is fairly well accepted that the existence of a well-done media piece increases the number of readers that a book has. It seems teenagers are often motivated to pick up a book because they've seen a movie or television production based on it. If they've enjoyed the film version, they're likely to want their pleasure reinforced by encountering the familiar characters and situations again in the book.

In the Honor Sampling, a large percentage of the early books that are included because they are presently assigned by adolescent literature professors or because they appeared on the A.L.A. "Still Alive in '75" list are those from which movies have been made. Undoubtedly these movies have helped to keep alive such titles as *Mr. and Mrs.*

If they've enjoyed the film version, they're likely to want to encounter the characters and situations in the book.

Bo Jo Jones (1967), *Red Sky at Morning* (1968), *The Andromeda Strain, Sounder,* and *Where the Lilies Bloom* (1969), and *Bless the Beasts and Children* (1970). In 1974, *The Autobiography of Miss Jane Pittman* was a prize-winning television special, and every year since 1973, *Go Ask Alice* garners a large viewing audience when it is shown. When Robb White's *Deathwatch* was adapted for television, the title was changed to *Savages* because two other movies already had similar-sounding titles. Unfortunately, a different name does not do as much to boost a book's readership.

Myth No. 9: Young Adult Literature Is Less Enduring Than Adult Literature

It's true that young adult literature does not have a *Moby Dick* or a *Crime and Punishment* to call its own. On the other hand, a great work by definition is individual and rare. Considering how new the phenomenon of young adult literature is, it would be astonishing indeed if there were a teenage book with the stature and enduring quality of *Moby Dick*. Books for young adults range from truly fine and imaginative works to outright trash. And although young adult literature includes books of widely varying quality, certainly the field has no monopoly on mediocrity or hack writing, which can be found in any area. It probably *is* fair to say, though, that as more freedom has been given to the writers and publishers of teenage books, this freedom has been used by good writers to produce better books, but poor writers have used it to hang themselves on every social ill they could find. The result has been a widening of the gap between the talented and the hack.

Many of the young adult books being published today are, admittedly, ephemeral. But the same can be said of most of what is published every year, whether intended for adults, children, or teenagers. Relatively little that is printed lasts for any length of time. More important, people read some books for information and others for their significance, but they also read much that has neither. There is nothing wrong with this. All of us read some of the time for entertainment and for relaxation. Today's young adult literature provides that, but it also provides an amazing amount of truly good literature.

The rejection, either in whole or in part, of these nine myths has shown what the best of young adult literature is not, but it seems appropriate to try turning these statements around and ending with a positive statement about what the best young adult literature is. First, it is written in a natural, flowing kind of language very much like that which young adults use orally. Although it is not simplified for easy reading, writers do avoid the long, drawn-out descriptions, the interweaving of multiple, complex plots, and the kind of pedantic or overblown language that is sometimes found in writing for adults. In the Honor Sampling the quality of the writing varies from good to excellent, but, in young adult literature as a whole, it varies from poor to excellent just as it does in writing aimed at any other audience.

Writers treat a wide variety of subject matter and themes, including many controversial ideas. And they choose their protagonists from minority groups as well as from the white middle-class majority. Like most adult and children's books, young adult literature usually supports the middle-class value system. And though recent books may push the boundaries out a little, they still point young readers toward the moral values and the behaviors deemed desirable by society. The protagonists, who can be either male or female, are relatively young (in their teens or early twenties) and are free from family responsibilities. And, finally, the production of a well-done media piece seems to promote the popularity of the book on which it is based.

Has contemporary young adult literature anything to offer teachers, librarians, or—most of all—students? Is young adult literature worth studying, given the multitudinous responsibilities we all have?

We believe the answer to both questions is an unqualified yes. Young adult literature was never intended to replace other forms of literature. It provides enjoyment, satisfaction, and literary quality while it brings life and hope and reality to young people. Some students may find it beyond their abilities, unfortunately, whereas other young people will have passed beyond it to great literature. Pigeonholing has always been tempting for teachers and librarians: it's easy to place students in neat categories so that we know who reads this kind of book and who that. Reality doesn't work that way. The teacher or librarian who force-feeds a steady diet of either great literature or teenage books, or any other particular kind of book, down the gullets of young readers proves that he or she knows nothing about them and cares as little about finding out. Susan Sontag reported in an interview in *The New York Times* for January 30, 1978, that she remembered all too well attending a "dreadful high school" where she was reprimanded for reading Immanuel Kant's *Critique of Pure Reason* instead of the assigned portion of the *Reader's Digest.* Responsible teachers and librarians individualize their work, recommending this book to that student, not because it's a classic or because everyone else has liked it, but because the student's own personality and interests are respected.

In order to fill this leadership role, adults must first understand what and who and where young adults are, and second they must know the books. There's only one way to know the books and that is to read them in their entirety, not just the reviews.

Young adult literature has come a long hard way in the last hundred years. Its progress has at times been doubtful, but the change in the last ten or so years is a harbinger of better things to come. Young adult literature is not the whole of literature, but it is an increasingly important part. The future teacher or librarian unfamiliar with young adult literature begins disadvantaged and, given the flow of the presses, is likely to remain so. This would be professionally irresponsible, but it would be a disaster for the students who will thus miss out on being introduced to the delights of reading for pleasure.

ACTIVITIES

1. Interview four adults who are in some way connected with education. Ask them to describe for you what young adult literature is. Write up a report of their opinions. Which, if any, of the myths appear in their descriptions? What evidence do they seem to be using for their opinions? Is there a correlation between how closely your informants work with young adult literature and how positive their feelings are about it? For example, does a high school reading teacher know more and feel more optimistic about young adult books than a college student preparing to teach history or a parent with children in high school?

2. Read two of the books on the Honor Sampling. In making your selection, show the list to a high-school student and ask for recommendations of books that the student has read and enjoyed or that friends have talked about. As you read the books, see if you enjoy them for the same reasons that the high-school students did.

3. Check the card catalogue of a local high school or public library to see how many of the books on the Honor Sampling are in the collection. Are there particular gaps that would reveal the personal preferences of those who do the purchasing? For example, are the adventure stories missing? Or the books about ethnic groups? Or

the ones that treat controversial topics? If the library is a general public library, does it have a young adult section? If so, are some of the books double-shelved in both the children's and the young adult sections; are others in both the young adult and the adult sections? Does it appear that the decision to shelve a book in a young people's section or in an adult section is made on the basis of which division of a publishing house it came from or is it made because of the nature of the topic and language?

This activity may be done as a class project with students responsible for visiting different libraries and reporting on books of designated years. Some interesting observations and comparisons can then be made about local public or school libraries.

NOTES

[1]Lou Willett Stanek, "Adults and Adolescents: Ambivalence and Ambiguity," *School Library Journal* 20 (February 1974): 21.

[2]Boyd R. McCandless and Richard H. Coop, *Adolescents: Behavior and Development,* 2d ed. (New York: Holt, Rinehart and Winston, Inc., 1979), p. 160.

[3]Robert E. Grinder and Theron Alexander, "Adolescence," in *The Academic American Encyclopedia* (Burbank: Arete Publishing Company, Inc., forthcoming).

[4]Erik H. Erikson, *Young Martin Luther, A Study in Psychoanalysis and History* (New York: W. W. Norton & Co., Inc., 1958), p. 14.

[5]"Trash for Teen-Agers: Or Escape from Thackeray, the Brontës, and the Incomparable Jane," *Louisville Courier-Journal,* June 17, 1951, quoted in Stephen Dunning, "Junior Book Roundup," *English Journal* 53 (December 1964): 702–3.

[6]J. Donald Adams, *Speaking of Books—and Life* (New York: Holt, Rinehart and Winston, Inc., 1965), p. 250–52.

[7]Jaap Tuinman, Michael Rowls, and Roger Farr, "Reading Achievement in the United States: Then and Now," *Journal of Reading* 19, No. 6 (March 1976): 455–63.

[8]Ibid., p. 463.

[9]Justin Wintle and Emma Fisher, eds., *The Pied Pipers: Interviews with the Influential Creators of Children's Literature* (Paddington Press, 1974), p. 194.

[10]Stephen Dunning, "A Definition of the Role of the Junior Novel Based on Analyses of Thirty Selected Novels" (Ph.D. diss., Florida State University, 1959), p. 317–18.

[11]Sheila Ray, "The Development of the Teenage Novel," in *Reluctant to Read?* ed. John L. Foster (London: Ward Lock Educational Publishers, 1977), p. 63.

2

Literary Aspects of
Young Adult Books

In beginning the systematic study of young adult literature, we quickly discover many of the same questions and considerations we face in studying *any* body of literature. Writers of young adult books work in much the same way as writers of other sorts of books. They have the same tools available to them, and largely the same intent: to evoke a response in a reader through words on a page. And young adult readers read with the same range of responses as any other group of readers.

In this chapter we will explore the kinds of literary devices and aspects of creative writing most likely to bring lasting satisfaction to young adult readers. Identifying with a story, not just through the eyes of the characters in it, but also through the eyes of the author, brings an added dimension of pleasure to literature. But the ability to enjoy a story on multiple levels is something that has to be developed over a long period of time. In fact, it is something that people continue to work on throughout their lives. That is why the principles discussed and the examples given in this chapter should be of as much interest to adults involved in this continuing process of developing their own skills of literary appreciation as to young readers just beginning to glimpse what is meant by "Literature with a capital L."

Some people speak of literature with a capital L to identify the kind of literature that is set apart from, or has a degree of excellence not found in, the masses of printed material that roll from the presses of the world each day. This type of literature rewards study, not only because of its content, but because of its style, the literary devices and techniques that are used, and the universality and permanence and at the same time the congeniality of the ideas expressed. It is on the question of universality and permanence that some critics have asked whether stories written specifically for young readers can be considered Literature. Their feeling is that if a story speaks only to readers of a certain age, then it cannot really have the kind of universality required in true literature. However, every adult has lived through an adolescence and continues to experience many of the doubts, leave-takings, embarkings on new roles, and sudden flashes of joy and wonder that are written about in books with protagonists between the ages of twelve and twenty-five. Books that show the uniqueness and at the same time the universality of such experiences are most often cited as Literature—*The Adventures of Huckleberry Finn, The Catcher in the Rye, Little Women,* and *Lord of the Flies,* for example. These books are often referred to as classics. They have proven themselves with different readers across different time periods. And they are the books that readers return to for a second and third reading, each time feeling rewarded.

In contrast to literature with a capital L there is formula literature and escape literature. In truth, all stories consist of variations on a limited number of plots and themes, but the difference between what is referred to simply as literature and what is referred to as formula literature is one of degree. Formula literature is almost entirely predictable. Many of the situation comedies, westerns, and adventure shows on television are formula pieces. So are many of the books that young people enjoy reading.

Because formula literature is highly predictable, the reader can relax and enjoy a story while expending a minimum of intellectual energy. For this reason, formula literature is often used as escape literature—something people read only for entertainment and relaxation with little or no hope of gaining insights or learning new information. Many of the paperbacks sold in airports and hospital waiting rooms were written as escape literature. Some people prefer to escape for a few hours with a murder mystery, others with a gothic, others with science fiction, and still others with a Harlequin romance. Much television programming meets many of the same needs as escape literature. There is nothing wrong with young people enjoying formula or escape literature either in books or on television, but, quite naturally, it is the goal of most of us who work with young readers to bring them to the stage where they can receive pleasure from all kinds of literature, including literature that is significant and lasting.

People who have devoted their lives to books and reading have discovered that the ability to appreciate literature at more complex and subtle levels is not a talent that some people are born with and others without. It is a skill developed over many years of reading, and there are quite definite stages that people go through as they make progress in developing this skill.

STAGES OF LITERARY APPRECIATION

In 1960, Margaret Early outlined three stages of reading growth, characterized by readers' responses, not by chronological age alone. She described the first stage as being that of unconscious enjoyment, a stage in which readers know what they like, but not why they like it. At this stage readers are easily delighted and undemanding. This stage has its beginnings in infancy when parents sing to their babies and share nursery rhymes and folktales. It continues as the primary stage of development through the beginning and middle years of elementary school where it fortifies youngsters as they learn decoding skills. For many young people this first stage is a natural and delightful time. For others, it is an early introduction into frustration, despair, and failure as they fall further and further behind in reading skills and get less and less pleasure from the ordinarily delightful activity of listening to stories and then reading them on their own. This stage of unconscious enjoyment is the beginning of literary appreciation. It cannot be by-passed if the reader is going to progress successfully to the second stage.

In the second stage, readers continue to enjoy literature on the first level of easy acceptance but are willing to exert considerable effort to enhance their own delight. They gradually move away from a simple interest in what happened in the story. They ask why. In both fiction and drama, they look for a logical development of character. They are no longer satisfied with stereotypes, and they demand that the characters be controlled by human motives. Typically, this stage of enjoying experiences vicariously—not merely listening but becoming part of the story—takes hold in late elementary and early junior high school. Young people read avidly and they read almost anything. Their interests cover a wide range and the purpose of reading is to inhabit, for a few hours, the body of someone else who does interesting things.

When readers reach the fullest level of literary appreciation, they respond with delight and know why they are delighted. They have learned to rely on their own discriminating judgment to help them choose reading that pleases them. Early writes that:

> A sign of maturity as a human being and as a reader is that a deeper feeling for mankind replaces narrow concern for oneself. The mature reader no longer seeks only *self*-knowledge in literature but, with the artist, digs at the wellsprings of life.

The main purpose in reading at this level is neither sociological nor psychological, but aesthetic. In reading a work of great literature, readers bring to it all their creative powers, the stream of their inner consciousness, all their living, and all the ideas of humanity that have become theirs through previous reading. Says Early: "In this sense, the art of reading is an extension of the creative process which produced the work of literature."[1]

Early adds that readers do not leave one stage when they enter another. A poor reader in the twelfth grade might consider Hemingway's *The Old Man and the Sea* exciting and good though precisely what was good or why it was good might escape him. A better reader might visualize herself in the tale and ask if the tale was probable or possible or if the actions of the old fisherman fit his character. But at the same time, she would enjoy the tale as simple adventure as well. A superior reader would enjoy the tale, ask questions about its external and internal logic, and then extend beyond that into questions of beauty and stylistic integrity and ways in which Hemingway might have probed more effectively or at least differently had he tried a different narrator or a different setting or any number of things. The superior reader participates with the writer in developing, and in effect rewriting, the novel.

Authors of the best young adult books use the same literary techniques—though perhaps to a different degree—as the authors of the best books for adults. As will be seen in the following chapters, these literary techniques can be discussed in many different ways. Two of the approaches that have proven to be the most useful include that of classification by genre and the analysis of such essential literary elements as plot, theme, character, point of view, tone, setting, style, and mode.

Interrelationships exist between genres and literary elements in that some genres are more apt than others to rely on or to emphasize particular literary elements. For example, setting is usually a more important part of a historical novel than of a romance, and an exciting plot is crucial to an adventure story, whereas good character development is crucial to a story of personal achievement. Figurative language is essential to poetry and good dialogue to drama, and so on. Because of these interrelationships, the following discussion of literary elements touches on genres as well.

The information given here is the sort you will need as a teacher or librarian to make your own judgments about books and to increase your own pleasure in reading them. It is also the sort of thing that you will hope to pass on to the young people with whom you work.

PLOT

In examining the books that become popular with young adults as compared to those that do not, a crucial difference often appears in the plotting. The plot of a story is the sequence of events in which the characters play out their roles in some kind of a conflict. It is what happens.

Elements of Plot

For most young readers, there needs to be a promise within the first few pages that something exciting is going to happen, that there is going to be a believable conflict. Authors use various techniques to get this message across to their readers, or to "hook" them. In Winifred Rosen's *Cruisin for a Bruisin* the narrative hook appears in the first three sentences in which the reader's interest is aroused simply by the topic and the author's candid manner of speaking about it:

> Lately I've begun to think that everyone is crazy. I'm not sure when it started, but since I turned thirteen—six months ago— I've been more and more sure that I understand less and less well what is really going on.
> Take sex, for example—not that I *ever* understood it, no matter how many people tried explaining it to me—but I never used to *worry* about it.

M. E. Kerr uses titles as narrative hooks, for example, *If I Love You, Am I Trapped Forever?* and *Is That You, Miss Blue?* Asking questions like this has the effect of bringing the reader directly into the middle of a story where the action is at its peak. The initial questions trigger other questions in the readers' minds and make them want to read the books to find the answers. We have a similar reaction when an author begins the story at an exciting part and then through a flashback fills in the necessary background information. Paul Zindel did this in *The Pigman*. Few readers put the book down after they get acquainted with two likable teenagers and then read John's statement:

Now Lorraine can blame all the other things on me, but she was the one who picked out the Pigman's phone number. If you ask me, I think he would have died anyway. Maybe we speeded things up a little, but you really can't say we murdered him.

Not murdered him.

An exciting plot is generally essential in adventure stories, fantasy, science fiction, and mysteries, less important in biographies, memoirs, and romances. The most exciting plots are the ones in which the action is continually rising, building suspense, and finally leading to some sort of a climax. Usually the book does not end right at the climax. Instead there is a brief subsiding and wrapping up of the details, which is called the denouement. In contrast to plots with rising action are those that are episodic in nature, that is, made up of episodes, all more or less of equal interest. These books have a minimum of suspense since the questions are answered or resolved in each episode.

Bette Greene's first two books for young readers illustrate the difference between an episodic plot and one with rising action. In *Philip Hall Likes Me. I Reckon Maybe*, readers follow Beth through such experiences as picketing Mr. Puterham's store, going in and out of the vegetable-selling business, finding that she is allergic to dogs, and winning a calf-raising contest. Although the incidents are related, they do not necessarily build on each other nor is there any one point in the book at which the reader's excitement is at a peak because everything is coming together.

In contrast, *Summer of My German Soldier* builds to a definite climax and then winds up with a well-developed denouement. During World War II, Patty Bergen, a young Jewish girl living in rural Arkansas, secretly befriends an escaped German prisoner of war. Except for Ruth, the family maid, he is the first person to show any respect or affection for Patty. Patty helps him escape on the train and everything in the book leads up to the climax, when her role in the affair is discovered. Readers have known

The author lays down hints that prepare the reader for what is going to happen.

all along that Patty would be punished, but they did not know how. This is what is told in the denouement. Readers also learn how Patty's parents reacted, how the townspeople reacted, and how Ruth reacted and what effect all of this had on Patty. Greene manages to communicate all of this by showing a scene in the reformatory in which Ruth comes to visit Patty. In this scene, readers find out pretty much what they expected. The denouement is no place for surprises or for new twists to be added to the plot.

A skilled author presents an exciting and interesting plot but not actually a surprising one. The author lays down hints that prepare the reader for what is going to happen. The reader may have an initial reaction of surprise at what has happened, but, in looking back on the situation, he or she should have the feeling that whatever happened was appropriate to the characters and the situation and therefore has verisimilitude or believability. It has been said that every story should have one—but no more than one—coincidence or unlikely happening. The reasoning behind this statement is that without something unusual, there wouldn't be a story. But as soon as there are two unusual happenings, then it becomes too obvious that this is something that happened in an author's mind rather than in the real world. The reader can feel manipulated in a situation like this.

One of the ways that authors prepare their readers for what is ahead is to use foreshadowing. Sometimes this is done so subtly that it influences the readers' expectations almost subconsciously. For example, in Jean Renvoize's *A Wild Thing,* the first night after the girl Morag finds the injured climber, she goes to her cave and brings back embers so that she can build a fire and keep him warm throughout the night. Renvoize wrote:

> At last, satisfied with her arrangements, she pulled the duffle over her and lay down with her head close to his, so that they were like a pair of Siamese twins joined only at the skull, or a nutcracker opened up and hinged around the fire.

The similes that Renvoize uses are both of things permanently or intricately joined. The reader is prepared by this foreshadowing to expect a permanent or intricate relationship to develop between Morag and the boy.

It is no longer uncommon for young adult authors to leave their stories with open endings. Traditionally readers have expected to know all the answers by the end of the book and to have the plot come to a tidy close, but with some of the new stories authors feel that this is an unrealistic expectation and so they are leaving it up to the reader to imagine the ending. This is what Alice Childress did in *A Hero Ain't Nothin' But a Sandwich* because she didn't think it was fair to predict either that Benjie would become a confirmed drug addict or that he would go straight. Boys in his situation turn either way and Childress wanted readers to think about this. Although stories with open ended plots are sometimes frustrating to young readers, they are interesting to read and discuss as a group because they force readers to ponder the story and come to conclusions.

Another modern trend that is frustrating to some readers and critics is that as authors strive for realism, they are forgetting about plot. Instead of writing stories, some critics say, they are writing case histories. Such books often have to do with a young person's struggle with drug or alcohol addiction, mental illness, conflict with parents, sexual problems, or problems with the law. When an author has not planned an exciting plot, it seems that the temptation is greater to rely on unsavory details. These are the books that are often criticized for their sensationalism.

To have an interesting plot, a story must have a problem of some sort. In adult books, several problems may be treated simultaneously, but in most of the books written specifically for young adults, as well as in those that they respond to from adult lists, the focus is generally on one problem. However, authors may include a secondary or minor problem to appeal to specific readers. For example, in most of Paul Zindel's books, the primary problem is one of personal growth and development on the part of either one or two protagonists. But he tucks in an unobtrusive element of love that will bring satisfaction to romantically inclined readers without being bothersome to the rest of his audience.

Types of Plots

Basically the problems around which plots are developed are of four types: protagonist against self, protagonist against society, protagonist against another person, and protagonist against nature.

Self Against Self.   A large portion of the rites-of-passage stories popular with young adults are of the protagonist-against-self type. Through the happenings in the book, the protagonist comes to some new understanding or level of maturity. For example, in Robin Brancato's *Winning*, paralyzed Gary Madden's struggle is in his own mind. Can he cope with his limitations and make the decision to build a meaningful life? In the title story of Norma Fox Mazer's *Dear Bill, Remember Me?* the girl comes to an honest appraisal of the relationship that she had with her big sister's boyfriend, and in Isabelle Holland's *Of Love and Death and Other Journeys*, the protagonist takes a new look at the father she has never known and decides that she can fashion a life for herself while living with him and his wife in an environment that is totally different from anything she has known. At the same time, she has to adjust to her mother's death and to leaving the friends who had been important to both her and her mother.

Self Against Society.   Protagonist-against-self stories are often, in part, protagonist-against-society stories. For example, in Sylvia Plath's *The Bell Jar* Esther Greenwood is struggling to understand herself, but the depression and the fears and doubts that she feels are brought on by her experience in New York as a college intern on a fashion magazine. Getting accepted for this position has been an important goal of hers, and she is disappointed because, when she achieves this goal, she finds that the work and the life that go with it seem frivolous and hollow.

Sue Ellen Bridgers' *Home Before Dark* is another book in which the protagonist is struggling both against herself and against society. Fourteen-year-old Stella has lived most of the life she can remember in the old white station wagon which her family used for traveling from one crop to the next. When finally Stella's father returns to the family farm that he had abandoned years before, Stella does not want to leave—ever. She refuses to leave even after her mother dies and her father remarries. As she explains:

> None of us ever owned anything until we came back to Daddy's home and Newton gave us the little house. But, somehow, I felt like it had always been ours. That land out there belonged to us no matter what anyone said. Daddy was born to it, and I was born to Daddy; so the land and the house were mine. They truly belonged to me, and I belonged to them, like I had known the house and land long before and had somehow forgotten about them for a while.

Finally Stella accepts the little house and the farm as being only one part of her life. They will always be there and she can come back to them, but she must go from them too, unless she wants to be trapped at a standstill while the rest of her family moves forward.

Several books that feature characters from "disadvantaged" homes and neighborhoods are also combinations of the protagonist-against-self and protagonist-against-society patterns. In these, the individuals' self-concepts as well as the problems they face are directly related to the society around them as in Nicholasa Mohr's *Nilda,* Rosa Guy's *The Friends,* and Sharon Bell Mathis' *Teacup Full of Roses.* Chaim Potok's *My Name Is Asher Lev* and *The Chosen* show boys who are trying to reach understandings of themselves, but these understandings are greatly affected by the Hasidic Jewish societies in which the boys were born and raised.

Robert Cormier's *The Chocolate War, I Am the Cheese,* and *After the First Death* all come close to being pure examples of plots in which the protagonists are in conflict with society. In *The Chocolate War,* almost everyone in the school—faculty and students alike—go along with the evil plan to force Jerry to conform. In *I Am the Cheese,* Adam is left friendless and vulnerable in an institution as the result of organized crime combined with government corruption. And in *After the First Death,* one young boy is betrayed by his father who is a military psychologist, while another is kept by his father in a terrible state of innocence in which he is trained as a terrorist and never allowed to experience human feelings of compassion, love, or fear. But the blame for the tragic consequences cannot be laid on the fathers' shoulders because each of them is a victim in his own way of the society to which he belongs. In a similar way, it is not a single individual, but a whole interrelated system that causes the conflicts in both Glendon Swarthout's *Bless the Beasts and Children,* which is about cruelty to both animals and to young boys who don't quite fit the standard mold, and in Peter Maas' *Serpico,* which is about corruption on the New York City police force.

Self Against Another. Sometimes there is a combination in which the protagonist struggles with self, and also with another person or persons. For example, in Judith Guest's *Ordinary People,* Conrad is struggling to gain his mental health after he attempts suicide, but this struggle is intricately tied in with the sibling rivalry that he felt with his older brother who was accidentally killed. And the sibling rivalry is intricately tied in with the relationship that exists between him and his parents.

A better example of protagonist against another person is Richard Peck's *Are You in the House Alone?* A high school girl is harassed and finally raped by a classmate, but even here society enters into it because one of the points being made is that society lets the rapist go and punishes the victim.

Person-against-person plots are seen in several books about parent and child relationships. In the true story of *Richie* by Thomas Thompson, the father actually kills his drug-addicted son. In Barbara Wersba's *Run Softly, Go Fast,* it is the father who dies, though not because of anything the son does. However, the death causes the son to attempt to analyze why he had such feelings of animosity for the man he used to love.

Adventure stories are often of the person-against-person type. In George A.

Woods' *Catch a Killer*, a young boy is kidnapped by a psychotic killer, and the plot centers around the efforts of a detective to trace the pair and save the boy. David Morrell's *First Blood* is a violent account of what happens when the antagonisms of a Viet Nam veteran are pitted against the antagonisms of the small town sheriff whom he challenges.

Self Against Nature. Among the most exciting of the protagonist-against-nature stories are accounts of true adventures such as Piers Paul Read's *Alive: The Story of the Andes Survivors*, Thor Heyerdahl's *The "RA" Expeditions*, and Dougal Robertson's *Survive the Savage Sea*.

Within recent years, several authors have done a reverse twist on the person-against-nature plot and have made nature the protagonist and people the antagonists. This is the beginning situation in Richard Adams' *Watership Down* and throughout *The Plague Dogs*. It is also what underlies the story in John Donovan's *Family* and in Robert C. O'Brien's *Z for Zachariah*.

THEME

Closely related to plot is theme. Theme in a book is what ties it all together and answers the questions: What does the story mean? What is it about? Theme should not be confused with a didactic moral tagged on at the end of a story, nor should it be confused with plot. Instead it is something that pervades the story and stays with the reader long after details of plot, setting, and even character have faded. Linguistic scholars talk about the deep structure of a sentence as compared to its surface structure. The surface structure is the exact words that are used, whereas the deep structure is the underlying meaning. Dozens of different surface structures could communicate the same idea, a message of love, for example. Plot and theme are related in the same way. A plot relates to a single story, whereas a theme is applicable to hundreds of stories.

Sometimes an author will be very explicit in developing a theme, even expressing part of it in the title as did both John Knowles, *A Separate Peace*, and S. E. Hinton, *The Outsiders*. At other times the theme is almost hidden so that young readers need help in finding it through discussion of the book with others who have read it. A book can have more than one theme, but usually the secondary theme(s) will be less important to the story. However, because of the experiences that a reader brings to a book, it may be a secondary theme that happens to impress a particular reader. A theme must be discovered by the reader. It can't simply be told or else it is reduced to a moral.

The kinds of themes treated in stories are determined by the mode in which the stories are written. (We discuss mode later in this chapter.) For example, themes of alienation, despair, futility, and hopelessness are treated in tragic and ironic stories. More optimistic themes appear in comic and romantic modes. It's in these modes that love conquers all, people achieve success, family members support each other, and young protagonists reach significant milestones on their way to maturity.

CHARACTER

The popularity of many books that do not have exciting or even interesting plots is a testament to the power of good characterization. When, through a writer's skill, readers identify closely with the protagonist, they feel as if they are living the experience. They become more interested in what is going on in the character's mind than they may be in what is happening to the character from the outside. For example, in Margaret Craven's *I Heard the Owl Call My Name*, a young priest, unaware that he is terminally ill, is sent to live in a remote Indian village. His superior thinks that in the region's "hardest parish" the young priest will have a better chance of learning all that a man needs to know before he dies. The young priest succeeds, but it is hard to believe that a sick man could live such a rugged and physically active life for almost two years without medical attention and without realizing that he is desperately ill. But, because the character is so well developed and the story is so gently told, most readers are willing to overlook this aspect as well as the coincidence of his being killed by a falling tree just after he has come to accept his impending death and just before he begins to suffer physically from the disease.

Character Development and Types

Because of the shorter length of most adolescent books, the author does not have space to develop fully more than a small cast of characters. There is usually a protagonist, an antagonist, and various supporting characters. The protagonist is usually the central character, the one with whom the reader identifies. Most commonly, this will be a young adult, perhaps a bit older than the reader, but not always. After reading a book with a fully developed protagonist, readers should know the character so well

---

Readers cannot rejoice in the arrival of a character unless they know where the character started.

---

that if a situation outside of the book were described, they could predict how this character would feel and act in the new situation. The reason they would be able to do this is that the author has developed a round character. Many sides—many different aspects—of the character have been shown. A major character can undergo changes in personality in ways a minor character cannot. Such changes are often the heart of the story, but, unless the character is well developed, they have no meaning. Readers cannot rejoice in the arrival of a character unless they know where the character started.

In contrast, many characters in literature are flat or stereotyped. As books (not just books for teenagers but for all ages) have gotten shorter and shorter, the literary element most affected has been characterization. For the sake of efficiency, authors have begun to rely more heavily on character types than on unique individuals.

Of course this is not entirely new. Since the beginning of literature, there have been archetypes that appear again and again. Archetypal characters include the wise and helpful older person who befriends and teaches a young protagonist, the villain or enemy, and the wicked or unsympathetic parent or stepparent. Archetypes differ from stereotypes in that they are usually main characters in the story. Stereotyped characters will be in the background with very little attention given to their development. The absent-minded professor, the nagging mother, and the "jock" are stereotypes. The hero who leaves home on a danger-fraught mission and returns as a stronger and better person is an archetype seen in stories as divergent as the Biblical story of Joseph, the modern *Dove* by Robin Graham, and *Home Before Dark* by Sue Ellen Bridgers. It is because this particular archetype is a part of most readers' backgrounds that we can have a good feeling at the end of Robert C. O'Brien's *Z for Zachariah*. As Ann Burden leaves the "safety" of Hidden Valley and ventures out into the radioactive world, readers feel confident that she will safely complete her quest and find other people with whom she can live and build a new society.

A critic is probably making a negative comment in saying that an author's characters are stereotyped, but, in reality, the conventions of writing make it necessary that at least some characters in nearly every story be stereotyped. The word "stereotype" comes from the printer's world where it was used to mean the process by which an image is created over and over again. It would be too ponderous for an author to have to build a unique personality for every background character. And it would be too demanding for a reader to respond to a large number of fully developed characters.

The use of stock characters was always accepted as part of the art of storytelling, but in the late 1960s and 1970s, as people's social consciousness grew, so did their dislike for stereotyping. Minority groups complained that their members were stereotyped in menial roles, feminists complained that women and girls always took a back seat to men and boys, and parents complained that they were presented as unimportant or even damaging to their children's lives. Justified as these complaints were (or are), it doesn't mean that writers can get along without stereotyping. But what they can do is to make a conscious effort to include as main characters the people who once were stereotyped only in minor roles. When these characters are playing main roles, the author can then take the necessary space to delineate individual qualities.

When an author is very successful at developing the characters in a book, readers get the feeling that the characters are real. They identify with them as friends and find it hard to believe that these "friends" live only between the covers of a book. Because of this involvement, readers often write to authors and request more information. This, along with financial success, sometimes inspires authors to write one or more sequels about the same characters.

However, a sequel for some reason is rarely as good as the original. Bette Greene says she hates sequels and swore she would never write one even when she received hundreds of letters asking her to continue the story of Patty Bergen and Ruth from

Summer of My German Soldier. Even though she had no intention of doing a sequel, every time she sat down to write, she found herself writing about Patty and Ruth. She finally gave in and wrote *Morning Is a Long Time Coming,* which was published in 1978, five years after the original story.

It took Scott O'Dell much longer to do a sequel to his popular *Island of the Blue Dolphins,* which won the prestigious Newbery Award given by the American Library Association to the most distinguished children's book of the year. *Island of the Blue Dolphins,* which appeared in 1960, was based on the true story of Karana, a Native American girl left alone on an island off the coast of California for nearly twenty years in the 1800s. The story ended with her rescue and arrival at a California mission. Many readers wanted to know what happened to Karana, but the real story would not have made a very good sequel because Karana died within a few months of her rescue. Finally O'Dell came up with an idea. He focused on Zia, a distant relative of Karana's. In this way he could be faithful to the historical fact of Karana's death and yet have a character with whom readers could identify. *Zia* appeared in 1976, sixteen years after the original. In the first book Karana is the main character, but in the sequel she is a foil. Her role in the story is to illuminate the personality and the struggles of Zia, the new protagonist.

Sequels differ from trilogies or other preconceived sets in that they are usually not planned when the original book is written. When a set is preplanned, as with Susan Cooper's or Anne McCaffrey's, the author will have plotted out the whole series. These sets of books grow out of interesting plots, whereas sequels are more apt to develop from interesting characterization.

Communicating Character

Authors use various techniques to achieve characterization. For example, they tell us what the characters do, what they say, what others say about them, what they think, and how they feel. In developing minor characters, authors are more likely to rely on communicating the physical qualities of a person (or an animal) because these can be written about with relative ease. One stereotype that people have complained about, justifiably, is a wicked or villainous characterization achieved through an ugly or deformed appearance, for example, Long John Silver in Robert Louis Stevenson's *Treasure Island.* Critics have pointed out that such characterization extends people's inclination to think in terms of "the good and the beautiful" and "the bad and the ugly."

The way people speak, aside from what they say, can be very revealing. Sometimes authors will have certain characters speak with a dialect or will have them use "different" words as Richard Adams did with the rabbits in *Watership Down.* This sets them apart, shows that they are somewhat different from the reader and therefore of special interest.

The writers of ethnic books often use touches of dialectal speech to communicate something about the background of their characters. But, because of difficulties in spelling, printing, and reading, few writers will do a whole book in dialect. Instead they will give only a hint. Native American speech is most often shown through loan translations (English words used in place of Native American ones) as in this sentence from

When the Legends Die by Hal Borland: "The Ute people have lived many generations, many grandmothers, in that land."

Black dialects are shown through vocabulary and grammatical constructions that are peculiar to black English. Black speech may also be shown through what is called eye dialect. A writer gives nonstandard spelling to words to show the reader that a dialect is being spoken. Many such spellings are actually phonetically accurate representations of standard speech as much as of nonstandard speech. The use of black dialect in fiction has increased in recent years as a reflection of black pride. June Jordan, Brenda Wilkinson, Maya Angelou, and Alice Childress are among black writers who code shift between standard and dialectal English. For example, in Childress' *A Hero Ain't Nothin' But a Sandwich,* Benjie talks about his parents' asking him if he wants to "go to the show, too?":

> They always say "too," and when they say it, I'm thinkin that me as the one more would be one too many. I always say, "No, I got me a TV thing I wanta see." But, dig it, who wanta be the extra one goin along to eyeball some picture bout Black people bein poor? I dig movies where people got high-rise hotels and where they be international spies wearin they fine suits and hoppin big planes from one airport to nother . . .

One of the advantages of books over movies and plays is that an author can more easily get inside the characters' minds and tell what they are thinking in greater detail. This is much harder to do when almost everything has to be communicated through dialogue. Characters often think things that they would not say to another person. A literary technique that is sometimes used to get around this problem both in stories and plays is the dramatic monologue. In this, the author has the character speak out in a direct and forceful way revealing things about both the speaker and the situation. If it is done in the form of a soliloquy, the speaker seems to be unaware of the audience. It is a kind of interior monologue, also called stream-of-consciousness, in which the words are written down as if they were not prepared for an outside reader. Sometimes they tumble out as disjointed or random thoughts, but at other times they may make coherent sense. They give the reader the feeling of coming into the middle of something. The beginning of Robert Cormier's *I Am the Cheese* is a good example of this kind of monologue:

> I am riding the bicycle and I am on Route 31 in Monument, Massachusetts, on my way to Rutterburg, Vermont, and I'm pedaling furiously because this is an old-fashioned bike, no speeds, no fenders, only the warped tires and the brakes that don't always work and the handlebars with cracked rubber grips to steer with. A plain bike—the kind my father rode as a kid years ago. It's cold as I pedal along, the wind like a snake slithering up my sleeves and into my jacket and my pants legs, too. But I keep pedaling, I keep pedaling.

This monologue serves as a narrative hook. It draws the reader into the midst of an intriguing story. The monologues most often seen in young adult literature are first-person stories in which this technique allows protagonists to speak frankly about their most intimate feelings. In Judy Blume's *Are You There God? It's Me, Margaret* the monologues are in the form of nighttime prayers. In Norma Fox Mazer's *I, Trissy,* a girl is practicing typing; in S. E. Hinton's *The Outsiders,* Ponyboy is writing his term paper; and in Paul Zindel's *The Pigman,* Lorraine and John take turns writing what they call their "memorial epic" because:

> It's just that some very strange things have happened to us during the last few
> months, and we feel we should write them down while they're still fresh in
> our minds. It's got to be written now before John and I mature and repress the
> whole thing.

Having characters do their own speaking is a forceful means of characterization, but the technique of having the protagonist tell the story through letters or a diary has been used so much in recent years that it is becoming trite. A better and less self-conscious technique that is growing in popularity is simply to have the protagonist tell the story in the first person with no apologies.

POINT OF VIEW

Point of view is expressed largely through the person who tells the story. A story has to be told from a consistent viewpoint. The storyteller has to decide just how far from the characters to stand, from which direction to illuminate their actions with sympathy, and when and if it is time to speak from inside one of them. The viewpoint that gives the storyteller the most freedom is the one called omniscient or "all knowing." With this viewpoint it is as if the writer is present in all the characters, knowing what is inside their minds. This was the viewpoint that Hannah Green used when she wrote *I Never Promised You a Rose Garden.* It would hardly have been believable for the girl Deborah to tell the story since throughout most of the book she is psychotic. Yet it is necessary that the readers be told what she is thinking since the real story takes place in her mind. Also, by using the third person omniscient viewpoint, Green could share the thoughts of the other patients, Deborah's psychiatrist, and her parents.

A writer has much less freedom if he or she decides to enter into the mind and body of one of the characters and stay there, that is, to write the book in the first person. It takes real skill on the writer's part to tell the story without slipping in facts or attitudes that would be unknown to the character whose voice is being used. First person narrators can describe other characters in an objective manner; that is, they can tell about whatever can be seen from the outside, but they cannot tell what is going on inside the minds of the other characters. A skilled writer can communicate a great deal about someone through presenting objective information. For example, Bette Greene's *Summer of My German Soldier* is consistently told in first person through the eyes of twelve-year-old Patty Bergen. Yet readers come away knowing something about Anton the soldier, quite a bit about Patty's parents, and a great deal about Ruth, the family's maid.

Another example of a first person story is Deborah Hautzig's *Hey, Dollface*. In this story the author wanted readers to know that the protagonist's parents had a happy marriage. If she had been writing from the point of view of the omniscient author, she could have just said so, but, since this was not the case, she had to figure out a way for Valerie, the protagonist, to communicate this information. This is how she did it:

Halfway back to my room I stopped. I wonder if she's ever been jealous or worried when Dad was away, I thought. I went back into the kitchen.

"Mom?"

"What?"

"Were you ever jealous?"

"Of what?"

I smiled. "Never mind." I went back to my room thinking nobody would believe me if I told them what a nice marriage my parents have. I'd trust Dad too. He always said Mom was the most beautiful woman in the world, even in the morning when she looked pasty and her hair was frazzled. They'd either say I was repressed and defensive or they just wouldn't believe it. Oh, well; I'll never get jaded, I said to myself as I flopped down on my bed.

One way to get around the limitation of having a first person book come all from the same viewpoint is to have first person chapters coming alternately from different people. M. E. Kerr used this technique in *I'll Love You When You're More Like Me* and so did Alice Childress in *A Hero Ain't Nothin' But a Sandwich*.

An author may choose to tell a story from the viewpoint of one of the relatively minor characters. Richard Peck has explained that he chooses to do this because the interesting stories are at the extreme ends of the normal curve. The exciting things are happening to the brilliant and successful students such as those that Norma Klein wrote about in *Love Is One of the Choices* or that Ursula K. Le Guin wrote about in *Very Far Away from Anywhere Else*. Or they are happening to the kids at the other end of the scale as in Fran Arrick's *Steffie Can't Come Out to Play* and S. E. Hinton's *That Was Then, This Is Now*. Peck says that these extreme characters are wonderful to write about, but they aren't the ones who will read his books. They are too busy, too involved in their own lives. It's the large group of students in between these extremes whose lives really aren't full of such highs and lows who will be reading the books. Therefore, what Peck does is to choose for a narrator someone from the middle group with whom readers can identify. He then tells the story through this person's eyes. For example in *Don't Look and It Won't Hurt*, it is the fifteen-year-old sister who tells the story of the pregnant and unmarried Ellen who goes to Chicago to have her baby. And in *Representing Super Doll*, it is the beauty queen's friend Verna who relates the story and who, in an example of wish fulfillment, is shown to be the real winner.

TONE

The tone of a book is determined by the author's attitude toward his or her subject, characters, and readers. It is difficult to pick out the exact elements that contribute to the tone of a book because many times the author is not even aware of them. Some people think that the most distinctive thing about young adult literature is its tone. They say they can pick up two books treating protagonists of the same age who are faced with similar problems, and, by reading a few pages, can tell that one has been written for a general adult audience while the other has been written for teenagers. If an author were speaking directly to you, tone would simply be communicated through the lilt of the voice, the lifting of an eyebrow, a twinkle in the eye, or a crease in the forehead. But when tone has to be communicated exclusively through the written word, then it is more complex.

Sometimes language reminiscent of the King James version of the Bible is used to lend weight and dignity to a book as in the titles *All Creatures Great and Small* by James Herriot, *Manchild in the Promised Land* by Claude Brown, and *The Chosen* by Chaim Potok. Or a different tone is established through using archaic or old-fashioned language. In *A Wild Thing*, author Jean Renvoize has the girl use quaint expressions when she talks to the boy she brings to her cave. For example, when he is complaining about not knowing the time or the date she says to him, "Work it out then, if it fashes ye so much." *Fash* is a Scottish word meaning "vex," and it may seem more archaic to American than to British readers. Nevertheless its use along with *ye* rather than *you* has the effect of setting the girl apart as somehow different from "the girl next door."

Some people think that the most distinctive thing about young adult literature is its tone.

The tone in *A Wild Thing* contrasts sharply with the humorous and irreverent tone that appears in many of the popular new books. Americans have always been fond of exaggeration or hyperbole and its use is one way of establishing a light, humorous tone. When writers use hyperbole, readers know that what they say is not true, but they nevertheless enjoy the far-fetched overstatement. An all-time childhood favorite that many adults still remember is Wanda Gag's story about the old man who says, "Hundreds of cats, thousands of cats, millions, and billions, and trillions of cats." Paul Zindel's title *Pardon Me, You're Stepping on My Eyeball!* is a more subtle hyperbole. In effect, it is saying, "Pardon me, but I am getting hurt. Although you don't seem to notice, you are stepping on me—and not just on my toe either—but clear up to my sensitive eyeball!"

Another literary technique that authors rely on when they are establishing the tone they desire is euphemistic wording. Euphemisms are words or phrases carefully chosen to avoid harsh or unpleasant concepts. In general, modern writers think it better to speak directly than to make the vague kinds of circumlocutions that used to be fashionable in writing. But still there are euphemisms that have literary impact. For example, the title *I Heard the Owl Call My Name* is more intriguing than a bald statement such as, "I knew I was going to die." And Hemingway's title *For Whom the Bell*

Tolls is both more euphemistic and euphonious than the question, "Who has died?"

A semantic area more susceptible to euphemism in adolescent than in adult literature is that of sex. Authors are constantly looking for ways to communicate sexual information without setting up a tone that would arouse "prurient interests"—or censors. This is why it is likely that in adolescent literature you will read about such parts of the body as the "fork of the thighs" as in Renvoize's *A Wild Thing*, "my special place" as in Blume's *Deenie*, and the "posterior fornix" as in Peck's *Are You in the House Alone?*

Euphemisms can be created because there are so many ways to denote or communicate the same basic information, but each variation will have a different connotation. It will trigger a different emotional response in the reader. In establishing tone, a skilled writer will take advantage of the connotations of words, but, because connotations are somewhat vague and will probably be interpreted differently by different readers, the author may not always be in total control of the message that reaches the readers. For example, some, but not all, readers who see the titles of R. R. Knudson's books: *Zanballer, Zanbanger, Zanboomer,* and *Fox Running* will think that sexual connotations were intended. Perhaps they were, but the books do not fulfill the promise as many readers would interpret it.

For certain kinds of books a reverent tone is appropriate, as, for example, a memoir about someone who has died. They are usually written in a loving tone by someone who was close to the person who died and who wants to pay tribute to or honor the person's memory. John Gunther's *Death Be Not Proud: A Memoir* telling about Gunther's teenage son's struggle against a fatal brain tumor has remained popular for three decades. Doris Lund's *Eric*, which tells about her seventeen-year-old son's four-year battle with leukemia, is, like Gunther's book, a sad but inspiring memoir. For memoirs to be successful the tone cannot be so worshipful that it becomes too sentimental.

Another pitfall that young adult authors must try to avoid is an overly didactic tone. Certainly it is the goal—conscious or unconscious—of most adults to teach worthwhile values to young people. Nevertheless, in literary criticism, calling a work "didactic" usually implies that the author has failed to establish an acceptable tone. The story seems to be created around a message instead of having a message or a theme grow naturally out of the story. Isabelle Holland's book *Hitchhike* was criticized as being overly preachy or didactic, for it appeared that the main reason she wrote the book was to warn girls against hitchhiking. Gertrude Samuels' book *Run, Shelley, Run!* appears to have been written for the didactic purpose of bringing the plight of homeless girls to the public's attention, and Jeannette Eyerly's *Bonnie Jo, Go Home* preaches a message about the unfairness of abortion laws in the 1960s.

Great literature always leaves the reader with something to think about. Lessons are taught, but they are subtle lessons, and the reader is left with the responsibility of analyzing what the writer has presented and of coming to a conclusion. *Lord of the Flies* is a book from which people learn a great deal, but it is not usually considered a didactic book because the author, William Golding, does not spell out the lesson for the reader. We might contrast Golding's nondidactic tone with the didactic message that appears in an introduction written by E. M. Forster to a 1962 edition of the same book:

> It is certainly not a comforting book. But it may help a few grownups to be less complacent and more compassionate, to support Ralph, respect Piggy, control Jack, and lighten a little the darkness of man's heart. At the present moment (if I may speak personally) it is respect for Piggy that seems needed most. I do not find it in our leaders.

Forster's comments could also be described as *editorializing*. Notice how he asked permission to express his personal opinion. Sometimes authors will editorialize, or give their own opinions, through the voice of a character as Susan Hinton did in *The Outsiders* when Ponyboy explains why he wrote his story:

> I could see boys going down under street lights because they were mean and tough and hated the world, and it was too late to tell them that there was still good in it, and they wouldn't believe you if you did. It was too vast a problem to be just a personal thing. There should be some help. Someone should tell their side of the story, and maybe people would understand then and wouldn't be so quick to judge a boy by the amount of hair oil he wore.

In reality, it is probably not so much that we dislike didactic tone as it is that we dislike that tone when the message is something with which we do not agree. If the message is reaffirming one of our beliefs, then we identify with it and enjoy the feeling that other people are going to be convinced of the "truth." It is partly because it was their message that teenagers responded so warmly to Hinton's book.

A nostalgic tone is a potential problem in much young adult literature. Nearly all books with teenage protagonists are of potential interest to young adult readers. But one of the things that keeps some of them from reaching a large young adult audience is that the authors have looked back at their own adolescence and have romanticized it. They are nostalgic about the good old days. But to a sixteen-year-old, "sweet sixteen" is nothing about which to be nostalgic. The tone comes through as condescension, which is unappealing to readers of any age.

SETTING

Setting—the context of time and place—is more important in some genres than in others. For example, it is often the setting, a time in the future or the far past or some place where people now living on this earth have never actually been, that lets readers know they are embarking on reading a fantasy. The special quality in J. R. R. Tolkien's *The Lord of the Rings* would not be possible were it not set in the mythical world of Middle Earth. Nor would many of the most popular pieces of science fiction be possible without their outer space or futuristic settings.

Historical fiction is another genre in which the setting is important to the story. *Summer of My German Soldier* could not have happened at any time other than during World War II. Without the war, there would not have been German prisoners in this country, nor would there have been the peculiar combination of public and private hysteria that worked on Patty Bergen's southern Christian community and her Jewish family. All of this makes it easy to think of *Summer of My German Soldier* as a historical novel. In contrast, Maureen Daly's *Seventeenth Summer* was set in approximately the same time period, but the crux of the story does not center around the war. It centers around a young girl's feelings toward the adult role that she is growing into and toward her first experience with love. Many girls who read *Seventeenth Summer* come away with the feeling that they are reading a slightly old-fashioned, but contemporary, novel.

In this book, we have rather arbitrarily chosen to label any book that is set during or prior to World War II as historical fiction. Often-read books whose settings make them fall clearly into the category of historical fiction are Jack Schaefer's *Shane*, Mark Twain's *The Adventures of Huckleberry Finn*, and Fred Gipson's *Old Yeller*. Of recent pieces of popular young adult fiction, the best example of how a story is controlled by its historical setting is probably Robert Newton Peck's *A Day No Pigs Would Die*. It is a family story set in the 1920s in a rural Vermont community of Shakers.

Kinds of Settings

There are basically two kinds of settings in stories; one is integral and the other is backdrop. When the setting is a part of the plot, then obviously it is integral as in the historical novels and fantasies mentioned earlier. It is also integral in any story—whether fictional or true—in which the plot or problem is person against nature. In stories of mountain climbing, survival, exploring, and other sorts of adventuring, the setting is actually the antagonist. It is interesting in and of itself just as a character would be.

Another kind of story in which the setting is integral is the regional story. For example, after reading James Michener's *Hawaii*, we want to visit Hawaii, or, if we live there, we want to learn more about it, and after reading *Caravans*, we have a new interest in Afghanistan. This is similar to the way we develop feelings for particular characters and want to get to know them better in a sequel or in a movie taken from the book. In some degree, nearly all realistic fiction is regional since the setting influences the story, but the term is usually applied to stories where the setting plays an unusually important part. For example Hal Borland's *When the Legends Die* and Frank Herbert's *Soul Catcher* are both regional stories about young Native American men whose searches for their own identities cannot be separated from the regions in which they grew up. Vera and Bill Cleaver also write regional stories including *Where the Lilies Bloom*, which is set in backwoods Appalachia, and *Dust of the Earth*, which is set in the Dakotas during the depression.

Traditionally most regional stories have had rural settings in which the protagonists are close to nature, but as the United States has changed to an urban society and realism has become more fashionable, cities also appear as important background settings as in Nicholasa Mohr's *El Bronx Remembered* and *In Nuevo York*. These are both collections of short stories that are held together by their common setting. Mohr communicates the Puerto Rican background of her stories through the touch of Spanish in the titles.

In contrast to stories with integral settings are those with backdrop settings. Stories of this type are set in a small town, an inner-city neighborhood, a modern suburb, or a high school. When authors establish this kind of setting, they are not particularly anxious to make it so clear-cut that it would be identifiable as only one particular place. They want to give enough details so that it comes alive, but to leave it vague enough that readers can imagine the story happening, for example, in their own town or at least in one they know.

The most common backdrop setting in young adult literature is that of a high school. Since school is the business—the everyday life—of teenagers, many of the books relate to school just as many adult books somehow relate to jobs and work. However, there is a difference in that adult jobs are extremely varied, but schools are pretty much the same. There may be boarding schools, exclusive day schools, military schools, and religious schools, as well as the "typical" public high school, but a school is still a school with its stairways, restrooms, lockers, cafeteria, classrooms, and parking lot. There are only so many ways to describe such places, which is one of the things that gives a sameness to books for this age group.

How Setting Works

But even in school-related stories in which the setting is pretty much a matter of backdrop, it is more important than many readers realize. Because of the length restrictions in books for this age group, setting is usually established quickly and efficiently. It continues to be developed throughout the story and to affect readers' reactions. A good example is Lois Duncan's *Killing Mr. Griffin*, which is about a group of high-school students who want to get even with a demanding teacher who has publicly humiliated them. They kidnap him, planning only to frighten and humble him, but he has a heart condition and dies.

The first line of the book establishes both the setting and the seriousness of the matter: "It was a wild, windy, southwestern spring when the idea of killing Mr. Griffin occurred to them." From here, Duncan goes on to describe the protagonist's walk across a playing field to the school building:

> Susan McConnell leaned into the wind and cupped her hands around the
> edges of her glasses to keep the blowing red dust from filling her eyes.
> Tumbleweeds swept past her like small, furry animals, rushing to pile in drifts
> against the fence that separated the field from the parking lot. The parked cars
> all had their windows up as though against a rainstorm. In the distance the
> rugged Sandia Mountains rose in faint outline, almost obscured by the pinkish
> haze.
>
> I hate spring, Susan told herself vehemently. I hate dust and wind. I wish
> we lived somewhere else. Someday—
> It was a word she used often—*someday*.

In less than half a page setting has already served three purposes. First, it has established a troubled mood; second, it has given basic information about where and who is going to be in the story; and, third, it has revealed something about the character of the protagonist. It has let readers know that she is dissatisfied with her life and will therefore be vulnerable to suggestions or opportunities to bring about changes.

Later in the book, setting serves other important purposes. We are shown Mr. Griffin at home offering to make breakfast for his pregnant wife and we see a different side of his personality so that we can feel truly sorry about his death. It would have been less credible if Duncan had tried to show us this different side of Mr. Griffin in the school setting where his students also could have seen it. By showing different characters in different settings, authors are able to reveal things to readers in such a way that the readers get the feeling of being in control of the situation because they know more than some of the characters do.

Settings can also act as symbols. They can provide a visible way to describe feelings that are very real even though they cannot be seen. For example, while the other boys are burying Mr. Griffin, David walks back to the two cars:

> He started first for Jeff's car and then, on impulse, opened instead the door of the Chevrolet and climbed in behind the steering wheel. In times past he had sometimes amused himself by contemplating how cars often seemed extensions of the people who owned them. There was Jeff's car, large and loud and flashy, and David's mother's, compact, economical and serviceable. Betsy's mother's Volkswagen was small and fitful, a nervous little automobile, painted bright yellow.
>
> Now, in Brian Griffin's car, he closed his eyes and tried to feel the presence of the man who had driven it, hoping for one last image of warmth and life. It did not come. The car was as cold and devoid of personality as the thing in the grave by the waterfall.

Mr. Griffin's car brings home to David the fact that Mr. Griffin is indeed dead. Sitting in the car he offers a prayer which is half a defense of himself and half a prayer for forgiveness, but hardly a blessing on the grave or the man whose body lies in it.

Even when the setting is a backdrop through most of the book, there may be places where it becomes integral as a part of the plot. This happens in Duncan's book in relation to the secret waterfall up in the mountains. One of the boys had found it with his former girlfriend. They were the only ones who ever went there so it seems an excellent place to take Mr. Griffin, and, when he dies, it also seems to be an excellent place to bury him. But the former girlfriend also remembers the place and just happens to go on a spring picnic with her new boyfriend. The two of them discover the evidence that leads the police to Mr. Griffin's body.

A setting does not really have to exist to play a part in a story. It might be just a dream of one of the characters, as when David and Sue imagine getting out of the whole problem by driving straight west to California and taking a ship to an uninhabited island. At one point, Sue confides that she has always had a dream of living by herself in a forest cabin by a peaceful lake instead of in a noisy, family household located in a dry and windy desert.

Setting may also serve as foreshadowing. For example, the night that everything comes to a climax (which incidentally is a bit overdone and melodramatic for our tastes), readers are prepared for something awful by the description of the weather:

> The wind began in the early afternoon. It rose slowly at first, but increased steadily. . . . The Sunday twilight was muted and pink, as the sun's last rays slanted through the thick, red air, and when dark came the wind did not drop but seemed to grow stronger, whining around the corners of houses and stripping the first new leaf buds from trees.

Being able to establish settings so that they accomplish multiple purposes is one of the most important skills a writer can develop. Successful writers use settings not only as parts of plot, but also to make the story live for readers, to help them visualize exactly what is happening, to illuminate character, to symbolize important feelings, and to establish moods.

STYLE

Style is the way a story is written as contrasted to what the story is about. It is the result or effect of combining the literary aspects we have already talked about.

An Individual Matter

No two authors have exactly the same style because with writing, just as with appearance, behavior, and personal belongings, style consists of the unique blending of all the choices each individual makes. From situation to situation, these choices may differ, but they are enough alike that the styles of particular authors such as Kurt Vonnegut, Jr., Richard Brautigan, and E. L. Doctorow will be recognizable from book to book. But style is also influenced by the nature of the story being told. For example, Ursula K. Le Guin used a different style when she wrote the realistic *Very Far Away from Anywhere Else* from the one she used when she wrote her science fiction *A Wizard of Earthsea*. Nevertheless, in both books she relied on the particular writing techniques that she likes and is skilled at using.

Authors' styles are influenced by such factors as their intended audience and their purpose in writing. For example, a nonfiction informative book will have a different style from that of an informative book that is written to persuade readers to a belief or an action. And, even after an author has made the decision to write a persuasive book, the style will be affected by whether the author chooses to persuade through humor, through a dramatic fictional account, or through a logical display of evidence.

The fact that the protagonists are young in most books for this age group also influences style. Probably the book that has had the greatest influence on writing style is J. D. Salinger's *The Catcher in the Rye.* Nearly every year, promotional materials or reviews compare five or six new young adult books to *Catcher.* Some of these comparisons are made on the basis of the subject matter, but the theme of a boy wavering between the innocence of childhood and the acceptance of the adult world—imperfect as it is—is not all that unusual. It is the style of the writing that makes Salinger's book so memorable, indeed such a milestone, and has inspired other authors to imitate the colloquial speech, the candid revelations of feelings, the short snappy dialogues, the instant judgments, and the emotional extremes ranging from hostility to great tenderness.

One of the most memorable scenes in the book is the one in which the young prostitute comes to Holden's hotel room, and he is so touched by her youth and innocence that he gives up the whole idea:

> She was very nervous, for a prostitute. She really was. I think it was because she was young as hell. She was around my age. I sat down in the big chair, next to her, and offered her a cigarette. "I don't smoke," she said. She had a tiny little wheeny-whiny voice. You could hardly hear her. She never said thank you, either, when you offered her something. She just didn't know any better.
> "Allow me to introduce myself. My name is Jim Steele," I said.
> "Ya got a watch on ya?" she said. She didn't care what the hell my name was, naturally. "Hey how old are you, anyways?"
> "Me? Twenty-two."
> "Like fun you are."
> It was a funny thing to say. It sounded like a real kid. You'd think a prostitute and all would say, "Like hell you are" or "Cut the crap" instead of "Like fun you are."

As the girl gets ready to leave, Holden observes that, "If she'd been a big old prostitute, with a lot of makeup on her face and all, she wouldn't have been half as spooky."

It is possible to describe the literary devices that are the basic ingredients of an author's style. But there is more to literary style than these various devices. Before a writer can be said to have a distinctive style, something has to click so that the devices blend together into a unified whole.

Figurative Language

Much of what determines a writer's style is how he or she uses figurative language. This is language that is interesting and important above and beyond the literal information it communicates. Writers use figurative language to set a mood, to surprise the reader, to create imagery, to make a passage memorable, and sometimes to show off their skill. Words used figuratively have different, or at least additional, meanings from those they have in standard usage. One type of figurative language—metaphors, symbols, allegories, and similes—stimulates the reader's mind to make comparisons. A second type appeals to the sense of sight or hearing. Examples include alliteration, assonance, rhyme, euphony, rhythm, and cadence. In the following sentence from Harold Brodkey's story, "Sentimental Education," both kinds of figurative language occur:

> Dimitri had a car, which Elgin borrowed—an old, weak-lunged Ford—and they could wheeze up to Marblehead and rent a dinghy and be blown around the bay, with the sunlight bright on Caroline's hair and the salt air making them hungry and the wind whipping up small whitecaps to make the day exciting.

The metaphor of the "weak-lunged Ford" that "wheezes" up to Marblehead helps the reader visualize the old car while the alliteration in "be blown around the bay" and "wind whipping up small whitecaps" and the rhyme in "sunlight bright" and "Caroline's hair and the salt air" affect the reader more subtly in establishing mood. The word "wheeze" is also an example of the figurative language device of onomatopoeia in which the sound of a word gives a hint of its meaning.

Metaphors are among the most common kinds of figurative language. In a metaphor basically dissimilar things are likened to another so that the reader gets a new insight. A fresh metaphor can be an effective device for making the reader an active instead of a passive participant. The reader has to become mentally involved in order to make associations that he or she has not thought of before. A metaphor can be very

---

A fresh metaphor can make the reader an active instead of a passive participant.

---

simple, consisting of only a word or two, as when, in *The Pigman*, John refers to "these two amoebae called Dennis Kobin and Norton Kelly," or it can be more involved as when in *Ordinary People*, Conrad is thinking ahead to studying with Jeannine and, ". . . it makes his skin ripple pleasantly, his stomach pull. A feeling you get going up in an elevator. *Shouldn't plan ahead like this shouldn't expect minutes hours and the elevator comes down you could hit the ground but what a trip.*" (Italics, the author's.)

A simile is a metaphor or comparison marked by such words as *like* and *as*. In *A Wild Thing* Jean Renvoize wrote, "Even the most important decision of her life, to run away, had been formed slowly and without real thought, as a stalagmite forms drop by drop into a cone," and, in *I Know Why the Caged Bird Sings*, Maya Angelou wrote, "The giggles hung in the air like melting clouds that were waiting to rain on me."

An allegory is an extended comparison or metaphor. It can be enjoyed on at least two levels. One is the literal or surface level on which the story is enjoyed simply for itself. On the second or deeper level, we can interpret and extend the meaning of the story, and it thereby becomes more interesting. It is in part the challenge of interpreting the allegory in William Golding's *Lord of the Flies* that makes it a good piece to read and discuss in a group.

An allegorical device that authors sometimes use is giving their characters symbolic names as Robert C. O'Brien did in *Z for Zachariah*. The title is taken from a Bible *ABC* book in which the first letter of the alphabet stands for Adam and the last for Zachariah. The symbolism suggests that if Adam was the first man on earth, Zachariah must be the last. The character's actual name is Mr. Loomis, which in the reader's mind may or may not be interpreted as a symbol of the fact that the book starts with his presence "looming" on the horizon. The girl in the book who carries a tremendous responsibility and at the end is left with the task of rebuilding a civilization is symbolically named Ann Burden. These names may influence readers' attitudes and enhance their pleasure without their being aware of it.

Allusions work in the same way. They are an efficient way to communicate a great deal of information because one reference in a word or a phrase triggers the readers' minds to think of the whole story or idea behind the allusion. Robert Cormier's title *I Am the Cheese* is an allusion to the old nursery song and game, "The Farmer in the Dell." Besides being efficient, allusions, like metaphors, are effective in forcing readers to become actively involved in making connections. A lazy or uninterested reader might not see any allusion in Cormier's title. Someone else, especially when discovering that the family's name is Farmer, would connect the title to the nursery rhyme and perhaps think of the last line, "And the cheese stands alone!" An even more thoughtful reader might carry it back one more step and think of the next to last line, "The rat takes the cheese." It is this last type of reader who may discover the most in Cormier's writing.

Personification and animalization refer to the attribution of human or animal qualities to inanimate objects. Robert Lipsyte's title *One Fat Summer* is an example. People and animals grow fat; summers do not. As with this example, it is often impossible to know whether the author was thinking of an animal or a person. In *The Pigman*, when John is talking about Mr. Pignati's death, he makes one reference that could be either to an animal or to a human, and then one that is clearly to a human. About the ambulance he says, "You could see the flashing dome going like crazy, pulsing like a heartbeat." And later when he is trying to analyze the whole situation, he says that it wasn't just Mr. Pignati who died, "Something in us had died as well. . . . And there was no place to hide—no place across any river for a boatman to take us." This latter example is an allusion to Greek mythology in which death is personified as a boatman taking people across the river Styx.

Although in literature symbols are communicated through words, they are more than words, which is why their meanings cannot be looked up in dictionaries. Also they are more complex than metaphors. For example, the semantic feature or meaning common to the word *thunder* and the metaphorical phrase *thunderous applause* is that of a big noise. But in Mildred Taylor's title *Roll of Thunder, Hear My Cry* there is no such simple explanation. The idea of noise is still there, but added to it is the idea of size and relativity. It is the power of all nature contrasted to the smallness of one human voice. Additionally, there's the negativeness, the ominous feeling that is communicated through the mention of a storm and the word *cry* which has a negative or at least a serious connotation as compared, for example, with *shout* or *yell*. Yet, in spite of this, the title has an optimistic ring to it, probably because the reader intuitively recognizes the strength of the voice behind the *my*. Weak characters hide under the bedcovers during a thunderstorm. Only the strong stand in the storm and yell back.

Symbolism can be a good subject for discussion with other readers because we all pick up different bits and pieces. What one reader will miss, another might find. It is almost like hunting for clues in a game. When all the clues are filled in, the total picture is much more meaningful than the separate pieces.

MODE

One way of discussing mode is in relation to the four story patterns that Northrop Frye has described: romance, tragedy, irony/satire, and comedy. Together these make up the story of everyone's life, and in literature as in life they are interrelated, flowing one into the other.

Many of M. E. Kerr's books are written predominantly in the romantic mode: the protagonist ends up a wiser, more experienced person with new understanding. In *Dinky Hocker Shoots Smack,* the romance is combined with a satirical treatment of the do-gooder, represented by Dinky's mother. She is so concerned with helping dope addicts that she fails to see that poor overweight Dinky needs some attention too. But the book ends optimistically with the reader feeling that Dinky's mother has come to a new insight.

If the book had ended with little or no hope for change, it would have been closer to irony, which is the mode of many of the books treated in Chapter 6, "The New Realism." Irony differs from tragedy in that it may be less intense, and, instead of having heroic qualities, the protagonist is an ordinary person, much like the reader. Ironic stories are basically negative. There is confusion, suffering, and injustice. The anonymous *Go Ask Alice,* John Donovan's *Wild in the World,* and Jean Renvoize's *A Wild Thing* are written in the ironic mode. The protagonists are helpless to change the forces of the world that gather against them.

Some critics would argue that these books are tragedies rather than ironies. Depending on one's definition of a hero, they may well be. Traditional literary tragedies have three distinct elements. First, there is a noble character who, no matter what happens, maintains the qualities that the society considers praiseworthy. Second, there is an inevitable force that works against the character, and, third, there is a struggle and an outcome. Robert Cormier's *I Am the Cheese* is a modern tragedy. The boy being interrogated throughout the book is the tragic hero. The inevitable force is corruption and government duplicity. And the outcome—in which the best that the boy can hope for is to live his life in a drugged and incoherent state—is indeed a tragedy. Yet the reader is left with some satisfaction and pride because there is a resiliency in the boy that keeps him, even when he is drugged, from totally surrendering to his highly skilled interrogators.

Another tradition sometimes considered essential in tragedy holds that the hero—worthy and admirable as he or she may be—has nevertheless contributed to the unfolding of the terrible events through some tragic flaw of character. With Cormier's book, the reader has the nagging feeling that maybe if the boy had not been so bright and so inquisitive (which were the characteristics that first brought trouble to his father) and had not found out his family's history, then maybe life could have gone on as before and Mr. Grey wouldn't have bothered with him. But at the same time, it is this brightness and persistence that keeps him from surrendering at the end.

The reader of a tragedy is usually filled with pity and fear—pity for the hero and fear for oneself that the same thing might happen. The intensity of this involvement causes the reader to undergo an emotional release as the outcome of the story unfolds. This release is known as catharsis and it has the effect of draining away dangerous human emotions, and it also fills the reader with a sense of exaltation or amazed pride in what the human spirit is called upon to undergo.[2]

Sheila Burnford's *Bel Ria* fits the definition of the comic mode in that it moves from ironic chaos to a renewal of human hope and spirit. It begins in the midst of war and death when a soldier and a small dog are brought together as the result of senseless killing. But as the story progresses, peace returns to both the human and animal characters and to the world. In the end, although the little dog dies, it is after a long, useful, and rewarding life. There is irony in the dog's death because it occurs just when its three masters are brought together, but it is almost as if the dog dies from happiness. The renewal and hope for the future is symbolized in the marriage of one of the masters and in the birth of the new baby.

The kind of information presented in this chapter is important and interesting for three reasons. First, it will help you to get more out of the reading you do throughout this course. Second, when you enjoy the books you read in this way and when you sharpen your insights into the authors' working methods, then you will be in a good position to share your insights with those young readers who are ready for them. You will also be better able to evaluate new books and to help young readers move along in developing their own abilities to evaluate and to receive pleasure at higher levels of reading appreciation. A third advantage to understanding literary terms and concepts is that they provide you with a handle for discussion. Without appropriate terminology, it will be very hard for you to carry discussions beyond the "I-like-it" and "I-don't-like-it" stage. It is much easier to appreciate and to understand what an author has done when you are acquainted with the technique and can give it a name. Knowing and using literary terms correctly will enable you to get maximum benefits from book discussions with both students and colleagues. It will also help you to read reviews and articles in magazines, journals, and other books with greater appreciation.

ACTIVITIES

1. Write your own reading autobiography. Tell about your first memories of receiving pleasure from books. Do you remember the first book you really liked? If so, what was it? When you started to choose books for yourself, did you read series books? How about books of a particular type, such as sports stories, horse stories,

or dog stories? What about informative books? Did you have one or more influential adults who encouraged you? If so, what did they do? Finally, analyze how your own stages of reading development measure up with those described by Margaret Early.

2. Read another book from the Honor Sampling. Write a one or two sentence description of each of the following: plot, theme, character, point of view, tone, setting, style, and mode.

3. Choose one of the young adult books you have read and take an in-depth look at the author's style. What makes it distinctive? Is it the dialogue? The descriptions? The figurative language? The tone? Or something else? Cite specific examples to support your generalizations.

NOTES

[1]Margaret Early, "Stages of Growth in Literary Appreciation," *English Journal* 49 (March 1960): 163–66.

[2]Glenna Davis Sloan, *The Child as Critic* (New York: Teachers College Press, 1975), pp. 19–21.

TITLES MENTIONED IN CHAPTER TWO

For information on the availability of paperback editions of these titles, please consult the most recent edition of *Paperbound Books in Print,* published annually by R. R. Bowker Company.

Adams, Richard. *The Plague Dogs.* Alfred A. Knopf, 1978.

———. *Watership Down.* Macmillan, 1975.

Alcott, Louisa May. *Little Women: Meg, Jo, Beth, and Amy. The Story of Their Lives. A Girl's Book.* Lee and Shepard, 1868.

Angelou, Maya. *I Know Why the Caged Bird Sings.* Random House, 1970.

Arrick, Fran. *Steffie Can't Come Out to Play.* Bradbury, 1978.

Blume, Judy. *Are You There God? It's Me, Margaret.* Bradbury, 1970.

———. *Deenie.* Bradbury, 1973.

Borland, Hal G. *When the Legends Die.* J. B. Lippincott, 1963.

Bridgers, Sue Ellen. *Home Before Dark.* Alfred A. Knopf, 1976.

Brown, Claude. *Manchild in the Promised Land.* Macmillan, 1965.

Burnford, Sheila. *Bel Ria.* Little, Brown, 1978.

Childress, Alice. *A Hero Ain't Nothin' But a Sandwich.* Coward, McCann, & Geoghegan, 1973.

Cleaver, Vera and Bill. *Dust of the Earth.* J. B. Lippincott, 1975.

————. *Where the Lilies Bloom.* J. B. Lippincott, 1969.

Cormier, Robert. *After the First Death.* Pantheon Books, 1979.

————. *The Chocolate War.* Pantheon Books, 1974.

————. *I Am the Cheese.* Pantheon Books, 1977.

Craven, Margaret. *I Heard the Owl Call My Name.* Doubleday, 1973.

Daly, Maureen. *Seventeenth Summer.* Dodd, Mead, 1942.

Donovan, John. *Family.* Harper & Row, 1976.

————. *Wild in the World.* Harper & Row, 1971.

Duncan, Lois. *Killing Mr. Griffin.* Little, Brown, 1978.

Eyerly, Jeannette. *Bonnie Jo, Go Home.* J. B. Lippincott, 1972.

Gipson, Fred. *Old Yeller.* Harper & Row, 1964.

Go Ask Alice. Prentice-Hall, 1971.

Golding, William. *Lord of the Flies.* G. P. Putnam's Sons, 1959.

Graham, Robin L. and Derek L. T. Gill. *Dove.* Harper & Row, 1972.

Green, Hannah. *I Never Promised You a Rose Garden.* Holt, Rinehart & Winston, 1964.

Greene, Bette. *Morning Is a Long Time Coming.* Dial, 1978.

————. *Philip Hall Likes Me. I Reckon Maybe.* Dial, 1974.

————. *Summer of My German Soldier.* Dial, 1973.

Guest, Judith. *Ordinary People.* Viking, 1976.

Gunther, John. *Death Be Not Proud: A Memoir.* Modern Library, 1953.

Guy, Rosa. *The Friends.* Holt, Rinehart & Winston, 1973.

Hautzig, Deborah. *Hey, Dollface.* William Morrow, 1978.

Hemingway, Ernest. *For Whom the Bell Tolls.* Charles Scribner's Sons, 1940.

————. *The Old Man and the Sea.* Charles Scribner's Sons, 1961.

Herbert, Frank. *Soul Catcher.* G. P. Putnam's Sons, 1972.

Herriot, James. *All Creatures Great and Small.* St. Martin's, 1972.

Heyerdahl, Thor. *The RA Expeditions.* Doubleday, 1971.

Hinton, S. E. *The Outsiders.* Viking, 1967.

————. *That Was Then, This Is Now.* Viking, 1971.

Holland, Isabelle. *Hitchhike.* J. B. Lippincott, 1977.

————. *Of Love and Death and Other Journeys.* J. B. Lippincott, 1975.

Kerr, M. E. *Dinky Hocker Shoots Smack.* Harper & Row, 1972.

————. *If I Love You, Am I Trapped Forever?* Harper & Row, 1973.

————. *I'll Love You When You're More Like Me.* Harper & Row, 1977.

————. *Is That You, Miss Blue?* Harper & Row, 1975.

Klein, Norma. *Love Is One of the Choices.* Dial, 1979.

Knowles, John. *A Separate Peace.* Macmillan, 1960.

Knudson, R. R. *Fox Running.* Harper & Row, 1975.

———. *Zanballer.* Delacorte, 1972.

———. *Zanbanger.* Harper & Row, 1977.

———. *Zanboomer.* Harper & Row, 1978.

Le Guin, Ursula K. *Very Far Away from Anywhere Else.* Atheneum, 1976.

———. *A Wizard of Earthsea.* Parnassus, 1968.

Lipsyte, Robert. *One Fat Summer.* Harper & Row, 1977.

Lund, Doris. *Eric.* J. B. Lippincott, 1974.

Maas, Peter. *Serpico.* Viking, 1973.

Mathis, Sharon Bell. *Teacup Full of Roses.* Viking, 1972.

Mazer, Norma Fox. *Dear Bill, Remember Me?* Delacorte, 1976.

———. *I, Trissy.* Delacorte, 1971.

Michener, James A. *Caravans.* Random House, 1963.

———. *Hawaii.* Random House, 1959.

Mohr, Nicholasa. *El Bronx Remembered.* Harper & Row, 1975.

———. *In Nueva York.* Dial, 1977.

———. *Nilda.* Harper & Row, 1973.

Morrell, David. *First Blood.* M. Evans, 1972.

O'Brien, Robert C. *Z for Zachariah.* Atheneum, 1975.

O'Dell, Scott. *Island of the Blue Dolphins.* Houghton Mifflin, 1960.

———. *Zia.* Houghton Mifflin, 1976.

Peck, Richard. *Are You in the House Alone?* Viking, 1976.

———. *Don't Look and It Won't Hurt.* Holt, Rinehart & Winston, 1972.

———. *Representing Super Doll.* Viking, 1974.

Peck, Robert Newton. *A Day No Pigs Would Die.* Alfred A. Knopf, 1972.

Plath, Sylvia. *The Bell Jar.* Harper & Row, 1971.

Potok, Chaim. *The Chosen.* Simon & Schuster, 1967.

———. *My Name Is Asher Lev.* Alfred A. Knopf, 1972.

Read, Piers Paul. *Alive: The Story of the Andes Survivors.* J. B. Lippincott, 1974.

Renvoize, Jean. *A Wild Thing.* Little, Brown, 1971.

Robertson, Dougal. *Survive the Savage Sea.* G. K. Hall, 1974.

Rosen, Winifred. *Cruisin for a Bruisin.* Alfred A. Knopf, 1976.

Salinger, J. D. *The Catcher in the Rye.* Little, Brown, 1951.

Samuels, Gertrude. *Run, Shelley, Run!* Thomas Y. Crowell, 1974.

Schaefer, Jack. *Shane.* Houghton Mifflin, 1949.

Stevenson, Robert Louis. *Treasure Island,* new ed. Charles Scribner's Sons, 1973.

Swarthout, Glendon. *Bless the Beasts and Children.* Doubleday, 1970.

Taylor, Mildred. *Roll of Thunder, Hear My Cry*. Dial, 1976.

Thompson, Thomas. *Richie*. Saturday Review Press, 1973.

Tolkien, J. R. R. *Lord of the Rings*. Houghton Mifflin, 1954–56.

Twain, Mark. *The Adventures of Huckleberry Finn*. Webster, 1884.

Wersba, Barbara. *Run Softly, Go Fast*. Atheneum, 1970.

Woods, George A. *Catch a Killer*. Harper & Row, 1972.

Zindel, Paul. *Pardon Me, You're Stepping on My Eyeball!* Harper & Row, 1976.

———. *The Pigman*. Harper & Row, 1968.

PART TWO

A Brief History of Young Adult Reading

3

1800-1900

A Century of Purity
with a Few Passions

Prior to 1800, literature read by children and young adults consisted largely of a few religious novels and many pietistic tracts. They advanced the belief that the young were merely small adults who must, like larger adults, accept the brevity of mortal life and God's judgment soon to come.

By 1800, the United States was no longer a much hoped for vision but a real and stable country. The attitude toward young people gradually changed during the first half of the nineteenth century because of several factors. Among them were our rapid national expansion in territory and population, widespread immigration, and the slow but certain evolution from agrarian to urban society. Developments in medical knowledge led to a decrease in infant mortality and longer life expectancy, which, along with slowly evolving changes in life-style, encouraged a more secular education and reduced the necessity for children to begin working at the age of thirteen or fourteen. The parental duty to prepare small adults for death slowly became an equally intense parental duty to prepare young people for the role of patriotic and Christian adults.

Perhaps the newer literature was still pious and somber, but it increasingly hinted at the possibility of humanity's experiencing a satisfying life here on earth. One could participate in responsibilities, work, family life, and even some joy before death. Books continued to reflect adult ideas and fashions but of this world, not merely the next.

It was a time of change, an early version of Toffler's "future shock," with cultural changes everywhere and ever more obvious. Society moved, often without noticing, from a simple society to one far more complex.

The abolitionist movement and the eventual legal emancipation of black people and the women's suffrage movement began our moral commitment to social consciousness. The westward expansion, the rise and decline of Indian wars in the west, and the growth of railroad transportation changed the country drastically. The Industrial Revolution joined with the growth of the cities to produce an increasingly urbanized society. Giants of industry appeared, and others lurked over the horizon. Cities had not yet produced anyone of the magnitude of a Boss Tweed, but corruption and slums were well on their way. Education became more popular and more accessible, not yet mass education, but education closer to the grasp of more people. The public library became an important part of many towns.

The Protestant ethic rode high. If God put mortals on earth to work hard to suit His purpose, it followed that there was nothing evil but much potential good in working hard for material success. Material success, so the argument went, implied wealth to advance God's plan on earth, and that easily led to idealism about and exalting of successful businessmen. The rise of men who were not necessarily from the best families but who were successful in the hard world of business fostered the spirit of democracy. Could anything be more democratic, less class-conscious, than the steady rise to conspicuous wealth of bright, energetic, gifted, and Christian young men?

Literature written specifically for young adults reflected the Protestant ethic and the need for hard work that would assure happiness and wealth. Protagonists in Horatio Alger's novels were so desperately imbued with it that they risked becoming crashing bores, but Alger's novels provided ideals and impetus for thousands of young men and women. There were no limits to the future of the young man willing to strive, for to strive was to succeed, according to popular belief.

Literature aimed at young women, and most adult women, emphasized home and family responsibilities, for women were expected to find solace and satisfaction in love, husband, children, and home. However, in some books there were subtle hints, and some not so subtle, that women had brains and feelings along with responsibilities.

More literature was written for young adults than ever before. An increasingly secularized society produced writers aware that love, adventure, work, and recreation existed in the real world of young people, and that these could provide useful themes in books. A new kind of novel began to appear that was aimed somewhat less obviously at moralizing and instructing and more at interesting the young adult. If moral lessons were still there, they were less direct, less immediate, less heavenly. Getting ahead in life, possibly even enjoying some aspects of life, became a central theme.

It was a changing time, an exciting time, a dangerous time to be alive. Life changed and literature changed and neither could go back to the simplicity of an earlier day. Some wept over the change, some worried over it, but most accepted its inevitability.

MORAL WRITERS AND MORAL BOOKS

While major writers, notably eighteenth-century novelists Henry Fielding, Tobias Smollett, and Laurence Sterne, were ignored and despised for their lack of obvious moral tone, other writers of the eighteenth and early nineteenth century became staples for the young.

Hannah More and her many tracts, especially *Repository Tracts* (1795-98) with its "The Shepherd of Salisbury," *Moral Sketches* (1819), and *Coelebs in Search of a Wife* (1809), became a necessary, sometimes soporific, but certainly moralistic part of every young person's reading. Almost equally popular was Maria Edgeworth whose *The Parent's Assistant* (1796), *Moral Tales for Young People* (1801), *Harry and Lucy* (1801), *Popular Tales* (1804), *Rosamund* (1821), *Frank* (1822), and *Harry and Lucy Concluded* (1825) sold well though none of them had the least literary merit compared to her *Castle Rackrent* (1800) for adults. Thomas Day remained popular for years through his edifying and moralizing *The History of Sanford and Mertom* (1783, 1786, 1789), one of the great exercises of literary persiflage of its time or any other time. Mason Locke Weems, better known as Parson Weems, published his popular if inaccurate and sugar-coated *A History of the Life and Death, Virtues and Exploits, of General George Washington* (1800), later altered to *The Life of Washington the Great* (1806), and finally altered to *The Life of George Washington* (1808).

But three books led all the rest in number of readers. John Bunyan's *The Pilgrim's Progress from This World to That Which Is to Come* (Part I, 1678; Part II, also 1678) was predictably popular, a religiously symbolic account of Christian, who flees his doomed city and journeys to the Celestial City. Pleased as adults could be with the pious lessons, Christian's travails through the Slough of Despond, the Valley of Humiliation, the Valley of the Shadow of Death, Vanity Fair, and the Country of Beulah were easily read by young people as melodrama and adventure. Religious, perhaps, but exciting nonetheless, a fictional ambiguity pleasing to both young and old insured the steady popularity of the book. Part II in which Christian's wife, Christiana, flees the city with similar adventures, was never as popular, but it was read.

Daniel Defoe was close behind Bunyan in popularity, not of course for *Moll Flanders* (1722) or *Roxanna* (1724), but for *The Life and Strange Surprising Adventures of Robinson Crusoe* (1719). It was based on the true story of Alexander Selkirk, marooned in 1704 at his own request on the uninhabited island of Juan Fernandez until his rescue in 1709. The life was strange, the adventures of Crusoe were surprising, and the book proved a permanent addition to libraries of both young and old, probably because the book was almost ostentatiously sermonistic and established that a civilized person, that is, white, could defeat a hostile environment and ignorant savages, nonwhites. Crusoe's ability to survive, to find a purpose for his existence, and to discover God everywhere pleased many while the numerous, practical details about housebuilding and gardening endeared him to others.

The third book remains something of an enigma. Jonathan Swift was hardly a model writer for pious young people. His *A Tale of a Tub* (1704) and his scatological poetry and prose made him an unlikely candidate for literary sainthood in early nineteenth-century America. *Gulliver's Travels* (1726) seemed as unlikely to gain admittance to American homes, but the book is such that it can be read by the young (usually in expurgated and emasculated editions) as a fantasy and by adults as misanthropic satire. Even then it remains puzzling that Lemuel Gulliver's travels to Lilliput and Brobding-nag did not merely escape attack but that they were highly praised. Presumably, young people did not realize how Gulliver put out the fire in the Queen's palace in Book I nor were they aware of some of the unpleasant aspects of Book II, much less the voyage to the land of the Houyhnhnms with its indictment of humans as Yahoos for their filth and evil.

These three books must have seemed refreshing indeed for young readers compared to two writers who wrote specifically for young people, Samuel Goodrich and Jacob Abbott.

Under the pen name Peter Parley, Goodrich wrote 170 books from 1827 through 1850, selling more than seven million copies. He revealed in his 1856 autobiography, *Recollections of a Lifetime, or Men and Things I Have Seen,* that as a child he had disliked fairy stories and Mother Goose rhymes because they were frightening and untrue. He liked *Robinson Crusoe* as an honest and moral book, but he loved Hannah More's "The Shepherd in Salisbury Plain" in *Repository Tracts* and later vowed to write American books emulating her work. His fiction certainly proved to be every bit as compelling as Hannah More's, just as surely as it was moral.

In 1827, he published his first book, *The Tales of Peter Parley about America.* Parley, an old man who is the focal point of this and all the remainder of the series, tells stories of New England and its history to admiring children who gather to hear him ramble on and on. In the next four years, Goodrich produced eleven other Peter Parleys, all emphasizing the American view of things and history.

Abbott studied for the Congregational ministry and later served as professor of mathematics and natural philosophy at Amherst and as a minister in Roxbury, Massachusetts. In 200 or more books Abbott set out with a vengeance to plant seeds of morality and education in the vineyard of childhood. Most famous were his twenty-eight Rollo books beginning in 1834. The title of the 1838 *Rollo at Work, or The Way for a Boy to Learn to Be Industrious* sounds the tenor and tone of the series. Perhaps less priggish than the Peter Parley books, they are sticky and stilted all the same, staggering in terms of what Abbott believed boys were intended to be—all serious, all decent,

Young adults read first and worried about the morality of the literature second.

kind, and thoughtful, all perfect or at least easily perfectible, all unreal and unlike any real boy this side of fiction. *Rollo at School* continues to mine this strain, but later books taking Rollo abroad (some unkind American readers maintained that that was where he should stay) are more entertaining since they force Rollo and Abbott to look for new territories and ideas. *Rollo on the Atlantic* (1853), *Rollo in London* (1855), *Rollo in Rome* (1858), and their ilk made Rollo seem a veritable boy Baedeker, but their sugar-coated geography lessons in the midst of a saccharin plot made them palatable and even popular.

The world had changed by the 1860s and young adults were being exposed (or exposing themselves) to far more secular literature. Morality was paraded forth in the

Susan Warner. *The Wide, Wide World,* 1850.

guise of sentimentalism and melodrama, but whether the morality was real or facade was open to question in the minds of many parents, educators, and clergymen. Young adults read first and worried about the morality of the literature second just as people have done throughout history.

DOMESTIC NOVELS

In 1855, Nathaniel Hawthorne wrote his publisher bitterly lamenting the state of American literature:

> America is now wholly given over to a d—d mob of scribbling women, and I should have no chance of success while the public taste is occupied with their trash—and should be ashamed of myself if I did succeed. What is the mystery of these innumerable editions of *The Lamplighter,* and other books neither better nor worse?—worse they could not be, and better they need not be, when they sell by the 100,000?[1]

The "trash" was the domestic novel, the best-selling literature from 1850 through the 1870s. Born out of a belief that humanity was redeemable, the domestic novel preached morality, woman's submission to man, the value of cultural, social, and political conservatism, a religion of the heart and the Bible, and the glories of genuine suffering.

Each novel concerns a young girl, usually orphaned and placed in the home of a relative or other benefactor, who soon meets a darkly handsome young man with dark shadows lurking in his past, a man not easily trusted but one eventually worth redeeming and loving. Melodramatic devices were commonplace—mysterious deaths, illnesses, sobbing women, malevolent men, instinctive benevolence, strange figures, forged letters, disappearing wills, frightened virgins, and somnambulism and trances—each novelist finding it necessary to provide greater thrills than her previous novel or that of any previous novelist. Domestic novels provided moral lessons in the midst of gothic thrills, but they soon created heroines with a love-hate feeling about men, ambivalently frightening, erotic, and attractive to female readers and puzzling if not appalling to male readers.

Heroines differed more in name than in characteristics. Uniformly submissive to, yet distrustful of their betters and men, they were self-sacrificing and self-denying beyond belief, interested in the primacy of the family unit and a happy marriage as the goal of all decent women. They abhorred sin generally, particularly divorce, drink, tobacco, and adultery.

Domestic novels were a product of the religious sentiment of the time, the espousal of traditional virtues, and the anxieties and frustrations of women trying to find a role in a changing society. They became weapons against a male-dominated society and the first American glimmer of feminist literature.

The promise and problems of domestic novels are apparent in the writings of Susan Warner, creator of the genre, and Augusta Jane Evans Wilson, whose *St. Elmo* was one of the all-time best sellers.

Writing under the pen name of Elizabeth Wetherell, Susan Warner produced more than twenty novels. *The Wide, Wide World* (1850), her best known novel, was claimed in the 1890s as one of the four most widely read books in England along with the Bible, *Pilgrim's Progress,* and *Uncle Tom's Cabin,* and was still read in the early 1900s. An abridged edition was published in England in 1911, and an edited and illustrated edition was published by the University of London Press in 1950.

Her manuscript was at first rejected by several New York publishers. George Putman was ready to send it back but decided to ask his mother to read it. The next morning she said, "If you never publish another book, George, publish this." Putman followed her advice, and the book was out in time to attract the Christmas trade. Sales were slow at first, though critical praise was high, but picked up and the first edition sold out in four months. Translations into French, German, Swedish, and Italian followed. English sales exceeded those of any previous American novel, and, by 1852, *The Wide, Wide World* was in its fourteenth edition.

The author's life paralleled that of her heroine, Ellen Montgomery. Warner's father was pathetically unable to provide, and the household was barren, bitter, and deadly serious. Ellen's family life is not so penurious, but her mother dies early and her father is consumed with serious business matters and determines to leave Ellen with Aunt Fortune Emerson. The aunt is not gladdened by the news and a mutual distaste develops. Ellen, to her aunt's displeasure, forms a firm, if platonic, friendship with Mr. Van Brunt, Fortune Emerson's intended, and an even more significant friendship with Miss Alice, daughter of the local minister, who showers Ellen with pity and piety and all that Ellen cannot find in her aunt's home. Unhappily for Alice, but happily for the moral good of the reader, Alice is doomed—probably she is too good for this world—and, in a deathbed scene highly admired by readers old and young, Alice dies. She is soon replaced by her brother John, a divinity student, who replaces Alice's sermons with his own. Later, Ellen's father dies, and tears flow before and after. In this first of many lachrymose domestic novels, Ellen cries at every turn: she "almost shrieked," "answered with a gush of tears," "burst into tears," "sobbed," "mingled bitter tears with eager prayers," "drew long, sobbing sighs," "watered the rock with tears," and "burst into violent grief." Warner's novel taught morality, the dangers of self-right-eousness, and the virtues of submission and religion. Despite its weepy and moralistic nature—perhaps because of it—it was incredibly successful. E. Douglas Branch called it, "The greatest achievement of any of the lady novelists."[2]

Augusta Jane Evans Wilson may well have been the most popular writer of the domestic school for her *St. Elmo* (1867). No other novel so literally touched the Ameri-can landscape—thirteen towns were named or renamed St. Elmo, as were hotels, rail-way coaches, steamboats, one kind of punch, and a brand of cigars. Every home seemed to have its copy. Edition after edition was printed, and some indication of the number of copies sold may be gauged by a notice in a special edition of *St. Elmo* that it was "limited to 100,000 copies." Only *Uncle Tom's Cabin* exceeded it in sales, and Wilson was more than once called by her admirers, the American Brontë. Men and women publicly testified that their lives had permanently changed for the better by reading the book.

Edna Earl, heroine of *St. Elmo* and the daughter of a village blacksmith, is or-phaned by the death of her father and bereft at the death of her grandfather. Rescued from a train wreck by snobbish and wealthy Mrs. Murray who sets out to raise Edna as her daughter, she finds herself in the same house with St. Elmo Murray, her benefac-tor's son, an evil and self-centered man who has not only killed another in a duel but has a well-deserved reputation as a seducer. St. Elmo takes one look at Edna and leaves home for four years. Pastor Allan Hammond becomes Edna's friend and teacher. When St. Elmo returns, Edna has Greek, Latin, Sanskrit, Chaldee, Hebrew, and Arabic firmly in hand. Fascinated by Edna, if not by her learning, St. Elmo falls in love, but she despises and rejects him. Edna turns to writing and becomes a successful novelist. The once arrogant and thwarted St. Elmo continues his courtship but is always rejected until he becomes a Christian and then a minister. They marry, another wicked man reformed by a good woman; another woman proves her innate superiority to man.

DIME NOVELS

Dime novels were as popular as domestic novels (and condemned as strongly) but had quite a different audience. James Fenimore Cooper's *Leatherstocking Tales* and some adventure writing of the early nineteenth century, tales of Indians, pirates, and myster-ies, influenced the subject matter of dime novelists. But it was left to Boston publisher

Maturin Murray Ballou (1820-95) to set the physical (and to some degree the emotional) pattern. His sensational novels were usually fifty pages, eight and a half inches by five inches, often illustrated with a lurid hand-colored woodcut. With wild tales by writers like Edward S. Ellis and Ned Buntline (soon to be staple writers of dime novels), they were a bargain at twenty-five cents.

Beadle and Adams Appear on the Scene

In 1858, Erastus Beadle and his brother Irwin, successful publishers of sheet music in Buffalo, moved to New York City, and, with Robert Adams, formed the firm of Beadle and Adams, destined for years to be the most successful purveyors of dime novels.

In June 1860, Beadle and Adams published Mrs. Ann S. Stephens' *Malaeska: The Indian Wife of the White Hunter,* probably with the help of Orville J. Victor, the resident editorial genius who guided many dime novels to success. Mrs. Stephens had originally published her novel in 1839 in *The Ladies' Companion,* which she edited, but the reprinting made Beadle and Adams famous and guaranteed her future employment as a dime novelist. Published in a salmon-colored wrapper, *Malaeska* was given the spectacular promotion readers soon associated with Beadle and Adams. On June 7, 1860, an advertisement appeared in the *New York Tribune:*

BOOKS FOR THE MILLIONS
A dollar Book for a dime!
128 pages complete, only ten cents!!!
MALAESKA
The
Indian Wife of the White Hunter
by Mrs. Ann Stephens
Irwin P. Beadle and Co., Publishers

Curious readers buying the six by four inches, 128-page book may have been uncertain about just what they were getting, but apparently what they got was good enough, for 65,000 copies were sold.

A bald plot summary makes the first dime novel appear incredibly melodramatic and crude. Malaeska marries a white hunter who, when he is dying, tells his Indian wife to take their child from the wilds of upper New York state to his wealthy parents in New York City. The parents accept the child, and Malaeska remains, for a time, known to him as his nurse. She tries to kidnap the boy to take him home but fails and goes back alone to the woods and her tribe. Her son, not knowing his parents, grows up hating Indians. Later, Malaeska identifies herself to him, and he commits suicide. She dies the next day on her husband's grave. Melodramatic it may have been, but it was also fast-moving, thrilling, exotic, and all for ten cents. Mass literature, priced for the masses, had arrived.

Other successes followed, but the eighth dime novel topped all previous efforts after an intriguing promotional campaign. On October 1, 1860, the *New York Tribune* carried this simple and intriguing ad, sans company, sans price, sans author:

Seth Jones is from New Hampshire.
Seth Jones understands the redskins.
Seth Jones answers a question.
Seth Jones strikes a trail.
Seth Jones makes a good roast.
Seth Jones writes a letter.
Seth Jones objects to sparking.
Seth Jones in his element.
Seth Jones takes an observation.
Seth Jones can't express himself.

On October 2, 1860, the *New York Tribune* carried another ad, still not listing the company involved.

Seth Jones; or, The Captives of the Frontier.
For sale at all the news depots.

Seth Jones was published that day to 60,000 readers. At least 500,000 copies were sold over the years in the United States alone, and it was translated into ten languages.

Edward S. Ellis. *Seth Jones,* 1860.

Contrary to later journals, which damned dime novels often without reading them, contemporary reviews were good, even at times enthusiastic. Four years after the publication of *Seth Jones*, reviewer William Everett wrote:

> Mr. E. S. Ellis' *Seth Jones* and *Trail Hunters* are good, very good. Mr. Ellis' novels are favorites and deserve to be. He shows variety and originality in his characters; and his Indians are human beings, and not fancy pieces.[3]

This book was not the first by Edward S. Ellis, who had written for Ballou, but *Seth Jones* made him famous and insured his financial success even after he stopped writing dime novels and turned to writing what turned out to be an incredible number of boys' books. *Seth Jones* takes place near the close of the eighteenth century. Seth, once a scout in the Revolutionary War, comes to Alfred Haverland's clearing in western New York state to announce that nearby Indians are ready for the warpath. In the attack, Haverland's sixteen-year-old daughter, Ina, is captured, and Seth, along with Ina's sweetheart, goes off on the rescue. At the end of the story Seth is revealed as aristocratic Eugene Morton in search of his lost fiancée. A double wedding, Seth and his love, Ina and hers, concludes the book.

Seth Jones would not have been enough to maintain Beadle and Adams' success by itself, but it served as a prototype, and dime novels numbering about 600 from this firm alone reaffirmed the success of *Seth Jones*. Beadle and Adams revolutionized some aspects of the publishing trade. They spent more money on advertising than other companies, they made advertising pay and made it respectable, and they knew how to merchandise their products.

Other Companies Get into the Act

Beadle and Adams did not long have a monopoly in their field. Success breeds competition as surely as it breeds success, and in 1863 Irwin Beadle left the firm accompanied by foreman George Munro to establish a rival publishing house. Beadle lasted only a short time, but for almost thirty years Munro's ten-cent novels were Beadle and Adams' chief competition. Other serious competition came from Norman Munro, George's brother, who started his firm in 1870, first using the name of Ornum (Munro spelled backward) and later, when the brothers became bitter enemies, using the family name. The entry of Frank Tousey into the market in 1878 was even more serious, and the competition of Street and Smith, beginning eleven years later, was the roughest of all. Street and Smith eventually became *the* dime novel company. Companies vied for public favor by producing rival fictional characters, George Munro's fictional detective "Old Sleuth" competing with Norman Munro's "Old Cap Collier," Frank Tousey's "Old King Brady," and Street and Smith's "Nick Carter." Beadle and Adams never developed a successful detective character and lost out in this limited field and finally in the broader market. By 1900, only two companies remained, Tousey and Street and Smith.

Dime Novel Characteristics

From 1860 until approximately 1875, dime novels cost ten cents, ran about 100 pages in small format (about seven by five inches), and were aimed at adults. By 1875, publishers discovered that boys were the most avid readers, though adults, too, bought them. Thereafter, publishers concentrated on the younger audience dropping the price to a nickel (though the public continued to call them dime novels, mostly out of habit) and cutting costs. The result was a nickel (or half-dime) novel of sixteen or thirty-two pages, usually part of a series and featuring one fictional hero, Diamond Dick, Fred Fearnot, Buffalo Bill, or some other equally fascinating and impossible character. The cover portrayed in lurid black and white (color came later) some heroic act of derring-do or a villainous performance of darkest evil.

Plots and Conventions of the Dime Novel

Action-packed dime novels grabbed hold of the reader's imagination from the first lines and never let go. Fast paced throughout with cliffhanging chapter endings and imaginative, if often far-fetched, thrills and chills, each surpassing the previous adventure, dime novels celebrated mystery, suspense, and the thrill of the chase. The prose was purple, the vocabulary merely seemed erudite, and literary allusions were common, but boys were not fooled. Dime novels were superior to anything else on the market, more readable than classics, more imaginative than other purple literature.

Daring Davy, the Young Bear Killer, or The Trail of the Border Wolf by Harry St. George (pen name for the prolific writer of dime novels and later boys' series books, St. George Rathbone), published as number 108 in Beadle's Half Dime Library on August 19, 1879, illustrates the *in medias res* opening so common to dime novels, the promised action, the purple prose, and the erudite vocabulary, all in the first brief paragraphs of the first chapter:

> "Then Davy Crockett must die!"
>
> The man who gave utterance to this emphatic sentence stood in the middle of a dilapidated old cabin that was almost entirely hidden in the heart of a dense forest. Giant trees grew all around it, their branches drooping so as to almost conceal the log hut from view.
>
> Outside the night breeze swept down the forest aisles, rustling the leaves in the passage and carrying many of them with it to the ground. The fair moon had wheeled up in the eastern heavens, and Jupiter was leading the march of the planets across the firmament. Now and then the melancholy howl of a wolf could be heard, sounding dismally through the silence of the night, and once a panther lent its shrill scream to awaken the echoes of the glen beyond, for the woods of old Tennessee were full of savage game at this early day.
>
> The scene inside the cabin was certainly wild enough to have pleased the most exacting.

Four men stood around a rickety table with drawn knives. The man who had just uttered that sentence of death was a perfect giant in point of size. He was known in the backwoods as Hercules Dan, and had been a hunter and trapper, living on what he could shoot and steal.

Two of the others possessed ill-favored faces, while the last did not condescend to show his features, which were completely hidden under a heavy hat, and a rough scarf which he had wound around his neck and the lower half of his face.

Six paragraphs into the tale and already we have threats, implied violence soon to become real, death, poetic writing (or what passed for it), and mystery. The remainder of the roughly 40,000-word novel (three columns of tiny print to the page) was no anticlimax.

Other stock characters in dime novels were the hero's closest friend, weaker but almost as decent, an older person who moved about spouting tiresome but supposedly wise sayings, and a comic black man, the butt of all humor, frequently superstitious but always servile and loyal, occasionally surprising the reader by proving far wiser and more courageous than anyone could have suspected.

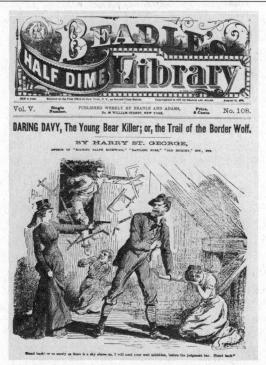

Harry St. George. *Daring Davy, The Young Bear Killer*, 1879.

Formulaic writing and stock characters were predictable and common, for dime novels never pretended to be great literature, and their use of standard characters, settings, and situations made readers comfortable. Today situation comedies, westerns, or mysteries on television do the same as they ease viewers into a relaxed state of expectation by providing elements, situations, and plot twists that have become satisfyingly traditional. Dime novels provided what dime novel readers wanted and demanded, rapid beginnings, implied and realized violence, periodic cliffhangers, contrived and fast endings, strained but possible coincidences, good versus evil, vengeance, purity, love, the sanctity of marriage, all for a nickel.

Beyond the excitement, they provided morality. Virtue victorious and villainy vanquished were the watchwords of dime novels. Thrills, of course, but morality had to be there too, and not just to make them acceptable to parents. Erastus Beadle sincerely believed that books should represent sound moral values, and the strict rules he imposed on his writers insured adventure and morality as this memo to his staff reveals:

So much is said, and justly, against a considerable number of papers and libraries now on the market, that we beg leave to repeat the following announcement and long-standing instructions to all contributors;

Authors who write for our consideration will bear in mind that—

We prohibit all things offensive to good taste in expression and incident—

We prohibit subjects or characters that carry an immoral taint—

We prohibit the repetition of any occurrence which, though true, is yet better untold—

We prohibit what cannot be read with satisfaction by every right-minded person—old and young alike—

We require your best work—

We require unquestioned originality—

We require pronounced strength of plot and high dramatic interest of story—

We require grace and precision of narrative, and correctness in composition.

Authors must be familiar with characters and places which they introduce and not attempt to write in fields of which they have no intimate knowledge.[4]

Some Dime Novel Types and Authors

Printed in editions running between 35,000 and 70,000 copies, depending on authors' reputations and the popularity of a particular series, dime novels sold in the millions. Beadle and Adams sold four million in 1865 only five years after the genre began. And Bragin notes:

Publishers never revealed their sales, but we estimate that the Tip Top Weekly Merriwell stories had a circulation up to a million copies weekly. We base this estimate on a talk we had with Mr. Harry Wolff, who stated that the Tousey story paper Happy Days, had circulation of 500,000 copies weekly, and that was, to use his words, "small potatoes," compared with the Street and Smith output.[5]

Many early dime novels were set in the West of the 1840s and 1850s, and some were set in an even earlier "west," for example, upper New York state in *Malaeska*. But with the opening of the West beyond the Mississippi River, the dime novel found a topic of insatiable interest. Fictional characters like Deadwood Dick, the James Boys, Pawnee Bill, Diamond Dick, and Young Wild West were introduced and lengthy series developed around them. Real people like Buffalo Bill, Wild Bill Hickock, and the James Brothers might not have been able to recognize themselves in the fiction written about them. It was mixed only occasionally with something bordering on the truth, but readers cared little in the midst of the heroic exploits.

Rivaling the popularity of the western dime novel was the detective story with such fictional heroes as Nick Carter, Old King Brady, Old Sleuth, Young Sleuth, and Cap Collier. Most famous of the writers of detective dime novels was Frederic Van Rensselaer Dey who wrote most of the Nick Carter novels. A dignified man, he was pleased with the success of Nick Carter—he wrote more than a thousand of them—because they were clean: "I never wrote one that could not have been read aloud to a Bible class."[6]

Two other kinds of dime novels that had many fans were the sports novels, with heroes like Frank Merriwell and Fred Fearnot, and the science fiction novels featuring Frank Reade, Frank Reade, Jr., Jack Wright, and Tom Edison, Jr.

Objections to Dime Novels and Objections to the Objections

By the 1870s schoolteachers, librarians, writers, and politicians were taking notice of dime novels, first attacking the sensationalism, sentimentality, and distance from reality, and later attacking the alleged power of dime novels to corrupt morals and to turn the young toward crime. In 1878, William Sumner itemized beliefs promulgated by dime novels and argued their potential corruptive influence, especially since dime novels were inexpensive and ubiquitous.[7] And in 1896 Theodore C. Burgess argued for stronger laws and more vigorous enforcement of laws already on the books to stave off the dime novel menace:

We have a law against the sale of that which is obscene, and it is worthy of consideration whether a law should not go one step farther—not a long one— and include such papers as the *Police Gazette* and those other forms of degrading literature known as the dime novel.[8]

A politician, either for the sake of morality or votes, tried to get such a bill through the New York Assembly in 1883. Part of the Honorable Abel Goddard's bill read:

> Any person who shall sell, loan, or give to any minor under sixteen years of age any dime novel or book of fiction, without first obtaining the written consent of the parent or guardian of such minor, shall be deemed guilty of a misdemeanor, punishable by imprisonment or by a fine not exceeding $50.[9]

One newspaper noted ironically that the bill would prohibit giving a copy of *Pilgrim's Progress* to a minor without first getting permission, and the length of the sentence, being indeterminant, might range from a few days to life if the judge were of the same persuasion as Goddard.[10]

Both librarians and schoolteachers discovered to their horror that dime novels were widely read by young people, revealing their own naiveté and ignorance about

The *Literary News* for May 1884 told of four youths in Milwaukee who organized a gang after reading some dime novels.

young people. Tales of the horror teachers and librarians felt when they uncovered dime novel addicts among the young were staples of the *Library Journal* and educational journals of the day.[11]

Then critics found startling proof that dime novels corrupted young adults and pushed them to the wrong side of the law. The *Literary News* for May 1884 told of four youngsters in Milwaukee who organized a gang after reading some dime novels. When frustrated in their plan to move west, the gang set fires about the city.[12] The 1883 *New York Herald* warned:

> Pernicious stories of the "dime novel" class continue to do their mischievous work. The latest recorded victim was a New London boy, aged fourteen, who shot himself during a period of mental aberration caused by reading dime novels.[13]

Dime novels also had defenders. William Everett writing in the prestigious *North American Review* in 1864 found them "unobjectionable morally, whatever fault be found with their literary style and composition. They do not even obscurely pander to vice, or excite the passions."[14] Writing in the *Library Journal* fifteen years later, Thomas Wentworth Higginson hardly overpraised dime novels, but his words were far more perceptive and honest than most commentators of the time:

I have turned over hundreds of dime novels in such places [book stalls] within a year or two, without finding a single word of indecency; they are overly sensational, and, so far as they deal with thieves and house-breakers, demoralizing; but they are not impure.[15]

Death of the Dime Novel

The end of the dime novel is impossible to attribute to any one factor. By 1900 Indian wars were over and with that came the end of contemporary western heroes. Dime novel detectives had been replaced by stories and books about Sherlock Holmes. If they didn't care for Holmes, readers could turn to detectives galore in the growing pulp magazine industry. Series books were now commonplace. The popular getting-ahead-in-life stories begun by Horatio Alger and continued by series books had few parallels in dime novels. The growing number of young people spending more years in school led to a demand for more realistic school and sports stories.

And so a pervasive, ubiquitous literature passed away. Many adults saw nothing in dime novels beyond potential harm and evil. Young adults knew better. Dime novels allowed them to people their lives with exciting characters doing fascinating things in a mildly realistic but mostly wildly romantic world. Of all literature written between 1860 and 1900, dime novels were probably the most widely read by young people seeking escape from an otherwise dull existence.

OTHER PAPERBACK BOOKS

Dime novels produced one significant offspring, the early paperback novel series costing a dime or less.

In 1864 Boston publisher James Redpath announced a series of dime books of high quality, each running from 96 to 124 pages, including Alcott's *On Picket Duty and Other Tales,* Balzac's *The Vendetta,* Swift's *Gulliver's Travels,* and Hugo's *Battle of Waterloo.*

By the 1870s attacks on the dime novel were common, and Chicago's Donnelly and Lloyd began its Lakeside Library with contemporary and classic books far superior, they argued, to sensational dime novels. Their high moral sense would have been more impressive had not most of their library been books pirated from England and the continent. Beadle and Adams retaliated by starting their Fireside Library, and soon Frank Leslie began his Home Library. Later George Munro published his Seaside Library (the first three titles were Mrs. Wood's *East Lynne,* Mulock's *John Halifax, Gentleman,* and Brontë's *Jane Eyre*), and Harper and Brothers began its Franklin Square Library. Paperback libraries cost little. Publishers needed to develop a stable of writers to create dime novel libraries, but Frank Tousey was able to save money by "borrowing" many, if not all, stories for his paperback series.

By 1877, fourteen libraries of inexpensive paperbacks offered many titles (George Munro reprinted almost 500 titles) and increasingly good literature. Beadle's Waverly

Library included novels by Mrs. Southworth and Mrs. Stephens, hardly the greatest literature, but it also published Dumas' *Camille*, Reade's *Peg Woffington*, Porter's *Thaddeus of Warsaw*, Goldsmith's *The Vicar of Wakefield*, and Bulwer-Lytton's *Leila*. Equally impressive, each novel in the Waverly Library cost only five cents from a newsdealer or six cents by mail.

THE POPULAR STORY WEEKLY

American weekly magazines containing large amounts of fiction began in 1837 when depression-hit publishers needed cheaper methods of producing books. They devised a scheme for printing books as newspapers, in many ways like modern Sunday supplements, on which they paid no taxes and which qualified for cheaper postage rates. Newspapers, irritated by what they considered unfair competition, started printing their own fiction supplements, at first for fifty cents, then twenty-five cents, and then six and one-quarter cents. By 1843, the Post Office Department changed the rules, charging book rates for supplements as well as for books and newspapers, but the cheap fiction supplements were well established.

In 1855, Francis S. Street and Francis S. Smith took over the *New York Weekly Dispatch*, and by 1857 they doubled the circulation with Smith's *The Vestmaker's Apprentice, or The Vampyres of Society*, a tale of villainy and virtue set against a background of greed, filth, and wickedness in New York City. Two years later, Street and Smith bought the *New York Weekly* outright for $40,000 though they had less than $100 between them. Within five years they paid off the debt. Their advertising methods teased the audience with hints of stories to come. To create interest for the forthcoming *Lillian the Wanderer, or The Perils of Beauty*, they announced:

> The heroine is a noble-souled and pure, but unfortunate orphan-girl, who is forced by circumstances to leave her home in Europe and come to this country. Upon arriving here, she falls into the clutches of [some] soulless ruffians, and her sufferings and narrow escapes from a fate worse than death are graphically sketched by the author. In the course of the Story, the reader is introduced both into the miserable hovel of poverty and into the mansion of luxury and wealth, and a clearer insight is had into all classes of society. The Story is written in the Author's best style and cannot fail to create a great sensation.[16]

Street and Smith published sea tales, adventures, and tales of suspense, but the most popular were about love and its tribulations. Mary Kyle Dallas' *Neglected Warning, or The Trials of a Public School Teacher*, doubtless well calculated to keep readers in suspense, but equally calculated to make schoolteachers question Street and Smith's sanity in running this story, which they claimed:

> will touch a sympathetic chord in the bosom of every reader, male or female. For who is not, either directly or indirectly, interested in those noble institutions, our public schools?[17]

The tale was not exactly about a typical schoolteacher, for at different times the heroine lay unconscious in the snow dressed only in her nightclothes, was locked in a church, had a friend who was buried alive and rose from his coffin at night, was rescued from a burning ship, and was married only to see her husband arrested for murder during the wedding ceremony.

As with the dime novel, critics found fault with the popular story weekly, especially the sensational stories and the glorification of impossible lives that readers could dream about but never approach. Critics worried that a maid or a working girl in a mill might waste time dreaming about a better life and the perfect man. In truth, popular story weeklies, like dime novels, provided escape literature to cheer up drab people leading drab lives. There was and is nothing wrong with that, critics to the contrary.

TWO MAJORS FOR MINORS: ALCOTT AND ALGER

Louisa May Alcott and Horatio Alger, Jr. were the first writers for young adults to gain national attention. Both wrote *Bildungsroman,* a novel of a young person growing from childhood to maturity. The similarity between the two stops almost as it begins. Alcott wrote about happy families; Alger wrote about broken homes. Alcott's novels were sometimes harsh but always honest. Alger's novels were romantic fantasies. Alcott's novels continue to be read for good reason. Except for the historian or the Alger buff, Alger's novels lie virtually forgotten.

The second daughter of visionary Amos Bronson Alcott, Louisa May Alcott lived her youth near Concord and Boston with a practical mother and a father who was brilliant, generous, and improvident.

After publishing *Hospital Sketches* (1863) based on her work in a Union hospital, she turned to writing thrillers, solely, she maintained, for money. Then, after an abortive effort to create dime novels, she wrote *Little Women,* her most enduring work. The reigning young adult's author of the time was Oliver Optic, the pen name of William T. Adams, and Boston publishers Roberts Brothers were eager to find a story for young adults that might offer competition to Optic's stories published by rival Boston publisher Lee and Shepard. Roberts' representative, Thomas Niles, had once told Alcott, "Stick to your teaching. You can't write," but as a publisher he had requested permission to reprint the successful *Hospital Sketches.* In September 1866 Niles suggested she write a girls' book, and in May 1868 he gently reminded her.

She sent a manuscript off to Niles who thought early parts of it dull, but other readers felt his judgment fallible, and the first part of *Little Women: Meg, Jo, Beth, and Amy. The Story of Their Lives. A Girl's Book* was published on September 30, 1868, with three illustrations and a frontispiece at $1.50 a copy. Slightly more than a month earlier, Alcott had read the proofs:

> August 26th—Proof of the whole book came. It reads better than I expected. Not a bit sensational, but simple and true, for we really lived most of it; and if it succeeds that will be the reason for it. Mr. N. likes it better now, and says some girls who have read the manuscripts say it is "splendid!" As it is for them, they are the best critics, so I should be satisfied.[18]

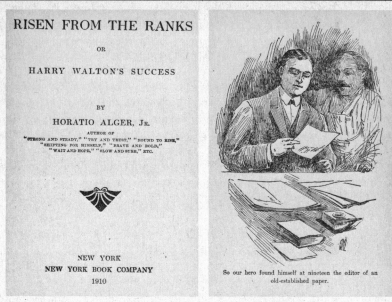

RISEN FROM THE RANKS

OR

HARRY WALTON'S SUCCESS

BY

HORATIO ALGER, JR.

AUTHOR OF

"STRONG AND STEADY," "TRY AND TRUST," "BOUND TO RISE,"
"SHIFTING FOR HIMSELF," "BRAVE AND BOLD,"
"WAIT AND HOPE," "SLOW AND SURE," ETC.

NEW YORK
NEW YORK BOOK COMPANY
1910

So our hero found himself at nineteen the editor of an
old-established paper.

Horatio Alger. *Risen from the Ranks,* 1874.

Little Women was well received by reviewers and sales were good here and in England. By early November 1868, she had begun work on the second part, and *Little Women or Meg, Jo, Beth and Amy. Part Second* was published on April 14, 1869.

The book was certainly the Alcott family story, the major difference being that an impractical and therefore unsympathetic father is replaced by an absent and therefore heroic father who is off with the Union Army. The March family survive happily without him, which is reminiscent of Alcott's thrillers in which women revenge themselves on men or prove them unnecessary.

The novel has vitality, joy, real life, and love generally devoid of sentimentality. It is, perhaps, a wistful portrait of a life Alcott wished she could have lived. The Civil War background is brilliantly subtle, pervading the book but rarely spoken. Indeed, the loneliness and never-ending quality of war is better expressed in *Little Women* than in many war novels for all their suffering, death, pain, and horror. Aimed at young adults, *Little Women* has maintained steady popularity with them and with younger children. Adults reread it to gain a sense of where they were when they were young.

Her later books were well received and remain favorites of many young adults today: *An Old-Fashioned Girl* (1870), *Little Men* (1871), *Eight Cousins* (1875), *Rose in Bloom* (1876), *Under the Lilacs* (1878), *Jack and Jill* (1880), and *Jo's Boys* (1886). None, however, were as successful as *Little Women*.

Son of an unctuous Unitarian clergyman who made the boy's childhood a nightmare of guilt and frustration, Horatio Alger spent his youth studying, in the process becoming known as "Holy Horatio." After graduation from Harvard at eighteen, Alger vacillated, entering and then leaving Harvard Divinity School, writing for the *Boston Transcript,* and teaching at a boys' school. Ordained a Unitarian minister in 1864, he served a Brewster, Massachusetts church only to leave two years later under a cloud of scandal, effectively hushed up at the time.[19] Already the author of seven books, Alger moved to New York City and began to write full time.

That same year he sent *Ragged Dick or Street Life in New York* to Oliver Optic's *Student and Schoolmate,* a goody-goody magazine for moral boys and girls. Optic knew salable pap when he saw it, and he bought Alger's work for the January 1867 issue. Published in 1867 or 1868 in hardback, *Ragged Dick* was the first of many successes for Alger and his publisher A. K. Loring in Boston and remains Alger's most readable novel, probably because it was the first from the mold that later turned totally predictable.

The plot, as in most Alger books, consisted of semiconnected episodes illustrating a boy's first steps towards maturity, respectability, and affluence. Ragged Dick, a young bootblack, sleeps "in a wooden box half full of straw." Grubby but not dirty, he smokes and gambles occasionally, but the reader immediately recognizes his essential goodness. On his way to work one day, he meets Mr. Greyson who gives him a quarter for a shine, says he cannot wait for change, and asks Dick to bring the fifteen cents to his office. Dick is the only one surprised, for Greyson sees in Dick what Alger assumes readers see, his inherent honesty and nobility. A few minutes later, Dick overhears Mr. Whitney talking to his nephew Frank, who is in need of a guide. Dick volunteers, to no one's surprise (except that of the reader who wonders why anyone would choose a totally unknown bootblack with whom to entrust his nephew). Mr. Whitney accepts, and the boys set out on a nine-chapter tour of the city, a handbook to the sights, sounds, and dangers of New York City.[20]

After Frank and Dick temporarily part, Dick vows a course of self-improvement with Frank as his model. When he returns the fifteen cents change to Mr. Greyson, the much-impressed Greyson asks Dick to attend the church where he teaches Sunday School. That same day, Dick befriends better-educated Henry Fosdick who, in return for sharing Dick's room, agrees to tutor him. He and Fosdick go to church and meet Greyson and his wife and their daughter, Ida, whom Dick clearly likes. Dick and Henry move steadily upward in the world, saving a bit each week and becoming more respectable every day. The novel, although wooden in style and episodically plotted, has touches of reality till this point. Alger, apparently unwilling or unable to move Dick slowly up the ladder of respectability, puts pluck aside and adds the infamous luck that characterized his novels. Dick and Fosdick find themselves on a ferry, a little boy falls overboard, and Dick, ignoring personal danger, follows the child into the water and saves him. A grateful father rewards Dick with new clothing and a job at ten dollars a week, a princely sum for the time. As the book closes, Alger cannot resist the temptation to gild the moral lily and at the same time sell a copy of the sequel:

> Here ends the story of Ragged Dick. As Fosdick said, he is Ragged Dick no
> longer. He has taken a step upward, and is determined to mount still higher.
> There are fresh adventures in store for him, and for others who have been

introduced in these pages. Those who have felt interested in his early life will find his history continued in a new volume, forming the second half of the series, to be called,—

Fame and Fortune:

or,

The Progress of Richard Hunter.

Some readers have incorrectly labeled Alger's books as "rags to riches," but the hero rarely achieves riches though he does find himself at the book's end on the lower rungs of the ladder of success. "Rags to respectability" would be a more accurate statement about Alger's work.

Alger wrote at least 119 novels, many of them popular until the early 1900s, selling altogether between sixteen million and seventeen million copies. Typical and revealing titles were *Luck and Pluck, or John Oakley's Inheritance* (1869), *Sink or Swim, or Harry Raymond's Resolve* (1870), *Bound to Rise, or Harry Walton's Motto* (1873), *Risen from the Ranks, or Harry Walton's Success* (1874), *Do and Dare, or A Brave Boy's Fight for Fortune* (1884), *Struggling Upward, or Luke Larkin's Luck* (1890).

OTHER EARLY SERIES WRITERS

The Boston publishing firm of Lee and Shepard established the format for young adult series. To the distress of teachers, librarians, and some parents, the series became *the* method of publishing most young adult novels, though it became far more sophisticated in Edward Stratemeyer's hands nearly forty years later. If sales are any index, readers delighted in Lee and Shepard's series just as they delighted in other series from other publishing houses. *Publishers' Trade List Annual* for 1887 contained sixteen pages listing 440 authors and 900 books under the Lee and Shepard logo. Series books clearly sold very well.

Four series writers were especially popular: Harry Castlemon, Oliver Optic, Martha Finley, and Susan Coolidge.

Under the pen name of Harry Castlemon, Charles Austin Fosdick wrote his first novel, *Frank the Young Naturalist* (1864), while in the Navy. Admiral David B. Porter agreed to read it and suggested Castlemon submit it to Cincinnati publisher Robert W. Carrol who answered with a $150 check, a letter of praise, and a recommendation that the author follow up with a series of five more books featuring Frank. Castlemon's career was off. He received $200 each for the remainder of the series, *Frank on a Gunboat* (1864), *Frank in the Woods* (1865), *Frank Before Vicksburg* (1865), *Frank on the Lower Mississippi* (1867), and *Frank on the Prairie* (1868), all under the "Gunboat Series" title. Other series followed.

Castlemon's approach was pragmatic. "Boys don't like fine writing. What they want is adventure, and the more of it you can get into 250 pages of manuscript, the better fellow you are."[21]

Typical of Castlemon's work is *Frank at Don Carlos' Ranch* (1871), second in the "Rocky Mountain Series." Archie, Frank's friend, stands before a large oil painting.

Something about the painting catches Archie's eye, he touches it, and a mysterious door opens. Archie's words and Castlemon's comment are the essence of Castlemon's style and the moral tone of his books:

> "Now I'd like to know what this means," thought he, pressing the knob harder than before. "This thing must be attached to a spring, because it comes back when I let go of it. Well—by—gracious!"
>
> It was very seldom indeed that Archie used any slang words, but sometimes, when he was greatly excited or astonished, he did like other boys—forgot all the good resolutions he had made regarding this bad habit.

Castlemon's popularity dimmed by 1900, but a Philadelphia librarian in 1925 woefully admitted Castlemon's novels were still read.[22]

Oliver Optic, pen name of William Taylor Adams, was a prolific writer, producing more than 100 books for young people under the Lee and Shepard banner. *The Boat Club* (1855), his first book and the first volume of the six book "Boat Club Series," ran through sixty editions and set a pattern for such series to follow as "The Army and Navy Series," "The Lake Shore Series," "The Onward and Upward Series," "The Great Western Series," "The Blue and the Gray Afloat Series," and "The Blue and the Gray on Land Series."

Kilgour maintains that Optic created mass-production writing for young people, which led librarians and teachers to attack Optic as they criticized few other authors.[23]

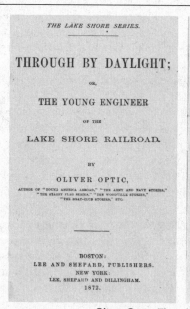

Oliver Optic. *Through by Daylight,* 1872.

Some bitterness may have stemmed from Optic's sales—he was a best-seller during his lifetime and afterwards—but adults never forgave him his fantastic plots and wooden dialogue.

If Optic is remembered at all today, it is for his quarrel with Louisa May Alcott who attacked his kind of book in her *Eight Cousins* (1875). In Chapter 8, Alcott describes four young men on a rainy Sunday afternoon reading and smoking. Mother appears and has nothing good to say about their choice of reading material, the sensational and unrealistic plots and the language. Optic saw the attack when the episode was first published in the August 1875 *St. Nicholas*. Optic defended himself in his *Oliver Optic's Magazine* for September 1875 by implying that Alcott may have borrowed the title for *Eight Cousins* from Amanda Douglas' *Seven Daughters*, published in his magazine, and by arguing that she mixed titles and plots and wildly exaggerated the stories. Optic concluded:

> Ah, Louisa, you are very smart, and you have become rich. Your success mocks that of the juvenile heroes you despise. Even the author of "Dick Dauntless" and "Sam Soaker," whoever he may be would not dare to write up a heroine who rose so rapidly from poverty and obscurity to riches and fame as you did; but in view of the wholesale perversion of the truth as we have pointed out, *ie* must ask you to adopt the motto you recommend for others— "Be honest and you will be happy," instead of the one you seem to have chosen: "Be smart and you will be rich."[24]

Attacks by reviewers, teachers, librarians, and even Alcott did not carry the day, for as late as 1900 Lee and Shepard's catalogue advertised 123 Oliver Optic novels.

Using the pen name Martha Farquharson, Martha Finley wrote the "Elsie Dinsmore" series, probably the most popular series of its time. In twenty-eight volumes, the series carried Elsie from childhood to grandmotherhood. A favorite with young women and a girl critics loved to hate, Elsie is persistently docile, pious, sincere, lachrymose, virtuous, humble, timid, ignorant, and good—irritatingly, pleasingly, or nauseatingly good.

Published in 1867 and running to an incredible number of editions after that, *Elsie Dinsmore* opens with virtuous and Christian Elsie awaiting the return of her beloved but long-absent father. Elsie has continual problems with a cold and indifferent father, Finley's way of demonstrating that children must love parents, no matter how blind the love must be, and that girls must love God and Jesus above all, no matter what the pressures. And if Elsie needs her love or faith to be tried, her father is unquestionably trying.

The most widely quoted episode, by those who loved or hated the book, occurs one Sunday when father asks Elsie to perform at the piano for guests. Elsie pleads, always in a pious and respectful tone, that the Sabbath forbids secular music, but father demands she remain at the piano until she is willing to play. Several hours pass while Elsie sits playing the martyr but never the piano. Suddenly, Elsie feels a pain and falls. A guest rushes to Elsie:

"A light! quick, quick, a light!" he cried, raising Elsie's insensible form in his arms; "the child has fainted."

One of the others, instantly snatching a lamp from a distant table, brought it near, and the increased light showed Elsie's little face, ghastly as that of a corpse, while a stream of blood was flowing from a wound in the temple, made by striking against some sharp corner of the furniture as she fell.

Seconds later, her soft eyes open and her first words are:

"Dear papa, are you angry with me?"

Next morning, a temporarily remorseful father visits Elsie:

"Elsie, do you know that you were very near being killed last night?"

"No, papa, was I?" she asked with an awestruck countenance.

"Yes, the doctor says if that wound had been made half an inch nearer your eye—I should have been childless."

His voice trembled almost too much for utterance as he finished his sentence, and he strained her to his heart with a deep sigh of thankfulness for her escape.

Piety reigns equally in *Elsie's Girlhood* (1872), in which Elsie incessantly cries, faints, loves, and prays; *Elsie's Motherhood* (1876); *Elsie's Children* (1877); *Elsie's Widowhood* (1880)—Elsie's husband was probably killed because he was an obstacle in plots; *Christmas with Grandma Elsie* (1888); and *Elsie in the South* (1899). Elsie moves from childhood to marriage to widowhood affirming the joys of fainting and crying, the American Dream fulfilled through piety, morality, and prayer.[25]

Susan Coolidge, pen name of Sarah Chauncey Woolsey, wrote fewer books than any other series writer. Only one of her series found wide favor, but it once rivalled Alcott's books. It is still published in England and reads well even today. *What Katy Did* (1872) features tomboy Katy Carr, her widowed doctor-father, and three sisters and two brothers. *What Katy Did at School* (1873) carries sixteen-year-old Katy on to boarding school where her escapades keep her in trouble. *What Katy Did Next* (1886) takes Katy off to Europe and a young naval officer. *Clover* (1888) and *In the Valley* (1891) conclude the series.

Coolidge's heroine resembles Alcott's Jo March in several ways. She is stubborn and sometimes willful but essentially good, loving, and caring. Katy is almost as attractive as Jo and sometimes more believable in her pranks. In 1978, the Public Broadcasting System produced six episodes of Katy's life, condensing too much too fast but proving that Coolidge's books deserve reading today, perhaps even a revival.

THE LITERATURE OF THE BAD BOY

Beginning with Thomas Bailey Aldrich's *The Story of a Bad Boy* in 1870, a literature developed around bad boys, flesh and blood, imperfect boys, tough on the outside and able to survive troubles in a world that was often rough and sometimes cruel.

The books were, except for Twain's, nostalgic books about old times, harking back to a golden age that had never been. Sometimes cruel and frequently confusing boyishness with barbarism, they were ultimately patronizing and backward-looking and, with the exception of Twain's, doomed to a relatively short life.

Thomas Bailey Aldrich was a prolific writer, but his reputation rests on *The Story of a Bad Boy*. Serialized in *Our Young Folks*, January to December 1869, and published as a book a year later, Aldrich's part-novel, part-autobiography became an immediate success with critics and readers. William Dean Howells began his review in the *Atlantic*:

> Mr. Aldrich has done a new thing in—we use the phrase with some gasps of reluctance, it is so threadbare and so near meaning nothing—American literature. We might go much farther without overpraising his pleasant book, and call it an absolute novelty, on the whole. No one else seems to have thought of telling the story of a boy's life, with so great desire to show what a boy's life is, and so little purpose of teaching what it should be; certainly no one else has thought of doing this for the life of an American boy.[26]

Aldrich's book was a novelty, but more important, it told the story of a boy as he was, or might be, not as he should have been. The book marked the beginning of realistic literature about boys, just as Alcott's *Little Women* had served the cause of young women only two years before.

The Story of a Bad Boy begins in New Orleans where Tom lives with his parents, though he is soon forced to return North where he will live with his grandfather. The story that stays with readers centers around Tom's gang, The Centipedes, the snowball fights, picnics, pranks of all sorts, and the girls whom members of the gang love. Aldrich illustrates with singular accuracy the social and moral values of the time, but other than Tom, the book falls back on stereotyped characterizations.

Newspaperman, writer, humorist, and later Governor of Wisconsin, George Wilbur Peck began writing about "Peck's Bad Boy" in *Peck's Sun*, his Milwaukee newspaper-family humor magazine, in 1882 and published *Peck's Bad Boy and His Pa* a year later. The crude jokes go beyond cruelty and the dialect becomes outlandish in later sequels.

Peck's Bad Boy and His Pa devotes separate chapters to the Bad Boy's pranks, often played on his father though the Boy does not discriminate. Two episodes will convey the book's spirit. In Chapter 11, the Boy douses his father's handkerchief with rum and wraps it around playing cards. Pa attends a prayer meeting where the preacher asks him to tell about his recent reformation. When Pa speaks, breaking into tears and taking out his handkerchief, cards fly and fumes spread. In Chapter 30, Pa comes home drunk. The Boy pretends to take him to a dissecting room where the Boy and his friends act as if they will cut him up as Pa wakes up and is horrified.

Peck had no subtlety, but his humor brought him readers far beyond any other writer of bad boy literature excepting Twain.

Mark Twain was the capstone of both bad boys' literature and nineteenth-century literature generally. *The Adventures of Tom Sawyer* (1876) and *The Adventures of*

Huckleberry Finn (1884) took the bad boy theme far beyond Aldrich or Peck. Humor, sometimes cruel, adventure, and other conventions of the bad boy books can be found in Twain, but compassion is mixed with cynicism, and there is none of the condescension or simplistic nostalgia of earlier bad boy books. As many critics have noted, *Huck Finn,* and to a lesser degree *Tom Sawyer,* are books young and old can read over and over on quite different levels, young adults for adventure and perhaps more, adults for insight and perhaps more.

Twain's problems with the censor are well known. Before *Huck Finn* was published in hardback, the February 1885 *Century Magazine* published extracts, but not all that Twain submitted. *Century* editor Richard Watson Gilder apparently found some material too harsh or too coarse and left out the preacher's harangue at the camp meeting and the lynching of Colonel Sherburn.[27]

After the publication of *Huck Finn,* the Concord (Massachusetts) Library banned the book as trashy, vicious, and unfit to be placed next to books by Emerson or Thoreau. Louisa May Alcott said, "If Mr. Clemens cannot think of something better to tell our pure-minded lads and lasses, he had best stop writing for them," a comment

---

The Brooklyn Public Library excluded *Tom Sawyer* and *Huck Finn* from their children's room as "bad examples for ingenuous youth" in 1905.

Twain felt would sell an additional 25,000 copies. The Concord Library was not alone in damning the book. *The Springfield Republican* wrote in 1885, "They [*Tom Sawyer* and *Huck Finn*] are no better in tone than the dime novels which flood the blood-and-thunder reading population. . . . Their moral tone is low, and their perusal cannot be anything less than harmful."[28] And the *St. Louis Republican* surveying the reading of young people in 1889 concluded its comments with:

> This also proves that there is growing up in this country a standard juvenile literature which is healthy and hopeful. There were but few lists containing books of a harmful tendency. It is not much to say that the books of the *Tom Sawyer* and *Huckleberry Finn* order were the worst mentioned.[29]

The Brooklyn Public Library excluded both books from their children's room as "bad examples for ingenuous youth" in 1905. Asa Don Dickinson, Librarian of Brooklyn College, pleaded that Twain's books be put back on the shelves, but "It was no use. The good ladies assured me in effect that Huck was a deceitful boy."[30] Dickinson sent an apologetic letter to Twain and received this reply.

Dear Sir:

I am greatly troubled by what you say. I wrote *Tom Sawyer* and *Huck Finn* for adults exclusively, and it always distresses me when I find that boys and girls have been allowed access to them. The mind that becomes soiled in youth can never again be washed clean; I know this by my own experience, and to this day I cherish an unappeasable bitterness against the unfaithful guardians of my young life, who not only permitted but compelled me to read an unexpurgated Bible through before I was 15 years old. None can do that and ever draw a clean sweet breath again this side of the grave. Ask that young lady—she will tell you so.

Most honestly do I wish I could say a softening word or two in defence of Huck's character, since you wish it, but really in my opinion it is no better than God's (in the Ahab chapter and 97 others) and those of Solomon, David, Satan, and the rest of the sacred brotherhood.

If there is an unexpurgated in the Children's Department, won't you please help that young woman remove Huck and Tom from that questionable companionship?[31]

WRITERS OF ADVENTURE TALES

Many important writers for young adults did not write series books. Most wrote fiction, for surveys reported that young adults liked fiction more than other literary genres, the favorites being adventure with boys, adventure and love stories with girls.[32] And tales of adventure, many of them first-rate, were easily found.

The past was a continual source of adventure. George Alfred Henty acquired fascination for and knowledge of foreign countries and their history as a newspaper reporter, and his eighty-odd historical-adventure tales read well even today once readers overcome some dated nineteenth-century diction. Of especial worth are *Beric, The Briton: A Story of the Roman Invasion* (1893), *When London Burned: A Story of the Plague and the Fire* (1895), and *Winning His Spurs: A Tale of the Crusades* (1892), but Henty is readable in any of his books. John Bennett is best remembered for *Master Skylark: A Story of Shakespeare's Time* (1897), a delightful account of young Nick Attwood, a golden-voiced boy singer who is involved in more than his share of adventure. Howard Pyle was known as an illustrator of young people's books as well as a writer, and *The Merry Adventures of Robin Hood* (1883) is still read. Even better were *Otto of the Silver Hand* (1888), set in medieval Germany, and *Men of Iron* (1892), a marvelously effective and exciting story of villainy and feudal rights in fifteenth-century England.

Piracy and smuggling have always appealed to our sense of adventure. John Meade Falkner wrote several books, but *Moonfleet* (1898) captivated readers, old and young, with its story of smuggling in Dorset, England, buried vaults, and a diamond with a curse. Only Robert Louis Stevenson, master of the genre, surpassed Falkner. Stevenson's *Kidnapped* (1886) is a thriller with a few faults, but *Treasure Island* (1883) is a jewel among adventure stories, popular then and with no loss of popularity now or in the foreseeable future.

Adventure among boys was the theme of three once-popular, now badly under-rated writers. Robert Michael Ballantyne is probably best known for *The Coral Island* (1858) since William Golding's *Lord of the Flies* (1955) parallels the earlier book and mentions it. *The Young Fur Traders* (1856) and *The Gorilla Hunters* (1861) were almost equally popular during the author's lifetime. Noah Brooks wrote biographies of Lincoln and a superb story of boys going west across the plains, *The Boy Emigrants* (1876). Best of the three was the prolific and yet excellent Kirk Munroe. Two of his best novels are *The Flamingo Feather* (1887), about early days in Florida, and *Derrick Sterling* (1888), a brilliant story of a young miner working his way up in life, Alger-like in theme but Dickensian in flavor.

The new adventure tales of mystery and detection were handled by the master, Arthur Conan Doyle, whose *Adventures of Sherlock Holmes* (1891) were first published for a delighted *Strand Magazine* audience. Later tales have not dimmed with time.

An even more exotic kind of adventure was the province of Jules Verne (1828–1905), whose science fiction and adventure tales *Twenty Thousand Leagues Under the Sea* (1872), *From the Earth to the Moon* (1873), and *Around the World in Eighty Days* (1874) delighted and confounded adult and young adult readers for many years.

FICTION AND LIBRARIES

The growth of public libraries in America presented opportunities for both the pleasure and education of the masses, but arguments about the purpose of public libraries arose almost simultaneously with the buildings themselves.

William F. Poole listed three common objections to the public library in the October 1876 *American Library Journal*[33] (soon to change its name to the *Library Journal*): the normal dread of taxes; the more philosophical belief that government had no rights except to protect people and property, that is no right to tax anyone to build and stock a public library; and concern over the kinds of books libraries might buy and circulate. In this third class of objection, Poole touched upon a problem that would rage for years thereafter, that is, whether a public library is established to provide assistance for scholars or for the masses. Poole believed the public library existed for the entire community or else there was no justification for a general tax.

Poole's words did not quiet critics who argued that the library's sole raison d'être was educational. Waving the banner of American purity in his hands, W. M. Stevenson maintained:

> If the public library is not first and foremost an educational institution, it has no right to exist. If it exists for mere entertainment, and for a low order of entertainment at that, it is simply a socialistic institution.[34]

Many librarians agreed.

The problem lay almost exclusively with fiction. Librarians, appalled by what they considered cheap, sensational, *pernicious* (a favorite word, much overused to describe the horror they felt) trash, anointed themselves to bring the unwashed masses to literary, if not personal, salvation.

But the debate over fiction and its propriety had begun much earlier.

Early Attacks on Fiction

The English novel originated by Richardson in his supposedly moral *Pamela* (1740) and continued by the more realistic, honest, and moral novels of Fielding led to some opposition in England but considerably more in America. Moral qualms became even stronger following the Revolutionary War, partly because of chauvinism but mostly from pietistic reasons, as novel reading became widespread and approached a national craze. Minor American authors warned youth of the dangers of the novel-reading habit. Mrs. Bloomsgrove, a novelist now forgotten for good reason, wrote to young women:

> Nothing can have a worse effect on our sex, than a free use of these writings which are the offspring of our modern novelists. Their only tendency is to excite romantic notions, while they keep the mind void of ideas, and the heart destitute of sentiment.[35]

Later novelists, perhaps to please moralists and defend themselves from potential attack and perhaps because they themselves wondered about the propriety and inherent decency of novels and novel reading, found occasion, paradoxically, to attack novel reading in their own novels. In the first domestic novel, Susan Warner's *The Wide, Wide World,* lachrymose heroine Ellen Montgomery is forbidden to read *Blackwood's Magazine* since it contains fiction.

Fiction Can Be Dangerous If Taken Internally

The second session of the 1876 American Library Association meeting in Philadelphia was devoted to "Novel-Reading." Controversy rose immediately, symptomatic of an argument to rage for years. A librarian announced that his rules permitted no novels in the library. His factory-worker patrons might ask for them, but he recommended other books and was able to keep patrons without supplying novels. To laughter, he said he never read novels so he "could not say what their effect really was."[36]

His sublimely ridiculous and condescending attitude toward library patrons was echoed by others. Librarians worried that catering to popular taste was dangerous, for "by supplying such books, a library fosters the taste that craves them, and it increases the demand."[37]

Laymen joined in. Thomas De Witt Talmage, a colorful and exceptionally popular Brooklyn Presbyterian Minister, frequently wrote and spoke on the dangers of the novel habit. He regarded novels, with but rare exceptions, as tools of Satan and perversity in print:

> A man who gives himself up to the indiscriminate reading of novels will be nervous, inane and a nuisance. He will be fit neither for the store, nor the

shop, nor the field. A woman who gives herself up to the indiscriminate
reading of novels will be unfitted for the duties of wife, mother, sister,
daughter. There she is, hair disheveled, countenance vacant, cheeks pale,
hands trembling, bursting into tears at midnight over the fate of some
unfortunate lover; in the daytime, when she ought to be busy, staring by the
half hour at nothing; biting her finger nails into the quick. . . . I could tell you
of a comrade that was great-hearted, noble, and generous. He was studying for
an honorable profession, but he had an infidel book in his trunk, and he said
to me one day: "De Witt, would you like to read it?" I said: "Yes, I would." I
took the book and read it only for a few minutes. I was really startled with
what I saw there, and I handed the book back to him and said: "You had
better destroy that book." No, he kept it. He read it, he re-read it. After
awhile he gave up religion as a myth. He gave up God as a nonentity. He gave
up the *Bible* as a fable. He gave up the Church of Christ as a useless
institution. He gave up good morals as being unnecessarily stringent. I have
heard of him but twice in many years. The time before the last I heard of him
he was a confirmed inebriate. The last I heard of him he was coming out of an
insane asylum—in body, mind and soul an awful wreck. I believe that infidel
book killed him for two worlds.[38]

Fiction and Young Adults

Librarians particularly worried about fiction's effect on young adults. Doubtless
they envied the plan devised by the Massachusetts Board of Education in 1840 providing leisure reading for young people but carefully excluding all fiction from its lists.
Librarians, generally, had no easy way out, for most of their libraries had fiction. The
problem was how to control it and restrict its use among young adults.

Poole argued in 1876 that the problem lay with parents who must regulate the
reading of young people.[39] But in the same volume of the *American Library Journal*,
William Kite lamented the dangers novels presented to young adults,[40] and library
literature did not relinquish the theme for some time.[41] Green posed the question, at
least a bit tongue in cheek, "Is it proper to have sensational novels and highly spiced
stories for the young in public libraries?"[42] and then answered, "They do good two
ways. They keep men and women and boys from worse reading. . . . They give young
persons a taste for reading."[43] James Mascarene Hubbard warred with trustees of the
Boston Public Library for years over the corruptive fiction he wanted removed.[44] *Library Journal* authors worried about the young adult fiction question while the battle
raged and even after 1900 when the war was over and fiction had become available to
young adults in most libraries.

Teachers worried almost as much as librarians. A principal of a large endowed
academy was approvingly quoted by a librarian for having said:

The voracious devouring of fiction commonly indulged in by patrons of the
public library, especially the young, is extremely pernicious and mentally
unwholesome.[45]

Similar complaints led some librarians to limit the number of books young adults could take out at one time. When Caroline M. Hewins surveyed library conditions in 1893, she found:

> 90 libraries allow them [young people] to change a book every day; one (subscription) gives them a dozen a day if they wish. 15 limit them to 2, and 3 to 3 a week, and 15 to only 1. Several librarians in libraries where children are allowed a book a day express their disapproval of the custom, and one has entered into an engagement with her young readers to take 1 book in every 4 from some other class than fiction.[46]

A gradual change from piety to morality led to literature that was more subtly if still surely didactic by 1900. Literature read by young adults, whether adult works or those written specifically for young adults—and the latter made great strides in quantity and quality—reflected the increasing freedom of writers. The development of inexpensive and ubiquitous dime novels, the popular story weeklies, and paperback libraries, along with more expensive but equally ubiquitous domestic novels, created a mass market of readers and led to an expanded national literacy. The rise of the public library permitted easier access to a greater quantity of literature just as it raised problems about the purpose of the library, especially for young adults. Series books, for better or worse, began. Expansion of literature written for young adults, and especially series books, lay only a few years away.

ACTIVITIES

1. Read Evelyn Geller's "The Librarian as Censor," *Library Journal* 101 (June 1, 1976): 1255-58 as background, and then read a few articles from early issues of the *Library Journal* on the question of restricting young adults from reading fiction in the library. Why do you suppose the restrictions applied almost exclusively to fiction? What arguments seem dated? What arguments might be used by a modern censor? Find a few articles in modern journals—like the *English Journal, School Library Journal, Top of the News, Wilson Library Bulletin,* or *Media and Methods*—on censorship and compare the reasoning of the contemporary and the old.
2. Locate a domestic novel (most university libraries are likely to have a few by Susan Warner and/or Augusta Wilson) and read the first few pages and perhaps skim a bit more. What kinds of style, diction, and plot devices or conventions are used that resemble modern best-selling gothics or romances? In what ways do these once-popular novels differ from popular novels of today? What about the domestic novel probably made it popular then?
3. Trying very hard to stay awake, read an Alger novel—several have been reprinted in the past few years. What elements about his books made them popular with young adults (and some adults)? If you were asked to write a brief introduction to

a modern reissue of the Alger novel, what would you want to say to the modern reader about Alger's popularity, his style, his message, his readability?

4. Read a dime novel to determine the style and formula. Compare it with a modern adventure novel, perhaps one by Peter Benchley or Ian Fleming or some other current favorite. What similarities and differences in plotting and characterization are evident? What aspects of the dime novel seem dated today? Which seem to have survived to be used by modern writers?

NOTES

[1]Caroline Ticknor, *Hawthorne and His Publisher* (Boston: Houghton Mifflin Co., 1913), p. 141.

[2]E. Douglas Branch, *The Sentimental Years, 1836-1860* (New York: Appleton, 1934), p. 131.

[3]William Everett, "Beadle's Dime Novels," *North American Review* 9 (July 1864): 308.

[4]Quentin Reynolds, *The Fiction Factory, or From Pulp Row to Quality Street* (New York: Random House, Inc., 1955), pp. 74-75.

[5]Charles Bragin, *Bibliography: Dime Novels 1860-1964* (New York: Privately printed, 1964), p. 2.

[6]Frederic Van Rensselaer Dey, "How I Wrote a Thousand 'Nick Carter' Novels," *American Magazine* 89 (February 1920): 19.

[7]William Sumner, "What Our Boys Are Reading," *Scribner's Monthly* 15 (March 1878): 681-85.

[8]Theodore C. Burgess, "Means of Leading Boys from the Dime Novel to Better Literature," *Library Journal* 21 (April 1896): 147.

[9]*Publisher's Weekly* 23 (April 28, 1883): 500.

[10]Ibid.

[11]See especially Burgess; Clement C. Young, "The Public Library and the Public School," *Library Journal* 21 (March 1896): 140-44; Arthur P. Irving, "Home Reading of School Children," *Pedagogical Seminary* 7 (April 1900): 138-40; "The Pawtucket Free Library and the Dime Novel," *Library Journal* 10 (May 1885): 105; and Ellen M. Cox, "What Can Be Done to Help a Boy to Like Good Books after He Has Fallen into the 'Dime Novel Habit'?" *Library Journal* 20 (April 1895): 118-19. There were many other examples.

[12]Quoted in Esther Jane Carrier, *Fiction in Public Libraries, 1876-1900* (New York: Scarecrow Press, 1965), p. 186.

[13]Quoted in *Library Journal* 8 (March-April 1883): 57.

[14]Everett, p. 308.

[15]T. W. Higginson, "Address," *Library Journal* 4 (September-October 1879): 359.

[16]Mary Noel, *Villains Galore . . . The Heyday of the Popular Story Weekly* (New York: Macmillan Publishing Company, Inc., 1954), p. 111.

[17]Ibid., pp. 112-13.

[18]Ednah D. Cheney, ed., *Louisa May Alcott: Her Life, Letters, and Journals* (Boston: Little, Brown and Company, 1901), p. 199.

[19]Edwin P. Hoyt, *Horatio's Boys: The Life and Works of Horatio Alger, Jr.* (Radnor, Pennsylvania: Chilton Book Company, 1974), pp. 1-6.

[20]See Eric Monkkonen, "Socializing the New Urbanites: Horatio Alger, Jr.'s Guidebooks," *Journal of Popular Culture* 11 (Summer 1977): 77-87, for a fine discussion of *Ragged Dick* as guidebook and handbook.

[21]Jacob Blanck, *Harry Castlemon, Boys' Own Author* (New York: R. R. Bowker Co., 1941), pp. 5-6.

[22]Samuel Scoville, Jr., "Rescue, Robbers, and Escapes," *Forum* 74 (July 1925): 86.

[23]Raymond L. Kilgour, *Lee and Shepard: Publishers for the People* (Hamden, Connecticut: The Shoe String Press, Inc., 1965), p. 270.

[24]Oliver Optic, "Sensational Books," *Oliver Optic's Magazine* 18 (September 1875): 718. For an account of the quarrel, see Gene Gleason, "What Ever Happened to Oliver Optic?" *Wilson Library Bulletin* 49 (May 1975): 647-50.

[25]For a somewhat different point of view, note Jacqueline Jackson and Philip Kendall, "What Makes a Bad Book Good: Elsie Dinsmore" in Francelia Butler, ed., *Children's Literature: Annual of the Modern Language Association Group on Children's Literature and the Children's Literature Association* 7 (1978): 45-67.

[26]*Atlantic* 25 (January 1870): 124.

[27]Robert Berkelman, "Mrs. Grundy and Richard Watson Gilder," *American Quarterly* 4 (Spring 1952): 66-72.

[28]Quoted in *Critic* 3 (March 28, 1885): 155.

[29]*Library Journal* 14 (November 18, 1889): 445.

[30]Asa Don Dickinson, "Huckleberry Finn Is Fifty Years Old—Yes; But Is He Respectable?" *Wilson Bulletin* 10 (November 1935): 183.

[31]Ibid.

[32]For examples, see *Library Journal* 8 (March-April 1883): 49-50, and Royal W. Bullock, "Some Observations on Children's Reading," *NEA Journal of Proceedings and Addresses, 1897* (Chicago: University of Chicago Press, 1897), pp. 1015-21.

[33]William F. Poole, "Some Popular Objections to Public Libraries," *American Library Journal* 1 (October 1876): 48-49.

[34]W. M. Stevenson, "Weeding Out Fiction in the Carnegie Free Library of Allegheny, Pa.," *Library Journal* 22 (March 1897): 135.

[35]Quoted in Tremaine McDowell, "Sensibility in the Eighteenth-Century American Novel," *Studies in Philology* 24 (July 1927): 395.

[36]"Novel Reading," *American Library Journal* 1 (October 1876): 98.

[37]George T. Clark, "Improper Books," *Library Journal* 20 (December 1895): 34.

[38]T. De Witt Talmage, *Social Dynamite, or The Wickedness of Modern Society* (Chicago: Standard Publishing Co., 1888) quoted in Neil Harris, ed., *The Land of Contrasts, 1880-1901* (New York: George Braziller, Inc., 1970), pp. 275, 278-79.

[39]Poole, pp. 49-50.

[40]William Kite, "Fiction in Public Libraries," *American Library Journal* 1 (February 1877): 277-79.

[41]For the best full discussion see Esther Jane Carrier, *Fiction in Public Libraries, 1876–1900* (New York: Scarecrow Press, 1965). See also one especially rich issue of *Library Journal* 4 (September–October 1879) with articles by Green, Clarke, Higginson, Atkinson, and Chamberlain.

[42]S. S. Green, "Sensational Fiction in Public Libraries," *Library Journal* 4 (September–October 1879): 347–48.

[43]Ibid., 348.

[44]See the following, only a few of many accounts of the running battle. J. M. Hubbard, "Fiction at the Boston Public Library," *Library Journal* 6 (July 1881): 205–6; "Editorial," *Library Journal* 6 (August 1881): 223; "Pernicious Reading in Our Public Libraries," *The Nation* 33 (November 10, 1881): 370–71; "Boston Public Library," *Library Journal* 6 (December 1881): 319; *Library Journal* 6 (January 1881): 11, 13; *Library Journal* 6 (March 1881): 45–47; J. M. Hubbard, *The Public Library and the School-Children: An Appeal to the Parents, Clergymen, and Teachers of Boston* (Boston: 1881); J. M. Hubbard, "How to Use a Public Library," *Library Journal* 9 (February 1884): 25–29; J. M. Hubbard, "Are Public Libraries Public Blessings?" *North American Review* 149 (September 1889): 339–46; "Editorial," *Library Journal* 14 (October 1889): 399.

[45]"Monthly Reports from Public Librarians upon the Reading of Minors: A Suggestion," *Library Journal* 24 (August 1899): 479.

[46]Caroline M. Hewins, "Report on the Reading of the Young," *Library Journal* 18 (July 1893): 252.

TITLES MENTIONED IN CHAPTER THREE

Abbott, Jacob. *Rollo at School.* 1839.

———. *Rollo at Work, or, The Way for a Boy to Learn to Be Industrious.* 1838.

———. *Rollo in London.* 1855.

———. *Rollo in Rome.* 1858.

———. *Rollo on the Atlantic.* 1853.

Alcott, Louisa May. *Eight Cousins.* 1875.

———. *Hospital Sketches.* 1863.

———. *Jack and Jill.* 1880.

———. *Jo's Boys.* 1886.

———. *Little Men.* 1871.

———. *Little Women: Meg, Jo, Beth, and Amy. The Story of Their Lives. A Girl's Book.* Lee and Shepard, 1868.

———. *Little Women or Meg, Jo, Beth and Amy. Part Second.* 1869.

———. *An Old-Fashioned Girl.* 1870.

———. *On Picket Duty and Other Tales.* 1864.

———. *Rose in Bloom.* 1876.

———. *Under the Lilacs.* 1878.

Aldrich, Thomas Bailey. *The Story of a Bad Boy.* 1870.

Alger, Horatio. *Bound to Rise; Or Harry Walton's Motto.* A. K. Loring, 1873.

———. *Do and Dare; Or, A Brave Boy's Fight for Fortune.* A. K. Loring, 1884.

———. *Fame and Fortune; Or, The Progress of Richard Hunter.* A. K. Loring, 1868.

———. *Luck and Pluck; Or, John Oakley's Inheritance.* A. K. Loring, 1869.

———. *Ragged Dick; Or, Street Life in New York.* A. K. Loring, @ 1867.

———. *Risen from the Ranks; Or, Harry Walton's Success.* A. K. Loring, 1874.

———. *Sink or Swim; Or, Harry Raymond's Resolve.* A. K. Loring, 1870.

———. *Struggling Upward; Or, Luke Larkin's Luck.* A. K. Loring, 1890.

Ballantyne, Robert Michael. *The Coral Island.* 1858.

———. *The Gorilla Hunters.* 1861.

———. *The Young Fur Traders.* 1856.

Bennett, John. *Master Skylark; A Story of Shakespeare's Time.* 1897.

The Bible.

Brontë, Charlotte. *Jane Eyre.* 1847.

Brooks, Noah. *The Boy Emigrants.* 1876.

Bunyan, John. *The Pilgrim's Progress from This World to That Which Is to Come.* 1678.

Castlemon, Harry. (real name: Charles Austin Fosdick). *Frank at Don Carlos' Ranch.* Robert W. Carrol, 1871.

———. *Frank Before Vicksburg.* Robert W. Carrol, 1865.

———. *Frank in the Woods.* Robert W. Carrol, 1865.

———. *Frank on a Gunboat.* Robert W. Carrol, 1864.

———. *Frank on the Lower Mississippi.* Robert W. Carrol, 1867.

———. *Frank on the Prairie.* Robert W. Carrol, 1868.

———. *Frank the Young Naturalist.* Robert W. Carrol, 1864.

Coolidge, Susan (real name: Sarah Chauncey Woolsey). *Clover.* 1888.

———. *In the Valley.* 1891.

———. *What Katy Did.* 1872.

———. *What Katy Did at School.* 1873.

———. *What Katy Did Next.* 1886.

Cooper, James Fenimore. *Leatherstocking Tales.* 1850.

Cummins, Maria. *The Lamplighter.* @ 1855.

Dallas, Mary Kyle. *Neglected Warning, or, The Trials of a Public School Teacher.* Street and Smith, n.d.

Day, Thomas. *The History of Sanford and Merton.* 1783, 86, and 89.

Defoe, Daniel. *The Life and Strange Surprising Adventures of Robinson Crusoe.* 1719.

———. *Moll Flanders.* 1722.

———. *Roxanna.* 1724.

Dey, Frederick Van Rensselaer. "Nick Carter" series.

Doyle, Arthur Conan. *The Adventures of Sherlock Holmes.* 1891.

Edgeworth, Maria. *Castle Rackrent.* 1800.

———. *Frank.* 1822.

———. *Harry and Lucy.* 1801.

———. *Harry and Lucy Concluded.* 1825.

———. *Moral Tales for Young People.* 1801.

———. *The Parent's Assistant.* 1796.

———. *Popular Tales.* 1804.

———. *Rosamund.* 1821.

Ellis, Edward S. *Seth Jones.* Beadle and Adams, 1860.

———. *Trail Hunters.* Beadle and Adams, 1862.

Falkner, John Meade. *Moonfleet.* 1898.

Farquharson, Martha (real name: Martha Finley). *Christmas with Grandma Elsie.* 1888.

———. *Elsie Dinsmore.* 1867.

———. *Elsie in the South.* 1899.

———. *Elsie's Children.* 1877.

———. *Elsie's Girlhood.* 1872.

———. *Elsie's Motherhood.* 1876.

———. *Elsie's Widowhood.* 1880.

Golding, William. *Lord of the Flies.* G. P. Putnam's Sons, 1959.

Henty, George Alfred. *Beric, The Briton. A Story of the Roman Invasion.* 1893.

———. *When London Burned. A Story of the Plague and the Fire.* 1895.

———. *Winning His Spurs. A Tale of the Crusades.* 1892.

More, Hannah. *Coelebs in Search of a Wife.* 1809.

———. *Moral Sketches.* 1819.

———. *Repository Tracts.* 1797–1798.

Mulock, Dinah Maria. *John Halifax, Gentleman.* 1857.

Munroe, Kirk. *Derrick Sterling.* 1888.

———. *The Flamingo Feather.* 1887.

Optic, Oliver (real name: William Taylor Adams). *The Boat Club.* Lee & Shepard, 1855.

Parley, Peter (real name: Samuel Goodrich). *Recollections of a Lifetime, or Men and Things I Have Seen.* 1856.

———. *The Tales of Peter Parley About America.* 1827.

Peck, George Wilbur. *Peck's Bad Boy and His Pa.* 1883.

Porter, Jane. *Thaddeus of Warsaw.* 1803.

Pyle, Howard. *Men of Iron.* 1892.

———. *The Merry Adventures of Robin Hood.* 1883.

———. *Otto of the Silver Hand.* 1883.

Reade, Charles. *Peg Woffington.* 1853.

St. George, Harry (real name: St. George Rathbone). *Daring Davy, The Young Bear Killer; Or, The Trail of the Border Wolf.* 1879.

Smith, Francis S. *The Vestmaker's Apprentice; Or, The Vampyres of Society.* 1857.

Stephens, Ann S. *Malaeska: The Indian Wife of the White Hunter.* Beadle & Adams, 1860.

Stevenson, Robert Louis. *Kidnapped.* 1886.

———. *Treasure Island.* 1883.

Stowe, Harriet Beecher. *Uncle Tom's Cabin.* 1852.

Swift, Jonathan. *Gulliver's Travels.* 1726.

———. *A Tale of a Tub.* 1704.

Twain, Mark (real name: Samuel Clemens). *The Adventures of Huckleberry Finn.* Webster, 1884.

———. *The Adventures of Tom Sawyer.* 1876.

Verne, Jules. *Around the World in Eighty Days.* 1874.

———. *From the Earth to the Moon.* 1873.

———. *Twenty Thousand Leagues Under the Sea.* 1872.

Weems, Mason Locke. *The Life of George Washington.* 1808.

———. *The Life of Washington the Great.* 1806.

———. *A History of the Life and Death, Virtues and Exploits, of General George Washington.* 1800.

Wetherell, Elizabeth (real name: Susan Warner). *The Wide, Wide World.* 1850.

Wilson, Augusta Jane Evans. *St. Elmo.* 1866.

Wood, Mrs. Henry. *East Lynne.* 1861.

SOME SUGGESTED READINGS

General Comments on Literature 1800–1850:

Blanck, Jacob. *Peter Parley to Penrod: A Bibliographical Description of the Best Loved American Juvenile Books.* New York: R. R. Bowker Co., 1938.

Blanck, Jacob. "A Twentieth-Century Look at Nineteenth-Century Children's Books" in *Bibliophile in the Nursery.* Edited by William Targ. Cleveland: World Publishing Co., 1957, pp. 427–51.

Crandall, John C. "Patriotism and Humanitarian Reform in Children's Literature, 1825–1860." *American Quarterly* 21 (Spring 1969): 3–22.

Kiefer, Monica. *American Children Through Their Books, 1700-1835.* Philadelphia: University of Pennsylvania Press, 1948.

MacLeod, Anna Scott. *A Moral Tale: Children's Fiction and American Culture, 1820-1860.* Hamden, Connecticut: Archon Books, 1975.

Rayward, W. Boyd. "What Shall They Read? A Historical Perspective." *Wilson Library Bulletin* 51 (October 1976): 146-53.

Sloane, William. *Children's Books in England and America in the Seventeenth Century.* New York: Columbia University Press, 1955.

Wishy, Bernard. *The Child and The Republic: The Dawn of Modern American Child Nurture.* Philadelphia: University of Pennsylvania Press, 1968.

General Comments on Literature, 1850-1900:

Branch, E. Douglas. *The Sentimental Years, 1836-1860.* New York: Appleton, 1934.

Cowie, Alexander. *The Rise of the American Novel.* New York: American Press, 1948.

Darling, Richard. *The Rise of Children's Book Reviewing in America, 1865-1881.* New York: R. R. Bowker Co., 1968.

Van Doren, Carl. *The American Novel.* New York: Macmillan Publishing Company, Inc., 1929.

The Domestic Novel:

Brown, Herbert Ross. *The Sentimental Novel in America, 1789-1860.* Durham, North Carolina: Duke University Press, 1940.

Hofstadter, Beatrice K. "Popular Culture and the Romantic Heroine." *American Scholar* 30 (Winter 1960-61): 98.

Papashvily, Helen Waite. *All the Happy Endings: A Study of the Domestic Novel in America, The Women Who Wrote It, The Women Who Read It, in the Nineteenth Century.* New York: Harper & Row, Publishers, Inc., 1956.

Pattee, Fred Lewis. *The Feminist Fifties.* New York: Appleton, 1940.

Susan Warner:

Denman, Frank. "How to Drive the Sheriff from the Homestead Door." *The New York Times Book Review,* December 24, 1944, p. 8.

Jordan, Alice M. "Susan Warner and Her Wide, Wide, World." *Horn Book* 10 (September 1934): 287-93.

Warner, Anna B. *Susan Warner.* New York: G. P. Putnam's Sons, 1904.

Augusta Jane Evans Wilson:

Calkins, Ernest Elmo. "St. Elmo, or, Names for a Best Seller." *Saturday Review of Literature,* December 16, 1939, p. 3.

Fidler, William Perry. *Augusta Evans Wilson 1835-1909.* University, Alabama: University of Alabama Press, 1951.

Maurice, Arthur Bartlett. "Best Sellers of Yesterday: Augusta Jane Evans' *St. Elmo.*" *Bookman* 31 (March 1910): 35-42.

Dime Novels (General):

Admari, Ralph. "Ballou, The Father of the Dime Novel." *American Book Collector* 4 (September-October 1933): 121-29.

Curti, Merle. "Dime Novels and the American Tradition." *Yale Review* 26 (June 1937): 761-68.

Dey, Frederic Van Rensselaer. "How I Wrote a Thousand 'Nick Carter' Novels." *American Magazine* 89 (February 1920): 19.

Jenks, George C. "Dime Novel Makers." *Bookman* 20 (October 1904): 108-14.

Johannsen, Albert. *The House of Beadle and Adams and Its Dime and Nickel Novels: The Story of a Vanished Literature.* 3 volumes. Norman: University of Oklahoma Press, 1950, 1962. A basic work in its field.

Leithead, J. Edward. "The Anatomy of Dime Novels: No. 1—Nick Carter." *Dime Novel Roundup,* September 15, 1964, pp. 76-79; and October 15, 1964, pp. 84-89. From his vast reading and collecting, Leithead wrote prolifically of dime novels in *Dime Novel Roundup,* still the best source of information about dime novels, and *American Book Collector* until his death in 1970. All his many articles are worth reading for their information and lively style.

Pearson, Edmund. *Dime Novels, or Following an Old Trail in Popular Literature.* Port Washington, New York: Kennikat Press, 1968; first published in 1929.

Reynolds, Quentin. *The Fiction Factory, or From Pulp Row to Quality Street.* New York: Random House, Inc., 1955.

Smith, Henry Nash. *Virgin Land: The American West as Symbol and Myth.* Cambridge: Harvard University Press, 1950.

Turner, E. S. *Boys Will Be Boys.* 3d ed. London: Michael Joseph, 1978. A book on Penny Dreadfuls, the English parallel to dime novels, but Chapter 10 is excellent on the American Frank Reade stories.

Dime Novels (Objections and Objections to the Objections):

Bishop, W. H. "Story-Paper Literature." *The Atlantic Monthly* 44 (September 1879): 383-93.

Burgess, Theodore C. "Means of Leading Boys from the Dime Novel to Better Literature." *Library Journal* 21 (April 1896): 144-47.

Comstock, Anthony. *Traps for the Young.* Edited by Robert Bremner. Cambridge: Harvard University Press, 1967; first published in 1883.

Cox, Ellen M. "What Can Be Done to Help a Boy to Like Good Books after He Has Fallen into the 'Dime Novel Habit'?" *Library Journal* 20 (April 1895): 118-19.

Harvey, Charles M. "The Dime Novel in American Life." *Atlantic* 100 (July 1907): 37-45.

Thurber, James. "Thix" in *The Beast in Me and Other Animals.* New York: Harcourt, Brace, World, 1948.

Sumner, William. "What Our Boys Are Reading." *Scribner's Monthly* 15 (March 1878): 681-85.

Popular Story Weeklies:

Bishop, W. H. "Story-Paper Literature," *The Atlantic Monthly* 44 (September 1879): 383-93.

Noel, Mary. *Villains Galore . . . The Heyday of the Popular Story Weekly.* New York: Macmillan Publishing Company, Inc., 1954.

Louisa May Alcott:

Cheney, Ednah D., ed. *Louisa May Alcott: Her Life, Letters and Journals.* Boston: Little, Brown, 1901.

Morrow, Honoré Willsie. *Father of Little Women.* Boston: Little, Brown, 1927.

Payne, Alma J. "Louisa May Alcott (1832-1888)," *American Literary Realism, 1870-1910* 6 (Winter 1973): 24-43. Excellent bibliographical material.

Salyer, Sandford. *Marmee: The Mother of Little Women.* Norman: University of Oklahoma Press, 1949.

Saxton, Martha. *Louisa May: A Modern Biography of Louisa May Alcott.* Boston: Houghton Mifflin Co., 1977.

Stern, Madeleine. *Louisa May Alcott.* Norman: University of Oklahoma Press, 1950. The most readable of all the biographies.

Horatio Alger, Jr.:

Alger, Horatio, Jr. "Writing Stories for Boys." *Writer* 9 (March 1896): 36-37.

Cawelti, John G. *Apostles of the Self-Made Man.* Chicago: University of Chicago Press, 1965, pp. 101-23.

Enslin, Morton. "Horatio Alger, Jr., after Seventy Years." *Dime Novel Roundup,* April 15, 1970, pp. 40-45; and May 15, 1970, pp. 50-55.

Falk, Robert. "Notes on the 'Higher Criticism' of Horatio Alger, Jr." *Arizona Quarterly* 19 (Summer 1963): 151-67.

Holland, Norman N. "Hobbling with Horatio; of the Uses of Literature." *Hudson Review* 12 (Winter 1959-60): 549-57.

Hoyt, Edwin P. *Horatio's Boys: The Life and Works of Horatio Alger.* Radnor, Pennsylvania: Chilton Book Company, 1974.

Seelye, John. "Who Was Horatio? The Alger Myth and American Scholarship." *American Quarterly* 17 (Winter 1965): 749-56.

Weiss, Richard. "Horatio Alger, Jr., and the Response to Industrialism" in *The Age of Industrialism in America: Essays in Social Structure and Cultural Values.* Edited by Frederic Cople Jahner. New York: The Free Press, 1968, pp. 304-16.

Wohl, R. Richard. "The 'Rags to Riches Story': An Episode of Secular Idealism" in *Class, Status, and Power: Social Stratification in Comparative Perspective.* 2d ed. Edited by Reinhard Bendix and Seymour Martin Lipset. New York: The Free Press, 1966, pp. 501-6.

Early Series Writers:

Harry Castlemon

Blanck, Jacob. *Harry Castlemon, Boys' Own Author: An Appreciation and Bibliography.* New York: R. R. Bowker Co., 1941.

Castlemon, Harry. "How to Write Stories for Boys." *Writer* 9 (January 1896): 4-5.

Martha Finley

Brown, Janet. *The Saga of Elsie Dinsmore.* Buffalo, N.Y.: University of Buffalo Press, 1945.

Jackson, Jacqueline, and Philip Kendall. "What Makes a Bad Book Good: Elsie Dinsmore" in Francelia Butler, ed., *Children's Literature: Annual of the Modern Language Association Group on Children's Literature and the Children's Literature Association* 7 (1978): 45-67.

Literature of the Bad Boy:

Geller, Evelyn. "Tom Sawyer, Tom Bailey, and the Bad-Boy Genre." *Wilson Library Bulletin* 51 (November 1976): 245-50.

Hunter, Jim. "Mark Twain and the Boy-Book in 19th-Century America." *College English* 24 (March 1963): 430-38.

Trensky, Anne. "The Bad Boy in Nineteenth-Century American Fiction." *Georgia Review* 27 (Winter 1973): 503-17.

Libraries:

Development of Libraries in America

Ditzion, Sidney. *Arsenals of a Democratic Culture: A Social History of the American Public Library Movement in New England and the Middle States from 1850 to 1900.* Chicago: American Library Association, 1947.

Shera, Jesse H. *Foundations of the Public Library.* Chicago: University of Chicago Press, 1949.

Thompson, C. Seymour. *Evolution of the American Public Library, 1653-1876.* Washington, D.C.: Scarecrow Press, 1952.

The Problem of Fiction

Carrier, Esther Jane. *Fiction in Public Libraries, 1876-1900.* New York: Scarecrow Press, 1965.

Geller, Evelyn. "The Librarian as Censor." *Library Journal* 101 (June 1, 1976): 1255-58.

Orians, G. Harrison. "Censure of Fiction in American Romances and Magazines 1789-1810." *PMLA* 52 (March 1937): 195-214.

Poole, William F. "Some Popular Objections to Public Libraries." *American Library Journal* 1 (October 1876): 45-51.

Restricting Fiction from Young Adults

Cohen, Max. "The Librarian as Educator, and Not a Cheap-John." *Library Journal* 13 (December 1888): 366-67.

Jones, Richard. "The Moral and Literary Responsibilities of Librarians in Selecting Books for a Public Library." *NEA Journal of Proceedings and Addresses, 1897* (Chicago: University of Chicago Press, 1897), pp. 1025-28.

Kite, William. "Fiction in Public Libraries," *American Library Journal* 1 (February 1877): 277-79.

Stevenson, W. M. "Weeding Out Fiction in the Carnegie Free Library of Allegheny, Pa." *Library Journal* 22 (March 1897): 133-35.

Young, Clement C. "The Public Library and the Public School." *Library Journal* 21 (April 1896): 140-44.

Loosening Restrictions on Young Adults

Cole, George Watson. "Fiction in Libraries: A Plea for the Masses." *Library Journal* 19 (December 1894): 18-21.

Green, S. S. "Sensational Fiction in Public Libraries." *Library Journal* 4 (September-October 1879): 345-55.

Hardy, George E. "The School Library a Factor in Education." *Library Journal* 14 (August 1889): 343-47.

Higginson, T. W. "Address." *Library Journal* 4 (September-October 1879): 357-59.

4

1900-1940

From the Safety of Romance to the Beginning of Realism

The first forty years of the twentieth century were times of change and challenge, aspiration mixed with frustration. The western frontier disappeared, and the country made the final change from an agrarian society to an urban one. It was a time of such disparate elements as ragtime and jazz, the Armory Show in New York and the Ashcan School of art, and the rapidly growing popularity of college football. World War I brought the certainty that it would end all wars. It led to the League of Nations and indirectly to women's suffrage. The spectre of communism appeared, movies became a popular art form, and Sacco and Vanzetti were tried. The labor movement grew along with Ford's production lines and cars, cars, cars: in 1900 only 13,824 cars were registered throughout the country; by 1919 there were more than 6,500,000; by 1929, more than 23,000,000. President Hoover came along, then the Wall Street crash of 1929 and Depression. By 1938, three million young people from sixteen through twenty-five were out of school and unemployed, and a quarter of a million boys were on the road. Franklin Delano Roosevelt introduced the "New Deal," and we watched the rise of Nazi Germany. When the end of the Depression seemed almost in sight, the New York World's Fair of 1939 became our optimistic metaphor for the coming of a newer, better, happier, and more secure world. World War II lay over the horizon, quite visible to some, ignored by most.

These forty years also witnessed many literary and pedagogical changes, among them new ways of assessing the reading interests of young adults, and the rise of English teaching as a discipline. There were further developments in series books, "junior" or "juvenile" divisions were started in publishing houses, and pulps and comics grew rapidly. Fashions changed in the kinds of books read by young adults too, just as they changed in everything else.

READING INTEREST STUDIES

Before 1900, librarians and English teachers published little about reading interests of young people. Many adults, intent on telling the young what to read, had scant interest in finding out what young adults cared about or liked to read. English teaching was a relatively new discipline—English was not given the time and attention accorded Latin and other school subjects until late in the nineteenth century—and teachers faced pressure from colleges to prepare the young for study and weighty matters. Recreational reading seemed vaguely time wasting, if not downright wicked. With the exception of a few articles like True's "What My Pupils Read,"[1] reading interests went largely unexplored. But after publication of the Vostrovsky study,[2] the first significant reading interest investigation, came the deluge. Simple and unsophisticated and naive they may have been, but they were still honest attempts to find out what young adults liked. From brief two or three page articles to books of several hundred pages, reading interest studies ranged from simple, direct status quo reports, especially earlier ones, to complex analyses of what young adults liked and why. Sometimes a wounded librarian or teacher would wax indignant about the dullness of the young and their lamentably mediocre tastes. Most reading interest studies, however, provided modern English teachers and librarians with helpful information that could be put to use in the classroom or library.

Findings of Reading Interest Studies

Generally, studies revealed that young adults read fiction far more than any other genre. They read books written specifically for them, series books from Stratemeyer's Literary Syndicate such as Tom Swift, Nancy Drew, Hardy Boys, Baseball Joe, and Ruth Fielding, and non-Stratemeyer series like Boys of Bob's Hill, Frank Merriwell, Roy Blakely, and Campfire Girls. They read adolescent books by Barbour, Heyliger, Pease, Terhune, Montgomery, Alcott, O'Brien, Seaman, and Altsheler. They read classics by Dickens, Scott, and Shakespeare. They read modern best sellers by Wright, Grey, Churchill, Curwood, Webster, Tarkington, McCutcheon, and many, many more.

In effect, they read many of the same writers and books reported in Irving Harlow Hart's "The Most Popular Authors of Fiction between 1900 and 1925,"[3] and they read best sellers selected by the Book-of-the-Month Club when it began in 1926 and the Literary Guild when it began a year later.

Some Reactions

Some investigators and readers reacted predictably and emotionally to reading interest studies. English teacher Alfred M. Hitchcock voiced fears that education and the reading public were hurtling steadily downward:

> Books, magazines, journals are written to catch the multitudes—the multitudes who are not very keenly intellectual, nor gifted with imagination, nor trained

to appreciate artistic form—the easy-going, pleasure-seeking, not over-ambitious, somewhat unmoral multitudes. There are notable exceptions, it is true; yet one cannot avoid the suspicion that many writers are content to give the public what the public wants, not what it needs. Reading the truly popular literature of the hour, in the manner in which it is commonly read by the young, can hardly be called an intellectual exercise. It does not challenge the mind; it does not invite the imagination. Too often it feeds the passions rather than the higher emotions. The youth who reads gets little; his moral and intellectual fiber is not strengthened.[4]

Reactions led some critics to bombast and wild metaphors, comparing reading to eating, and arguing as Montrose J. Moses did, "A continual diet of one type of book is likely permanently to injure the taste."[5] The "you-are-what-you-eat-and-you-are-what-you-read" metaphor became increasingly tiresome in articles by librarians and teachers over the years.

The argument over the possible harm that might come from series books, or popular literature sometimes called "subliterature," has raged for years, and the end is unlikely to precede the millennium. In the lengthy *Winnetka Graded Book List*, partly concerned with the reading of junior high students, Washburne and Vogel did not list all books reported; "Books that were definitely trashy or unsuitable for children, even though widely read, have not been included in this list."[6] Enough people were apparently curious about the trashy or unsuitable books to lead the authors to add two supplements.[7] Predictably, *Elsie Dinsmore* was among the damned, but so were Edgar Rice Burroughs' *Tarzan of the Apes*, Eleanor Porter's *Pollyanna*, Gene Stratton Porter's *Freckles* and *A Girl of the Limberlost*, Zane Grey's westerns, and books from the Ruth Fielding and Tom Swift series. No surprises there, but surprises did pop up. Many popular girls' mysteries by Augusta Huill Seaman were excluded from the original list, but others of her titles, seemingly no better or worse, were approved or recommended. Strangely, Mark Twain's *Tom Sawyer Abroad* was among the unwashed and disapproved. So was Mary Roberts Rinehart's *The Circular Staircase*. Arthur Conan Doyle's *The Adventures of Sherlock Holmes* was recommended, but *The Hound of the Baskervilles* was not acceptable. Such puzzlements must have disturbed readers looking for that most impossible of tools, a list applicable to all teachers, schools, libraries, and students.

Other critics seemed less concerned about the souls of the young even if trash were part of the diet. Critic and English professor William Lyon Phelps argued that reading some relatively poor literature was not only not harmful but almost inevitable for most young readers:

> I do not believe the majority of these very school teachers and other cultivated mature readers began in early youth by reading great books exclusively; I think they read Jack Harkaway, an Old Sleuth, and the works of Oliver Optic and Horatio Alger. From these enchanters they learned a thing of tremendous importance—the delight of reading. Once a taste for reading is formed, it can be improved. But it is improbable that boys and girls who have never cared to read a good story will later enjoy stories by good artists.[8]

In a book aimed at future English teachers, Reed Smith agreed with Phelps and doubt-less horrified some librarians and English teachers:

> It is better for a boy to read Nick Carter or Frank Merriwell than not to read at all; and it is much better for him to read *Tarzan of the Apes* and *The Shepherd of the Hills* and like them than to read *Vanity Fair* and *Moby Dick* and hate them.[9]

Girls' Books and Boys' Books

Teachers and librarians frequently commented that girls' books, particularly up to the middle 1930s, were inferior to boys' books. Franklin T. Baker wrote that girls' books of 1908 were "numerous and . . . often painfully weak" lacking "invention, action, humor"[10] with the obvious exception of Alcott. Two years later Clara Whitehill Hunt agreed that many girls' books were empty, insipid, and mediocre.[11] As late as 1935, a writer could still object to the dearth of good fiction for girls. Reviewing some interesting nonfiction for boys, Julia Carter broke in with what appeared to be an exasperated parenthetical obiter dictum:

> Will someone please tell me why we expect the *boys* to know these things and still plan for the girls to be mid-Victorian, and consider them hoydens beyond reclaiming, when instead of shrieking and running like true daughters of Eve, they are interested in snakes and can light a fire with two matches?[12]

Yet only two years later, writers like Caroline Dale Snedeker, Cornelia Meigs, Jeanette Eaton, Mabel Robinson, and Elizabeth Forman Lewis were producing enough quality girls' literature to encourage Alice M. Jordan to write:

> There was a time not long ago when the boys had the lion's share in the yearly production of books intended for young people. So writers were urged to give us more stories in which girls could see themselves in recognizable relationship to the world of their own time, forgetting perhaps that human nature does not change and the vital things are universal. Yet, none the less, the girls had a real cause to plead and right valiantly the writers have responded.[13]

Critics believed then, as they continued to do for years thereafter, that girls would read boys' books but boys would never read girls' books. Logosa accepted boys' books as "more sincere, vigorous, wholesome, and free from affectation."[14] Boys' books con-sistently outsold girls' books—publishers could count on that—until the first Nancy Drews appeared on the market. At least part of the problem of stereotyping girls' and boys' books lay with stereotypes of boys' and girls' roles as expressed by two writers. Clara Vostrovsky, author of the first significant reading interest study, went back to ancient times for her stereotypes suggesting that it was "probable" that the differences in reading interests between boys and girls lay "in the history of the race."[15] Psychologist G. Stanley Hall predicated the reading interests of girls and boys on psychological differences:

> Boys love adventure, girls sentiment. . . . Girls love to read stories about girls which boys eschew, girls, however, caring much more to read about boys than boys to read about girls. Books dealing with domestic life and with young children in them girls have almost entirely to themselves. Boys, on the other hand, excel in love of humor, rollicking fun, abandon, rough horse-play, and tales of wild escapades. Girls are less averse to reading what boys like than boys are to reading what girls like. A book popular with boys would attract some girls, while one read by most girls would repel a boy in the middle teens. The reading interests of high-school girls are far more humanistic, cultural and general, and that of boys is more practical, vocational, and even special.[16]

The simple truth, perhaps too obvious and discomforting to be palatable to some parents, English teachers, and librarians, was that boys' books were generally far superior to girls' books. That had nothing to do with the sexual or psychological nature of boys or girls, but rather with the way authors treated their audience. Many authors insisted on making girls good and domestic and dull (if a heroine were allowed some freedom to roam outside the house, she soon regretted it or grew up, whichever came

Boys rarely read girls' books, but girls did not necessarily like the books any better.

first), perhaps because they thought parents and librarians wanted books that way. Boys were allowed outside the house to find work and responsibilities, of course, but also to find adventure and excitement in their books. Of course, boys rarely read girls' books, but girls did not necessarily like the books any better. One girl, not fitting the Vostrovsky or Hall stereotypes, preferred *Captains Courageous* to a girls' book because it had "so much more pep."[17] And she was right; it did.

Motion Pictures and Books

From the time motion pictures became a popular medium, librarians and teachers debated the value of films and worried that they would lead people, especially young adults, away from books. As early as 1918, one writer argued that motion pictures were more powerful and created more vivid impressions on the young than books, but he also felt movies would lead to "an increased demand for fiction dealing with the stories exhibited."[18] Eleven years later, Cleveland librarian Marilla Waite Freeman pointed out the number of potential library tie-ins with current movies like *The Covered Wagon, Ben-Hur, Scaramouche, Show Boat,* and *Seventh Heaven.*[19] A year later, Duffus acknowledged a fact many librarians and teachers had come to accept, "A motion picture production may send the circulation of the book from a little more than nothing to a million or more a year."[20] By 1940, Hollywood's influence on young adults' reading interests and tastes was acknowledged, accepted, and praised for the good it could do for books, libraries, and classrooms:

> Hollywood has a tremendous influence on reading tastes of youth today. Comprehensive surveys made in all libraries indicate that good movies made from books definitely stimulate reading of the book. Release of motion pictures made from books will often have immediate effect in the school library. Dust is blown off some of the older volumes, or books classified as "too dry," "not interesting," and they are removed from the shelf for reading and re-reading. There is often renewed interest in the classics. Such books as Dickens, *Tale of Two Cities;* Wyss, *Swiss Family Robinson;* Brontë, *Wuthering Heights;* Austen, *Pride and Prejudice;* Roberts, *Northwest Passage;* Kipling, *The Light That Failed;* Du Maurier's *Rebecca;* Fields' *All This, And Heaven Too* have been put in steady circulation.[21]

THE DEVELOPING AND CHANGING ENGLISH CLASSROOM

By 1900, both the school library and the public library played significant roles in helping young adults find reading materials. Although many libraries reflected the traditional belief that classics should be the major reading of youth, young adults could find in many other libraries a variety of materials they liked, not trash, but certainly popular books.

That would have rarely been true of English teachers, saddled as they were with the responsibility of preparing young adults for college. College entrance examinations virtually forced secondary English teachers to feed their students a steady diet of great literature, not because great books were necessarily enjoyable or satisfying but because college exams were predicated on a study of the classics. High schools then hardly touched the masses of young adults, enrolling a mere one of twenty-five young people. They were regarded by most college teachers and many secondary teachers as preparatory schools, institutions to prepare students not for life but for college. Given these circumstances, the chances of students' discovering much joy and excitement in literature or in finding contemporary books in English classes were minimal.

The attention paid to poetry and nonfiction prose was hardly surprising, but some teachers argued for the use of the often ignored novel in the classroom. An Illinois committee surveying English teachers found novels all too rarely used, recommended their use, and then added a warning not to overuse them.

> The novel is conspicuous by its absence. The literary history of the Nineteenth Century shows no names more remarkable than those of Scott, Dickens,

Thackeray, and Eliot, to say nothing of Hawthorne, Cooper, and Cable. These men are celebrated for fiction. The novel has become a factor in our life. It is instructive and propagandist; it teaches psychology; preaches a new religion, or attacks the old; gives lessons in sociology; reforms old abuses; satirizes new follies; and continually retells the old but ever new story of human life. It forms the greater part of our reading, if library statistics are to be trusted, and certainly is most potent in its influence on human conduct. It therefore belongs in the English course of the high school. Perhaps one is enough; certainly five seems too large a number.[22]

Unhappily, the study of literature was often reserved for the senior year, as William E. Mead lamented in *The Academy* (a journal that is far and away the best source of information about English teaching prior to the *English Journal*).

Most high schools give but a single year to literature, and that at the end of the course. To leave the average boy to the forlorn hope of reaching the last year of the high school before giving him an insight into literature is practically to condemn him for life to a taste for third-rate prose and third-rate poetry. He may pick up a knowledge of literature by himself, but we need not expect him to be very grateful to his teachers.[23]

College Entrance Examinations Ride High

Early entrance exams for college simply required some proof of writing proficiency, but in the years 1869 and 1870, Harvard began using Milton's *Comus* and Shakespeare's *Julius Caesar* as alternative books for the examination. Four years later Harvard required a short composition based on a question from one of the following works: Shakespeare's *The Tempest, Julius Caesar,* and *The Merchant of Venice,* Goldsmith's *The Vicar of Wakefield,* or Scott's *Ivanhoe* and *The Lay of the Last Minstrel.*

In 1894, the prestigious Committee of Ten on Secondary School Studies presented its report, and English became an accepted discipline in the schools, if not yet as respectable as Latin. Chaired by controversial Harvard President Charles W. Eliot, the Committee was appointed by the National Educational Association in July, 1892 and met later that year to determine the nature, limits, and methods appropriate to many subject matters in secondary school.[24] Samuel Thurber of The Boston Girls' High School was unable to promote his belief that a high school curriculum should consist almost entirely of elective courses, but as chairman of the English Conference, his report both liberalized and dignified the study of English. Thurber wrote that one of the chief objectives of English teaching was to "cultivate a taste for reading, to give the pupil some acquaintance with good literature, and to furnish him with the means of extending that acquaintance."[25] Thurber and his committee urged that English be studied five hours a week for four years. Further, the English Conference urged uniform college entrance examinations be established throughout the country.

The result was the publication of book lists, mainly classics, to be the basis of entrance examinations. Books such as Shakespeare's *Twelfth Night* and *As You Like It,*

Milton's Books I and II from *Paradise Lost,* Scott's *The Abbott* and *Marmion,* Thackeray's *English Humorists,* Irving's *Bracebridge Hall,* or Dobson's *Eighteenth Century Essays* virtually became the English curriculum as teachers, inevitably concerned with their students' entry into college, increasingly adapted the English curriculum to fit the list. Not all teachers believed that the enjoyment of reading had anything to do with teaching English, and those who did were given little leeway in their choice of classroom books. Thurber worried about teaching literature too mature for young adults and the inevitable dichotomy between school reading and voluntary reading or real reading, that "dismal gulf" between the study of literature and reading outside the school:

> Not a month ago I saw a boy of fourteen pass through a similar experience. I had just taken from a class *The Lady of the Lake* and put into their hands Stevenson's *Treasure Island.* At the close of the hour an astonished, excited voice said to me: "I—I've read this book!" "Well, and what of that?" "Why, I didn't know we studied *this kind of a book* in school."[26]

Thurber's point was well taken. Teachers labored under the responsibility for preparing students to pass college entrance exams. Their responsibility did not necessarily extend to encouraging students to enjoy reading or to extend reading beyond the required text.

Alfred Hitchcock certainly presented *the* widely held point of view at the time about literature and college entrance examinations when he wrote:

> To say that with one or two exceptions the present college requirements are all absurdly inappropriate is hardly respectful to the college professors, and the hundreds of high-school teachers who sanction them. It may take years of experimenting to find the best way of presenting the *Conciliation Speech* and Milton's lyrics; it certainly requires more skill to handle the Milton lyrics than it does to play with the works of G. A. Henty. Not only must pupils work; teachers must work too.
>
> Those who recommend the abolishment of the present college requirements, and the substitution of much easier and inferior classics to be studied in a wholly agreeable way, show very little faith in the ability of the average teacher to make his work profitable, and still less faith in the hardihood of the average pupil. A love for literature which can be blighted by the *Conciliation Speech* or the *Essay on Milton* is hardly worth coddling.[27]

The National Council of Teachers of English (NCTE) Begins

Out of the growing protest about college entrance exams, a group of English teachers attending a National Education Association English Table formed a Committee on College Entrance Requirements in English to assess the problem through a national survey of English teachers. The Committee uncovered a not unexpected hostility to colleges ill-advised and presumptuous enough to try to control the secondary English curriculum through the guise of entrance examinations. John M. Coulter, a professor at the University of Chicago, tried to sound that alarm to college professors, without much success:

> The high school exists primarily for its own sake; and secondarily as a preparatory school for college. This means that when the high-school interest and the college interest come into conflict, the college interest must yield. It also means that the function of a preparatory school must be performed only in so far as it does not interfere with the more fundamental purpose of the high school itself. It also means that independent dictation by colleges, either directly or indirectly, must be changed to adaptation to what the high school can do or ought to do, as determined by the high schools themselves. The high school must be regarded as an autonomous, not subordinate, institution.[28]

Some irate teachers recognized that the problem of college control would hardly be the last issue to face English teachers and formed the nucleus of the National Council of Teachers of English. The First Annual Meeting in Chicago on December 1 and 2, 1911[29] was largely devoted to resentment about actions of the National Conference on Uniform Entrance Requirements, particularly because that body had representatives from twelve colleges, two academies, and only two public high schools (principals, not English teachers). Wilbur W. Hatfield, soon to edit the *English Journal* and then at Farragut High School in Chicago, relayed instructions from the Illinois Association of Teachers of English on two responsibilities NCTE should recommend:

1. To include in its list for class reading, study, or whatever you choose to call it, some books of the last ten years. Our present custom of using only old books in the classroom leaves the pupil with no acquaintance with the literature of the present day, from which he is sure to choose his reading after graduation.
2. To appoint a committee to compile a list of comparatively recent books suitable for home reading by the pupils.[30]

Later Actions of English Teachers

James Fleming Hosic's 1917 report on the *Reorganization of English in Secondary Schools*,[31] part of a larger report on reorganization of all subject matter fields and all published under the aegis of the U.S. Bureau of Education, looked at books and teaching in ways that must have seemed muddle-headed, perverted, or perverse to traditionalists. Looking at literature for the tenth, eleventh, and twelfth grades, Hosic chose words that pleased many, puzzled others, and alienated some:

> The literature lesson should broaden, deepen, and enrich the imaginative and emotional life of the student. Literature is primarily a revelation and an interpretation of life; it pictures from century to century the growth of the human spirit. It should be the constant aim of the English teacher to lead pupils so to read that they find their own lives imaged in this larger life, and

attain slowly, from a clearer appreciation of human nature, a deeper and truer understanding of human nature. . . . It should be the aim of the English teacher to make [reading] an unfailing resource and joy in the lives of all.[32]

To encourage this, Hosic provided several pages listing books for study and general reading. Classics were included but so were modern works such as Churchill's *Richard Carvel*, Jackson's *Ramona*, London's *Martin Eden*, Norris' *The Pit*, and Wister's *The Virginian* for the tenth grade; Allen's *The Kentucky Cardinal*, Farnol's *The Broad Highway*, Kipling's *The Light That Failed*, and Johnston's *To Have and To Hold* for the eleventh grade; and Galsworthy's *Justice*, Synge's *Riders to the Sea*, Hauptmann's *The Sunken Bell*, and Deland's *The Awakening of Helena Richie* for the twelfth grade.[33] Teachers terrified by the contemporary reality reflected in these books—and perhaps equally terrified by the possibility of throwing out age-old lesson plans and tests on classics—had little to fear. In many schools, nothing changed.

Dora V. Smith reported in 1933[34] that the most widely studied full-length works in secondary schools were classics. *Silas Marner* led the list followed by *Julius Caesar*, *Idylls of the King*, *Tale of Two Cities*, and *Lady of the Lake*. Most such required books were taught at interminable length, teachers seemingly smitten by what came to be known as the "intensive" method, four to six weeks—sometimes even more—of detailed examination per work while horrified or bored students vowed never to read anything once they escaped high school. Coryell offered proof that the "intensive" method produced no better test results and considerably more apathy toward literature than the "extensive" method in which students read assigned works faster. The latter gave them time for many other works and they enjoyed literature far more.[35] Her research had a negligible effect on most classroom teachers as did most other significant research.

However, the work of two college professors in the 1930s influenced more English teachers. A 1936 study by Lou LaBrant on the value of free reading at the Ohio State University Laboratory School revealed that students with easy access to different kinds of books and some guidance read more, enjoyed what they read, and moved upward in literary sophistication and taste.[36] Earlier, Dora V. Smith found English teachers knew next to nothing about books written for adolescents. She corrected the situation at the University of Minnesota, establishing the first course in adolescent literature.[37] Later, she wrote:

We must provide teachers who know books first-hand and recognize their place in the lives of boys and girls. It is fair neither to young people nor to their teachers to send out from our colleges and universities men and women trained alone in Chaucer and Milton and Browning to compete with Zane Grey, Robert W. Chambers, and Ethel M. Dell. At the University of Minnesota we have instituted a course in adolescent literature which aims to supplement the necessary training in the classics given by the English department with this broader knowledge of good books, old and new, for boys and girls and for intelligent, cultured men and women—books not commonly judged worthy of academic consideration.[38]

EDWARD STRATEMEYER'S LITERARY SYNDICATE

Whatever disagreements librarians and English teachers may have had over the years about books suitable for young adults, they ineffectively bonded together and loudly opposed the books produced by Edward Stratemeyer and his numerous writers. Edward Stratemeyer founded the most successful industry ever built around adolescent reading. Sometime in 1886, Stratemeyer took time off from working for his stepbrother and wrote an 18,000 word serial, *Victor Horton's Idea*, on brown wrapping paper and mailed it to *Golden Days*, a Philadelphia weekly boys' magazine. A check for seventy-five dollars arrived shortly, and Stratemeyer's success story was underway. By 1893 Stratemeyer was editing *Good News*, Street & Smith's boys' weekly, building circulation to more than 200,000. In addition to editing a few other boys' magazines, his work at Street & Smith made his name known to the public, particularly young adults. Even more important, he came to know staff writers such as William T. Adams, Edward S. Ellis, and Horatio Alger, Jr. When Optic and Alger died leaving some uncompleted manuscripts, Stratemeyer was asked to finish the last three Optic novels, and he completed (or possibly wrote from scratch) at least eleven and possibly as many as eighteen Alger novels.

His first hardback book published under his own name was *Richard Dare's Venture, or Striking Out for Himself* (1894), the first in a series he titled "Bound to Succeed." By the close of 1897, Stratemeyer had six series and sixteen hardcover books in print.

A major breakthrough came in 1898. After Stratemeyer sent a manuscript about two boys on a battleship to Lothrop and Shepard, one of the most successful publishers of young adult fiction, Admiral Dewey won his great victory in Manila Bay, and a Lothrop reader asked Stratemeyer to place the boys at the scene of Dewey's victory. He rewrote and returned the book shortly, and *Under Dewey at Manila, or, The War Fortunes of a Castaway* hit the streets in time to capitalize on all the publicity. Not one to miss an opportunity, Stratemeyer used the same characters in his next books, all published from 1898 to 1901 under the series title "Old Glory." Using the same characters in contemporary battles in the Orient, Stratemeyer created another series called *Soldiers of Fortune* published from 1900 through 1906.

By this time Stratemeyer had turned to full-time writing and was being wooed by the major publishers of his day, notably Grosset & Dunlap and Cupples & Leon, for he had a formula for writing books that appealed to young adults. For a time he turned to stories of school life and sports, the "Lakeport" series (1904-1912), the "Dave Porter" series (1905-1919), and the most successful of his early series, the "Rover Boys" (thirty books from 1899 to 1926), books so popular they were shipped to Canada, Australia, and England, translated into German and Czechoslovakian, and sold somewhere between five or six million copies across the world.

But Stratemeyer aspired to greater things. Some time between 1906 and 1910, he approached both his publishers suggesting they reduce the price of his books to fifty cents. The publishers may have been shocked to find an author willing to sell his books for less money, but, as they soon realized, mass production of fifty-centers increased their revenue and Stratemeyer's royalties almost geometrically.

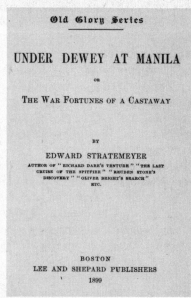

OH, LUKE! SEE THE STARS AND STRIPES! Page 183

Edward Stratemeyer. *Under Dewey at Manila*, 1898.

But an even greater breakthrough came, at roughly the same time, when he evolved the idea of his Literary Syndicate, perhaps modeled loosely after Alexandre Dumas' fiction factory in which Dumas and sixty or more anonymous assistants produced 277 books. Stratemeyer was aware that he could create plots and series faster than he could possibly write them. Details of the Stratemeyer Syndicate are fuzzy, but the general outline is clear. Stratemeyer advertised for writers who needed money, and then sent them sketches of settings and characters along with a chapter-by-chapter outline of the plot. Writers had a few weeks to fill in the outlines, and when the copy arrived, Stratemeyer tightened the prose and checked for discrepancies with earlier volumes of the series. Then the manuscript was off to the printer and checks went out to the writers, from fifty to one hundred dollars depending upon the writer and the importance of the series.

Possibly we may never know all the Syndicate authors. Stratemeyer wrote the books appearing under his own name and presumably those under the pen names Arthur M. Winfield or Captain Ralph Bonehill. Leslie McFarlane[39] wrote the first twenty-six Hardy Boys and three of the Dana Girls, Howard Garis[40] (better known for his Uncle Wiggily stories) wrote the first thirty-five Tom Swift books, and Harriet Adams, Stratemeyer's daughter, wrote many of the Dana Girls and virtually all the Nancy Drew books.

Stratemeyer books had common formulaic elements that held readers through book after book. The first lines promised adventure and the rest of the chapters delivered thrills page after page. Andrew Svenson, Harriet Adams' partner in the Syndicate until his death, summarized both the technique and the power of the Stratemeyer Syndicate books:

> The trick in writing children's books is to set up danger, mystery and excitement on page one. Force the kid to turn the page. I've written page one as many as 20 times. Then in the middle of each chapter there's a dramatic point of excitement and, at the chapter's end a cliffhanger.[41]

Readers of any books featuring Baseball Joe, Tom Swift, the Hardy boys, or Nancy Drew will remember that heart-stopping, chapter ending sentence, "Watch out, Joe!" (or Tom, or Frank, or Nancy). Heroes and heroines were trustworthy, resilient, strong, courageous, and likable. Perhaps most important, they proved the equal, if not the superior, of adults. It is no accident that Nancy Drew, the most successful of all the many Stratemeyer Syndicate protagonists, represents all the characteristics her young readers most admired, the most significant being her love of mysteries and her ability to solve puzzles totally befuddling adult characters.

The use of hooks typified most series books. Early in the opening chapters in any but the initial volume of a series, a hook to the previous volume or volumes would appear. In the last paragraph or two of the last chapter, another hook would be thrown out to attract readers to the next volume:

> As Helen relaxed from her recent adventures, she thought to herself, "How peaceful it will be to spend a few weeks at the farm just enjoying myself." Helen could not foresee that in only a few weeks she would find a mysterious bracelet and be caught up again in a mystery that would puzzle her and amaze her friends.

Finally, roughly halfway through the second chapter of many series books, action was suspended to summarize the preceding volumes, no great problem in the second or third volume, but as series ran to many volumes, summaries became highly compressed and almost frantic. In *Ruth Fielding and Her Greatest Triumph, or Saving Her Company From Disaster* (1933), the twenty-ninth of the series, the author wrote a page and a half of breathless summary:

> Ruth's life was not unlike a thrilling moving picture scenario. As the reader learns in the first volume of the series, *Ruth Fielding at the Red Mill*, the girl came as an orphan to live at the picturesque red mill of old Jabez Potter and Aunt Alvirah Boggs, his faithful housekeeper. There she had grown up, and learned to know Helen Cameron and her brother Tom, and had met Chess Copley.
>
> In time Ruth listened to Tom's insistent plea that they become engaged, while Helen gave her promise to Chess. Yet neither girl was to think seriously of marriage for years to come, and with college days intervening, good times and exciting adventures were always at hand.

During her college days Ruth had shown marked ability as a scenario writer and moving picture actress. Eager to "try her wings," she had induced Mr. Hammond, president of the Alectron Film Corporation, to give her a real opportunity. Her first venture was a marked success and after that she organized her own film company, with Tom as the efficient treasurer.

Marriage had not terminated Ruth's career, for Tom was a sensible husband and proud of his wife's renown and prestige. Helen, not to be outdone by her chum, had become the wife of Chess Copley. While her interests had not centered in business, she too had discovered that marriage by no means spelled the end of adventure.

At the birth of Baby June, Ruth had given up her moving picture work, but only for a short time. The discovery that a rival company was endeavoring to exploit an inexperienced actress and make the public believe it was Ruth Fielding, had brought her back to Hollywood. For a time her reputation had been threatened and many persons had believed that Ruth Fielding was no longer the great actress she once had been. Her attempt to discover the identity of her strange "twin" and outwit the men who had plotted her downfall, is related in the book, *Ruth Fielding and Her Double*.

If all that weren't enough to outline the life of this truly remarkable young woman, the summary ignores the many mysteries Ruth solved, her work in the Red Cross and on the front lines of World War I, and her trips across the country.

"THE NATIVES PROSTRATED THEMSELVES UPON THE SANDS IN WORSHIPFUL ATTITUDE."
"Ruth Fielding and Her Greatest Triumph."   (See page 196)

Ruth Fielding and Her Greatest Triumph

OR

Saving Her Company From Disaster

BY

ALICE B. EMERSON

AUTHOR OF "RUTH FIELDING OF THE RED MILL," "RUTH FIELDING AT GOLDEN PASS," "RUTH FIELDING AT CAMERON HALL," "RUTH FIELDING CLEARING HER NAME," "RUTH FIELDING AND HER DOUBLE," ETC.

ILLUSTRATED

NEW YORK
CUPPLES & LEON COMPANY
PUBLISHERS

Alice B. Emerson. *Ruth Fielding and Her Greatest Triumph*, 1933.

Attacks on Stratemeyer were not long in coming. Librarian Caroline M. Hewins criticized both Stratemeyer's books and the journals that praised his output:

> Stratemeyer is an author who mixes "would" and "should," has the phraseology of a country newspaper, as when he calls a supper "an elegant affair" and a girl "a fashionable miss," and follows Oliver Optic closely in his plots and conversations.[42]

Most librarians supported Hewins, but the effect of librarians' attacks hardly affected Stratemeyer's sales. A far more stinging and effective attack came in 1913. Chief Boy Scout executive James E. West was disturbed by the deluge of what he thought inferior books and urged the Library Commission of the Boy Scouts of America to establish a carefully selected and recommended library to protect young men. Not long afterward, Chief Scout Librarian Franklin K. Mathiews urged Grosset & Dunlap to make better books available in fifty-cent editions—to compete with Stratemeyer—and on November 1, 1913 the first list appeared in a Boy Scout publication, "Safety First Week."

But that was not enough to satisfy Mathiews. In 1914, Mathiews wrote his most famous article under the sensational title, "Blowing Out the Boy's Brains," a loud, angry, and vituperative attack, sometimes accurate but often unfair. Mathiews' most famous sentence was widely quoted: "I wish I could label each one of these books: 'Explosives! Guaranteed to Blow Your Boy's Brains Out.'"[43] The attack was mildly successful for the moment though how much harm it did to Stratemeyer's sales is open

"Oh, do help Sammy!" begged Tess, with clasped hands.   Page 214

Grace Brooks Hill. *The Corner House Girls on a Tour,* 1917.

to question. Stratemeyer went on to sell more millions of books.[44] When he died in 1930, his two daughters ran the Syndicate and daughter Harriet Adams continues it till this day.

Grosset & Dunlap and Cupples & Leon, Stratemeyer's publishers, were only two of the many publishers of series books. Henry Altemus, M. A. Donahue, Barse & Hopkins, A. L. Chatterton, Reilly & Lee, Street & Smith, and Sully & Kleintiech ground them out, but so did quality publishers of adult books: Appleton-Century; Crowell; Dodd & Mead; Farrar & Rinehart; Harper & Brothers; Holt; Houghton Mifflin; Lippincott; Little, Brown; McKay; Putnam; and Scribner. Later, five publishers—Goldsmith, Saalfield, Whitman, Winston, and World—reprinted many of the more popular series.

Series covered everything young adults care about from adventure, to scouting, the circus, Indians, mysteries, prehistoric times, science fiction, and every war in which we were involved. Thousands of volumes were printed and millions of copies sold.

Series books were inevitably moral. Whatever parents, teachers, or librarians might have objected to about the unrealistic elements of the books or the poor literary quality, they would have agreed that the books were clearly on the side of good and right, if simplistically and unrealistically so. Series books—and many adult books as well—repeatedly underlined the same themes. Sports produced truly manly men. Foreigners were not to be trusted. School, education, and life should be taken seriously. The outdoor life was healthy, physically and psychologically. Good manners and courtesy were essential for moving ahead. Work in and of itself was a positive good and would advance one in life. Anyone could defeat adversity, any adversity, *if* that person

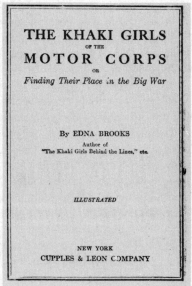

WAVING HIS ARMS, HE BELLOWED TO THE CROWD TO
"STAND BACK. GIVE US A CHANCE."
The Khaki Girls of the Motor Corps.   *Page 172*

THE KHAKI GIRLS
OF THE
MOTOR CORPS
OR
Finding Their Place in the Big War

By EDNA BROOKS
Author of
"The Khaki Girls Behind the Lines," etc.

ILLUSTRATED

NEW YORK
CUPPLES & LEON COMPANY

Edna Brooks. *The Khaki Girls of the Motor Corps*, 1918.

had a good heart and soul. The good side (ours and God's) always won in war. Evil and good were clearly and easily distinguishable. And good always triumphed over evil (at least by the final chapter).

THE COMING OF THE "JUNIOR" OR "JUVENILE" NOVEL

Though countless books had been published and widely read by young adults for years, the term "junior" or "juvenile" was first applied to young adult literature during the early 1930s.

Rose Wilder Lane's novel *Let the Hurricane Roar* had been marketed by Longmans, Green, and Company as an adult novel. A full-page blurb on the front cover of the February 11, 1933 *Publishers Weekly* bannered THE BOOK THAT MAKES YOU PROUD TO BE AN AMERICAN! and quoted an unnamed reader, presumably an adult, saying, "Honestly, it makes me ashamed of cussing about hard times and taxes." The tenor of the ad and ones to follow suggest an adult novel likely to be popular with young adults as well. It had been the same with the earlier serialization of the novel in the *Saturday Evening Post*, and also with the many favorable reviews. But, sometime later in 1933, Longmans, Green began to push the novel as the first of their series of "Junior Books," as they termed them.

That the company was tempted to attract young adults to Lane's novel is not difficult to understand. Daughter of Laura Ingalls Wilder, Lane wrote of lives and a threatening frontier world she had known in a compelling manner certain to win readers and admirers among young adults. *Let the Hurricane Roar* tells of newly married David and Molly and their life on the hard Dakota plains. David works as a railroad hand for a time, Molly waits for her baby to arrive, and both strive for independence and the security of owning their own fifty-acre homestead. When they do reach that dream and the baby is born, all looks well, but David overextends his credit, grasshoppers destroy the wheat crop, and no employment can be found nearby. David heads East to find work and later breaks his leg, leaving Molly isolated on the Dakota plain for a winter. Neighbors flee the area, and Molly battles loneliness, blizzards, and wolves before David returns. In summary, *Let the Hurricane Roar* sounds melodramatic, but it is not. In a short, quiet, and loving work, Lane made readers care about two likable young adults living a tough life in a hostile environment. The book's popularity is attested to by its twenty-six printings between 1933 and 1958 and a recent reissue in paperback under the title *Young Pioneers*.

The development of publishing house divisions to handle books lying in limbo between children's and adults' books grew after *Let the Hurricane Roar*, though authors of the time were sometimes unaware of the "junior" or "juvenile" branches as John R. Tunis was when he tried to market *Iron Duke* in 1934 and 1935. After sending the manuscript to Harcourt, Tunis was invited into the president's office. Mr. Harcourt clearly did not want to talk about the book, but instead took the startled author directly to the head of the Juvenile Department. He explained that Harcourt wanted to publish the book as a juvenile, much to Tunis' bewilderment and dismay, since he had no idea what a "juvenile" book was. Thirty years later he still had no respect for the term. "That odious term juvenile is the product of a merchandising age."[45]

PULPS AND COMICS AND STUFF

Hardcover books had four rivals for young adult readership during the first forty years of the twentieth century: pulp magazines, comic strips, comic books, and Big-Little Books. All four were disliked and attacked by many teachers, librarians, and parents. All four were widely read by young adults.

Pulp Magazines

Frank Munsey began his magazine *Argosy* in 1891 for adults, but it proved popular with young and old alike. By 1903 Street & Smith had begun publishing *Popular Magazine* aimed at rivaling *Argosy*, but rapidly developed a stable of pulp magazines (so-called because of the high fiber content used in the cheap paper) for specialized interests—*Detective Story, Western Story, Love Story, Sports Story,* and *Sea Stories*. Other

---

Pulps were often ridiculed, usually by people who never read them.

---

pulps followed: *Top-Notch, Flying Aces, Real Love, Battle Stories, True Love, Spy Stories, All-Western, Ranch Romances, Sweetheart Stories,* and *Lariat,* producing some popular heroes like Clarence E. Mulford's Hopalong Cassidy, Walter Gibson's The Shadow, Richard Wormser's Nick Carter, and Lester Dent's Doc Savage. Long after the death of pulp fiction, writer Jack Smalley explained the two basics of all pulp stories, "All you needed to sell a story to the pulps was a good title and an arresting lead paragraph."[46]

Pulps were often ridiculed, usually by people who never read them. Two recent collections of pulp stories suggest a higher quality of writing than is usually suspected. *The Fantastic Pulps*[47] includes stories by Stephen Crane, Jack London, Upton Sinclair, Sinclair Lewis, Dashiell Hammett, MacKinlay Kantor, and Ray Bradbury among others. *Hard-Boiled Detective: Stories from "Black Mask Magazine," 1920–1951*[48] features such writers as Dashiell Hammett, Raymond Chandler, Erle Stanley Gardner, and George Harmon Coxe.

Comic Strips

When James Swinnerton began his "Little Bears" in 1892 in the *San Francisco Examiner,* he surely was unaware that he had created an art form soon to be emulated by other artists and read by people of all ages. A year later bitter rivals Joseph Pulitzer of the *New York World* and William Randolph Hearst of the *New York Journal* were feuding, as usual. Pulitzer purchased a four-color rotary press to reprint artworks in his Sunday supplement. The rotary press did not work well, but the Sunday editor suggested it would work for comic art, so Pulitzer went to Richard F. Outcault who created a comic strip, "Down in Hogan's Alley." One character stood out in all the slum scenes, a strange-looking boy with an oriental face, a bald head, and only one tooth. Due to a freakish printing accident, the boy appeared in bright yellow and thus was born on February 16, 1896, the best remembered early comic strip, "The Yellow Kid." A year later, Rudolph Dirks began "The Katzenjammer Kids," and comic strips were here to stay.

By 1900 the comic strip formula was established—dialogue was contained in balloons, strips had sequential narratives, from one drawing to the next, but generally developed only one joke, and they presented a continuity from day to day or week to week that readers could depend on.

Winsor McCay's "Little Nemo in Slumberland," the most innovative of the early strips, pictured surrealistic but magnificently drawn dreams of a six-year-old boy. In 1911 the greatest of all comic strips began, George Herriman's "Krazy Kat." Herriman's work set an imposing and almost impossible to surpass standard of creativity, whimsy, and humor for other writers. Krazy was a strange, androgynous creature hated by Ignatz Mouse who threw brick after brick at Krazy only to be caught by Offisser B. Pupp.

George McManus' "Bringing up Father" in 1913 brought Maggie and Jiggs to the nation and served as the first domestic comic strip. Later popular comic strips were Fontaine Fox's "Toonerville Folks" (1913), Sydney Fisher's "The Gumps" (1917), Frank King's "Gasoline Alley" (1919)—the first comic strip to advance characters chronologically and still one of the great comic strips—Harold Gray's "Little Orphan Annie" (1924), Philip Newlan and Richard Calkins' "Buck Rogers" (1929), Chic Young's "Blondie" (1930), Chester Gould's "Dick Tracy" (1931), Martha Orr's "Apple Mary" (1932)—in 1940 called "Mary Worth's Family" and in 1944 simply "Mary Worth"— Alex Raymond's magnificently drawn "Flash Gordon" (1934), Al Capp's "Li'l Abner" (1934), Bill Holman's wacky "Smokey Stover" (1935), Jerry Siegel and Joe Shuster's "Superman" (1938), and Walt Kelly's loving contribution to American folklore and culture, "Pogo" (1949).

Comic Books

Comic books began as an offshoot of comic strips. A collection of "The Yellow Kid" strips was published in March 1897, and reprints of other comic strips were offered at least through the early 1920s. In 1922, a reprint magazine, *Comic Monthly*, began, each month given to reprints of a different comic strip, and in 1929, George Delacorte published thirteen issues of *The Funnies*, the first four-color comic books.

In 1933, 10,000 copies of *Funnies on Parade* were published by Eastern Color Printing Company in New York and distributed as a premium by Procter & Gamble. Later that same year, M. C. Gaines convinced Eastern that other companies could use the gimmick for premiums, and Eastern printed *Famous Funnies: A Carnival of Comics*, reprints of Sunday color comics, in quantities of more than 100,000. Sure of success, Gaines asked Eastern to print 35,000 copies of *Famous Funnies, Series 1*, a sixty-four page book that sold for ten cents in chain stores.

National Periodical Publications' *New Fun* (after the first issue, entitled *More Fun*) in 1935 was the first comic book to publish original material, not merely reprints. Later that year Walt Disney began his *Mickey Mouse Magazine* (in 1940 to become *Walt Disney's Comics and Stories*), a combination of reprinted and original material.

Detective Comics in 1937 was the first themed nonreprint comic book. Published by National Periodical Publications, the company soon became known in the trade as DC Comics. DC's *Action Comics* began in June 1938 with a character soon to become part of American mythology, "Superman," who began as one of several strips but was soon given his own separate publication. Later comic heroes included Batman, who appeared first in DC's *Detective Comics* #27 in 1939. The Sub-Mariner and the Human Torch debuted in *Marvel Comics* that same year, Captain Marvel started in Fawcett's *Whiz Comics* in 1940, and Wonder Woman appeared in DC's *All-Star Comics* #8 a year later.

By the close of 1941, over 160 comic book titles were distributed monthly selling more than twelve million copies. A year later *Crime Does Not Pay* brought realistic crime stories to readers. In 1950 William M. Gaines, son of M. C. Gaines, began several new horror comics, *Crypt of Terror, The Vault of Horror, Weird Science,* and *Two-Fisted Tales.*

The suspicion of parents, teachers, librarians, and other critics that comic books had a potentially evil influence on the young led to formation of a U.S. Senate Subcommittee, chaired by Estes Kefauver, to investigate detrimental effects of comic books. It also led to an investigation by psychologist Frederic Wertham resulting in a bitter attack on crime, horror, and hero comics:

> Slowly, and at first reluctantly, I have come to the conclusion that this chronic stimulation, temptation, and seduction by comic books, both their content and their alluring advertisements of knives and guns, are contributing factors to many children's maladjustment.
>
> All comic books with their words and expletives in balloons are bad for reading, but not every comic book is bad for children's minds and emotions. The trouble is that "good" comic books are snowed under by those which glorify violence, crime and sadism.
>
> At no time, up to the present, has a single child ever told me as an excuse for a delinquency or for misbehavior that comic books were to blame. Nor do I nor my associates ever question a child in such a way as to suggest that to him. If I find a child with fever, I do not ask him "What is the cause of your fever? Do you have measles?" I examine him and make my own diagnosis. It is our clinical judgment, in all kinds of behavior disorders and personality difficulties of children, that comic books do play a part.[49]

A selection of titles from the Emanuel Haldeman-Julius library of Little Blue Books.

After the Senate Subcommittee Report[50] and the furor surrounding Wertham's impassioned book, publishers, fearful of pressures to come, staved off some of the fury by creating a Comics Code Authority banning profanity, nudity, excessive violence and horror, portrayal of crime as attractive, and disrespect for established authority. The Code also recommended less slang and better grammar in comics. Presumably, critics, teachers, librarians, and parents were pacified. Few young people probably noticed anything very different in the comics, and things soon headed back to normal.

Big-Little Books

Less significant than pulps, comic strips, or comic books, Big-Little Books still were widely read (and today bring a nice sum for sound copies). Published originally by Whitman in cardboard covers, they normally had one page of text facing a full-page illustration. Sizes varied from approximately three inches by three inches to those slightly larger. Selling for ten cents and usually featuring a new adventure of a popular comic strip or movie hero, they appealed both to those who liked comic books and to those presumably a little more literate. The first Big-Little Book, *The Adventures of Dick Tracy,* was printed in 1932, and hundreds followed based on comic strips such as "Flash Gordon," "Skippy," "Terry and the Pirates," "Moon Mullins," or "Apple Mary"; on movies, movie characters, or actors such as "Our Gang," "Donald Duck," Gene Autry, Jackie Cooper, or Johnny Mack Brown; and other sources such as *The Three Musketeers, Tom Swift and His Magnetic Silencer,* or Edgar Bergen and Charlie McCarthy.

THE LITTLE BLUE BOOKS

All too little has been written about the work of Emanuel Haldeman-Julius (1889–1951) and his incredible and influential library of Little Blue Books. Basing his operation in Girard, Kansas, Haldeman-Julius sold roughly five hundred million copies from his library of about two thousand titles, many purchased by young adults with—or without—parental permission. Although he lived in the heart of the Bible belt and was always controversial, he gained the respect of many midwesterners earnestly—sometimes desperately—seeking education. A rationalist and an atheist, he had an ingrained belief in the educational perfectibility of humanity if people had inexpensive good books readily available. Haldeman-Julius began battling ignorance, superstition, and misunderstanding by publishing a library of small, paperbound books at twenty-five cents each. He soon discovered enough interested readers to drop the price to fifteen cents, then ten cents, and finally five cents, selling them in bulk by mail. Two-page ads in newspapers and magazines such as *Saturday Evening Post, Popular Mechanics, Ladies Home Journal,* and *The New York Times Book Review* brought him first orders and repeat business. The blue-covered books dealt with an incredible variety of subjects. The scope of these five-cent books was without parallel in American publishing. Using that amazing nickel, one could purchase titles as different as Poe's *The Fall of the House of Usher,* Darrow's *Debate on Capital Punishment, The Diary of Samuel Pepys,* Doyle's *Sherlock Holmes Problem Stories,* Verne's *Five Weeks in a Balloon, Nature Poems of Wordsworth, An Encyclopedia of Sex, Famous $12,000 Prize-Winning Tongue-Twisters,* and Haldeman-Julius' own *The Art of Reading.* He even published Will Durant's *The Story of Philosophy* (1926) in a dozen or so booklets. A mixed but impressive bag.

Haldeman-Julius' contribution to American education was profound. He made books and education available for thousands of Americans denied more than a few years of formal education.

A FEW BOOKS YOUNG ADULTS LIKED

Books popular with young adults fall into six reasonably discrete categories, each a mixture of good (or adequate) books and bad (or dismal) books. Some deserve reading today; others deserve the interment already decently provided.

And a Little Child Shall Lead Them (Though God Knows Where)

Among the most popular books prior to World War I were those featuring a small child, usually a girl, who significantly changed those people around her. At their best, they showed an intriguing youngster humanizing sterile or cold people. At their worst

" FLUNG HERSELF INTO HER AUNT'S SCANDALIZED, UNYIELD-
ING LAP."

Eleanor H. Porter. *Pollyanna*, 1913.

(and they often were) they featured a child rapturously happy and miraculously even-dispositioned who infected an entire household—or even a community—with her messianic drive to improve the world through cheer and gladness.

The type began promisingly with Kate Douglas Wiggin's *Rebecca of Sunnybrook Farm* (1904). Nothing Wiggin wrote surpassed Rebecca, which sold more than a million and a quarter copies between 1904 and 1975. Living in a small town during the 1870s, the optimistic heroine is handed over to two maiden aunts while her parents cope with a large family. She is educated despite her imperfections, high spirits, and rebelliousness, and at the close of the book seems cheerfully on her way upward to a better life. Wiggins' book preaches acceptance of the status quo, not surprising for the time, but the heroine does get herself into believable scrapes, the book does not overly sentimentalize either itself or the world, and humor is more common than sadness or preaching. The book deserved its success, just as it deserves reading today.

Anne of Green Gables (1908) by Lucy Maud Montgomery was a worthy successor to Rebecca. As in Wiggin's book, Anne travels to an alien society. Here, a childless couple who wants to adopt a boy gets Anne by mistake. Anne changes the couple for the better, but they also change her, and Anne's delightfully developed character goes far to remedy any defects in the book. Docile as she tries to be (and occasionally succeeds), she is alive, charming, and impulsive. When the book ends, Anne is believably ready to take on responsibilities.

Wiggin and Montgomery generally managed to skirt the sea of sentimentalism, that fatal syrupy deep beloved by bad writers. Occasionally, Rebecca and Anne waded out dangerously far, but their common sense, their impulsiveness, their love of laughter, and their ability to laugh at themselves saved them and brought them back to shore. After them came the disaster, authors and characters so enamored of humanity, so convinced that all people were redeemable, so stickily and uncomplainingly sweet and good that they drowned in goodness while readers either drowned with them or gagged.

Jean Webster's *Daddy-Long-Legs* (1912) was sticky enough in its picture of a college girl who falls in love with her benefactor. Gene Stratton Porter was worse in her *Freckles* (1904), *A Girl of the Limberlost* (1909), *Laddie* (1913), and *Michael O'Halloran* (1915) where sentiment is all and coincidence and a good heart solve all problems.

But it was left to Eleanor Porter to write the genre's magnum opus and destroy it with *Pollyanna* (1913). *Pollyanna* is usually remembered as a children's book, but it began as a popular adult novel, eighth among best sellers in 1913 and second in 1914. So sickeningly sweet is the heroine that countless adults and young people could rightfully credit her with their diabetes. Orphaned Pollyanna comes to the house of rich Aunt Polly, who scorns her. Lovely but wholesome Pollyanna plays her "glad game," befuddling Nancy, the maid. Nancy asks Pollyanna to explain the game:

> "Why, it's a game. Father taught it to me, and it's lovely," rejoined Pollyanna. "We've played it always, ever since I was a little, little girl. I told the Ladies' Aid, and they played it—some of them."
>
> "What is it? I ain't much on games, though."
>
> Pollyanna laughed again, but she sighed, too; and in the gathering twilight her face looked thin and wistful.
>
> "Why, we began it on some crutches that came in a missionary barrel."
>
> "*Crutches!*"
>
> "Yes. You see I'd wanted a doll, and father had written them so; but when the barrel came the lady wrote that there hadn't any dolls come in, but the little crutches had. So she sent 'em along as they might come in handy for some child, sometime. And that's when we began it."
>
> "Well, I must say I can't see any game about that," declared Nancy, almost irritably.
>
> "Oh, yes; the game was to find something about everything to be glad about—no matter what 'twas," rejoined Pollyanna, earnestly. "And we began right then—on the crutches."
>
> "Well, goodness me! I can't see anythin' ter be glad about—gettin' a pair of crutches when you wanted a doll!"
>
> Pollyanna clapped her hands.
>
> "There is—there is," she crowed. "But *I* couldn't see it, either, Nancy, at first," she added, with quick honesty. "Father had to tell it to me."
>
> "Well, then, suppose *you* tell *me*," almost snapped Nancy.
>
> "Goosey! Why, just be glad because you *don't—need—'em!*" exulted Pollyanna, triumphantly. "You see it's just as easy—when you know how!"

To the loathing of some sensible people, the "Glad Game" raged across the country. But Pollyanna does more than laugh at personal misfortunes. She reunites once-happy and now miserable lovers and friends, saves Aunt Polly from a loveless life, eliminates gloom for miles around, rescues the miserable, and gladdens everybody, just everybody.

Hearth, Home, and Responsibility (with Bits of Sin)

Stories of motherhood and true love were popular with young adults and adults. At times, little hints (and sometimes broad brushstrokes) of sin, redeemed or otherwise, made the stories more palatable.

Alice Hegan Rice could easily have created an ocean of treacle in *Mrs. Wiggs of the Cabbage Patch* (1901), but instead she portrayed an optimistic family led by an indomitable mother in the midst of a Louisville slum without making either seem unbelievable. Her publisher doubted the book would sell and printed only 2000 copies for the first edition. Once they were rapidly picked up, he admitted his guess was wrong and began turning out 40,000 copies a month. The book was a best seller and remains in print today.

Several writers were unable to keep large doses of sentimentalism and goodness from their books, though no rival for sweetness per page arose to worry Gene Stratton Porter or Eleanor Porter. John Fox, Jr., wrote of his beloved Cumberland Mountains and the coming of civilization and machines in *The Little Shepherd of Kingdom Come* (1903) and *The Trail of the Lonesome Pine* (1908). Harold Bell Wright moved to the Ozarks in search of better health and found interesting people, God, and a deep belief in muscular Christianity. He began preaching in a schoolhouse and spent the next twelve years

---

If the sanctity of the home and the love of God sold well, sin was equally attractive.

---

moving from pastorate to pastorate. *The Shepherd of the Hills* (1907) and *The Calling of Dan Matthews* (1909) made money by attacking the hypocrisy of formalized religion, especially in big cities. By then Wright had left the pulpit for full-time writing and later books were consistent best sellers endorsed by ministers and attacked by literary critics. The first printing of *The Winning of Barbara Worth* (1911) ran to 175,000 copies, and the advertising and printing for *Their Yesterdays* (1912) was even greater. *When a Man's a Man* (1916) and *The Re-creation of Brian Keith* (1919) are typically Wright, strong on theme and sermonistic to a fault. Brief bits of plot and stereotyped characters are manipulated to ensure that readers understand Wright's point about God and the church.

Simple love stories were popular. Grace Livingston Hill sold more than four million copies in a lifetime writing such novels as *The Girl from Montana* (1907), *Exit Betty* (1920), and *Rainbow Cottage* (1934). Prolific English novelist Florence Barclay produced a best seller in America with *The Rosary* (1910) in which an incredible but plain young woman has faith in her blind sweetheart and sings the popular song of the time, "The Rosary," to help him onward and upward.

If the sanctity of the home and the love of God sold well, sin was equally attractive. In 1907, Elinor Glynn published *Three Weeks,* portraying the queen of a mythical European country who forgets her husband and duties for a glorious three weeks' sex romp with a handsome Englishman. Readers realized that it was nothing more than romanticized pornography, the love scenes on the tigerskin rug justified their feelings, and sales rose. What the book lacked in psychological probing, it compensated for with pages of physical probing. Just as sin-laden and equally popular was *The Sheik* (1921) by Edith Maude Hull. The abduction of self-centered Diana Mayo by the sensual Sheik and his rough treatment of her excited millions. The film version starring Rudolph Valentino was superior to the book. For many readers, young and old, these books broke conventions long overdue for destruction, and they were widely read, albeit often covertly.

Moving Westward

The closing of the West heightened interest in an exciting, almost magic, era. A few writers, aiming specifically at young adults, knew the West so well that they became touchstones for authenticity in other writers. George Bird Grinnell wrote *Pawnee Hero Stories and Folk Tales* (1889) and *By Cheyenne Campfires* (1926) and established an honest and generally unsentimentalized portrait of Indian life. Both he and Charles A. Eastman often appeared on reading interest studies as boys' favorites. Eastman's autobiography, *Indian Boyhood* (1902), was often justifiably praised for its sense of time and place. Joseph Altsheler (1862–1919) wrote more conventional adventure tales of the West, often lapsing into melodrama, but he was for some time a favorite for *The Young Trailers* (1907), *The Last of the Chiefs* (1909), and *The Horsemen of the Plains* (1910).

The first really great writer to focus on the West and its mystique of violence and danger mixed with open spaces and freedom was Owen Wister, whose *The Virginian: A Horseman of the Plains* (1902) provided a model of colloquial speech and romantic and melodramatic adventure for novels to follow. "When you call me that, *smile!*" was endlessly quoted by boys for years thereafter. Andy Adams was a far more trustworthy guide to the West in *The Log of a Cowboy: A Narrative of the Old Trail Days* (1903), but the public was clearly more interested in thrills and spills than it was in accuracy. Zane Grey fulfilled whatever need the public had with his incredibly romantic pictures of life in the older days of the West in *The Spirit of the Border* (1906) and *The Wanderer of the Wasteland* (1923). The best of his books—certainly the most-remembered and probably the epitome of the overly romanticized western—was *Riders of the Purple Sage* (1912) filled with classic elements: the mysterious hero, the innocent heroine, evil villains, and the open land. Criticized as Grey has been by librarians and teachers—who seem in

A leap in the nick of time.
(See page 261.)

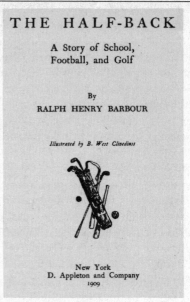

THE HALF-BACK

A Story of School,
Football, and Golf

By
RALPH HENRY BARBOUR

Illustrated by B. West Clinedinst

New York
D. Appleton and Company
1909

Ralph Henry Barbour. *The Half-Back*, 1899.

general to have read little or nothing of his work—he was and is read, and his books stay in print. Anyone who wishes to know what the western dream was should read Grey.

Rah Rah for the School and Fair Play

With more young adults attending school and with the steadily rising popularity of sports—especially college football and professional baseball—more school-sports stories appeared. For many teachers and professors then and now, academic excellence and sports are mutually exclusive terms. Some people worried that football was too rough; many that it would distract from studies. We may associate the term "football fever" with modern times, but it was used at the turn of the century when one educator fretted about sports:

> I noticed two years ago, when the football fever was raging, that it was generally believed that a college's success in football drew students to it, and that some schools thought it necessary to make football a leading feature in their "fit for college."[51]

William Gilbert Patten was not the first writer of sports novels, but he was the first to introduce a regular, almost mythic, sports character known throughout America—Frank Merriwell. In 1895 Ormond Smith (of Street & Smith) urged Patten, one of his stable of dime novelists, to write a school and sports series with lots of adventure.

Under the pen name of Burt L. Standish, Patten created heroic Frank Merriwell and in two weeks wrote a story that appeared as "Frank Makes a Foe" in *Tip Top Weekly* in 1896. Circulation of *Tip Top Weekly* boomed and Patten and Frank Merriwell were hits. Several hundred stories about Frank followed, and Patten later combined a number of them into hardback books. A natural leader, an incredible boxer, an expert duelist, an exemplary baseball player, and an all-round great guy, Frank is also decent, heroic, modest, and everything a mother could wish for in a son. One episode near the end of *Frank Merriwell at Yale* (1903) illustrates Frank's charisma and charm in turning bad guys into good guys. A boxer-hood-bad-guy tries unsuccessfully to waylay Frank; later, he recognizes Frank's greatness when our hero nobly asks the boxer to go straight. The bad guy immediately sees the light:

> I t'ink ye're right, an' I'm going ter try ter do it. I allus did hate ter work, but if I kin get any kind of a job I'm going ter try it once more. I don't know w'y it is, but jes' being wid youse makes me want ter do der square t'ing.

Although they did not create any heroes as well known as Frank Merriwell, three much better writers stand out for their more realistic sports books.

Owen Johnson wrote for adults, but *The Varmint* (1910) and *The Tennessee Shad* (1911), about sports and pranks at Lawrenceville School, were widely read by boys. *Stover at Yale* (1911) is about sports, but more significant to Johnson were his attacks on Yale's problems, snobbery, social clubs, fraternities, senior societies, and anti-intellectualism.

Ralph Henry Barbour wrote an incredible number of fine books, beginning with *The Half-Back* (1899), presenting believable boys in believable situations at school playing the sports of different seasons. Dated as his books are by rule changes, they are still readable. Rarest of all for the time, Barbour presented few villains. His books became repetitious over the years as he used the same formula—a boy attending school and learning who and what he is and what he might become through sports—but the formula was Barbour's invention. His theme was stated in the dedication to *The Half-Back*: "To Every American Boy Who Loves Honest, Manly Sports." He steadfastly and sincerely believed that sports presented opportunities and challenges for every boy, a belief predicated on three acts of faith: schools must have school spirit, school spirit comes from sports, and sports must be amateur and free of any taint of commercialism or professionalism. He reflected the philosophy of Walter Camp, father of football and writer of several sports novels—*Danny Fists* (1913) is his best—who wrote:

> If you are enough of a man to be a good athlete, and some one asks you to use that athletic ability on their behalf, don't take money for it, or anything that amounts to pay. . . .
>
> You don't want your boy "hired" by any one. If he plays, he plays as a gentleman, and not as a professional; he plays for victory, not for money; and whatever bruises he may have in the flesh, his heart is right, and he can look you in the eye as a gentleman should.[52]

To Barbour sports were significant in a boy's life, but they were a part of life, not all of it. He would never have understood Knute Rockne's words, "After the Church, football is the best thing we have." Barbour's concern about encroaching professionalism in school and college football is illustrated in *The Spirit of the School* (1907). A young, likable boy, who happens also to be a good athlete, is paid to attend Beechcroft. The coach does not approve but he does nothing about the boy or the situation. A few members of the football squad know, but when others find out, dissension arises. A vote is taken and the amateur spirit is restored to the academy with Barbour's complete approval.

William Heyliger followed in the same pattern with *Bartley: Freshman Pitcher* (1911). But Barbour's concerns were sports and school, whereas Heyliger wrote more varied books: school and sports stories in his *St. Mary's* series, *Fairview High* series, and *Lansing* series; and ground-breaking vocational stories in *High Benton* (1919), *High Benton, Worker* (1921), *Dan's Tomorrow* (1922), *Steve Merrill, Engineer* (1935), *You're on the Air* (1941), and *Top Lineman* (1943).

School stories for girls never achieved a similar volume or readership, but a few authors had loyal readers. Laura Elizabeth Richards was best known for *Peggy* (1899) in which a poor girl goes to school and becomes a school hero in basketball. Marjorie Hill Allee was author of three books about girls at college, *Jane's Island* (1931), *The Great Tradition* (1937), and *Little American Girl* (1938). *The Great Tradition* intrigued young adults with its mixture of romance, college life, and the spirit of research among five young graduate students at the University of Chicago.

Strange Deeds and Far Lands

Young adults, then and now, read tales of adventures as avidly as adults. No other literary genre has been as often used or as persistently successful with readers.

The public's fancy near the turn of the century was taken by a craze for adventure-romance set in imaginary countries: Anthony Hope, pen name of Anthony Hope Hawkins, created the passion for never-never lands in *The Prisoner of Zenda* (1894) loosely modeled after Robert Louis Stevenson's *Prince Otto* (1885). Englishman Rudolph Rassendyl, hunting in Ruritania at a crucial time, learns that he closely resembles King Rupert. Rassendyl agrees to foil the machinations of evil plotters, falls in love with the lovely Princess Flavia, but does his duty and nobly leaves the country alone having done his all. Twenty-six printings within the year proved he was a hero to Americans.

American author George McCutcheon pushed the tale of the mythical kingdom to its limits. In *Graustark: The Story of a Love Behind a Throne* (1901) romance is all, adventures are thrilling beyond real life, and Americans cannot be beaten by anyone. Twenty-nine year old American Grenfell Lorry falls in love with lovely Miss Guggenslocker, despite her name. He finds she is, in reality, Princess Yetive of Graustark, and plots against her are brewing. He learns that Graustark's debt must be paid by her marriage to the prince of a neighboring country. Lorry foils plots, battles enemies, and wins the princess. Told he cannot marry Yetive since he is only a commoner, he says:

> I am not a prince, as you are saying over and over again to yourself. Every born American may become the ruler of the greatest nation in the world—the United States. His home is his kingdom; his wife, his mothers, his sisters are his queens and his princesses; his fellow citizens are his admiring subjects if he is wise and good. In my land you will find the poor man climbing to the highest pinnacle, side by side with the rich man. . . . We recognize little as impossible. Until death destroys this power to love and to hope I must say to you that I shall not consider the Princess Yetive beyond my reach.

And he marries her. Five sequels followed, none as successful as the original but all more than merely respectable sellers.

As the day of adventure fantasy waned, other authors turned to more conventional themes of adventure, notably survival against great odds. John Buchan produced his most enduring work in *The Thirty-Nine Steps* (1915), the tale of an innocent, naive, and not especially bright young man caught in a world of spying and intrigue. Alfred Hitchcock's 1935 film (and two later ones by other directors) helped to maintain the popularity of a book solidly entrenched as a classic of adventure literature.

Survival at sea against nature and fellow man was the theme of Charles Nordhoff and James Norman Hall in several books, notably the Mutiny trilogy about Captain William Bligh, Fletcher Christian, the mutineers, and those loyal to their king in *Mutiny on the Bounty* (1932), *Men Against the Sea* (1934), and *Pitcairn's Island* (1934).

That same sense of the sea, its beauty, its deadliness, and its boredom, pervades many books by Howard Pease, especially those about Tod Moran. *The Tattooed Man* (1926), *The Ship Without a Crew* (1934), *The Black Tanker* (1941), and *Heart of Danger* (1947) were widely read for their excitement and Pease's clear understanding and love of the sea.

Rarest of all adventure writers is the one who creates a popular myth as Edgar Rice Burroughs did in *Tarzan of the Apes* (1914). In that and later books, Tarzan was rarely treated with any courtesy by teachers or librarians, but the ape-man myth attracted readers in vast numbers. *Tarzan* sold more than thirty-five million copies in the 1920s and 1930s. The sequels added more sales, and the many movies starring several different Tarzans made the character and its author household names.

Reality Can Sell

Although other types of books usually outsold realistic portrayals of the state of humanity, some books critical of society and its institutions were good sellers.

Margaret Deland broke first ground in her appraisal of a young minister seeking truth and struggling against his Calvinist background in *John Ward, Preacher* (1888). Slightly more sentimental, but even more popular, was her study of a woman living in sin yet seeking salvation for a young orphan in *The Awakening of Helena Richie* (1906).

Booth Tarkington, best known to young adults for *Penrod* (1914) and the condescending *Seventeen* (1902), produced a number of best-selling portraits of humanity,

warts and all. Good as *The Turmoil* (1915) and *The Midlands* (1924) are, his most enduring (and oddly endearing) books of middle-America have proved to be *The Magnificent
Ambersons* (1918), a picture of the fall of a young man, and *Alice Adams* (1921), the tale
of a dangerous dreamer. Different as the two books are, both show Tarkington analyzing the American dream and questioning its reality.

Later iconoclastic writers proved equally popular with young adults. Sinclair Lewis destroyed the myth of the purity of small towns in *Main Street* (1921), the myths
about small-town businessmen in *Babbitt* (1922), and the myths about small-minded
evangelists in *Elmer Gantry* (1927), but he did not destroy his readers' faith in the
process. What he did do was challenge readers to think and convince them that an
unexamined idea or belief was seductive and potentially dangerous.

What Lewis began, John Steinbeck carried forward for many readers. Lewis attacked men and ideas, Steinbeck attacked institutions and society; Lewis despised men,
but Steinbeck loved his fellows. Steinbeck may be, as it has been claimed, less a writer
than a social propagandist, but, given the social conditions of the 1930s, Steinbeck
brought—and continues to bring—a strident voice to social issues. The number of his
books that remain popular because of parallel social conditions today (it is difficult for
young adults to read Steinbeck purely as a critical social historian) is impressive. *Tortilla Flat* (1935); *In Dubious Battle* (1936), which is surely his best book; and *The Red Pony*
(1937) are sympathetic depictions of loneliness and the importance of family loyalty
just as much as they are studies of social ills, past and present.

Fewer writers of the time turned to racial issues. Du Bose Heyward's *Porgy* (1925)
is probably better known in the George Gershwin opera, *Porgy and Bess,* but both that
book and *Mamba's Daughters* (1929) portrayed blacks pushed about by whites and
poverty yet able to keep their dignity. Joseph Gollomb, unfortunately largely forgotten
today, wrote four books about a large racially troubled city high school, *That Year at
Lincoln High* (1918), *Working Through at Lincoln High* (1923), *Up at City High* (1945), and
Tiger at City High (1946).

Elizabeth Foreman Lewis deserves to be remembered for her honest and compassionate portraits of life in China, which she knew at first hand. She won the Newbery
Award for her 1932 *Fu of the Upper Yangtze* and its picture of an ambitious young
apprentice to a coppersmith, but readers who care about integrity and good writing will
find almost equal rewards in *Ho-Ming, a Girl of New China* (1934) and *To Beat a Tiger*
(1956).

Young adult literature and books read by young adults underwent many changes
from 1900 to 1940. Teachers and librarians took more interest in assessing types and
titles of books read by young adults. The Stratemeyer Syndicate turned the creation of
series stories from a small-scale operation to a major industry. If teachers and librarians
heartily disapproved of Stratemeyer's series and other series, young adults read them
avidly, though by 1940 most series books were dead except for the lively Hardy Boys
and the even healthier Nancy Drew. Publishers added "Junior" or "Juvenile" divisions.
Fiction of the time moved slowly and sometimes clumsily from the innocence of *Pollyanna* and *Graustark* to serious and nonromanticized books. Life seemed relatively sure,
easy, simple, and safe in 1900; the First World War and the Depression dispelled that

myth. When the Depression of the 1930s was ending, World War II and a very different world were just over the horizon, and a different kind of literature was soon to appear for young adults.

ACTIVITIES

1. Read one of the Stratemeyer Syndicate books still popular, a Nancy Drew or Hardy Boys mystery. What assumptions about adults, young adults, and values are inherent in the book? What ingredients—or assumptions—made the book popular? What keeps it popular? Why do you suppose some teachers and librarians have criticized these two series, even banning them from schools and libraries at times? If possible, interview several librarians and teachers to learn what they feel about Nancy Drew or the Hardy Boys and why they feel as they do. Talk to a few young adults to find out why Nancy Drew or the Hardy Boys are still popular. Talk to a few adults your own age to find what their reactions were (and are) to Nancy Drew or the Hardy Boys.

2. Read a few comic books presently popular with young adults (ask some young friends which comic books are popular or ask jobbers or dealers for the titles/series that sell well). What makes the comic book popular? If possible, find a reader of the comic book (after you have read it) to compare notes—don't try to convert the young adult to anything, at least not now. What does the reader see in the comic that you did or did not? Why? How? What assumptions about humanity and values does the comic book make, obviously or covertly?

3. Read some articles from early issues of the *English Journal* or *Academy* or the *Library Journal.* What was it like to be a librarian or English teacher in the good old days? What professional problems did they have in common with you? What problems seem significantly different? Why? How? What kinds of books seemed to be popular then? How do they differ from popular books today?

NOTES

[1]M. P. True, "What My Pupils Read," *Education* 14 (October 1893): 99–102.

[2]Clara Vostrovsky, "A Study of Children's Reading Tastes," *Pedagogical Seminary* 6 (December 1899): 523–35.

[3]*Publishers Weekly,* 107 (February 21, 1925): 619–22.

[4]Alfred M. Hitchcock, "The Relation of the Picture Play to Literature," *English Journal* 4 (May 1915): 296.

[5]Montrose J. Moses, "Dietary Laws of Children's Books," *Bookman* 51 (July 1920): 590.

[6]Carleton Washburne and Mabel Vogel, *Winnetka Graded Book List* (Chicago: American Library Association, 1926), p. 5.

[7]Carleton Washburne and Mabel Vogel, "Supplement to the Winnetka Graded Book List," *Elementary English Review* 4 (February 1927): 47–52; and 4 (March 1927): 66–73.

[8]William Lyon Phelps, "The Virtues of the Second-Rate," *English Journal* 16 (January 1927): 13–14.

[9]Reed Smith, *The Teaching of Literature in the High School* (New York: American, 1935), p. 7.

[10]Franklin T. Baker, *A Bibliography of Children's Reading* (New York: Teachers College, Columbia University, 1908), pp. 6–7.

[11]Clara Whitehill Hunt, "Good and Bad Taste in Girls' Reading," *Ladies' Home Journal* 27 (April 1910): 52.

[12]Julia Carter, "Let's Talk about Boys and Books," *Wilson Bulletin for Librarians* 9 (April 1935): 418.

[13]Alice M. Jordan, "A Gallery of Girls," *The Horn Book Magazine* 13 (September 1937): 276.

[14]Hannah Logosa, "Elements in Reading Guidance," *Public Libraries* 27 (March 1922): 147.

[15]Vostrovsky, p. 535.

[16]G. Stanley Hall, "Children's Reading: As a Factor in Their Education," *Library Journal* 33 (April 1908): 124–25.

[17]Fannie M. Clark, "Teaching Children to Choose," *English Journal* 9 (March 1920): 142.

[18]Orrin C. Cocker, "Motion Pictures and Reading Habits," *Library Journal* 43 (February 1918): 68.

[19]Marilla Waite Freeman, "Tying Up with the Movies: Why? When? How?" *Library Journal* 54 (June 15, 1929): 519–24.

[20]Robert Luther Duffus, *Books: Their Place in a Democracy* (Boston: Houghton Mifflin Co., 1930), p. 117.

[21]Louise Dinwiddie, "Best Sellers and Modern Youth," *Library Journal* 65 (November 15, 1940): 958–59.

[22]W. H. Ray et al., "English in the High School," *Academy* 4 (May 1889): 187.

[23]William E. Mead, "A Ten Years' Course in Literature," *Academy* 2 (March 1887): 55.

[24]*Report of the Committee of Ten on Secondary School Studies* (New York: American, 1894). For details about conditions leading to the Committee of Ten's formation, the Committee's deliberations, and its influence see two excellent studies, Edward A. Krug, *The Shaping of the American High School* (New York: Harper & Row, Publishers, Inc., 1964) and Theodore R. Sizer, *Secondary Schools at the Turn of the Century* (New Haven: Yale University Press, 1964).

[25]Samuel Thurber, "Report of English Conference" in *Report of the Committee of Ten on Secondary School Studies* (New York: Appleton, 1894), p. 86. Thurber was both a brilliant teacher and writer whose comments, especially in *School Review* and *Academy*, deserve attention today.

[26]Samuel Thurber, "Voluntary Reading in the Classical High School from the Pupil's Point of View," *School Review* 13 (February 1905): 170.

27Alfred M. Hitchcock in the discussion following a reading of Lilian B. Miner, "Voluntary Reading in the English High School," *School Review* 13 (February 1905): 188-89.

28J. M. Coulter, "What the University Expects of the Secondary School," *School Review* 17 (February 1909): 73.

29"Proceedings of the First Annual Meeting, Chicago, December 1 and 2, 1911," *English Journal* 1 (January 1912): 30-45.

30Wilbur W. Hatfield, "Modern Literature for High School Use," *English Journal* 1 (January 1912): 52.

31*Reorganization of English in Secondary Schools,* Department of the Interior, Bureau of Education, Bulletin 1917, no. 2 (Washington: Government Printing Office, 1917).

32Ibid., p. 63.

33Ibid., pp. 76-84.

34Dora V. Smith, *Instruction in English,* Bulletin, 1932, no. 17. National Survey of Secondary Education, Monograph no. 20 (Washington: Government Printing Office, 1933).

35Nancy Gillmore Coryell, *An Evaluation of Extensive and Intensive Teaching of Literature: A Year's Experiment in the Eleventh Grade,* Teachers College, Columbia University, Contributions to Education, no. 275 (New York: Teachers College, Columbia University, 1927).

36Lou LaBrant, *An Evaluation of the Free Reading Program in Grades Ten, Eleven, and Twelve for the Class of 1935,* The Ohio State University School, Contributions to Education No. 2 (Columbus: Ohio State University, 1936). See also Lou LaBrant, "The Content of a Free Reading Program," *Educational Research Bulletin* 16 (February 17, 1937): 29-34.

37Dora V. Smith, "Extensive Reading in Junior High School: A Survey of Teacher Preparation," *English Journal* 19 (June 1930): 449-62.

38Dora V. Smith, "American Youth and English," *English Journal* 26 (February 1937): 111.

39Leslie McFarlane, *Ghost of the Hardy Boys* (New York: Two Continents Publishing Group, Inc., 1976), a delightful account of the days McFarlane spent working for Stratemeyer.

40Roger Garis, *My Father Was Uncle Wiggily* (New York: McGraw-Hill Book Co., 1966).

41Quoted by Ed Zuckerman, "The Great Hardy Boys' Whodunit," *Rolling Stone,* September 9, 1976, p. 39.

42Caroline M. Hewins, "Book Reviews, Book Lists, and Articles on Children's Reading: Are They of Practical Value to the Children's Librarian?" *Library Journal* 26 (August 1901): 58. Attacks on series books, but especially Stratemeyer's books, persisted thereafter in library literature. Mary E. S. Root prepared a list of series books not to be circulated by public librarians, "Not to Be Circulated," *Wilson Bulletin for Librarians* 3 (January 1929): 446, including books by Alger, Finley, Castlemon, Ellis, Optic, and others, the others being heavily Stratemeyer. Two months later, Ernest F. Ayres responded, "Not to Be Circulated?" *Wilson Bulletin for Librarians* 3 (March 1929) 528-29, objecting to the cavalier treatment accorded old favorites and sarcastically adding,

"Why worry about censorship so long as we have librarians?" Attacks continue today. Librarians and English teachers to the contrary, the Syndicate clearly is winning, and students seem to be pleased.

[43]Franklin K. Mathiews, "Blowing Out the Boy's Brains," *Outlook* 108 (November 18, 1914): 653.

[44]For years the most frequently quoted source of information on Stratemeyer's Syndicate was the biased "For It Was Indeed He," *Fortune* 9 (April 1934): 86. The article deserves attention even today but it should be balanced with other materials either objective or biased on Stratemeyer's side, for example, John T. Dizer, Jr., "Boys' Books and the American Dream," *Dime Novel Roundup* 37 (February 15, 1968): 12–17, and 37 (March 15, 1968): 29–31; John T. Dizer, Jr., "Fortune and the Syndicate," *Boys' Book Collector* 2 (Fall 1970): 146–53, and 2 (Winter 1971): 178–86; and a nostalgic and enjoyable look at series books, Arthur Prager, *Rascals at Large, or The Clue in the Old Nostalgia* (New York: Doubleday, 1971).

[45]John Tunis, "What Is a Juvenile Book?" *The Horn Book Magazine* 44 (June 1968): 307.

[46]Jack Smalley, "Amazing Confessions of a Pulpeteer," *Westways* (June 1974): 20.

[47]Peter Haining, ed., *The Fantastic Pulps* (New York: Vintage Books, 1975).

[48]Herbert Ruhn, ed., *The Hard-Boiled Detectives: Stories from "Black Mask Magazine" 1920–1951* (New York: Vintage Books, 1977).

[49]Frederic Wertham, *Seduction of the Innocent* (New York: Holt, Rinehart and Winston, Inc., 1954), p. 10.

[50]*Comic Books and Juvenile Delinquency,* Interim Report of the Committee on the Judiciary (Washington, D.C.: Government Printing Office, 1955).

[51]E. L. Godkin, "The Illiteracy of American Boys," *Educational Review* 13 (January 1897): 6.

[52]Walter Camp, *Book of College Sports* (New York: Century, 1893), pp. 2–3.

TITLES MENTIONED IN CHAPTER FOUR

Adams, Andy. *The Log of a Cowboy: A Narrative of the Old Trail Days.* 1903.

Allee, Marjorie Hill. *The Great Tradition.* 1937.

———. *Jane's Island.* 1931.

———. *Little American Girl.* 1938.

Allen, James Lane. *The Kentucky Cardinal.* 1894.

Altsheler, Joseph. *The Horsemen of the Plains.* 1910.

———. *The Last of the Chiefs.* 1909.

———. *The Young Trailers.* 1907.

Appleton, Victor (Stratemeyer Syndicate pseudonym). Tom Swift series.

Barbour, Ralph Henry. *The Half-Back.* 1899.

———. *The Spirit of the School.* 1907.

Barclay, Florence. *The Rosary.* 1910.

Buchan, John. *The Thirty-Nine Steps.* 1915.

Burroughs, Edgar Rice. *Tarzan of the Apes.* 1914.

Burton, Charles Pierce. Boys of Bob's Hill series.

Camp, Walter. *Danny Fists.* 1913.

Chadwick, Lester (Stratemeyer Syndicate pseudonym). Baseball Joe series.

Churchill, Winston. *Richard Carvel.* 1899.

Deland, Margaret. *The Awakening of Helena Richie.* 1906.

———. *John Ward, Preacher.* 1888.

Dixon, Franklin W. (Stratemeyer Syndicate pseudonym). The Hardy Boys series.

Doyle, Arthur Conan. *The Adventures of Sherlock Holmes.* 1891.

———. *The Hound of the Baskervilles.* 1902.

Du Maurier, Daphne. *Rebecca.* 1938.

Durant, Will. *The Story of Philosophy.* 1926.

Eastman, Charles A. *Indian Boyhood.* 1902.

Emerson, Alice B. (Stratemeyer Syndicate pseudonym). *Ruth Fielding and Her Double.* Cupples & Leon, 1932.

———. *Ruth Fielding and Her Greatest Triumph, Or, Saving Her Company from Disaster.* Cupples & Leon, 1933.

———. *Ruth Fielding at the Red Mill.* Cupples & Leon, 1913.

Farnol, Jeffrey. *The Broad Highway.* 1910.

Farquharson, Martha (real name: Martha Finley). Elsie Dinsmore series.

Fitzhugh, Percy Kees. Roy Blakely series.

Fox, John. *The Calling of Dan Matthews.* 1909.

———. *The Little Shepherd of Kingdom Come.* 1903.

———. *The Trail of the Lonesome Pine.* 1908.

Frey, Hildegarde G. Campfire Girl series.

Galsworthy, John. *Justice.* 1910.

Glynn, Elinor. *Three Weeks.* 1907.

Gollomb, Joseph. *That Year at Lincoln High.* 1918.

———. *Tiger at City High.* 1946.

———. *Up at City High.* 1945.

———. *Working Through at Lincoln High.* 1923.

Grey, Zane. *Riders of the Purple Sage.* 1912.

———. *The Spirit of the Border.* 1906.

———. *The Wanderer of the Wasteland.* 1923.

Grinnell, George Bird. *By Cheyenne Campfires.* 1926.

———. *Pawnee Hero Stories and Folk Tales.* 1889.

Heyliger, William. *Bartley: Freshman Pitcher.* 1911.

———. *Dan's Tomorrow.* 1922.

———. Fairview High series.

———. *High Benton.* 1919.

———. *High Benton, Worker.* 1921.

———. Lansing series.

———. St. Mary's series.

———. *Steve Merrill, Engineer.* 1935.

———. *Top Lineman.* 1943.

———. *You're on the Air.* 1941.

Heyward, Du Bose. *Mamba's Daughters.* 1929.

———. *Porgy.* 1925.

Hill, Grace Livingston. *Exit Betty.* 1920.

———. *The Girl from Montana.* 1907.

———. *Rainbow Cottage.* 1934.

Hope, Anthony (real name: Anthony Hope Hawkins). *The Prisoner of Zenda.* 1894.

Hull, Edith Maude. *The Sheik.* 1921.

Jackson, Helen Hunt. *Ramona.* 1884.

Johnson, Owen. *Stover at Yale.* 1911.

———. *The Tennessee Shad.* 1911.

———. *The Varmint.* 1910.

Johnston, Mary. *To Have and To Hold.* 1900.

Keene, Carolyn (Stratemeyer Syndicate pseudonym). Dana Girls series.

———. Nancy Drew series.

Kipling, Rudyard. *Captains Courageous.* 1897.

———. *The Light That Failed.* 1890.

Lane, Rose Wilder. *Let the Hurricane Roar.* Longmans, Green, 1933.

———. *The Young Pioneers* (reissue of *Let the Hurricane Roar*). McGraw-Hill, 1976.

Lewis, Elizabeth Forman. *Fu of the Upper Yangtze.* 1932.

———. *Ho-Ming, A Girl of New China.* 1934.

———. *To Beat a Tiger.* 1956.

Lewis, Sinclair. *Babbitt.* 1922.

———. *Elmer Gantry.* 1927.

———. *Main Street.* 1921.

London, Jack. *Martin Eden.* 1909.

McCutcheon, George. *Graustark: The Story of a Love Behind a Throne.* 1901.

Montgomery, Lucy Maud. *Anne of Green Gables.* 1908.

Nordhoff, Charles and James Norman Hall. *Men Against the Sea.* 1934.

———. *The Mutiny on the Bounty.* 1932.

————. *Pitcairn's Island.* 1934.

Norris, Frank. *The Pit.* 1903.

Pease, Howard. *The Black Tanker.* 1941.

————. *Heart of Danger.* 1947.

————. *The Ship Without a Crew.* 1934.

————. *The Tattooed Man.* 1926.

Porter, Eleanor. *Pollyanna.* 1913.

Porter, Gene Stratton. *Freckles.* 1904.

————. *A Girl of the Limberlost.* 1909.

————. *Laddie.* 1913.

————. *Michael O'Halloran.* 1915.

Rice, Alice Hegan. *Mrs. Wiggs of the Cabbage Patch.* 1901.

Richards, Laura Elizabeth. *Peggy.* 1899.

Rinehart, Mary Roberts. *The Circular Staircase.* 1908.

Roberts, Kenneth. *Northwest Passage.* 1937.

Scott, Sir Walter. *The Abbott.* 1820.

————. *Ivanhoe.* 1819.

————. *The Lady of the Lake.* 1810.

————. *The Lay of the Last Minstrel.* 1805.

————. *Marmion.* 1808.

Sheldon, Charles. *In His Steps.* 1896.

Standish, Burt L. (real name: William Gilbert Patten). Frank Merriwell series.

————. *Frank Merriwell at Yale.* 1903.

Steinbeck, John. *In Dubious Battle.* 1936.

————. *The Red Pony.* 1937.

————. *Tortilla Flat.* 1935.

Stevenson, Robert Louis. *Prince Otto.* 1885.

————. *Treasure Island.* 1883.

Stratemeyer, Edward. Bound to Succeed series.

————. Dave Porter series.

————. Lakeport series.

————. Old Glory series.

————. *Richard Dare's Venture, Or, Striking Out for Himself.* 1894.

————. Rover Boys series.

————. Soldiers of Fortune series.

————. *Under Dewey at Manila, Or, The War Fortunes of a Castaway.* 1898.

————. *Victor Horton's Idea.* 1886.

Tarkington, Booth. *Alice Adams.* 1921.

———. *The Magnificent Ambersons*. 1918.

———. *The Midlands*. 1924.

———. *Penrod*. 1914.

———. *Seventeen*. 1902.

———. *The Turmoil*. 1915.

Tunis, John R. *Iron Duke*. 1938.

Twain, Mark (real name: Samuel Clemens). *Tom Sawyer Abroad*. 1894.

Webster, Jean. *Daddy-Long-Legs*. 1912.

Wiggin, Kate Douglas. *Rebecca of Sunnybrook Farm*. 1904.

Wister, Owen. *The Virginian: A Horseman of the Plains*. 1902.

Wright, Harold Bell. *The Re-Creation of Brian Keith*. 1919.

———. *The Shepherd of the Hills*. 1907.

———. *That Printer of Udell's*. 1903.

———. *Their Yesterdays*. 1912.

———. *When a Man's a Man*. 1916.

———. *The Winning of Barbara Worth*. 1911.

SOME SUGGESTED READINGS

General Comments on Literature 1900-1940:

Greene, Suzanne Ellery. *Books for Pleasure: Popular Fiction 1914-1945*. Bowling Green, Ohio: Bowling Green University Popular Press, 1974.

Hackett, Alice Payne and James Henry Burke. *80 Years of Best Sellers, 1895-1975*. New York: R. R. Bowker Co., 1977.

Hart, Irving Harlow. "Best Sellers in Fiction During the First Quarter of the Twentieth Century." *Publishers Weekly*, February 14, 1925, pp. 525-27.

Hart, James D. *The Popular Book: A History of America's Literary Taste*. Berkeley: University of California Press, 1950.

Mott, Frank Luther. *Golden Multitudes: The Story of the Best Sellers in the United States*. New York: Macmillan Publishing Company, Inc., 1950.

Sample, Hazel. *Pitfalls for Readers of Fiction*. Chicago: National Council of Teachers of English, 1940.

Reading Interest Studies:

Anderson, Roxanna E. "A Preliminary Study of the Reading Tastes of High School Pupils." *Pedagogical Seminary* 19 (December 1912): 438-60.

Belsen, Danylu, chairman. "The Reading Interests of Boys." *Elementary English Review* 3 (November 1926): 292-96.

"Books Boys Like Best." *Publishers Weekly,* October 23, 1915, pp. 1315-45.

Brink, William G. "Reading Interests of High School Pupils." *School Review* 47 (October 1939): 613-21.

Charters, W. W. "What's Happened to Boys' Favorites?" *Library Journal,* 74 (October 15, 1949): 1577. An especially intriguing article as it sums up five surveys, all in *Library Journal,* in 1907, 1917, 1927, 1937, and, finally, 1949.

Eaton, H. T. "What High School Students Like to Read." *Education* 43 (December 1922): 204-9.

Jordan, Arthur Melville. *Children's Interests in Reading.* 2d ed. Chapel Hill: University of North Carolina Press, 1926.

Low, Florence B. "The Reading of the Modern Girl." *Nineteenth Century* 59 (February 1906): 278-87.

Popkin, Zelda. "The Finer Things in Life." *Harper's Magazine* 164 (April 1932): 602-11.

Scoggin, Margaret C. "Do Young People Want Books?" *Wilson Bulletin for Librarians* 11 (September 1936): 17.

Smith, Franklin Orin. "Pupils' Voluntary Reading." *Pedagogical Seminary* 14 (June 1907): 209-22.

Terman, Lewis M. and Margaret Lima. *Children's Reading: A Guide for Parents and Teachers.* New York: Appleton, 1927.

Vostrovsky, Clara. "A Study of Children's Reading Tastes." *Pedagogical Seminary* 6 (December 1899): 523-35.

Waples, Douglas and Ralph D. Tyler. *What People Want to Read About: A Study of Group Interests and a Survey of Problems in Adult Reading.* Chicago: American Library Association, 1931.

Washburne, Carleton and Mabel Vogel. *Winnetka Graded Book List.* Chicago: American Library Association, 1926.

Washburne, Carleton and Mabel Vogel. "Supplement to the Winnetka Graded Book List." *Elementary English Review* 4 (February 1927): 47-52; and 4 (March 1927): 66-73.

Young Adult Literature:

Cadogan, Mary and Patricia Craig. *You're a Brick, Angela! A New Look at Girls' Fiction from 1839 to 1975.* London: Gollancz, 1976.

Lerman, Leo. "An Industry within an Industry." *Saturday Review of Literature,* November 8, 1941, pp. 3-7.

Mearns, Hughes. "Bo Peep, Old Woman, and Slow Mandy: Being Three Theories of Reading." *New Republic,* November 10, 1926, pp. 344-46.

Smith, Dora V. "American Youth and English." *English Journal* 26 (February 1937): 99-113.

Smith, Dora V. "Extensive Reading in Junior High School: A Survey of Teacher Preparation." *English Journal* 19 (June 1930): 449-62.

English Teaching:

Cole, William Morse. "The Vital in Teaching Secondary English." *School Review* 14 (September 1906): 469-83.

Hatfield, Wilbur W., ed. *An Experience Curriculum in English.* New York: Appleton, 1935.

Hosic, James Fleming, chairman. *Reorganization of English in Secondary Schools.* Department of the Interior, Bureau of Education, Bulletin 1917, no. 2. Washington: Government Printing Office, 1917.

Smith, Dora V. *Evaluating Instruction in Secondary School English.* Chicago: National Council of Teachers of English, 1941.

Thurber, Samuel. "Report of the English Conference" in *Report of the Committee of Ten on Secondary School Studies.* New York: American, 1894, pp. 86-95.

Thurber, Samuel. "Voluntary Reading in the Classical High School." *School Review* 13 (February 1905): 168-79.

College Entrance Requirements:

Applebee, Arthur N. *Tradition and Reform in the Teaching of English: A History.* Urbana, Illinois: National Council of Teachers of English, 1974.

Crowe, John M.; Mrs. E. K. Broadus; and James Fleming Hosic. "Report of the Conference Committee on High-School English." *School Review* 17 (February 1909): 85-88.

Hosic, James Fleming. "A Brief Chapter of Educational History Together with a Summary of the Facts So Far Obtained by a Committee of the National Education Association and a List of References." *English Journal* 1 (February 1912): 95-121.

Scott, Fred Newton. "College-Entrance Requirements in English." *School Review* 9 (June 1901): 365-78.

Stout, John Elbert. *The Development of High-School Curriculum in the North Central States from 1860 to 1918.* Chicago: University of Chicago Press, 1921.

Thomas, Charles Swain, ed. *Examining the Examination in English: A Report on the College Entrance Requirements.* Harvard Studies in Education, no. 17. Cambridge: Harvard University Press, 1931, pp. 1-15.

Free Reading:

LaBrant, Lou. "The Content of a Free Reading Program." *Educational Research Bulletin* 16 (February 17, 1937): 29-34.

LaBrant, Lou. *An Evaluation of the Free Reading Program in Grades Ten, Eleven, and Twelve for the Class of 1935, the Ohio State University School.* Contributions to Education No. 2. Columbus: Ohio State University Press, 1936.

The Stratemeyer Literary Syndicate:

Abrahamson, Richard F. "They're Reading the Series Books, So Let's Use Them; or Who Is Shaun Cassidy?" *Journal of Reading* 22 (March 1979): 523-30.

Dizer, John T., Jr. "Fortune and the Syndicate." *Boys' Book Collector* 2 (Fall 1970): 146-53; and 2 (Winter 1970): 178-86.

"For It Was Indeed He." *Fortune,* April 1934, p. 86.

Kuskin, Karla. "Nancy Drew and Friends." *The New York Times Book Review,* May 4, 1975, pp. 20-21.

Mason, Bobbie Ann. *The Girl Sleuth: A Feminist Guide.* Old Westbury, New York: Feminist Press, 1975.

McFarlane, Leslie. *Ghost of the Hardy Boys: An Autobiography of Leslie McFarlane.* New York: Two Continents Publishing Group, Inc., 1976.

Prager, Arthur. "Edward Stratemeyer and His Book Machine." *Saturday Review,* July 10, 1971, p. 15.

Prager, Arthur. "The Secret of Nancy Drew—Pushing Forty and Going Strong." *Saturday Review,* January 25, 1969, p. 18.

Zuckerman, Ed. "The Great Hardy Boys' Whodunit." *Rolling Stone,* September 9, 1976, pp. 37-40.

Mathiews and Stratemeyer:

Mathiews, Franklin K. "Blowing Out the Boy's Brains." *Outlook,* November 18, 1914, pp. 652-54.

Mathiews, Franklin K. "The Influence of the Boy Scout Movement in Directing the Reading of Boys." *Bulletin of the American Library Association* 8 (January 1914): 223-28.

Mathiews, Franklin K. "Why Boys Read 'Blood and Thunder' Tales." *Elementary English Review* 2 (October 1925): 280-82.

Melcher, Frederic. "The Story of 'Book Week.' " *Elementary English Review* 7 (October 1930): 191.

Series Books:

Deane, Paul C. "The Persistence of Uncle Tom: An Examination of the Image of the Negro in Children's Fiction Series." *Journal of Negro Education* 37 (Spring 1968): 140-45.

Dizer, John T., Jr. "Boys' Books and the American Dream." *Dime Novel Roundup,* February 15, 1968, pp. 12-17; and March 15, 1968, pp. 29-31.

Garis, Roger. *My Father Was Uncle Wiggily.* New York: McGraw-Hill Book Company, 1966.

Girls' Series Books: A Checklist of Hardback Books Published 1900-1975. Minneapolis: Children's Literature Research Collections, University of Minnesota Library, 1978. A most handy research help.

Hudson, Harry K. *A Bibliography of Hard-Cover Boys' Books.* Rev. ed. Tampa, Florida: Data Print, 1977. The prototype for the *Girls' Series Books* listed above and *the basic book* in studying series books.

Kilgour, Raymond L. *Lee and Shepard: Publishers for the People.* Hamden, Connecticut: The Shoe String Press, Inc., 1965.

MacDonald, J. Frederick. "The 'Foreigner' in Juvenile Series Books, 1900-1945." *Journal of Popular Culture* 8 (Winter 1974): 534-48.

Prager, Arthur. *Rascals at Large, or The Clue in the Old Nostalgia.* New York: Doubleday & Co., Inc., 1971.

Root, Mary E. "Not to Be Circulated." *Wilson Bulletin for Librarians* 3 (January 1929): 446. See the response by Ernest F. Ayres, "Not to Be Circulated?" *Wilson Bulletin for Librarians* 3 (March 1929): 528-29.

Scoggin, Margaret C. "Junior Books for the Stepping-Stone Reader." *Wilson Bulletin for Librarians* 9 (December 1934): 209-11.

Soderbergh, Peter A. "Bibliographical Essay: The Negro in Juvenile Series Books, 1899-1930." *Journal of Negro History* 58 (April 1973): 179-82.

Yost, Edna. "The Fifty-Cent Juveniles." *Publishers Weekly*, June 18, 1932, 2405-8.

Yost, Edna. "Who Wrote the Fifty-Cent Juveniles?" *Publishers Weekly*, May 20, 1933, 1595-98.

Pulps:

Goulart, Ron. *An Informal History of the Pulp Magazine.* New Rochelle, New York: Arlington House, 1972.

Wilkinson, Richard Hill. "Whatever Happened to the Pulps?" *Saturday Review*, February 10, 1962, p. 60.

Comics and Comic Books:

Couperie, Pierre. *A History of the Comic Strip.* New York: Crown Publishers, 1968.

Daniels, Les. *Comix: A History of Comic Books in America.* New York: Outerbridge and Dienstfrey, 1971.

Robinson, Jerry. *The Comics: An Illustrated History of Comic Strip Art.* New York: G. P. Putnam's Sons, 1974.

Wertham, Frederic. *Seduction of the Innocent.* New York: Holt, Rinehart and Winston, Inc., 1954.

Haldeman-Julius and His Little Blue Books:

Herder, Dale M. "Haldeman-Julius, the Little Blue Books, and the Theory of Popular Culture." *Journal of Popular Culture* 4 (Spring 1971): 881-91.

Herder, Dale M. "The Little Blue Books as Popular Culture: E. Haldeman-Julius' Methodology" in Russell B. Nye (ed.), *New Dimensions in Popular Culture.* Bowling Green, Ohio: Bowling Green University Popular Press, 1972, pp. 31-42.

Mordell, Albert. *The World of Haldeman-Julius.* New York: Twayne, 1960.

5

1940-1966

From Certainty to Uncertainty in Life and Literature Courtesy of Future Shock

Nineteen forty began uncertainly as we moved from the Depression into a prewar economy and employment market. Our involvement in World War II began with heavy losses in the Pacific, drafts, and Gold Star mothers, and proceeded to victory at Iwo Jima, North Africa, and Omaha Beach. From a hatred of Communism before 1941 we moved to a temporary brotherhood during World War II. Then came Yalta, the Iron Curtain, blacklisting, and Senator McCarthy. We went from the A-Bomb to the H-Bomb to germ warfare to napalm. First our heroes were John Wayne, Clark Gable, and Loretta Young, then youthful idols such as Marilyn Monroe and James Dean. We became increasingly permissive sexually—or so it seemed to many people. Music went from "Your Hit Parade" to folk music to rock and roll to the Beatles and the Rolling Stones, and Dick Clark beamed on from his "American Bandstand" every year. We entertained ourselves with radio drama, then Milton Berle and "I Love Lucy," and on to "Studio One," "See It Now," and "The Defenders." We went from "Li'l Abner" to "Pogo," and from Bob Hope to Mort Sahl. Among the problems of the time were school integration, racial unrest, the civil rights movement, riots in the streets, and women's rights. We went from violence to more violence, with the assassinations of John Kennedy and Malcom X. The economy swung from inflation to recession and back again. We started with World War II, for which the nation united; then we went to the Korean War, with the nation unsure; and we ended with the Vietnam War, and an increasingly divided nation. The twenty-five years between 1940 and 1965 revealed a country separated by gaps of all kinds: generational, racial, technological, cultural, and economic.

MORE READING INTEREST STUDIES

By 1940, reading interest studies were fixtures in educational journals, and increasingly they did not merely report findings but they interpreted results and questioned the kind of literature used in the schools. In 1946, George W. Norvell briefly reported on his long-range study, "Our data shows clearly that much literary material being used in our schools is too mature, too subtle, too erudite to permit its enjoyment by the majority of secondary-school pupils."[1] In his preliminary work and his book-length report,[2] Norvell arrived at six implications for secondary schools: (1) assigned material should be enjoyable to young adults; (2) "in addition to the study in common, there [should] be much wide reading through which young people may enjoy the materials which appeal to them individually"; (3) teachers should refrain from choosing materials to please themselves and place the students' interests first; (4) three-fourths of the selections currently used should be replaced by more interesting materials; (5) new programs should find materials to interest boys usually bored by the present curricula; and (6) "to increase reading skill, promote the reading habit, and produce a generation of book-lovers, there is no factor so powerful as interest."[3]

Others supported Norvell's contention that young adults' choices of voluntary reading rarely overlapped books widely respected by more traditional English teachers. In 1947 Marie Rankin surveyed eight public libraries in Illinois, Ohio, and New York to discover the most consistently popular books with adolescents. Helen Boylston's *Sue Barton, Senior Nurse* led the list; others from the top ten were probably not known to many English teachers.[4] Twelve years later, Stephen Dunning surveyed fourteen school and public librarians asking them to report on junior novels popular with students. Librarians listed the top ten as Maureen Daly's *Seventeenth Summer*, Henry Gregor Felsen's *Hot Rod*, Betty Cavanna's *Going On Sixteen*, Rosamund Du Jardin's *Double Date*, Walter Farley's *Black Stallion*, Sally Benson's *Junior Miss*, Mary Stolz's *The Sea Gulls Woke Me*, Rosamund Du Jardin's *Wait For Marcy*, James Summers' *Prom Trouble*, and John Tunis' *All-American*.[5]

Fiction consistently ranked high with young adults. An admittedly unscientific sampling of thirteen reading interest surveys—out of innumerable ones made between 1940 and 1966—revealed a wide variety of titles by many authors, but they were almost entirely fiction.[6]

Near the height of the outpouring of published studies, Jacob W. Getzels assessed the value of reading interest surveys and found most of them wanting in "precision of *definition*, rigor of *theory*, and depth of *analysis*."[7] He was, of course, right. Most reports were limited to a small sample from a few schools—often only one school—and little was done except to ask students what they liked to read. From a scientific point of view, most were hopelessly deficient.

But the studies did have some value. They gave librarians and teachers insight into books young adults liked, and, by extrapolation, books they might like. They suggested which tastes were current and which were changing, which books were being read and which were losing popularity. More important yet, they gave insights into young adults and their interests, not just in reading but in other areas as well, and that suggested all sorts of activities in schools and libraries to attract recalcitrant read-ers. They brought hope to librarians and teachers that no matter how reluctant readers were in school, somewhere out there somebody was reading, a hope that—as any librarian or teacher knows on Friday afternoon or the day after Christmas vacation—needs constant rekindling.

These surveys need to be made every year by English teachers and librarians to assess—or reassess—where students are. Few of these surveys will be published, but they will all be helpful.

G. Robert Carlsen summarized the reading interests discovered up to 1954 and argued that books could help to fulfill three broad areas of young adult needs:

> Young people need assurance of the status of human beings. With the end of childhood, children are painfully stirred by a desire to find that they as indi-viduals are important creations of God, capable of infinite development. . . .
>
> A second area of need in the developing adolescent is for assurance of his own normality. . . . Young people need to test their reactions, to experiment with them to find out whether or not they are normal human beings; but they do not want to reveal their own abnormality to others—if abnormality it is—by asking direct questions. . . .
>
> A third need of young people that seems to govern their reading choices, particularly in the later period, is a need for role-playing. With the developing of their personality through adolescence, they come to a semi-integrated picture of themselves as human beings. They want to test this picture of themselves in many kinds of roles that it is possible for a human being to play and through testing to see what roles they may fit into and what roles are uncongenial.[8]

Dwight L. Burton reminded English teachers that their goal was to bring young adults into contact with books—good books and mediocre books and classics, books of all kinds—and that doing that would demand some significant changes in the tradi-tional curriculum:

> If we are to prove that there is always a book for every student, then we must drop our concern with teaching any certain book. We must concern ourselves with any book, however ephemeral, which in any way can rekindle a flagging spirit or provide meaning for a searching mind. We need not worry about whether or not we are teaching "good" literature.[9]

HAVIGHURST'S DEVELOPMENTAL TASKS

The work of Robert J. Havighurst at the University of Chicago was helpful to teachers and librarians in both reading interests and bibliotherapy. Havighurst maintained that at various stages in life (infancy and early childhood, middle childhood, adolescence, adulthood, and old age) certain tasks are imposed by society upon each of us. Havighurst did not argue that the tasks were good or bad, just that they existed, and a person unable or unwilling to perform the tasks at roughly the appropriate time would be rejected or ostracized, or, worse yet, pitied by society.

He first listed five adolescent tasks[10] and later expanded them to ten:

1. Achieving new and more mature relations with agemates of both sexes.
2. Achieving a masculine or feminine social role.
3. Accepting one's physique and using the body effectively.
4. Achieving emotional independence of parents and other adults.
5. Achieving assurance of economic independence.
6. Selecting and preparing for an occupation.
7. Preparing for marriage and family life.
8. Developing intellectual skills and concepts necessary for civic competence.
9. Desiring and achieving socially responsible behavior.
10. Acquiring a set of values and an ethical system as a guide to behavior.[11]

Implications for helping young adults find books illustrating or illuminating the ten developmental tasks were obvious. Some misguided librarians and English teachers tried desperately to fit students into developmental tasks independent of who or what

---

Paperbacks as we know them first entered the mass market in 1938 when Pocket Books issued Pearl Buck's *The Good Earth.*

---

or where they were. But Havighurst could not forestall fools—no one can achieve that most impossible of tasks—and good librarians and teachers found much in Havighurst to help them.[12]

BIBLIOTHERAPY COMES TO THE SCHOOLS

In writing his account of the use of books as part of his treatment for psychiatric patients in 1929, Dr. G. O. Ireland used the term *bibliotherapy,*[13] a new term for librarians and English teachers. The word soon caught on, and by the late 1930s and early 1940s articles dealing with bibliotherapy became almost commonplace. A 1939 author asked, "Can There Be a Science of Bibliotherapy?"[14] and was answered a year later:

The science of bibliotherapy is still in its infancy, yet public libraries are featuring readers' advisory services, and hospital libraries are on the increase. All school librarians who practice individual reading guidance are participating, perhaps unconsciously, in a program of bibliotherapy.[15]

By the 1950s, bibliotherapy was firmly entrenched in the schools. Philosophically, it was related to and justified by Aristotle's *Poetics* and the theory of emotional release through catharsis, a theory with remarkably little support save many unverifiable personal testimonials.

One clear and easy application of bibliotherapy was the free reading program (sometimes too clear and too easy for the inept amateur psychologist/English teacher who, finding a new book in which the protagonist had acne, sought out the acne-ridden kid in class saying, "You must read this—it's about you." Not, incidentally, an apocryphal story). Lou LaBrant, popularizer of free reading, sounded both a recommendation and a warning when she wrote:

> Certainly I can make a much wiser selection of offerings if I understand the potential reader. . . . The first step has been taken when we have some assurance that the book or short selection which we recommend or teach will have a hearing; that it will come within the understanding of the young reader because it deals with problems with which he is conversant and that it will hold some appeal to him because he, like the author of the piece, is concerned with a certain aspect of living.
>
> This does not mean, as some have interpreted, that a young reader will enjoy only literature which answers his questions, tells him what is to be done. It is true, however, that young and old tend to choose literature, whether they seek solutions or escape, which offers characters or situations with which they can find a degree of identification.[16]

With all the problems inherent in some uses of bibliotherapy, few would argue with Frank Ross' appraisal of its contemporary potential and danger:

> This kind of fitting the book to the reader has always been the librarian's creed. . . . The teacher probably can do it better because he knows his students better, better sometimes than the parents do. One caution should be kept in mind. . . . Only after weeks of observing the student in his class performance, in his compositions, and in his conferences should anyone begin bibliotherapy.[17]

THE RISE OF PAPERBACKS

Some young adult readers might assume paperbound books have always been with us. But, despite the success of dime novels and libraries of paperbacks in the late 1800s, paperbacks as we know them first entered the mass market in 1938 when Pocket

Books offered Pearl Buck's *The Good Earth* as a sample volume in mail-order tests.[18] In the spring of 1939, a staff artist created the first sketch of Gertrude the Kangaroo with a book in her paws and another in her pouch. It became Pocket Books' trademark. A few months later, the company issued ten titles in 10,000 copy editions, all remaining best sellers for years: James Hilton's *Lost Horizon*, Dorothea Brande's *Wake Up and Live*, William Shakespeare's *Five Great Tragedies*, Thorne Smith's *Topper*, Agatha Christie's *The Murder of Roger Ackroyd*, Dorothy Parker's *Enough Rope*, Emily Brontë's *Wuthering Heights*, Samuel Butler's *The Way of All Flesh*, Thornton Wilder's *The Bridge of San Luis Rey*, and Felix Salten's *Bambi*. *The Good Earth* became the eleventh title. By the close of 1939, Pocket Books had published twenty-four other titles that sold more than one and a half million copies. In 1940, the company published fifty-three more titles selling more than four and a half million copies. Success for paperbacks was assured.

Avon began publishing in 1941, Penguin (in the United States) entered in 1942, and Bantam, New American Library, Ballantine, Dell, and Popular Library began publishing in 1943. By 1951, sales had reached 230 million paperbacks annually.

Phenomenal as the growth was, paperbacks were slow to appear in schools although a look at an early edition of Bowker's *Paperbound Books in Print* reveals an incredible number of titles available in areas from philosophy to adolescent books. That did not prevent some librarians from complaining that paperbacks did not belong in libraries because they were difficult to catalogue and attractive to steal. It did not prevent some teachers and principals from maintaining that paperback covers were lurid and contents little more than pornography. They sometimes took them from libraries or students and tore the paperbacks apart enthusiastically. In 1969 (and later in some schools) paperbacks were as serious a disciplinary matter as pornography:

> "I'd rather be caught with Lady Chatterley in hardcover than *Hot Rod* in paperback," a precocious high school junior in New York City told me earlier this year. "Hard covers get you one detention, but paperbacks get you two or three," he explained.
>
> Curriculum change is painfully slow in inner city schools where change is most needed. But even in the ghetto, changing perceptions of paperback books are making this high school junior's report a rare phenomenon. It seems that paperbacks are beginning to make the education scene. Having served its fifty years in educational purgatory, the paperback is becoming an acceptable "innovation" which, I suppose, means that it is no longer a true innovation.[19]

The innovation was overdue. Students had long before discovered the value of paperbacks. Paperbacks were ubiquitous, comfortably sized, and inexpensive, and students bought their own libraries while some teachers and librarians wondered where all their customers had gone. Part of the early enthusiasm for paperbacks and acceptance in the schools came from the creation of the Scholastic Book Clubs[20] and the many editions of the Readers' Choice Catalogues. As Grosset and Dunlap, Tempo Books, Pyramid Publications, and Archway Books competed with Scholastic, schools opened paperback book stores for sales to excited secondary students. Later Dell's Yearling and Mayflower books would become the major suppliers of books written specifically for young adults, but by 1966 paperbacks were very much a part of young adults' lives, a point amply demonstrated by Daniel Fader's brilliant *Hooked on Books.*[21]

There is no apparent end for paperback possibilities in the young adult market. Enthusiastically assessing the growth by 1977, Ray Walters noted that reader enjoyment and literacy itself depends upon the success of the paperback industry:

> The mass-market houses aren't alone in hoping that their crusade will succeed. After all, if Americans don't learn to read and enjoy books when they're young, what future is there for writers, publishers, booksellers, librarians—and book review editors?[22]

CHANGES AND GROWTH IN YOUNG ADULT LITERATURE

In 1941, Leo Lerman surveyed the growth of juvenile literature, defined as "books upon every conceivable subject for boys and girls ranging in age from six months to eighteen years," from 1920 to 1940. Noting that during that twenty year span, 14,536 juvenile books had been printed, Lerman concluded, "Children's books have become big business—an industry within an industry."[23] Lerman might have been surprised by the growth of young adult literature in the years that followed, particularly with the development of paperback books.

More important than mere quantity, the quality of young adult literature rose steadily, if at times hesitatingly and uncertainly, from 1941 to 1965. Series books, so popular from 1900 to 1940, died out—except for the Stratemeyer Syndicate stalwarts Nancy Drew, the Hardy Boys, and one new series, Tom Swift, Jr.—killed by increasing reader sophistication and the wartime scarcity of paper. Their replacements were not always great advances, but young adult books did improve steadily.

Much young adult literature of the 1940s and 1950s celebrated those wonderful high school years. Books seemed at times to concentrate exclusively on concerns with dating, parties, class rings, working on the school newspaper, preparing for the school prom, senior year, the popular crowd (or learning to avoid it), and teen romance devoid of realities like sex. That accounted for titles such as *Boy Trouble, Girl Trouble, Prom Trouble, Teacher Trouble, Practically Fifteen, Going on Sixteen, Almost Seventeen, A Girl for Michael, A Boy for Debbie, A Touchdown for Harold, A Horse for Sheila.* Books often sounded alike, looked alike, and read alike, but they were unquestionably popular.

Plots were usually simple, simplistic, and too-often simpleminded. One or two characters might be slightly developed, but other characters were merely sketched or tossed in as stock figures or stereotypes. Major characters faced a dilemma (joining a school sorority, playing football unfairly, joining the popular crowd, going to an all-night dance), adult figures stood by hoping the protagonists would come through morally unscathed, and after a bit of hesitation or uncertainty, the morals of the community and the goodness of young adults were reaffirmed. Books dealt almost exclusively with white, middle-class values and morality. Endings were almost uniformly happy and bright, and readers could be certain that neither their morality nor their intelligence would be challenged.

Taboos may never have been written down, but they were clear to readers and writers. Certain things were not to be mentioned—obscenity, profanity, suicide, sexuality, sensuality, homosexuality, protests against anything significant, social or racial injustice, or the ambivalent feelings of cruelty and compassion inherent in young adults and all real people. Some things could be mentioned, but rarely and then introduced by implication rather than direct statement and only then as bad examples for thoughtful, decent young adults: pregnancy, early marriage, drugs, smoking, alcohol, school dropouts, divorce, alienation of young adults. Consequently, the books were generally innocuous and pervaded by a saccharine didacticism. They taught good, adult-determined attitudes: life is rewarding for the diligent worker and difficult for the slacker; a virtuous life is not merely its own reward but leads to a richer life here on earth; serious dilemmas deserve serious attention by adults who then tell young adults how to handle the problems but not to think for themselves till later; fast driving kills, fast marriages do not last, fast money is evil money, fast actions will surely be regretted, and fast dates are dangerous. Good boys and girls must accept adult and societal rules as good and just without question; young people would survive all those funny preoccupations and worries of adolescence and emerge as thoughtful, serious adults.

Despite all those unwritten rules and qualifications, some writers transcended the taboos and qualifications even in the 1940s and 1950s. Truth did reign in a number of books by writers Florence Crannell Means, John Tunis, Maureen Daly, Esther Forbes, Henry Gregor Felsen, Paul Annixter, and Mary Stolz.

Reviewing young adult literature in 1960, Stanley B. Kegler and Stephen Dunning could write: "Books written for adolescents are improving in quality. Books of acceptable quality have largely replaced poorly written and mediocre books."[24] Three years later, they queried editors of young adult books and found taboos still operating if lessening: "There are few house rules regarding taboos—other than those dictated by 'good taste and common sense.' "[25] One editor responded:

I see very little change in taboos in the past ten years. There are franker discussions of the problems of sex in nonfiction.

Another wrote:

I think the number of narrow-minded taboos—smoking, drinking, swearing, etc.—have diminished. A creative author works best in "responsible" freedom. If an author is serious and responsible, and if we are, and if we together work within the areas of honest good taste, it is difficult to see how we can offend.

By the middle of the 1960s many, though hardly all, taboos had disappeared as unwritten restrictions.[26] Most authors had learned that in young adult literature, as in all literature, good books do not set out deliberately to break taboos although some bad books seem to try to do so. Good books take up life and real problems and follow characters and emotions as they wend their way through reality, touching on taboos where necessary. A few authors seemed deliberately to court taboo subjects, notably

Jeanette Eyerly with *Drop-Out* (1963), her dropout and early marriage novel; *A Girl Like Me* (1966), her pregnancy novel; *Radigan Cares* (1970), her political novel; and *Bonnie Jo, Go Home* (1972), her abortion novel. Indeed that led to legitimate criticism of some writers for writing a "drug" novel or a "suicide" novel or a "pregnancy" novel. Some adolescent novels have been so thoroughly tied to one social or emotional ill that they are not novels about people but about things. That may increase their sales, but it diminishes their chances of survival. Good books focus on people with problems. Bad books focus on problems that seem incidentally to involve people.

As young adult literature moved into the middle and late 1960s, novels presented more complex plots with better developed human beings enmeshed in real problems with no easy ways out. More use of sophisticated literary techniques, particularly in point of view, led to more honest and realistic literature. Happy endings were not precluded, but they were not required. More humor was apparent, not mere sophomoric silliness. Fewer taboos intruded, but good books remained very much on the side of the angels, their didacticism more subtle and sometimes entirely missed by unsophisticated readers. Themes were more mature and complex as almost every subject area opened up for inquiry: alienation, death, loneliness, society's values, mental health, and illness, both physical and social. Novels reflected the increasing sophistication of readers and the complexity of the time. Most important, reality entered the world of books, just as it had always been a part of young adults' lives.

NINE OUTSTANDING WRITERS FOR YOUNG ADULTS

Of authors popular with young adults, nine stand out for their psychological perception and exceptional writing talent.

Florence Crannell Means

Means was popular in the 1930s, and her popularity held up well into the 1940s and later. *A Candle in the Mist* (1931), about a young orphan boy who traveled with a family to Minnesota in 1871, mixed history with suspense and revealed a talented writer, but later books revealed even more talent. *Tangled Waters* (1936), the story of a fifteen-year-old Navajo girl on her Arizona reservation, was her first successful effort at characterizing a minority. Her first black adolescent appears in *Shuttered Windows* (1938). Sixteen-year-old Harriet Freeman grows up in Minneapolis and then chooses to live for a year with her great-grandmother on an island off the South Carolina coast. Formulaic as the plot is and paternalistic as the tone was by today's standards, the book conveyed a sense of worth and dignity about black people rare in young adult or adult literature for that time. *The Moved Outers* (1945), a story of Japanese-Americans forced into relocation camps during World War II, may appear dated and mild by today's standards, but it still has power. Means was unable to avoid drawing the too-obvious moral about the danger of an increasingly totalitarian America, but her heart was in the right place. Her message was more powerful at the time than we now can realize, given the rabid anti-Japanese climate persisting even after World War II.

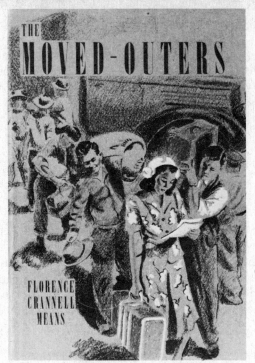

Florence Crannell Means. *The Moved-Outers*, 1945.

Later books, *Tolliver* (1963), *It Takes All Kinds* (1964), and *Our Cup Is Broken* (1969) are worth reading and establish Means as an important writer, one worth reading and even studying for the mirror she holds up to prejudice.

John Tunis

Newspaperman Tunis published his first young adult novel, *Iron Duke*, in 1938. After four years of athletics at a small high school, Jim Wellington (the Iron Duke) wants desperately to enter the athletic big time at Harvard. His efforts are, at first, realistically unsuccessful, but the book is really a character study involving athletics, not just another sports story. What his first book promises, *All-American* (1942) delivers. The novel is dated by the changes that have taken place in football and in society, but it is a remarkable work for its time. Ronald Perry plays football for the Academy team and is partially responsible for injuring a local high school opponent in a crucial game. His Academy friends don't worry about the incident, but Perry cannot live with his guilt at the Academy. He leaves to go where he finds that he is even less wanted, the local high school. There he learns some important lessons about racism and reality. The football team slowly accepts him, but, after a successful season, an invitation to a postseason game in the South requires that a black athlete stay home. Perry leads a

John Tunis. *All-American,* 1942.

quiet and tentative revolt, joined by a few of his teammates. To his surprise, he finds that things do happen and may even change when people care. *All-American* seems somewhat paternalistic now, but for the time and the society then, it was a remarkable, even radical novel for young adults.

Yea! Wildcats (1964) mixes basketball with incipient totalitarianism in a small town. *A City for Lincoln* (1945) is also nominally a basketball story, but Tunis' liberal inclinations and didacticism produced a study of American politics, one of his least successful novels for young adults and one of his most intriguing for adults. A more successful account of basketball mania, *Go, Team, Go!* (1954), is perhaps the best novel ever written about public pressure on a coach who cares about more than merely winning. *Silence Over Dunkerque* (1963) contains nothing remotely athletic, but it is a good straightforward picture of the horrors and cruelty of war. Possibly his most successful book appeared in 1967. *His Enemy, His Friend* is a brilliant fusion of war and its aftermath and sports. A German soldier during World War II is forced to order the execution of some townspeople. Years later, the son of one of those executed opposes the soldier's team in a soccer match.

Tunis occasionally let his moral outrage and sensitivity carry him away, but at his best he wrote the finest sports stories since Ralph Henry Barbour. Tunis knew the power of athletic glory for good and for evil, and he knew what locker rooms smell like. His vision of the physical and moral aspects of athletics is impressive and endures with readers even after plots can no longer be remembered.

Maureen Daly

Daly published only one novel for young adults, but unlike almost all other young adult novels of its time, it endures. *Seventeenth Summer* (1942) is about shy, unnoticed Angie Morrow and her love for Jack Duluth in the summer before she is to set off for college. Very little happens in the novel, but very little happens during any one summer in most of our lives. Angie falls in love, she dates, and her relationship with Jack leads to misunderstandings and frustrations, mostly sexual. And at the close of the book, she and Jack part, sadly, as most first lovers do.

But it is not the plot so much as certain aspects of the story that make *Seventeenth Summer* different. In addition to portraying a young boy and girl sensitively and honestly, Daly shows a society in which drinking beer and even smoking will not inevitably lead to damnation, not even for young adults. At one point, Jack takes Angie to a roadhouse where they see a male pianist with painted fingernails. Angie innocently asks Jack to explain, and Jack stutters, looks embarrassed, and offers no satisfactory answer, but the adult reader recognizes what Angie does not.

Some critics, librarians, and English teachers are deeply and even personally offended by Angie's innocence. They maintain that she could never have been *that* innocent, or that naive, gullible, and unsuspecting. Innocence and sophistication are difficult to define at best. Some sophisticated young adults even today, more than thirty years after Angie, wear a veneer of worldliness that, if penetrated even the tiniest bit, reveals a frightened innocent.

Possibly, say the accusers, but even so, Angie certainly wasn't typical of her time, not even of that 1942 world where good was good and bad was bad and never the twain could meet. Other girls of the time, so the reasoning goes, weren't all that innocent. They would have been aware of the physical implications (and consequences) of love, even first love.

But Daly never claimed Angie was typical—only the critics claim that. Angie was an individual, not a representative of seventeen-year-old girls in 1942. Writers, at least serious writers, create individuals out of the masses, not to represent the masses. And Angie is an individual.

Esther Forbes

Primarily a historian, in fact a winner of the Pulitzer Prize for history in 1942 for *Paul Revere and the World He Lived In*, Forbes wrote one still-popular novel for young adults. *Johnny Tremain* (1943) sets fourteen-year-old Johnny in pre-Revolutionary War times. A cocky apprentice to a silversmith and clearly a young genius in the making, Johnny cripples his hand. Partly because of that and partly because of the fervor of the time, he becomes involved with patriots Sam Adams, John Hancock, and Paul Revere.

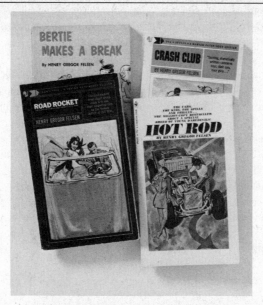

A selection of titles by Henry Gregor Felsen.

The spirit of the time is well captured by historian Forbes, but readers who care little about history can still find an engrossing and exciting tale about Johnny, his injury, his friends, and war.

Forbes did not write again for young adults, but the number of readers who continue to enjoy *Johnny Tremain* is wide indeed.

Henry Gregor Felsen

Felsen began writing for young adults with several World War II books, *Navy Diver* (1942), *Submarine Sailor* (1943), *He's in the Coast Guard Now* (1943), and *Pilots All* (1944). His first three major books concern short, fat Bertie in *Bertie Comes Through* (1947), *Bertie Takes Care* (1948), and *Bertie Makes a Break* (1949). Probably read by young adults because Bertie's troubles have hilarious results, the books are still a fascinating study of adolescent failure.

After a singularly dull stab at a vocational novel, *Davey Logan, Intern* (1950), Felsen wrote *Two and the Town* (1952) about a young couple forced to marry because the girl is pregnant. Old-hat today and twenty years ahead of its time then, the book could safely have been placed in the hands of any young adult by any parent as a sure warning of the consequences of "doing it," for Felsen preached endlessly and was morally merciless to the boy and girl. With all that, *Two and the Town* broke ground in young adult literature by treating pregnancy honestly and seriously. What the reactions of young adults or parents might have been is largely conjectural, for many librarians skirted the issue of censorship by not buying the book. Contemporary reviewers recognized that the book might cause trouble. One began:

> Many libraries will not buy this, and others will treat it with kid gloves, but we need it. Factual pamphlets and books treating sex miss the emotions of error and repair that this book, written for and about youth, presents.[27]

Felsen's fame began with publication of *Hot Rod* (1950), and two other similar books, *Street Rod* (1953) and *Crash Club* (1958). *Hot Rod* is still in print and still widely read, though its didacticism is strong, particularly in the scene near the end in which accident victims are buried. Despite this, the story of Bud Crayne, his fondness for speeding, and his comeuppance and eventual salvation at the hands of Patrolman Ted O'Day had and has wide appeal. Few writers so intently didactic have been so widely read. Presumably, young adults learned long ago how to endure the moral lessons of their elders and still survive.

Paul Annixter

Under the Annixter pen name, Howard A. Sturtzel wrote many novels, often with his wife Jane Sturtzel, but his most exceptional book is *Swiftwater* (1950), a remarkable tale of excitement, symbolism, and ecology mixed with, alas, some stereotyped characters. Cam Calloway feels a kinship with the wild geese near his Maine farm, and his feelings and his love are emulated by his son Bucky. Something of a footloose wanderer, Cam dreams more than he acts. Bucky is both dreamer and actor, and his drive to find roots for himself and his mother and to establish a wild game preserve for his beloved geese becomes the heart of the novel. Much has been made of the early scenes between Bucky and the wolverine, with the animal symbolizing evil, perhaps too much so. However, individual chapters of the novel are excellent short stories in their own right, and the whole novel is a most convincing, honest, and well-written novel for young adults. Its wide readership is deserved whether it is enjoyed as an adventure story, an initiation story, or as an early ecological manifesto.

Jack Bennett

South African journalist Bennett wrote three novels for young adults, two of them among the best of the time. In *Jamie* (1963), set on a large South African farm, Jamie wants to be like his father. The opportunity to become a man comes early when Jamie's father is killed by a maddened water buffalo. Jamie vows to kill the animal, and that vow becomes almost a mania.

Mister Fisherman (1965) may remind readers of Theodore Taylor's *The Cay*, but Bennett's story of a young white boy helped by an old black fisherman to survive at sea is a better book.

Bennett's third novel, *The Hawk Alone* (1965), is an excellent study of white hunter Gord Vance. Vance had done everything and had shot everything. When he discovers he has outlived his time, that he is no longer a man, only a myth and a legend, Vance realizes that his hunting days are over. He knows he serves no valuable function, not even for himself, and he decides that suicide is the answer. Realistic, insightful, and extraordinarily well written, *The Hawk Alone* deserves far more readers than it has ever received.

James Summers

Popular as Summers' books were at the time they were written and productive as he continues to be, Summers is almost a forgotten writer. Capable of writing charming fluff such as *Girl Trouble* (1953), *Trouble on the Run* (1956), and *Off the Beam* (1956), all eminently forgettable, he could also write most sensitively. *Operation ABC* (1955) is almost a case study of a football hero, apparently successful in everything, who literally cannot read and fears college because he would be unmasked as a fraud. *The Wonderful Time* (1957) shows a nineteen-year-old returning to high school after a stretch in the

Jack Bennett. *Jamie*, 1963.

Mary Stolz. *A Love, or a Season,* 1954.

Army and trying desperately to fit into a world that is no longer his. *The Shelter Trap* (1962) is about some gifted students who decide to live for a short time in a fallout shelter. *The Iron Doors Between* (1968) features Vic Shan recently released from a California State Reformatory with a future as uncertain as his past. *You Can't Make It by Bus* (1969) is about an intelligent Chicano high-school student in an American society that will not accept him as a first-class citizen.

Summers has a wonderful ability to capture American youth, but his chief asset as a writer is also his major liability: his incredible ear for young adult jargon. Unhappily, by the time any of his books is published, the jargon is not merely dated, but dead.

His two best books are *Ring Around Her Finger* (1957), a study of a young marriage from the point of view of the boy, and *The Limit of Love* (1959), a remarkably effective delineation of a sexual love affair. Ronnie Jordan knows she has missed two periods, and boyfriend Lee Hansen worries and blames Ronnie for ruining his life. In the weeks that follow, the mess leaves them emotionally bankrupt and no longer in love, but Lee emerges as a boy and Ronnie as a real woman ready to face problems and her own responsibilities. *The Limit of Love* is now dated, but it was a book far ahead of its time. Many schools would not purchase it because of its picture of two nice kids sexually involved by an author who does not place blame on either.

Mary Stolz

Stolz is, simply put, our most consistently artistic writer for young adults. Richard S. Alm spoke for teachers and librarians when he wrote that Stolz is "versatile and most skilled . . . (and) writes not for the masses who worship Sue Barton but for the rarer adolescent."[28] She joined the literary scene with her first novel, *To Tell Your Love* (1950), an introspective and moving portrait of a young girl waiting vainly all summer for a phone call from the boy she loves.

Later books fulfill the promise of her first novel. *The Sea Gulls Woke Me* (1951) deals with a protected girl and a domineering mother; *In a Mirror* (1953) concerns an overweight girl seeking to face her problem; *Ready or Not* (1953), and its sequel *The Day and the Way We Met* (1956), tells of girls in a lower-middle class environment; and *Rosemary* (1955) is about a college town and a local girl who cannot go to college.

Her two finest works are *Pray Love, Remember* (1954), a remarkable story of popular, lovely, and cold Dody Jenks who does not like her family or herself, and *A Love, or a Season* (1964) in which love between Harry and Nan threatens to get out of hand and become too passionate before they can handle it or themselves. Readers today may find *A Love, or a Season* a bit naive, but some girls presumably still have serious doubts about capriciously hopping into bed, no matter how intense the love may seem.

BOOKS POPULAR WITH YOUNG ADULTS

Reading of young adults fell loosely into six areas, some containing many popular titles, some only a few.

Career Books March On

Fiction allowing, even encouraging, young adults to examine careers was hardly new in the 1940s. Francis Rolt-Wheeler wrote twenty volumes of career fiction beginning with *The Boy with the U.S. Survey* in 1909 and ending with *The Boy with the U.S. Aviators* in 1929.

But the deluge of vocational books sugar-coated with fiction began in the 1930s and carried on until the 1950s. Almost every job was covered. Journalism by Emma Bugbee's *Peggy Covers the News* (1936) and William Heyliger's *Ritchie of the News* (1933), librarianship by Lucile Fargo's *Marian—Martha* (1936) and Mary Provines' *Bright Heritage* (1939), fashion designing by Adele de Leeuw's *Gay Design* (1942) and Christie Harris' *You Have to Draw the Line Somewhere* (1964), secretarial work by Blanche Gibbs and Georgiana Adams' *Shirley Clayton, Secretary* (1941) and Harriet Carr's *Confidential Secretary* (1958), television work by Dorothy McFadden's *Lynn Decker: TV Apprentice* (1953) and Ruth Milne's *TV Girl Friday* (1957), and on and on. Hardly an occupation escaped the eagle eyes of publishers and writers eager to insure that every young adult, of whatever vocational persuasion, should have at least one novel about his or her field. Presumably no author penned any book-length fiction about garbage collectors or hangmen, but had any youngster expressed an interest in those fields, some author prompted by a publisher would have churned out *Robert Gimstock: Sanitation Expert* or *Hanging Them High with Harold*.

Without question, books about nursing led popularity polls with girls, and Helen Dore Boylston was the most popular of the writers. Her Sue Barton series ran to seven volumes from *Sue Barton, Student Nurse* (1936) to *Sue Barton, Staff Nurse* (1952) and is still readable, albeit dated. Curiously, Sue Barton seems more popular today in Great Britain. Boylston's chief rival, in a field where authors' names generally meant little and changed as publishers sought another vocational interest, was Helen Wells, whose Cherry Ames nursing series ran to twenty volumes and whose Vicki Barr flight stewardess series ran to thirteen books.

Lucille G. Rosenheim's *Kathie, The New Teacher* (1949) reveals both the strengths and weaknesses of vocational novels. Kathie Kerber, new seventh-grade teacher at Hillcrest, meets in one year all the problems and prejudices that a teacher with bad luck would perhaps meet in the first ten years of teaching. She encounters romance, intolerant students, a sneak thief, the town skinflint, sentimental parents, and much more. Everything comes too fast and too easily, and impossible problems are rapidly disposed of because Kathie cares and has a good heart. With all that, the book may have given some readers an idea of what teaching is all about, although a bit melodramatically.

Whatever freshness the vocational novel may once have had, by the 1940s it was a formula and little more. Four or five characters were certain to appear: a decent and attractive, if sometimes shy, hero/heroine just graduating from high school or college and needing a job desperately; one or two friends of different temperaments—two men if the book was directed at girls since romance was doomed to raise its head; a villain or at the very least a crotchety older person who puts temporary obstacles in the professional path of the protagonist; and an older and wiser person who helps the protagonist to advance. Early in the book the insecure hero/heroine suffers a mixture of major and minor setbacks, but, undaunted, the protagonist wins the final battle and a place in her or his profession. The novel almost certainly passes rapidly and lightly over the job's daily grind, focusing instead on the high points, the excitement and events that make any job potentially, if rarely, dramatic. Many vocational books were widely read for that drama, although it certainly distorted the accuracy of information provided.

Adventure and Suspense

There was no diminution of interest in adventure or suspense though the interest was largely fulfilled by various kinds of war books until at least the later 1940s.

Young adult war literature at first tended to be nonfiction such as Carl Mann's *He's in the Signal Corps Now* (1943) or Betty Peckham's *Women in Aviation* (1945), or it consisted of military-vocational novels such as Martha Johnson's *Ann Bartlett, Navy Nurse* (1941) or Elizabeth Lansing's *Nancy Naylor, Flight Nurse* (1944).

True stories about battles and survivors were ultimately more popular. Richard Tregaskis was widely popular for the blood, death, and heroism of *Guadalcanal Diary* (1943), but by far the most respected and beloved of war reporters was Ernie Pyle whose *Here Is Your War* (1943), *Brave Men* (1944), and the posthumous *Last Chapter* (1946) won admirers for his journalistic skills and personal courage. Two accounts of heroism are still read today, not as museum pieces, but as exciting and effectively told accounts of men caught in war who find depths of courage and personal values within themselves that they might not otherwise have believed. They are Robert Trumbull's *The Raft* (1942), about three Navy fliers forced down in the Pacific, and Quentin Reynolds' *70,000 to One* (1946), about an American airman on a small Pacific island with 70,000 Japanese troops.

Of the many novels published about World War II, something more than mere bravado and jingoism could be found in John Hersey's *A Bell for Adano* (1944), John Horne Burns' sadly neglected but masterful *The Gallery* (1947), Norman Mailer's *Naked and the Dead* (1948), and James Jones' *From Here to Eternity* (1951), though his *The Pistol* (1959) and *The Thin Red Line* (1962) are better novels. Herman Wouk's *The Caine Mutiny* (1951) proved more popular even though (or perhaps because) it was little more than a proestablishment paean to blind conformity.

Of the many books about the war, the most quietly appealing and subtly horrifying were those about innocent people caught up in the holocaust. Christine Arnothy's experiences as a young Hungarian girl during the horrors of Russian and German invasions were captured in *I Am Fifteen and I Do Not Want to Die* (1956). Anne Frank's *The Diary of a Young Girl* (1952) deserved to be the best seller that it is. By 1975 her book had sold more than five million copies, the majority in paperback. A diary that covers the two years Anne and her family spent secreted in the abandoned half of an old building, Anne Frank's story captures the foreboding and doom of war and concentration camps as no other book does.

Elie Wiesel shows what could be the aftermath of Anne Frank's story, not the waiting for but the reality of concentration camp life in *Night* (1960). In Transylvania, near the end of 1941, Wiesel nears his twelfth birthday and wishes to become a scholar like his father. Soon, police round up all foreign Jews, loading them into cattle cars. All seems temporarily well with native Jews until 1944 when German troops enter Hungary and begin mass Jewish deportation. Wiesel records the journey to Birkenau, then to Buchenwald, and the killing and dying. Despite blood and horror, *Night* is a story of a man struggling to find belief in God as the world goes mad. *Dawn* (1961) continues the life of one eighteen-year-old concentration camp survivor in a Jewish terrorist group dedicated to freeing Israel from English rule. *Dawn*, ironic both in title and situations, portrays a mad world as frightening as the autobiographical *Night*.

Perhaps as a reaction to the realities of war, the most popular series of books for both adults and young adults during the 1950s and 1960s centered about that dreaded and fascinating operative, James Bond, Agent-007. In *From Russia with Love* (1951), *Casino Royale* (1954), *Dr. No* (1959), *Goldfinger* (1959), *Thunderball* (1961), *You Only Live Twice* (1964), and *The Man with the Golden Gun* (1965), Ian Fleming caught the mood of the time, eager for escapist excitement tinged with what appeared to be realities. Cardboard sexist figure or not, Bond captured readers' imaginations and proved even more popular in film form.

Love, Romance, Passion, and Sex

Interest in tender feelings persisted, though the moments grew less tender and more tempestuous early in this period.

Writers for young adults contributed several fine romances. Margaret E. Bell wrote of an earlier, more innocent, time in Alaska in *Love Is Forever* (1954) about a young and often troubled marriage. Vivian Breck, pen name of Vivian Breckenfield, wrote a fine adventure story in *High Trail* (1948) and a superior study of young marriage in *Maggie* (1954). One of the most popular books, and one still read and most readable, is Benedict and Nancy Freedman's *Mrs. Mike* (1947), the story of Mike Flannigan and Kate O'Fallen who marry and move to the dangers of the northern Canadian wilderness.

Perhaps the ideal romance of the time was *Green Dolphin Street* (1944) by Elizabeth Goudge, a writer who had long produced sensitive studies of small-town life in England but nothing approaching a best seller in America. *Green Dolphin Street* had everything working for it—a young and handsome man in love with one of a pair of sisters. He leaves and writes home his wishes, but the wrong sister accepts. The true love, apparently thwarted by his unfaithfulness, becomes a nun. Passion, love, and adventure are all handled well by a first-rate writer.

Kathleen Winsor was also one of a kind, though what one and what kind was widely debated. When her *Forever Amber* (1944) appeared, parents worried, censors paled, and young adults smiled. Winsor's book was hardly the first to be banned in Boston, but her publisher was adept at turning what appeared to be a defeat into a major victory, gloriously announcing in papers far and wide that the contents were indeed too shocking for Bostonians but not too strong for other cities. City fathers in many towns urged that it be banned, but most readers were only curious, not salacious, and *Forever Amber* sold more than a million and a half copies in three years. Generally, young adults ignored the fuss and read the book.

The uproar that greeted Amber and her affairs was much the same as the one that awaited Grace Metalious and *Peyton Place* (1956). Again parents and community leaders did not keep young people from reading the book avidly for all its unraveling of family scandals and multitudinous affairs in a small New England town. Nine million copies sold the first year, and a sequel, *Return to Peyton Place* (1959), a movie, and a television series insured that virtually every young adult in the United States knew the book. A few brave English teachers acknowledged its existence, but many principals feared morality would deteriorate in their schools should even one copy of *Peyton Place* be found. The world survived.

Teachers were less sure morality could survive the onslaught that followed only a few years later in the form of Irving Wallace and books like *The Chapman Report* (1960), which capitalized on the Kinsey report, *The Prize* (1962), and *The Man* (1964). But worse was yet to come, though some young adults would have said better, with the appearance of Harold Robbins, pen name of Harold Rubins, and *The Carpetbaggers* (1961) and *The Adventurers* (1966), two potboilers and sexual thrillers Robbins wrote when his best book, *A Stone for Danny Fisher* (1952), went almost unnoticed.

Society's Problems

Young adults, especially in the last year or two of high school, have often been receptive to books about human dilemmas stemming from the ways society functions or malfunctions. Society changed rapidly and drastically from 1940 through 1966, and malfunctions seemed almost the norm and the human consequences deeply disturbing.

Of increasing concern to many young adults was their growing awareness that the democracy announced in our Constitution was more preached than practiced. As the censorship applied to John Steinbeck's *The Grapes of Wrath* (1939) and *Of Mice and Men* (1937) lessened—though it never entirely disappeared—young readers read of the plight of migrant workers and learned that all was not well with our country.

Many were deeply bothered by Alan Paton's stories of racial struggles in South Africa, *Cry the Beloved Country* (1948) and Paton's most mature study of love in the midst of injustice, *Too Late the Phalarope* (1953). Still more were touched by the sentiment and passion of Harper Lee's *To Kill a Mockingbird* (1960). Viewed as dated and patronizing by some critics today, *Mockingbird* was for many young adults the first book they had read about racial problems in the South, a book that gave them a hero in the gentle but strong Atticus Finch and some understanding of the American dream gone sour. For some, Lee's novel served as a sympathetic introduction to black people.

Literature about blacks was not difficult to find before World War II, but literature by blacks was another matter. After 1945, black literature became easier to find. Perhaps the war itself, which spotlighted Hitler's fervent belief in racism, contributed to the growing awareness of the state of blacks and the rise of black writing. Perhaps the GI Bill of Rights after the war helped as some blacks were allowed education hitherto denied them for economic reasons. Whatever the exact causes, blacks increasingly and rightfully became literary and moral forces to be reckoned with and young adults often took notice.

Richard Wright and his books served as bitter prototypes for much black literature. *Native Son* (1940) shocked some blacks and many whites with the stored-up anger of Bigger Thomas, and *Black Boy* (1945) was both Wright's autobiography and his denouncement of America.

The greatest black novel, and one of the greatest novels of any kind of the last fifty years, is *Invisible Man* (1952) by Ralph Ellison. Existentialist in tone, *Invisible Man* is at different times bawdy (the incest scenes remind readers of Faulkner without being derivative), moving, frightening, but always stunning and breathtaking. Ellison begins by describing the black as the figuratively invisible man:

I am an invisible man. No, I am not a spook like those who haunted Edgar Allan Poe; nor am I one of your Hollywood-movie ectoplasms. I am a man of substance, of flesh and bone, fiber and liquids—and I might even be said to possess a mind. I am invisible, understand, simply because people refuse to see me. Like the bodiless heads you see sometimes in circus sideshows, it is as though I have been surrounded by mirrors of hard, distorting glass. When they approach me they see only my surroundings, themselves, or figments of their imagination—indeed, everything and anything except me.

Invisible Man is Ellison's only novel. His collection of essays, *Shadow and Act* (1964), is significant for any young adults who care about good prose or about understanding Ellison's ideas.

Several white writers were popular with young adults for their statements about racial dilemmas. Lillian Smith was attacked for her novel *Strange Fruit* (1944), the story of a marriage of a black and a white. A court decision banning the book temporarily made a few reactionaries happy, but the book's national reception and sales were good enough to distress racists. John Howard Griffin suffered some censorship for his novel

---

At first, simplistic books portrayed kind whites taking young blacks into tow and getting them started on the right path.

The Devil Rides Outside (1952) though less than he experienced with his popular and sometimes reviled *Black Like Me* (1961), his account of temporarily becoming black and traveling through much of the South suffering indignities common to blacks. Griffin's book may have become dated, though not so much as some think, but the accusations of some blacks that the book was paternalistic seem ill-advised and revisionist. David Westheimer developed a sweet-sour romance between a pregnant white girl and a young black lawyer in trouble with the law in *My Sweet Charlie* (1965).

Three black nonfiction writers remain popular. Claude Brown painted a stark picture of black ghetto life in *Manchild in the Promised Land* (1965), and, despite anguished cries from many parents about the "filth" in the book, Brown's book appears to have a permanent place in the literature of oppression and freedom. Malcolm X and Alex Haley, the latter better known for *Roots,* painted a no more attractive picture in *The Autobiography of Malcolm X* (1965). The most enduring work may prove to be Eldridge Cleaver's *Soul on Ice* (1968), an impassioned plea by a black man in prison, in a prison of concrete and a prison of the mind, who wrote to save himself.

Writings about blacks aimed at young adults were not long in coming. They were, at first, simplistic books either encouraging young blacks to cooperate with whites since whites had the power or portraying kind whites taking young blacks into tow and getting them started on the right path. Typical were novels by Jesse Jackson:

Call Me Charley (1945), *Anchor Man* (1947), *Charley Starts from Scratch* (1958), and *Tessie* (1968). Catherine Marshall's *Julie's Heritage* (1957) differentiated so little between whites and blacks that it was hard for readers to recognize Julie as a black with somewhat special problems.

Lorenz Graham brought realistic black characters to young adult literature. If *South Town* (1958) with its characters seeking a better life in the North seems dated today, *North Town* (1965) is still believable as it moves the Williams family and son David, the major character, into conflict with both whites and blacks. *Whose Town?* (1969) brings David more problems as he sees his best friend shot by a white man. Graham's books probed for answers but did not provide any easy ones.

Nat Hentoff has written good topical books that quickly become dated, for example his story of Vietnam and draft resistance, *I'm Really Dragged But Nothing Gets Me Down* (1968), and his somewhat lesser study of radical teachers and high school revolutions, *In the Country of Ourselves* (1971). His first novel for young adults was a superb story of a white boy trying to break into the black world of jazz, *Jazz Country* (1965). It is an unusual topic, and perhaps neither blacks nor whites are comfortable with the theme or the characters, which is sad because Hentoff is a remarkable, compassionate, and honest writer. *Jazz Country* is a major work.

Of the nonfiction writings for young adults about blacks, Shirley Graham has provided several good biographies: *There Was Once a Slave: The Heroic Story of Frederick Douglass* (1947), probably her best book; *Your Most Humble Servant: The Story of Benjamin Banneker* (1949), her most intriguingly different story; *The Story of Phillis Wheatley: Poetess of the American Revolution* (1949); and *Booker T. Washington: Educator of Hand, Head, and Heart* (1955). Elizabeth Yates won applause for *Amos Fortune, Free Man* (1950) and the Newbery Prize a year later, but her account of a slave who gained freedom in 1801 and fought the rest of his life for freedom for other blacks has been attacked by some black groups as paternalistic, a word much overused by black critics who assume that any white writer is inherently incapable of writing about blacks.

Personal Problem and Initiation Novels

Intrigued and concerned as many young adults were about social issues and dilemmas, something far more immediate constantly pressed in upon them—their own personal need to survive in an often unfriendly world. As one youngster said, "What do they mean, 'What am I going to do when I grow up?' First I have to survive and that's a problem with school and parents and my girl friend."

Survival was hardly the theme of many popular writers for girls. The watchword for Janet Lambert was acceptance. She preached the doctrine of happiness, sentimentalism, and acceptance in *Star Spangled Summer* (1941), in which the lonely daughter of a millionaire spends a summer on an army post finding herself and ennobling those around her, much as Pollyanna did years before.

After Lambert there was a deluge of girls' books detailing their emotional traumas, but almost entirely ignoring their physical concerns. Betty Cavanna wrote many romances of youth engaged in dating and early love, but they contained nothing remotely resembling passion. Her characters were stereotypes and her plots repetitious but *Going on Sixteen* (1946) remained popular for years. *Paintbox Summer* (1949) about an art colony and two loves for one girl was her best book, melodramatic and a bit flossy but still effective at times. Far worse was Rosamund Du Jardin whose books have interchangeable titles, incredibly undramatic or unbelievable plots, and wooden dialogue. Nevertheless, books such as *Practically Seventeen* (1949), *Wait for Marcy* (1950), and *Double Feature* (1953) were avidly read. Typical of Du Jardin's books is *Senior Prom* (1957), which finds Marcy struggling to decide whether to date noble but poor Rick or flashy but rich Bruce for that most important activity, the senior dance. Marcy is also worried about befriending an old man others have warned her against. She proves true to her trust and her essential goodness by deciding to date Rick (Bruce dates another in desperation and has a bad car accident, presumably in retribution) and to befriend the old man (who soon dies, willing her $15,000).

Superior to the earlier authors, Anne Emery certainly preached acceptance of the status quo, especially acceptance of parental rules, but she offered better books that proved popular with young adult women. With an exception here or there, her books eschew real controversy yet they appear to focus on real social concerns: *Going Steady* (1950), *Sorority Girl* (1952), and her best book *Married on Wednesday* (1957).

At the same time conventional girls' books appeared, Mina Lewiton dealt with far more suspect, even controversial, topics. *The Divided Heart* (1947) was an early study of the impact of divorce on a young woman, and *A Cup of Courage* (1948) was an honest and groundbreaking account of alcoholism and its destruction of a family. Later, Zoa Sherburne proved more enduring with her portrait of alcohol's effect in *Jennifer* (1959), though her best and most likely to last book is *Too Bad About the Haines Girl* (1967), a superb novel about pregnancy, honest and straightforward without being unduly preachy.

But something far more significant and enduring appeared during the same years that the personal problem novel seemed supreme. The *Bildungsroman*, a novel about the initiation, maturation, and education of a young adult, began to grow in appeal. The number of such books, most of them originally published for adults but soon read by young adults, appearing from 1940 onward was prodigious.

One of the first, now nearly forgotten, was Dan Wickenden's *Walk Like a Mortal* (1940). Seventeen-year-old Gabe McKenzie learns that he will never achieve his longed-for excellence in athletics, and he accepts his excellence in journalism as a substitute. His neurotic mother and dull father are verging on separation and Gabe must accept the fact of his own conflicting loyalties. Girls found an equally appealing and honest book in Betty Smith's *A Tree Grows in Brooklyn* (1943).

But no book won the young adult favor or the adult opposition that J. D. Salinger's *The Catcher in the Rye* (1951) did. Still the most widely censored book in American schools, and still hated by people who assume that a disliked word (*that* word) corrupts an entire book, *Catcher* has been avidly read ever since it became a selection of the Book-of-the-Month Club. Holden Caulfield may indeed be what so many have accused him of being, vulgar and cynical and capable of seeing only the phonies around him, but he is also loyal and loving to those he sees as good or innocent. His struggle to preserve innocence leads him to the brink and a mental breakdown. *Catcher* is many things, literary, profane, sensitive, cynical. For many young adults it is the most honest and human story they know about someone they recognize—even in themselves—a young man caught between childhood and maturity and unsure which way to go. Whether *Catcher* is a masterpiece like James Joyce's *Portrait of an Artist as a Young Man* depends on subjective judgment, but there is no question that Salinger's book captured—and continues to capture—the hearts and minds of countless young adults as no other book has.

Most teachers and librarians would have predicted just as long a life for John Knowles' *A Separate Peace* (1961) and William Golding's *Lord of the Flies* (1955), but fame and longevity are sometime things, and despite many articles in the *English Journal* about the literary and pedagogical worth of both books, they seem to be in a state of decline. Knowles' account of Gene Forrester and his close friend raised fascinating questions about loyalty, friendship, and responsibility. Golding's book, pessimistic as it is, had great appeal for young adults with its story of young English boys stranded on a desert island and learning that civilization can too easily degenerate into barbarism. Though some facets of the book appear at first to resemble clichés out of some badly written imitation of *Treasure Island,* the bloodlust and horrifying realities soon involve readers. It may be a gloomy picture but it is an honest and possible vision, disturbingly so.

Sports and Cars

Sports stories continued to be popular with some young adults, though aside from John Tunis no writer of any great talent appeared between 1940 and 1966.

Nonfiction was not yet as popular as it would later become, but one of the best books of the time was the autobiography of Boston Red Sox outfielder Jim Piersall, *Fear Strikes Out* (1955), telling about his life as an athlete and his mental breakdown. Almost equally worthwhile was Roy Campanella's *It's Good to Be Alive* (1959) dealing with his life as a catcher and his adjustment to a tragic and almost fatal car accident.

Occasionally, a good sports book appeared, but, oddly enough, the few quality books were rarely about popular sports like football, baseball, or basketball. Bob Allison's *The Kid Who Batted 1.000* (1951) is about baseball, but more than that, it is a genuinely amusing story of a young man with only one athletic talent, the ability to foul off pitch after pitch. Philip Harkins' *Knockout* (1950) and Frank O'Rourke's *The Last Round* (1956) were fine novels about boxing, though neither found a large number of fans.

Two authors were the best of the crop. John F. Carson's basketball novels convey a love of the game and an understanding of the power of athletics for good or evil. They are *Floorburns* (1957), *The Coach Nobody Liked* (1960), and *Hotshot* (1961). C. H. Frick, pen name of Constance Frick Irwin, used clever plot twists to make her sports novels different. *Five Against the Odds* (1955) features a basketball player stricken with polio, *Patch* (1957) is about a runner who loves running for its own sake, not because it may lead to winning anything, and *The Comeback Guy* (1961) focuses on a too-popular, too-successful young man who gets his comeuppance and works his way back to self-respect through sports.

More popular at the time than sports stories were car books, especially hot rod stories. Henry Gregor Felsen led all the rest with *Hot Rod* (1949), but also popular were Philip Harkins' *Road Race* (1953) and William Gault's *Thunder Road* (1952) and *Road Race Rookie* (1962).

THE RISE OF CRITICISM OF YOUNG ADULT LITERATURE

Today, we take criticism of young adult literature for granted in journals such as *Top of the News, School Library Journal, English Journal, Wilson Library Bulletin, The Horn Book Magazine, Children's Literature in Education, The Lion and the Unicorn,* and *Interracial Books for Children Bulletin,* but it developed slowly. In the 1940s, journals provided little information and less criticism of young adult literature, excepting book lists, book reviews, and occasional references to a few authors or titles in articles on reading interests or raising young peoples' literary tastes. A teacher and author as gifted as Dwight L. Burton could devote considerable space in 1947 to the worth of Daly's *Seventeenth Summer* or Wickenden's *Walk Like a Mortal,* but Burton's perceptive comments were more appreciative than critical.[29] Given the times and the attitude of many teachers and librarians, appreciation or even recognition may have been more important than criticism.

Appreciation or even recognition may have been more important than criticism.

Four years later, Burton wrote the first criticism of young adult novels, again concerned with Daly and Wickenden, but this time injecting criticism along with appreciation and commenting on more titles, among them Paul Annixter's *Swiftwater,* Betty Cavanna's *Going on Sixteen,* and Madeleine L'Engle's *The Small Rain.*[30] Concluding his article, Burton identified the qualities of the good young adult novel and prophesied its potential and future:

> The good novel for the adolescent reader has attributes no different from any good novel. It must be technically masterful, and it must present a significant synthesis of human experience. Because of the nature of adolescence itself, the good novel for the adolescent should be full in true invention and imagination. It must free itself of Pollyannism or the Tarkington-Henry Aldrich-Corliss Archer tradition and maintain a clear vision of the adolescent as a person of complexity, individuality, and dignity. The novel for the adolescent presents a ready field for the mature artist.[31]

In 1955 Richard S. Alm provided even greater critical coverage of the young adult novel.[32] He agreed with critics that many writers presented "a sugar-puff story of what adolescents should do and should believe rather than what adolescents may or will do and believe,"[33] but he argued that if writers like Janet Lambert and Helen Boylston wrote airy exercises in superficialism, other writers provided young adults with books of greater psychological accuracy and literary merit. Not only did Alm cite specific authors and titles he found good, for example, Maureen Daly's *Seventeenth Summer*, Henry Gregor Felsen's *Two and the Town*, Mildred Walker's *Winter Wheat*, Mary Stolz's *To Tell Your Love*, and Esther Forbes' *Johnny Tremain*, he painted their strengths and weaknesses in clear strokes and concluded by offering teachers some questions that might be useful in analyzing the merit of young adult novels.

A year later, Emma L. Patterson began her fine study of the origin of young adult novels, "The junior novel has become an established institution."[34] Her command of history, her knowledge of trends in young adult novels, her awareness of shortcomings and virtues of the novels, and her understanding of the place of young adult novels in schools and libraries made her article essential reading for librarians and teachers.

But, despite the leadership of Burton, Alm, and Patterson, helpful criticism of young adult literature was slow in coming. But biting criticism of the worst of young adult novels was soon forthcoming. Only a few months after Patterson's article, Frank G. Jennings' "Literature for Adolescents—Pap or Protein?"[35] appeared. The title was unambiguous, but if any reader had doubts about where Jennings stood, the doubt was removed with the first sentence, "The stuff of adolescent literature, for the most part, is mealy-mouthed, gutless, and pointless." The remainder of the article added little to that point, and if Jennings did overstate his case, Burton, Alm, Patterson, and other sensible supporters would have agreed that much young adult literature, like much adult literature, was second-rate or worse. Jennings' article was not the first broadside attack, and it certainly would not be the last.[36]

After that small trickle of criticism came a slightly larger trickle. The *English Journal* provided some criticism by Edwards,[37] Petitt,[38] and an excellent 1967 summary of trends in young adult literature by Davis.[39] The *Library Journal* offered surprisingly little criticism of young adult literature even after starting *Junior Libraries* on September 15, 1954, and before changing the title to *School Library Journal* in September, 1961. Only Dunning's 1959 article[40] seems worth reading today. In the 1960's, *School Library Journal* provided a little more criticism, an article by Daigon[41] and several excellent comments by Broderick,[42] the best of the bunch. *The Horn Book Magazine* published four worthwhile articles: the earliest is that by Lewis,[43] but Cameron's,[44] Townsend's,[45] and Karl's[46] deserve readers today. Disappointingly, Karl's 1966 article[47] was the only critical article to appear in the *Wilson Library Bulletin*.

Much of the literature written for young adults from 1940 through 1966 goes largely and legitimately ignored today. Books by once popular writers like Janet Lambert, Jesse Jackson, or Margaret Bell gather dust.

But some writers for young adults between 1940 and 1966 are still read, perhaps by an audience younger than originally intended, but often by readers as old as their first ones. Mary Stolz is still read, but then the same is true of Maureen Daly, Esther Forbes, and Henry Gregor Felsen.

More important than mere longevity is the effect these authors had on books appearing after 1966. Readers before then could not have anticipated S. E. Hinton's *The Outsiders* or Paul Zindel's *The Pigman*, which were to appear in only a year or two, much less Isabelle Holland's *The Man Without a Face*, Norma Klein's *Mom, The Wolfman and Me*, Rosa Guy's *Ruby*, or Robert Cormier's *The Chocolate War*, all to be published in the next ten or eleven years. But the iconoclastic, taboo-breaking novels today would not have been possible had it not been for earlier novels that slowly broke ground and prepared readers, teachers, and librarians (and even some parents) for contemporary novels. Society's changes, of course, inevitably lead to changes in literature, but changes in young adult literature can be attributed in large part to authors like Tunis, Means, Annixter, Daly, and Stolz.

ACTIVITIES

1. Some people have suggested that Havighurst's developmental tasks are now dated, sexist, and elitist. Reread the brief section on developmental tasks in this chapter and read some of the original words in Robert J. Havighurst's *Human Development and Education* (New York: Longmans, Green, 1953). Do you feel the modern-day critics are correct? What are the initiation rites or developmental tasks our society presently demands of its young adults? How do young adults (or parents, teachers, or librarians) know that? How have they changed since Havighurst wrote his developmental tasks?

2. Read a novel by one of the outstanding writers from 1940 to 1966, for example John Tunis' *All-American*, Maureen Daly's *Seventeenth Summer*, Henry Gregor Felsen's *Hot Rod*, Paul Annixter's *Swiftwater*, Esther Forbes' *Johnny Tremain*, or Mary Stolz's *Pray Love, Remember*. Review the book in terms of the audience of its time and the audience of contemporary young adults. What values are promulgated by the author? Are those values worthwhile or germane to young adults today?

3. Read an article or two on the uses of bibliotherapy in classrooms and libraries today, for example, articles suggested in Corinne W. Riggs's *Bibliotherapy: An Annotated Bibliography* (Newark, Delaware: International Reading Association, 1971). What are the values and potential problems in bibliotherapy? What contemporary books would be useful with what kinds of students? How would you go about using any book as bibliotherapy, either in a classroom or a library?

NOTES

[1]George W. Norvell, "Some Results of a Twelve-Year Study of Children's Reading Interests," *English Journal* 35 (December 1946): 532.

²George W. Norvell, *The Reading Interests of Young People* (Boston: D. C. Heath & Co., 1950). See also the revised edition, *The Reading Interests of Young People* (Lansing: Michigan State University, 1973).

³Norvell, "Some Results . . . ," p. 536.

⁴Marie Rankin, *Children's Interests in Library Books of Fiction,* Teachers College, Columbia University, Contributions to Education, no. 906 (New York: Teachers College, Columbia University, 1947).

⁵Stephen Dunning, "The Most Popular Junior Novels," *Junior Libraries* 5 (December 15, 1959): 7-9.

⁶In order of publication, the thirteen are: Glenn Myers Blair, "The One Hundred Books Most Enjoyed by Retarded [in reading proficiency] Readers in Senior High School," *English Journal* 30 (January 1941): 42-47; David H. Russell, "Reading Preferences of Young Adolescents in Saskatchewan," *English Journal* 30 (February 1941): 131-36; Ethel L. Cornell, "The Voluntary Reading of High School Pupils," *American Library Association Bulletin* 35 (May 1941): 295-300; Ruth Strang, "Reading Interests," *English Journal* 35 (November 1946): 477-82; Reverend Edward F. Donahue, "Leisure-Time Reading Interests of Catholic High School Boys," *Catholic Educational Review* 45 (November 1947): 525-33; Ethel M. Anderson, "A Study of Leisure-Time Reading of Pupils in Junior High School," *Elementary School Journal* 48 (January 1948): 258-67; Florence Powell, "Students' Choice," *Library Journal* 76 (March 15, 1951): 488-90; Paul I. Lyness, "Patterns in the Mass Communications Tastes of the Young Audience," *Journal of Educational Psychology* 42 (December 1951): 449-67; Walter Barbe, "A Study of the Reading of Gifted High-School Students," *Educational Administration and Supervision* 38 (March 1952): 148-52; Marion W. Taylor and Mary A. Schneider, "What Books Are Children Reading?" *Chicago School Journal* 38 (January-February 1957): 155-60; Paul A. Witty, "A Study of Pupil Interests, Grades 9, 10, 11, 12," *Education* 82 (October 1961): 100-110; Beryl I. Vaughan, "Reading Interests of Eighth-Grade Students," *Journal of Developmental Reading* 6 (Spring 1963): 149-55; and "YA's Disclose Favorite Reading, Library Uses, in Westchester Survey," *School Library Journal* 12 (April 1966): 68.

⁷Jacob W. Getzels, "The Nature of Reading Interests: Psychological Aspects" in *Developing Permanent Interests in Reading,* ed. Helen M. Robinson, Supplementary Education Monographs, no. 84, December 1956 (Chicago: University of Chicago Press, 1956): p. 5.

⁸G. Robert Carlsen, "Behind Reading Interests," *English Journal* 43 (January 1954): 7-10.

⁹Dwight L. Burton, "There's Always a Book for You," *English Journal* 38 (September 1949): 374.

¹⁰Gladys B. Johnson, "Books and the Five Adolescent Tasks," *Library Journal* 68 (May 1, 1943): 350-52.

¹¹Robert J. Havighurst, *Human Development and Education* (New York: Longmans, Green, 1953), p. 111-56.

¹²See one of several examples, Alice R. Brooks, "Integrating Books and Reading with Adolescent Tasks," *School Review* 5 (April 1950): 211-19.

¹³G. O. Ireland, "Bibliotherapy: The Use of Books as a Form of Treatment in a Neuropsychiatric Hospital," *Library Journal* 54 (December 1, 1929): 972-74.

[14]Alice I. Bryan, "Can There Be a Science of Bibliotherapy?" *Library Journal* 64 (October 15, 1939): 773-76.

[15]William A. Heaps, "Bibliotherapy and the School Librarian," *Library Journal* 65 (October 1, 1940): 789.

[16]Lou LaBrant, "Diversifying the Matter," *English Journal* 40 (March 1951): 135.

[17]Frank Ross, "Bibliotherapy," *Media and Methods* 5 (January 1969): 36.

[18]Frank L. Schick, *The Paperbound Book in America: The History of Paperbacks and Their European Background* (New York: R. R. Bowker Co., 1958), p. 128. A fascinating work.

[19]S. Alan Cohen, "Paperbacks in the Classroom," *Journal of Reading* 12 (January 1969): 295.

[20]For a 1971 status report on the Scholastic Book Club, see Annette Grant, "Reading What They Wanna Read," *The New York Times Book Review*, February 21, 1971, p. 8.

[21]Daniel Fader, *Hooked on Books* (New York: Berkley Publishing Corp., 1966), revised as *Hooked on Books: Program and Proof* in 1968, and updated in 1976 as *The New Hooked on Books*.

[22]Ray Walters, "Paperback Talk," *The New York Times Book Review*, November 13, 1977, p. 90.

[23]Leo Lerman, "An Industry Within an Industry," *Saturday Review of Literature* 24 (November 8, 1941): 3.

[24]Stanley B. Kegler and Stephen Dunning, "Junior Book Roundup—Literature for the Adolescent, 1960," *English Journal* 50 (May 1961): 369.

[25]Stanley B. Kegler and Stephen Dunning, "Junior Book Roundup," *English Journal* 53 (May 1964): 392.

[26]The debate over what should or should not be offered in classes or on library shelves continues and there seems little likelihood of abatement. One librarian worried about people who fill "shelves with garbage and sewage" in 1967 and continued, "Then you need sensible censorship indeed," without defining precisely (or even generally) *garbage, sewage,* or *sensible.* See *Wilson Library Bulletin* 42 (December 1967): 369.

[27]*Library Journal* 77 (July 1952): 1216.

[28]Richard S. Alm, "The Glitter and the Gold," *English Journal* 44 (September 1955): 320.

[29]Dwight L. Burton, "Books to Meet Students' Personal Needs," *English Journal* 36 (November 1947): 469-73. See also G. Robert Carlsen, "Literature and Emotional Maturity," *English Journal* 38 (March 1949): 130-38, and Isabel V. Eno, "Books for Children from Broken Homes," *English Journal* 38 (October 1949): 457-58 for similar articles.

[30]Dwight L. Burton, "The Novel for the Adolescent," *English Journal* 40 (September 1951): 363-69.

[31]Ibid., p. 369.

[32]Richard S. Alm, "The Glitter and the Gold," *English Journal* 44 (September 1955): 315.

[33]Ibid.

[34]Emma L. Patterson, "The Junior Novels and How They Grew," *English Journal* 45 (October 1956): 381.

[35]*English Journal* 45 (December 1956): 526-31.

[36]See for examples, Alice Krahn, "Case Against the Junior Novel," *Top of the News* 17 (May 1961): 19-22; Esther Millett, "We Don't Even Call Those Books!" *Top of the News* 20 (October 1963): 45-47; and Harvey R. Granite, "The Uses and Abuses of Junior Literature," *Clearing House* 42 (February 1968): 337-40.

[37]Margaret Edwards, "Let the Lower Lights Be Burning," *English Journal* 46 (November 1957): 461.

[38]Dorothy Petitt, "A Search for Self-Definition: The Picture of Life in the Novel for the Adolescent," *English Journal* 49 (December 1960): 616-26, and "The Junior Novel in the Classroom," *English Journal* 52 (October 1963): 512-20.

[39]James Davis, "Recent Trends in Fiction for Adolescents," *English Journal* 56 (May 1967): 720-24.

[40]Stephen Dunning, "The Most Popular Junior Novels," *Junior Libraries* 5 (December 1959): 7-9.

[41]Arthur Daigon, "The Novel of Adolescent Romance: Theme and Value in Teen-age Fiction," *School Library Journal* 12 (April 1966): 36-40.

[42]Dorothy Broderick, "The Twelve-Year-Old 'Adult' Reader," *School Library Journal* 11 (May 1965): 17-23, and "A Study in Conflicting Values," *School Library Journal* 12 (May 1965): 17-24.

[43]C. S. Lewis, "On Three Ways of Writing for Children," *The Horn Book Magazine* 39 (October 1963): 459-69.

[44]Eleanor Cameron, "Of Style and the Stylist," *The Horn Book Magazine* 40 (February 1964): 25-32.

[45]John Rowe Townsend, "Didacticism in Modern Dress," *The Horn Book Magazine* 43 (April 1967): 159-64.

[46]Jean Karl, "A Children's Editor Looks at Excellence in Children's Literature," *The Horn Book Magazine* 43 (February 1967): 31-41.

[47]Jean Karl, "The Real and the Unreal," *Wilson Library Bulletin* 41 (October 1966): 162-67.

TITLES MENTIONED IN CHAPTER FIVE

For information on the availability of paperback editions of these titles, please consult the most recent edition of *Paperbound Books in Print,* published annually by R. R. Bowker Company.

Allison, Bob and F. E. Hill. *The Kid Who Batted 1.000.* Doubleday, 1951.

Annixter, Paul. *Swiftwater.* A. A. Wyn, 1950.

Arnothy, Christine. *I Am Fifteen and I Do Not Want to Die.* E. P. Dutton, 1956.

Bell, Margaret Elizabeth. *Love Is Forever.* William Morrow, 1954.

Bennett, Jack. *The Hawk Alone.* Little, Brown, 1965.

———. *Jamie.* Little, Brown, 1963.

———. *Mister Fisherman.* Little, Brown, 1965.

Boylston, Helen Dore. *Sue Barton, Senior Nurse.* John Lane, 1950.

———. *Sue Barton, Staff Nurse.* Little, Brown, 1952.

———. *Sue Barton, Student Nurse.* Little, Brown, 1936.

Brande, Dorothea. *Wake Up and Live.* World, 1941.

Breck, Vivian. *High Trail.* Doubleday, 1948.

———. *Maggie.* Doubleday, 1954.

Brown, Claude. *Manchild in the Promised Land.* Macmillan, 1965.

Buck, Pearl S. *The Good Earth.* John Day, 1931.

Bugbee, Emma. *Peggy Covers the News.* Dodd, Mead, 1936.

Burns, John Horne. *The Gallery.* Harper & Row, 1947.

Campanella, Roy. *It's Good to Be Alive.* Little, Brown, 1959.

Carr, Harriet. *Confidential Secretary.* Macmillan, 1958.

Carson, John F. *The Coach Nobody Liked.* Farrar, Straus & Giroux, 1960.

———. *Floorburns.* Farrar, Straus & Giroux, 1957.

———. *Hotshot.* Farrar, Straus & Giroux, 1961.

Cavanna, Betty. *Going on Sixteen.* Ryerson, 1946.

———. *Paintbox Summer.* Presbyterian Board of Christian Education, 1949.

Christie, Agatha. *The Murder of Roger Ackroyd.* Grosset & Dunlap, 1940.

Daly, Maureen. *Seventeenth Summer.* Dodd, Mead, 1942.

De Leeuw, Adele Louise. *Gay Design.* Macmillan, 1942.

Du Jardin, Rosamond. *Boy Trouble.* Longmans, 1953.

———. *Double Feature.* Longmans, 1953.

———. *Practically Seventeen.* Longmans, 1949.

———. *Senior Prom.* J. B. Lippincott, 1957.

———. *Wait for Marcy.* Longmans, 1950.

Ellison, Ralph. *Invisible Man.* Random House, 1952.

———. *Shadow and Act.* Random House, 1964.

Emery, Anne. *Going Steady.* Westminster, 1950.

———. *Married on Wednesday.* Ryerson, 1957.

———. *Sorority Girl.* Westminster, 1952.

Eyerly, Jeanette. *Bonnie Jo, Go Home.* J. B. Lippincott, 1972.

———. *Drop-Out.* J. B. Lippincott, 1963.

———. *A Girl Like Me.* J. B. Lippincott, 1966.

———. *Radigan Cares.* J. B. Lippincott, 1970.

Fargo, Lucile Foster. *Marian-Martha.* Dodd, Mead, 1936.

Farley, Walter. *Black Stallion.* Random House, 1944.

Felsen, Henry Gregor. *Bertie Comes Through.* E. P. Dutton, 1947.

———. *Bertie Makes a Break.* E. P. Dutton, 1949.

———. *Bertie Takes Care.* E. P. Dutton, 1948.

———. *Crash Club*. Random House, 1958.

———. *Davey Logan, Intern*. E. P. Dutton, 1950.

———. *He's in the Coast Guard Now*. MacBride, 1943.

———. *Hot Rod*. E. P. Dutton, 1950.

———. *Navy Diver*. E. P. Dutton, 1942.

———. *Pilots All*. Harper & Row, 1944.

———. *Street Rod*. Random House, 1953.

———. *Submarine Sailor*. E. P. Dutton, 1943.

———. *Two and the Town*. Charles Scribner's Sons, 1952.

Fleming, Ian. *Casino Royale*. Macmillan, 1954.

———. *Dr. No*. Macmillan, 1958.

———. *From Russia with Love*. Macmillan, 1957.

———. *Goldfinger*. Macmillan, 1959.

———. *The Man with the Golden Gun*. New American Library, 1965.

———. *Thunderball*. Viking, 1961.

———. *You Only Live Twice*. Clarke, Irwin, 1964.

Forbes, Esther. *Johnny Tremain*. Houghton Mifflin, 1943.

———. *Paul Revere and the World He Lived In*. Houghton Mifflin, 1942.

Frank, Anne. *Anne Frank: The Diary of a Young Girl*. Doubleday, 1952.

Freedman, Benedict and Nancy. *Mrs. Mike*. Coward, McCann & Geoghegan, 1947.

Frick, Constance H. *The Comeback Guy*. Harcourt Brace Jovanovich, 1961.

———. *Five Against the Odds*. Harcourt Brace Jovanovich, 1955.

———. *Patch*. Harcourt Brace Jovanovich, 1957.

Gault, William. *Thunder Road*. E. P. Dutton, 1952.

———. *Road Race Rookie*. E. P. Dutton, 1962.

Gibbs, Blanch L. and Georgiana Adams. *Shirley Clayton, Secretary*. Dodd, Mead, 1941.

Golding, William. *Lord of the Flies*. Coward, McCann & Geoghegan, 1955.

Goudge, Elizabeth. *Green Dolphin Street*. Coward, McCann & Geoghegan, 1944.

Graham, Lorenz. *North Town*. Thomas Y. Crowell, 1965.

———. *South Town*. Follett, 1958.

———. *Whose Town?* Thomas Y. Crowell, 1969.

Graham, Shirley. *Booker T. Washington: Educator of Hand, Head, and Heart*. Julian Messner, 1955.

———. *The Story of Phillis Wheatley: Poetess of the American Revolution*. Julian Messner, 1949.

———. *There Was Once a Slave: The Heroic Story of Frederick Douglass*. Julian Messner, 1947.

———. *Your Most Humble Servant: The Story of Benjamin Banneker*. Julian Messner, 1949.

Griffin, John Howard. *Black Like Me*. Houghton Mifflin, 1961.

————. *The Devil Rides Outside.* William Collins Sons, 1952.

Harkins, Philip. *Knockout.* Holiday House, 1950.

————. *Road Race.* Thomas Y. Crowell, 1953.

Harris, Christie. *You Have to Draw the Line Somewhere.* Atheneum, 1964.

Hentoff, Nat. *I'm Really Dragged But Nothing Gets Me Down.* Simon & Schuster, 1968.

————. *In the Country of Ourselves.* Simon & Schuster, 1971.

————. *Jazz Country.* Harper & Row, 1965.

Hersey, John Richard. *A Bell for Adano.* Alfred A. Knopf, 1944.

Heyliger, William. *Ritchie of the News.* Appleton-Century, 1933.

Hilton, James. *Lost Horizon.* Grosset & Dunlap, 1933.

Jackson, Jesse. *Anchor Man.* Harper & Row, 1947.

————. *Charley Starts from Scratch.* Harper & Row, 1958.

————. *Tessie.* Harper & Row, 1968.

Johnson, Martha. *Ann Bartlett, Navy Nurse.* Thomas Y. Crowell, 1941.

Jones, James. *From Here to Eternity.* Scribner, 1951.

————. *The Pistol.* Scribner, 1959.

————. *The Thin Red Line.* Scribner, 1962.

Knowles, John. *A Separate Peace.* Macmillan, 1960.

Lambert, Janet. *Star-Spangled Summer.* E. P. Dutton, 1941.

Lansing, Elizabeth. *Nancy Naylor, Flight Nurse.* Thomas Y. Crowell, 1944.

Lee, Harper. *To Kill a Mockingbird.* J. B. Lippincott, 1960.

L'Engle, Madeleine. *The Small Rain.* Vanguard, 1945.

Lewiton, Mina. *A Cup of Courage.* Robert McKay, 1948.

————. *The Divided Heart.* Robert McKay, 1947.

McFadden, Dorothy. *Lynn Decker: TV Apprentice.* Dodd, Mead, 1953.

Mailer, Norman. *The Naked and the Dead.* Clarke, Irwin, 1948.

Malcolm X. *The Autobiography of Malcolm X.* Grove, 1965.

Mann, Carl. *He's in the Signal Corps Now.* McBride, 1943.

Marshall, Catherine. *Julie's Heritage.* Longmans, 1957.

Means, Florence Crannell. *A Candle in the Mist.* Houghton Mifflin, 1931.

————. *It Takes All Kinds.* Houghton Mifflin, 1964.

————. *The Moved Outers.* Houghton Mifflin, 1945.

————. *Our Cup Is Broken.* Houghton Mifflin, 1969.

————. *Shuttered Windows.* Houghton Mifflin, 1930.

————. *Tangled Waters: A Navajo Story.* Houghton Mifflin, 1936.

————. *Tolliver.* Houghton Mifflin, 1963.

Metalious, Grace. *Peyton Place.* Julian Messner, 1956.

————. *Return to Peyton Place.* Julian Messner, 1959.

Milne, Ruth. *TV Girl Friday.* Little, Brown, 1957.

O'Rourke, Frank. *The Last Round.* William Morrow, 1955.

Parker, Dorothy. *Enough Rope.* Sun Dial, 1940.

Paton, Alan. *Cry the Beloved Country.* Charles Scribner's Sons, 1948.

———. *Too Late the Phalarope.* Charles Scribner's Sons, 1953.

Peckham, Betty. *Women in Aviation.* Thomas Nelson, 1945.

Piersall, James Anthony and Albert Hirshberg. *Fear Strikes Out.* Little, Brown, 1955.

Provines, Mary Virginia. *Bright Heritage.* Longmans, 1939.

Pyle, Ernie. *Brave Men.* Holt, Rinehart & Winston, 1944.

———. *Here Is Your War.* Holt, Rinehart & Winston, 1943.

———. *Last Chapter.* Holt, Rinehart & Winston, 1946.

Reynolds, Quentin James. *70,000 to One.* Random House, 1946.

Robbins, Harold. *The Adventurers.* Simon & Schuster, 1966.

———. *The Carpetbaggers.* Simon & Schuster, 1961.

———. *A Stone for Danny Fisher.* Alfred A. Knopf, 1952.

Rolt-Wheeler, Francis William. *The Boy with the U.S. Aviators.* Lothrop, Lee & Shepard, 1929.

———. *The Boy with the U.S. Survey.* Lothrop, Lee & Shepard, 1909.

Rosenheim, Lucille G. *Kathie, the New Teacher.* Julian Messner, 1949.

Salinger, J. D. *The Catcher in the Rye.* Little, Brown, 1951.

Sherburne, Zoa. *Jennifer.* William Morrow, 1959.

———. *Too Bad About the Haines Girl.* William Morrow, 1967.

Smith, Betty. *A Tree Grows in Brooklyn.* Harper & Row, 1943.

Smith, Lillian. *Strange Fruit.* Reynal, 1944.

Smith, Thorne. *Topper.* Sun Dial, 1942.

Steinbeck, John. *The Grapes of Wrath.* Viking, 1939.

———. *Of Mice and Men.* Viking, 1937.

Stolz, Mary Slattery. *The Day and the Way We Met.* Harper & Row, 1956.

———. *In a Mirror.* Harper & Row, 1953.

———. *A Love, or a Season.* Harper & Row, 1964.

———. *Pray Love, Remember.* Harper & Row, 1954.

———. *Ready or Not.* Harper & Row, 1953.

———. *Rosemary.* Harper & Row, 1955.

———. *The Sea Gulls Woke Me.* Harper & Row, 1951.

———. *To Tell Your Love.* Harper & Row, 1950.

Summers, James. *Girl Trouble.* Westminster, 1953.

———. *The Iron Doors Between.* Westminster, 1968.

———. *The Limit of Love.* Ryerson, 1959.

———. *Off the Beam.* Westminster, 1956.

———. *Operation ABC.* Westminster, 1955.

————. *Prom Trouble*. Ryerson, 1954.

————. *Ring Around Her Finger*. Westminster, 1957.

————. *The Shelter Trap*. Westminster, 1962.

————. *Trouble on the Run*. Ryerson, 1956.

————. *The Wonderful Time*. Ryerson, 1957.

————. *You Can't Make It by Bus*. Westminster, 1969.

Tregaskis, Richard William. *Guadalcanal Diary*. Random House, 1943.

Trumbull, Robert. *The Raft*. Holt, Rinehart & Winston, 1942.

Tunis, John R. *All-American*. Harcourt, Brace and Co., 1942.

————. *A City for Lincoln*. Harcourt, Brace and Co., 1945.

————. *Go, Team, Go!* William Morrow, 1954.

————. *His Enemy, His Friend*. William Morrow, 1967.

————. *Iron Duke*. Harcourt, Brace and Co., 1938.

————. *Silence over Dunkerque*. William Morrow. 1962.

————. *Yea! Wildcats*. Harcourt, Brace and Co., 1944.

Wallace, Irving. *The Chapman Report*. Simon & Schuster, 1960.

————. *The Man*. Simon & Schuster, 1964.

————. *The Prize*. Simon & Schuster, 1962.

Westheimer, David. *My Sweet Charlie*. Doubleday, 1965.

Wickenden, Dan. *Walk Like a Mortal*. William Morrow, 1940.

Wiesel, Eliezer. *Dawn*. Hill & Wang, 1961.

————. *Night*. Hill & Wang, 1960.

Wilder, Thornton. *The Bridge of San Luis Rey*. Harper & Row, 1927.

Winsor, Kathleen. *Forever Amber*. Macmillan, 1944.

Wouk, Herman. *The Caine Mutiny*. Doubleday, 1951.

Wright, Richard. *Black Boy*. Harper & Row, 1945.

————. *Native Son*. Harper & Row, 1940.

Yates, Elizabeth. *Amos Fortune, Free Man*. Aladdin, 1950.

SOME SUGGESTED READINGS

General Comments on Literature, 1940-1966:

Alm, Richard. "The Glitter and the Gold." *English Journal* 44 (September 1955): 315.

Burton, Dwight. *Literature Study in the High Schools*. 3d. ed. New York: Holt, Rinehart and Winston, Inc., 1970.

Burton, Dwight. "The Novel for the Adolescent." *English Journal* 40 (September 1951): 363-69.

Carlsen, G. Robert. "Forty Years with Books and Teen-Age Readers." *Arizona English Bulletin* 18 (April 1976): 1-5.

Davis, James E. "Recent Trends in Fiction for Adolescents." *English Journal* 56 (May 1967): 720-24.

Edwards, Margaret A. "The Rise of Teen-Age Reading." *Saturday Review*, November 13, 1954, p. 88.

Epstein, Jason. "Good Bunnies Always Obey: Books for American Children." *Commentary* 35 (February 1963): 112-22.

Hackett, Alice Payne and James Henry Burke. *80 Years of Best Sellers, 1895-1975*. New York: R. R. Bowker Co., 1977.

Hart, James D. *The Popular Book: A History of America's Literary Taste.* Berkeley: University of California Press, 1950.

Hentoff, Nat. "Getting Inside Jazz Country." *The Horn Book Magazine* 42 (October 1966): 528-32.

Jennings, Frank G. "Literature for Adolescents—Pap or Protein?" *English Journal* 45 (December 1951): 526-31.

Johnson, James William. "The Adolescent Hero: A Trend in Modern Fiction." *Twentieth Century Literature* 5 (April 1959): 3-11.

Nordstrom, Ursula. "Honesty in Teenage Novels." *Top of the News* 21 (November 1964): 35-38.

Rosenblatt, Louise M. *Literature as Exploration.* 3d ed. New York: Noble and Noble, Publishers, Inc., 1977.

Rosenheim, Edward W., Jr. "Children's Reading and Adults' Values" in *A Critical Approach to Children's Literature.* Edited by Sara Innis Fenwick. Chicago: University of Chicago Press, 1967, pp. 3-14.

Reading Interest Studies:

Anderson, Esther M. "A Study of Leisure-Time Reading of Pupils in Junior High School." *Elementary School Journal* 48 (January 1948): 258-67.

Anderson, Scarvia B. *Between the Grimms and "The Group": Literature in American High Schools.* Princeton: Educational Testing Service, 1964.

Barbe, Walter. "A Study of the Reading of Gifted High-School Students." *Educational Administration and Supervision* 38 (March 1952): 148-54.

Broehl, Frances. "New Influences in the Field of Recreational Reading." *English Journal* 30 (April 1941): 281-86.

Carlsen, G. Robert. "Behind Reading Interests." *English Journal* 43 (January 1954): 7-12.

Carlsen, G. Robert. "For Everything There Is a Season." *Top of the News* 21 (January 1967): 103-10.

Dunning, Stephen. "The Most Popular Junior Novels." *Junior Libraries* 5 (December 1959): 7-9.

Edwards, Margaret A. "A Time When It's Best to Read and Let Read." *Wilson Library Bulletin* 35 (September 1960): 43-45.

Getzels, Jacob W. "The Nature of Reading Interests: Psychological Aspects" in *Developing Permanent Interest in Reading.* Edited by Helen M. Robinson. Supplementary Education Monographs, no. 84. Chicago: University of Chicago Press, 1956, pp. 5-9.

Lapides, Linda P. "Unassigned Reading: Teen-Age Testimonies I and II: A Decade of Teen-Age Reading in Baltimore, 1960-1970." *Top of the News* 27 (April 1971): 278-91.

Nelms, Ben F. "Reading for Pleasure in Junior High School." *English Journal* 55 (September 1966): 676-81.

Norvell, George W. *The Reading Interests of Young People.* Boston: D.C. Heath & Co., 1950.

Norvell, George W. "Some Results of a Twelve-Year Study of Children's Reading Interests." *English Journal* 35 (December 1946): 531-36.

Petitt, Dorothy. "A Search for Self-Definition: The Picture of Life in the Novel for the Adolescent." *English Journal* 49 (December 1960): 616-26.

Plotz, Helen. "The Rising Generation of Readers." *The New York Times Magazine,* August 5, 1956, p. 44.

Rankin, Marie. *Children's Interests in Library Books of Fiction.* Teachers College, Columbia University Contributions to Education, no. 906. New York: Teachers College Press, 1947.

Scanlan, William J. "One Hundred Most Popular Books of Children's Fiction Selected by Children." *Elementary English* 25 (February 1948): 83-97.

Scoggin, Margaret C. "Young People's Reading Interests Not Materially Changed in Wartime." *Library Journal* 68 (September 15, 1943): 703-6.

Soares, Anthony T. "Salient Elements of Recreational Reading of Junior High School Students." *Elementary English* 40 (December 1963): 843-45.

Havighurst's Developmental Tasks:

Brooks, Alice. "Integrating Books and Reading with Havighurst's Developmental Tasks." *School Review* 58 (April 1950): 211-19.

Havighurst, Robert J. *Developmental Tasks and Education.* New York: Longmans, Green, 1948.

Havighurst, Robert J. *Human Development and Education.* New York: Longmans, Green, 1953.

Johnson, Gladys B. "Books and the Five Adolescent Tasks," *Library Journal* 68 (May 1, 1943): 350-52.

Bibliotherapy:

Bryan, Alice I. "Can There Be a Science of Bibliotherapy?" *Library Journal* 64 (October 15, 1939): 773-76.

Darling, Richard L. "Mental Hygiene and Books: Bibliotherapy as Used with Children and Adolescents." *Wilson Library Bulletin* 32 (December 1957): 293-96.

Dreyer, Sharon Spredemann. *The Bookfinder: A Guide to Children's Literature about the Needs and Problems of Youth Aged 12–15.* Circle Pines, Minnesota: American Guidance Service, 1977.

Heaps, Willard A. "Bibliotherapy and the School Librarian." *Library Journal* 65 (October 1, 1940): 789–92.

Lindeman, Barbara, and M. Kling. "Bibliotherapy: Definitions, Uses, and Studies." *Journal of School Psychology* 7 (1968–69): 34–41.

Riggs, Corinne W., ed. *Bibliotherapy: An Annotated Bibliography.* Newark, Delaware: International Reading Association, 1971.

Russell, David H., and Caroline Schrodes. "Contributions of Research in Bibliotherapy to the Language Arts Program." *School Review* 58 (September 1950): 335–42; and 58 (October 1950): 411–20.

Paperbacks:

Butman, Alexander; Donald Reis; and David Sohn, eds. *Paperbacks in the Schools.* New York: Bantam Books, Inc., 1963.

Enoch, Kurt. "The Paper-Bound Book: Twentieth-Century Publishing Phenomenon." *Library Quarterly* 24 (July 1954): 211–25.

Fader, Daniel. *The New Hooked on Books.* New York: Berkley Publishing Corp., 1976.

Lewis, Freeman. "The Future of Paper-Bound Books." *Bulletin of the New York Public Library* 57 (October 1953): 506–15.

Lewis, Freeman. "Paper-Bound Books in America." *Bulletin of the New York Public Library* 57 (February 1953): 55–75.

Schick, Frank L. *The Paperbound Book in America: The History of Paperbacks and Their European Background.* New York: R. R. Bowker Co., 1958.

Career Books:

Edwards, Anne. "Teen-Age Career Girls." *English Journal* 42 (November 1953): 437–42.

Forrester, Gertrude. *Occupational Literature: An Annotated Bibliography.* New York: H. W. Wilson Co., 1971.

Splaver, Sarah. "The Career Novel." *Personnel and Guidance Journal* 31 (March 1953): 371–72.

PART THREE

Modern
Young Adult
Reading

6

The New Realism

Of Life and
Other Sad Songs

The books featured in this chapter are sometimes referred to as "problem novels," and in many ways they make up what people consider to be the main body of modern young adult literature. Anyone really looking at the field or even browsing through this textbook will realize that young adults are reading many other kinds of books. But the new realism receives the lion's share of attention because it is new and different and sometimes controversial. Never before have books of this type been written for young readers.

What is distinctive about the new realism is that the best of it treats candidly and with respect problems that belong specifically to young adults in today's world. As we pointed out in Chapter 1, adolescence as a unique period of life is a fairly recent development coinciding with the development of complex industrial societies. The problems that go along with modern adolescence did not exist in the nineteenth century, so, of course, they were not written about. At least in this one area, there is ample justification for books directed specifically to a young adult audience because there is a difference in the kinds of real-life problems that concern adults and those of interest to young adults.

Many critics are pleased that juvenile literature has "come of age," but others are not so enthusiastic. Sheila Egoff, in the 1979 May Hill Arbuthnot lecture, quoted from the Book of Matthew: "What profiteth a man if he shall gain the whole world and lose his own soul?" Then she stated, "I am very much afraid that in contemporary children's literature, when it gained the whole world of adult freedom and power and vast expansion of subject matter, it lost some of its soul—its identity as a separate and distinctive branch of writing."[1]

She outlined four reasons for the appeal of the problem novel. "One explanation—or perhaps claim is the more accurate word—is that the problem novel has therapeutic value." Today many young people have severe problems, she reasoned, and perhaps by reading about similar cases they are helped to find solutions to their own problems. Or at least they find comfort in the fact that they are not alone. Second, for those children whose lives are not filled with such problems there is the appeal of the exotic. Said Egoff: "Just as adult, upper-class suburbanites find *The Godfather* absorbing, so well brought up girls may find a kind of romance and excitement in the 'hard-boiled' naturalism of the problem novels." (Girls far outnumber boys in this reading audience.) A third theory Egoff developed was that "the problem novel wins its audience by flattery. Children want to feel grown-up and problem novels offer to youngsters—in simple language that they can perfectly well follow—the implication that they are ready to deal with issues and themes that are indisputably 'adult.'" She cited the movie makers who have long attracted juvenile audiences by labeling movies "for mature viewers." As the fourth reason, she explained "the appeals of the *p*'s— prurience and peer pressure":

> How welcome it must be to find between the covers of a book both words and subjects that have been considered taboo and may still be so in an individual child's home or school environment. While they may give the child a delicious *frisson*, they also spell respectability. . . . Not to have read Judy Blume seems as socially unacceptable as not being familiar with the latest "in" television show.

Egoff worries that the trend toward realism is so exaggerated that young readers will turn away from it just as they turned away from the didacticism of earlier years. She thinks the recent popularity of the Hardy Boys and Nancy Drew books—which was not caused by, but preceded and went along with the creation of the television series— is a result of readers not being able to find in current books the entertainment and the escape that they want.

WHAT ARE THE PROBLEMS?

What are some of the problems faced by today's youth? A look at any newspaper can provide some clues, but if all we knew of teenagers came from newspapers, we might well think that all young people drink heavily, run away from home, expect contraceptives on demand, commit crimes, and kill themselves. We know this isn't true, but it *is* true that young people today find themselves having to make decisions regarding their own values and behavior in a bewilderingly complex society. Choices exist today that didn't exist even a few years ago: psychoactive drugs are readily available, if not legal; abortion is legal under many circumstances; a college education is no longer considered the panacea it once was; the traditional structure of marriage and family is being challenged as never before. This is not to say that these are the first teenagers in history with difficult decisions to make, just that every generation of young people has a special set of problems unique to the age. The teenagers of the 1980s are no exception.

SUGGESTIONS FOR EVALUATING THE PROBLEM NOVEL

A good problem novel usually has:	A poor problem novel may have:
A strong, interesting, and believable plot centering around a problem that a young person might really have.	A totally predictable plot with nothing new and interesting to entice the reader.
	Characters that are cardboard-like exaggerations of people who are too good or too bad to be believed.
The power to transport the reader into another person's thoughts and feelings.	More characters than the reader can comfortably keep straight.
Rich characterization. The characters "come alive" as believable with a balance of good and negative qualities.	Many stereotypes.
	Lengthy chapters or descriptive paragraphs that add bulk but not substance to the book.
A setting that enhances the story and is described so that the reader can get the intended picture.	A preachy message. The author spells out the attitudes and conclusions with which he or she wants each reader to leave the book.
A worthwhile theme. The reader is left with something to think about.	Nothing that stays with the reader after the book has been put down.
A smoothness of style that flows steadily and easily, carrying the reader along.	A subject that is of interest only because it is topical or trendy.
	Inconsistent points of view. The author's sympathies change with no justification.
A universal appeal so that it speaks to more than a single group of readers.	Dialogue that sounds forced and/or inappropriate to the characters.
A subtlety that stimulates the reader to think about the various aspects of the story.	"Facts" that do not jibe with those of the real world.
	Unlikely coincidences or changes in characters' personalities for the sake of the plot.
A way of dealing with the problem so that the reader is left with insights into either society or individuals or both.	Exaggerations which result in sensationalism.

Another way of looking at the problems of teenagers is through the developmental tasks that R. J. Havighurst outlined. His definition of a developmental task was:

> a task which arises at or about a certain period in the life of the individual,
> successful achievement of which leads to his [or her] happiness and to success
> with later tasks while failure leads to unhappiness in the individual,
> disapproval by the society, and difficulty with later tasks.[2]

The discussion of books in this chapter will show a close relationship between these tasks (described in Chapter 5) and the problems that are written about. As listed, the tasks seem relatively simple, but a discussion of the books and the various alternatives they explore will illustrate that they aren't so simple after all.

A rather common observation about adolescent reading has been that young people are looking for mirror images of themselves. In relation to realistic fiction, this may be only partially true. A more accurate analogy could be made to the wedding custom in Afghanistan where the bride and groom say their vows while facing a large mirror, rather than each other. Traditionally at the age of twelve a girl begins wearing a *chaderi* so that her face is covered to everyone outside her immediate family. Marriages are arranged and when the *mullah* declares the couple husband and wife, the girl removes her *chaderi*. But instead of looking at each other, the bride and groom satisfy their curiosity by staring intensely in the mirror. Of course they see themselves in the mirror, but what they are really examining is the other person. This does not mean that they are above egocentricity. On the contrary, they are being understandably selfish in trying to answer such questions as, "What is this person like?" "How do I look in relation to this person?" "How should I act toward him (or her)?" and "How will my life be affected?"

Being blatantly curious and openly staring face-to-face would not be culturally acceptable so the mirror (which, incidentally, is given to the couple as their first piece of household furniture) serves a purpose similar to that of books in the lives of adolescent readers. It puts a frame around someone who, in relation to the viewer, is of intense interest, and it makes it acceptable to stare.

Young readers use books as the Afghans use their wedding mirrors. The author acts as the mirror, absorbing directly from life what is of importance and then reflecting this information back to the viewer so that it can be openly examined as true life never could be. What teenagers are interested in examining in this mirroring of life are the forces that stand between them and independence. They are asking, "Who is this person, what is this force that may touch my life?" "What is going to be the balance of power between me and it?" and "How can I best keep from becoming a victim?"

Are problem novels realistic? Realism is experientially true. It can be defined as an author's honest attempt to depict people in ordinary situations without sentimentalizing or glossing over anything. In order to understand the nature of the problem novel, it is necessary to look not only at the subject matter but also at how the subject matter influences writing styles and at how one book lays the groundwork for others.

THE GROUND-BREAKING BOOKS

If we were to try to pinpoint the birth of the new realism, the year would probably be 1967, when S. E. Hinton's *The Outsiders,* Ann Head's *Mr. and Mrs. Bo Jo Jones,* and Jean Thompson's *House of Tomorrow* appeared. These were followed in 1968 by Paul Zindel's *The Pigman* and Richard Bradford's *Red Sky at Morning.* In the next year came William Armstrong's *Sounder,* Vera and Bill Cleaver's *Where the Lilies Bloom,* and John Donovan's *I'll Get There. It Better Be Worth the Trip.*

These books had a new candor to them. Hinton wrote about the Socs and the Greasers, and it was the Greasers whose story she told. Prior to this, it had nearly always been stories about the society kids in their white middle-class neighborhoods that found their way into adolescent fiction. Both Head and Thompson wrote about unmarried girls who were pregnant. In Head's book, the girl marries the father, but in Thompson's book the father is already married and the girl goes to a home for unwed mothers.

In Zindel's *The Pigman* an alienated boy and girl make friends with a lonely old man who can't admit that his wife has died. The three of them share true feelings of love and carefree playfulness, but in the end the old man dies tragically, and the boy and girl are left to ponder their role in his death and what it all means. In *Red Sky at Morning,* southerner Josh Arnold and his mother go to a little town in New Mexico where they are to wait out the Second World War. While living there, Josh gains at least a partial understanding not only of his Mexican American neighbors but also of himself. Some people—mostly adults—were shocked by the language in this book.

The next three books continued the trend of pushing away from safe, middle-class settings. *Sounder* is a grim historical piece about a poverty-stricken black family of tenant farmers. In *Where the Lilies Bloom,* which is set in the Tennessee mountains, fourteen-year-old Mary Call struggles to keep her orphaned brothers and sisters together after they secretly bury their father. And in *I'll Get There. It Better Be Worth the Trip,* Davy, who has been raised by his grandmother, has to move to New York to live with an alcoholic mother that he hardly knows and certainly does not understand.

These eight books of the late 1960s exemplify several of the characteristics that during the 1970s came to be associated with the problem novel for young adults. There are basically four ways, besides the subject matter, in which these books differ from earlier books. First, there is the choice of *characters.* Unlike previous books for young people, the protagonists come mostly from lower-class families. This ties in with the second major difference, which is that of *setting.* Whereas most earlier books are set in idyllic and pleasant suburban homes, the settings in these books are often portrayed as harsh, difficult places to live. In order to get the point across about the characters and where and how they live, authors used colloquial *language,* which is the third major difference. Authors began to write the way people really talked. For example, in dialogue, they used swear words and ungrammatical constructions. That the general public allowed this change in language in most cases is significant. It shows that people were drawing away from the idea that the main purpose of fictional books for young readers is to set an example of proper, middle-class behavior.

The fourth difference also relates to this change in attitude, and that is the change in *mode*. As more and more people began to think that the educational value of fiction is to extend young readers' experiences and to give them opportunities to participate vicariously in more roles and activities than would be either desirable or possible in real life, the possibility arose for a change in the mode of the stories. In the old days most of the books—at least most of the books approved of by educators—were written in the comic and romantic modes. These were the books with the happy endings. As long as we believed that children would model their lives after what they read, then of course we wanted them to read happy stories because a happy life is what we all want for our children. But the problem novel is based on a different philosophy. One idea behind it is that young people will have a better chance to be happy if they have realistic expectations about life—if they know both the bad and the good about the society in which they live. Because of this, problem novels are written in the ironic—or sometimes the tragic—mode.

One of the newest definitions of irony is "a tennis serve that you can't return." You can admire its perfection, its appropriateness, and even the inevitability of the outcome, but you just can't cope with it. There's a refreshing honesty to stories that show readers they aren't the only ones who get served that kind of ball and that the human spirit, though totally devastated in this particular set, may rise again to play another match.

THE CHOCOLATE WAR AS A PROBLEM NOVEL

The book that we have chosen as an example of the best of modern realism for young adults is Robert Cormier's *The Chocolate War* (1974). It contains the kind of realism that many other books had been just leading up to. Its message about conformity and human manipulation is all the more powerful because the young protagonist is so vulnerable. The religious symbolism that pervades the book serves as a contrasting backdrop to the terrible evil that pervades Trinity High School where the protagonist is a freshman. The opening paragraph is the simple line: "They murdered him." Readers, who at first might think the reference is to Jesus, soon find that it is to fourteen-year-old Jerry Renault who is being "tested" to see if he has enough guts to get on the football team.

The story begins and ends on the athletic field where the shadows of the goal posts resemble "a network of crosses, empty crucifixes." On Jerry's third play at Trinity High he is "hit simultaneously by three of them." He blinks himself back to consciousness and jumps to his feet:

> intact, bobbing like one of those toy novelties dangling from car windows, but erect.
>
> "For Christ's sake," the coach bellowed, his voice juicy with contempt. A spurt of saliva hit Jerry's cheek.
>
> Hey, coach, you spit on me, Jerry protested. Stop the spitting, coach.
>
> What he said aloud was, "I'm all right, coach," because he was a coward about

stuff like that, thinking one thing and saying another, planning one thing and doing another—he had been Peter a thousand times and a thousand cocks had crowed in his lifetime.

What happens is that in the course of the book Jerry gets the courage to think and do the same thing. He refuses to sell fifty boxes of chocolates that the corrupt teacher, Brother Leon, has assigned to each student. For the first ten days of the candy campaign, he simply follows the orders of the Vigils, a gang who in the words of their head man, Archie Costello, "*were* the school." But when the ten days are up and the Vigils order Jerry to do a reverse and to participate in the selling campaign, he dares to say no.

At first Jerry is a hero, but because this threatens the power of the Vigils, Archie uses his full potential in people management to turn the student body against Jerry. When all the chocolates except Jerry's are sold, Archie arranges a boxing match between Jerry and a bully who is trying to work his way into the Vigils. It is supposed to be set up "with rules. Fair and square," but what Archie really masterminds is a physical and psychological battering much worse than anything Jerry underwent at football practice.

The last chapter of the book could have begun with the same line as the first chapter—"They murdered him"—only this time it would have been more than a metaphor. Although Jerry is probably going to recover physically from a fractured jaw and internal injuries, his spirit has been murdered. In the midst of the fight:

> a new sickness invaded Jerry, the sickness of knowing what he had become,
> another animal, another beast, another violent person in a violent world,
> inflicting damage, not disturbing the universe but damaging it. He had allowed
> Archie to do this to him.

And after the fight when the pain—"Jesus, the pain"—brings Jerry back to consciousness, the reader sees how changed he is because of what he tries to tell his friend Goober:

> They don't want you to do your thing, not unless it happens to be their thing,
> too. It's a laugh, Goober, a fake. Don't disturb the universe, Goober, no matter
> what the posters say.

In selecting *The Chocolate War* as a touchstone example, we asked ourselves several questions about the book. These same or similar questions could be asked when evaluating almost any problem novel. First, does the book make a distinctive contribution? Does it say something new or does it convey something old in a new way? And if so, is it something of value?

Robert Cormier was praised by *The Kirkus Reviews* because he dared to "disturb the upbeat universe of juvenile books" with *The Chocolate War*. He did not compromise by providing a falsely hopeful conclusion, nor did he sidestep the issue by leaving it open for readers to imagine their own happy ending. Until Cormier, most writers for young readers had opted for one of these two approaches. Yet Cormier was not being "difficult" just for the sake of being different. When he was questioned at the 1976 National Council of Teachers of English convention about his motives in writing such a pessimistic book for young readers, he answered that he had written three other novels and numerous short stories all with upbeat endings and that in *The Chocolate War* he was simply providing a balance. He then went on to say that today's young readers are a television generation. They have grown up thinking that every problem can be solved within a half-hour or an hour at the most, with time out for commercials. It's important for people to realize that all problems are not that easily solved. In real life there are some problems that may never be solved and others whose solutions will demand the utmost efforts of the most capable people in the world.

The plot of a book must be examined to see how closely it grows out of the characters' actions and attitudes. Is it an idea that could easily have been dropped into another setting or onto other characters? With Cormier's book, there wouldn't have been a story without the unique but believable personalities of both Jerry and Archie, as well as of Brother Leon. The problem was not so bizarre or unusual that it overshadowed the characters, nor were the characters such unusual people that readers could not identify with them or imagine themselves having to deal with people like them. It is because the characters at first appear to be such ordinary people that readers are drawn into the story. The theme is similar to that in Golding's *Lord of the Flies,* but because Golding's book is set on a deserted island in the midst of a war it could be dismissed as unrealistic. Cormier's book has an immediacy that is hard to deny. The problem is a real one that teenagers can identify with on the first or literal level, yet it has implications far beyond one beaten-up fourteen-year-old and 20,000 boxes of stale Mother's Day candy.

It's common in evaluating a book to question the role of the setting. Is it just there or does it contribute something to the mood or the action or to revealing characterization? In *The Chocolate War* the story would not have been nearly so chilling without the religious setting. It provided contrast. In some ways the evil in Archie is less hideous than that in Brother Leon, the corrupt teacher who enlists Archie's help in making his unauthorized investment pay off. The brother hides behind his clerical collar and his role of teacher and assistant headmaster, whereas Archie only identifies himself as a nonbeliever in the so-called "Christian ethic." For example, when his stooge Obie asks him how he can do the things he does and still take communion, he responds, "When you march down to the rail, you're receiving the Body, man. Me, I'm just chewing a wafer they buy by the pound in Worcester."

Another question especially relevant in respect to books for young readers is the respect the author has for the intended audience. Cormier showed a great deal of respect for his readers: nowhere did he write down to them. The proof of his respect for them is in some of the subtle symbolization that he worked into the story and the care with which he developed his style. For example, the irony of the whole situation is exemplified in the gang's name, the *Vigils.* The word is cognate with *vigilant* and *vigorous,* which certainly Archie is, but its origin is in religious language where it meant the keeping of a watch on the night preceding a religious holiday. Today, vigil lights are candles placed devotionally before a shrine or image. This is comparable to the way that the members of the gang stand before Archie, who basks in the glow of their admiration. Another example of Cormier's subtlety is the fact that Archie's name has such meanings as "principal or chief" as in archvillain, "cleverly sly and alert," and "at the extreme, that is, someone or something most fully embodying the qualities of its kind."

A question that has to be asked somewhere in the evaluation process is whether or not anyone is reading the book. G. Robert Carlsen said that if he were giving prizes for the best book published each year for young adult readers, in 1974 he would have given first place to James Baldwin's *If Beale Street Could Talk* and second place to *The Chocolate War* even though *The Chocolate War* is really the better book. His reasoning for putting it second instead of first was that teenagers were not reading it in large enough numbers. In his experience it was a book better loved by critics than by teenagers. Lou Willett Stanek also reported that the teenage readers with whom she visited were uncomfortable with the portrayal of the boys in the school as basically evil. Her sample readers could accept the evil in Brother Leon and maybe in Archie, but not in the whole student body. In spite of these reactions, it is obvious that someone is reading *The Chocolate War*. In its first year as a paperback (1975) it went through three printings, and when, in 1977, a survey was taken of 160 college classes in adolescent literature, it tied with Paul Zindel's *The Pigman* as being assigned reading in the most classes.[3]

Cormier showed respect for his readers. Nowhere did he write down to them.

Nearly all writers for teenagers make certain adjustments to attract a reading audience. Some authors will say that they write strictly for themselves and it's immaterial to them whether or not anyone reads their books. This is probably either an exaggeration or an ego-defense mechanism. The physical act of typing up a manuscript and mailing it off to an editor is so demanding that someone writing only for personal fulfillment would not be likely to go through the effort. Besides, literature consists of a two-way process in which the reader brings thoughts and feelings to be intertwined with those of the author. If no one is reading a book, then only half the process is taking place. Reader reactions are important, especially when it is mainly adults who purchase the books that will be offered to youngsters.

But how far an author bends to attract an audience usually affects the quality and the honesty of a book. Richard Peck says that young readers do not really want realism. Instead they want romance masked as realism. They want to identify with teenage protagonists who accomplish something that in real life teenagers probably couldn't do on their own.

Betsy Byars, in a speech at the University of Iowa, said that the first thing she does when planning a book is to get rid of all the parents so that the children can feel they are accomplishing things on their own. This seems to be a commonly agreed upon convention and one which Cormier followed. Jerry's mother had died of cancer and his father is preoccupied, "sleepwalking through life." With the other characters there is simply no mention of parents or family. It could be argued that this isn't realism, especially in view of the fact that Robert Cormier got the inspiration for his book when he casually gave his own son a ride back to his private high school to return, without incident, a carton full of chocolates that he did not want to sell. For most of the teenage protagonists who appear in modern fiction to be without parents or with very inadequate parents may not be "realistic," but it is nevertheless a common motif in the problem novel.

CATEGORIES OF CONCERN IN PROBLEM NOVELS

Parent/Child Relationships

Although in many problem novels, parents are left out or ignored, there is another group of books in which the parent plays a central role. In most of these, one or both of the parents *is* the problem. This relates to the one really major task faced by every young adult and that is achieving independence, making the switch from being someone's daughter or son to being an individual in her or his own right.

The new realism has brought about noticeable changes in this area. Imperfect parents may have previously appeared in books featuring youth but written for adults, but in the late 1960s and 1970s books written and published for teenagers began to show parents who are not merely slightly flawed. They give immoral advice, as in Paul Zindel's *My Darling, My Hamburger;* they are alcoholic, as in Patricia Dizenzo's *An American Girl;* they are cruel, as in Bette Greene's *Summer of My German Soldier;* they are always quarreling, as in Judy Blume's *It's Not the End of the World;* they abandon their children, as in P. A. Engebrecht's *Under the Haystack;* and they are preoccupied and selfish, as in John Ney's *Ox* books. The appearance of parents like these in juvenile novels made it easier for adult novels featuring imperfect parents to find their way into young adult collections. For example, Marjorie Kellogg's *Like the Lion's Tooth* is a very grim story of family love gone awry. It is about a group of molested and battered youngsters who give each other badly needed moral support and psychological help.

When the parents are obviously flawed as in these books, the circumstances push the protagonists from the family nest and thereby force them to establish their own identities. In M. E. Kerr's *Is That You, Miss Blue?* Flanders Brown is sent to a boarding school when her mother runs off with a younger man. This trauma starts her on her way to being her own person. In Hila Colman's *Sometimes I Don't Love My Mother* a seventeen-year-old girl must separate herself from her newly widowed mother, and in Anne Snyder's *First Step,* Cindy begins to break free from the psychological hold that her alcoholic mother has had on her. One of the most powerful explorations of a child breaking free from a parent is Barbara Wersba's *Run Softly, Go Fast.* Dave Marks supposedly writes the book just after his father has died. In it he explores their love-hate relationship and what it has meant to his own values and beliefs.

Three books that came out in 1978 present different life-styles but very similar problems. They are Richard Peck's *Father Figure,* Ernest J. Gaines' *In My Father's House,* and Walter Dean Myers' *It Ain't All for Nothin'.* In each book there is a broken family in which one or more sons have been separated from their fathers for a period of years when something happens to cause the sons to return to their fathers. The stories recount the faltering steps they go through in establishing their new relationships. Peck's very readable book is about contemporary, white middle-class protagonists; Gaines's book is set in the South and reveals much about the pain of transition that blacks have undergone within the last few decades. Myers' book, which is less grim and more suitable for younger readers, is set in the inner city. A young boy whose grandmother has grown too old and sick to care for him must go and live with his father, a two-bit criminal who welcomes the boy chiefly for his welfare check. The main interest in the story is the boy's growing awareness of what his father is and his realization that he does not need to be the same. Other interesting books that focus on father-son relationships include Robert Cormier's *After the First Death,* Paul Zindel's *Confessions of a Teenage Baboon,* Paula Fox's *Blowfish Live in the Sea,* and M. E. Kerr's *The Son of Someone Famous.*

There aren't as many books of this type with female protagonists. In an interesting article entitled "Growing Up Female: The Literary Gaps," Lou Willett Stanek lamented the small number of books that honestly look at mother-daughter relationships. The reason that this was the case in earlier years, she says, is that it was

---

There aren't many books that honestly look at mother-daughter relationships.

---

extremely hard for women to have families and to be writers. Most of those who did succeed in becoming writers—Jane Austen, George Eliot, Virginia Woolf, and the Brontë sisters, for example—had no children. Today it is still a relatively unexplored area, ironically because of the feminist movement, which in trying to open up new options for girls, has cast a slightly negative tone over the whole idea of motherhood. Stanek wrote:

> Since the mother-child relationship is the only irreversible role, it seems that an exploration of this relationship, as one of many options, should be offered to young women. This does not mean that schools should be selling idealized motherhood. The holiest icon, the Virgin Mary and the Babe—sacred mother and innocent child—has raised as many false expectations as the myth of "and they got married and lived happily ever after."[4]

She marks it as a positive step that mothers of daughters, including Norma Klein, Judy Blume, Betty Miles, and Norma Fox Mazer, are now writing for young readers. There are some interesting mother-daughter relationships in the writings of these women. One of the most memorable is in Mazer's story of a daughter dying of cancer, "Guess

Whose Friendly Hands," which is published in *Dear Bill, Remember Me?* In Klein's *Mom, The Wolfman and Me,* there is a wonderful friendship between Brett and her mother. The problem is that Brett fears they will lose this if her mother marries.

Even more rare than effective books about mothers and daughters are books about opposite-sex parent-child relationships. It's hard to find books that honestly explore mother-son or father-daughter relationships.

Body and Self

Books that treat problems related to accepting and using one's physical body effectively will be treated in several sections of this text. When the physical problem is relatively minor, or is at least one that can be solved, then it might be treated more as an accomplishment-romance (for example, Robert Lipsyte's *One Fat Summer* in Chapter 7). Informative books, sports books, and biographical accounts also deal with physical problems. In the kind of book we are talking about here, problems with the physical body are often treated as a secondary or minor theme. In fact, it is almost an obligatory element in realistic fiction for the young protagonist to express dissatisfaction with his or her appearance. This is understandable since there is hardly anyone who has a

---

It is almost an obligatory element in realistic fiction for the young protagonist to express dissatisfaction with his or her appearance.

---

perfect body or who hasn't envied others for their appearance or physical skill. This is a special problem for adolescents because their bodies are changing so fast that they have not yet had time to adjust to them. One theory about the identity crisis that teenagers go through is that it is closely tied in with their new physical appearance. The reason they spend so much time looking in mirrors is to reassure themselves that, "Yes, this is me!"

In 1970, Judy Blume surprised the world of juvenile fiction by writing a book that gave major attention to the physical aspect of growing up. Margaret Simon in *Are You There God? It's Me, Margaret* worries because her breasts are small and because she's afraid she will be the last one in her crowd to begin menstruating. A later Blume book, *Then Again, Maybe I Won't* features Tony Miglione and his newly affluent family. He too worries about his developing body. In fact, he carries a jacket even on the warmest days so that he will have something to hide behind in case he has an erection. These books are read mostly by younger adolescents. But Blume's *Deenie* is read by both junior and senior high students. It is about a pretty teenager whose mother wants her to be a model. But it is discovered that she has scoliosis and must wear an unsightly back brace. An especially interesting aspect of the book, which goes unnoticed by many readers, is that Deenie worries that her back problem might be related to the fact that she masturbates.

What has made Blume's books so popular is their refreshing candor about worries that young people really do have. Another plus is that physical development is not treated separately from emotional and social development. This is why Blume's books are more fun to read (and more controversial) than are factual books about the development of the human body.

But the problem novel has not stopped with treating the more or less typical problems of growing up. It has gone on to explore such physical problems as drug addiction in, for example, *Go Ask Alice*, S. E. Hinton's *That Was Then, This Is Now*, Sharon Bell Mathis' *Teacup Full of Roses*, and Alice Childress' *A Hero Ain't Nothin' But a Sandwich*. Teenage alcoholism is the subject of Sandra Scoppettone's *The Late Great Me* and Robert Wagnen's *Sarah T.—Portrait of a Teen-Age Alcoholic*.

Death is another formerly taboo subject that appears in the problem novel. In John Donovan's *Wild in the World* the members of an isolated farm family die one by one. Jean Renvoize's *A Wild Thing* ends with the lonely death of the protagonist. And in Charles P. Crawford's *Three-Legged Race*, three teenage patients in a hospital—one with leukemia—develop a supportive friendship. Another story in which leukemia plays a part is Gunnel Beckman's *Admission to the Feast*. In it nineteen-year-old Annika Hallin accidentally learns from a substitute doctor that she has leukemia. She flees by herself to her family's summer cottage where she tries to sort out her reactions:

> I don't think I understood it until last night . . . that I, Annika, . . . will just be put away, wiped out, obliterated. . . . And here on earth everything will just go on. . . . I shall never have more than this little scrap of life.

It is almost harder to write a believable and yet not totally depressing story about someone who is not going to die but who has a severe physical problem that cannot be cured. Robin Brancato succeeded in doing this in her book *Winning*. It is the story of English teacher Ann Treer and an injured high-school football player, Gary Madden. When the book opens, he has not been told that he is permanently paralyzed. Ann has reluctantly agreed to tutor him at the hospital, and she is surprised when he asks her to bring him some books from the library:

> "Which ones?"
> "Books—that I could read—that we could read when you're here."
> "O.K. What books?"
> "Books about what's wrong with me. You know, about spine injuries."

She protests that surely he ought to ask his doctor who would not only know what books to recommend but could also give him whatever information he needs. But Gary doesn't want to ask the doctor; in fact, he doesn't want anyone to know that he is curious so Ann agrees:

"I'll do what I can," she said. "You mustn't count on me, though. I don't know what books I can get."

Gary smiled ironically. "Just get one that widens my view of the world."

"So you do see the value of books!" Ann said.

"Yeah. They tell us about ourselves."

As Ann Treer leaves, she ponders why Gary has chosen her to be his agent in confirming his suspicions and concludes that it is:

because she wasn't as likely to judge him as the doctor was, probably. Not about to measure his manhood as his friends might. Because she hadn't borne him, with all the pain and expectations surrounding that. Because she didn't worship him and hanker for him, as Diane did.

The value of such fictional treatments as the ones cited in this section is that they involve the reader in the problem from many different viewpoints. A relationship is shown between physical and emotional problems. For example, one of the strong points of Brancato's book is that it shows the ripple effect of Gary's accident: how it changes his friends, his parents, his girlfriend, and his teacher. In one brief moment their definition of winning is changed forever. In the new situation, surviving—just wanting to survive—means winning, and readers cheer with Gary when he makes it through the depression that causes some of his hospital mates to commit suicide.

Sex and Sex Roles

We will give some examples of the different kinds of sex-related problems treated in fiction here, but for a fuller discussion of books treating sex see the appropriate sections in Chapter 7 ("The Love Romance"), Chapter 11 ("Books About Sex"), and Chapter 13 ("Sex: Because It's There").

In nearly all books about growing up, sexual maturity probably plays some part, but what has surprised or offended many people about the new problem novels is that they have gone into such specific details and into problem areas far removed from the idealistic dreams that we have for our young people. The mental anguish and social punishment that accompanies a nontraditional sexual preference are dealt with in John Donovan's *I'll Get There. It Better Be Worth the Trip*, Lynn Hall's *Sticks and Stones*, Isabelle Holland's *The Man Without a Face*, and Sandra Scoppettone's *Trying Hard to Hear You*. The physical, emotional, and societal aspects of rape are treated in two popular books: Richard Peck's *Are You in the House Alone?* and Patricia Dizenzo's *Why Me?* Abortion is the subject of Jeannette Eyerly's melodramatic *Bonnie Jo, Go Home*. It also appears in Norma Klein's two books *It's Not What You Expect* and *Love Is One of the Choices* with much less emphasis on the trauma of it.

Premarital pregnancy is the problem in Ann Head's *Mr. and Mrs. Bo Jo Jones*, Zoa Sherburne's *Too Bad About the Haines Girl*, Jean Thompson's *House of Tomorrow*, Margaret Maze Craig's *It Could Happen to Anyone*, Nora Stirling's *You Would if You Loved Me*,

Jeannette Eyerly's *A Girl Like Me*, Patricia Dizenzo's *Phoebe*, Paul Zindel's *My Darling, My Hamburger*, and John Neufeld's *For All the Wrong Reasons*. W. Keith Kraus analyzed these novels in "Cinderella in Trouble: Still Dreaming and Losing" and concluded that "the old double standard is reinforced by the so-called new realism."[5] He compared the wish-fulfillment nature of the stories to the old romances in which the girl is at the beginning an outsider who is discovered by a popular athlete. As she begins to date, a whole new social world opens up to her. But the dating leads to petting, and then to sex, and finally pregnancy and unhappiness. He lamented that "the sexual act itself is never depicted as joyful, and any show of intimacy carries a warning of future danger."

Many new problem novels go into areas far removed from the idealistic dreams we have for our young people.

An equally interesting aspect of the whole matter of sex is that of what Havig-hurst labels as "achieving a masculine or feminine social role." When he first outlined the adolescent developmental tasks during the 1950s, there was nothing very contro-versial about the idea that boys and girls should aspire to their proper sex roles, but today such a statement sets many people's teeth on edge. On one side of the issue are those who say that finding one's sex role is nothing more than finding one's self. They believe that there is no such thing as an innately male or an innately female role, that these roles have evolved in cultures from people's tendencies to exaggerate and to classify and categorize. They say that the few physical differences between males and females that do exist have been magnified and that successive generations have been taught to make their behavior fit the stereotypes. On the other side of the issue are people who believe that a society is in grave danger when it begins tampering with the patterns of development that the human race has been traveling in for thousands of years.

The confusion and disagreement regarding sex roles is not just an adult problem that youth does not have to think about. On the contrary, it is probably more impor-tant to them than to most adults whose lifestyles and obligations are already so estab-lished that all they can comfortably do is play the game out to its conclusion. In light of this, the best of the current writers are presenting honest portrayals of all kinds of relationships and roles and then hoping that young readers can observe and make choices that will best fit their own personalities and needs.

Rosa Guy's trilogy, *The Friends, Ruby*, and *Edith Jackson*, exemplifies one of these alternative explorations that would not have been presented to young readers a gen-eration ago. The first book in the group treats an unlikely but believable friendship between Phyllisia and Edith who are both rejects in the social structure of their Harlem neighborhood. Phyllisia is too good for the neighborhood. Her family has immigrated from the West Indies and her overly strict restaurant-owner father constantly instills in her a feeling of superiority. He is horrified when Phyllisia brings home poor "ragamuffin" Edith with her ragged coat, holey socks, turned-over shoes, and matted hair. Edith's mother is dead and her father has disappeared. She is trying to hold together her family of four little sisters and two brothers. One unusual thing about the book is that it treats the friendship of two girls with the same kind of serious respect with which boys' friendships have traditionally been written about. In most earlier books, girls' friendships always broke up as soon as boys appeared on the scene.

The second book in Guy's trilogy, *Ruby*, focuses on Phyllisia's sister who is two years older than Edith and Phyll. It includes the story of a lesbian relationship between Ruby and a beautiful classmate. *Publishers Weekly* described the book as "a sensitive novel in which adolescent homosexuality is viewed as nothing so frightening, but perhaps just a way-step toward maturity." In *Edith Jackson*, the protagonist is looking forward to her eighteenth birthday when she hopes to be free of foster homes and The Institution so that she can try again to set up a home for her sisters. But, by the end of the book, the girls are scattered, and Edith realizes that it is her own life she must plan. She has had a brief love affair with a handsome Harlem playboy almost twice her age and is excited at finding herself pregnant. But in the end of the book, she has decided that the mature thing to do is to have an abortion.

A difficulty inherent in the problem novel is that it looks at life from a basically negative stance and in many ways presents an unbalanced set of options. For example, critics ask, how can young readers get insights into the kinds of men and women they want to be and into preparing for marriage and family life when most of the parents in these books are so unsuccessful? The lack of positive role models, particularly adult males and females in family roles, is definitely a problem with the new realism. Writers have presented a much wider range of successful role models who are themselves young adults.

Friends and Society

Books in this category are tied in closely with books that deal with several of the other developmental tasks including the ones about relations with agemates, masculine and feminine social roles, preparing for a career, developing an ideology, and achieving socially responsible behavior.

People used to identify the major problem here as "finding one's place in society," but, today, young people, prodded by adults who were college students in the late 60s and early 70s, are inclined to ask not only how can I fit in, but also how can I change society to fit my needs and the needs of others? Teenage protagonists do not imagine themselves bringing overnight changes to society, but they are very much concerned with injustice and how often young people are the victims of it. Examples of books dealing with this problem include Robert Cormier's *I Am the Cheese,* showing an ominous relationship between organized crime and corrupt government; Virginia Hamilton's *M. C. Higgins, the Great,* D. R. Sherman's *The Lion's Paw,* and Robb White's

Deathwatch, all dealing with disregard for nature; and William Armstrong's *Sounder,* Louise Meriwether's *Daddy Was a Number Runner,* and Jessamyn West's *The Massacre at Fall Creek,* showing the victimization of minorities.

The question of just what is socially responsible behavior is at the root of several interesting books featuring members of minority groups. Some of them are Frank Herbert's *Soul Catcher,* Marilyn Harris' *Hatter Fox,* and Ernest Gaines' *The Autobiography of Miss Jane Pittman.* Society's system of institutions and social workers whose job is to "control" young people's lives when families cannot do the job is brought into question in such books as June Jordan's *His Own Where* and Vera and Bill Cleaver's *Where the Lilies Bloom.* In these books the young protagonists are trying desperately to stay free from such control. Whether or not a thirty-year-old retarded man should be institutionalized is just one of the issues considered in Sue Ellen Bridger's *All Together Now.*

Religion's potential as a controlling force is probably greater than that of any other social institution, and for this reason Chaim Potok's books about Hasidic Jewish families are especially interesting. In spite of the fact that adolescents are concerned about the role of religion in their lives, many writers shy away from treating the subject for fear of offending believers of one faith or another. M. E. Kerr's *Is That You, Miss Blue?* touches on the subject of religion in a relatively light way, but it is valuable in providing an acceptable vehicle for examining and discussing religious values. For example, when one popular high-school biology teacher resigned mid-year to devote full time to distributing Gideon Bibles, his surprised students were very curious, but they certainly did not feel comfortable enough to discuss with him his motives and beliefs. With the help of M. E. Kerr they could openly stare at someone else's very religious teacher and ask the question they really wanted to ask their biology teacher: "Is that the real you?"

It is not just adult society that is scrutinized in these books. Many of them focus on the difficulty of establishing relationships with other teenagers. *The Chocolate War* is not the first or only book to explore negative peer pressure and the power that a gang can hold over individuals. This is one of the areas where the answers to life's questions are very different for adults and for young people. Very few adults are worried about having their lives controlled by a group of teenage toughs, but most high school students—even the outwardly sophisticated ones—have twinges of fear about fellow students like Urek, the antagonist in Sol Stein's *The Magician.* In this book the protagonist is sixteen-year-old Ed Japhet who "could be fairly called an accomplished magician." But after he provides the intermission entertainment at a school dance, Urek and his followers beat him severely because Urek is jealous of Ed's success. The close of the book is ironic because Ed ends up killing Urek and Ed's schoolteacher father phones the same unethical lawyer who had gotten Urek off scot-free in the beginning. Other books that explore teenage gangs and violence include Frank Bonham's *Durango Street,* Kin Platt's *Headman,* and S. E. Hinton's *Rumble Fish.*

Theodore Weesner's *The Car Thief* is different in that readers identify with the boy who steals the cars rather than with the victims. He is sixteen-year-old Alex Housman, and readers meet him the night he decides to go to his first high-school dance. He has to take two buses and walk three quarters of a mile to get there. This takes him two hours, and then, when he arrives, no one acknowledges his presence. They even check in a book to make sure he is a student at Central High School:

> He did not stay long. When he left, on his way to the door, sidestepping politely through the dancers, he had to pause once to let a couple not looking avoid bumping into him. He smiled lightly over this, as if over something cute, something youthful, but if they had bumped into him, and if he had had a knife, he could have ripped their throats with it. Out in the parking lot he took his first car, a Chevrolet Bel Air with keys hanging in the ignition.

A somewhat less disturbing aspect of fitting into society is that of gaining financial independence. For young people this is a two-pronged issue. In the first place, they must somehow get enough money right now to achieve the degree of independence that in their peer group is considered status. In some groups this may be only the money needed to buy soda pop and an occasional ticket to the movies. In other groups the desired goal is to have enough money to pay for clothing, entertainment, and transportation and thus remove them from parental control.

Achieving this kind of immediate financial independence usually means having a part-time job. There is room for more books about this aspect of young adults' lives. Hundreds of thousands of teenagers have jobs in fast food restaurants, but in books in which young people have tried to earn their own living the setting has usually been a rural one. Kristin Hunter's *The Soul Brothers and Sister Lou* is interesting because it shows how a group of black, city youth get the chance to become professional musicians. But in exchange, "lest they become has-beens at seventeen," they have to trade in the fun of improvisation for discipline and perfection.

The second and probably more significant aspect of gaining financial independence has to do with the future. Young adults must choose and prepare for the way they will earn their living in years to come. Making this choice brings about all kinds

In the 1960s the American work ethic was openly challenged by young adults.

of conflicts and problems, particularly between parents, who may have one set of goals, and young people, who may have quite another set, or even no goals at all. In the 1960s the American work ethic was openly challenged by young adults. Middle-class parents were shocked when their children expressed a preference for first choosing a life-style and a place to live and then finding a job to fit those choices.

Another big change brought about by a changing culture is that making a career choice is no longer reserved only for males. Nine out of ten young adult females today will at some time during their lives work outside of the home. The acceptance of this is seen in such books as Norma Klein's *Mom, the Wolfman and Me* and Ursula K. Le

Guin's *Very Far Away from Anywhere Else,* which both include strong female characters with career ambitions. Sidney Offit's *What Kind of Guy Do You Think I Am?* is an interesting reversal of the old stereotype of the woman earning her PHT for "Putting Hubby Through." Eighteen-year-old Ted Cooper decides to forgo his own college plans—they weren't really his, they were his family's—so that he can support his brilliant girlfriend while she finishes up at Princeton.

In realistic fiction the choice of a future career will more often appear as a sub-theme, for example, as part of a parent-child conflict, than as the only issue in the book. An example of this is Chaim Potok's *My Name Is Asher Lev.* It is about a young Jewish boy who persists in his dream to be an artist in spite of the great disappointment this brings to his traditional father who views art as superfluous. A reader who wishes to focus directly on the problem of choosing a career will be more likely to turn to the informative books presented in Chapter 11 or to the biographical-career type books discussed in Chapter 10.

When people say that adolescent literature is a recent development, it is probably the books in this chapter that they are thinking about. Although these books are commonly referred to as the "new realism," the term isn't very accurate. First, many of the books are not realistic. Perhaps the events could have happened to someone, but in the abbreviated space that they have, authors tend to cram in more bad things than would be likely to happen to an individual. And, second, realism appears in many books other than the kinds presented here. For example, a romance might be realistic in its depiction of feelings, a historical novel might be realistic in the details it presents about time and place, and a fantasy might be realistic in its portrayal of believable characters. So the label of "new realism" doesn't fit perfectly. Neither does the label of "problem novel," as in every story that has a plot, there is a problem of some kind.

In the absence of a single term to identify these books, we will conclude this chapter with a brief description of their characteristics. First, they have to contain a significant, contemporary problem treated in a serious and candid fashion. The action usually points in toward the protagonist rather than out toward the world. Because adults and young people face quite different problems, these books are much more likely than are the books discussed in some of the other chapters to appeal exclusively to young readers. None of the protagonists in the books mentioned in this chapter are over twenty-one. And, finally, many of the problems treated (and much of the language used) were taboo in books for young readers until recent years. Some of these books are highly topical, trendy, and sensational. In fact, it is in this genre that both the best and the worst of young adult literature can be found.

ACTIVITIES

1. Read *The Chocolate War* and write an analysis of it based on Havighurst's developmental tasks. How many of them appear somewhere in the book? How are they treated? Which ones get the most attention? Are any of them totally ignored?

2. Read one of the problem novels and analyze the degree to which it is realistic, that is, true to life. You might interview a counselor, a social worker, or a young adult who has had experience with this particular problem. If the book differs from reality, tell how and conjecture on why. Is the author trying to teach a lesson? Make the story more exciting? Simplify it for the sake of brevity? Or something else?

3. Read several books that treat a similar theme, for example, drugs, pregnancy, handicaps (either mental or physical), gangs, or parent-child relationships. Write a paper showing what the books have in common. Some of the questions that you might try to answer include: Are there new stereotypes that have developed? Does each book offer something distinctive? Would you recommend that young adults read all of them, some of them, or none of them? Which is written at the highest level of literary quality? Which at the highest level of popular appeal? Which book is likely to last the longest, and which is the most trendy?

NOTES

[1]Sheila Egoff, "May Hill Arbuthnot Honor Lecture: Beyond the Garden Wall," *Top of the News* 35 (Spring 1979): 257-71.

[2]R. J. Havighurst, *Human Development and Education* (New York: Longmans, Green, 1953), p. 2.

[3]They each had 35; *The Catcher in the Rye* had 21; *The Outsiders,* 19; *A Separate Peace,* 18; *A Day No Pigs Would Die,* 13; and *A Hero Ain't Nothin' But a Sandwich,* 11.

[4]Lou Willett Stanek, "Growing Up Female: The Literary Gaps," *Media and Methods* (September 1976): pp. 46-48.

[5]W. Keith Kraus, "Cinderella in Trouble: Still Dreaming and Losing," *School Library Journal* (January 1975): pp. 18-22.

RECOMMENDED TITLES

For information on the availability of paperback editions of these titles, please consult the most recent edition of *Paperbound Books in Print,* published annually by R. R. Bowker Company.

Parent/Child Relationships

Arundel, Honor. *The Terrible Temptation.* Thomas Nelson, 1971.

Bach, Alice. *A Father Every Few Years.* Harper & Row, 1977.

Blume, Judy. *It's Not the End of the World.* Bradbury, 1972.

Bridgers, Sue Ellen. *Home Before Dark.* Alfred A. Knopf, 1976.

Donovan, John. *I'll Get There. It Better Be Worth the Trip.* Harper & Row, 1969.

———. *Remove Protective Coating a Little at a Time.* Harper & Row, 1973.

Elfman, Blossom. *The Sister Act.* Houghton Mifflin, 1978.

Engebrecht, P. A. *Under the Haystack.* Thomas Nelson, 1973.

Fox, Paula. *Blowfish Live in the Sea.* Bradbury, 1970.

Gaines, Ernest J. *In My Father's House.* Alfred A. Knopf, 1978.

Greene, Bette. *Summer of My German Soldier.* Dial, 1973.

Hamilton, Virginia. *Arilla Sun Down.* Greenwillow, 1976.

Heide, Florence Parry. *Growing Anyway Up.* J. B. Lippincott, 1976.

Kerr, M. E. *Dinky Hocker Shoots Smack.* Harper & Row, 1972.

———. *The Son of Someone Famous.* Harper & Row, 1974.

Mazer, Harry. *The Dollar Man.* Delacorte, 1974.

———. *Guy Lenny.* Delacorte, 1971.

Moggach, Deborah. *You Must Be Sisters.* St. Martin's, 1979.

Myers, Walter Dean. *It Ain't All for Nothin'.* Viking, 1978.

Peck, Robert Newton. *A Day No Pigs Would Die.* Alfred A. Knopf, 1972.

Platt, Kin. *Chloris and the Creeps.* Chilton, 1973.

Richard, Adrienne. *Pistol.* Little, Brown, 1969.

Snyder, Anne. *First Step.* Holt, Rinehart & Winston, 1975.

Stallworth, Anne. *This Time Next Year.* Vanguard, 1972.

Stolz, Mary. *The Edge of Next Year.* Harper & Row, 1974.

———. *Leap Before You Look.* Harper & Row, 1972.

Wersba, Barbara. *Run Softly, Go Fast.* Atheneum, 1970.

Winthrop, Elizabeth. *A Little Demonstration of Affection.* Harper & Row, 1975.

Yep, Lawrence. *Child of the Owl.* Harper & Row, 1977.

Zindel, Paul. *Confessions of a Teenage Baboon.* Harper & Row, 1977.

Body and Self

Arundel, Honor. *The Blanket Word.* Thomas Nelson, 1973.

Bach, Alice. *Mollie Make-Believe.* Harper & Row, 1974.

Beckman, Gunnel. *Admission to the Feast.* Holt, Rinehart & Winston, 1972.

Blume, Judy. *Are You There God? It's Me, Margaret.* Bradbury, 1970.

———. *Deenie.* Bradbury, 1973.

———. *Then Again, Maybe I Won't.* Bradbury, 1971.

Brancato, Robin. *Winning.* Alfred A. Knopf, 1977.

Childress, Alice. *A Hero Ain't Nothin' But a Sandwich.* Coward, McCann & Geoghegan, 1973.

Crawford, Charles P. *Three-Legged Race.* Harper & Row, 1974.

Dixon, Paige. *May I Cross Your Golden River.* Atheneum, 1975.

Donovan, John. *Wild in the World.* Harper & Row, 1971.

Gerson, Corinne. *Passing Through.* Dial, 1978.

Go Ask Alice. Prentice-Hall, 1971.

Green, Hannah. *I Never Promised You a Rose Garden.* Holt, Rinehart & Winston, 1964.

Guest, Judith. *Ordinary People.* Viking, 1976.

Kellogg, Marjorie. *Tell Me That You Love Me, Junie Moon.* Farrar, Straus & Giroux, 1968.

Kingman, Lee. *Head Over Wheels.* Houghton Mifflin, 1978.

Levenkrou, Steven. *The Best Little Girl in the World.* Contemporary Books, 1978.

Lowry, Lois. *A Summer to Die.* Houghton Mifflin, 1977.

Mathis, Sharon Bell. *Teacup Full of Roses.* Viking, 1972.

Neufeld, John. *Lisa Bright and Dark.* S. G. Phillips, 1969.

Plath, Sylvia. *The Bell Jar.* Harper & Row, 1971.

Platt, Kin. *The Boy Who Could Make Himself Disappear.* Chilton, 1968.

———. *Hey Dummy.* Chilton, 1971.

Renvoize, Jean. *A Wild Thing.* Little, Brown, 1971.

Savitz, Harriet May. *The Lionhearted.* John Day, 1975.

Scoppettone, Sandra. *The Late Great Me.* G. P. Putnam's Sons, 1976.

Wagnen, Robert. *Sarah T.—Portrait of a Teen-Age Alcoholic.* Ballantine, 1976.

Windsor, Patricia. *The Summer Before.* Harper & Row, 1973.

Sex and Sex Roles

Beckman, Gunnel. *Mia Alone.* Viking, 1975.

Chambers, Aidan. *Breaktime.* Harper & Row, 1979.

Christman, Elizabeth. *A Nice Italian Girl.* Dodd, Mead, 1976.

Dizenzo, Patricia. *Phoebe.* McGraw-Hill, 1970.

Elfman, Blossom. *The Girls of Huntington House.* Houghton Mifflin, 1972.

Fritzhand, James. *Life Is a Lonely Place.* M. Evans, 1975.

Guy, Rosa. *Ruby.* Viking, 1976.

Hall, Lynn. *Sticks and Stones.* Follett, 1972.

Head, Ann. *Mr. and Mrs. Bo Jo Jones.* G. P. Putnam's Sons, 1967.

Hoffman, Alice. *Property Of.* Farrar, Straus & Giroux, 1977.

Holland, Isabelle. *Man Without a Face.* J. B. Lippincott, 1972.

Klein, Norma. *It's Not What You Expect.* Pantheon, 1973.

———. *Love Is One of the Choices.* Dial, 1979.

Offit, Sidney. *What Kind of Guy Do You Think I Am.* J. B. Lippincott, 1977.

Peck, Richard. *Are You in the House Alone?* Viking, 1976.

Rosen, Winifred. *Cruisin for a Bruisin.* Alfred A. Knopf, 1976.

Scoppettone, Sandra. *Trying Hard to Hear You.* Harper & Row, 1974.

Sherburne, Zoa. *Too Bad About the Haines Girl.* William Morrow, 1967.

Thompson, Jean. *House of Tomorrow.* Harper & Row, 1974.

Zindel, Paul. *My Darling, My Hamburger.* Harper & Row, 1969.

Friends and Society

Armstrong, William. *Sounder.* Harper & Row, 1972.

Bethancourt, T. Ernesto. *New York City Too Far from Tampa Blues.* Holiday House, 1975.

Bonham, Frank. *Cool Cat.* E. P. Dutton, 1977.

———. *Durango Street.* E. P. Dutton, 1965.

———. *Viva Chicano.* E. P. Dutton, 1970.

Bradford, Richard. *Red Sky at Morning.* J. B. Lippincott, 1968.

Bridgers, Sue Ellen. *All Together Now.* Alfred A. Knopf, 1979.

Cleaver, Vera and Bill. *Where the Lilies Bloom.* J. B. Lippincott, 1969.

Cormier, Robert. *After the First Death.* Pantheon, 1979.

———. *The Chocolate War.* Pantheon, 1974.

———. *I Am the Cheese.* Pantheon, 1977.

Danziger, Paula. *Can You Sue Your Parents for Malpractice?* Delacorte, 1979.

———. *The Cat Ate My Gymsuit.* Delacorte, 1974.

———. *The Pistachio Prescription.* Delacorte, 1978.

DeJongh, James and Charles Cleveland. *City Cool.* Random House, 1978.

Gaines, Ernest J. *The Autobiography of Miss Jane Pittman.* Dial, 1971.

Golding, William. *Lord of the Flies.* G. P. Putnam's Sons, 1959.

Guy, Rosa. *Edith Jackson.* Viking, 1978.

———. *The Friends.* Holt, Rinehart & Winston, 1973.

Hamilton, Virginia. *M. C. Higgins the Great.* Macmillan, 1974.

———. *Zeely.* Macmillan, 1967.

Harris, Marilyn. *Hatter Fox.* Random House, 1973.

Hentoff, Nat. *I'm Really Dragged But Nothing Gets Me Down.* Simon & Schuster, 1968.

Herbert, Frank. *Soul Catcher.* G. P. Putnam's Sons, 1972.

Hinton, S. E. *The Outsiders.* Viking, 1967.

———. *Rumble Fish.* Delacorte, 1975.

———. *That Was Then, This Is Now.* Viking, 1971.

Holland, Ruth. *The Room.* Delacorte, 1973.

Holman, Felice. *Slake's Limbo.* Charles Scribner's Sons, 1974.

Hunter, Kristin. *The Soul Brothers and Sister Lou.* Charles Scribner's Sons, 1968.

Jordan, June. *His Own Where.* Thomas Y. Crowell, 1971.

Kerr, M. E. *Is That You, Miss Blue?* Harper & Row, 1975.

Knowles, John. *A Separate Peace.* Macmillan, 1960.

Levoy, Myron. *Alan and Naomi.* Harper & Row, 1977.

Mazer, Harry. *The War on Villa Street.* Delacorte, 1978.

Mazer, Norma Fox. *A Figure of Speech.* Delacorte, 1973.

McCannon, Dindga. *Peaches.* Lothrop, Lee & Shepard, 1974.

Meriwether, Louise. *Daddy Was a Number Runner.* Prentice-Hall, 1970.

Mohr, Nicholasa. *El Bronx Remembered.* Harper & Row, 1975.

———. *In Nueva York.* Dial, 1977.

———. *Nilda.* Harper & Row, 1973.

O'Dell, Scott. *Kathleen, Please Come Home.* Houghton Mifflin, 1978.

Platt, Kin. *Headman.* Greenwillow, 1975.

Potok, Chaim. *The Chosen.* Simon & Schuster, 1967.

———. *In the Beginning.* Alfred A. Knopf, 1975.

———. *My Name Is Asher Lev.* Alfred A. Knopf, 1972.

Salinger, J. D. *The Catcher in the Rye.* Little, Brown, 1951.

Samuels, Gertrude. *Run, Shelley, Run!* Thomas Y. Crowell, 1974.

Sherman, D. R. *The Lion's Paw.* Doubleday, 1975.

Stein, Sol. *The Magician.* Delacorte, 1971.

Swarthout, Glendon. *Bless the Beasts and Children.* Doubleday, 1970.

Taylor, Mildred. *Roll of Thunder, Hear My Cry.* Dial, 1976.

Townsend, John Rowe. *Good-bye to the Jungle.* J. B. Lippincott, 1967.

———. *Trouble in the Jungle.* J. B. Lippincott, 1969.

Weesner, Theodore. *The Car Thief.* Random House, 1972.

Zindel, Paul. *The Pigman.* Harper & Row, 1968.

7

The Old Romanticism

Of Wishing and Winning

A kind of story that serves as a counterbalance to the depressing realism of the problem novel is the romance. Romances were among the very first stories to be told. People like to hear them because they have happy endings, and the tellers of romances are willing to exaggerate just enough to make the stories more interesting than real life. A basic part of the romance is a quest of some sort. In the course of the quest, the protagonist will experience doubts and will undergo severe trials, but he or she will be successful in the end. This success will be all the more appreciated because of the difficulties that the protagonist has suffered. The extremes of suffering and succeeding are characteristic of the romance. In good moments, it is like a happy daydream, but in bad moments it resembles a nightmare.

The word *romance* comes from the Latin adverb *romanice* which means "in the Latin manner." It is with this meaning that Latin, Italian, Spanish, and French are described as romance languages. The literary meaning of *romance* grew out of its use by English speakers to refer to French dialects, which were much closer to Latin than was their own Germanic language of English. Later it was used to refer to Old French and finally to anything written in French.

Many of the French stories that were read by English speakers were tales about knights who set out on such bold adventures as slaying dragons, rescuing princesses from ogres, and defeating the wicked enemies of a righteous king. Love was often an element in these stories, for the knight was striving to win the hand of a beloved maiden. So, today, when a literary piece is referred to as a romance, it usually contains either or both adventure and love.

The romance is appealing to teenagers because it is matched in several ways to their roles in life. The symbols that are used often relate to youthfulness and hope, and, in keeping with this, many of the protagonists, even in the traditional and classic tales, are in their teens. Modern young adults are at an age when they leave home or anticipate leaving to embark on a new way of life. It is more likely to be called "moving out" than "going on a romantic quest," but the results are much the same. And seeking and securing a "true love" usually—but not always—takes up a greater proportion of the time and energy of the young than of middle-aged adults. And the exaggeration that is part of the romantic mode is quite honestly felt by young people. Never at any other stage of life do people feel their emotions quite so intensely. It was noticing this intensity about his own children that led Robert Cormier to begin writing about young protagonists. He observed that in one afternoon at the beach, they could emotionally go through what to an adult would be a whole month of experience.

Another teenage characteristic particularly appropriate to the romantic mode is the optimism of youth. Whether or not young people, either as a group or as individuals, are really more optimistic than their elders, they are presumed to be so, and a writer doing the same story for adults might be more tempted to present it as irony than as romance.

THE ADVENTURE-ROMANCE

The great satisfaction of the adventure-romance lies in its wish fulfillment, as when David slays Goliath, when Cinderella is united with the noble prince and given the fitting role of queen, and when Dorothy and Toto find their way back to Kansas. In every culture there are legends, myths, and folk and fairy tales which follow the pattern of the adventure-romance. In the Judeo-Christian culture, the Biblical story of Joseph is a prime example. Early in life, he is chosen and marked as a special person. When his brothers sell him as a slave to the Egyptian traders, he embarks on his quest for wisdom and knowledge. The climax of the story comes years later during the famine that brings his brothers to Pharaoh's palace. Without recognizing Joseph, they beg for food. His forgiveness of them and his generosity to them is final proof of his worthiness.

It is a distinguishing feature of the adventure-romance that the happy ending is achieved only after the hero has proven his or her worth by undergoing a crisis or an ordeal. Usually as part of the ordeal the hero must make a sacrifice, must be wounded, or must leave some part of his or her body, even if it is only sweat or tears. The real loss is that of innocence, but it is usually symbolized by a physical loss as in Norse mythology when Odin gives one of his eyes to pay for gaining wisdom, or in J. R. R. Tolkien's *Lord of the Rings* when Frodo, who has already suffered many wounds, finds that he can't throw the ring back and so must let Gollum take his finger along with the ring. What is purchased with the suffering of the hero is nearly always some kind of wisdom, even though wisdom is not what the hero set out to find.

The adventure-romance has elements applicable to the task of entering the adult world, which all young people anticipate. The story pattern includes the three stages of formal initiation as practiced in many cultures. First, the young and innocent person is separated both physically and spiritually from the nurturing love of friends and family.

Then, during this separation, the hero, who embodies noble qualities, undergoes a test of courage and stamina that may be either mental, psychological, or physical. In the final stage the young person is reunited with former friends and family in a new role of increased status.

One Fat Summer as Adventure-Romance

How this archetypal initiation rite can be translated into a modern, somewhat realistic story for young adults is shown through Robert Lipsyte's *One Fat Summer* (1977). It is the story of a quest for self-respect. When the protagonist begins it, he is quite unaware of the magnitude of his undertaking. As part of the quest, he is isolated from his family. The suffering that he undergoes is something that no one else could do for him, but it makes the victory that much sweeter.

The story begins on the Fourth of July with fourteen-year-old Bobby Marks feeling sorry for himself at the Rumson Lake Community Association Carnival. He hates summertime because that is when his family moves out to Rumson Lake where everybody takes off his clothes and the other kids can see "your thick legs and your wobbly backside and your big belly and your soft arms. And they laugh." Bobby weighs more than 200 pounds. He doesn't know how much more because he always bails out when the pointer on the bathroom scale starts to climb past the 200 pound mark.

What happens in the book is that Bobby takes a job as an underpaid and over-worked yard boy. He does it only so he won't have to be a camp counselor or a mother's helper on the beach where people would see his fat and laugh at him. By the

---

What is purchased with the suffering of the hero is nearly always wisdom, though wisdom is not what the hero seeks.

---

end of the summer, Bobby weighs 175 pounds, which isn't exactly thin, but it isn't what anyone would call fat either. His loss of weight is his tangible reward, but, more important than this is his coming to know himself and to understand, at least partially, the motives of the half-dozen people who play significant roles in his life that summer. This understanding brings him relief from the fears that had haunted him during all the summers his family had spent at Rumson Lake.

Bobby does not lose weight or come to these understandings without the central struggle or ordeal that is at the heart of all romances. His physical ordeal is the task of keeping Dr. Kahn's huge hillside lawn immaculate. In the eyes of the world cutting a lawn may not seem like the kind of Herculean task that would qualify for a romantic quest, but for Bobby it was such:

The longer I cut, the bigger the lawn seemed to get. A friend of my father's once showed us his color movies of a mule trip down into the Grand Canyon. He said that the farther down he went, the bigger the canyon seemed to get. From the top, it looked like just a huge hole, but as he descended, the walls of the canyon seemed to flatten back and the hole became another world. It was something like that with the lawn. . . .

I tried to go faster, but then I went over a stone. Clang. The blade batted it against a tree. Thud. I got panicky. The rest of the afternoon was a blur. The heat was pounding into the ground and my clothes stuck to me. My underwear was strangling me. Sweat pouring down my forehead stung my eyes and blinded me. My hands and feet were burning. My lungs were bursting.

As befits the mode of romance, the place that Bobby works is both idyllic and far removed from the small houses and cottages that make up the middle-class beach community that he is accustomed to. Dr. Kahn's house is on the other side of the lake, and at first Bobby's family and friends do not know that he is working. When Bobby first looks at Dr. Kahn's lawn it is "like a velvet sea, a green velvet sea that flowed up from the gray shore of the county road to surround a great white house with white columns. The house looked like a proud clipper ship riding the crest of the ocean."

A more important challenge than that of the lawn is the one that Bobby meets in the ex-Marine Willie Rumson who is the kind of villain that appears in nearly all romances. It is in keeping with the romance pattern that the characters, other than the protagonist, are one-sided. They are either villains or angels. Since a romance is essentially the story of one person's achievement and development, everything else is a condensation. For the sake of efficiency, the personalities of the supporting characters are shown through symbols, metaphors, and significant details, all of which highlight the qualities that are important to the story. (Dr. Kahn, Bobby's employer, is presented as such a negative stereotype, though, that some readers have been offended.)

It is not usually the villain whom the hero has to defeat ultimately, but the villain stands in the way of the real accomplishment and gives the hero an enemy upon whom to focus. Without some scary, nightmarish, and usually life-threatening incident, the happy ending could not be appreciated. At first, Willie and his friends just tease Bobby calling him "The Crisco Kid" because he's "fat in the can," and asking him if he has a license to drag that trailer behind him. But then Willie can't get a job, and he decides that he wants to be Dr. Kahn's yard worker. He demands that Bobby quit the job, and, when it becomes apparent that he won't, Willie and his buddies get mean.

In keeping with the form of the romance it is significant in the ordeal that follows that Bobby experiences something similar to what in the traditional romance would have been a vision. He has been stripped of his clothes and left on an island in the lake. Symbolically the peaceful setting of the lake has changed into something fearsome. The night "exploded with thunder and lightning and the wind drove nails of rain" into his naked body. Bobby is lying in the mud and puddles where they dumped him and he thinks he's going to drown, but then he hears a voice.

"On your feet, Marks."

I looked around. I saw no one in the darkness.

"Stand up."

The voice was familiar.

"Up. Get up."

Lightning hit the water, the black sky parted like curtains at high noon, flooding the island with light. But there was no one there.

"I SAID GET UP. YOU CAN DO IT, BIG FELLA."

The water touched my lips. Be so easy now to relax into the soft mud, get it over with.

"ON YOUR FEET. YOU'RE NOT GONNA LET THOSE BASTARDS KILL YOU. YOU BEAT THE LAWN, YOU CAN BEAT THEM. YOU'RE TOUGH. YOU RAN, YOU FOUGHT, YOU'LL DO IT AGAIN. YOU'LL DO IT TILL YOU WIN."

I recognized the voice.

Captain Marks, Commander Marks, Big Bob Marks.

It was me.

I stood up.

Another element of the romance is that the protagonists put forth efforts on their own behalf. By standing up, Bobby proves that he is willing to do this and is, therefore, worthy of outside help. As it often does in the romance, the outside help comes from an unexpected source. A cousin of Willie's arrives in a canoe and takes Bobby back to Rumson Beach. All that Bobby loses in the ordeal is a sock. What he finds is a new kind of confidence. This prepares him for the final confrontation with Willie Rumson, which, fortunately for Bobby, turns out to be an underwater fight. Bobby has the advantage because all his life he has swum underwater to keep people from seeing how fat he is. Bobby wins the fight, but this physical act is only a symbolic way of showing the emotional victory that Bobby achieves over his own misunderstandings and fears.

The whole experience gives him enough confidence to face Dr. Kahn at last and ask him for the pay that was originally advertised for the job:

He stared at me. Just like he did the very first time, a lifetime ago. But those shotgun eyes didn't scare me anymore.

"You should pay me for this summer," said Dr. Kahn. "I've watched you change from a miserable fat boy into a fairly presentable young man. On my lawn. On my time."

"You didn't do it, Dr. Kahn. I did it."

This last statement sums up a prime requisite for a modern young adult romance. The hero has to accomplish the task and it has to be one that readers can respect and at the same time imagine themselves accomplishing.

Other Stories of Accomplishment

Isabelle Holland's story *Heads You Win, Tails I Lose* has a similar theme to *One Fat Summer*, only it is not as believable. With the help of pills stolen from her mother's dresser drawer, the protagonist loses enough weight within six weeks to transform her from a pudgy, unpopular adolescent into a thin, pretty girl who for the first time is being asked on more dates than she can accept.

Despite the lack of believability, the wish-fulfillment nature of the story is so powerful that Holland says it outsells several of her better books including the highly acclaimed *Man Without a Face*. Some adults have objected to this kind of portrayal of the romantic quest. They understand the need to show in some tangible way that the young person has made an accomplishment, but they fear that young readers will interpret the physical achievement literally rather than figuratively. Teenagers are already overly concerned about their physical bodies and any defects that they might have. Most physical defects—even many cases of obesity—cannot be changed. They would therefore prefer stories in which the protagonist comes to terms with the problem and adjusts to it or compensates for it. Mildred Lee's *The Skating Rink* is such a story. Tuck Faraday stutters, and, because of this, he withdraws into such a shell that everyone assumes that he is stupid. Then Pete Degley comes to town and builds a roller skating rink. He likes the shy Tuck, who hardly ever speaks, and recognizes his need to do something special. He trains Tuck as a skater, and, on opening night, Tuck's dreams are fulfilled as he performs with Pete Degley's wife in front of the whole community.

In referring to the genre, probably the term *accomplishment-romance* would be more accurate than *adventure-romance* because the stories don't always involve an adventure or a trip, but they do involve an accomplishment of some kind. The significant accomplishment is usually a mental one even if, for the sake of the story, it is dramatized as a physical one. When there is no symbolization, then it is more likely that the author will have to show the protagonist suffering actual defeat or death. This would result in irony or tragedy rather than romance. The tone the author uses also can change a story from romance to irony or tragedy. Although romance has its share of somber moments, the overall tone must be relatively light and optimistic. For example, Holden Caulfield sets out on a quest, but J. D. Salinger's *The Catcher in the Rye* does not qualify as a romance. It is too grim. The same could be said for Hannah Greene's *I Never Promised You a Rose Garden* and Judith Guest's *Ordinary People*. These three books contain many of the elements of the traditional romance including worthy young heroes who set out to find wisdom and understanding. In the course of the stories, they make physical sacrifices but these are real rather than symbolic, for example, the suicide attempts in the latter two titles. The wise and kindly psychiatrists are modern realistic counterparts to the white witches, the wizards, and the helpful gods and goddesses who in the traditional romances have always been there to aid and instruct worthy young heroes much as Merlin did with young Arthur. The difference between the traditional helpers in romances and the modern ones in realistic stories is that the realistic ones lack magic; they must rely on hard painstaking work. This is what is communicated by the title *I Never Promised You a Rose Garden*. Deborah Blau's psychiatrist says this to her when she wants to warn the young girl that even when she is "cured" and has left the mental institution, life will still be full of problems. If Greene's book had been a romance, then there would have been no mention of this fact. Readers could have pictured Deborah leaving the institution and living "happily ever after."

The important role of physical effort and danger in the romantic mode has caused people to assume falsely that the adventure romance is an exclusively male story. But, of course, in real life it isn't only males who experience physical danger, even though cultural expectations have caused society to place males, more than females, in dangerous situations. This has naturally affected the genre and reader's expectations. For example, Irene Hunt wrote two stories, one about a boy and one about a girl traveling the route to maturity. One was a war story (*Across Five Aprils*) and the other one was the story of an orphan raised by an unmarried school teacher (*Up a Road Slowly*). It is to be expected that she would put the male protagonist in the war story and the female protagonist in the gentler, home-oriented story.

An unusual war-related story in which a thirteen-year-old girl achieves personal maturity by actually going on a romantic quest is T. Degens' *Transport 7-41-R*. The story is set in Germany one year after the end of World War II. The girl's parents, who for physical and/or psychological reasons can no longer afford to have her at home, arrange papers saying that she is a former resident of Cologne so that she will be given a place on the train as a returning refugee. Her parents are supposedly sending her to

The significant accomplishment is usually a mental one, even if it is dramatized as a physical one.

a school, but she's not even sure it exists, and her own goal is to find her older brother Jochen. She imagines that once she is with him, everything will be wonderful. During the train trip she grows close to an elderly couple, the Lauritzens. Midway, the wife dies and the girl assists the old man in keeping his wife's death a secret because the whole reason for his trip was to take her "home" and give her a real burial. The girl helps the old man to succeed in his promise to his wife, but in the process she has to give as a bribe to the cemetery attendant her leather boots, which were the only things of value she owned. This is her symbolic sacrifice.

The story doesn't have a totally happy ending, but the girl is nevertheless in a far better position than at the beginning of the journey. She is no longer all alone. She has a companion and a purpose in life. She is not going to give up her independence or her search for her brother, but neither is she going to live in limbo waiting for him to come and make everything wonderful. She has come to the realization that it is up to her. And the story ends with her and the old man leaving the cemetery knowing that they have a lot of work to do.

This acceptance of the compromised dream is another element of the romance pattern that is particularly meaningful to young adults. Many of them are just beginning to achieve some of their life-long goals, and they are finding that the end of the rainbow, which is a symbolic way of saying such things as "When I graduate," "When we get married," "When I'm eighteen," or "When I have my own apartment," is illusory. Like the characters in the romances, they are not sorry that they have ventured for they have indeed found something worthwhile, but it is seldom the pot of gold that they had imagined.

Jean George's *Julie of the Wolves,* which is read by younger adolescents, is a classic example of the romantic quest ending in a compromised dream. Julie's separation from her Eskimo family and friends is a result of her running away from the retarded Daniel who was planning to make her his wife in fact as well as in name. She sets out with the vague and unrealistic goal of running away to her pen pal in San Francisco. As she gains wisdom this changes to a decision to live in the old ways. Amaroq, the great wolf, lends "miraculous" help to her struggle for survival on the Arctic tundra. The climax comes when she learns that her father still lives and that she has arrived at his village. But she is disillusioned when she finds that he has married a "gussack" and pilots planes for hunters. She slips away to return to the tundra, but that night when the temperature falls far below zero and "the ice thundered and boomed, roaring like drumbeats across the Arctic," Tornait, Julie's golden plover who has been her faithful companion, dies in spite of all that Julie does to save him.

Tornait is the last symbol of Julie's innocence and as she mourns his death she comes to accept the fact that the life of both the wolf and the Eskimo is changing and she points her boots toward her father and the life that he now leads. Through her quest, she gains the understanding that her life must change, but she also gains something unexpected. She learns a great deal about her native land and the animals whose home it is. Readers are optimistic that Julie will not forget what she has experienced and that she will have some part in protecting it, though perhaps not to the degree that she would have desired.

Virginia Hamilton's *M. C. Higgins the Great* is another example of the compromised dream. A young boy must settle for less than he wants because of the selfishness of adults who pay little heed to ecology. Strip miners have threatened the security of M. C.'s Appalachian family by taking the coal from the top of the mountain on which their home is located. A great spoil is gradually creeping toward the house. M. C. thinks the family should leave and move to the city. He envisions his mother becoming a famous singer, but a young girl who is travelling through helps M. C. to get a more realistic view of the family's chances of being transformed through his mother's singing. M. C. decides that there is something worth saving in his family heritage and their third-generation home on the mountain. He begins building a retaining wall behind the house.

A part of the book that makes it especially interesting as a romance is the role played by M. C.'s steel pole with the bicycle seat mounted on top. It is while sitting on this pole and contemplating the surrounding countryside that M. C. comes to his realization. In traditional romances, the protagonist usually receives the vision or insight "in a high or isolated place like a mountain top, an island, or a tower."[1] M. C.'s pole fills these qualifications and is at the same time unique and intriguing. It is also significant that M. C. earned his pole through his own physical efforts. His father gave it to him for swimming the Ohio River.

Since the pattern of the romance has been so clearly outlined by critics, and since its popularity has passed the test of time with honors, it would seem to be a very easy story to write. The plot has already been worked out. All an author needs to do is develop a likable protagonist, figure out a quest, fill in the supporting roles with stock characters, and then supply a few interesting details. But it is far from being this simple. Sometimes, as in dance, the things that look the simplest are in fact the hardest to execute. To be effective, they must look as though they are effortless—simply floating on air—but achieving such an effect is never easy. The plot must not be so obvious that a reader will recognize it as "the same old thing." The really good author will develop a unique situation that on the surface will appear to be simply a good story. Its appeal as a romantic quest should be at a deep almost subconscious level, with readers experiencing a sense of déjà vu. It is as if their own life story is being told because the romantic quest is everyone's story. All people are searching for answers to the great questions of life.

Characterization is especially important in relation to the protagonist in an accomplishment- or adventure-romance. Readers must be able to identify with the hero. As *Julie of the Wolves* proves, this does not mean that the hero has to live in the same life style or even have the same conflicts as the reader. But it does mean that the emotions must be ones that the reader can understand, and the author has to present them in such a way as to create empathy.

In spite of the fact that the adventure-romance is one of the most common patterns in books for young adults, relatively few titles are listed in this chapter. This is because there are not many books that are adventure-romances and nothing more. It is more common for the elements of the adventure-romance, that is, the worthy young hero embarking on a quest in which wisdom is gained, to be worked into other genres. Obviously this pattern is crucial to the books featured in Chapter 10 on heroes. Many science fiction and fantasy stories are also based on this pattern as shown in Chapter 9. When the adventure itself seemed to overshadow the accomplishment, the books were included in Chapter 8 as adventure or suspense stories.

THE LOVE-ROMANCE

The love-romance is of a slightly different nature, but it shares many characteristics with the adventure-romance. They both are symbolically associated with youth and with springtime. There is an ordeal or a problem to be overcome followed by a happy ending. The "problem" is invariably the successful pairing of a likable young couple. An old definition of the love-romance pattern is, "Boy meets girl, boy loses girl, boy wins girl." This is a fairly accurate summary except that with teenage literature it is the other way around. Most of them are told from the girl's point of view. She is the one who meets, loses, and finally wins a boy.

The tone of the love-romance is lighter than that of the adventure-romance. In a love story the protagonist neither risks nor gains as much as in an adventure. Notwithstanding *Romeo and Juliet,* people seldom die, emotionally or physically, because of young love. For this reason, the love-romance tends to be less serious in its message. Its power lies in its wish fulfillment.

Seventeenth Summer and *Forever* as Love-Romances

As both an illustration of the love-romance and a demonstration of how little the pattern has changed over the past three-and-a-half decades, we will compare Maureen Daly's *Seventeenth Summer* (1942) to Judy Blume's *Forever* (1975). Both of these books have been, and continue to be, extremely popular. Although their titles appear to be opposite in meaning, they really say the same thing because "forever" carries with it an understood negation. The point of Blume's book is that the love affair is not "forever," just as Daly's point is that the romance is only for one significant summer.

Both books are about a quest. In *Forever* it begins when Katherine meets Michael symbolically on New Year's Eve, and in *Seventeenth Summer* it begins when Angie meets Jack "at the very beginning of the summer." It is part of the pattern that the important positive events in the stories are set in idyllic surroundings. Jack has his boat and the beach house at the lake. Michael is a skier, and the first time he and Katherine make love is when they go to his sister's ski cabin in Vermont with "beautiful fresh snow everywhere and miles and miles of woods."

Both Jack and Michael are in the vanguard of what was considered socially acceptable when the books were written. Jack smokes a pipe and drinks beer. For 1942, this was almost revolutionary in a teenage book. What Blume does to characterize Michael as more "worldly" than Katherine is to show that in the past Michael smoked pot but has made a decision against it for the future. Another indication of Michael's worldliness is the fact that he has had VD, which he got from a girl in Maine. Because it is important in wish fulfillment that the girl be the first one the boy has ever loved, Blume is careful to show that this was purely a physical thing. Michael did not even know the girl's name, so he couldn't get in touch with her to let her know she had it. The girls are portrayed as being more innocent because they are the real protagonists, and it is important that they embody the virtues held noblest by society.

Few boys have read *Seventeenth Summer;* more have read *Forever,* but it too is basically a girl's book. When it became a best seller, many adult males in the profession: librarians, high-school English teachers, and college instructors of adolescent literature read it. For some of them it was the first love-romance they had read seriously, and their reactions to the individual book were tied in with reactions to the genre or type. It made many of them feel uncomfortable and they snickered about it at professional meetings. One frequently quoted comment was, "The only character whose name I can remember is a penis called Ralph."

The stories are definitely female oriented. It is not just a coincidence that the protagonists in both *Seventeenth Summer* and *Forever* have only sisters, no brothers. The little sisters represent what Angie and Katherine used to be. Angie's older sisters and Katherine's two friends, Sybil and Erica, are foils in the stories. Their experiences with boys make the protagonists' romances seem so much better in contrast. The fathers in each family play very small roles. In contrast, the mother-daughter relationships are rather fully developed as warm and mutually supportive. Interestingly, Judy Blume dedicated her book to her daughter, and Maureen Daly dedicated hers to her mother.

About the only characters with whom male readers can identify are the boyfriends, and there are cultural attitudes that make this less than desirable. As already shown, Daly and Blume were careful to characterize the boys as "good catches." The crux of the problem is that people don't want to be "caught" or "hooked." For a teenage boy this is a disquieting idea, but for a girl the daydream of having a boy "fall" for her is the modern day counterpart to having a fairy godmother come and grant three wishes. As Angie explains:

> It's funny what a boy can do. One day you're nobody and the next day you're the girl that some fellow goes with and the other fellows look at you harder and wonder what you've got and wish that they'd been the one to take you out first. And the girls say hello and want you to walk down to the drugstore to have Cokes with them because the boy who likes you might come along and he might have other boys with him. Going with a boy gives you a new identity—especially going with a fellow like Jack Duluth.

In both books the girls are the ones to initiate the end of the romance. In *Seventeenth Summer,* Angie has always planned to leave and go to college at the end of the summer; in *Forever,* Katherine meets Theo and in a relatively painless fashion transfers her affections from one boy to another. In spite of this independence on the part of the girls, they have only the vaguest of goals for their own lives. When Angie is talking to Jack, trying to instill in him a greater ambition, she encourages him to "read a lot," but her only suggestion for herself is that, "I could brush my hair every night." And at Michael's family graduation party, when one of his uncles asks Katherine what she wants to do with her life, all she can answer is that she wants to be happy "and make other people happy too."

Variations on the Love-Romance

It was probably to keep the emphasis on the romances that the authors made Angie and Katherine so here-and-now oriented. But this is not an absolute for a love-romance. For example, an interesting contrast is Ursula K. Le Guin's *Very Far Away from Anywhere Else.* In this book the two protagonists are each interested in future careers and in the course of their relationship they come to some significant understandings about themselves and what they want to do. For this reason it is hard to decide whether to identify this book as an accomplishment-romance or a love-romance. It is narrated by seventeen-year-old Owen Thomas Griffiths, a high-school intellectual who dreams of becoming a truly great scientist. Through his friendship with Natalie Field, a talented musician pursuing her own dream of becoming a composer, he faces up to the pressures felt by many teenagers who for one reason or another are outside of the mainstream. The opening of the book reads:

> If you'd like a story about how I won my basketball letter and achieved fame, love, and fortune, don't read this. I don't know what I achieved in the six months I'm going to tell you about. I achieved something, all right, but I think it may take me the rest of my life to find out what.

The pattern of the love story is even more static than that of the adventure- or accomplishment-romance, so it would be natural to ask what it is that makes one story better than another or keeps love stories from being interchangeable—as indeed, many of them are.

The answer is that the same qualities that make any other piece of fiction outstanding may serve to make the love-romance special. It may be that the author has done an exceptionally good job with characterization, with plot, with setting, or with style or tone. Of these, probably the most important is characterization. If readers do not feel that they know the man and woman as individuals, then they can't identify with them and consequently won't care whether they make it or not. For example, the great success of Erich Segal's *Love Story* was based not so much on the fact that it was a sad story as on the fact that readers felt the sadness because they had come to know Jennifer and Oliver. Every day there are equally sad stories to be found in the obituary columns of newspapers, but casual readers do not shed tears as they do in reading about Jennifer's death. Jennifer and Oliver are believable and likable. The dialogue between them rings true and has a range to it that is not often found. It goes from the tender and touching to the irreverent and shocking that was so much in vogue during the late 1960s.

The plot may be more exciting than usual. When this happens, it is usually because there is an outside force trying to keep the young people apart. In Sarah Patterson's *The Distant Summer*, it is World War II that is the threat. Kathie is the sixteen-year-old daughter of an English rector, and Johnny is an American pilot who wanders into her father's church to play the organ. The surprise ending is that their love survives through incredible odds even as Johnny flies daily bombing raids, and then through the next thirty years of what is apparently quite ordinary living.

The characterization is excellent, but the bonus for readers is that they can vicariously live not just the love story but also a part of World War II that they probably have never thought about.

Having something extra like this will not save a weak story, but it will add interest to a strong one. Jessamyn West's *The Massacre at Fall Creek* is a well-liked piece of historical fiction. It illustrates how a love story that is integrated into a larger story can be more interesting because of the dual plot. Readers get to know the young couple through the part they play in the first American court case (Fall Creek, Indiana, 1824) in which white men were tried, convicted, and executed for killing native Americans.

A well-developed setting may add variety and interest to what otherwise would be a typical love story. For example, in 1971 June Jordan's *His Own Where* proved that a well-written love story could be just as satisfying set in an inner city as in the suburbs. The young couple create their own idyllic setting by running away to a cemetery where they make their home in a neglected caretaker's room. And in 1977, Brenda Wilkinson's story about young and black *Ludell and Willie* was made special by its early 1960s setting in Waycross, Georgia.

Another quality that might make a love story stand out—at least temporarily—is a new twist or philosophy. Changing social attitudes in the late 1960s and early 1970s opened up whole new vistas for authors who wanted to write love stories. Not all of the themes are new, but there is a new freedom to treat them openly in books for young readers. For example, Katie Letcher Lyle's *Fair Day and Another Step Begun* is a modern retelling of an old English ballad "Childe Waters." It is the story of a young pregnant girl who pursues the twenty-two-year-old father of her child until the baby is born, and he acknowledges his responsibility and accepts the newborn infant as his own.

Several writers have taken the standard stories and done reverse twists on them. One of the most popular is Norma Klein's *It's OK If You Don't Love Me.* Sophisticated New Yorker, Jody, seduces Lyle, a shy and straight tennis player, who has moved from the Midwest to New York for his senior year. Another turnabout is Jeannette Eyerly's *He's My Baby, Now,* in which the teenage father of an illegitimate baby does not want the baby given up for adoption. In the end the boy realizes that for the sake of everyone's lives, this is the best solution. Because of the difficulty of the decision, this book should perhaps be categorized as an accomplishment- rather than as a love-romance.

Love-romances can be sad as long as they aren't too grim. One of the sad ones is Barbara Wersba's *In the Country of the Heart.* It is told through the voice of a young writer who five years earlier had an affair with an older woman poet. Their relationship began when he sought her out to be his mentor not knowing that she was terribly sick and had come home to die. This story is read through tears, but Wersba's other romance, *Tunes for a Small Harmonica* is read through smiles if not outright giggles. It is easier to describe sixteen-year-old J. F. as looking like a teenage cab driver—which she is not—than as either a boy or a girl. But underneath the short haircut, the wrinkled jeans, and the Tappan Zee High School jacket, she is all girl, and she falls in love with thirty-year-old Harold Murth. He was her poetry teacher, a wan and pale, and apparently poverty-stricken scholar. She takes it upon herself to raise $1,000 by playing her harmonica on the streets of New York so that he can go to Cambridge and finish his dissertation. It's Christmas Eve when for the first time in her teenage years she gets all dressed up in preparation for making her magnificent offering. Along with the $1,000 she also plans to give him her virginity. But when she arrives at his apartment, she finds, much to her disappointment, that his spartan existence is by choice. He is not only a wealthy man, he is also a married man. She is saved from a Christmas Day suicide by an invitation to interview for a part in a movie. She is at first thrilled, but then comes to the realization that the director, who is a cousin of Harold Murth's, really isn't interested in her. He is interested in her "differentness." He wants to make a fast buck on the fact that she is a freak:

> Because I *was* a freak, I decided suddenly. I didn't look like anybody else. And I never had. I had spent my whole life worrying about being a peculiar person, when that was what I was *meant* to be in the first place. So screw it, I thought furiously. If I am a freak at least I'll be an honest freak and not use my freakiness to become some goddam movie star. . . .

J. F. goes home a wiser woman, which makes this another one of the books straddling the border between the accomplishment-romance and the love-romance.

So many of the love stories that came out in the 1970s were reversals or alternatives to the traditional love story that in 1978 Norma Klein could do another reversal by writing a more or less straight romance under the title *Love Is One of the Choices.* It is the story of two best friends who at the end of high school each develop intimate relationships with the men they love. One of them chooses to marry and become pregnant right away, but the other one gets pregnant, refuses to marry, and has an abortion.

Changing values and attitudes also make it likely that less self-conscious novels will be written about homosexual relationships. But readers and authors bring to this topic such strong feelings that any story of love between two people of the same sex is likely to be too "heavy" to qualify as romance. However, Deborah Hautzig's *Hey, Dollface* is perhaps light enough. Valerie Hoffman and Chloe Fox are new sophomores at an exclusive girls' high school. Their developing friendship reminds readers of that of Gene and Finny in *A Separate Peace* and of Davy and Altschuler in *I'll Get There. It Better Be Worth the Trip.* Valerie and Chloe are surprised to discover that the warm affection they feel for each other is somehow tied in with their sexuality. The book has an open ending, which is appropriate in that no one can accurately predict what the future holds for two young teenagers who have both a beautiful friendship and a current of excitement between them quite unlike anything either one has experienced before.

Who Reads Them and Why?

It is impossible to evaluate the love-romance without taking into consideration the purpose for which someone chooses to read a particular title. If it is as escape fantasy, then the best book is the one with the happiest ending and the most idealized characters. But if the purpose is to find out what having a boy or girl friend is really like, then the best book is the one that presents the fullest and most honest picture. There is a special problem with love-romance because it is not out-and-out make-believe. Many young readers take these books quite seriously, yet several of their time-honored conventions are unrealistic. For example, when a romance flounders, there is always another boy, or the promise of another boy, waiting nearby as Danny is in Irene Hunt's *Up a Road Slowly*. The protagonist had already rejected him. Nevertheless he hangs around doggedly, and, sure enough, Julie comes to understand what the reader knew all along. The second boy is far superior to the first.

Another unrealistic convention is that, for some unexplained reason, a popular boy will suddenly take a look at a shy and previously unnoticed girl and fall in love with her. The impression given is that this happens at least once to everyone, and that, when it happens, the couple will live happily ever after.

The trends toward realism in general and the feminist movement in particular have cast long shadows over the love-romance. Many of its hallowed conventions are simply incompatible with these new ways of thinking. This means that fewer love-romances are being written today. Yet librarians report that many of the old ones are among the books most often checked out, for example, *Jean and Johnny* by Beverly Cleary, *Diane's New Love* by Betty Cavanna, and the *Dinny Gordon* stories by Anne Emery. It is possible that young people keep reading the old romances because no one

The trends toward realism in general and the feminist movement in particular have cast long shadows over the love-romance.

is providing them with new ones that are as appealing. The clash of feminist ideas with the old romantic ones has also caused a kind of polarization. Librarians say that many adult women who have rejected the new realism come in seeking teenage romances. They want to read love stories like the ones they remember from their youth. One of the amazing publishing stories of the late 1970s is that of the Harlequin romances, mass-produced paperbacks sold through a book club as well as at newsstands. They are advertised under red hearts and such slogans as, "Remember how it was when you first fell in love." One young adult specialist in a library reports that many of her patrons read them as avidly as do adult women. She hastens to add that she doesn't purchase them. Almost every week someone donates a grocery bag full.

The reason that the librarian did not want us to think that she had purchased the Harlequin romances is that most of the mass-produced love-romances are basically sexist. They have a clear-cut division between males and females and the roles that each must play. The boy is the one who must "fall" for the girl. In these stories this is something that just happens to him, almost as if he had been shot with Cupid's arrow or had drunk a love potion. He approaches the girl, who is at first resistant or at least reluctant to admit an interest. But the boy persists, and then the girl "falls" for him. The interest in the romance is built up by this seesawing back and forth between the pair. Depending on the point of view, it is almost as if the girl and boy are protagonist and antagonist. Underlying the conflict is the idea that males and females are basically at war and trying to conquer each other.

Another problem in many romances, especially those written for teenagers, is that authors tend to gloss over the part that sex plays in such relationships. Ironically it's love at first sight, which must imply a physical, that is, a sexual attraction, yet the boys are portrayed as being almost platonically interested in the girl's thoughts and feelings.

Robert Unsworth writing in *School Library Journal* decries the dearth of books that give an unbiased treatment to the part that male sexuality plays in the growing-up process of all boys. He cites a statement of the protagonist, Alan Bennett, in M. E. Kerr's *If I Love You, Am I Trapped Forever?* Alan, who tells the story in first person, starts out by saying, "I'm not going to describe in detail the very personal things that take place between me and Leah. I'm not writing this book for a bunch of voyeurs." Unsworth comments that:

> It is fear of censorship, not voyeurism, which plagues too many young adult
> novels to a degree where the image of the male in the juvenile novel is
> woefully incomplete. Leaving sex out of a novel that purports to examine male
> maturation and growth is like writing a cookbook without mentioning food.[2]

He goes on to say that "We do not need explicit sex in teenage fiction any more than we need the head-in-the-sand approach to sexuality that seems to be the current norm. There is a middle ground." Books that he commends for including at least some honest mention of male sexual development are Judy Blume's *Then Again, Maybe I Won't*, Robert Cormier's *The Chocolate War*, Mildred Lee's *Fog*, and Don Moser's *A Heart to the Hawks*.

The problem with the romances is that they are set down in a world that has established two sets of rules: one for women and one for men. Jessie Potter, director of the National Institute for Human Relationship in Chicago, observes that:

> The folklore that surrounds us as we grow up teaches us to expect that we
> will find the right person to love, and that we will not have any problems with
> intimacy, communication, and sex. Nothing could be further from the truth.
>
> For the most part, boys have been and are still being taught that to be a
> man means to turn off their feelings, act out of impersonal rationality, force
> their wills upon others, and be aggressive. And girls are still learning that to
> be a woman means to be soft and emotional, submissive and withholding.
>
> Having learned these lessons well from early childhood, aggressive men
> and withholding women are doomed to anger, frustration, and incredible pain
> in their search for joyful sex and intimacy.[3]

Even without this double set of rules love could hardly live up to the expectations that people have for it. In one part of their minds, many adults as well as teenagers long to return to the time when they were small enough to be carried around in the arms of loving parents who adored them and provided both physical and emotional warmth and security. But in another part of their minds they know they are too big for this and can never return to the helplessness of babyhood. The next best thing is to have someone who is worthy of trust and respect fall in love with them. The dream for both sexes is that this lover will provide the old parental warmth and security, but in a new way.

In this dream, especially for women, sex may play a small part. In most romances, love is the more dominant theme, but romances that ignore sex or treat it in such a glossed-over way that it bears little resemblance to reality present an unfair picture to both sexes. High-school girls who naturally long for the glamour and excitement of going out with the neatest boy in school (which is nearly always the case in the teenage romances) are also apt to be somewhat frightened by the newness of sex and by the lessons they have been given all their lives on the need for abstinence and "purity." Because of this, the romances that portray love without sex are especially appealing to girls. They are wish fulfilling in presenting relationships that on the surface have all that the media make look so desirable without the adult responsibilities that come with sexual involvement.

But these same "pure" stories may be very threatening to boys because they present males who are being warm and gentle and open with little or no mention of sexual feelings. The idealized boys in romantic fiction reveal emotions in ways that run counter to the macho image with which males have traditionally been raised. It is probably because of this, that many boys are uncomfortable about reading romances.

An interesting corollary can be seen in the pornography that is rejected by most females but embraced by many males. Pornography is at the opposite end of the scale from romances. It stresses the physical aspects of sex with very little emphasis on the emotional involvement of love. Pornography is wish fulfilling for males in that the females are usually shown as desiring sexual relationships without requiring any "romancing."

This preference that males show for pornography over romances would be more understandable if the preference were for adventure/suspense stories that portray actions in which only or mostly males participate. The preference that females show for romances over pornography would also be more understandable if the stories were about mother/child relationships or some other distinctively female role. But when the crux of a story is a male/female relationship, as it is in love stories, then stories that are honest should be acceptable to both sexes.

People who enjoy romances simply as a form of escape are justifiably irritated at discussions such as this, which imply that these stories should be accurate in every detail. They point out that no one goes around demanding that every adventure/ suspense story resemble the real-life activities that most people will experience. The majority of the stories that people read are exaggerated in some way. Fiction does not portray only or exactly what will happen to most people or it wouldn't be fiction.

But the point in relation to the romanticized love stories is that people—especially young girls—are socialized to think that "true love" is the one dream that is in the realm of possibility for everyone. The love-romance is held up to females as the guarantee of a happily-ever-after future, especially by the advertising industry. But critics complain that channeling teenage girls' wishes for the future into love-romances is setting them up for disappointments in two ways. First, the kinds of romances that are pictured do not happen to everyone. There simply are not that many "perfect" boys who are going to commit themselves to girls. And even the girls who do have boy friends are made to feel slightly ashamed or embarrassed because they do not compare favorably to the ones in the romances. Real boys are not as open about their love nor are they as platonically interested in girls' thoughts and problems as are the boys in the romances.

The second way in which girls will be disappointed is that they will learn—perhaps too late—that having a boy friend or getting married is not all that is necessary for a fulfilling life. Girls need to plan their futures beyond the altar. The idea that teenage boys should go to "prep schools" and teenage girls to "finishing schools" is rather antiquated. Both males and females need to be preparing for the life that is ahead of them.

What this means in relation to the adults who guide the reading of youth is that they should do what they can to let girls know that many of the romances are a kind of fantasy. They may be fun to read, but they should be counterbalanced with realistic

Adults should let girls know that many of the romances are a kind of fantasy.

books and with discussions of how romances compare to what the readers know about real life and to the "beautiful people" images that are projected in the media. It is unfortunate that because boys do not like to read romances, they are seldom read in classroom settings and discussed in groups. Peer opinions would be valuable in helping girls and boys assess both the appeal and the accuracy of love-romances.

Romances that have exotic settings are perhaps less apt to be taken seriously by readers than are the ones that are outwardly realistic. For example, many of the gothics have similar elements to the modern romances, but readers can enjoy them imaginatively much as they do murder mysteries and science fiction. Most readers recognize them as being exaggerations. Also some of the gothics have women protagonists who are interesting and successful beyond the confines of the romance. For example, in Barbara Michael's stories the woman does not always end up marrying the man. She sometimes chooses to go and do her own thing. Michael's gothics are popular partly because of this unusual twist and partly because she adds touches of humor and hints of the supernatural. The gothics of Phyllis Whitney, Mary Stewart, and Victoria Holt are also popular because they allow girls to escape into a kind of fantasy in which they can enjoy the satisfaction of the romance, plus occasional chills and thrills, all the time knowing that the stories are imagined.

In a similar way, both critics and readers can be more relaxed about sex roles and expectations when they are reading historical romances. We can sit back and imagine ourselves as Scarlett O'Hara enjoying the love of Rhett Butler, but we don't really expect our lives to be like Scarlett's and Rhett's. Because the identification is not quite as close as in modern stories, and because there is usually an element of adventure in the historical novels, this kind of love story is more apt to be enjoyed by males as well as by females. For example, some boys read Rose Wilder Lane's *The Young Pioneers*, Pearl S. Buck's *The Good Earth*, and Marilyn Durham's *The Man Who Loved Cat Dancing*, which was described in the Best Books list of the Young Adult Services Division of A.L.A. as "a western, a relentless character study, a violent tragedy, but—most of all—a love story." Other historical fiction that contains elements of the romance will be discussed in Chapter 8.

In relation to the love-romance, probably the most significant development over the last decade has been the teenage love-romance that is written to and read by both boys and girls. Paul Zindel has written such stories in *Pardon Me, You're Stepping on My Eyeball!* and *The Undertaker's Gone Bananas*. So has M. E. Kerr with her *I'll Love You When You're More Like Me* and *If I Love You, Am I Trapped Forever?* These stories include significant boy/girl relationships but they differ from the more traditional romances in several ways. First, there is something more to the story than the relationship. Just as in real life, the love relationship is there with all of its emotional importance, but it is part of a bigger story. Second, the story is not told only from the girl's viewpoint. As a special ploy to attract male readers (authors know that girls already read love stories), these new romances are often narrated by the boy. Or there's a mix as in Kerr's *I'll Love You When You're More Like Me* in which the boy and girl write alternate chapters. A third difference is that there is no indication of either partner exploiting or manipulating the other as often happens in exaggerated romances and pornography. In those stories that appeal to both sexes, no one is out to "make a catch." Instead the couple works together to solve some kind of a mutual problem or to achieve a goal of some sort.

Both the adventure-romance and the love-romance are psychologically very satisfying. More than any other genre, they are especially well matched to the particular stage of life that is young adulthood. The stories are optimistic and wish fulfilling. Their basic pattern resembles the real-life activities of young people who are moving from childhood into adulthood. Romances incorporate the successful completion of a quest in which the protagonist is elevated in status. But usually more important than the respect earned from others is the feeling of self-respect and self-confidence that the young hero gains in the course of the story. All of these things work together to insure that the books treated in this chapter will be among the most popular in the young adult section of any library.

ACTIVITIES

1. Read a modern adventure-romance and see how many of the following elements from traditional romances that you can find: (a) a worthy young hero; (b) a journey (literal or symbolic); (c) a villain; (d) physical danger; (e) a sacrifice symbolized by some physical damage to the protagonist's body or to something valued by the protagonist; (f) an older, wiser person who lends assistance; (g) an idyllic setting

near the end of the story; (h) a sudden insight or realization that comes in this idyllic setting; (i) an accomplishment that gives the protagonist new status with both adults and peers.

2. Read one of the love-romances written by Beverly Cleary, Betty Cavanna, Ann Emery, or Rosamund Du Jardin. In an attempt to empathize with young readers, engage in a "willing suspension of disbelief" and note the incidents of wish fulfillment that are incorporated in the story. As a class, discuss whether or not adults should try to lead young readers to recognize the unrealistic wish fulfillment nature of these stories. Some of the reasons for doing this were given in the chapter, but other viewpoints to consider include whether these stories are just something that young teens will outgrow, whether you would be insulting their level of taste and therefore destroying a desirable rapport, and whether these elements should be attacked in stories when they appear daily in television commercials, advertisements, movies, songs, and human interest newspaper stories. You might compare the wish fulfillment seen in the romances to that seen in the headlines of tabloid newspapers. What does this show about human nature?

3. Read one of the books by M. E. Kerr or Paul Zindel that features both a male and a female protagonist. There is usually a love-relationship between the two. Write a one-page paper in which you show how this relationship differs from that in the more common love-romances that are read mainly by girls.

NOTES

[1]Glenna Davis Sloan, *The Child as Critic* (New York: Teachers College Press, 1975), p. 33.

[2]Robert Unsworth, "Holden Caulfield, Where Are You?" *School Library Journal* (January 1977): pp. 40–41.

[3]Jessie Potter, "An Open Letter to American Women about Men," *Voice of Youth Advocates* 1, (June 1978): 7–8.

RECOMMENDED TITLES

For information on the availability of paperback editions of these titles, please consult the most recent edition of *Paperbound Books in Print*, published annually by R. R. Bowker Company.

Adventure-Romances

Benchley, Nathaniel. *Only Earth and Sky Last Forever.* Harper & Row, 1972.

Borland, Hal G. *When the Legends Die.* J. B. Lippincott, 1963.

Bridgers, Sue Ellen. *Home Before Dark*. Alfred A. Knopf, 1976.

Clark, Ann Nolan. *Year Walk*. Viking, 1975.

Cleaver, Vera and Bill. *Dust of the Earth*. J. B. Lippincott, 1975.

———. *The Queen of Hearts*. J. B. Lippincott, 1978.

———. *Where the Lilies Bloom*. J. B. Lippincott, 1969.

———. *The Whys and Wherefores of Littabelle Lee*. Atheneum, 1973.

Craven, Margaret. *I Heard the Owl Call My Name*. Doubleday, 1973.

Degens, T. *Transport 7–41–R*. Viking, 1974.

Farley, Carol. *The Garden Is Doing Fine*. Atheneum, 1975.

Feagles, Anita MacRae. *Me, Cassie*. Dial, 1968.

Freedman, Benedict and Nancy. *Mrs. Mike*. Coward, McCann & Geoghegan, 1947.

George, Jean Craighead. *Julie of the Wolves*. Harper & Row, 1972.

Greene, Bette. *Philip Hall Likes Me. I Reckon Maybe*. Dial, 1974.

Hall, Lynn. *Sticks and Stones*. Follett, 1972.

Hamilton, Virginia. *M. C. Higgins, the Great*. Macmillan, 1974.

Holland, Isabelle. *Heads You Win, Tails I Lose*. J. B. Lippincott, 1973.

———. *Of Love and Death and Other Journeys*. J. B. Lippincott, 1975.

Hunt, Irene. *Across Five Aprils*. Follett, 1964.

Lee, Mildred. *Fog*. Seabury, 1972.

———. *The Skating Rink*. Seabury, 1969.

Lipsyte, Robert. *The Contender*. Harper & Row, 1967.

———. *One Fat Summer*. Harper & Row, 1977.

Mazer, Norma Fox. *Dear Bill, Remember Me?* Delacorte, 1976.

Meyer, Carolyn. *C. C. Poindexter*. Atheneum, 1978.

Moon, Michael E. *John Medicinewolf*. Dial, 1979.

Myers, Walter D. *Fast Sam, Cool Clyde, and Stuff*. Viking, 1975.

O'Dell, Scott. *Island of the Blue Dolphins*. Houghton Mifflin, 1960.

———. *Zia*. Houghton Mifflin, 1976.

Peck, Robert Newton. *Eagle Fur*. Alfred A. Knopf, 1978.

Potok, Chaim. *The Chosen*. Simon & Schuster, 1967.

———. *My Name is Asher Lev*. Alfred A. Knopf, 1972.

Powers, John R. *Do Black Patent Leather Shoes Really Reflect Up?* Contemporary Books, 1975.

Love-Romances

Baldwin, James. *If Beale Street Could Talk*. Dial, 1974.

Blume, Judy. *Forever*. Bradbury, 1976.

Buck, Pearl S. *The Good Earth.* John Day, 1931.

Cleaver, Vera and Bill. *Trial Valley.* J. B. Lippincott, 1977.

Daly, Maureen. *Seventeenth Summer.* Dodd, Mead, 1942.

Durham, Marilyn. *The Man Who Loved Cat Dancing.* Harcourt Brace Jovanovich, 1972.

Goldman, William. *The Princess Bride.* Harcourt Brace Jovanovich, 1973.

Greene, Bette. *Morning Is a Long Time Coming.* Dial, 1978.

Hautzig, Deborah. *Hey, Dollface.* William Morrow, 1978.

Hunt, Irene. *Up a Road Slowly.* Follett, 1966.

Hunter, Mollie. *The Stronghold.* Harper & Row, 1974.

Jordan, June. *His Own Where.* Thomas Y. Crowell, 1971.

Kerr, M. E. *If I Love You, Am I Trapped Forever?* Harper & Row, 1973.

———. *I'll Love You When You're More Like Me.* Harper & Row, 1977.

———. *Love Is a Missing Person.* Harper & Row, 1975.

Klein, Norma. *It's OK If You Don't Love Me.* Dial, 1977.

———. *Love Is One of the Choices.* Dial, 1979.

Lane, Rose Wilder. *The Young Pioneers.* McGraw-Hill, 1976.

Le Guin, Ursula K. *Very Far Away from Anywhere Else.* Atheneum, 1976.

Lockley, Ronald. *Seal-Woman.* Bradbury, 1975.

Lyle, Katie Letcher. *Fair Day and Another Step Begun.* J. B. Lippincott, 1974.

Mazer, Norma Fox. *Up in Seth's Room.* Delacorte, 1979.

McKay, Robert. *Dave's Song.* Meredith Press, 1969.

Mitchell, Margaret. *Gone with the Wind.* Macmillan, 1936.

Newman, Daisy. *I Take Thee, Serenity.* Houghton Mifflin, 1975.

Ney, John. *Ox Under Pressure.* J. B. Lippincott, 1976.

Patterson, Sarah. *The Distant Summer.* Simon & Schuster, 1976.

Peyton, K. M. *The Beethoven Medal.* Thomas Y. Crowell, 1972.

Raucher, Herman. *The Summer of '42.* G. P. Putnam's Sons, 1971.

Rosen, Winifred. *Cruisin for a Bruisin.* Alfred A. Knopf, 1976.

Said, Kurban. *Ali and Nino.* Hutchinson, 1970.

Segal, Erich. *Love Story.* Harper & Row, 1970.

Speare, Elizabeth. *Witch of Blackbird Pond.* Houghton Mifflin, 1958.

Townsend, John Rowe. *Goodnight Prof, Dear.* J. B. Lippincott, 1971.

Wersba, Barbara. *The Country of the Heart.* Atheneum, 1975.

———. *Tunes for a Small Harmonica.* Harper & Row, 1976.

West, Jessamyn. *Massacre at Fall Creek.* G. K. Hall, 1975.

Westheimer, David. *My Sweet Charlie.* Doubleday, 1965.

Wilkinson, Brenda. *Ludell and Willie.* Harper & Row, 1977.

Windsor, Patricia. *The Summer Before*. Harper & Row, 1973.

Wood, Phyllis A. *Song of the Shaggy Canary*. Westminster, 1974.

Zindel, Paul. *Pardon Me, You're Stepping on My Eyeball!* Harper & Row, 1976.

———. *The Undertaker's Gone Bananas*. Harper and Row, 1978.

8

Excitement and Suspense

Of Sudden Shadows

Something perverse in us delights in excitement, suspense, and danger. We take great joy in scaring the wits out of each other when we are young. At eight or nine or ten (and older) we regale friends with stories of boogeymen and spooks—anything to make our listeners' blood chill and their hands sweat. When we go camping on dark nights, we tell ghost stories so that we can feel superior while that delicious sense of fear runs rampant among us all, especially the storyteller.

Every culture has its share of folktales well calculated to make goosebumps rise and bad children behave, tales embodying terror, mystery, fear, the spectral, the inexplicable, the impossible, the deadly—in short, all the things that we fear. Halloween is, ambivalently, a time of fun and a time of terror, and there is no fun without the terror.

And when we grow up do we put away childish terrors? Of course not. We seek horror movies, and, if the latest reincarnation of Bela Lugosi or Peter Cushing or Christopher Lee or Boris Karloff doesn't chill us with a shiver of fright, we feel cheated. We visit an amusement park, not to sit sedately (and maturely) on some merry-go-round, but to head for the latest thrill-a-minute, life-threatening, a-nurse-is-in-attendance-should-anyone-have-a-heart-attack rides. We beg someone to stay up with us until 2:00 A.M. to watch an old movie that scared us to death when we were younger.

Why are we so eager to feel fear? Why do we take a secret delight in the race car driver who seems near a skid on a bad track? Why do we watch the tightrope walker flirt with death?

Is it because our lives are so mundane and dull that vicarious danger may be all we can have? Is it because we fear death and are pleased to tempt it and escape for the moment? Do we benefit somehow from watching someone face impossible odds and emerge victorious, a feat we see less and less often in the real world? Perhaps adventure, excitement, and suspense allow us the luxury of catharsis. If it is not an Aristotelian purging of emotions, at least it is a purging of drives and fears, of monsters and enemies that we might centuries ago have been able to attack directly in bloody battles. Denied those outlets today, we gladly pay people to provide them for our reading and viewing pleasure.

In tales of excitement and stories from the past we can revel in times when evil was evil, good was good, and each was clearly and easily distinguishable. These tales make us certain that humanity will not merely survive, but that its courage deserves to survive.

ADVENTURE STORIES

Humanity over the ages has taken pleasure and psychological refuge in tales like the *Odyssey*, the *Iliad*, *Beowulf*, *Sir Gawain and the Green Knight*, *Don Quixote*, and *Ivanhoe*. Some adventure tales have more than excitement, but the excitement is enough to please us much of the time.

Early filmmakers knew that. Cliffhanging serials, an American innovation, were predicated on excitement and suspense, for example *The Adventures of Kathlyn* (1913), *The Hazards of Helen* (1914), *The Mysteries of Myra* (1916), and the most famous *The Perils of Pauline* (1914). Chills at every possible moment and terror around every corner frightened the masses who loved living through each minute of fear.

"Once upon a time" are magic words. Even if they are not stated exactly that way they spin open every adventure and imply action and excitement. We may care about the people, but it is really the action that is all-important along with the violence, real or implied. And the greater of these is the implied violence, the things we fear will happen. Pace and tempo force action to come faster and speed us into the tale and its complications. The first lines can push us into the plot, witness the first paragraph of Robbie Branscum's *Me and Jim Luke*, especially the first line:

> I knew the hand was dead the minute it touched my naked shoulder next to my overall strap. I couldn't have moved if my life depended on it, and I reckoned it did. I sort of froze, and at the same time I felt like messing all over myself. I tried to holler, but no matter how wide I got my mouth open no sound came out. I could see the light of the lantern Jim Luke carried get further and further away, and finally it was plumb out of sight. The moon was plenty bright enough to see by, but Lord I didn't want to see the thing that had hold of me. I knew if I did, I would die for sure.

Few readers could stop reading there.

But adventure stories demand more than action and speed, important as those elements are. The writer must provide a brief character sketch of at least the hero and

SUGGESTIONS FOR EVALUATING ADVENTURE STORIES

A good adventure story has most of the positive qualities generally associated with good fiction. In addition it usually has:	A poor adventure story may have the negative qualities generally associated with poor fiction. It is particularly prone to have:
A likable protagonist with whom young readers can identify.	A protagonist who is too exaggerated or too stereotyped to be believable.
An adventure that readers can imagine happening to themselves.	Nothing really exciting about the adventure.
Efficient characterization.	Only stereotyped characters.
An interesting setting that enhances the story without getting in the way of the plot.	A long drawn-out conclusion after the climax has been reached.
Action that draws readers into the plot within the first page or so of the story.	

the villain. If we are to care about them, we must know them as believable people. But, because we are primarily interested in the action, we are not likely to be pleased by descriptive or reflective passages that would delay the story. What the author must do is to reveal the characters primarily in terms of the plot: what could happen, what has happened, what might happen, and how do all of these tie together?

We want surprises and turns of the screw throughout. Heroes become entrapped, and the way out of danger leads only to further jeopardy. Of the three basic conflicts, adventure tales will usually center on person against person instead of person against nature or person against self, although the latter will receive some attention as the hero faces frustration and possible failure. Heroes must be people we can admire and care about. Even though we may not like them at first, we must begin to worry with and live with and identify with them. Villains, no matter what their motivations (and we may temporarily sympathize with them), must be crafty, clever, devious, and cruel, worthy opponents holding all the best cards and certain to win, or so it seems—and we may cheat and flip a few pages or even peek at the end of the book, to reassure ourselves of what we must know, that good wins out.

Of all literary devices, the most significant in adventure tales is verisimilitude. With all the unlikely plot twists of adventure tales, the author must provide realistic details galore to reassure us, despite our inner misgivings, that the actions are possible. We want to believe that the hero's frustrations and the cliffhanging episodes could really have happened. Without that, the story cheats, and that we cannot tolerate, no matter how much we try.

A love interest is unlikely in adventure tales. Perhaps there is a love left behind, but none during the tribulations. A girl and a boy may flee together, and sex is possible—some writers would appear to believe that sexual scenes are obligatory—but only as a momentary diversion. Rarely are they significant in the story.

Robb White's *Deathwatch* epitomizes the elements of adventure stories: person vs. person, person vs. nature, and person vs. self conflicts, tension, thrills and chills on each page, and a likable hero frustrated at every turn by an inventive, devious, and cruel villain.

The first brief paragraphs take us into the tale and introduce the two actors:

> "There he is!" Madec whispered. "Keep still!"
> There had been a movement up on the ridge of the mountain. For a moment something had appeared between the two rock outcrops.
> "I didn't see any horns," Ben said.
> "Keep quiet!" Madec whispered fiercely.

We know *Deathwatch* has something to do with hunting, but we have no reason to believe that hunting will become an ominous metaphor. We recognize that the name Madec has a harsh sound and that it seems vaguely related to the word *mad*, again without recognizing how prescient we are. Within the next few pages, we learn how carefully White has placed the clues before us. Ben crouches with his little .22 Hornet and watches Madec with his "beautifully made .358 Magnum Mauser action on a Winchester 70 stock with enough power to knock down an elephant—or turn a sleeping Gila monster into a splatter" and remembers that Madec had been willing to shoot at anything that moved:

> Madec huddled over the gun. There was an intensity in his eyes far beyond that of just hunting a sheep. It was the look of murder.

And murder is there. Before long, Madec takes a shot at a bighorn sheep, but it turns out to be an old desert prospector, now quite dead, and he asks Ben to quash the incident and forget it ever happened. Ben refuses, and the book is off and running. So is Ben, running for his life, without gun, water, or food, amid hostile desert mountains and sand and a killing sun.

Madec personifies the maddened but incredibly crafty villain, able to read Ben's mind and forestall his attempts to get clothes or weapons or water. Madec is a worthy opponent. We know that Ben will win—what kind of mad or hostile world would allow Madec to win—but we wonder. And at each of Madec's devious turns to stop Ben from escape, we doubt just as we should in a good adventure novel. Ben changes from a rational, calm young man to a frightened, desperate animal and then to a cold and dangerous person who must think as Madec thinks to win out over the villain. Madec begins with all the power on his side: guns, water, food, and wealth. Given reality, we know he should win, but, given our sense of rightness and justice, he cannot be allowed to win. Ben has little interest in right or wrong after a few pages. His interest is more elemental, simple survival until he can escape.

Many adventure stories focus on survival against nature. Harry Mazer's *Snow Bound* features spoiled fifteen-year-old Tony LaPorte, who is trying to prove something by running away from home in his mother's old car. He stops to pick up hitchhiker Cindy Reichert, who is neither impressed with him nor with his driving ability. He sets out to impress her and ends up driving off the road in a blinding snowstorm. How they survive despite cold, wild dogs, and no food, and how they change makes a rattling good tale that's especially fun to read when the summer temperature reaches 100 degrees in the shade.

William Judson's *Cold River* brings shivers to the reader no matter what the season. In 1921, Tim, his older stepsister Lizzy, and their father are lost in the Adirondack Mountains. When their father dies of pneumonia, the two young adults are truly lost without survival skills and without a clear understanding of where they are. But survive they do despite wild animals, cold, and a predatory human. *Cold River* is a particularly intriguing narrative for it is told by Lizzy in her sixties looking back on the most thrilling time of her life, not nostalgically but realistically and bravely. All in all, it's a superb tale of humanity's indomitable drive to live.

True accounts of mountain climbing fall into a slightly different category of person against nature story. The hero goes forth to seek the adventure, to openly challenge nature. Few acts of courage (foolhardiness) appeal more to young adults. Why does a climber struggle against snow, ice, rocks, precipices, uncertainty, and loneliness? Sir Edmund Hillary's classic answer, "Because it's there," suffices at least for the moment. Anyone who collects stamps or goes camping or runs for the sheer fun of it learns soon enough that it is impossible to explain the lure of the hobby to the uninitiated.

Part of the appeal of these books rests on the exotic and faraway settings that add to the adventure. This is one reason why Hillary's book *From the Ocean to the Sky*, which tells of his trip up the Ganges River, is as interesting as his mountain climbing books, which include *High Adventure: The Crossing of Antarctica* and *No Latitude for Error: Schoolhouse in the Clouds*.

Conventionally, certain elements are often found in books on mountaineering: a glossary, maps, photographs, details about preparations. But a mountain climbing book is not a textbook; readers want to know what the climbers' thoughts are. People who are willing to read a whole book will not be satisfied with Hillary's "because it's there" response. They want to know what the authors believe, and what they think during the long hours of toil and solitude on the mountain. Unless a book provides such answers, it fails.

In 1894, John Muir tried to answer these questions in his classic *The Mountains of California*. In 1953 Maurice Herzog also tried in *Annapurna: First Conquest of an 8000-Meter Peak*. David Roberts deals with the subject in two books, *The Mountain of My Fear* and *Deborah: A Wilderness Narrative*. In the first book Roberts tells of four Harvard students who want to be first to scale the western face of Mt. Huntington in Alaska. Roberts provides ample detail, but more significantly he attempts to explore what mountains signify in his universe. In *Deborah* he comes closer to explaining who and what he is and what mountains mean. *Deborah* is a painful book, for we see, not the death of a person, but the death of a long and close friendship. *The Hall of the Mountain*

King by Howard H. Snyder describes a twelve-man attempt in 1967 to scale 20,320-foot Mount McKinley, the highest peak in North America. Snyder's book is painful too. A glance at the dust jacket reveals that only five of the men came back, partly because of bad weather, but mostly because of poor human judgment.

Three books celebrate the mountains. Chris Bonington's *Annapurna South Face* tells of the ascent in 1970. Its photographs are stunning and worth the price of the book. In *High Odyssey: The First Solo Winter Assault of Mount Whitney and the Muir Trail Area*, Eugene A. Rose describes a 1928 trek of Orland Bartholomew. Miriam Underhill's *Give Me the Hills* describes her lifelong love affair with climbing in Europe and North America and her struggles in leading the first all-woman assault on the Matterhorn in the Alps.

Person against person has been a theme in many adventures, and William Goldman's *Marathon Man* is a thrilling and violent example. A young man whose only dream is to become a runner watches his world fall apart when his brother is killed and

Person against person has been a theme in many adventures.

he becomes inadvertently involved in an international spy ring. Frederick Forsyth's two books, *The Day of the Jackal* and *The Odessa File,* are excellent thrillers. The first is concerned with the effort to stop the Jackal from assassinating Charles de Gaulle; the latter with a German reporter attempting to get into a secret organization shielding former Nazi SS officers so that he can learn the whereabouts of the sadistic ex-commandant of the infamous Riga Camp.

Michael Crichton's *The Great Train Robbery* is a delightfully old-fashioned thriller with robber extraordinaire Edward Pierce determined to get away with a gold shipment on a supposedly impregnable railroad train in 1855. Based on a real robbery, which the Victorians called "The Crime of the Century," Crichton's book focuses on the step-by-step preparations for the robbery by a clever and surprisingly witty criminal. The humor distinguishes this book from its fellows.

A few adventure stories pit animals against humans as in Berton Roueche's *Feral.* This book forcefully reveals aspects of both animals and humans that we would rather not think about. Jack and Amy Bishop move from crowded New York City to a peaceful village on Long Island. One of their first steps is getting a pet cat, Sneakers; when they return to the city, one of their last steps is abandoning Sneakers near a home with children so she will be adopted. When they return to their quiet country home some time later, they soon learn that feral cats are running wild, not the Sneakers variety, but vicious, killer cats. Before long the horror strikes, and the town is virtually under siege. Making household pets monstrous is no easy task in a nation of animal lovers, but Roueche succeeds. When cats surround the Bishop home, they call the police who do not recognize the desperation in Jack Bishop's voice. One policeman arrives, and Jack tells what happens:

I could hear a turmoil of cats from down behind the car. There was a rise of broad blue shoulders and a bloody blonde head. He came stumbling, half crawling, around the front end of the car. He was hung with cats, and his face was running blood. . . .

He half turned back, he seemed to be listening, and started down the driveway. I yelled. I yelled at the top of my voice. He heard me. He stopped and faced around. He wiped a bloody hand across his bloody face, he took a step toward the house, and stopped again. His feet were tangled in cats. He wiped his hand again across his face, across his eyes. There was a streak of mangy yellow—and a cat was on his arm. It flowed to his shoulder. He struck at it with his revolver. He struck and missed and the revolver flew out of his hand. The cat lunged for his face. He grabbed and got it in his hands, got it around the neck. He tore it squirming, writhing, hissing loose. It clawed at his hands, at his neck, at his face. He twisted it away and threw it into the pack at his feet. But it took his balance with it. He pitched to his knees. I had one last glimpse of his face—what was left of his face. Then the cats were on him.

Joan Phipson used a similar problem in her book *The Cats* which is set in her native Australia. Two boys are kidnapped and taken to an old deserted house in a territory of cats gone feral and dangerous.

A story such as Peter Benchley's *Jaws* is not quite so shocking because people have never considered sharks lovable. Ron Faust's *The Burning Sky* is in the same category. It features a bankrupt rancher-hunting guide who sets up an illegal hunting trip for a rich Texan and his family, but instead of hunting the mountain cats as planned, the humans soon begin preying on each other. Oliver Lange's *Red Snow* is another exciting animal story, set in a small New Mexican town terrorized by a mountain lion.

WESTERNS

The appeal of the American West is as old as the first explorer who saw it and marveled. Dime novels of the 1870s and 1880s exalted the wildness and vitality of things western—miners and cowboys and mountain men and soldiers and outlaws. Ned Buntline (pen name of Edward Zane Carroll Judson) lived a wild life of his own, but it paled in 1869 when he met William F. Cody. This meeting laid the foundation for his career as a writer of westerns. He wrote a number of Buffalo Bill dime novels starting with *Buffalo Bill, The King of Border Men,* published in the December, 1869, *New York Weekly.* The meeting also changed Cody's life. He went from near obscurity to national fame thanks to Buntline, an imaginative writer not especially concerned about facts or truth.

Years later radio recognized the appeal of the western, mostly in children's shows such as "Sky King" and "The Lone Ranger." And, at times, modern television has seemed to thrive on such programs as "Gunsmoke," "Have Gun, Will Travel,"

"Wagon Train," "Rawhide," "Wanted, Dead or Alive" and "Maverick." For many small towns in the 1920s and 1930s, films *were* westerns, especially the early serials starring John Wayne.

Owen Wister's *The Virginian: A Horseman of the Plains* (1902) set the pattern for years thereafter with its quiet and noble hero, a schoolmarm heroine, the hero's weak friend, a bad-guy villain, gunfights, rustlers, cowboys, cattle drives, violence, and revenge. Andy Adams' *The Log of a Cowboy: A Narrative of the Old Trail Days* (1903) added verisimilitude to the responsibility of the western author. Adams' fictional account of a trail drive was based on some experience and some research and brought reality to the western. Commercially successful western writers advanced the quality of western novels not a whit, but they unquestionably made westerns far better known and they advanced—or perpetuated—a number of western conventions. The most honest were by Eugene Manlove Rhodes—*Stepsons of Light* (1921), *Paso Por Aqui* (1927), and *The Proud Sheriff* (1935). The most romantic, popular, and famous writer was Zane Grey with *The Heritage of the Desert* (1910), *Riders of the Purple Sage* (1912), *The Rainbow Trail* (1915), *The Call of the Canyon* (1924), and *The Thundering Herd* (1925).

But amazing numbers of first-class writers lived and breathed the West and wrote accurate, nonromantic, honest novels, for example Oliver LaFarge with *Laughing Boy* (1929) and the better but less well known *The Enemy Gods* (1937). A. B. Guthrie's scope is best seen in his coverage of the western movement in *The Way West* (1949). Charles L. McNichol's *Crazy Weather* (1944) is a tale of two boys, one Mojave Indian and one white, heading up the Colorado River in search of their manhood. Jack Schaefer's *Shane* (1949) is probably the most widely used western novel in secondary schools, and its romantic vision of the loner-hero has become a part of western mythology. Frank Waters, one of the most significant of western writers, deserves readers for all sorts of reasons. He has written one of the most sensitive of Indian novels in *The Man Who Killed the Deer* (1942). Two of his nonfiction works convey Indian ways and beliefs better than any other western books, *Masked Gods* (1950) and *Book of the Hopi* (1963).

Conventions of the western are so set that any commercial writer who ignored them would be laughed out of the bookstore. The setting is obviously the West, probably some time from 1880 on through 1895, the high point of cowboy life. Civilization meets the frontier, and the vastness of the West will receive at least lip service. Excitement and adventure permeate the novel (attacks, rustlers, lynchings, bank holdups, gunfights, and so forth), and violence is more likely to be present than implied. Nostalgia for the old days usually appears. The hero (a marshal, cowboy, mountain man, wagon master) will be moral, almost puritanical; he may drink, but, when it comes to shooting and women and little children and schooling, morality triumphs. After *Shane*, it should surprise no one that many heroes are loners: gunfighters come to put the small town aright and bring justice to all through killing the yellow varmint who shot down the old storekeeper. Others in the cast are likely to include the hero's sidekick, a gunfighter (the hero's friend may be a former gunfighter or a dying one, shades of Doc Holliday), a trail boss or a ranch owner, a saloon girl or two, several bad guys (easily identifiable by their language or irreverence or appearance), a heroine (once usually the schoolmarm, now more likely to be the ranch owner's daughter or an outlaw's daughter), some painted women, and assorted townspeople or rovers to make crowd noises. Actions will come fast and be set at a mine or on Front Street (sometimes even at the O.K. Corral) or in a saloon. There will be a fight over a woman or an old grudge or a card game or a claim or sheep or cattle or the division of the loot in a robbery or who's fastest in a draw, or over anything two men might argue about. All western towns have small boys who idolize the latest hero or the latest gunfighter. All are visited by trail drivers (cattle trails were, according to convention, as wide as the whole West to have encompassed all the towns in books that mention trail drives). All have deadlines visitors must not cross at peril to their lives.

Ferol Egan's *The Taste of Time* employs several of these conventions just as it invents other incidents. Seventy-year-old Jedediah Wright, New York farmer, has watched his wife die and waits for his own death to come. Then he realizes life may not quite be over yet, and, to the consternation of his family, he takes off for the wild West to live a little before he dies. Having no idea how to get wherever it is he is going, Jed joins up with two young men. Their battles with Indians and settlers, the death of one

Today, writers of westerns often turn to the contemporary West.

young man at the hands of a couple of desperadoes, and their move on to the gold territory fits into the conventions, but there is far more to the book. Jed is anything but the usual westbound youth, and his keen common sense and his willingness to live and learn are not typical of westerns. Neither is his friendship with an educated Chinese man, Lem. The fact that this relationship is not tolerance but total acceptance is unusual for the time and for the western novel. His marriage to a young Indian girl (who comes with the mining claim Jed and Lem purchase) is touching and believable despite the discrepancy in their ages. Perhaps we are all moved to discover an old man who does not nibble at life, but rips it off in big chunks and hungers for more.

Well-told novels of the American Indian include Benjamin Capps' *A Woman of the People* about Helen Morrison, who is captured by Comanches and over the years becomes a part of their way, one of the people. It's a fine book as Capps' books usually are. Dorothy Johnston's *Buffalo Woman* is about the meaning of womanhood in the Oglala tribe. From the time Whirlwind is thirteen her tribe suffers hardships and she cries out, "Everything is wrong. The world is upside down." And Lynn Gessner's *Navajo Slave* is about a Navajo boy kidnapped by Utes and sold into slavery to rich Spanish landowners.

Three fine novels about western badmen are Charles O. Locke's *The Hell Bent Kid* about a decent youngster, Tot Lohman, who kills a cowboy in a dance brawl and then finds it difficult to escape the retribution of the victim's family. E. L. Doctorow's *Welcome to Hard Times* is about the Man from Boise, a brutal gunslinger who lays low the town of Hard Times. When the people finally succeed in putting it back together, he returns to devastate it once more out of sheer love of destruction. Gary Jennings's often funny *The Terrible Teague Bunch* is about four misfits, all of them rather nice, who decide to rob a train. The obstacles they encounter are believable, and their attempts to become outlaws are amusing, touching, and sometimes savage.

In a genre that would seem antithetical to humor, four books stand out. David Wagoner's *The Road to Many a Wonder* is the frustrating road two very young newlyweds follow to reach a gold claim near Denver. Robert Flynn's *North to Yesterday* sometimes borders on a lampoon, but mostly it's wryly amusing and quixotic. Similar to Flynn's book is Robert Day's *The Last Cattle Drive* about a contemporary Kansas rancher who, fed up with the high price of paying truckers to haul his beef, sets out to drive the cattle to Kansas City. Bill Gulick's *Liveliest Town in the West* is set in sleepy, dull, ignored-by-everyone Dustville. The public relations editor of the *Dustville Clarion* decides to put the town on the map by creating a hero of such accomplishments and proportions that tourists will flock to the town. The book, though silly at times, is for the most part a good-natured spoof by an accomplished writer of more traditional westerns.

Once, the western meant the old West. Today, writers have turned to the contemporary West, perhaps to use it simply as a setting, more likely to show today's decadent or lost West compared to the vital West of yesterday. Larry McMurtry's *The Last Picture Show*, brilliantly filmed by Peter Bogdanovich, is literally about the last time a movie is shown in a small town drying up through lack of interest. McMurtry's *Leaving Cheyenne* and *Horseman, Pass By* (filmed under the title *Hud*) are equally pained novels about the once potent but now increasingly tame Texas prairies.

Contemporary authors write of the Indian today, emasculated by white society. James Welch's *Winter in the Blood* is set on a Montana ranch and is about the bleakness faced by a Native American as he examines his life in search of some meaning for today and some hope for tomorrow. Marilyn Harris' *Hatter Fox* is almost equally cynical about today and tomorrow. Seventeen-year-old Navajo Hatter Fox is in jail and Dr. Teague Summer tries to help. When she is sent to a reformatory, he follows in hopes of keeping her out of a mental institution. It is one of the favorites of young adults. N. Scott Momaday's *House Made of Dawn* is about Abel before and after World War II on his Indian reservation with his grandfather. The bitterest critic, and often the funniest and most effective with his wicked satiric pen, is Vine Deloria, Jr., whose *Custer Died for Your Sins: An Indian Manifesto* savagely attacks whites, especially missionaries, for the sins committed in the name of progress, advancement, and acculturation.

Two oddities deserve mention. Clair Huffaker's *The Cowboy and the Cossack* is set not in the West but in Siberia where fifteen American cowboys and fifteen Russian cossacks ride herd on a 4,000-mile trail drive in 1880. Huffaker is a fine writer and the offbeat topic is well handled. Richard Brautigan's *The Hawkline Monster: A Gothic Western* is bawdy and irreverent and very funny if readers are willing to mix the western and cowboys with the gothic and a monster. Brautigan fans, and there are many of them, who liked *Trout Fishing in America, In Watermelon Sugar,* and especially *Willard and His Bowling Trophy: A Perverse Mystery* will like *The Hawkline Monster.*

Many of the conventions of the western are so similar to the conventions of young adult books as described in Chapter 1 that there is really little need for westerns written especially for readers of this age. For example, many characters are familiar types and the hero is relatively young or is at least a loner not encumbered by family responsibilities. The achievement is a worthy one with which young readers can identify. The plot is straightforward, and the vocabulary and syntax are not overly complex. This means that with westerns, more than with most genres, teenage readers will adopt as their own the books that are published for the general adult audience.

MYSTERIES

Daniel's detection of the guilty in the story of Susanna in the Apocrypha is arguably the first detective story. But the modern mystery began with Poe's "The Murders in the Rue Morgue" in 1841. Soon after, dime novel detectives like Old King Brady, Old Sleuth, Young Sleuth, Cap Collier, and, foremost of them all, Nick Carter, popularized detective and mystery stories in the United States. But the first truly great literary detective after Poe's C. Auguste Dupin appeared in 1887 when Sherlock Holmes strode across the pages of Arthur Conan Doyle's *A Study in Scarlet* accompanied by faithful and always befuddled Dr. Watson.

Why are mysteries so popular? They are often unrealistic, even some of the best of them. They demand a deep suspension of our disbelief, and we gladly give it. We know that mysteries are games, and we love games. We hope, so we say, to beat the detective to the culprit, but we rarely do, and, when it does happen, we feel cheated.

The characteristics of the traditional murder mystery are well known and relatively fixed. Devotees are more interested in variations on a theme than in violations of the rules, and variations seem endless.

There must be a crime. A short story may settle for a robbery or blackmail, but a novel must include a murder; whatever lesser crimes the writer wishes to toss in are fine as long as there is one murder, sometimes more. The murder takes place after a chapter or two are spent introducing the characters, including the probable victim and those who might wish his or her death. Soon after the murder, perhaps before, a detective enters, though he or she may not be an official police officer. Clues are scattered, the investigation of several suspects proceeds, and then the detective solves the case and explains the solution. A denouement may follow, or the book may end almost abruptly, for the work is done and the puzzle solved. The plot is a complex interweaving of suspicion, motives, and clues, but the characters are often simple, undeveloped, stick-figures, save in the best writers of mysteries. We care more about the detectives and the way they work through the puzzles than we do about the people involved.

The hard-boiled mystery differs in some significant ways. The detective is usually a male. He is privately employed and has no altruistic motives. He enters a case for pay, not love of the chase or the puzzle as is common in traditional mysteries. The traditional detective/solver of the crime is often optimistic, even cheerful. Not so the private eye. Working out of a cheerless office, he is tired and cynical, having seen too much of the seamy side of life to feel hope for anything. He has a quiet dignity that he may easily wisecrack about, but the dignity is there. He believes in justice, but he is not above going outside the law to finish a job. Indeed, he is cynical about the courts, the system, and the establishment and may not seem higher on a moral scale than the person pursued. He is impatient with class distinctions. Most important, while he may be involved in a mystery, he is likely to view detective work as hard and routine, not cerebral. The traditional detective is bright and sees what others do not see. The private eye knows that any bright person could do the job by sticking with it long enough and doing the necessary legwork. The traditional mystery may have some violence after the murder, but generally post-murder violence is little more than implied. But in the private detective's world and the hard-boiled mystery novel, violence comes with the territory.

Most prolific of young adult mystery writers is Jay Bennett. *Deathman, Do Not Follow Me,* his first book, begins as a fine study of alienated Danny Morgan. Unhappily, once the reader cares about Danny, a silly mystery intrudes and the book falls apart. But two of his later books are more successful. *The Long Black Coat* and *The Dangling Witness* won Edgar Awards for the best juvenile mysteries for 1973 and 1974. The *Birthday Murderer* continues Bennett's highly popular string of mysteries.

His most hard-boiled work is *Say Hello to the Hit Man.* Fred Morgan, an apparently typical college student with a girl friend, a job, and a future, is the son of a crime syndicate leader. Fred dislikes his father and will not acknowledge him. By the second page, we know something is terribly wrong when a phone call begins:

> "Hello," he said.
>> "Fred Morgan?" A man's voice low and quiet.
>> "Yes?"
>> It was a voice he had never heard before.
>> "Got a message for you, Fred. Say hello to the Hit Man."
>> Fred began to tremble. He couldn't speak. Outside a sudden breeze came
> up and rustled the clothesline.
>> "You're going to die," the voice said.

Out of desperation, Fred seeks his father's help, several people become suspects, and, though the ending is vaguely reminiscent of Hammett's *The Maltese Falcon,* it has a character of its own.

Bennett's mysteries more commonly hinge on implied violence and real threats than on actual murders. Active violence, Bennett seems to say, is less threatening than the possibility of imminent violence, and he's right because threats from unknown or shadowy sources are insidious and may go on forever whereas the event, the actual violence, is real and can be handled, assuming, of course, that you are not dead.

Charles Crawford's *Letter Perfect* is similar to Lois Duncan's *Killing Mr. Griffin.* Three bored students plan a perfect crime as a joke but it loses its humor and turns into serious blackmail. Both novels are concerned with the very real peer pressure students face daily.

A recent mystery by popular writer Ellen Raskin, *The Westing Game,* is a rare young adult novel in that it is a genuinely involving puzzle based on Samuel Westing's will and some clues given to sixteen people. They will inherit the bulk of Westing's estate if they can solve the puzzle. Besides, heroine Turtle Alice Tabitha-Ruth Wexler is an appealing girl. A book from another favorite, Paul Zindel's *The Undertaker's Gone Bananas*, is typical clever Zindel, accurate observations, zany characters, and witty dialogue, eminently forgettable as all his work has been since *My Darling, My Hamburger*. Bobby Perkins, school outcast and inveterate prankster, almost convinces his girl friend Lauri Geddes that the undertaker, Mr. Hulka, has killed his wife. Lauri doubts but not so much as do the police, and Bobby becomes the boy who cried wolf as he and Lauri discover evidence that Hulka is a killer and soon to become their pursuer.

The offbeat detective can be found in Henry Winterfeld's *Detectives in Togas* and its sequel *Mystery of the Roman Ransom*, both set in ancient Rome with schoolboys playing detectives. Harry Kemelman has written seven popular mysteries about Rabbi David Small and his Talmudic reasoning powers, *Friday the Rabbi Slept Late, Saturday the Rabbi Went Hungry, Sunday the Rabbi Stayed Home, Monday the Rabbi Took Off, Tuesday the Rabbi Saw Red, Wednesday the Rabbi Got Wet,* and *Thursday the Rabbi Walked Out*. What the good man does next with no days left remains a mystery in itself at the moment. Tony Hillerman's *The Blessing Way, Dance Hall of the Dead,* and *The Listening Woman* have Navajo Joe Leaphorn as a detective working on various tribal reservations and handling delicate matters of tribal religions and myths, all convincing, accurate, and good mysteries, to boot.

Julian Symons' *The Blackheath Poisonings: A Victorian Murder Mystery* is accurately titled. In a late nineteenth-century London suburb, two families of toymakers watch three people die of arsenic poisoning. Symons' book is a mystery but also a comment on and a revelation of a time and a place and some fascinating human beings who, quite accidentally, are fictional. Donald Zochert's *Murder in the Hellfire Club* begins with

---

The "perfect crime" in juvenile mysteries is not a crime at all but is instead some sort of a puzzle.

---

a murdered porter found dead in a locked room and Ben Franklin, American and citizen of the world, playing detective. The plot is intricate, the characterization of the eighteenth-century Franklin excellent indeed—Zochert even coins some pseudo-Poor Richard epigrams—and the atmosphere of the rakish Hellfire Club is believable and accurate. Zochert's use of an actual historical figure as a fictional detective is in the same tradition as, though not derived from, Lillian de la Torre's employment of Dr. Samuel Johnson, the great dictionary maker, in two collections of short stories, *Dr. Sam: Johnson, Detector* and *The Detections of Dr. Sam: Johnson*.

Finally, Sherlock Holmes imitators never die though imitations are sometimes abortions or abominations. Three recent, rather good ones are Nicholas Meyer's *The Seven-Per-Cent Solution* (sending Holmes to Vienna and Freud) and *The West End Horror* (leaving Holmes in London along with G. B. Shaw and others), and Michael Dibdin's *The Last Sherlock Holmes Story* (featuring Holmes and Jack the Ripper).

Perhaps the basic appeal of mysteries goes beyond the game into something elemental. All of us wish harmony restored whenever we are threatened with chaos. We yearn, sometimes secretly, to play Hamlet and put the world aright. Mysteries allow us to do that vicariously. Something is out of joint—a murder—and the good of society is threatened. The detective steps in and puts the world back into order, right is restored, and light reigns, at least for a time.

There are some differences in mysteries written specifically for young readers and those written for the general public. In the ones published for young readers, the crimes are going to be less violent, especially if they are committed by a young person. Murder, for example, will probably not be premeditated, but instead will be the result of an accident or a prank gone awry. It is because of this reluctance to have young protagonists involved in "real" crimes, that mysteries written specifically for young people are a relatively recent addition to the field. The "perfect crime" in juvenile mysteries is not a crime at all but is instead some sort of a puzzle. It's partly because she was clever enough to come up with a truly intriguing mystery without any real villains that Ellen Raskin won the Newbery Award for *The Westing Game.*

STORIES OF THE SUPERNATURAL

The supernatural appeals to us because there is always the threat of the unknown striking in secret ways and in secret places. Fear of the unknown may go back to prehistoric times when cave shadows and lightning mystified and darkness was a threat. Humanity has always demanded answers, even to impossible and irrational questions, and the unknown could only be explained sensibly—or so it must have seemed—in terms of superior but unnatural elements and beings. Such explanations must have especially satisfied heroes forced to fight such unnatural things. Fighting the unbelievable and inexplicable is far more challenging, and winning would be more pleasing, losing more acceptable.

Even with our modern knowledge and sophistication, we have held onto our fascination with the inexplicable. We delight in chambers of horrors, tunnels of terror, or haunted houses. We claim to be rational yet read the astrology columns daily. We mock the superstitions of others yet allow ourselves a pet one or two, joking to others that we do not mean to be taken seriously when we toss salt over our shoulders, refuse to walk under a ladder, avoid black cats, and knock on wood. Oddly enough, we follow superstitions at times without recognizing them, assuming that certain customs have always existed without inquiring why. Black is often assumed to be the appropriate dress for funerals since it is dark and gloomy and demonstrates respect or solemnity, or so we reason. We may not be aware that black was worn at some time lost in history because spirits, sometimes malignant or perhaps just indignant, lingered near the corpse for a time. Wearing black made the living difficult for evil or irritated spirits to see. As long as the spirits were around, danger lurked, hence long mourning periods. Somehow, that simple belief developed into the customs we follow even yet.

Greek and Roman literature extensively used supernatural elements. So did Shakespeare much later. Whether he believed in witches and ghosts and things that go bump in the night is conjectural. Certainly, some of the Elizabethan audience did.

The gothic novel of terror through the unexplainable (at least unexplained) began with Horace Walpole's *The Castle of Otranto* in 1764. The early phase of supernatural novels culminated in Mary Shelley's *Frankenstein* (1818), which brought enlightenment and concern for humanity into what had been a school of writing devoted to pure fright. The romantic poets' interest in supernatural events led to Coleridge's "The Rime of the Ancient Mariner," surely regarded by many high-school students as one of the all-time great curses.

Television, despite the frequent excellence of Rod Serling's "Twilight Zone," has never capitalized on the supernatural, perhaps because it is too literal a medium, perhaps because of inadequate budgets. Radio, appealing more to the imagination, indeed, forcing listeners to use their imaginations, had a natural affinity for the supernatural. Horror movies such as *Dracula, The Mummy,* and *Dead of Night* have always attracted crowds.

Supernatural thrillers have ground rules fans know and they expect authors to abide by them. Settings are usually in some eerie, haunted house or the scene where some strange event took place years ago. Some thrillers are set in the more mundane world, say a brownstone house in New York City, but the mundane will not remain calm and average for long as frightening events unroll and strange people come out to play. Darkness is essential; usually it is physical darkness, but the darkness of the soul in broad daylight will do nicely. The hero—either male or female—will be good, at first oblivious to the evil around but increasingly aware of the climate of fear that pervades. Often a wife or a husband will sell out to evil and entice the spouse to join in a black mass. Rituals or ceremonies are essential. There are family curses or pacts made with the devil by witches who are identifiable because they cannot be seen in mirrors or photographs or because they carelessly leave behind a mark or token that is a sign of their work, for example, a lock of hair from the victim, a waxen image, or a burnt candle.

In Lois Duncan's *Summer of Fear,* Rachel Bryant's family is notified that some relatives have died in a car accident, except for the seventeen-year-old daughter, Julia. The young girl, looking strangely mature for seventeen, arrives and changes the lives of everyone in the family. Rachel, the narrator, suspects, without quite knowing why, that Julia is different. How different she learns later:

> Julia was a plain, thin girl with long, black hair that hung halfway to her waist. Her brows were heavy, her face narrow and sallow, but her *eyes*—even now, thinking back upon that moment, I cannot begin to describe my first impression of her eyes. They were deep and dark and filled with secrets. Haunted eyes. Haunting eyes. They were the strangest eyes I had ever seen.

Rachel does not care for Julia, but the most distrustful member of the family is Trickle, the dog, who growls at Julia. According to legend, animals have insight into who is and who is not normal. Trickle is not long for this world, but then neither is anyone who gets in Julia's way. A burned wax image, stranger and stranger eyes, Julia's inability to be photographed, and more contribute to Rachel's awakening, Julia's downfall, and a fine supernatural thriller.

Exorcism appears frequently in tales of the supernatural, and in none more so than in William Blatty's *The Exorcist* in which a mother and a priest set out to save twelve-year-old Regan MacNeil from satanic possession. A less successful exorcism is seen in Jay Anson's supposedly true tale, *The Amityville Horror*. In December 1975, George Lee Lutz, wife Kathleen, and three children move into a Long Island home valued far beyond their budget but selling for surprisingly little. They later learn that one year earlier a particularly gruesome mass murder had taken place there. Each night after they move in strange things happen—a red-eyed pig is seen at a window, noises begin at 3:15 A.M. (the time of the murders), flies infest the sewing room, and the family dog—animals, remember, have second sight in these things—will not enter the house. A priest attempts to exorcise the spirits, but bad things happen to him and the family moves out.

There are several other popular supernatural thrillers. William Goldman's *Magic* is about a failed magician who makes a pact with the devil. Thomas Page's *The Spirit* is about Indian John Moon, formerly a Green Beret in Vietnam, who returns to his mountains to search for a spirit to guide and protect him. He finds Bigfoot whom he

---

Darkness is essential; usually it is physical darkness, but the darkness of the soul in broad daylight will do nicely.

---

follows and for whom he willingly kills. Penelope Lively's *The Ghost of Thomas Kempe* is about young James who discovers a small greenish glass bottle containing the ghost of Kempe. He releases the one-hundred-year-old spirit and then must face up to the problem of evil that surrounds him. Gene Wolfe's *The Devil in a Forest* is about an English medieval village in cahoots with a bandit. It is struggling to rid itself of the superstitions to which it still clings.

Humor seems at odds with the supernatural, but three novels are both supernatural and very funny. Richard Peck's *The Ghost Belonged to Me* shows young Alexander learning to believe in the reality of Inez Dumaine's ghost. A sequel, *Ghosts I Have Been*, features Blossom Culp learning to adjust to her own psychic powers. The title of Peter Beagle's *A Fine and Private Place* comes from Marvell's poem "To His Coy Mistress":

> The grave's a fine and private place,
> But none, I think, do there embrace.

The grave is also, in Beagle's touching and amusing novel, a lively, sometimes odd, and usually funny place. A living human talks to the dead, the dead find a kind of love after death, and a delightfully tough old raven thinks the whole thing is wacky. The raven brings food to the human who lives there, constantly complains about flying because he is getting along in years, and one day finds an unorthodox answer to tired wings. He hops a ride on a truck:

He had never done such a thing before. Because he was too arrogant to walk, too heavy for telephone wires, and too unpopular for bird sanctuaries, an amazingly large portion of his life had been spent in the air. He felt no particular pride in having been born a bird, and he subscribed to no avian code of ethics, but he had never seen a bird make use of human transportation, and pioneers made him nervous.

The decision had to be made quickly. His wings felt like flatirons, and the truck was pulling farther and farther ahead. The raven glanced quickly around, saw nobody, hesitated, felt oddly guilty, said, "Ah, screw it," raised one last small chinook of flapping, and fell, gasping, into the back of the truck.

"By God," he said aloud, "this is the way to travel. Damned if I ever fly another stroke."

Obviously this is not your run-of-the-mill supernatural thriller, but then that is the point about good supernatural books. Each one has to be different. Since they are exploring the unknown, they need to do it in previously unknown ways. Because young adults are curious and in many ways more open than adults in conjecturing and exploring new ideas, the supernatural is especially appealing to many of them. Treading on spooky ground is a social experience, and teenagers delight in rounding up a group of friends to go together to see a scary movie, swap stories, and discuss the possibilities of ghosts, goblins, and even griffins.

HISTORICAL FICTION

Most of us read historical novels because we are curious about other times and other places and other people, but we are likely to be disappointed if the books lack adventure, mystery, and general excitement. Movies like *Gone with the Wind, The Three Musketeers, Bonnie and Clyde,* and *Little Big Man* pique the interest of viewers heretofore ignorant of a particular time and place, just as popular television shows like *Centennial, Roots, Little House on the Prairie,* and *Upstairs, Downstairs,* attract viewers in the millions. History sells, as any publisher knows, but history sells better if adventure, mystery, and suspense are integral parts.

Certainly best-selling historical fiction in America has not been short on excitement. For examples one can look at Sir Walter Scott's *Waverly* (1814), James Fenimore Cooper's *The Deerslayer* (1841), Alexandre Dumas' *The Count of Monte Cristo* (1844), Lew Wallace's *Ben Hur* (1880), Mary Johnston's *To Have and To Hold* (1900), Rafael Sabatini's *Scaramouche* (1921), Hervey Allen's *Anthony Adverse* (1938), and Thomas Costain's *The Silver Chalice* (1953).

As in any other subgenre, historical novels have their conventions. A historical novel should be steeped in accurate pictures of the people, events, totems, and taboos of a time, the food, the clothing, customs, transportation, literature, music, houses, smells, games, vocations, and religions. Enthusiasts will forgive no anachronism no matter how small. The novel should give a sense of history's continuity, a feeling for the flow of history from one period into another that will for good reason be different from the period before. It should tell a lively story with a sense of impending danger, mystery, or romance that moves the action, and action there must be.

Usually a historical novel focuses on one major character and carries this person from birth or early childhood through marriage or the time of majority. The major figure may be involved with real historical figures and will certainly be caught up in real happenings. The hero presents a picture of the time better than any schoolbook history. Readers will have a more compassionate or more perceptive view of history capturing the essence of the time and place chosen. The protagonist acts as a mediator between us and the history we do not know or have forgotten.

Two English historical novelists lead all the rest. Leon Garfield began with *Jack Holborn* in 1965, and that book set the tone and place for all his novels to follow. All are set in the eighteenth century and most are about orphans searching for a heritage and a home. *The Sound of Coaches* has a particularly fine opening that catches the sights, feelings, and sounds of the time:

> Once upon a winter's night when the wind blew its guts out and a fishy piece of moon scuttled among the clouds, a coach came thundering down the long hill outside of Dorking. Its progress was wild and the coachman and his guard rocked from side to side as if the maddened vehicle was struggling to rid itself of them before going on to hell without the benefit of further advice. Even the passing landscape conspired to increase the terror of the journey, and the fleeting sight of a gibbet—its iron cage swinging desolately against the sky—turned the five passengers' thoughts towards the next world . . . of which destination there'd been no mention in Chichester where they'd booked their passage.

Once the five passengers, the coachman, and the guard (who turns out to be the coachman's wife) reach Dorking a young girl has a baby and dies leaving an orphan behind but no identity for mother or child. At first annoyed, then involved, and finally moved, the passengers all become parents of one sort or another, though Mr. Chichester and his wife raise the child whom they name Sam. The first part of the book is Sam's growth until age thirteen and his insatiable desire to be a coachman. The second and third parts tell of his journey to London, his apprenticeship as an actor in a quarrelsome and rather poor acting troupe, and his search for his father. Garfield reminds readers of Fielding's wit and humor and youthful exuberance as seen in *The History of Tom Jones, A Foundling* (1749) and of Smollett's love and compassion and generosity in his *The Expedition of Humphry Clinker* (1771).

Garfield's eighteenth century is a lusty, squalid, swollen, ugly, bustling world filled with adventure and has some beautifully developed humor mixed with dramatic moments. Typically eighteenth century, the story deals with an orphan searching for identity, reality versus illusion, daylight versus dreams, flesh versus fantasy. Garfield's ability to characterize major or even minor figures is amazing, but his one-sentence sketches of characters that appear only once are equally impressive. Of one man, he writes, "He was one of those gentlemen who affect great gallantry to all the fair sex

---

SUGGESTIONS FOR EVALUATING HISTORICAL FICTION

A good historical novel usually has:	A poor historical novel may have:
A setting that is integral to the story.	A story that could have happened any time or any place. The historical setting is for visual appeal and to compensate for a weak story.
An authentic rendition of the time, place, and people being featured.	
An author who is so thoroughly steeped in the history of the period that he or she can be comfortably creative without making mistakes.	Anachronisms in which the author illogically mixes up people, events, speaking styles, social values, or technological developments from different time periods.
Believable characters with whom young readers can identify.	Awkward narration and exposition as the author tries to teach history through the characters' conversations.
Evidence that even across great time spans people share similar emotions.	Oversimplification of the historical issues and a stereotyping of the "bad" and the "good" guys.
References to well-known events or people, or other clues through which the reader can place the happenings in their correct historical framework.	Characters who fail to come alive as individuals who have something in common with the reader. They are just stereotyped representatives of a particular period.
Readers who come away with the feeling that they know a time or place better. It is as if they have lived in it for at least a few hours.	

---

except their wives." Of a prostitute he writes, "A face full of beauty spots, with grave-yard dust between." And about the protagonist in *The Sound of Coaches*, the reader is told, "although jealousy was ordinarily foreign to Sam's nature, they did, on occasion, talk the same language." And Garfield's epigrams are often most effective, for example, "Many a man is made good by being thought so."

The other outstanding writer of historical fiction for young adults is Rosemary Sutcliff, who has published several novels about Roman Britain and several others about the early days of Britain. Using subtly developed characters always true to a particular time and place, she has produced a body of literature that is deserving of attention, probably because she is deeply committed to the past and to making it intelligible, warts and all, to her readers. Her Roman Britain novels begin with *The Eagle of the Ninth* set in 125 A.D. when Marcus sets out to trace the lost Ninth Hispana Legion. This is Sutcliff's favorite novel and her best. It is followed by *The Silver Branch*, about Saxon mercenaries beginning to nibble at Roman heels, and *The Lantern Bearers*, which takes place after almost four hundred years of occupation as Roman troops leave England. *The Capricorn Bracelet* links the Roman Britain novels to her Britain novels by means of a bracelet passed down from one member of a family to the next between 61 A.D. and 383 A.D. This book is followed by *The Mark of the Horse Lord,* about a former Roman slave and gladiator; *Warrior Scarlet,* set in the Bronze Age; *Song for a Dark Queen,* about Queen Boadicea or Boudicca; *The Shield Ring,* which tells of the Vikings in Britain; *Sword at Sunset,* about Artos or King Arthur; *Knight's Fee,* set after the Battle of Hastings; *Simon,* about the English Civil War and Cromwell; and *Rider on a White Horse,* set after that war.

Most of Sutcliff's books are about a romantic dying cause, never romanticized, but viewed with just the slightest hint of a nostalgic sigh that comes, not from the novelist, but from a historian who cares deeply about her subject and her people.

There are many other good writers of historical fiction for young people including some of those cited in Chapter 10. Two views of slave trading are seen in Hester Burton's *To Ravensrigg* and Paula Fox's *The Slave Dancer.* Burton's book is told from a British point of view and centers on Emmie Hesket, an orphan. It is both a mystery and an indictment of slavery and the slave trade. Fox is more direct in indicting slavery. The protagonist Jessie Bollier at age thirteen is kidnapped to play his fife on a slave ship to keep slaves in shape so that they will bring better prices. Fox's book has been attacked, mostly by revisionists who object to a white boy telling a tale so painful and heinous to blacks, and to other people as well. Surely Jessie's viewpoint is not that of a modern person, but then neither is Huck Finn's or Jo March's or Henry David Thoreau's or Shakespeare's. *The Slave Dancer* is Fox's statement of horror at our cruelty to each other performed in the name of progress, and it is an honest and somber and powerful truth, well told. The controversy illustrates a problem area that is particularly common to historical books.

Nathaniel Benchley's *Beyond the Mists* amusingly and accurately tells of the time of Viking raids on Britain and the rise of Christianity in Scandinavia. Historical novels are often weak in humor, and Benchley's novel stands out in contrast. Gunnar, sole survivor of a Viking raiding party, returns to Norway to find the King has been baptized and is anxious to secure the safety of all other souls through mass baptisms. As Gunnar tells it:

> I was impressed, as he'd intended me to be, but there was something that nagged at my mind. "About this mass baptism," I said, "Have all these people come to you asking to be baptized? I mean, does a whole community suddenly get the urge, all at the same time?"
>
> "In a manner of speaking, yes," he replied. "We take the troops, and round the people up. Those who are slow to accept the Lord Jesus wind up in the fjord anyway."
>
> "Oh," I said. "I see."
>
> "Yes," said the King. "Later on, of course, they're grateful for their salvation." He'd been leaning forward, and now he sat back to indicate a change of subject. "What do you intend to do?" he asked.
>
> "Oh, I'll be baptized," I said quickly. "No problem there."

A variation in the historical novels is Anne Eliot Crompton's *A Woman's Place*. Told in five sections, the novel recreates the woman's place (a farmhouse) in 1750, 1800, 1850, 1900, and 1950 with different families and descendants interweaving in an intricate and ordered plot. Least satisfying for the last episode, Crompton's book presents a series of crises and yields a sense of history's continuity that is surprisingly rare in too many historical novels. Not so much a variation as it is simply a fine novel, E. L. Doctorow's *Ragtime* is about the ragtime era, and the prose itself has a syncopated ragtime beat. The ragtime orchestration allows wholly new and important characters to enter halfway through the novel just as ragtime music allows new melodies to emerge throughout. It is not, as some people thought, a new kind of story mixing historical figures with fictional figures—Shakespeare and others had done that long before Doctorow—but it is an effectively written novel about illusions and dreams at war with reality and life. Coalhouse Walker's story and his madly great vision of changing the world caught some militants' attention, but the whole novel deserved wide readership.

A weakness, some maintain, of the historical novel is that it removes readers from reality today and keeps them in the past. That is not true of better historical novels like those cited in the last few pages. These books are filled with interesting characters, fast-moving plots, and vivid settings. In other words, they are absorbing stories. They catch readers up in a period of history and then send them back to the present more aware of where they came from, perhaps a little more curious about their roots and their prospects. Historical novels show us both real and fictional characters trying, as we all must, to work out problems and human dilemmas. These characters may have lived in circumstances far different from our own, but they had similar feelings and problems. By understanding that, we enrich our own lives and spirits.

As the books cited in this section have shown, excitement and suspense stories and historical fiction provide wonderful opportunities for living in someone else's shoes. Readers feel emotions they could get in no other way whether it is the exhilaration of being on top of a magnificent mountain, the satisfaction of winning against incredible odds, or just the weak-kneed relief that comes from living through a harrowing experience.

But with some recent stories, authors provide a bonus. They give the reader something to ponder after the story is finished. It may relate to ecology and what happens when old and new cultures clash. Or it may relate to unfairness and the need for human dignity as shown in some of the recent books about Native Americans, or it may illustrate the political and emotional interrelatedness of people in today's world as shown in stories about terrorists. But whatever the problem, the real mark of success in such stories is the degree to which the author can involve the reader's emotions.

ACTIVITIES

1. Because of the excitement and the suspense, the stories in this section are excellent material for book talks. Read three of the books and prepare book talks on them. If you need help, look ahead to Chapter 12 for suggestions.

2. From the books that you read in relation to this chapter, select one that has not been made into a movie but that you think would be good on the screen. Describe the setting you envision, the music, and the actors. Are there major changes that you would make to accommodate a different medium? Tell why you think it would make a good movie.

3. It is commonly said that characterization is relatively weak in the adventure story. Think back to a problem novel or an accomplishment-romance that you read earlier and compare the characterization with that in one of the adventure stories that you read for this chapter. In which story was it stronger, that is, which protagonist do you feel you know the best? How did the authors reveal character? Were there revelations of character all the way through or only at the beginning? Considering the different purposes of each author, how well did they succeed in getting you acquainted with the respective protagonists?

4. Read a historical novel and write an evaluation of it. You might use the chart on page 246 to stimulate your thinking. But, as you write your evaluation, remember that such charts or lists can never be more than starting points. Every book is unique and the chart is a generalization. Feel free to go beyond the ideas presented in the charts or to disagree with them according to the particular book you are evaluating.

RECOMMENDED TITLES

For information on the availability of paperback editions of these titles, please consult the most recent edition of *Paperbound Books in Print,* published annually by R. R. Bowker Company.

Adventure Stories

Adams, Richard. *The Plague Dogs.* Alfred A. Knopf, 1978.

Adlard, Mark. *The Greenlander.* Summit, 1979.

Aldridge, James. *The Marvelous Mongolian.* Little, Brown, 1974.

Benchley, Peter. *Jaws.* Doubleday, 1974.

Bickel, Lennard. *Mawson's Will.* Stein and Day, 1977.

Branscum, Robbie. *Me and Jim Luke.* Doubleday, 1971.

Burnford, Sheila. *Bel Ria.* Little, Brown, 1978.

———. *The Incredible Journey.* Little, Brown, 1961.

Caras, Roger. *The Custer Wolf: Biography of an American Renegade.* Little, Brown, 1966.

Charriere, Henri. *Papillon.* William Morrow, 1970.

Clark, Mary Higgins. *A Stranger Is Watching.* Simon & Schuster, 1978.

Clark, Mavis Thorpe. *If the Earth Falls In.* Seabury, 1975.

Cohen, Peter Zachary. *Deadly Game at Stony Creek.* Dial, 1978.

Conrad, Barnaby and Niels Mortensen. *Endangered.* G. P. Putnam's Sons, 1978.

Crichton, Michael. *The Great Train Robbery*. Alfred A. Knopf, 1975.

Deighton, Len. *SS-GB*. Alfred A. Knopf, 1979.

Dickinson, Peter. *Annerton Pit*. Little, Brown, 1977.

Eckert, Allen W. *Incident at Hawk's Hill*. Little, Brown, 1971.

Elder, Lauren and Shirley Streshinsky. *And I Alone Survived*. E. P. Dutton, 1978.

Ellis, Mel. *The Wild Horse Killers*. Holt, Rinehart & Winston, 1976.

Faust, Ron. *The Burning Sky*. Playboy, 1978.

Feeley, Pat. *Best Friend*. E. P. Dutton, 1977.

Fenner, Phyllis R., ed. *Perilous Ascent: Stories of Mountain Climbing*. William Morrow, 1970.

Forbes, Colin. *Avalanche Express*. E. P. Dutton, 1977.

Forsyth, Frederick. *The Day of the Jackal*. Viking, 1971.

———. *The Odessa File*. Viking, 1972.

Gallico, Paul. *The Poseidon Adventure*. Coward, McCann & Geoghegan, 1969.

Godey, John. *The Snake*. G. P. Putnam's Sons, 1978.

———. *The Taking of Pelham One Two Three*. G. P. Putnam's Sons, 1973.

Goldman, William. *Marathon Man*. Delacorte, 1974.

Harris, Thomas. *Black Sunday*. G. P. Putnam's Sons, 1975.

Haston, Dougal. *In High Places*. Macmillan, 1973.

Hillary, Edmund. *From the Ocean to the Sky*. Viking, 1979.

———. *Nothing Venture, Nothing Win*. Coward, McCann, & Geoghegan, 1975.

Houston, James. *Frozen Fire*. Atheneum, 1977.

Hubank, Roger. *North Wall*. Viking, 1978.

Judson, William. *Cold River*. Mason/Charter, 1974.

Lange, Oliver. *Red Snow*. Seaview, 1978.

Lawrence, R. D. *The North Runner*. Holt, Rinehart & Winston, 1979.

Ludlum, Robert. *The Holcroft Covenant*. Dial, 1978.

———. *The Matarese Circle*. Richard Marek, 1979.

MacInnes, Helen. *Above Suspicion*. Little, Brown, 1941.

———. *Prelude to Terror*. Harcourt Brace Jovanovich, 1978.

———. *The Salzburg Connection*. Harcourt Brace Jovanovich, 1968.

———. *The Snare of the Hunter*. Harcourt Brace Jovanovich, 1974.

MacLean, Alistair. *Breakheart Pass*. Doubleday, 1974.

———. *Circus*. Doubleday, 1975.

Mazer, Harry. *Snow Bound*. Delacorte, 1973.

Messner, Reinhold. *The Big Walls*. Oxford University, 1978.

Morrell, David. *Testament*. M. Evans, 1975.

Peck, Richard. *Through a Brief Darkness*. Viking, 1973.

Phipson, Joan. *The Cats*. Atheneum, 1976.

Poole, Josephine. *Touch and Go.* Harper & Row, 1976.

Roberts, David. *Deborah: A Wilderness Narrative.* Vanguard, 1970.

———. *The Mountain of My Fear.* Vanguard, 1968.

Rose, Eugene A. *High Odyssey: The First Solo Winter Assault of Mt. Whitney and the Muir Trail Area.* Howell-North, 1974.

Roth, Arthur. *The Iceberg Hermit.* Four Winds, 1974.

Roueche, Berton. *Feral.* Harper & Row, 1974.

Salter, James. *Solo Faces.* Little, Brown, 1979.

Sherman, D. R. *The Lion's Paw.* Doubleday, 1975.

Sleator, William. *Blackbriar.* E. P. Dutton, 1972.

Snyder, Howard H. *The Hall of the Mountain King.* Charles Scribner's Sons, 1973.

Southall, Ivan. *Ash Road.* Greenwillow, 1978.

Stewart, Mary. *The Moon-Spinners.* William Morrow, 1963.

Tanerbaum, Robert and Philip Rosenberg. *Badge of the Assassin.* E. P. Dutton, 1979.

Taylor, Theodore. *Teetoncey.* Doubleday, 1974.

Thiele, Colin. *Fight Against Albatross Two.* Harper & Row, 1976.

———. *Fire in the Stone.* Harper & Row, 1974.

———. *The Hammerhead Light.* Harper & Row, 1977.

———. *The Shadow on the Hills.* Harper & Row, 1978.

Trevor, Elleston. *The Theta Syndrome.* Doubleday, 1977.

Vliet, R. G. *Rockspring.* Viking, 1974.

White, Robb. *Deathwatch.* Doubleday, 1972.

Wibberley, Leonard. *Flint's Island.* Farrar, Straus & Giroux, 1972.

Westerns

Benedict, Rex. *Good Luck, Arizona Man.* Pantheon, 1972.

———. *Goodbye to the Purple Sage: The Last Great Ride of the Sheriff of Medicine Creek.* Pantheon, 1973.

———. *Last Stand at Goodbye Gulch.* Pantheon, 1974.

———. *The Ballad of Cactus Jack.* Pantheon, 1975.

Bradford, Richard. *Red Sky at Morning.* J. B. Lippincott, 1968.

Brautigan, Richard. *The Hawkline Monster: A Gothic Western.* Simon and Schuster, 1974.

Capps, Benjamin. *The Trail to Ogallala.* Duell, 1964.

———. *Woman Chief.* Doubleday, 1979.

———. *The Woman of the People.* Duell, 1966.

Clements, Bruce. *The Faces of Abraham Candle.* Farrar, Straus & Giroux, 1969.

Day, Robert. *The Last Cattle Drive.* G. P. Putnam's Sons, 1977.

Decker, William. *To Be a Man.* Little, Brown, 1967.

Deloria, Vine. *Custer Died for Your Sins: An Indian Manifesto.* Macmillan, 1969.

Doctorow, E. L. *Welcome to Hard Times.* Simon and Schuster, 1960.

Egan, Ferol. *The Taste of Time.* McGraw-Hill, 1977.

Flynn, Robert. *North to Yesterday.* Alfred A. Knopf, 1967.

Forman, James. *People of the Dream.* Farrar, Straus & Giroux, 1972.

Garfield, Brian. *Wild Times.* Simon and Schuster, 1979.

Gessner, Lynne. *Navajo Slave.* Harvey House, 1976.

————. *Danny.* Harvey House, 1978.

Grove, Fred. *The Great Horse Race.* Doubleday, 1977.

————. *Bush Track.* Doubleday, 1978.

Gulick, Bill. *The Liveliest Town in the West.* Doubleday, 1969.

Hall, Oakley. *The Bad Lands.* Atheneum, 1978.

Harris, Marilyn. *Hatter Fox.* Random House, 1973.

Henry, Will. *The Bear Paw Horses.* J. B. Lippincott, 1973.

————. *From Where the Sun Now Stands.* Random House, 1960.

————. *One More River to Cross.* Random House, 1967.

————. *Maheo's Children.* Chilton, 1968.

————. *Summer of the Gun.* J. B. Lippincott, 1978.

Hill, Ruth. *Hanta Yo.* Doubleday, 1979.

Houston, Robert. *Bisbee '17.* Pantheon, 1979.

Huffaker, Clair. *The Cowboy and the Cossack.* Trident, 1973.

Jennings, Gary. *The Terrible Teague Bunch.* W. W. Norton, 1975.

Johnston, Dorothy. *Buffalo Woman.* Dodd, Mead, 1977.

L'Amour, Louis. *Down the Long Hills.* Bantam, 1968.

Locke, Charles O. *The Hell Bent Kid.* W. W. Norton, 1957.

Manfred, Frederick. *Conquering Horse.* McDowell, Obolensky, 1959.

————. *Lord Grizzly.* McGraw-Hill, 1954.

————. *Riders of Judgment.* Random House, 1957.

McMurtry, Larry. *Horseman, Pass By.* Harper & Row, 1961.

————. *The Last Picture Show.* Dial, 1966.

————. *Leaving Cheyenne.* Harper & Row, 1963.

Momaday, N. Scott. *House Made of Dawn.* Harper & Row, 1968.

————. *The Way to Rainy Mountain.* University of New Mexico Press, 1969.

Purdum, Herbert R. *A Hero for Henry.* Doubleday, 1961.

————. *My Brother John.* Doubleday, 1966.

Richard, Adrienne. *Pistol.* Little, Brown, 1969.

Rockwood, Joyce. *Long Man's Song.* Holt, Rinehart & Winston, 1975.

Schellie, Don. *Me, Cholay & Company: Apache Warriors.* Four Winds, 1973.

Wagoner, David. *The Road to Many a Wonder.* Farrar, Straus & Giroux, 1974.

Welch, James. *Winter in the Blood.* Harper & Row, 1974.

Mysteries

Ball, John. *In the Heat of the Night.* Harper & Row, 1965.

Barry, Nora. *Sherbourne's Folly.* Doubleday, 1978.

Bennett, Jay. *The Birthday Murderer.* Delacorte, 1977.

———. *The Dangling Witness.* Delacorte, 1974.

———. *Deathman, Do Not Follow Me.* Meredith, 1968.

———. *The Long Black Coat.* Delacorte, 1973.

———. *Say Hello to the Hit Man.* Delacorte, 1976.

Branscum, Robbie. *Johnny May.* Doubleday, 1975.

Brown, Roy. *The Cage.* Seabury, 1977.

———. *Find Debbie!* Seabury, 1976.

———. *The Swing of the Gate.* Seabury, 1978.

Christie, Agatha. *And Then There Were None.* Dodd, Mead, 1940.

———. *By the Pricking of My Thumbs.* Dodd, Mead, 1968.

———. *The Murder at the Vicarage.* Dodd, Mead, 1930.

———. *Murder in Retrospect.* Dodd, Mead, 1942.

———. *A Murder Is Announced.* Dodd, Mead, 1950.

———. *The Murder of Roger Ackroyd.* Dodd, Mead, 1926.

———. *Murder After Hours.* Dodd, Mead, 1946.

Corlett, William. *The Dark Side of the Moon.* Bradbury, 1977.

Crawford, Charles. *Letter Perfect.* E. P. Dutton, 1977.

Cromie, Alice. *Lucky to Be Alive.* Simon and Schuster, 1979.

Dibdin, Michael. *The Last Sherlock Holmes Story.* Pantheon, 1978.

Duncan, Lois. *Daughters of Eve.* Little, Brown, 1979.

———. *Killing Mr. Griffin.* Little, Brown, 1978.

Ellis, Mel. *No Man for Murder.* Holt, Rinehart & Winston, 1973.

Francis, Dick. *Enquiry.* Harper & Row, 1969.

———. *Slayride.* Harper & Row, 1973.

Freeling, Nicolas. *The Widow.* Pantheon, 1979.

Garfield, Brian. *The Threepersons Hunt.* M. Evans, 1974.

Greenburg, Dan. *Love Kills.* Harcourt Brace Jovanovich, 1978.

Hillerman, Tony. *The Blessing Way.* Harper & Row, 1970.

———. *Dance Halh kf the Dead.* Harper & Row, 1973.

———. *The Listening Woman.* Harper & Row, 1978.

Hinkemeyer, Michael T. *The Fields of Eden.* G. P. Putnam's Sons, 1977.

Hughes, Dorothy B. *Ride the Pink Horse.* Duell, Sloan, 1946.

James, P. D. *The Black Tower.* Charles Scribner's Sons, 1975.

———. *Death of an Expert Witness.* Charles Scribner's Sons, 1977.

———. *A Mind to Murder.* Charles Scribner's Sons, 1967.

———. *Shroud for a Nightingale.* Charles Scribner's Sons, 1971.

———. *An Unsuitable Job for a Woman.* Charles Scribner's Sons, 1972.

Kemelman, Harry. *Friday the Rabbi Slept Late.* Crown, 1964.

———. *Monday the Rabbi Took Off.* G. P. Putnam's Sons, 1972.

———. *Saturday the Rabbi Went Hungry.* Crown, 1966.

———. *Sunday the Rabbi Stayed Home.* G. P. Putnam's Sons, 1969.

———. *Thursday the Rabbi Walked Out.* William Morrow, 1978.

———. *Tuesday the Rabbi Saw Red.* Arthur Fields, 1973.

———. *Wednesday the Rabbi Got Wet.* William Morrow, 1976.

le Carre, John. *The Spy Who Came in from the Cold.* Coward, McCann & Geoghegan, 1964.

———. *Tinker, Tailor, Soldier, Spy.* Alfred A. Knopf, 1974.

Lovesey, Peter. *Waxwork.* Pantheon, 1978.

MacDonald, John D. *The Dreadful Lemon Sky.* J. B. Lippincott, 1975.

Macdonald, Ross. *Sleeping Beauty.* Alfred A. Knopf, 1973.

Meyer, Nicholas. *The Seven-Per-Cent Solution.* E. P. Dutton, 1974.

———. *The West End Horror: A Posthumous Memoir of John H. Watson, M.D.* E. P. Dutton, 1976.

Peyton, K. M. *A Midsummer Night's Death.* Collins World, 1979.

Queen, Ellery (pseudonym of Frederic Dannay and Manfred B. Lee). *Calamity Town.* Little Brown, 1942.

———. *The Greek Coffin Mystery.* Stokes, 1932.

Raskin, Ellen. *The Westing Game.* E. P. Dutton, 1978.

Ray, Mary. *The Ides of April.* Farrar, Straus & Giroux, 1975.

Rendell, Ruth. *No More Dying Then.* Hutchinson, 1971.

———. *A Sleeping Life.* Doubleday, 1978.

———. *Some Lie and Some Die.* Hutchinson, 1973.

Snyder, Zilpha Keatley. *The Egypt Game.* Atheneum, 1967.

Storr, Catherine. *The Chinese Egg.* McGraw-Hill, 1975.

Symons, Julian. *The Blackheath Poisonings: A Victorian Murder Mystery.* Harper & Row, 1978.

Torre, Lillian de la. *The Detections of Dr. Sam: Johnson.* Doubleday, 1960.

———. *Dr. Sam: Johnson, Detector.* Alfred A. Knopf, 1946.

Townsend, John Rowe. *The Intruder.* J. B. Lippincott, 1970.

Winterfeld, Henry. *Detectives in Togas.* Harcourt Brace Jovanovich, 1956.

———. *Mystery of the Roman Ransom.* Harcourt Brace Jovanovich, 1977.

Zindel, Paul. *The Undertaker's Gone Bananas.* Harper & Row, 1978.

Zochert, Donald. *Murder in the Hellfire Club.* Holt, Rinehart & Winston, 1979.

Stories of the Supernatural

Anson, Jay. *The Amityville Horror*. Prentice-Hall, 1977.

Baker, Lucinda. *Walk the Night Unseen*. G. P. Putnam's Sons, 1977.

Beagle, Peter. *A Fine and Private Place*. Viking, 1960.

Blatty, William P. *The Exorcist*. Harper & Row, 1971.

Clapp, Patricia. *Jane-Emily*. Lothrop, Lee & Shepard, 1969.

Coyne, John. *The Piercing*. G. P. Putnam's Sons, 1979.

Cullinan, Thomas. *The Bedeviled*. G. P. Putnam's Sons, 1978.

Duncan, Lois. *A Gift of Magic*. Little, Brown, 1971.

———. *Summer of Fear*. Little, Brown, 1976.

Goldman, William. *Magic*. Delacorte, 1976.

Gordon, John. *The Ghost on the Hill*. Viking, 1977.

Greaves, Margaret. *Stone of Terror*. Harper & Row, 1974.

Hamilton, Virginia. *Justice and Her Brothers*. Greenwillow, 1978.

Harris, Marilyn. *The Conjurers*. Random House, 1974.

Hjortsberg, William. *Falling Angel*. Harcourt Brace Jovanovich, 1978.

King, Stephen. *The Shining*. Doubleday, 1977.

Konvitz, Jeffrey. *The Sentinel*. Simon and Schuster, 1974.

Lawrence, Louise. *The Wyndcliffe*. Harper & Row, 1977.

Leach, Christopher. *Rosalinda*. Frederick Warne, 1978.

Lively, Penelope. *The Ghost of Thomas Kempe*. E. P. Dutton, 1973.

Marasco, Robert. *Burnt Offerings*. Delacorte, 1973.

Maybury, Anne. *Walk in the Paradise Garden*. Random House, 1972.

McGraw, Elois Jarvis. *A Really Weird Summer*. Atheneum, 1977.

Millhiser, Marlys. *The Mirror*. G. P. Putnam's Sons, 1979.

Page, Thomas. *The Spirit*. Wade Rawson, 1977.

Peck, Richard. *The Ghost Belonged to Me*. Viking, 1975.

———. *Ghosts I Have Been*. Viking, 1977.

Poole, Josephine. *Moon Eyes*. Little, Brown, 1967.

Sefton, Catherine. *The Haunting of Ellen*. Harper & Row, 1975.

Severn, David. *The Girl in the Grove*. Harper & Row, 1974.

Sherburne, Zoa. *Why Have All the Birds Stopped Singing?* William Morrow, 1974.

Siddons, Anne Rivers. *The House Next Door*. Simon and Schuster, 1978.

Smith, Martin Cruz. *Nightwing*. W. W. Norton, 1977.

Snyder, Zilpha Keatley. *Heirs of Darkness*. Atheneum, 1978.

———. *The Truth about Stone Hollow*. Atheneum, 1974.

Storr, Catherine. *The Chinese Egg*. McGraw-Hill, 1975.

Straub, Peter, *Ghost Story*. Coward, McCann & Geoghegan, 1979.

Westall, Robert. *The Devil on the Road*. Greenwillow, 1979.

Wolfe, Gene. *The Devil in a Forest*. Follett, 1976.

Historical Fiction

Banks, Lynn Reid. *Sarah and After*. Doubleday, 1977.

Behn, Harry. *The Faraway Lures*. World, 1963.

Benchley, Nathaniel. *Beyond the Mists*. Harper & Row, 1975.

Bunting, Eve. *The Haunting of Kildoran Abbey*. Frederick Warne, 1978.

Burnford, Lolah. *The Vision of Stephen*. Macmillan, 1972.

Burton, Hester. *Castors Away!* World, 1963.

———. *Kate Ryder*. Thomas Y. Crowell, 1975.

———. *To Ravensrigg*. Thomas Y. Crowell, 1977.

Clavell, James. *Shōgun*. Atheneum, 1975.

Collier, James and Christopher Collier. *The Bloody Country*. Four Winds, 1976.

Crompton, Anne Elliot. *A Woman's Place*. Little, Brown, 1978.

Doctorow, E. L. *Ragtime*. Random House, 1975.

Fast, Howard. *The Immigrants*. Houghton Mifflin, 1977.

Flanagan, Thomas. *The Year of the French*. Holt, Rinehart & Winston, 1979.

Fox, Paula. *The Slave Dancer*. Bradbury, 1973.

Garfield, Leon. *The Apprentices*. Viking, 1978.

———. *Black Jack*. Pantheon, 1969.

———. *The Confidence Man*. Viking, 1979.

———. *Devil-in-the-Fog*. Pantheon, 1966.

———. *Jack Holborn*. Pantheon, 1965.

———. *The Pleasure Garden*. Viking, 1976.

———. *The Prisoners of September*. Viking, 1975.

———. *Smith*. Pantheon, 1967.

———. *The Sound of Coaches*. Viking, 1974.

———. *The Strange Affair of Adelaide Harris*. Pantheon, 1971.

Gedge, Pauline. *Child of the Morning*. Dial, 1977.

Goldman, William. *The Princess Bride*. Harcourt Brace Jovanovich, 1972.

Harner, Michael and Alfred Meyer. *Cannibal*. William Morrow, 1979.

Haugaard, Erik Christian. *Cromwell's Boy*. Houghton Mifflin, 1978.

———. *A Messenger for Parliament*. Houghton Mifflin, 1976.

Hunt, Irene. *No Promises in the Wind*. Follett, 1970.

Hunter, Mollie. *The Stronghold*. Harper & Row, 1974.

Keith, Harold. *This Obstinate Land*. Thomas Y. Crowell, 1977.

Lampman, Evelyn Sibley. *Bargain Bride*. Atheneum, 1977.

McCullough, Colleen. *The Thornbirds.* Harper & Row, 1977.

Michener, James A. *Centennial.* Random House, 1974.

O'Dell, Scott. *The Hawk That Dare Not Hunt by Night.* Houghton Mifflin, 1975.

Plaidy, Jean. *The Widow of Windsor.* G. P. Putnam's Sons, 1978.

Pope, Elizabeth Marie. *The Perilous Gard.* Houghton Mifflin, 1974.

Renault, Mary. *The King Must Die.* Pantheon, 1958.

———. *The Praise Singer.* Pantheon, 1978.

Sisson, Rosemary Anne. *Will in Love.* William Morrow, 1977.

Sutcliff, Rosemary. *Blood Feud.* E. P. Dutton, 1977.

———. *The Capricorn Bracelet.* Henry Z. Walck, 1973.

———. *The Eagle of the Ninth.* Henry Z. Walck, 1954.

———. *Knight's Fee.* Henry Z. Walck, 1961.

———. *The Lantern Bearers.* Henry Z. Walck, 1959.

———. *The Mark of the Horse Lord.* Henry Z. Walck, 1965.

———. *Rider on a White Horse.* Coward, McCann & Geoghegan, 1959.

———. *The Shield Ring.* Henry Z. Walck, 1957.

———. *The Silver Branch.* Henry Z. Walck, 1958.

———. *Simon.* Henry Z. Walck, 1954.

———. *Song for a Dark Queen.* Thomas Y. Crowell, 1979.

———. *Sword at Sunset.* Coward, McCann & Geoghegan, 1963.

———. *Warrior Scarlet.* Henry Z. Walck, 1958.

Walsh, Jill Patton. *The Emperor's Winding Sheet.* Farrar, Straus & Giroux, 1974.

West, Jessamyn, *The Massacre at Fall Creek.* Harcourt Brace Jovanovich, 1975.

9

Science Fiction, Fantasy, and Utopias

Of Wondrous Worlds

Most of us, young or old, need occasionally to go outside of ourselves, to dream, to travel, to see things we have never seen, things that may exist, things that could never exist. We may even create our own imaginary land peopled with creations fashioned in our own image or in the images of people or things or animals we admire. Some of those creations are inevitably derivative. Heaven knows how many young people have read an Oz book and then devised an Oz world or read *Winnie the Pooh* or *A Wind in the Willows* and devised amazingly parallel worlds of friendly animals and cozy interiors.

That need may account, as we grow older, for part of our continued enthusiasm for fantasy and science fiction. Sigmund Freud offered another explanation:

> Remote times have a great attraction—sometimes mysteriously so—for the imagination. As often as mankind is dissatisfied with its present—and that happens often enough—it harks back to the past and hopes at last to win belief in the never forgotten dreams of a Golden Age.[1]

Fantasy and science fiction permit us to see golden worlds of the past and the future, and utopias allow us to see how our contemporary problems are perhaps solvable. Without dreams we die, yet most of us realize that to live permanently in fantasy, science fiction, and utopia is to remain childlike and increasingly childish. But, on the other hand, if we accept the real world as the only possibility, we will damn ourselves to a stifling existence. Perhaps it is because young adults have not yet been squelched by society that they are able to respond wholeheartedly to the kinds of books presented in this chapter. Many of them are in the process of examining the life-styles and the society around them, so they are more keenly interested than are adults in looking at the alternatives in science fiction, fantasy, and utopia.

SCIENCE FICTION

Science fiction enjoys great popularity today, but that has not always been the case. A visit to the paperback racks in a bookstore fifteen or twenty years ago would probably have revealed no section devoted to science fiction. What existed would have been buried in the fiction department. Today, the average bookstore devotes considerable space to science fiction, partly because it has become respectable, mostly because it has become extraordinarily popular. Perhaps the film *Star Wars* created some appeal, but more of it came from the continued and popular work of science fiction writers like Ray Bradbury, Isaac Asimov, Arthur C. Clarke, Robert A. Heinlein, Ursula K. Le Guin, Robert Silverberg, Poul Anderson, Frederick Pohl, and C. M. Kornbluth. Publishers, hardback and paperback, have recognized the market for science fiction, and several have created science fiction divisions.

Ray Bradbury argues that the appeal is understandable because science fiction is important literature, not merely popular but second-rate material. Opening his essay, "Science Fiction: Why Bother?" he compares himself to a fourth-rate George Bernard Shaw who makes an outrageous statement, and then tries to prove it. The statement that he makes is that "Science-fiction is the most important fiction being written today."[2] He adds that it is not "*part* of the Main Stream. It *is* the Main Stream."

Carl Sagan, the Cornell University astronomer-author, has added his testament, writing that it was science fiction that brought him to science. Kurt Vonnegut, Jr. has also applauded science fiction through his character Eliot Rosewater, protagonist in *God Bless You, Mr. Rosewater, or Pearls Before Swine*. Stumbling into a convention of science fiction writers, Rosewater drunkenly tells them how much he loves them because they are the only ones who:

> know that life is a space voyage, and not a short one, either, but one that'll last for billions of years. You're the only ones with guts enough to really care about the future, who really notice what machines do to us, what wars do to us, what cities do to us, what big, simple ideas do to us, what tremendous misunderstandings, mistakes, accidents and catastrophes do to us.[3]

He goes on to praise them for being "zany enough to agonize over time and distances without limit, over mysteries that will never die, over the fact that we are right now determining whether the space voyage for the next billion years or so is going to be Heaven or Hell."

But why does science fiction appeal to young adults? First and probably most important, it is exciting reading. Science fiction may have begun with the rocket-to-the-moon kind of book, but it has advanced far beyond that. Nevertheless, it is still exciting material to read, on many levels. Science fiction writers recognize their readers' maturity and sophistication, and they refuse to write down to anyone. Science fiction allows young adults to read imaginative fiction without being accused of reading kiddie books, fairy tale stuff. Science fiction presents real heroes to readers who find their own world depressingly devoid of people worth admiring, heroes doing important and brave acts, going to frontiers, even pushing back those frontiers. This is especially

SUGGESTIONS FOR EVALUATING IMAGINATIVE LITERATURE

A good piece of imaginative literature has most of the positive qualities generally associated with good fiction. In addition it usually has:

A smooth, unhackneyed way of establishing the imaginative world.

An originality of concept. Without this originality, it cannot accurately be labelled *fantasy*.

Enough relationship to the real world so that the reader is led to look at the world in a new way or from a new viewpoint.

Something that stimulates readers to participate in the author's creative thinking and to carry the story further in their own minds.

A rigorous adherence to the "rules" of the imaginative world so that the story is internally consistent even though it may break with the physical laws of this world as they are now known.

A poor piece of imaginative literature has the negative qualities generally associated with poor fiction. In addition it may have:

An awkward transition between reality and fantasy.

A reliance on trite stereotypes already created by other writers of science fiction or fantasy.

No relationship to the real world or to human nature.

Inconsistencies within the story. The author unpredictably changes the behavior of the characters or relies on unexpected magical solutions to solve problems.

important for readers living in a world and time that seems to have no frontiers left. Science fiction obviously appeals to young adults growing up with moon shots and the Apollo space program, and whose entertainment includes *Star Trek*, *2001: A Space Odyssey*, and *The Invasion of the Body Snatchers*. Maybe most important, science fiction writers respect young readers and see them as intellectually curious, which is praise of a very high order indeed.

Science fiction has a history and a heritage. Over 100 years ago Jules Verne provided such science fiction stories as *Journey to the Center of the Earth* (1864), *From the Earth to the Moon* (1865), and *Round the Moon* (1870). The first American science fiction story was Edward S. Ellis' dime novel *The Huge Hunter; or The Steam Man of the Plains*, which appeared in 1869. *Frank Reade Jr., and His Steam Wonder* (a locomotive that needed no rails) appeared in 1879. It was the first of 187 science fiction dime novels written by Louis Senarens, who signed his books "Noname." He was less than eighteen years old when he wrote the first one.

Edward Stratemeyer's Literary Syndicate produced thirty-eight volumes of the Tom Swift series, but those are usually more adventure than science. The Syndicate also produced the Great Marvel series. These nine volumes, written by Howard Garis under the name of Roy Rockwood, included *Lost on the Moon, or In Quest of the Field of Diamonds* (1911) and *By Air Express to Venus, or Captives of a Strange Planet* (1929).

The development of modern science fiction begins with Hugo H. Gernsback. (The Hugo Awards given each year for excellence in science fiction writing honor his name.) An electrical engineer, in 1908 he started *Modern Electrics,* the first magazine devoted to radio. In 1911 finding a few extra pages, he wrote a serialized story, *Ralph 124C/41 +: A Romance of the Year 2660,* which was a utopian vision of the future with inventions and innovations. Because of its success, Gernsback included more stories of the future. In 1926 he began *Amazing Stories,* the first issue containing fiction by Poe, Wells, and Verne. In 1929 he lost control of *Amazing Stories* and began *Science Wonder Stories* and coined the term "science fiction." He demanded a too-literal and sterile scientific accuracy in stories, which made them formula-ridden and repetitive, but he did offer a market for a kind of science fiction story. When *Amazing Stories'* title was changed to *Amazing Science Fiction,* and when two more major magazines appeared, *Fantasy and Science Fiction* and *Analog,* science fiction writers had publications and a market to aim at, both of which became increasingly liberal and willing to accept different writers and different approaches. Many of today's science fiction writers first published in one of these three magazines.

Three writers had appeared during this time in book form and were to have a strong influence on writers who followed. One of these was H. G. Wells with *The Time Machine* (1895), *The Invisible Man* (1897), and *The War of the Worlds* (1898). It is the latter that caused such a furor when Orson Welles dramatized it on radio's Mercury Theater on the night of October 30, 1938. Another of his books, *The First Men in the Moon* (1901), gained a wide audience. What is important about Wells is that he also wrote straight novels of literary repute; consequently, his science fiction novels were not regarded as mere sensational entertainments ground out by an anonymous hack writer.

The second influential writer is Olaf Stapledon, whose three novels were highly regarded, though not nearly so widely read as Wells'. They included *Last and First Men: A Story of the Near and Far Future* (1930), *Last Men in London* (1932), and *The Star Maker* (1937). C. S. Lewis doubtless brought the greatest respectability to early science fiction writing. As a professor and noted literary critic, Lewis may have been thought odd for writing theological science fiction in his three still-read books, *Out of the Silent Planet* (1938), *Perelandra* (1943), and *That Hideous Strength* (1945), but no one questioned his literary ability.

But science fiction became more significant and found a larger audience during and after the Second World War. Part of its increased prestige came from the fact that science fiction writers had predicted both the atomic age and the computer revolution. Attitudes in society changed so that people were more willing to consider alternatives and to reappraise the structure of society. And the paperback industry flourished, which made it possible for large segments of society to have access to both novels and science fiction magazines. With more science fiction books available for growing numbers of readers, fan magazines (usually called *fanzines*) such as *Locus* and newsletters solidified the popularity of science fiction.

Sure proof that science fiction had become mature and respectable appeared in December 1959 when the prestigious (and occasionally stuffy) Modern Language Association began a science fiction newsletter, *Extrapolation*. Colleges and secondary schools offered courses in science fiction. Respectable publications, even literary magazines, began to recognize the existence of science fiction writers. Science fiction had grown up. Not only could uneducated, simple-minded readers read it on their level; college professors could read it on their level.

Robert A. Heinlein defined science fiction as:

> speculative fiction in which the author takes as his first postulate the real world as we know it, including all established facts and natural laws. The result can be extremely fantastic in content, but it is not fantasy; it is legitimate—and often very tightly reasoned—speculation about the possibilities of the real world.[4]

According to this definition, science fiction must conform to natural law. True, a novel can be based on quite different laws of another planet, but those laws must be clear and consistent. No dragons need apply for work in science fiction—they are the province of fantasy. The limitation has never proved onerous for science fiction writers, many of whom are engineers, scientists, or doctors.

There are other conventions. Characters voyage out into space facing all sorts of dangers: melodramatic ones such as space pirates and gunfighters, scientific ones based on our physical laws or some variation. Other planets often have some sort of intelligent life, though the form may differ drastically from that on Earth. Contemporary problems are often seen from several hundred years in the future, and that view of overpopulation, religious bickering, sexual disharmony, or political machinations may give readers some perspective on our own time. Prophecies are not a requirement of science fiction, but some of the richest books, notably those of Isaac Asimov and Arthur C. Clarke, have been prophetic. In many science fiction stories, Earth is a dying planet, or it is already dead, if not decently interred.

Ray Bradbury's *The Martian Chronicles* is widely known and widely taught in secondary schools, deservedly so. Bradbury has no interest in how people locomote from Earth to Mars, but he has great interest in what people have done to Earth and what some of them propose to do to Mars. Indeed, the novel is not about Mars so much as it is about people's selfishness and propensity for destruction here on Earth.

Basically a collection of short stories tied together fairly loosely, *The Martian Chronicles* has the advantage of presenting various moods and messages in several different forms. The book opens with a brief section entitled "January 1999 Rocket Summer" and the reader is off into space. "April 2000: The Third Expedition" is one of the most effective adventure portions of the book. The expedition is fearful of what they may meet:

The rocket landed on a lawn of green grass. Outside, upon this lawn, stood an iron deer. Further up on the green stood a tall brown Victorian house, quiet in the sunlight, all covered with scrolls and rococo, its windows made of blue and pink and yellow and green colored glass. Upon the porch were hairy geraniums and an old swing which was hooked into the porch ceiling and which now swung back and forth, back and forth, in a little breeze. At the summit of the house was a cupola with diamond leaded-glass windows and a dunce-cap roof! Through the front window you could see a piece of music entitled "Beautiful Ohio" sitting on the music rest.

It's not the usual Martian town.

A change in mood from the adventure tale is "June 2001: And the Moon Be Still as Bright," an ecological commentary on our drive to destroy everything, including ourselves. Then we go to an amusingly nasty commentary on the sterility and meanness of censors in "April 2005: Usher II."

The theme of alien invaders once so common in science fiction is largely neglected today. Two science fiction stories of the 1950s, both worth reading today, offer unusual twists on the theme. Jack Finney's *The Body Snatchers*, probably better known as *The Invasion of the Body Snatchers*, from the 1956 and 1978 film versions, shows a quiet

---

The theme of alien invaders once so common in science fiction is largely neglected today.

---

alien invasion in which people are slowly replaced by their mirror images grown in large pods. John Wyndham's *The Midwich Cuckoos* is set in an idyllic small English village isolated from the rest of the world for a short time during which all residents are sedated. Later, all the women in Midwich find themselves pregnant. When the babies arrive, there is real reason for concern. Wyndham's book was filmed in 1960 as *Village of the Damned.*

Science fiction has attempted to detail and explore other cultures. The finest exponent of that theme is C. J. Cherryh. *Brothers of Earth* covers the past history, language, and culture of a future people on a distant planet. Similarly, her first two in a proposed series, *Faded Sun: Kesrith* and *Faded Sun: Shon'jir*, continue this theme.

Overpopulation and intense crowding are themes of Lester del Rey's *The Eleventh Commandment* in which the Church, spurred on by the words "Be fruitful and multiply," turns the planet into an overpopulated hell. John Brunner's *The Dreaming Earth* touches on overpopulation, mechanization, and drugs used to make miserable people believe they are happy. John Hersey's *My Petition for More Space* is set in some vaguely future time in an intensely crowded world. Sam Poynter waits for days in a long, crowded line in New Haven to reach the petition window to ask for more space—each person is allotted an area eight feet by twelve feet. Every place is full of people:

> Every square inch of concrete and asphalt is taken up. . . . It takes a walker
> fifteen or twenty minutes to move a single block. This is the familiar
> suffocating physical crush of the morning hours: breast touches shoulder
> blade, hip rubs hip, one's shoes are scuffed by others' shoes.

Technology and the fear of technology is a theme used by several authors. James Blish's *Cities in Flight*, four novels collected under one title, shows an overpopulated Earth in which entire cities are mechanized with a device called a spindizzy and raised from Earth to become monstrous intergalactic hoboes. John Christopher's *The Prince in Waiting* takes place after the "Disaster" overtakes civilization. A committee of Seers communicates with the spirits, and machines are hated. Christopher's theme is continued in the sequels, *Beyond the Burning Lands* and *The Sword of the Spirits*. Anne McCaffrey's *The Ship Who Sang* emphasizes the valuable functions of technology. Physically handicapped people find a release as their brains literally become the heart of computer systems. Leigh Brackett's *The Long Tomorrow* attacks those people who would endorse any technology. She pictures a society that fears technology and has returned to a simple life on the land. Any knowledge of machines is forbidden. Len, a young boy, revolts and leaves home searching for freedom.

Another common theme is the revolt against conformity. A. E. van Vogt's *Slan* is about a society that fears people who can communicate over long distances by telepathy. His comments on them, the slans, and their pariah status clearly reflects any society that fears a group because it is different. Robert Silverberg's *The World Inside* is set in 2381. It is a life without restrictions on childbirth or sex. What is severely restricted is travel outside the mammoth skyscrapers in which people are assigned to live, presumably happily. John Christopher's *Wild Jack*, set in the twenty-third century, shows a conformist society with a few thousand people living in London and constantly besieged by savages from the outside. Written in Russia in 1920–21, and still not published there, Yevgeny Zamyatin's *We* pictures a world of Reason where one citizen, D-503, finds he has a soul and he wishes to be allowed to exercise it. In *House of Stairs*, William Sleator shows young people in a highly elaborate experiment, manipulated first this way and then that, in a Skinnerian world gone mad. Of all books on this theme, Ray Bradbury's *Farenheit 451* makes the strongest statement. Firefighters of the future do not, in Bradbury's book, stop fires, they begin them and the chief target is printed paper. One of the firefighters has qualms and has kept some books. The reader recognizes that the protagonist is due for a change in attitude and personal safety as he goes over to the other side.

Religion has been used as a theme less frequently than one might guess, but four books have focused on it. Walter M. Miller's *A Canticle for Leibowitz* shows a feudal society forming after a nuclear war leads people away from machines and back to belief in God. Robert McKay's *Skean* places 114-year-old ornithologist Skean in the middle of a cosmic game played for the universe by two opponents. Skean is not sure which is God and which is Satan, if, indeed, that is who they are. In Frank Herbert's *Dune* a young alien is ultimately confirmed as the religious leader of nomadic natives on a desert planet. *The Mote in God's Eye* by Larry Niven and Jerry Pournelle tells about a first contact from another galaxy who dies. Earth must send an emissary speedily to avert war and destruction.

Science fiction is inherently serious, and humor throughout a book is rare though certain kinds do appear. Christine Nostlinger's *Konrad* begins with Mrs. Bartolotti receiving a package from a factory containing her son, Konrad. He is nauseatingly perfect in every way to the consternation of his classmates and almost everyone else. Frederick Pohl and C. M. Kornbluth's *The Space Merchants* is a delicious and wicked satire on advertising and how very little it changes over the years.

With all the hundreds of science fiction writers, three writers have clearly become the most significant. Isaac Asimov has written over 200 books, but the Foundation trilogy, consisting of *Foundation, Foundation and Empire,* and *Second Foundation,* and nearly thirty years old, remains his best-known work. Set in the year 12,000 of the Galactic Era, it shows psychohistorians plotting the reactions of groups of people into the future. Arthur C. Clarke's *Childhood's End* is often listed as one of the masterworks of science fiction, though it has been less widely read than others of Clarke's works. Clarke envisages an Earth controlled by Masters who never appear but who manipulate events and people and seem to promise all good things. In *Imperial Earth,* Clarke comments from the future, looking back at how science fiction has helped advance and forecast it. And in *Rendezvous with Rama,* Clarke shows a mysterious, invading artificially-created cylinder world all too briefly examined by humans. The third major writer, Robert A. Heinlein, is probably best known for *Stranger in a Strange Land,* a book about a young man raised on Mars who finds Earth's civilization strange. Heinlein's many other books are also worth reading. *Red Planet: A Colonial Boy on Mars* was written for young adults, but the story of a young academy student on Mars who gets into scrapes but manages to stop a war is charming reading by any standards. *Methuselah's Children* seems far from reality, but its story of the selective secret breeding of long-lived people to create an even longer-living race may not be as remote as we might wish.

FANTASY

In 1972 Patrick Merla noted that young adult literature was becoming more realistic and adult literature more fantastic:

> the paradox of "reality" for children versus "fantasy" for adults may be double-edged—children looking for facts to help them cope with an abrasive environment while adults probe a deeper, archetypal reality that can transform society altogether. A paradox not merely bemusing or amusing, but one that betokens a renascence of the wish to live humanely: a wealth of profound possibilities for mankind.[5]

Things have changed little for adults since Merla made that observation, and many young adults are reading fantasy as well. *The New York Times Book Review* for January 7, 1979, listed two books of fantasy among the top five best selling nonfiction books. Number two was *Gnomes* with a text by Wil Huygen and illustrations by Rien Poorvliet, and number five was *Faeries* written and illustrated by Brian Froud and Alan Lee.

Testimony to the therapeutic value of fantasy for men, women, and children is not difficult to find. Whatever worries we might have that fantasy somehow wars with reason are unnecessary, says folklorist and fantasy writer J. R. R. Tolkien:

> Fantasy is a natural human activity. It certainly does not destroy or even insult Reason; and it does not either blunt the appetite for, nor obscure the perception of, scientific verity. On the contrary, the keener and the clearer is the reason, the better fantasy it will make. If men were ever in a state in which they did not want to know or could not perceive truth (facts or evidence) then Fantasy would languish until they were cured.[6]

Theologian Harvey Cox in comparing fantasy with festivity argues that fantasy is essential and that it allows people to relive and anticipate, to remake the past and create whole new futures:

> Fantasy is the richest source of human creativity. Theologically speaking, it is the image of the creator God in man. Like God, man in fantasy creates whole worlds *ex nihilo*, out of nothing.
>
> Yet, despite its importance, our era has dealt very shabbily with fantasy. In many other cultures fantasy has been carefully nurtured and those with unusual abilities at fantasy honored. In ours, we have ignored fantasy, deprecated it, or tried to pretend it wasn't really there. After all, we are "realists."[7]

And *Psychology Today* agrees that fantasy is essential in our lives. In an interview, science fiction writer Ray Bradbury said:

> The ability to "fantasize" is the ability to survive. It's wonderful to speak about this subject because there have been so many wrong-headed people dealing with it. We're going through a terrible period in art, in literature and living, in psychiatry and psychology. The so-called realists are trying to drive us insane, and I refuse to be driven insane. . . . We survive by fantasizing. Take that away from us and the whole damned race goes down the drain.[8]

What is the appeal of fantasy to young adults? First, it is, like science fiction, in many ways thrilling escapist literature. It is more than that, but any reader knows full well that fantasy allows the reader to leave the present and go to another world where evil and good are easier to determine, and where heroes can be found. The heroes of fantasy are young, but youth does not preclude manhood and womanhood; it encourages, even demands, speeded up maturity; at fourteen the boys are men and the girls women. Fantasy writers do not condescend to readers, and in demonstrating that young adults can be wise and heroic, they indirectly compliment readers and create more of them. Perhaps the strongest appeal of fantasy lies in its mythic nature, either recreating old myths in new guises or creating entirely new mythologies and legends. This appeals to us almost insidiously; it's like a recollection of our prehistoric existence.

Robert H. Boyer and Kenneth J. Zahorski define high fantasy by first explaining that it does not consist of ghost stories, animal fables, folk tales, or satirical farces. Instead, high fantasy consists of:

> fairy tales, those ancient and new stories which take place in the mysterious other world of faerie, such as *Beowulf* or J. R. R. Tolkien's *The Hobbit;* myth tales, stories whose setting is the realm in which gods and men have commerce, as in the Welsh *Mabinogion* or in Lloyd Alexander's *The Foundling and Other Tales of Prydain.*[9]

Conventions in fantasy have been well established. First, and most important, is the quest. Someone, probably a young person, alone or accompanied by friends goes off on a quest to protect someone or some country from the powers of evil. The quest may be ordained or required or may, occasionally, be self-determined. Good and evil may be confused at various points, but there is a power of good and a power of evil and the youthful protagonist will recognize the distinction, though not necessarily immediately.

Fantasy is clearly related to mythology, especially the Welsh *Mabinogion* and the Arthurian legend, or it parallels one or the other. Fantasy is a world of magic. It need not conform to our physical, scientific laws. But whatever laws or languages or living beings (dragons, trolls, hobbits, and so forth) are created must be consistent throughout a book. Colors may be important as symbols, but light and dark clearly are symbolic. By the close of the book, the youthful protagonist, who usually begins in a lowly

---

Perhaps the strongest appeal of fantasy lies in its mythic nature.

---

job, has achieved something, though it may not be what he wanted most or what he felt was most important for himself or his country. But rarely is evil totally vanquished; evil may be banished or may look defeated, but the possibility of its return always looms ahead. The quest itself entails all kinds of obstacles, physical as well as emotional or mental. If any one thing typifies the quest, it is travel, usually over a tremendously long distance and sometimes taking years. Finally, the author creates a new world that the reader can see before him in the form of a map, usually opposite the title page. The author may create a new language, and some words will become part of the reader's lexicon.

Forerunners of contemporary fantasy writers are E. R. Eddison, whose *The Worm Ouroboros* attracted readers in the 1920s, and Lord Dunsany and H. P. Lovecraft, writers of both fantasy and horror stories. J. R. R. Tolkien began modern fantasy writing with two books still widely read, almost cult books for many people. *The Hobbit, or There and Back Again* began in 1933 as a series of stories Tolkien told to his children about a strange little being, Bilbo the Hobbit. He developed the story and published the book in 1937. More famous is his trilogy *The Lord of the Rings* published in America from 1954 to 1956. Tolkien's love of languages led him to create a language, Elvish, for his own amusement and for the book. Appendices to *The Lord of the Rings* are devoted to a history of Middle-Earth, its language, and its geography. An extension of Tolkien's work, published posthumously in 1977, *The Silmarillion*, was number one on *The New York Times* list of best-selling fiction for several weeks in 1977, amazing for a work of fantasy, but the work itself was a disappointment to many readers of Tolkien. Tolkien created, or, at the very least, exemplified most of the virtues and many of the conventions of fantasy. As such, he is important. But his greatest importance lies in the excellence of *The Lord of the Rings*, which can be read and reread an infinite number of times.

Lloyd Alexander's five-volume series, frequently referred to as "The Chronicles of Prydain," about Taran, the Assistant Pig-Keeper, is one of the finest fantasies written for young adults. The opening book, *The Book of Three*, introduces the major characters, especially the lowly Taran, and sends him on a mission to save Prydain, his land, from evil. He is seeking his own identity as well, for no one knows his heritage. His impatience early in the book to be a hero is understandable if vexing to the old enchanter, Dallben, who feels responsible for Taran. The old man counsels patience, "for the time being":

> "For the time being!" Taran burst out. "I think it will always be for the time being, and it will be vegetables and horseshoes all my life."
>
> "Tut," said Dallben, "there are worse things. Do you set yourself to be a glorious hero? Do you believe it is all flashing swords and galloping about on horses? As for being glorious . . ."
>
> "What of Prince Gwydion?" cried Taran. "Yes! I wish I might be like him."
>
> "I fear," Dallben said, "that is entirely out of the question."
>
> "But why?" Taran sprang to his feet. "I know if I had the chance . . ."
>
> "Why?" Dallben interrupted. "In some cases," he said, "we learn more by looking for the answer to a question and not finding it than we do from learning the answer itself."

Taran, youthful impetuousness and righteous indignation aglow, is bored by Dallben's philosophy and wants action, and action he gets soon enough. In *The Black Cauldron*, Taran journeys to face evil Arawn, and in *The Castle of Llyr* he and friends save

Princess Eilonwy from an evil enchantress. In *Taran Wanderer*, he searches for his parentage, and he begins to learn how to accept that most dreadful of things, failure. In the concluding book, *The High King*, the Sword of Dyrnwyn falls into the hands of Arawn, and once more Taran and Prince Gwydion and friends march against evil. Evil is difficult to conquer temporarily and impossible to conquer permanently, as Taran learns.

Taran's quest is his theme, but Alexander's theme is Taran's growth into manhood. From a child who admires Prince Gwydion for his derring-do, Taran grows into a man who recognizes the Prince as a symbol of good, perhaps the power of good. From a child who idealizes Princess Eilonwy, he grows into a man who can woo and win her. (Incidentally, the romance in fantasies may have attraction for young males who cannot openly read love stories but who can read quest books full of adventure.) From a child who sees the quest as adventure leading to heroism, Taran grows into a man who recognizes that heriosm requires making choices between good and evil and continuing the quest wherever it takes him. As Taran prepares to set out once more, Dallben says,

> "The tasks you set yourself are cruelly difficult. There is no certainty you will accomplish even one, and much risk you will fail in all of them. In either case, your efforts may well go unrewarded, unsung, forgotten. And at the end, like all mortals, you must face your death; perhaps without even a mound of honor to mark your resting place."
>
> Taran nodded. "So be it," he said. "Long ago I yearned to be a hero without knowing, in truth, what a hero was. Now, perhaps, I understand it a little better. A grower of turnips or a shaper of clay, a Commot farmer or a king—every man is a hero if he strives more for others than for himself alone. Once," he added, "you told me that the seeking counts more than the finding. So, too, must the striving count more than the gain."

Lamenting the young adults who would not read Alexander or had not found him, Betty Whetton wrote in 1972:

> Perhaps Alexander erred in thinking he wrote for youngsters. He may well, however, share with Tolkien and Lewis the acclaim of those born before the early '50's and who may really be at heart Assistant Pig Keepers.[10]

Ursula Le Guin's *The Earthsea Trilogy* may have found more readers than Alexander. Opening with Sparrowhawk, son of a bronzesmith, who is given his true name of Ged from the great wizard, Le Guin takes Ged in *A Wizard of Earthsea* through a series of trials both psychological and physical that force him to learn and mature. In *The Tombs of Atuan*, Le Guin focuses on young Arha and her training as the future priestess of the Tombs. Learning her responsibilities to the divinities, she encounters Ged, and they escape, both developing as adults. *The Farthest Shore* again focuses on Ged who learns, as Archmage of Roke, that true magic is no longer to be found in the kingdom. He sets out to test ancient prophecies.

Three fantasies, somewhat different than Alexander or Le Guin, deserve mention. One, Antoine de Saint-Exupery's *The Little Prince*, has been a favorite with discerning readers for years. An airplane pilot, down in the Sahara Desert with engine problems, encounters a little boy who asks, "If you please—draw me a sheep." The Little Prince, from a planet no larger than a house, wanders from planet to planet seeking friendship and love. On Earth he meets a fox who shares his secret with the prince, "It is only with the heart that one can see rightly; what is essential is invisible to the eye."

The quest is perhaps the single most common theme in fantasy.

The second is Peter Beagle's lovely book, *The Last Unicorn*. Assisted by the magician Schmendrick and accompanied by Molly Grue, the lonely unicorn seeks others of its kind. Beagle's masterful description of the unicorn opens the book.

The unicorn lived in a lilac wood, and she lived all alone. She was very old, though she did not know it, and she was no longer the careless color of sea foam, but rather the color of snow falling on a moonlit night. But her eyes were still clear, and unwearied, and she still moved like a shadow on the sea.

Beagle's humor is always strong and dependable. Schmendrick is incapable of telling any story without some elaboration. Stopping at one town early in the quest to find the unicorn's fellows, he tells of his early adventures.

During the meal Schmendrick told stories of his life as an errant enchanter, filling it with kings and dragons and noble ladies. He was not lying, merely organizing events more sensibly.

The third is Robin McKinley's *Beauty*, a retelling of the old legend of Beauty and the Beast. Differing from the older version in a few details here and there, none significant, McKinley's Beauty is strong and unafraid and loving. When her father tells her that he has been condemned to death by the Beast for stealing a rose, Beauty gladly agrees to go in place of her father:

"He cannot be so bad if he loves roses so much."
"But he is a Beast," said Father helplessly.
I saw that he was weakening, and wishing only to comfort him, I said, "Cannot a Beast be tamed?"

McKinley's version may lack the surrealistic quality of Jean Cocteau's film, but in many ways it compares most favorably. It is a fine fantasy about reality.

The theme of time travel is common to much fantasy. Robert Nathan's *Portrait of Jennie* is a romantic favorite about an artist meeting a young girl who influences his painting. As he ages rapidly, he tries to puzzle out who and what she is. Poul Anderson recreates the fall of the Lost Continent in *The Dancer from Atlantis,* and introduces people pulled back from the twentieth century trying to repair a time machine to return to their own era. Andre Norton's *Wraiths of Time* presents a young black archeologist who goes back to the Nubian kingdom of Meroe and is forced to impersonate a princess. Prince Stephen is imprisoned by his father for befriending an enemy, and, when he is tortured, he is suddenly released to the year 1822 in Lolah Burford's *The Vision of Stephen.*

The quest is perhaps the single most common theme in fantasy. Anne McCaffrey's *Dragonsong* shows young Menolly who desperately wants to become a Harper. In *Dragonsinger* Menolly comes closer to her dream. Katherine Kurtz' three-volume series, *Deryni Rising, Deryni Checkmate,* and *High Deryni,* is about an occult race, now outlawed, who once ruled Gwynedd. In Susan Cooper's "The Dark Is Rising" series, Will Stanton goes on several quests.

Arthurian legend was a passion for T. H. White. His *The Sword in the Stone* and *The Once and Future King,* both concerned with Arthur and his knights of the Round Table, have become classics. Mary Stewart departed from her romances to write three books about Merlin from the time of his oath until Arthur becomes a man in *The Crystal Cave, The Hollow Hills,* and *The Last Enchantment.*

Welsh legends have been the source of many fantasies, and the inspiration for others. Of the many books derived from Welsh legends, none has been more critically praised than Alan Garner's *The Owl Service* in which three young people reenact the Welsh myth of Flower-Face taken from "Math Son of Mathony" in the *Mabinogion.* For two critics, Garner's book represented a major growth in young adult literature:

> *The Owl Service* is perhaps the first really *adult* children's book; the first book, that is, in which childish sensibilities are not deferred to, in which the author has not felt that his audience needs, above all, to be protected.[11]

Animal fantasy is also common. Walter Wangerin, Jr.'s *The Book of the Dun Cow* recreates the story of Chaunticleer the Rooster with extremely effective comic touches. The legend of the half-seal/half human is used in three fine books. Ronald Lockley's *Seal-Woman* reflects his knowledge of nature and tells of Shian and her love for a human who eventually loses out to her call from the sea. Rosemary Harris' *The Seal-Singing* tells of three girls who relive an old family story about a woman who sang seals to their death. And Mollie Hunter's *A Stranger Came Ashore* portrays fearful Scottish people unsure whether Finn Learson is a man or a seal-man.

The flashing swordsman school of fantasy with its daring feats, beautiful women, and frequent skirmishes with death is represented by Leigh Brackett's *The Book of Skaith: The Adventures of Eric John Stark.* Fritz Leiber's *Swords and Ice Magic* presents two blustering swordsmen heroes pursuing maidens and dangers.

Humor is found here and there in books of fantasy, but two books emphasize it. Leonard Wibberley's *The Mouse That Roared* satirizes war. The tiny Duchy of Grand Fenwick declares war on the United States knowing that it will lose, but also knowing that it is certain to receive aid and assistance afterwards. To the country's surprise and horror, Grand Fenwick wins the war. Thomas Berger's *Arthur Rex* is a loving and amusing look at Arthurian legend. Berger assumes that the violence inherent in the Arthurian tales is real, spilling real blood, and that the chased maidens are not always all that chaste. It is a delightful but slightly derisive parody.

Before leaving fantasy, one other type of book should be mentioned as appealing to young adults. These are the children's fantasies including Lewis Carroll's *Alice in Wonderland*, Margery Williams' *The Velveteen Rabbit*, and A. A. Milne's *Winnie the Pooh*. Young adults return to these sometimes out of nostalgia, sometimes because they missed them when they were young, and sometimes just because they exemplify all that is so appealing about fantasy. It allows us to escape for a few hours into another world and then returns us to our own with new insights and appreciation.

UTOPIAS

It is the more thoughtful and more intellectual young adult who enjoys reading utopias. Utopias generally lack some of the excitement and fast-moving plots that are integral parts of other stories. The writer of adventure, fantasy, and science fiction is first a storyteller and second a bearer of a message. But the writer of utopian books thinks first of the message and then devises a story to carry the message. Another factor that limits the appeal of utopian books is that they are usually based on dissatisfaction with present conditions. It is true that many young adults are dissatisfied with society, but they are probably not dissatisfied with the same degree of anger as are adult writers of utopian stories. This means that they may miss some of the allusions. In spite of these drawbacks, the idealism of youth is so strong that many young readers are attracted to books presenting utopian visions.

The centuries-long appeal of utopias is suggested by the Greek origin of the word, which includes two meanings: "no place" and "good place." Most of us, in idle moments, dream of a perfect land, a perfect society, a perfect place that would solve all of our problems and, if we are properly altruistic, all the world's problems as well. Few of us will have opportunity to do more than dream. That may explain why we are intrigued with those who carry the dream one step forward and write a plan, a book about that dream, making concrete in print a possible utopia.

In his *Republic* in the fifth century B.C., Plato presented his ideal world offering specific suggestions for educating the ruling class, for with wise philosopher-kings, the people would prosper, intellectual joys would flourish, and the land would be safe, or so the theory went.

Later utopias were geared less to the ruling class and more to a society that would preserve peace and create harmony and happiness for the people. Sir Thomas More's *Utopia* (1516) argued for the mental equality of the sexes, simple laws understandable to all, and common ownership of everything. Whether More meant his book as any sort of practical plan is doubtful, but he probably did intend it as a criticism of English life. Most utopias reflect both an author's enthusiasm for certain ideas and practices and an abhorrence of others.

During the 1800s such writers as Samuel Butler, William Morris, William Dean Howells, and Edward Bellamy wrote utopian novels. And in the United States people sought satisfaction through various utopian schemes in such places as Harmony, Pennsylvania; New Harmony, Indiana; Brook Farm, Massachusetts; Fruitlands, Massachusetts; Oneida, New York; Nauvoo, Illinois; and Corning, Iowa.

But twentieth-century writers produced more dystopias (diseased or bad lands) than utopias. Unlike utopias, which are written to offer us the possibility of a better world, dystopias warn us of society's drift toward a horrifying world lying just over the horizon. They are sometimes misinterpreted as prophecies alone, but such books as Aldous Huxley's *Brave New World* and *Brave New World Revisited,* George Orwell's *Animal Farm* and *1984,* and Anthony Burgess' *A Clockwork Orange* are part prophecy, part warning.

Among the recent writers of utopian stories is Ernest Callenbach whose *Ecotopia: The Notebooks and Reports of William Weston* begins with the assumption that the northwest part of the United States secedes in 1980. In 1999 reporter William Weston is allowed to visit as the first outsider. As Callenbach's title suggests, the new country is predicated on ecology and on 1960s communal ideas.

Actual utopian communities have been used in several novels. Elizabeth Howard's *Out of Step with the Dancers* shows a celibate Shaker religious community in 1853 through the eyes of young Damaris as she accompanies her converted father to a strange new life. The problem of religious pacificism confronted with the Civil War is

The writer of utopian books thinks first of the message and then devises a story to carry the message.

the subject of Janet Hickman's *Zoar Blue* about the German separatist community of Zoar, Ohio. Lynn Hall's excellent *Too Near the Sun* centers on sixteen-year-old Armel Dupree and his Icarian community near Corning, Iowa. His older brother, to the shame of the family, has left the community to seek the outside world. Armel now wonders if he should not do the same, particularly as he sees an ideal community composed of considerably less than ideal people.

A good book that should be better known is Benjamin Capps' *The Brothers of Uterica.* Brother Jean Charles Bossereau leads a group into Texas to establish a utopian community based on religious freedom, universal suffrage, community-owned land, care of the old, and reward for hard work. The premise of the community is stated in item eleven of the "Goals of Our Common Faith" in the New Socialist Colonization Company. "We seek a life ordered by reason and good will; we expect to find such a life amid the beauties and common virtues of nature." Nature fails to cooperate, and people both in and out of the community lack reason and good will as well as common sense, so the venture fails.

Communes so popular in the 1960s persist today; witness Raymond Mungo's *Total Loss Farm: A Year in the Life* and Richard Wizansky's *Home Comfort: Life on Total Loss Farm*, both extolling the joys and satisfactions of this Vermont farm and explaining why some find peace and some find little and leave. Psychologist B. F. Skinner's utopian suggestions and criticisms of our contemporary life in *Walden Two* served as a basis for the Twin Oaks Community experiment in Virginia that is described by Kathleen Kinkade in *A Walden Two Experiment: The First Five Years of Twin Oaks Community*. Two novels about farm communes are Edward Connolly's *Deer Run* and Chester Aaron's *Hello to Bodega*.

Robert Coover examines the madness of some cults in *The Origin of the Brunists*. A mining explosion kills ninety-seven people but one man, Giovanni Bruno, lives, and he decides God has saved him to proclaim the approaching end of the world. Thousands follow him. The death of the mind and the dangers of cults are examined in Robin F. Brancato's *Blinded by the Light*. Gail Brower infiltrates a cult to locate her older brother. The novel, particularly the last part, has elements of a spy thriller.

Nature is the utopia of many who see it as a soothing balm capable of moving and changing humanity burdened with artificiality. Utopian writers today view wilderness as the salvation of humanity. This is in contrast to nineteenth-century writers and pioneers who often considered it valuable only because it afforded people an opportunity to replace it with farms and cities ordained by God. Edward Abbey expresses the new philosophy by writing:

> A man could be a lover and defender of the wilderness without ever in his lifetime leaving the boundaries of asphalt, powerlines, and right-angled surfaces. We need wilderness whether or not we ever set foot in it. We need a refuge even though we may never need to go there.[12]

Abbey's *Desert Solitaire: A Season in the Wilderness* and *The Journey Home: Some Words in Defense of the American West* celebrate the wilderness and the possibility of some human growth for good in the the wilderness. Other, sometimes quite different, exaltations of nature and wilderness are Annie Dillard's *Pilgrim at Tinker Creek*, Peter Matthiessen's *The Snow Leopard*, John Nichols' *If Mountains Die*, Ann Zwinger's *Run, River, Run: A Naturalist's Journey Down One of the Great Rivers*, Colin Fletcher's account of his walking the length of the Grand Canyon, *The Man Who Walked Through Time*, and Taylor Morris' sometimes frightening, sometimes glorious hike from New Hampshire to Nova Scotia with a band of college students, *The Walk of the Conscious Ants*.

Concerns with nature's utopia and what we are doing to befoul it in the name of progress are seen in three young adult novels, Betty Cummings' *Let a River Be* and Jean Craighead George's *Hook a Fish, Catch a Mountain* and *Going to the Sun*. That excellent stylist John McPhee writes of archconservationist David Brower and Brower's three encounters with a mining engineer, a land developer, and a dam builder in *Encounters with the Archdruid.* Anyone interested in nature as humanity's hope should read the work of Joseph Wood Krutch, a transplanted easterner who loved the West. A handy collection of his essays is *The Best Nature Writing of Joseph Wood Krutch.*

The American West, probably because it still has large areas of wilderness quite different from anything seen in the East, seems especially suited to utopian writings of a mystical nature. The books of Carlos Castaneda fall into this category. His books such as *The Teachings of Don Juan: A Yaqui Way of Knowledge* and *A Separate Reality: Further Conversations with Don Juan* have appealed to some high-school students, but mostly to adults and college students. They are based on the wisdom and teachings of a Yaqui Indian medicine man/sorcerer who introduces the author to the wisdom of the peyote cult. As a result, the author sets out on a quest to become "a man of knowledge" and in the process experiences strange and fascinating worlds of thought and perception.

Although there are certainly exceptions, young adults are basically optimistic and imaginative. They have not lived long enough to have lost their natural curiosity, nor have most of them been weighed down by such problems as failing health, heavy family responsibilities, and dreams gone bankrupt. They are an especially good audience for the books treated in this chapter.

The three types of books have in common an optimism. Even the dystopian books leave readers grateful for the world as it is as opposed to what it might be. The other quality that the books have in common is that they start with life as we know it and then stretch the imagination. They are free swinging yet anchored in varying degrees to the real world. The most firmly attached are the utopian stories because they are written by people with a serious message about what society could be if only individuals did their part. Next are the science fiction stories, which are also based on real life, that is, on the laws of nature. The difference between science and science fiction is that science fiction writers take scientific theories and put them to use without waiting for the long years of tedious testing and proving. The genre furthest removed from the confines of the real world of today is fantasy. But, even here, the characters have much in common with humans. Deep down, whether they are dragons, hobbits, or assistant pig keepers, their feelings are those that readers can understand.

We need to dream, all of us, not to waste our lives but to enrich them, for to dream is to recognize humanity's possibilities. In a world and time hardly characterized by undue optimism, the genres treated here offer us hope, not the sappy sentimental hope of "everything always works out for the best," but realistic hope based on our noblest dreams of survival. If we go down, we do it knowing that we have cared and dreamed and found something for which we are willing to struggle.

ACTIVITIES

1. It is sometimes said that the new gods in America are science and technology. Some of our stories support this idea. In the James Bond books and movies, for

example, the superspy frequently receives "miraculous" help from modern technology. Another example is the hero who is half-god and half-human. Today we have heroes from Frankenstein to the Bionic Man who are half-human and half-technology. Read one of the recommended science fiction books and make notes on incidents or statements that reflect or support the idea that modern readers place an almost religious faith in science and technology.

2.   Interview a young adult asking him or her to describe an ideal community or way to live. Read one of the utopian novels and compare the portrayal given in the book with the one described by the young person. How were they the same? How were they different? Do you think the person you interviewed would have enjoyed the book you read? Why or why not?

3.   Read one science fiction, one utopian, and one fantasy book. Examine the techniques that the authors used to establish the fact that the stories were not realistic. Write a comparison showing what the three authors did similarly and what they did quite differently. Did they make transitions returning the reader to the real world? Did they use time as a clue? Did they rely on traditional motifs or did they invent new circumstances and incidents?

NOTES

[1]Sigmund Freud, *Moses and Monotheism,* trans. Katherine Jones (New York: Vintage Books, 1939), p. 89.

[2]Ray Bradbury, "Science Fiction: Why Bother?" in *Teacher's Guide: Science Fiction* (New York: Bantam Books, Inc., n.d.), p. 1.

[3]Kurt Vonnegut, Jr., *God Bless You, Mr. Rosewater, or Pearls Before Swine* (New York: Delacorte Press, 1965), p. 27.

[4]Robert A. Heinlein, "Ray Guns and Rocket Ships," *Library Journal* 78 (July 1953): 1188.

[5]Patrick Merla, " 'What Is Real?' Asked the Rabbit One Day," *Saturday Review* 55 (November 4, 1972): 49.

[6]J. R. R. Tolkien, *The Tolkien Reader* (New York: Ballantine Books, Inc., 1966), pp. 74-75.

[7]Harvey Cox, *The Feast of Fools: A Theological Essay on Festivity and Fantasy* (Cambridge: Harvard University Press), p. 59.

[8]Mary Harrington Hall, "A Conversation with Ray Bradbury and Chuck Jones," *Psychology Today* 1 (April 1968): 28-29.

[9]Robert H. Boyer and Kenneth J. Zahorski, eds., *The Fantastic Imagination: An Anthology of High Fantasy* (New York: Avon Books, 1977), p. 2.

[10]Betty Whetton, "Who Will Read Prydain?" *Arizona English Bulletin* 14 (April 1972): 53.

[11]Mary Cadogan and Patricia Craig, *You're a Brick, Angela! A New Look at Girls' Fiction from 1839 to 1975* (London: Gollancz, 1976), p. 371.

[12]Edward Abbey, *Desert Solitaire: A Season in the Wilderness* (New York: Ballantine Books, Inc., 1968), p. 148.

RECOMMENDED TITLES

For information on the availability of paperback editions of these titles, please consult the most recent edition of *Paperbound Books in Print,* published annually by R. R. Bowker Company.

Science Fiction

Anderson, Poul. *War of the Wing-Men.* Ace, 1958.

Asimov, Isaac. *Foundation.* Doubleday, 1951.

———. *Foundation and Empire.* Doubleday, 1952.

———. *Second Foundation.* Doubleday, 1953.

Balmer, Edwin and Philip Wylie. *When Worlds Collide.* J. B. Lippincott, 1932.

———. *After Worlds Collide.* J. B. Lippincott, 1933.

Bethancourt, T. Ernesto. *Instruments of Darkness.* Holiday House, 1979.

Blish, James. *They Shall Have Stars.* New Directions, 1957.

———. *A Life for the Stars.* G. P. Putnam's Sons, 1962.

———. *Earthman Come Home.* G. P. Putnam's Sons, 1955.

———. *The Triumph of Time.* Avon, 1958.

Brackett, Leigh. *The Long Tomorrow.* Ballantine, 1974.

Bradbury, Ray. *Fahrenheit 451.* Ballantine, 1953.

———. *The Illustrated Man.* Doubleday, 1951.

———. *The Martian Chronicles.* Doubleday, 1950.

Brunner, John. *The Dreaming Earth.* Pyramid, 1963.

Cherryh, C. J. *Brothers of Earth.* Doubleday, 1976.

———. *Faded Sun: Kesrith.* Doubleday, 1978.

———. *Faded Sun: Shon'jir.* Doubleday, 1978.

Christopher, John. *The Prince in Waiting.* Macmillan, 1970.

———. *Beyond the Burning Lands.* Macmillan, 1971.

———. *The Sword of the Spirits.* Macmillan, 1972.

———. *Wild Jack.* Macmillan, 1974.

Clarke, Arthur C. *Childhood's End.* Ballantine, 1953.

———. *Imperial Earth.* Harcourt Brace Jovanovich, 1976.

———. *Rendezvous with Rama.* Harcourt Brace Jovanovich, 1973.

Crichton, Michael. *The Andromeda Strain.* Alfred A. Knopf, 1969.

Del Rey, Lester. *The Eleventh Commandment.* Stockwell, 1961.

Dick, Philip K. *The Man in the High Castle.* G. P. Putnam's Sons, 1962.

Finney, Jack. *The Body Snatchers.* Dell, 1955.

———. *Time and Again.* Simon and Schuster, 1970.

Freedman, Nancy. *Joshua Son of None.* Delacorte, 1973.

Gerrold, David. *When Harlie Was One.* Ballantine, 1975.

Heinlein, Robert A. *Methuselah's Children.* Gnome, 1958.

———. *Red Planet: A Colonial Boy on Mars.* Charles Scribner's Sons, 1951.

———. *Stranger in a Strange Land.* G. P. Putnam's Sons, 1961.

Herbert, Frank. *Dune.* Chilton, 1965.

Herbert, Frank and William Ransom. *The Jesus Incident.* G. P. Putnam's Sons, 1979.

Hersey, John. *My Petition for More Space.* Alfred A. Knopf, 1974.

Hoover, H. M. *The Delikon.* Viking, 1977.

———. *The Lost Star.* Viking, 1979.

Lawrence, Louise. *Star Lord.* Harper & Row, 1978.

Le Guin, Ursula K. *The Dispossessed.* Harper & Row, 1974.

———. *The Left Hand of Darkness.* Ace, 1969.

Mark, Jan. *The Ennead.* Thomas Y. Crowell, 1978.

McCaffrey, Anne. *The Ship Who Sang.* Walker, 1969.

McClure, Jones. *Cast Down the Stars.* Holt, Rinehart & Winston, 1978.

McIntyre, Vonda N. *Dreamsnake.* Houghton Mifflin, 1978.

McKay, Robert. *Skean.* Thomas Nelson, 1976.

Meredith, Richard D. *We All Died at Breakaway Station.* Ballantine, 1969.

Miller, Walter M. *A Canticle for Leibowitz.* J. B. Lippincott, 1959.

Niven, Larry and Jerry Pournelle. *The Mote in God's Eye.* Simon and Schuster, 1974.

Norton, Andre (pseudonym of Alice Mary Norton). *Dark Piper.* Harcourt Brace Jovanovich, 1968.

———. *Moon of Three Rings.* Viking, 1966.

Nostlinger, Christine. *Konrad.* Franklin Watts, 1977.

Nourse, Alan E. *The Bladerunners.* David McKay, 1974.

O'Brien, Robert C. *Z for Zachariah.* Atheneum, 1975.

Pohl, Frederick and C. M. Kornbluth. *The Space Merchants.* Ballantine, 1953.

Russ, Joanna. *The Two of Them.* G. P. Putnam's Sons, 1978.

Silverberg, Robert. *Shadrack.* Bobbs-Merrill, 1976.

———. *The World Inside.* Doubleday, 1971.

Simak, Clifford D. *Mastodonia.* Ballantine, 1978.

Sleator, William. *House of Stairs.* E. P. Dutton, 1974.

Smith, E. E. "Doc" (Edward E. Smith). *Triplanetary.* Fantasy Press, 1948.

Stableford, Brian M. *Halcyon Drift.* Daw, 1972.

Tiptree, James, Jr. (pseudonym of Alice Sheldon). *Star Songs of an Old Primate Tree.* Ballantine, 1978.

Townsend, John Rowe. *The Visitors.* J. B. Lippincott, 1977.

Van Vogt, A. E. *Slan.* Simon and Schuster, 1940.

Wetanson, Burt and Thomas Hoobler. *The Hunters.* Doubleday, 1978.

Wyndham, John. *The Midwich Cuckoos.* Ballantine, 1958.

Zamyatin, Yevgeny. *We.* Viking, 1972.

Science Fiction—Anthologies

Boucher, Anthony, ed. *A Treasury of Great Science Fiction,* two vol. Doubleday, 1959.

Bova, Ben, ed. *The Science Fiction Hall of Fame: The Greatest Science Fiction Novellas of All Time.* Doubleday, 1973.

Knight, Damon, ed. *100 Years of Science Fiction.* Simon and Schuster, 1968.

————. *A Science Fiction Argosy.* Simon and Schuster, 1972.

Lucie-Smith, Edward, ed. *Holding Your Eight Hands: An Anthology of Science Fiction Verse.* Doubleday, 1969.

Mansfield, Roger, ed. *The Starlit Corridor: Modern Science Fiction Short Stories and Poems.* Pergamon, 1967.

Phillips, Robert, ed. *Moonstruck: An Anthology of Lunar Poetry.* Vanguard, 1974.

Sargent, Pamela, ed. *Women of Wonder: Science Fiction Stories by Women About Women.* Random House, 1975.

————. *More Women of Wonder: Science Fiction Novelettes by Women About Women.* Random House, 1976.

————. *The New Women of Wonder: Recent Science Fiction Stories by Women About Women.* Random House, 1978.

Silverberg, Robert, ed. *Science Fiction Hall of Fame: The Greatest Science Fiction Stories of All Time.* Doubleday, 1970.

Fantasy

Alexander, Lloyd. *The Black Cauldron.* Holt, Rinehart & Winston, 1965.

————. *The Book of Three.* Holt, Rinehart & Winston, 1964.

————. *The Castle of Llyr.* Holt, Rinehart & Winston, 1966.

————. *The High King.* Holt, Rinehart & Winston, 1968.

————. *Taran Wanderer.* Holt, Rinehart & Winston, 1967.

Anderson, Poul. *The Dancer from Atlantis.* Doubleday, 1971.

Beagle, Peter. *The Last Unicorn.* Viking, 1969.

Berger, Thomas. *Arthur Rex.* Delacorte, 1978.

Brackett, Leigh. *The Book of Skaith: The Adventures of Eric John Stark.* Ballantine, 1974-76.

Brooks, Terry. *The Sword of Shannara.* Ballantine, 1977.

Burford, Lolah. *The Vision of Stephen.* Macmillan, 1972.

Cooper, Susan. *The Dark Is Rising.* Atheneum, 1973.

———. *Greenwitch.* Atheneum, 1974.

———. *The Grey King.* Atheneum, 1975.

———. *Over Sea, Under Stone.* Harcourt Brace Jovanovich, 1966.

———. *Silver on the Tree.* Atheneum, 1977.

de Larrabeiti, Michael. *The Borribles.* Macmillan, 1978.

Finney, Charles. *The Circus of Dr. Lao.* Viking, 1935.

Farmer, Penelope. *A Castle of Bone.* Atheneum, 1972.

Froud, Brian and Alan Lee. *Faeries.* Harry N. Abrams, 1978.

Garner, Alan. *The Owl Service.* Henry Z. Walck, 1967.

———. *Red Shift.* Macmillan, 1973.

Harris, Rosemary. *The Seal-Singing.* Macmillan, 1971.

Hunter, Mollie. *A Stranger Came Ashore.* Harper & Row, 1975.

Huygen, Wil (illustrated by Rien Poorvliet). *Gnomes.* Harry N. Abrams, 1977.

Ipcar, Dahlov. *A Dark Horn Blowing.* Viking, 1978.

Jones, Diana Wynne. *Charmed Life.* Greenwillow, 1978.

———. *Drowned Ammet.* Atheneum, 1978.

Kurtz, Katherine. *Deryni Rising.* Ballantine, 1970.

———. *Deryni Checkmate.* Ballantine, 1972.

———. *High Deryni.* Ballantine, 1973.

Le Guin, Ursula K. *A Wizard of Earthsea.* Parnassus, 1968.

———. *The Tombs of Atuan.* Atheneum, 1971.

———. *The Farthest Shore.* Atheneum, 1972.

Leiber, Fritz. *Swords and Ice Magic.* Ace, 1977.

Lockley, Ronald. *Seal-Woman.* Bradbury, 1975.

Lynn, Elizabeth A. *The Dancers of Arun.* G. P. Putnam's Sons, 1979.

Matheson, Richard. *What Dreams May Come.* G. P. Putnam's Sons, 1978.

Mayne, William. *Earthfasts.* E. P. Dutton, 1966.

McCaffrey, Anne. *Dragonsong.* Atheneum, 1976.

———. *Dragonsinger.* Atheneum, 1977.

———. *Dragondrums.* Atheneum, 1979.

McKillip, Patricia A. *The Forgotten Beasts of Eld.* Atheneum, 1974.

———. *Harpist in the Wind.* Atheneum, 1979.

McKinley, Robin. *Beauty.* Harper & Row, 1978.

Nathan, Robert. *Portrait of Jennie.* Alfred A. Knopf, 1940.

Nichols, Ruth. *Song of the Pearl.* Atheneum, 1976.

Norton, Andre. *Wraiths of Time.* Atheneum, 1976.

Reamy, Tom. *Blind Voices.* G. P. Putnam's Sons, 1978.

Saint-Exupery, Antoine de. *The Little Prince.* Harcourt Brace Jovanovich, 1943.

Stewart, Mary. *The Crystal Cave.* William Morrow, 1970.

———. *The Hollow Hills.* William Morrow, 1973.

———. *The Last Enchantment.* William Morrow, 1979.

Storr, Catherine. *Winter's End.* Harper & Row, 1979.

Tolkien, J. R. R. *The Hobbit, or There and Back Again.* Houghton Mifflin, 1937. Revised edition published in 1965.

———. *The Lord of the Rings.* Houghton Mifflin, 1954-56.

———. *The Silmarillion.* Houghton Mifflin, 1977.

Wangerin, Walter, Jr. *The Book of the Dun Cow.* Harper & Row, 1978.

Wharton, William. *Birdy.* Alfred A. Knopf, 1978.

White, T. H. *The Once and Future King.* G. P. Putnam's Sons, 1940.

———. *The Sword in the Stone.* G. P. Putnam's Sons, 1939.

Wibberley, Leonard. *The Mouse That Roared.* Little, Brown, 1955.

Wrightson, Patricia. *The Dark Bright Water.* Atheneum, 1979.

———. *The Ice Is Coming.* Atheneum, 1977.

Utopias

Aaron, Chester. *Hello to Bodega.* Atheneum, 1976.

Abbey, Edward. *Desert Solitaire: A Season in the Wilderness.* McGraw-Hill, 1968.

———. *The Journey Home: Some Words in Defense of the American West.* E. P. Dutton, 1977.

Brancato, Robin F. *Blinded by the Light.* Alfred A. Knopf, 1978.

Burgess, Anthony. *A Clockwork Orange.* W. W. Norton, 1963.

Callenbach, Ernest. *Ecotopia: The Notebooks and Reports of William Weston.* Bantam, 1975.

Capps, Benjamin. *The Brothers of Uterica.* Meredith, 1967.

Connolly, Edward. *Deer Run.* Charles Scribner's Sons, 1971.

Coover, Robert. *The Origin of the Brunists.* Viking, 1977.

Corlett, William. *Return to the Gate.* Bradbury, 1977.

Cummings, Betty Sue. *Let a River Be.* Atheneum, 1978.

Dillard, Annie. *Pilgrim at Tinker Creek.* Harper's Magazine Press, 1974.

Fletcher, Colin. *The Man Who Walked Through Time.* Alfred A. Knopf, 1968.

George, Jean Craighead. *Going to the Sun.* Harper & Row, 1976.

———. *Hook a Fish, Catch a Mountain.* E. P. Dutton, 1975.

Gilman, Charlotte Perkins. *Herland.* Pantheon, 1979. (First published as a magazine serial in 1915.)

Hall, Lynn. *Too Near the Sun.* Follett, 1970.

Hallahan, William H. *Keeper of the Children.* William Morrow, 1978.

Herzog, Arthur. *Make Us Happy.* Thomas Y. Crowell, 1978.

Hickman, Janet. *Zoar Blue.* Macmillan, 1978.

Howard, Elizabeth. *Out of Step with the Dancers.* William Morrow, 1978.

Kinkade, Kathleen. *A Walden Two Experiment: The First Five Years of Twin Oaks Community.* William Morrow, 1973.

Krutch, Joseph Wood. *The Best Nature Writing of Joseph Wood Krutch.* William Morrow, 1970.

Mathiessen, Peter. *The Snow Leopard.* Viking, 1978.

McPhee, John. *Encounters with the Archdruid.* Farrar, Straus & Giroux, 1971.

Morris, Taylor. *The Walk of the Conscious Ants.* Alfred A. Knopf, 1972.

Mungo, Raymond. *Total Loss Farm: A Year in the Life.* E. P. Dutton, 1971.

Nichols, John. *If Mountains Die.* Alfred A. Knopf, 1979.

Sandroff, Ronni. *Fighting Back.* Alfred A. Knopf, 1978.

Skinner, B. F. *Walden Two.* Macmillan, 1948.

Thomson, David. *In the Shining Mountains: A Would-Be Mountain Man in Search of the Wilderness.* Alfred A. Knopf, 1979.

Wizansky, Richard. *Home Comfort: Stories and Scenes of Life on Total Loss Farm.* Saturday Review Press, 1973.

Wood, Allen Tate and Jack Vitek. *Moon-Struck: A Memoir of My Life in a Cult.* William Morrow, 1979.

Zwinger, Ann. *Run, River, Run: A Naturalist's Journey Down One of the Great Rivers.* Harper & Row, 1975.

10

Life Models

Of Heroes
and Hopes

The word *hero* may conjure up a picture of Robin Hood or perhaps John Wayne leading a group of Marines in a charge up a hill. All societies and cultures have had heroes who embody the values and virtues of their culture. Before written records, storytellers kept alive—and probably improved on—the stories of their feats. With the beginning of writing and later of printing, their stories have been recorded. There are real-life heroes who are the subjects of biographies and fictional heroes who are the subjects of every form of literature. The Greeks gave us their gods and those who confronted the gods, Prometheus, Oedipus, and Antigone. Writers have presented heroes as different as Shakespeare's Juliet, Dostoyevsky's Raskalnikov, Ibsen's Dr. Stockmann, Cervantes' Don Quixote, and Mitchell's Scarlett O'Hara. These fictional characters have always competed with living heroes, then or now, like Muhammad, Mary, Galileo, Napoleon, Copernicus, Jefferson, Queen Victoria, Golda Meir, and on and on.

WHO ARE THE HEROES? WHO NEEDS THEM?

We have heroes because we need to have people to admire, even at times to worship. In 1941 Dixon Wecter wrote, "Hero-worship answers an urgent American need."[1] Seventeen years later Arthur Schlesinger wrote in "The Decline of Greatness," that he was worried because now that hero worship was no longer fashionable, "then our instinct for admiration is likely to end by settling on ourselves. The one thing worse for democracy than hero worship is self-worship."[2] And in 1978 Henry Fairlie agreed with Schlesinger when he said, "A society that has no heroes will soon grow enfeebled."[3]

Who are the heroes of young adults? In the last few years various polls have been published suggesting that we are losing our giants, or at least that young adults do not seem to admire giants. A 1976 survey—with a questionable polling approach—announced the top fifty heroes of young Americans. The top ten of both boys and girls were O. J. Simpson, Elton John, Neil Armstrong, John Wayne, Robert Redford, Chris Evert, Mary Tyler Moore, Billie Jean King, Henry Kissinger, and Joe Namath.[4] If some of those names were not troubling, others on the list were more than slightly surprising: Ralph Nader was number 16; Billy Graham, 19; Cher, 20; George Wallace, 25; Mick Jagger, 27; Loretta Lynn, 34; Gloria Steinem, 39; and Rod McKuen, 41. Number 44 was horrifying—Charles Manson. Jonas Salk appeared as number 45, and even that high a listing may have surprised the pollsters. Another poll that year announced the five Americans whom high-school students most admired: Richard Nixon, Henry Kissinger, Betty Ford, Gerald Ford, and Billy Graham.[5] A Scholastic Magazine poll of personal heroes from more than 14,000 secondary students in 1977 revealed Farrah Fawcett-Majors as the hero of the year followed by Jerry Lewis, Nadia Comaneci, and "none."[6] "None" was the most popular choice among high-school students but not among junior-high students.

Such polls as these may say more about the effects of modern mass media than about people's needs and desires in relation to heroes. For one thing, attitudes may not be as different today as we think they are. Centuries ago, or even a few decades ago, there were no national pollsters around asking the same question and expecting to get the same answer from coast to coast. When people are asked to identify their heroes, they know that they are expected to name someone who will be recognized by the asker. This means they have to name a national figure. Two hundred and seventeen million people live in the United States. It is only through the mass media—television, radio, newspapers, and magazines—that anyone can become known by that many people. Notice how many of those listed in the polls are professional media people. They are politicians and entertainers. They devote their lives to learning how to make the media work for them in getting their names and faces before the public. The competition is keen because in the "global village," so aptly labelled by Marshall McLuhan, there is an inexhaustible supply of potential celebrities. The public can barely remember their names much less what they've done, which one hopes is at least a partial explanation for the inclusion of such names as Charles Manson.

The people young adults admire may be very different from the people whose names they would write down as celebrities. They may look up to a neighbor, a teacher, a favorite aunt, or some other adult with whom they've had enough interaction to feel confident that the person is sincere and has qualities that are truly admirable. With media heroes people are understandably skeptical because so many of them have turned out to be different from the image that they present to the public. And the prying eye of the media that creates a hero can quite easily deflate that same hero.

The need for a hero is a persistent theme running through young adult novels. M. E. Kerr's several books are concerned with the protagonist's search for someone to admire who will not be a betrayer. *If I Love You, Am I Trapped Forever?* is a superior portrayal of a handsome, brilliant, popular young man, Alan Bennett, anxiously seeking a father or an adult outside his family whom he can trust and find heroic. His struggle to stay cool so that no one will recognize his confusion and insecurity are touching and believable. *Gentlehands* is less effective, but the rather unlikeable Buddy

Boyle's love for wealthy Skye Pennington and his admiration for his grandfather, Frank Trenker, are well-handled. One early scene should be recognizable and understandable to young adults eager to find heroes in whose glory they can bask. Buddy has taken Skye to his grandfather's house to show off the culture Buddy feels is lacking in his mother's and father's house. Trenker sees through Buddy's actions and amused says:

> "Do you think you impressed her, Buddy?"
> "Well, *you* did." I mumbled, and his remark had made my face red.
> He didn't say anything, so I said, "It was borrowed glory, I guess."
> "I'm happy to lend it to you," he said.
> "Thanks." . . .
> "You know, Buddy," my grandfather finally said, "you can get there on your own once you're pointed in the right direction."
> "Get where?" I said, but I knew what he was talking about. He knew I knew, too, and didn't even bother explaining where.
> "I'd be happy to point you, if that's what you want," he said.

Only a few minutes later, Trenker tries to show his grandson that winning what he wants, whatever it is, is possible: "Obstacles are challenges for winners, and excuses for losers."

Young adults, and, for that matter, all of us, need to find heroes worth admiring, worth emulating. Unhappily, we may be attracted to people with charisma, today's magic word. We may seek someone who talks, acts, and thinks the way we do. What we should seek, and do in our better moments, are heroes with dignity, who are above the crowd, and who are admirable but not necessarily likable. Looking up to the kinds of heroes presented in the following sections is something that we all need in order to survive and to make survival worthwhile.

An interesting theory holds that storytelling began when cavemen came back from a hunt and told about their exploits. If they had nothing to tell, they made up something, and the art of fiction was born. When an exceptionally brave storyteller dared to confess that he had been frightened and had called out for help from a superior being, the religious element entered into storytelling. And when a hunter or warrior showed unusual bravery or skill, his fellows bragged about him and perhaps exaggerated as they recounted the experience. It was in this way that the hero tale developed. These stories told of physically dangerous exploits that took place in a short span of time in predominantly masculine groups.

Women, who gave birth to children and provided the child's first nourishment, were given primary responsibility for the care of the young. Throughout the ages they stayed close to home while the men went forth to do battle with the elements, with animals, or with other humans. When they returned home, the waiting women and children provided a receptive audience for their stories.

This heritage has made people think of heroic adventure as being a male activity. One sign that people think it unusual for a woman to play this role is the coinage and the continued use of the word *heroine* to refer to a female, who, considering her sex, is doing something unexpected. But today the definition of *hero* is changing as are the roles that women play. Because of this we are quite satisfied to refer to both males and females as *heroes*. There have always been heroic women, but to a large extent they have been admired and honored for how well they raised their children. This is all well and good and nothing that we want to change, but, from a literary standpoint, raising children takes such a long time that it doesn't make for a very exciting hero tale. Besides, a mother's success is usually judged by the accomplishments of her children, and then the primary attention is focused on them.

There were occasional stories in the past about women doing exciting, physical things, but these were the exception. They were interesting because of the reverse twists, as in, for example, the Greek legend about the Amazons and the old German folktale about Molly Whuppie who outwits the giant. Today we are much more likely to have hero tales about women who are interesting, not just because they are women, but because, by anyone's standards, they have done something admirable.

There were occasional stories about women doing exciting, physical things, but these were the exception.

It's true that men's bodies have a higher proportion of muscle tissue than do women's, but this isn't as important as it used to be. For example, the differences in strength between male and female pale into insignificance when they are compared to the power of a jet engine, a gun, or a Caterpillar tractor. In modern societies, machines do the largest proportion of the physical work, and the machines are made so that either men or women can operate them. Perhaps one of the reasons for modern people's intense interest in sports is that this is one area in which the relatively insignificant differences between the physical strength of one individual and another are still important.

Medical technology has also brought about tremendous changes. First, it has learned to save the lives of babies and children so that a woman no longer needs to have eight children in the hope of raising four of them. Second, it has developed birth-control techniques so that couples can choose when and how often they want to give birth to children. And third, it has made such overall improvements in health and maternity care that women's life expectancies have increased twenty years within the last two generations.

All of this means that women today have something their grandmothers never had: TIME! They have time to engage in pursuits in addition to motherhood and time to write about these pursuits. This is bringing about a change in the publishing world so that now it is much easier than it was a decade ago to find books featuring female heroes both in and out of family contexts. However, the books tend to have a different focus from those featuring males, and, in some areas, we had to look very hard to find good books about female heroes. A decade ago it would have been impossible to present a balanced chapter. Today it was a challenge. Ten years from now, we hope it will be nothing out of the ordinary.

CURRENT TRENDS IN BIOGRAPHIES

When checking the biography shelves of almost any library, readers will probably find a predominance of biographies about white males. In contrast, when checking catalogues of newly published books, readers will find more biographies about minorities and women. During the 1970s, the imbalance became so obvious, particularly in school textbooks, that publishers took steps to correct the situation. Textbooks were revised and many trade books were published to serve as supplementary classroom material. New biographies were written about such people as Paul Robeson, Mahalia Jackson, Cesar Chavez, Duke Ellington, Maria Tallchief, Louis Armstrong, and W. E. B. DuBois. Several companies sponsored series, of which one of the most notable is the Thomas Y. Crowell "Women of America" series edited by Milton Meltzer. Authors also worked hard to find contemporary women and members of minorities whose stories could be told. And they looked into history to find individuals whose stories would be interesting even if they had not been famous.

Sometimes when there was not enough historical information available or when it was desirable to provide young readers with information about a large number of people quickly, collective biographies were published. Some were put together under obvious themes, for example Robert A. Liston's *Women Who Ruled: Cleopatra to Elizabeth II* and William Loren Katz's *Black People Who Made the Old West.*

When the authors take a less obvious theme and search out stories to support it, the books may be more interesting. That is what Julius Lester did in *Long Journey Home: Stories from Black History.* His goal was to present "the many whose individual deeds are seldom recorded and who are never known outside their own small circles of friends and acqaintances." Sally Van Wagenen Keil did a similar thing when she wrote *Those Wonderful Women in Their Flying Machines: The Unknown Heroines of World War II,* and Margery Facklam wrote *Wild Animals, Gentle Women,* which consists of journalistic accounts of twelve women who succeeded in different jobs as ethologists. Nearly everyone has heard of Jane Goodall but perhaps not of the other women whose work is equally interesting. For example, Belle Benchley joined the San Diego Zoo in 1925 as a bookkeeper. By 1927, she was the zoo's director, but, considering the state of the zoo, this was not a particularly momentous career step. It was Benchley who, in the years between 1927 and 1953, when she retired, made the zoo the world-famous spot that it is today. Hettie Jones chose blues music as her theme when she wrote *Big Star Fallin' Mama: Five Women in Black Music,* presenting the stories of Ma Rainey, Bessie Smith, Billie Holiday, Mahalia Jackson, and Aretha Franklin.

Collective biographies present librarians and teachers with the added responsibility of finding some way to let potential readers know who is featured in these books. In the case of women and minorities where there is a lack of material and where students probably have an inadequate background of information, librarians might consider inserting a cross reference in the card catalogue under the name of the individual. Some librarians have been able to enlist volunteer help for this task. Another way to focus attention on people featured in collective biographies is to make a display highlighting their names and giving some indication of the area of their accomplishments.

The ancient Greeks enjoyed both their stories about the gods of Mount Olympus and the hero tales about the mortal descendants of these gods. But the hero tales had an added attraction that helped listeners to identify with the protagonists. Unlike the gods, who live forever, the heroes had one human parent, which meant that they were mortal and could be killed. In any undertaking, the most that the gods could risk was their pride, but the heroes could lose their lives.

A comparison could be made to modern literature. Fiction is more or less like the stories about the gods. As long as it is fiction, we know in the back of our minds that the author can always bring the protagonist out alive. But with true hero tales, that is, biographies, the protagonists risk their lives just as readers would have to do in the same situation. This adds an extra degree of credibility and intensity because the reader thinks, "If this happened to someone else, then it might happen to me."

Judging from lists of "best" or "favorite" books, biographies come the closest of any nonfiction to remaining popular for a long time and to being considered literature with a capital L. For example, on the Honor Sampling, given in Appendix A, over fifty percent of the nonfiction books are biographical in nature. One of the reasons that biographies have a good chance of succeeding is that the writers have the best of two worlds. They can present the uniqueness and authenticity of one person's life and, at the same time, emotions and problems that all humans face.

Traditionally, biographies—especially those for young readers—were written about heroic figures who were thought worthy of emulation. In some of these books from the past, biographers built their subjects up to almost god-like proportions. But the result of stressing only the noble qualities of heroes was sometimes discouraging to readers. People are well acquainted with their own weaknesses, and, when they are told only about the strengths of their heroes, they conclude that heroes are of quite another breed. Today's biographies for young adults are likely to be written more objectively, providing a balance of both strengths and weaknesses. They demonstrate how the subject and the reader share similar emotions. Both have fears and insecurities and both succumb to temptations and vanities. After reading a good biography, the reader feels a kinship with the subject, not so much in spite of as because of the character's human frailties.

The desire for feeling a kinship with the subject of a biography has also influenced the choice of subject. The people featured in the kinds of biographies that are popular today represent a broad spectrum of society. Many have worked to become good writers to share their experiences and feelings as did Tim O'Brien in his introspective memoir about being a foot soldier in Vietnam. His book, *If I Die in a Combat Zone, Box Me Up and Ship Me Home,* explores the complex issues of courage, cowardice, and morality in war. Others are of special interest because they give readers insights into cultures or experiences different from their own. *The Education of Little Tree* by

Forest Carter tells about his experience as an orphaned five-year-old who was taken to live in his Cherokee grandparents' log cabin. The place was Tennessee and the year was 1930, and what he learned was the Cherokee ethic of living. In *I Once Knew an Indian Woman*, Ebbitt Cutler tells about a woman he knew forty years ago when he was a child in Canada. She emerges as a savior for her people. *Tisha: The Story of a Young Teacher in the Alaskan Wilderness* by Anne Hobbs as told to Robert Specht takes place in 1927 when Hobbs went to teach in Chicken, Alaska. Several writers have recently

SUGGESTIONS FOR EVALUATING BIOGRAPHIES

A good biography usually has:	A poor biography may have:
A subject of interest with whom the author and, therefore, the readers feel intimately acquainted.	A subject who happens to be of current interest but whose life the author has no real commitment to or knowledge of beyond that available in any good public library.
Documentation of sources and suggestions for further reading—both done inconspicuously so as not to interfere with the story.	An adulatory tone which makes the person too good to be true.
New and/or unusual sources of original information.	Sensationalism, that is, a focus on the negative aspects of the subject's life. A debunking of a historically respected character without adequate documentation of the reasons that the author's viewpoint differs from history's perception.
Accurate facts about setting and characters.	
A central theme or a focus point that has been honestly developed from the author's research.	None of the interesting detail that makes the story of a person's life unique.
In-depth development of the character so that readers understand the way in which the subject shaped his or her own life. Things did not just happen to the person.	A disproportionate emphasis on the history and the circumstances surrounding this subject's life so that the reader does not get acquainted with the person. (One biography of Golda Meir is really the story of modern Israel using Mrs. Meir as an attention-getting device and a selling point for libraries looking for biographies of strong women.)
Use of language that is appropriate to the historical period and the literary style of the book.	
Information showing how the subject was thought about by contemporaries.	

written autobiographical novels of this type, for example, Judy Blume's *Starring Sally J. Freedman as Herself,* about a young Jewish girl growing up just after World War II, and Eleanor Wong Telemaque's *It's Crazy to Stay Chinese in Minnesota,* about a meeting of the Far East and Middle West during the 1940s.

Under the old philosophy of writing about heroes who would serve as role models for young people, authors shied away from doing books about contemporaries. They conservatively waited until history had judged a person's worth. It is true that writing about a living subject is taking a risk. For example, writers who in the late 1960s wrote laudatory biographies of Richard M. Nixon did not get their fair share of royalties when in the 1970s Watergate made these books seem quaint, or worse. It is not that there couldn't be a laudatory biography about Nixon, but it would need to take Watergate into account. Nevertheless the same forces that have made young readers hungry for information about all kinds of subjects have made them want to know about the people they see on television and in magazines and newspapers. Someone whose name is already known has a head start in garnering interest for a personal book. And today's authors often focus largely on one aspect of someone's life. They no longer feel it necessary to start with the subject's birth and carry the story through to the end. For example, many young readers who like the poetry of Rod McKuen would probably be interested in his book *Finding My Father: One Man's Search for Identity,* and moviegoers who have admired Shirley MacLaine would be likely to pick up her book about her 1973 tour of the People's Republic of China, *You Can Get There from Here.*

Another characteristic of biographies that is important to young adults is the age of the protagonists. If the subjects are young—in their teens or early twenties—the book is more likely to be read and enjoyed. This is probably one of the reasons that Steven Gaines' *Marjoe: The Life of Marjoe Gortner* is popular. Marjoe was a child evangelist whose career seemed washed up by the time he was fourteen. Stevie Wonder, another person who had a career when he was still a teenager, is described in *The Story of Stevie Wonder* by James Haskins. His real name is Steveland Morris and, in spite of being blind, he managed to become one of the most popular singers in the country. A book that might not be classified as pure biography but which nevertheless tells the story of people's lives is *Heaven Is a Playground* by Rick Telander. It takes readers into the lives of talented black youths whose love of basketball is the central hope they have for the future.

A book's popularity is determined, not so much by the level of the subject's achievement, as it is by the degree to which the author is skilled in recreating quite ordinary events and in openly sharing the emotions that go along with them. For example, a mild-mannered English veterinarian, James Herriot, won both teen-age and adult readers when he opened up his heart and soul in *All Creatures Great and Small* and its sequels *All Things Bright and Beautiful* and *All Things Wise and Wonderful.* Two other books that reveal the inner workings of the authors' minds are *Doing My Own Time* by Richard H. Shoblad, a prisoner who recounts the change that came over him when he decided to redirect his life, and *Report from Engine Co. 82* by New York City fireman Dennis E. Smith who describes the emotional as well as the physical side of his job.

Another item that correlates with popularity is the age of the writer of an autobiography. Some are surprisingly young. Robin Graham was only sixteen when he set sail in a sloop to circle the world. He tells his story (with the help of Derek L. T. Gill) in *Dove.* Mark Vonnegut was little more than a teenager when he became schizophrenic. He tells the story of his fight to return to reality in *The Eden Express.* Athlete Bruce Jenner, who won a gold medal at the Montreal Olympics, tells the story of his four years of training in *Decathlon Challenge: Bruce Jenner's Story.*

It is probably because today's young adults are accustomed to the here-and-now approach of television that they seem to want everything "direct from the horse's mouth." They like the authenticity that is implicit in interviews, personal statements, and autobiographies. With today's sophisticated system of ghostwriters and extensive editorial support, it is possible for many more people to tell their personal stories. The custom of having autobiographies ghostwritten or written "with" someone else is so common that when Lauren Bacall wrote her biography she attracted attention by giving it the ambiguous title of *Lauren Bacall by Myself.*

As writers of biographical pieces compete to make their stories interesting, they use many of the techniques of the fiction writer. In fact, it is practically impossible with current books to draw a clear-cut line between fiction and biography. Sometimes titles lend more confusion than clarity as is the case with Ernest J. Gaines' *The Autobiography of Miss Jane Pittman.* It is not an autobiography at all, or even a biography. Rather it is historical fiction whose author used the format of a young reporter interviewing a very old woman to lend a feeling of authenticity to the story. Other books will be about real persons and real events that have been extensively researched; nevertheless the author will choose to label the book a "novel." That is what Rhoda Lerman did with *Eleanor.* The book is set in the four years following Eleanor Roosevelt's discovery that Franklin loved someone else. Even though readers will probably interpret the story as "biographical," the author, by choosing to call it a novel, allowed herself a degree of freedom that she would not have had if she were doing a biography.

In general, it is not this kind of imagined historical biography that appeals to young readers. Instead what they like are more detailed accounts than they can find on television or in newspapers and magazines of the lives of interesting contemporaries or near-contemporaries. Examples of books in this category are *Buried Alive: The Biography of Janis Joplin* by Myra Friedman, *Muhammad Ali* by Wilfrid Sheed, and *Judy Garland* by Anne Edwards.

Because of their interest in reading about contemporaries who are in the news and since they have free access to books written for the general public, some of the most popular biographies among young adults are not about worthy role-models. Colin Mackenzie's *Biggs* is the story of Ron Biggs who is "the world's most wanted man" because of his part in Britain's great train robbery. *Helter Skelter* by Vincent Bugliosi and Curt Gentry is the story of Charles Manson and how he made a band of runaways into murderers. The popularity of this last title troubled many adults who were uncomfortable with the idea that their children were looking at Charles Manson as a hero. However, more than one psychologist offered reassurance by explaining that reading about someone does not necessarily mean that the reader wants to follow in that person's footsteps. It is more likely to be curiosity than hero worship that is at play. As humans we are drawn to examining and pondering our dual natures. We peer into the evil nature of something truly horrible in the same way that we peer into a great chasm or over the ledge of a skyscraper. We have no intention of falling or jumping over, yet the fact that someone did, makes us shudder because we recognize the possibility. Should we expect young adults to be any different from adults in being fascinated by the horrors of the world? The flourishing business that tabloid newspapers do attests to the fact that people are fascinated by those who have done terrible things. In an article entitled, "Is TV Exploiting Tragedy?" Sally Bedell stated that each of the television renditions—the documentary-dramas—of the tragedies of the 1970s (the Charles Manson murders, the Patricia Hearst kidnapping, the Israeli raid on Entebbe, and Watergate) garnered at least one-third of the viewing audience, which is a very high percentage. Brandon Stoddard, president of the ABC motion-pictures unit, has said that "merely labeling a TV-film a true story can add millions to a network's audience."[7] The networks after much inner turmoil decided against doing dramatized versions of the lives of Jim Jones, cult leader who directed the Guyana suicide-murders, and of David Berkowitz, the "Son of Sam" killer.

The problem comes in deciding who is an out-and-out villain and who is an antihero. One of the literary contributions of the last century has been the development of stories featuring protagonists who are quite ordinary, or even less than ordinary, but who nevertheless appeal to readers. These anti-heroes, even though they do not have traditional heroic qualities, are admired because the reader feels a strong sense of

The debunking biography takes a popular hero down from his or her pedestal.

identification and empathizes with their attempts to cope. But people such as Charles Manson, Jim Jones, and David Berkowitz are not anti-heroes. They do not represent meek, humble, and confused people trying their hardest to understand life. As Stoddard said when he explained the decision of the network not to tell Berkowitz's story, "it would have been incredibly exploitative. He was a very sick man. . . . When you try to examine the psyche of an individual who is that abnormal, it is difficult to find insights that are useful to the average American."[8] It is this latter kind of insight that is provided in the best stories of the anti-hero.

Before leaving the anti-hero, we should also mention the debunking biography. This is another fairly recent trend in which a popular hero is taken down from his or her pedestal. Although such books are certainly "anti-hero," they differ somewhat from what is usually meant by anti-hero in literary terminology. The subject of a debunking biography is not written about sympathetically, whereas an anti-hero is. *Mommie Dearest* is a debunking biography of Joan Crawford written by her adopted daughter, Christina, and *An Untold Story* is a debunking biography of Eleanor Roosevelt written by her son, Elliot.

Jim Bouton's *Ball Four: My Life and Hard Times Throwing the Knuckleball in the Big Leagues* was not the first nor will it be the last iconoclastic sports story telling in detail the salaries, disputes, foolishness and stupidity of other baseball players. Bouton's work put baseball mania and baseball worship in some sort of perspective, but with our need for heroes—real heroes, of course—Bouton may have offered us more honesty than we needed or wanted. Honesty may be an overrated virtue at times. That heroes are human is a truism. That all their sins and warts need public exposure may be open to question. Books like *Ball Four* are antidotes for too much hero worship. Not to read debunking books is to miss one facet of humanity, but to read only debunking books is to produce only debunkers, and that we already have in sufficient number.

To summarize, biographies and personal statements are among the most popular of current nonfiction writing. Although there are many traditional biographies featuring both historical and contemporary men who have made outstanding contributions, today there are also many newly written biographies featuring heroic women and members of minority groups. Biographical pieces are also being written by quite ordinary citizens, including young adults, whose main contribution is their ability to reveal their inner feelings about the unique aspects of their own lives. To make the biographies interesting, writers are using many of the same literary techniques that fiction writers use. And although most biographies are written about someone who is admired, the presentations are balanced giving both the negative and positive qualities of the subjects. As with modern fiction, readers show a preference for realism over romanticizing. Most biographical pieces provide young readers with worthy role-models, which is as important today as it ever was.

TYPES OF HEROES

Quiet Heroes

Fiction abounds with quiet heroes worth admiring and emulating. They reassure us that although we are mortal a few individuals find ways to transcend their mortality to leave behind a record. In books of this type, attention is usually paid to character development, particularly of the quiet hero. Others in the book reflect or comment on the hero. The books often are episodic with particular episodes focusing on problems confronting the heroes and forcing them into decisions that will clarify the values or beliefs they live by. Heroes are frequently pushed to a physical or psychological precipice to establish their beliefs and their innate superiority to other people. Quiet heroes carry burdens, but they do it quietly, not dramatically. What the magician Schmendrick said in Peter Beagle's *The Last Unicorn* about great heroes is almost equally true of quiet heroes: "Great heroes need great sorrows and burdens, or half their greatness goes unnoticed." With quiet heroes, their greatness often does go unnoticed by their friends and neighbors, but not by readers. If quiet heroes have anything bordering on a tragic flaw, it is not the Aristotelian flaw but that of modern humanity, the kind that Arthur Miller described as nothing but an unwillingness to remain passive in the face of what is conceived to be a challenge to one's dignity, one's image of rightful status.

Only the passive, only those who accept their lot without active retaliation, are "flawless." Most of us are in that category.

But there are among us today, as there always have been, those who act against the scheme of things that degrades them. . . .[9]

Papa in Robert Newton Peck's *A Day No Pigs Would Die* has great dignity. Financially poor he may be, but spiritually and heroically he is rich. The narrator, Rob, sometimes does not understand his father and worries about him, but he always respects him, knowing instinctively that Papa has dignity and stature. As he tries to explain to a neighbor:

> Papa works all the time. He don't never rest. And worse than that, he works inside himself. I can see it on his face. Like he's been trying all his life to catch up to something. But whatever it is, it's always ahead of him, and he can't reach it.

Papa is not passive. He fights to maintain his dignity, his image of his rightful status.

Two crucial scenes establish Papa's humanity, willingness to admit error, and dignity. The first is for many readers the ugliest episode in the book. A weasel has been caught and Papa puts the weasel and a dog, Hussy, in a barrel to teach the dog to hate and kill weasels. Rob protests to no avail until the weasel is dead and the dog nearly so. Rob says:

> "She's dying. And if you got any mercy at all . . . you'll do her in. Right now. She killed the weasel. Isn't that what you wanted to have her do, with all it's sport? She's crazy with hurt. And if you don't kill her, I will."

Although the neighbor warns the boy to mind his tongue, Papa agrees with Rob. After killing the dog, Papa says:

> "I swear. I swear by the Book of Shaker and all that's holy, I will never again weasel a dog. Even if I lose every chicken I own."

The second crucial episode is near the end of the book when Rob and Papa discover that Rob's pet pig, Pinky, is sterile. Given the Depression and the sad state of family finances, Pinky must die to give them food for the winter. Rob cannot, for a moment, accept the inevitability and necessity of Pinky's death:

> "Oh, Papa. My heart's broke."
> "So is mine," said Papa. "But I'm thankful you're a man."
> I just broke down, and Papa let me cry it all out. I just sobbed and sobbed with my head up toward the sky and my eyes closed, hoping God would hear it.
> "That's what being a man is all about, boy. It's just doing what's got to be done."

A Day No Pigs Would Die is not about the "cult of kill," as one critic claimed, but about a quiet hero and a boy who reveres his father-hero. Papa does not want to kill, but he knows when killing has to be done, and he knows what being responsible is all about.

Some books focus on the quiet hero by comparing the person with his contemporaries. Two books offer interesting contrasts about police work. Peter Maas' *Serpico* is a cop who deeply believes in what he does. Hated by criminals and other policemen for rooting out corruption, Frank Serpico was ostracized, but he offers a model for young adults who fear what might happen to them socially if they don't go along with everyone else. Robert Daley's *Prince of the City: The True Story of a Cop Who Knew Too Much* presents the other side of the coin focusing on the members of the Special Investigative Unit of the New York City Police Department and their betrayal of duty through bribery, illegal phone taps, withholding dope for their own sale, and perjury. The honesty of Serpico compared to the corruption of the Special Investigative Unit will undoubtedly shock some, but the contrast between them represents two sides of the same coin, one heroic, one evil.

Two recent black novels present the young and the old facing ignorance and prejudice. Gaines' *The Autobiography of Miss Jane Pittman* demonstrates the tenacity of a woman who has lived 110 years both as slave and free woman and who faces black militancy in the 1960s fearlessly and quietly. Mildred D. Taylor's *Roll of Thunder, Hear My Cry* introduces us to a rural Mississippi family during one frighteningly chaotic year in the Depression when the Logan children face prejudice and terror and fight back in their own quiet but effective way.

Other quiet heroes are rugged individualists, not afraid to be different and misunderstood throughout their lives. Alan Sillitoe's *The Loneliness of the Long-Distance Runner* is about a Borstal (reform school) boy forced to run the long-distance races to win admiration for the institution and its warden. He loves running, but at the close of the book he is forced to make a decision between what is right for him and what is expected of him by others. Ken Kesey's *One Flew Over the Cuckoo's Nest* gives us McMurphy, an antiestablishment leader in a revolt to bring humanity to a mental institution. His conflicts with Big Nurse are almost classic encounters of the quiet hero. Whether he loses or wins at the end is something young adults love to talk about.

Edward Abbey is a personal and literary exponent of quietly (sometimes not too quietly) fighting back at the establishment. *The Brave Cowboy* shows the last of a dying breed, a living anachronism. John W. Burns rides his horse, Whisky, into Duke City to free a friend from jail. Failing in that—the friend is willing to serve his term—Burns breaks out and faces modern technology, cars, and high-powered rifles. Better known under its film title, *Lonely Are the Brave,* Abbey's novel shows us one side of some quiet heroes. A more destructive side, but in some minds no less heroic, is in Abbey's *The Monkey Wrench Gang.* Three men and a woman set out to destroy all the technological devices—dams, power transformers, drill rigs, and the like—they can find in northern Arizona and southern Utah to put humanity back in its place so nature can reign. As one of the men, Seldom Smith, says, "Somebody has to do it." Another Abbey book, *Fire on the Mountain,* carries a similar message. Rancher John Vogelin and his twelve-year-old grandson stand off, for a time, the United States Air Force who want to take over their ranch as part of a missile range.

In some books, the quiet hero faces the inevitability of death. John Donovan's *Wild in the World* and Gunnel Beckman's *Admission to the Feast* have already been described in Chapter 6, and Margaret Craven's *I Heard the Owl Call My Name* was used as an example in Chapter 2. Glendon Swarthout's *The Shootist* is melodramatic, but the portrait of a dying gunfighter in a West that no longer knows him or needs him is convincing. John Bernard Books's decision to go out fighting, dying as he had lived, is true to his character.

In treating death, nonfiction books seem to have an added power to them. In a mid 1970s nationwide survey of nonfiction books popular with young adults, the ten books mentioned as favorites by the most respondents were all accounts of someone's struggle for survival. Given in the order of votes received, they are *Alive: The Story of the Andes Survivors; Eric; Brian's Song; Bermuda Triangle; Go Ask Alice; I Am Third; Anne Frank: The Diary of a Young Girl; Death Be Not Proud: A Memoir; Dove;* and *Brian Piccolo: A Short Season.*

Death appeared in all but one of these top ten books. It seems ironic that teenagers who are supposedly on the threshold of their lives are so interested in death. The strong interest shown in survival stories may stem from the fact that teenagers are about to establish their independence and they may be assessing their own chances for physical and emotional survival. In most of the books, even when death occurs there is

---

Few young adults know how ugly and demeaning war can be.

---

a spiritual or emotional victory. Or perhaps death wins only a partial victory as in *Alive.* Forty-six people board the chartered plane for its ill-fated flight from Uruguay to Chile. Ten weeks later sixteen emerge from the frozen heart of the Andes. In *Eric* Doris Lund writes about her son and his struggle with leukemia during which he managed to prolong his life two years past the doctor's prediction. During those years he was captain of a college soccer team, he had a love affair, he went scuba diving, and he traveled with a buddy across the United States in an old van.

Three of the books were intertwined in a way that would not have been likely in the days before modern mass media. They dealt with the death from cancer of the popular young football star Brian Piccolo. The favorite of the three was *Brian's Song* by William Blinn, which was based on the television movie of the same name. The movie was taken from a chapter entitled "Pick" in Gayle Sayers' book *I Am Third.* Sayers was Piccolo's team roommate. A separate book on the same subject is *Brian Piccolo: A Short Season* by Jeannie Morris. Author Morris was the wife of Brian's friend and teammate, Johnny Morris, and she began working with Brian when he was hospitalized. They made tape recordings in an attempt to stave off boredom.

Recent books that treat death include William Buchanan's *A Shining Season,* which tells how a twenty-four-year-old runner spent his last eighteen months of life; Elaine Ipswich's *Scott Was Here,* which is a tribute to the author's teenage son who struggled for five years against a terminal illness; and *Ellen: A Short Life Long Remembered,* which was chosen as a favorite by students reading in the University of Iowa Books for Young Adults program.

· Quiet heroes may also be those who have overcome or compensated for handicaps. Helen Keller's *The Story of My Life* is almost a classic. Tom Sullivan's *If You Could See What I Hear* is an upbeat, personal account of blindness, and *The Other Side of the Mountain* is the story of the rehabilitation of Jill Kinmont, a skier who fell while she was practicing for the Olympics and was permanently paralyzed. *Wheelchair Champions: A History of Wheelchair Sports* by Harriet May Savitz is a factual book about a relatively new kind of sports event.

Marie Killilea's *Karen* and its sequel *With Love from Karen* are inspirational accounts of a child with cerebral palsy and a family who provides a loving and supportive environment for their remarkable daughter. Mary MacCracken's *Lovey: A Very Special Child* is the story of a disturbed child whose teacher finally had the satisfaction of reaching her.

Books about quiet heroes are a relatively new kind of book, but they appeal to readers who have had enough experience in the world to become somewhat skeptical of the flamboyant hero. The need for this kind of skepticism sometimes is itself the subject of young adult novels. The protagonist in the story finds a hero, but is then disillusioned to learn that the hero has clay feet. Rafaèl Yglesias' *The Game Player* is one of the most distinguished of these books. Howard Cohen is a shy young man fascinated by Brian Stoppard's drive and ability to win every game no matter what it is: baseball, football, acting, chess, sex, poker, or bridge. Brian is the game player who derives singularly little pleasure from playing but immense, cold joy from psyching out other players and winning. Even though the denouement is a bit anticlimactic, Yglesias' book is an impressive study of a man for whom all life is a game. The quiet hero in the book is Howard Cohen who comes to recognize that there is more to heroism than winning.

Heroes in War

War is kept before us in the daily papers and in newscasts. If that were not enough, it is difficult to watch the late movie without seeing one actor or another gallantly saving us from this or that enemy as they bravely fight for America.

Why are we so continually preoccupied with war, bloodshed, and death? Perhaps because war is inherently frightening and evil and, in the minds of too many of us, inevitable. The Bible is full of battles, and so is the *Odyssey* and the *Iliad*. War serves as the background for *Antigone* just as it has for *The Red Badge of Courage, A Farewell to Arms, The Caine Mutiny, A Bell for Adano,* and *Naked and the Dead.* War has influenced musicians and artists; or perhaps it would be fairer to say that war has horrified them and left an indelible mark.

Young adults know that war is significant though few know how ugly and demeaning it can be. Perhaps realistic stories about war will serve to acquaint readers with some of the horrors of it and show how easily people can forget their humanity. War novels must, obviously, have a war at the center. The war need not be raging at that moment since the authors may choose to write of war's effect, direct or indirect, on the protagonists or on people they know. The story is likely to include physical or psychological suffering. Death lurks at the doorstep, or did once, and it still may emotionally for one or more characters. Often the war, present or past, seems to be happening in slow motion, focusing on people or events or horrors. Or the reverse may happen: events may be telescoped eliminating the trivial or nonessential to force readers (and sometimes characters) to see the realities of war more intensely. But there must not be a romanticized view of war. For jousting and glorious battles, fair maids and heroic heroes, one reads Sir Walter Scott, but for accurate and honest accounts of what war was like and the desolation it spread, one goes to other sources. Today a romanticized portrayal of war would seem offensive and dishonest to readers.

In 1961, critic J. Donald Adams told how he had come across a new book and read it in a single sitting. He wrote:

> Another kind of book of the same length might well have taken me longer, but this was one of compelling narrative power, of unflagging interest. It was Howard Fast's *April Morning*, a story of the battle of Lexington as seen through the eyes of a 15-year-old boy who took part in it. When I had finished it, I said to myself, "This is an even better book than Crane's *Red Badge of Courage*." I still think so.[10]

All comparisons are invidious, and many suffer in the light of another day. Whether or not Fast's book about the Revolutionary War is superior to Crane's book about the Civil War is food for the critics' feast, not ours. What is true is that Fast's *April Morning* added another to the list of superior war stories. It centers on fifteen-year-old Adam Cooper, who is no hero but a mortal. He knows the rightness of war until he is in the thick of it, and then he wonders at the carnage and the stupidity, but still sees its necessity. In eight sections taking readers from the afternoon of April 18, 1775, through the evening of April 19, *April Morning* explores the family relationships of Adam and his father, his mother Sarah, his beloved Granny and the girl he loves.

Adam is unquestionably superstitious and headstrong, but his chief defect is his youth and his immaturity. The first two are forgotten and the last two disappear when Adam's father is shot by British redcoats and Adam is off and running, not to war, not for vengeance, but for safety. He is filled with fear, "saturated with it, sick with it." The lines had disappeared and the men and boys were running "in every direction that was away from the British."

> I tripped and fell into the drainage ditch, banged my head hard enough to shake me back to some reality, pulled myself up, and saw Samuel Hodley standing above me with a ragged hole in his neck, the blood pouring down over his white shirt. We looked at each other, then he fell dead into the ditch. I vomited convulsively, and then, kneeling there, looked back across the commons.

Adam discovers what needs to be learned, that war is a messy and dirty business, but that he has survived and may yet survive to the end of the war. Much later, Adam meets the press, a reporter from the *Boston Advertiser*, who will not be put off. When

Adam says he is too tired to know what the truth is, the reporter glibly replies, "A patriot always knows what the truth is." He does and Adam does not, no more than anyone who has been at the center of war, or even at the edges, knows the truth. To know the truth about war is to have the objectivity born of total ignorance or total uninvolvement. Failing that, one must be a general or a politician.

It would be unfair and inaccurate to call Adam a hero, at least in the usual sense. But Adam is a war hero in some important ways. He survives, he does what he has to do, and he tries to make sense out of the horror, to understand what the war is all about. And it is about him, whether he wants it to be or not. He is a part of the war, like it or not.

Jennifer Johnston's *How Many Miles to Babylon?* is about World War I and two Irishmen, Alexander Moore, who is upper-class, and Jerry Crowe, who comes from peasant stock. War breaks out and they enlist, Alex as an officer and gentleman, Jerry as an enlisted man. Their friendship almost endures the trench slaughter until official-dom takes over and the men are divorced from humanity and each other. In slightly more than 150 pages of tightly packed prose, Johnston makes us keenly aware of soldiers crowded in a trench and what they can and cannot do.

Two other World War I novels deserve attention. Although neither are recent in publication, both are contemporary in honesty and feeling. William March's *Company K*, the greatest war novel ever written, consists of sketches and stories about all the men in that company from Private Joseph Delaney on to Private Sam Ziegler, nothing more, but taking a page or two for each soldier, March vividly paints hell and war and what it does to men. The publication of Dalton Trumbo's *Johnny Got His Gun* in 1939 was badly timed. That year, with fear of Hitler surrounding us, was not the best time to publish—much less sell—a detailed portrait of the hell caused by war, but, since World War II, Trumbo's book has become a classic account of a war-induced basket case.

One study of war that introduced a phrase into our lexicon was Joseph Heller's *Catch-22*, a masterful, very funny, and also very sad look at the lunacy of war and the mad logic of the military mind.

Of all writers for young adults, James Forman stands out as the best war novelist. His books come closer than most to catching the misery and stink of war coupled with the pathos of real people caught up in events they cannot comprehend or manage. Perhaps most significant, Forman's novels give us heroes, believable ones, in the midst of war, acting as heroes might, unsure, frightened, bewildered, and horrified. Yet his characters have strength and nobility. They would probably deny the last adjective, but they would be wrong. *Ceremony of Innocence*, his best book, is based on an actual episode, but even had it not been factually documented, readers would have believed the events could have happened. We need to be able to think that people like Sophie and Hans Scholl, a sister and brother, had the courage in 1942 Germany to produce and disseminate leaflets attacking Nazism, no matter how sure their fate.

The Traitor takes place a few years earlier, but the story of Pastor Eichhorn and his two sons, Paul (a foster son), who is willing to fight Nazism, and Kurt, who is an ardent Nazi, is equally believable and almost as compelling. Forman's other novels include

Horses of Anger about a young German soldier beginning to question the Nazi philosophy, *The Survivor* about a family in the way of war with little chance of survival, *Ring the Judas Bell* about civil war in 1940s Greece, *My Enemy, My Brother* about Palestine and hatred, *Follow the River* about the son of a Nazi prison doctor following the spirit of Ghandi in India after the war, and *A Fine, Soft Day* about the religious war in Northern Ireland.

The roles of males and females are quite different in war stories, but that doesn't mean that women and girls are any less heroic than men and boys. Few people could argue with the real life heroism of Anne Frank, or that of Johanna Reiss whose book about her three years of hiding in *The Upstairs Room* is popular with younger adolescents. Another well-liked book is the story of Jeanne Wakatuski and her family's internment during World War II because they were Japanese. *Farewell to Manzanar* takes its title from the name of the camp in the east Sierras to which Jeanne's family was sent along with hundreds of other Japanese-Americans. There is no denying the heroism of this family and many others like them.

Michele Murray's *The Crystal Nights* is not quite so dramatic. Relatives escape a German concentration camp and come to join a Connecticut family. The heroism is made up of daily sacrifices rather than one grand and glorious act. In Jean Little's *Listen for the Singing*, a young refugee from Germany becomes involved with the Canadian civil defense, and in Mara Kay's *In Face of Danger* another young girl lodges with a Germany family in 1938. The landlady's son is a fanatic Nazi, but his mother harbors two Jewish girls in the attic. A different perspective on World War II was presented in 1977 when Ilse Koehn published her true story of growing up in Nazi Germany without knowing that she was part Jewish, *Mischling, Second Degree: My Childhood in Nazi Germany.*

I'm Deborah Sampson by Patricia Clapp is especially interesting because it is based on the true story of a young girl who fought bravely in the Revolutionary War under the name of Robert Shurtlieff. Fictional stories treated in other sections of this text that have elements of war-related heroism include Bette Greene's *Summer of My German Soldier*, Sarah Patterson's *That Distant Summer*, and T. Degen's *Transport 7-41-R.*

Books about innocents caught in war are legion. Some of the better ones are Joseph Bor's *The Terezin Requiem* and Fania Fenelon's *Playing for Time*, both about concentration camp orchestras so professional that even the Nazis were astounded. Jerzy Kosinski's *The Painted Bird* is about a little boy abandoned by his parents who lives first with this family and then with that. He survives through imagination and sheer courage.

Traditional heroes in war novels are less common than many readers might expect. Perhaps because war produces devastation and chaos, and because of Vietnam, readers have become too troubled by the whole concept of war to join in open admiration for someone who participates wholeheartedly. Within a single generation, there has been almost a complete reversal of the old idea of a war hero. Today, in war, as in many other aspects of life, it is the quiet hero, the survivor against incredible odds, who is admired.

Sports Heroes

Both adults and young adults have been fascinated by sports and sports heroes as far back as the Olympic games in ancient Greece. Today, spectator and participatory sports are the most popular recreation activities in the United States. Everyday millions of people are out jogging, playing tennis, swimming, or golfing. Millions more are playing team sports in leagues organized by churches, city recreation departments, private clubs, and schools. Viewing audiences for major sports events are phenomenal. All in all, sports play an unprecedented role in American life. Given our national mania most of us would be shocked—or horrified—if the current president of Cornell University repeated what his predecessor said in 1873 about a proposed football game against the University of Michigan. "I will not permit 30 men to travel 400 miles merely to agitate a bag of wind."

Sports, more than any other important facet of American life, is youth oriented making it of special interest to young adults. In many sports, athletes reach their peak when they are still in their teens or early twenties, leading to powerful sense of identification. Other than in sports, could young people dream of the success and fame that Nadia Comaneci and Tracy Austin achieved at age fourteen? And it is not just at this superstar level that sports provide young people with chances to succeed. There are thousands of levels between that of world fame and the ten-year-old who wins the most-improved-player trophy on the local Little League team. Sports are emphasized so much in the American growing-up process that it would be an unusual child who had not been pressured—by parents or peers—to try out for some sort of team.

The "game" is a microcosm of the American system; it is life in miniature.

Parents and schools often encourage children to participate in sports because, in addition to providing good physical exercise, sports are thought to be one way to teach life's principles. Sports provide an outlet in which people can play out conflicts within the security of rules. The "game" is, supposedly, a microcosm of the great American system.

Until recently, most young women were denied the experience of playing and working and learning together on an organized school sports team.[11] That denial, women's groups have argued convincingly, hampers females in their careers. Women sensitive to criticism and apt to give up when they do not immediately succeed, so goes the argument, became that way because they were not allowed to learn about defeat and the art of recovering and bouncing back to try again. But the exclusion of women from sports is rapidly changing, and women who feel they missed an important part of their youth are encouraging their daughters to participate in swimming, basketball, soccer, archery, golf, tennis, gymnastics, softball, and even football. There is always a lag between a social change and its appearance in books, but changes can be seen. In three recent romances—Judy Blume's *Forever* and Norma Klein's *It's Okay if You Don't Love Me* and *Love Is One of the Choices*—the protagonists are all skilled and competitive tennis players. (We sometimes forget that Nancy Drew was and is a fine athlete.)

Sports books, fictional or nonfictional, have some common elements. A description of the game itself—rules, training, crowds, thrills—has increasingly been expanded to include the players and what the game does to the players. Rather than a simple accounting of one inning or one quarter after another, emphasis may be on the toughening, the character-developing aspects of the sport. At the heart of much sports fiction is an examination of the price of fame, the transitory nature of glory, and the doomed temptation to make glory endure. Another common theme is the camaraderie of the players and the mystical bond between them that is beyond rational explanation.

Early sports books were written to teach boys the same kinds of things that they could learn through ideal sports participation. The purity of sports at the turn of the century was exemplified by Ralph Henry Barbour and his novels. Barbour deeply believed in hard play, fair play, and the amateur spirit and dedicated his 1900 novel *For the Honor of the School* "To That School, Wherever It May Be, Whose Athletics Are Purest." Dated though his books now seem, he was serious in his belief that school spirit was inevitably coupled with both athletic and academic excellence. He and other young adult writers preached this doctrine from the turn of the century until the 1940s.

Despite the love affair Americans have had with sports, surprisingly little serious fiction about sports has emerged. Barring a boxing tale by Hemingway, some outlandish and funny stories by Damon Runyon, and some amusing but ironic (and at times savage and cynical) stories by Ring Lardner, only four major novels and one major drama concerned with sports have been published: Bernard Malamud's *The Natural* (1952), Mark Harris' *Bang the Drum Slowly* (1956), Robert Coover's *The Universal Baseball Association, Inc., J. Henry Waugh, Prop.* (1968), Don DeLillo's *End Zone* (1972), and Jason Miller's play, *That Championship Season* (1972). The traditional sports novel for young adults, once so common, has now all but disappeared. Ralph Henry Barbour and William Heyliger, along with all their imitators, are no longer read. John Tunis' novels filled with heroes and realistic games played by characters who reeked of sweat lie sedately on library shelves, and the books of the late 1950s and early 1960s written by John F. Carson and H. D. Francis are going out of print. Perhaps, kindly old Pop Dugout, wily with his world of sports wisdom and warm genial backpatting, was never very real, but somehow that sentimental fiction of the past had a charm that we have lost and with it many sports heroes for young readers.

To attract young readers, current sports fiction must have something not provided either in the old sports stories or in the real-life stories featured in the current media.

Robert Lipsyte's *The Contender* is an example of an outstanding and popular book with an extra touch far beyond the traditional sports novel. Black school dropout Alfred Brooks is despised by his former friends for working at a Jewish owned grocery store and for refusing to help them rob the store. Escaping from them one day, Alfred drops into Donatelli's gym and is curious about boxing. Donatelli agrees to help, and after that the world is a school to Alfred. He learns his Jewish employer was once a promising fighter, he finds that some former friends ridicule his role as a fighter but that some younger boys admire him, and he discovers that training and boxing are rough and sometimes unrewarding. Alfred learns that crowds want to see blood and pain. Most important, he learns that he can be a contender in life, if not in boxing. Alfred does not set out to be a hero or find a hero, but, to his surprise, he succeeds in both. *The Contender* offers far more than an initiation into the arcane, and often forbidden or forbidding, world of prize fighting. It offers far more than a believable glimpse into a black world. The book is about young adults searching for acceptance and dignity.[12]

Another extra in recent sports fiction is the inclusion of women as protagonists. Little fanfare or prepublication advertising greeted the appearance of R. R. Knudson's *Zanballer* in 1972, but high-school girls soon discovered it, and its popularity climbed steadily. Librarians reported that it nearly always inspired requests for "another book like this one." Unhappily, the books that followed, *Zanbanger* (1977) on basketball and *Zanboomer* (1978) on baseball, were contrived and far less successful for adults, though young adults read them almost as avidly as *Zanballer*. The first of the series focuses on football. Zan Hagen attends Lee High School and is appalled when she discovers the girls' P.E. classes have been shifted to the old Home Economics room while the gym is being remodeled for the forthcoming boys' basketball season. The girls are expected to do folk dancing, dodging around the old sinks and leftover gas stove outlets. Zan finally manages to convince the boys' coach to let her and the friends she can either entice or browbeat train in the same way as the football players. But Zan is not satisfied with just training. She wants to go on to real football competition.

Her cohort and mentor is Arthur Rinehart who outlines strategy and acts as her attorney, her spy, her coach, and her friend. Rinehart's part in the stories disappoints some women who are delighted to find a strong female protagonist in believable sports stories but who dislike the fact that much of her success comes from Rinehart's help. Christy Tyson, young adult specialist in the Mesa (Arizona) Public Library, defends Rinehart's role. She has found that quite a few boys read and enjoy the *Zan* series, and she thinks they would not if it weren't for Rinehart. She points out that the role he plays of supportive, intellectual friend is as nontraditional for a male as is Zan's role of assertive athlete for a female. She believes more books touching on this kind of social change are needed. When they appear, they will be read and enjoyed by both boys and girls.

Knudson has written a more serious book, *Fox Running*. This story of two Olympic-level runners who learn from each other is especially good in portraying a supportive and relaxed relationship between two women with a common interest but widely different backgrounds. The girl known as Fox Running is an Apache who has been trained since childhood by her grandfather. Readers who enjoy Knudson's books might like Thomas J. Dygard's *Winning Kicker*, the story of Kathy Denver, a crackerjack place-kicking specialist, who earns a place on the Higgins High School football team.

Biographies, interviews, and reminiscences are replacing young adult sports novels. These books take up where magazine articles and television programs leave off. For example, Bill Bradley's autobiographical *Life on the Run* conveys the spirit of basketball, weighing the love of the game and team camaraderie against constantly being on the go and the boredom of waiting at airports and motels. The portraits of Bradley's fellow New York Knicks as players and as people are impressive. What emerges from the book is not simply one basketball game after another but the sweat, pain, anxiety, friendships, loneliness, and the talk of players. Bradley explains why he, an all-American player at Princeton University and a Rhodes Scholar at Oxford, turned professional. It was during his second year in England when:

> after not touching a basketball for nine months, I went to the Oxford gym simply for some long overdue exercise. There I shot alone. . . . A feeling came over me that stirred something deep inside. I realized that I missed the game. . . . I knew that never to play again, never to play against the best, the pros, would be to deny an aspect of my personality perhaps more fundamental than any other.

But he does far more than explain why he returned to basketball; he explains why professional athletes care about the game and their teammates.

Some books talk about our persistent need for sports heroes whose lives and accomplishments are worthy of admiration and even emulation. Maury Allen's *Where Have You Gone, Joe Dimaggio? The Story of America's Last Hero* explains why Dimaggio was an authentic hero and why we all need heroes when so few can be found today. William Brashler's *Josh Gibson: A Life in the Negro Leagues* is a loving and sometimes frightening account of what it was like to play in those circumstances. In the course of the story, the picture of a great human being and athlete emerges. Another picture of a black man fighting his way to the top is Joe Louis' autobiography, *Joe Louis: My Life*. The unusual friendship that develops between a shy black athlete and a Southern white is told in two young adult favorites: Gale Sayers' *I Am Third* and Jeannie Morris' *Brian Piccolo: A Short Season*. The changing role of the sports hero is described in a nostalgic glance back at the sports heroes of another time, James V. Young and Arthur F. McClure's *Remembering Their Glory: Sports Heroes of the 1940's*.

Some interesting looks into women's sports include Lynn Haney's *The Lady Is a Jock;* Grace Lichtenstein's *A Long Way Baby: Behind the Scenes in Women's Pro Tennis;* and Karen Folger Jacob's *Girlsports*, which features athletes between nine and seventeen. Billie Jean King's informative *Tennis to Win* is read in part because she is a hero in gaining respect and equality for women's tennis.[13]

Three books are concerned with sports scandals, heroes gone wrong and hero worship gone sour. Eliot Asinof's *Eight Men Out: The Black Sox and the 1919 World Series* tells of the great Chicago White Sox team that sold out and particularly of the much-admired Shoeless Joe Jackson who had a lifetime batting average of .365. Two books about the basketball scandals of the early 1950s are Stanley Cohen's *The Game They Played* and Charles Rosen's *Scandals of '51: How the Gamblers Almost Killed College Basketball*.

A few master writers have gone beyond the games, the players, and the rules to the very essence of the game. John McPhee's *Levels of the Game* is a beautifully crafted book by the best nonfiction writer in America today about a Forest Hills tennis match between Arthur Ashe and Clark Graebner. Readers bored by tennis will have some understanding of why tennis attracts so many people after reading this book. Roger Angell, a fine baseball writer, collected his *New Yorker* articles in two superb books, *The Summer Game* and *Five Seasons: A Baseball Companion.* George Plimpton's *One More July* conveys the feelings Bill Curry had during his last year playing center for the Green Bay Packers. Pat Jordan may not be the writer McPhee or Angell or Plimpton is, but two books, *The Suitors of Spring* and *A False Spring,* get across his abiding love affair with baseball. He explains what it meant, professionally and personally, to play minor league baseball and to know that he would never go any further. His more recent *Chase the Game* is especially interesting because it tells of three young adults who almost make it out of the ghetto by playing basketball.

The transitory nature of sports fame is found in Martin Ralbovsky's *Destiny's Darlings: A World Championship Little League Team Twenty Years Later.* The author describes the Little League team from Schenectady, New York, and their World Championship game on August 27, 1954. He interviewed many of the players twenty years

---

A few master writers have gone beyond the games, the players, and the rules to the very essence of the game.

---

later and contrasts the early glory with their later lives, more than a bit reminiscent of A. E. Housman's "To an Athlete Dying Young." Jay Acton's *The Forgettables* is about a virtually unknown sport in America, minor league football, and the Pottstown Pennsylvania Firebirds, a few players on the way up, a few on the way down, and most of them going no place. Acton's book is a sad commentary on an understandable but hopeless drive to prolong college fame to the point where it becomes foolish and almost unendurable.

A few sports books deserve reading because of their originality. Two collections of science fiction short stories will appeal to both sports and science fiction fans, Martin Greenberg's *Run to Starlight: Sports Through Science Fiction* and Terry Carr's *The Infinite Arena: Seven Science Fiction Stories About Sports.* William Harrison's *Roller Ball Murder,* a collection of short stories, has the title story set in the future when companies rather than countries control the world. To stave off human frustration and to allow people to maim and even kill vicariously, a blood-lust sport is devised that is fast, exciting, and deadly. Patricia Nell Warren's *The Front Runner* centers on track and includes a fine distance runner, a track coach, and homosexual love—a brilliant book.

Moe Berg: Athlete, Scholar, Spy by Louis Kaufman, Barbara Fitzgerald, and Tom Sewell is poorly written, but it is a fantastic and seemingly impossible biography of a former Princeton scholar and linguist who in 1934 went to Japan as a catcher on a visiting United States all-star baseball team along with players like Babe Ruth and Lou Gehrig. In his role as a spy, he took numerous photographs, many of them of Japanese armaments and industry, surprising for a baseball-playing tourist.

Sports books are too often uncomfortably "rah-rah" and sometimes too consumed with the heroes of the game. But some books do convey the feeling and love for the game that the great soccer star, Pele, talked about at the end of his playing days:

> Because of its universal appeal, I believe soccer can unite all the peoples of the world. Its theme is so vast it can fill the world with understanding, peace and love. I know this because I have been a missionary of soccer for 22 years.
>
> After all these years in soccer, I have come to realize that through soccer we can all be brothers. Soccer's appeal and magnitude is such that it ignores race, religion and politics. Soccer has one real goal and that is to create friendship.[14]

Heroes exist both in real life and in fiction. We read about quiet heroes, sports heroes, and even some war heroes. They do not wear medals. They do not parade, except perhaps to the sound of their own drums, but they exist in and out of books. Henry James said that life was a slow, reluctant march into enemy territory. Heroes know this, but it does not deter them. One of the characters in Jerzy Kosinski's *The Devil Tree* said:

> Of all mammals, only a human being can say "no." A cow cannot imagine itself apart from the herd. That's why one cow is like any other. To say "yes" is to follow the mass, to do what is commonly expected. To say "no" is to deny the crowd, to be set apart, to reaffirm yourself.

That person is the hero.

In Sam Peckinpah's film, *Ride the High Country* (1962), two aging former U.S. Marshals down on their luck are given one last chance to bring a shipment of gold down from a mountain mining town. Gil Westrum plans to take the gold and run; society owes him that, or so he says. Steve Judd refuses to play along, and when Westrum asks him why, Judd can only answer, "All I want is to enter my house justified."

That's all any hero could ask, to live a life of integrity, humanity, and dignity based upon what he or she believes in deeply. That's all, but it's everything. Such heroes do exist, heroes willing to die for something they believe in, more important, heroes willing to live to fight for their beliefs. We all need heroes to help us stumble through the dark to find the light as they have, to falter and fail and win out in some measure as they have. We may not need the grandiose heroes of old so much as we need people like ourselves who can achieve an immortality within a family or a community. As teachers and librarians we have both the responsibility and the opportunity to bring books that reveal these facts to young adults.

ACTIVITIES

1. Find a topic or theme and read one biographical account and one fictional account. For example, read Robert Lipsyte's novel *The Contender* and his biography *Free to Be Muhammad Ali*, or read a biography of Eleanor Roosevelt and the novel *Eleanor*. Compare the two books. What different techniques or kinds of incidents were there? How did the dialogues differ? Was one stronger on plot and the other stronger on character development? Which did you enjoy the most? Tell why? From which one did you learn the most? Did you learn different kinds of things?
2. Choose a particular group of people that has been somewhat overlooked in books. Prepare an annotated bibliography of books that you think would appeal to young adults looking for heroes in this group. Check publisher's catalogues for recent releases as well as researching such standard guides as *Books in Print, Subject Index to Children's Books,* and guides to literature about particular ethnic groups or women.
3. Visit a local public or high-school library. Study the collective biographies and then devise a plan that you could use to inform students about the people who are featured in these books. If practical, actually produce a promotional bulletin board, display, handout, or other piece of educational material that could be used in the library in conjunction with promoting these books.

NOTES

[1]Dixon Wecter, *The Hero in America: A Chronicle of Hero-Worship* (New York: Charles Scribner's Sons, 1941), p. 1.

[2]Arthur Schlesinger, Jr., "The Decline of Greatness," *Saturday Evening Post* 231 (November 1, 1958): 70.

[3]Henry Fairlie, "Too Rich for Heroes," *Harpers Magazine* 257 (November 1978): 33.

[4]Mary Susan Miller, "Who Are the Kids' Heroes and Heroines?" *Ladies' Home Journal* 93 (August 1976): 108-9.

[5]Gordon A. Sabine, "Richard Nixon Ranked First By Teens," *Phoenix Gazette* ("Marquee" supplement), October 2, 1976, p. 4.

[6]Rick Ratliff, "An 'Angel' Emerges as Hero of Teens," *Chicago Tribune*, January 4, 1977, I, 15.

[7]Sally Bedell, "Is TV Exploiting Tragedy?" *TV Guide*, June 16-22, 1979, p. 5.

[8]Ibid., p. 6.

[9]Arthur Miller, "Tragedy and the Common Man" in *Aspects of the Drama*, ed., Sylvan Barnet, Morton Berman, and William Burto (Boston: Little, Brown, 1962), p. 64-65.

[10]J. Donald Adams, "Speaking of Books," *The New York Times Book Review*, May 14, 1961, p. 2.

[11]See Joanna Bunker Rohrbaugh, "Femininity on the Line," *Psychology Today* 13 (August 1979): 30-42 for a discussion of sports and women.

[12]See John Simmons, "Lipsyte's *Contender*: Another Look at the Junior Novel," *Elementary English* 49 (January 1972): 116-19 for a most perceptive article on the book and its value to teachers.

[13]Comments on the need for more, and better, sports books for young women can be found in Patricia Campbell, "Women in Sports in Children's Books: Wealthy, White and Winning," *Interracial Books for Children Bulletin*, vol. 10, no. 4 (1979), pp. 3-10.

[14]Pele, "Pele's Farewell: What Soccer Has Meant," *The New York Times*, September 25, 1977, V, 5.

RECOMMENDED TITLES

For information on the availability of paperback editions of these titles, please consult the most recent edition of *Paperbound Books in Print*, published annually by R. R. Bowker Company.

Biographies

Agee, James. *Letters of James Agee to Father Flye*. Houghton Mifflin, 1971.

Angelou, Maya. *Gather Together in My Name*. Random House, 1974.

————. *I Know Why the Caged Bird Sings*. Random House, 1970.

————. *Singin' and Swingin' and Gettin' Merry Like Christmas*. Random House, 1976.

Bacall, Lauren. *Lauren Bacall by Myself*. Alfred A. Knopf, 1978.

Baez, Joan. *Daybreak*. Dial, 1968.

Bentley, Phyllis. *The Brontës and Their World*. Charles Scribner's Sons, 1979.

Blume, Judy. *Starring Sally J. Freedman as Herself*. Bradbury, 1977.

Brown, Claude. *Manchild in the Promised Land*. Macmillan, 1965.

Bugloisi, Vincent and Curt Gentry. *Helter Skelter: The True Story of the Manson Murders*. W. W. Norton, 1974.

Carter, Forest. *The Education of Little Tree*. Delacorte, 1979.

Clark, Steven. *Fight Against Time: Five Athletes—A Legacy of Courage*. Atheneum, 1979.

Clarke, Mary Stetson. *Bloomers and Ballots: Elizabeth Cady Stanton and Women's Rights*. Viking, 1972.

Cleaver, Eldridge. *Soul on Ice*. McGraw-Hill, 1968.

Conot, Robert. *A Streak of Luck: The Life and Legend of Thomas Alva Edison*. Simon and Schuster, 1979.

Crawford, Christina. *Mommie Dearest*. William Morrow, 1978.

Cutler, Ebbitt. *I Once Knew an Indian Woman*. Houghton Mifflin, 1973.

Douglas, William O. *Go East, Young Man: The Early Years*. Random House, 1974.

Edwards, Anne. *Judy Garland*. Simon and Schuster, 1975.

Facklam, Margery. *Wild Animals, Gentle Women*. Harcourt Brace Jovanovich, 1978.

Flack, Dora and Lula Parker Betenson. *Butch Cassidy, My Brother.* Brigham Young University Press, 1976.

Fox, Ray Errol. *Angela Ambrosia: The Story of a Girl's Winning Fight for Life.* Alfred A. Knopf, 1979.

Friedman, Marcia. *The Story of Josh.* Ballantine, 1975.

Friedman, Myra. *Buried Alive: The Biography of Janis Joplin.* William Morrow, 1973.

Gaines, Steven S. *Marjoe: The Life of Marjoe Gortner.* Harper & Row, 1973.

Gillespie, Dizzy and Al Fraser. *To Be or Not to Bop.* Doubleday, 1979.

Giovanni, Nikki. *Gemini.* Bobbs-Merrill, 1971.

Gordon, Barbara. *I'm Dancing as Fast as I Can.* Harper & Row, 1979.

Graham, Robin Lee and Derek L. T. Gill. *Dove.* Harper & Row, 1972.

Gray, Madeline. *Margaret Sanger: A Biography of the Champion of Birth Control.* Richard Marek, 1979.

Gridley, Marion E., ed. *American Indian Women.* Hawthorn, 1974.

Gunther, John. *Death Be Not Proud: A Memoir.* Random House, 1953.

Haskins, James. *Barbara Jordan.* Dial, 1977.

———. *James Van Derzee: The Picture-Takin' Man.* Dodd, Mead, 1979.

———. *The Life and Death of Martin Luther King.* Lothrop, Lee & Shepard, 1977.

———. *The Story of Stevie Wonder.* Lothrop, Lee & Shepard, 1976.

Herriott, James. *All Creatures Great and Small.* St. Martin's, 1972.

———. *All Things Bright and Beautiful.* St. Martin's, 1974.

———. *All Things Wise and Wonderful.* St. Martin's, 1977.

Hobbs, Anne with Robert Specht. *Tisha: The Story of a Young Teacher in the Alaskan Wilderness.* St. Martin's, 1976.

Hoenig, Gary. *Reaper: The Inside Story of a Gang Leader.* Bobbs-Merrill, 1975.

Houston, Jeanne Wakutsuki and James D. *Farewell to Manzanar.* Houghton Mifflin, 1973.

Johnson, William Oscar and Nancy P. Williamson. *"Whatta-Gal": The Babe Didrikson Story.* Little, Brown, 1977.

Jones, Hettie. *Big Star Fallin' Mama: Five Women in Black Music.* Viking, 1974.

Jordan, Barbara and Shelby Hearon. *Barbara Jordan: A Self-Portrait.* Doubleday, 1979.

Keil, Sally Van Wagener. *Those Wonderful Women in Their Flying Machines: The Unknown Heroines of World War II.* Rawson Associates, 1979.

Lawick-Goodall, Jane Van. *In the Shadow of Man.* Houghton Mifflin, 1971.

———. *My Friends the Wild Chimpanzees.* National Geographic Society, 1967.

L'Engle, Madeleine. *The Summer of the Great-Grandmother.* Farrar, Straus & Giroux, 1974.

Lerman, Rhoda. *Eleanor.* Holt, Rinehart & Winston, 1979.

Libby, Bill. *The Reggie Jackson Story.* Lothrop, Lee & Shepard, 1979.

Louis, Joe with Edna and Art Rust. *Joe Louis: My Life.* Harcourt Brace Jovanovich, 1978.

Lund, Doris. *Eric.* J. B. Lippincott, 1974.

Mackenzie, Colin. *Biggs: The World's Most Wanted Man.* William Morrow, 1975.

Mackenzie, Midge. *Shoulder to Shoulder.* Alfred A. Knopf, 1975.

MacLaine, Shirley. *You Can Get There from Here.* W. W. Norton, 1975.

Malcolm X. *The Autobiography of Malcolm X.* Grove, 1965.

Manley, Seon and Susan Belcher. *O, Those Extraordinary Women! or the Joys of Literary Lib.* Chilton, 1972.

McKuen, Rod. *Finding My Father: One Man's Search for Identity.* Coward, McCann & Geoghegan, 1976.

Mead, Margaret. *Blackberry Winter.* William Morrow, 1972.

Moody, Anne. *Coming of Age in Mississippi.* Dial, 1968.

Morris, Jeannie. *Brian Piccolo: A Short Season.* Rand McNally, 1971.

Nelson, Mary Carroll. *Maria Martinez.* Dillon, 1972.

Parks, Gordon. *Choice of Weapons.* Harper & Row, 1966.

Powers, John R. *Do Black Patent Leather Shoes Really Reflect Up?* Contemporary Books, 1975.

Roosevelt, Elliot. *An Untold Story.* G. P. Putnam's Sons, 1973.

Sabin, Francene. *Women Who Win.* Random House, 1975.

Sanders, Marion K. *Dorothy Thompson: A Legend in Her Time.* Houghton Mifflin, 1973.

Sayers, Gale. *I Am Third.* Viking, 1970.

Sayre, Anne. *Rosalind Franklin and DNA.* W. W. Norton, 1975.

Schoor, Gene. *Babe Didrikson: The World's Greatest Woman Athlete.* Doubleday, 1977.

Shoblad, Richard H. *Doing My Own Time.* Doubleday, 1972.

Siegel, Beatrice. *Alicia Alonso: The Story of a Ballerina.* Frederick Warne, 1979.

Smith, Dennis E. *Report from Engine Co. 82.* McCall Books, 1972

————. *The Final Fire.* Saturday Review Press, 1975.

Telemaque, Eleanor Wong. *It's Crazy to Stay Chinese in Minnesota.* Nelson, 1978.

Terrell, John Upton and Donna M. Terrell. *Indian Women of the Western Morning: Their Life in Early America.* Dial, 1974.

Thomas, Piri. *Down These Mean Streets.* Alfred A. Knopf, 1967.

Vecsey, George. *One Sunset a Week.* Saturday Review Press, 1974.

Vonnegut, Mark. *The Eden Express.* Praeger, 1975.

Quiet Heroes

Abbey, Edward. *The Brave Cowboy.* Dodd, Mead, 1956.

————. *Fire on the Mountain.* Dial, 1962.

————. *The Monkey Wrench Gang.* J. B. Lippincott, 1975.

Bales, William Alan. *The Seeker.* McGraw-Hill, 1976.

Beckman, Gunnel. *Admission to the Feast.* Holt, Rinehart & Winston, 1971.

Berry, Wendell. *The Memory of Old Jack.* Harcourt Brace Jovanovich, 1973.

Böll, Heinrich. *The Lost Honor of Katharina Blum.* McGraw-Hill, 1975.

Bolt, Robert. *A Man for All Seasons.* Random House, 1962.

Brecht, Bertolt. *Galileo.* Grove Press, 1966.

Craven, Margaret. *I Heard the Owl Call My Name.* Doubleday, 1973.

Daley, Robert. *Prince of the City: The True Story of a Cop Who Knew Too Much.* Houghton Mifflin, 1979.

Dickinson, Peter. *Tulku.* E. P. Dutton, 1979.

Dodd, Wayne. *A Time of Hunting.* Seabury, 1975.

Donovan, John. *Wild in the World.* Harper & Row, 1971.

Gaines, Ernest J. *The Autobiography of Miss Jane Pittman.* Dial, 1971.

Godden, Rumer. *In This House of Brede.* Random House, 1969.

Guy, Rosa. *Ruby.* Viking, 1976.

Haley, Alex. *Roots.* Doubleday, 1976.

Hamilton, Virginia. *Zeely.* Macmillan, 1967.

Heidish, Marcy. *A Woman Called Moses.* Houghton Mifflin, 1976.

Hunter, Kristin. *The Lakestown Rebellion.* Charles Scribner's Sons, 1978.

Keller, Helen. *The Story of My Life.* Doubleday, 1954.

Kellog, Marjorie. *Like the Lion's Tooth.* Farrar, Straus & Giroux, 1972.

Kerr, M. E. *Gentlehands.* Harper & Row, 1978.

———. *If I Love You, Am I Trapped Forever?* Harper & Row, 1973.

———. *Is That You, Miss Blue?* Harper & Row, 1975.

———. *The Son of Someone Famous.* Harper & Row, 1974.

Kesey, Ken. *One Flew Over the Cuckoo's Nest.* Viking, 1962.

Kingman, Lee. *Head over Wheels.* Houghton Mifflin, 1978.

Maas, Peter. *Serpico.* Viking, 1973.

McKay, Robert. *Dave's Song.* Meredith, 1969.

Ney, John. *Ox: The Story of a Kid at the Top.* Little, Brown, 1970.

———. *Ox Goes North: More Trouble for the Kid at the Top.* Harper & Row, 1973.

———. *Ox Under Pressure.* J. B. Lippincott, 1976.

Peck, Richard. *Father Figure.* Viking, 1978.

Peck, Robert Newton. *A Day No Pigs Would Die.* Alfred A. Knopf, 1973.

Ryan, Cornelius and Kathryn M. Ryan. *A Private Battle.* Simon and Schuster, 1979.

Saint-Exupery, Antoine de. *Wind, Sand and Stars.* Harcourt Brace Jovanovich, 1939.

Savitz, Harriet May. *The Lionhearted.* John Day, 1975.

———. *Wheelchair Champions: A History of Wheelchair Sports.* Thomas Y. Crowell, 1978.

Sillitoe, Alan. *The Loneliness of the Long-Distance Runner.* Alfred A. Knopf, 1959.

Sullivan, Tom. *If You Could See What I Hear.* Harper & Row, 1975.

Swarthout, Glendon. *Bless the Beasts and Children.* Doubleday, 1970.

———. *The Shootist.* Doubleday, 1975.

Taylor, Mildred. *Roll of Thunder, Hear My Cry.* Dial, 1976.

Wersba, Barbara. *Run Softly, Go Fast.* Atheneum, 1970.

Wibberley, Leonard. *The Last Stand of Father Felix.* William Morrow, 1974.

Yglesias, Rafael. *The Game Player.* Doubleday, 1978.

Heroes in War

Bawden, Nina. *Carrie's War.* J. B. Lippincott, 1973.

Benchley, Nathaniel. *Bright Candles.* Harper & Row, 1974.

———. *A Necessary End.* Harper & Row, 1976.

Bor, Joseph. *The Terezin Requiem.* Alfred A. Knopf, 1963.

Burton, Hester. *In Spite of All Terror.* World, 1969.

Caidin, Martin. *The Last Dogfight.* Houghton Mifflin, 1974.

Clapp, Patricia. *I'm Deborah Sampson.* Lothrop, Lee & Shepard, 1977.

Collier, James Lincoln and Christopher Collier. *The Winter Hero.* Four Winds, 1978.

Cooper, Susan. *Dawn of Fear.* Atheneum, 1970.

Dank, Milton. *The Dangerous Game.* J. B. Lippincott, 1977.

———. *Game's End.* J. B. Lippincott, 1979.

Degens, T. *Transport 7-41-R.* Viking, 1974.

Epstein, Leslie. *King of the Jews.* Coward, McCann & Geoghegan, 1978.

Fast, Howard. *April Morning.* Crown, 1961.

Fenelon, Fania. *Playing for Time.* Atheneum, 1977.

Forman, James. *Ceremony of Innocence.* Hawthorn, 1970.

———. *A Fine, Soft Day.* Farrar, Straus & Giroux, 1978.

———. *Follow the River.* Farrar, Straus & Giroux, 1975.

———. *Horses of Anger.* Farrar, Straus & Giroux, 1967.

———. *My Enemy, My Brother.* Hawthorn, 1969.

———. *Ring the Judas Bell.* Farrar, Straus & Giroux, 1965.

———. *The Survivor.* Farrar, Straus & Giroux, 1976.

———. *The Traitors.* Farrar, Straus & Giroux, 1968.

Frank, Anne. *The Diary of a Young Girl.* W. W. Norton, 1957.

Friedlander, Säul. *When Memory Comes.* Farrar, Straus & Giroux, 1979.

Graham, Gail. *Cross-Fire.* Pantheon, 1972.

Greene, Bette. *Summer of My German Soldier.* Dial, 1973.

Hanser, Richard. *A Noble Treason: The Revolt of the Munich Students Against Hitler.* G. P. Putnam's Sons, 1979.

Heller, Joseph. *Catch-22.* Simon and Schuster, 1961.

Houston, Jeanne Wakatsuki and James D. Houston. *Farewell to Manzanar.* Houghton Mifflin, 1973.

Johnston, Jennifer. *How Many Miles to Babylon?* Doubleday, 1974.

Kay, Mara. *In Face of Danger.* Crown, 1977.

Kerr, Judith. *The Other Way Round.* Coward, McCann & Geoghegan, 1975.

————. *A Small Person Far Away.* Coward, McCann & Geoghegan, 1979.

————. *When Hitler Stole Pink Rabbit.* Coward, McCann & Geoghegan, 1972.

Koehn, Ilse. *Mischling, Second Degree: My Childhood in Nazi Germany.* Greenwillow, 1977.

Kosinski, Jerzy. *The Painted Bird.* Houghton Mifflin, 1965.

Little, Jean. *Listen for the Singing.* E. P. Dutton, 1977.

Ludlum, Robert. *The Rhinemann Exchange.* Dial, 1974.

March, William. *Company K.* Sagamore Press, 1957. First printed 1933.

Mazer, Harry. *The Last Mission.* Delacorte, 1979.

McGivern, William P. *Soldiers of '44.* Arbor House, 1979.

Montagu, Ewen. *Beyond Top Secret Ultra.* Coward, McCann & Geoghegan, 1978.

Murray, Michele. *The Crystal Nights.* Seabury, 1973.

O'Brien, Tim. *Going After Cacciato.* Delacorte, 1978.

————. *If I Die in a Combat Zone, Box Me Up and Ship Me Home.* Delacorte, 1973.

Orgel, Doris. *The Devil in Vienna.* Dial, 1978.

Patterson, Sarah. *The Distant Summer.* Simon & Schuster, 1976.

Reiss, Johanna. *The Upstairs Room.* Thomas Y. Crowell, 1972.

————. *The Journey Back.* Thomas Y. Crowell, 1976.

Richter, Hans Peter. *Friedrich.* Holt, Rinehart & Winston, 1970.

Rose, Anne. *Refugee.* Dial, 1977.

Sachs, Marilyn. *A Pocket of Seeds.* Doubleday, 1972.

Southall, Ivan. *Seventeen Seconds.* Macmillan, 1974.

————. *What About Tomorrow?* Macmillan, 1977.

Trumbo, Dalton. *Johnny Got His Gun.* J. B. Lippincott, 1939.

Tunis, John. *Silence Over Dunkerque.* William Morrow, 1962.

Uhlman, Fred. *Reunion.* Farrar, Straus & Giroux, 1977.

Van Stockum, Hilda. *The Borrowed House.* Farrar, Straus & Giroux, 1975.

Walsh, Jill Paton. *Dolphin Crossing.* Macmillan, 1967.

————. *Fireweed.* Farrar, Straus & Giroux, 1970.

Westall, Robert. *The Machine Gunners.* Greenwillow, 1976.

Wojciechowska, Maia. *Till the Break of Day.* Harcourt Brace Jovanovich, 1972.

Woodford, Peggy. *Backwater War.* Farrar, Straus & Giroux, 1975.

Zei, Aliki. *Wildcat Under Glass.* Holt, Rinehart & Winston, 1968.

Heroes in Sports

Acton, Jay. *The Forgettables*. Thomas Y. Crowell, 1973.

Allen, Maury. *Where Have You Gone, Joe Dimaggio? The Story of America's Last Hero*. E. P. Dutton, 1975.

Angell, Roger. *Five Seasons: A Baseball Companion*. Simon and Schuster, 1977.

———. *The Summer Game*. Viking, 1972.

Ashe, Arthur with Frank Deford. *Arthur Ashe, Portrait in Motion*. Houghton Mifflin, 1975.

Asinof, Eliot. *Eight Men Out: The Black Sox and the 1919 World Series*. Holt, Rinehart & Winston, 1977.

Bouton, Jim. *Ball Four: My Life and Hard Times Throwing the Knuckleball in the Big Leagues*. World, 1970.

Bradley, Bill. *Life on the Run*. Quadrangle, 1976.

Brashler, William. *The Bingo Long Traveling All-Stars and Motor Kings*. Harper & Row, 1973.

———. *Josh Gibson: A Life in the Negro-Leagues*. Harper & Row, 1978.

Buchanan, William J. *A Shining Season*. Coward, McCann & Geoghegan, 1978.

Carr, Terry. *The Infinite Arena: Seven Science Fiction Stories About Sports*. Nelson, 1977.

Chavoor, Sherman and Bill Davidson. *The 50-Meter Jungle*. Coward, McCann & Geoghegan, 1973.

Cohen, Stanley. *The Game They Played*. Farrar, Straus & Giroux, 1977.

Coover, Robert. *The Universal Baseball Association, Inc., J. Henry Waugh, Prop*. Random House, 1968.

Cope, Myron. *The Game That Was*. Thomas Y. Crowell, 1974.

Creamer, Robert W. *Babe: The Legend Comes to Life*. Simon & Schuster, 1974.

DeLillo, Don. *End Zone*. Houghton Mifflin, 1972.

Dolan, Edward F. Jr. and Richard B. Lyttle. *Janet Guthrie: First Woman Driver at Indianapolis*. Doubleday, 1977.

Dygard, Thomas J. *Winning Kicker*. William Morrow, 1978.

Falls, Joe. *The Boston Marathon*. Macmillan, 1977.

Fixx, James F. *The Complete Book of Running*. Random House, 1977.

Fox, Larry. *The O. J. Simpson Story: Born to Run*. Dodd, Mead, 1974.

Gibson, Althea. *I Always Wanted to Be Somebody*. Harper & Row, 1958.

Gifford, Frank with Charles Mangel. *Gifford on Courage*. M. Evans, 1976.

Greenberg, Martin. *Run to Starlight: Sports Through Science Fiction*. Delacorte, 1975.

Gutman, Bill. *Modern Women Superstars*. Dodd, Mead, 1977.

Haney, Lynn. *The Lady Is a Jock*. Dodd, Mead, 1973.

Harris, Mark. *Bang the Drum Slowly*. Alfred A. Knopf, 1956.

Harrison, William. *Roller Ball Murder*. William Morrow, 1974

Heward, Bill. *Some Are Called Clowns: A Season with the Last of the Great Barnstorming Baseball Teams*. Thomas Y. Crowell, 1974.

Jacobs, Karen Folger. *Girlsports*. Bantam, 1978.

Jenner, Bruce and Phillip Finch. *Decathlon Challenge: Bruce Jenner's Story*. Prentice-Hall, 1977.

Johnston, Jack. *In the Ring and Out*. Two Continents, 1978. First published in 1927.

Jordan, Pat. *Broken Patterns*. Dodd, Mead, 1977.

————. *Chase the Game*. Dodd, Mead, 1979.

————. *A False Spring*. Dodd, Mead, 1975.

————. *The Suitors of Spring*. Dodd, Mead, 1973.

Kahn, Roger. *The Boys of Summer*. Harper & Row, 1972.

Karras, Alex and Herb Gluck. *Even Big Guys Cry*. Holt, Rinehart & Winston, 1977.

Kaufman, Louis; Barbara Fitzgerald; and Tom Sewell. *Moe Berg: Athlete, Scholar, Spy*. Little, Brown, 1974.

Kieran, John; Arthur Daley; and Pat Jordan. *The Story of the Olympic Games: 776 B.C. to 1976*. Rev. ed. J. B. Lippincott, 1977.

King, Billie Jean with Kim Chapin. *Billie Jean*. Harper & Row, 1974.

————. *Tennis to Win*. Harper & Row, 1970.

Knudson, R. R. *Fox Running*. Harper & Row, 1975.

————. *Zanballer*. Delacorte, 1972.

————. *Zanbanger*. Harper & Row, 1977.

————. *Zanboomer*. Harper & Row, 1978.

Knudson, R. R. and P. K. Ebert, eds. *Sports Poems*. Dell, 1971.

Kramer, Jerry. *Instant Replay: The Green Bay Diary of Jerry Kramer*. World, 1968.

LeFlore, Ron and Jim Hawkins. *Breakout*. Harper & Row, 1978.

Lichtenstein, Grace. *A Long Way Baby: Behind the Scenes in Women's Pro Tennis*. William Morrow, 1974.

Lipsyte, Robert. *The Contender*. Harper & Row, 1967.

————. *Free to Be Muhammed Ali*. Harper & Row, 1979.

Louis, Joe. *Joe Louis: My Life*. Harcourt Brace Jovanovich, 1978.

Malamud, Bernard. *The Natural*. Harcourt Brace Jovanovich, 1952.

McPhee, John. *Levels of the Game*. Farrar, Straus & Giroux, 1969.

McWhirter, Norris and Ross McWhirter. *Guinness Sports Record Book*. 4th ed. Bantam, 1976.

Michener, James A. *Sports in America*. Random House, 1976.

Miller, Jason. *That Championship Season*. Atheneum, 1972.

Morris, Jeannie. *Brian Piccolo: A Short Season*. Rand McNally, 1972.

Nyad, Diana. *Other Shores*. Random House, 1978.

O'Connor, Philip T. *Stealing Home*. Alfred A. Knopf, 1979.

Pele and Robert L. Fish. *My Life and the Beautiful Game.* Doubleday, 1977.

Peterson, Robert W. *Only the Ball Was White.* Prentice-Hall, 1970.

Plimpton, George. *One More July.* Harper & Row, 1977.

Ralbovsky, Martin. *Destiny's Darling: A World Championship Little League Team Twenty Years Later.* Hawthorn Books, 1974.

Rodgers, Pepper and Al Thorny. *Pepper.* Doubleday. 1976.

Rosen, Charles. *Scandals of '51: How the Gamblers Almost Killed College Basketball.* Holt, Rinehart & Winston, 1978.

Russell, Bill. *Go Up for Glory.* Noble, 1968.

Russell, Bill and Taylor Branch. *Second Wind: The Memoirs of an Opinionated Man.* Random House, 1979.

Sayers, Gale. *I Am Third.* Viking, 1970.

Sheed, Wilfrid. *Muhammed Ali: A Portrait in Words and Photographs.* Thomas Y. Crowell, 1975.

Skehan, Everett M. *Rocky Marciano: Biography of a First Son.* Houghton Mifflin, 1977.

Smith, Robert. *Babe Ruth's America.* Thomas Y. Crowell, 1974.

Sobel, Ken. *Babe Ruth and the American Dream.* Random House, 1974.

Telander, Rick. *Heaven Is a Playground.* St. Martin's, 1977.

Toomay, Pat. *The Crunch.* W. W. Norton, 1975.

Warren, Patricia Nell. *The Front Runner.* William Morrow, 1974.

Whiting, Robert. *The Chrysanthemum and the Bat.* Dodd, Mead, 1977.

Young, James V. and Arthur F. McClure. *Remembering Their Glory: Sports Heroes of the 1940's.* Barnes, 1978.

11

Informational Books

Of Tantalizing Topics

Informational books are sometimes treated as an unwelcome or at least unrecognized stepchild of literature. When we took a survey of books studied in 200 adolescent literature classes, very few informational books appeared on the combined list of assigned books. Yet every year hundreds of fine informational books are published for young readers, and many of them make it to the annual best book lists. For example, on the 1979 "Best Books for Spring" list published in *School Library Journal*, ten out of nineteen titles recommended for young adults were nonfiction. English teachers generally pay less attention to nonfiction than do reading teachers and librarians, but even in the University of Iowa's poll published yearly in *The English Journal*, approximately one-fourth of the titles are nonfiction.

Awards are seldom given for nonfiction writing, yet the good nonfiction writer has to be more skilled in many ways than the fiction writer. The structure of a short story or a novel is such that most readers have the experiential and reading background necessary to anticipate what is coming in a story. If the author leaves something out, the readers can fill it in, perhaps without even realizing what they have done. But supplying the missing information from nonfiction is not so easy. When a step or an ingredient is missing in a how-to book, the result can only be frustration and disappointment.

Reviewing sources are beginning to pay more attention to nonfiction, but they are hampered because the typical reviewer may not have the expertise to judge the accuracy of information. Reviewers are therefore a bit more hesitant to evaluate a piece of nonfiction. Most reviewing sources have room to treat only a small portion of the books that are actually published in a year. Reviewers have to make choices, and, as each reviewer shows a slight preference for fiction, the cumulative effect is that fiction receives the lion's share of attention. This lopsidedness is aggravated further by the fact that many reviewers, especially those working with educational journals, come from the English literature or English teacher tradition, and they naturally tend to pick books that would be used in conjunction with English classes rather than biology, home economics, social studies, industrial arts, or business classes.

While pondering the differences between the books that make it to the best book lists and those that are ignored, we wrote to George A. Woods, children's book review editor of *The New York Times Book Review* and asked him how he decided on nonfiction titles deserving review space. He responded first in the negative by telling what he does *not* consider worthy of critical attention:

> Let us assume that nonfiction is bad and sad, particularly in the lower age group. You know, First Book of Doorknobs, Let's Visit the Sanitary Sewage Disposal Plant, etc. Most of it at the lower levels is a paste job, a ripoff, repetitious, inane, perhaps easily sold to schools and libraries but sure as hell not to me. In the areas you are restricted to, [grades] six to twelve, things are only a little better. Do you realize the innumerable biographies of Pele, baseball and football players, Heinrich Schliemann and the archaeology of Troy; accounts of the Civil War, WW II; episodes from American history; dinosaurs; rocketry; death; teenage acne, etc. For my purposes, too much of what is published as nonfiction smacks of being in school. Indeed isn't most of it acknowledged as being supplemental reading to the curriculum?[1]

He then went on to say that the criteria on which he selects the informational books to be featured in his reviews are mostly his own "gut-level" reactions. "What I respond to as being new or far better than what we have had before, what has a majesty of language, is unique, aids a child's understanding, makes him an eyewitness to history."

Milton Meltzer makes a case for the consideration of nonfiction as literature on the grounds that the best of it fits both the dictionary definition of literature and of art. He quotes author Jane Langton who, as a judge for one of the important annual awards, had to come up with her own criteria for nonfiction. She decided that for a book to be worthy of recognition it has to "exude some kind of passion or love or caring."[2] It has to have literary quality and the potential for leaving a mark on the reader, changing him or her in some way. To this, many critics add that the really good book will stimulate young readers to want to know more about the topic. Their appetites will be whetted.

In the mid-1970s, James Haskins, a writer of informational books for young readers, conducted a study of the nonfiction written for older children and adolescents between 1950 and 1975. To his surprise, he found that he had not made just a partial study but had covered practically the whole development of nonfiction for young readers. Prior to the 1950s what was published for young readers was in the main either fiction (novels and short stories), poetry, or textbook material to be used in school. No one thought that young readers would be interested in factual books unless they were forced to study them as part of their school work.

One of the things that happened in the 1950s to change all this was that the Russians launched Sputnik, and we in America launched ourselves on a gigantic education explosion. We were in the midst of the Cold War and were sincerely frightened that Russia was scientifically and technologically ahead of us, and so we began to put new emphases on education and the learning of factual material. In 1961, Congress passed the National Defense Education Act, which gave millions of dollars to school libraries. At first, the money was specifically earmarked for the purchase of science and math books. These books were not textbooks but supplements to the curriculum to be used by students independently. Publishers stumbled over each other in trying to fill their catalogues with books that would not only qualify for purchase under the Act but would also excite young readers enough to take the books out or purchase them on their own.

Another change in society that contributed to the increased popularity of nonfiction is the knowledge explosion of the last few decades. Today there is simply more information to be shared between writer and reader. It is this fact, more than any other, that is responsible for the wide variety of books available.

The influence of the mass media can be seen in both the subjects that are written about and in the format and design of many books. They are amply illustrated with full-page photographs and planned for browsing and skimming, as well as more attentive reading. Another significant trend is that authors of informative books are making use of the attention-getting and attention-holding devices that have traditionally belonged to writers of fiction. The chief advantages of the new informative books over the mass media are that there are so many of them and that they can be found quickly by the people who happen to be interested in a particular topic. There is no waiting for a program to be aired, and there is less chance of disappointment over skimpy information or unanswered questions.

Rather than attempting to be comprehensive in this chapter, we have decided to present a sampling that will give some idea of the many types of books available and the different approaches within each type. One of the reasons that it is almost impossible to be comprehensive in this area is that there is such a rapid turnover. Many of the books that are popular this year, will be out-of-date next year or the year after. It is also somewhat harder to agree on what a good informational book is as compared to a good piece of fiction. With fiction, there is the general purpose of providing the reader with an imaginative experience. It is fairly easy to judge the success with which a book does this. But it is different with informational nonfiction books. As will be shown, there are so many different types and so many different approaches that judging one book against another is almost impossible.

Each book has to be judged according to its purpose and often the purposes are so different that it is like the old problem of comparing apples and oranges. Sometimes a book will be successful simply because it is different—more like a mango than either an apple or an orange. For example, Rien Poorvliet and Wil Huygen's *Gnomes* defies classification, but young readers respond warmly to it. They like the illustrations and the descriptions of gnome folklore, but they also respond on a deeper level, recognizing an underlying utopian theme.

The important thing about informational books is that there are so many of them with so many different purposes, that in this one area it is truly possible to individualize. The challenge is in finding and matching the right books to the right readers.

TOPICS OF SPECIAL INTEREST

Books About the World Around Us

The biggest continuing need in the book business is for good writers of informative nonfiction. In a world where there is much more information than any single person can learn in a lifetime, there is a great need for writers who can present it in a clear and straightforward manner so that it can be assimilated as efficiently as possible.

In the past it was commonly held that the nonfiction writer's job was to interest young readers in whatever subject was being treated. Writers therefore took a casual, almost leisurely approach telling all the "fascinating" facts they could dig up. They bent over backward to be entertaining. But today, young readers, especially teenagers whose time is more limited than that of many adults, do not want to casually meander through a morass of facts and opinions. They want books that are streamlined and to the point, or at least organized so that information can be looked up. For example, more than one teenager has complained about going to the library to get a book on bicycles to find out how to fix a bike. It is disappointing to have to read through two or three chapters on the history of bikes before coming to what is needed. Many teenagers lack skills in skimming and analyzing indexes and headings, so authors need to be extra careful to organize and label their writing clearly. They should also put the basic information first so that readers can understand the points that are being made.

People read and write books about the whole wide wonderful world simply because it's there. Each author captures a tiny portion of it and puts it between the covers of a book where readers can go and extract the gold. The subjects of such books are as varied as the world. For example, a writer might focus on pop culture, which Roger C. Sharpe does in *Pinball!*; on the world of dance, which Nancy Reynolds does in *Repertory in Review;* or on great classic paintings, which Ariane Ruskin Batterberry does in *The Story of Art.*

People never outgrow their love for picture books. Teenagers enjoy browsing through David Macaulay's intricate drawings in *Pyramid, Cathedral,* and *Underground* and through the photographs in Gary Smith's *Windsinger* and Alden Robertson's *The Wildhorse Gatherers. Linda's Pictures* is a collection of pictures taken by Paul McCartney's wife, who is a professional photographer. The book features the Beatles, as well as other rock groups. Two other music books that are appealing because of their in-depth portraits and numerous photographs are *The Rolling Stone Illustrated History of Rock and Roll* and Tony Palmer's *All You Need Is Love: The Story of Popular Music.* Other books with impressive photographs include Abigail Heyman's *Growing Up Female: A Personal Photo-Journal,* which has brief diary-like entries accompanying each picture. *How to See* by George Nelson is a photographic essay comparing shapes and objects in nature with those made by humans. *Bear's Heart* by Burton Supree with Ann Ross is made up of drawings by an American Indian who was taken to a Florida prison-school to be educated over a hundred years ago, and *Self Reliance: Ralph Waldo Emerson* is a photographic interpretation by Gene Dekovic of some of Emerson's writings.

The mass media, mainly television, but also the movies and radio have created interests that go deeper than the kind of information that can be given under the tightly controlled limitations of public programing. Some of these interests relate to the media themselves. For example, *Fantastic Television* by Gary Gerani and Paul Schulman

The media often present only the surface facts of intriguing social issues. It's up to authors to explore them further.

is especially suited to young adults because it is a pictorial presentation of the beginnings of television, especially the programs of the 1950s and 1960s that students have seen in countless reruns. Similarly *Heroes of the Horrors* by Calvin Thomas Beck is appealing to teenagers because it presents the most horrible movies of all time, many of which readers will remember, and it gives the life stories of such "monstrous" heroes as Lon Chaney, Boris Karloff, and Vincent Price.

The media often present only the surface facts of some intriguing social issues. It's up to authors to explore them further. One such area is ecology and appreciation for nature. Books about animals are favorites in this area, which should not be surprising considering Americans' feelings for animals. Most of us love to go to zoos; bird watching is a firmly established pastime; we picket stores selling furs from endangered animals; and we spend millions each year for pet food.

Books that build on this fondness for animals include Rosemary Collett's *My Orphans of the Wild,* which tells how the Collett family for years has rescued injured wild animals. Robert L. Behme and his family raised two abandoned coyote pups and disproved many myths, which he tells about in *Shasta and Rogue: A Coyote Story.* The death of a pet can be a moving experience as shown in Sonia Levitin's *Reigning Cats and Dogs* and in Gavriil Troyepolsky's *Beem.*

The other side of human nature in relation to animals is shown in several books that document people's cruelty. Cleveland Amory's *Man Kind? Our Incredible War on Wildlife* is almost a prosecuting attorney's list of charges against needless slaughter in the name of sport or because of our belief in folktales about the coyote's or wolf's evil nature. Hope Ryden's *God's Dog* is a defense of the coyote. Farley Mowat's *A Whale for the Killing* is an indictment of people who watched a female fin whale strand herself in a cove and then tormented her until she died. Barry Holstun Lopez's *Of Wolves and Men* damns us for our ignorance in accepting legends about wolves and for exterminating them so successfully.

A quite different area of social concern is that of crime and justice. Interest in this area is reflected in Elinor Lander Horwitz's *Capital Punishment* and Barbara Habenstreit's

"To My Brothers Who Did a Crime . . .": Former Prisoners Tell Their Own Stories in Their Own Words. A book about justice related to the women's movement is Susan Brownmiller's *Against Our Will: Men, Women, and Rape.* Andrea Medea and Kathleen Thompson's *Against Rape* treats the same subject, but not with historical detail. Dale Carlson's *Girls Are Equal Too: The Women's Movement for Teenagers* is an introduction to feminism for junior-high students; Elizabeth Janeway's *Between Myth and Morning: Women Awakening* is good for older students.

There are hundreds of books providing information that the history books did not have room for. Webb Garrison wrote *Lost Pages from American History,* which presents interesting, but little known, stories. Maisie and Richard Conrat wrote *Executive Order 9066: The Internment of 110,000 Japanese Americans.* Dee Brown is most famous for his *Bury My Heart at Wouded Knee: An Indian History of the American West* (a simplified version is entitled *Wounded Knee*). His more recent *Hear That Lonesome Whistle Blow: Railroads in the West* lacks the drama of the Wounded Knee story, but it is equally well written. Milton Meltzer is the one writer who has done the most in this area with books particularly slanted to young readers. Among his better known titles are *Violins and Shovels: The WPA Arts Projects, Bound for the Rio Grande: The Mexican Struggle 1845–1850,* and *Never to Forget: The Jews of the Holocaust.* Miriam Gurko wrote *The Ladies of Seneca Falls: The Birth of the Woman's Rights Movement,* and Linda Grant De Pauw wrote *Founding Mothers: Women of America in the Revolutionary Era.* Doris Faber's *The Perfect Life: The Shakers in America* and Carolyn Meyer's *Amish People: Plain Living in a Complex World* give insights into little-known groups of people. This is typical of many books written in the hope that they can serve as supplements to general history and social studies textbooks that treat only the major groups.

Another area that both adult and young adult readers are finding interesting is old age. As examples of the tremendous difference in tone and point of view that nonfiction writers use, three books will be briefly described. They are *Gramp* by Mark and Dan Jury, *Old Is What You Get* by Ann Zane Shanks, and *When I Grew Up Long Ago* by Alvin Schwartz.

Gramp is the most controversial of the three. It is a photographic essay prepared by the college-age grandsons of Frank Tugend. The book covers the last three years of Tugend's life during which he was senile. When their grandfather's condition was such that he could not be left alone, different family members took turns staying with him. The boys, who had been enthusiastic photographers since childhood, took pictures to relieve their boredom, and eventually they had the idea of doing a book on the whole experience. They began to keep notes and tape record the comments of family members and friends (including the doctor). Two aspects of the book are controversial. Tugend had begged not to be taken to a nursing home or a hospital and his family kept the promise. When, after three years of senility, he removed his false teeth and said he wasn't going to eat any more, neither his family nor his doctor did anything to force food or drink on him. He died within a few weeks. The other controversial thing about the book is its frankness. There are pictures of nudity, conversations about toilet accidents, and people's less than noble reactions to a man who embarrasses them. Some people condemn the book as being degrading and disrespectful. Others praise it for its honesty and completeness. One reader agreed that the book was painful but was

SUGGESTIONS FOR EVALUATING INFORMATIVE NONFICTION

A good piece of informative writing usually has:

A subject of interest to young readers, written about with zest. Information that is up-to-date and accurate.

New information, or information organized in such a way as to present a different point of view than in previously available books.

A reading level, vocabulary, and tone of writing that are at a consistent level appropriate to the intended audience.

An organization in which basic information is presented first so that chapters and sections build on each other.

An index and other aids to help readers look up facts if they want to return to the book for specific information or to glean ideas and facts without reading the entire book.

Adequate documentation of the sources of information, including some original sources.

Information to help interested students locate further readings on the subject.

In how-to books, clear and accurate directions including complete lists of the equipment and supplies needed in a project.

Illustrations that add interest as well as clarity to the text.

A competent author with expertise in the subject matter.

A poor piece of informative writing may have:

Obsolete or inaccurate information and/or illustrations. Even one such occurrence causes the reader to lose faith in the rest of the book.

Evidence of "cutting-and-pasting" in which the author merely reorganized previously prepared material without developing anything new in content or viewpoint.

Inconsistencies in style or content, for example, college level vocabulary but a childish or cute style of writing.

An awkward mix of fiction and nonfiction techniques through which the author unsuccessfully tries to slip information in as an unnoticed part of the story.

A reflection of out-of-date or socially unfair attitudes, for example, a history book that presents only the history of white upper-class males with a title and introduction that give the impression that it is a comprehensive history of the time period being covered.

A biased presentation in which only one side of a controversial issue is presented with little or no acknowledgement that many people hold different viewpoints.

In how-to books, frustrating directions that oversimplify and/or set up unrealistic expectations so that the reader is disappointed in the result.

grateful for it because it provided the kind of information that no one would know without undergoing a similar experience. When families are just entering such a situation, they need all the honest information they can find in order to make the best decisions.

In class discussions on the book there seems to be a correlation between the age of the reader and the attitude toward the book. College-age students seem to feel more comfortable with the book than do older students who are working as teachers and librarians. Perhaps young students are so much further away from old age that they do not identify personally with Mr. Tugend, or perhaps, like the grandsons, they are more accustomed to the tell-it-like-it-is idea.

Ann Zane Shanks' book *Old Is What You Get* presents an almost opposite visual image of old age. It is a composite book with photographs and statements by many old people and also by teenagers. The pictures taken by the author are mostly portraits in which people are dressed up and smiling. Shanks talks to both old and young with candor and sincerity about such subjects as remarriage, nursing homes, life-style, growing old, fears, and friends. In a section on attitudes, Fred Wooley, age 68, states:

> You finally see the light about old people when you reach forty. You see
> you're going to be old in another thirty years and then you hope people are
> going to be kind to you. My generation respected our grandparents; our
> parents made certain of that. I don't know if I loved them, but I feared them.

And Susan Robinson, age 88, is quoted:

> I was finished bringing up the children, and I felt I could relax a bit. And I
> said to myself, "You are no longer a young woman and you can't be giddy or
> carry on. You have to be reserved. You're an old woman of fifty." Then one
> day I said, "What a dope I am, this is my time to live. I'm through with all my
> responsibilities. The children are grown and now I can go and do." And I did.
> I still wear everything the young people wear, within reason. I don't let myself
> feel old.

In the same section Dayna Bowen, age 15, writes:

> I've never thought about being older than twenty. Of course, I've thought
> about getting married and things like that, but I never see myself living alone.
> I want to be around people even if I do get very old. . . . Even if I become
> totally and completely disabled, I'd want to teach school, teach music,
> something. . . . I think no matter how old I get, there's never going to be a
> time when I can't make somebody smile. That's worth a whole lot to me.

Alvin Schwartz also interviewed old people in *When I Grew Up Long Ago*, but he did not focus on their present lives and thoughts. He went to 156 people who remembered living between 1890 and 1914 and he talked with them about their memories. He edited the comments for clarity or brevity but assures the reader that they are very close to the informant's exact phrasing. They range in length from half a page to only a sentence or two organized under such topics as crime, games, learning the facts of life, celebrating holidays, superstitions, the appearance of Halley's comet in 1910, and the San Francisco earthquake in 1906. An especially interesting part of the book is his description of how he set about planning the book, doing the background research, and collecting the interviews. Two sample entries from the "Facts of Life" section are quoted below:

> We had this doctor book. It was a great big thick book, and it had all the cures for everything that could ever happen to you. But it also had pictures of all the different parts of the body. So we were not allowed to look at this doctor book. My parents kept it on the shelf in their clothes closet under the quilts.
> But on Wednesdays Mother was not at home in the afternoons. That was when the Ladies' Aid met at the church. So Wednesdays after school, my sister and I would look at the doctor book. We took turns. One of us would look, and the other would watch to see if Mother was coming.
>
> Laramie, Wyoming, 1910

> When my brother was born I didn't even realize Mother was going to have a baby. People used to wear so much clothing I guess I never really noticed. But I didn't have any idea where babies came from, and I was fifteen. When I got to be a little older, a friend of the family explained it to me.
>
> Brooklyn, New York, 1900

These three books are good illustrations of the influence of the media, particularly television, on not only the subject matter but also the design and format of modern nonfiction. They present the thoughts and experiences of quite ordinary people. They are organized so that readers can either study them thoroughly, skim casually, or drop in and out much as viewers do with television programs. Two of the three are heavily illustrated with photographs. *Gramp* is put together much like a documentary drama whereas *When I Grew Up Long Ago* and *Old Is What You Get* resemble a combination of talk show and on-the-spot interview. Writers and designers of nonfiction books know that they must compete for the attention of their readers, and they are adopting many of the techniques used by their chief competitor, television.

Books About Physical and Mental Health

When young people go to the shelves of libraries in search of books about health, it is most often in search of an answer to a specific problem, for example:

Am I pregnant? Do I have diabetes? What's mononucleosis? How serious is scoliosis? What happens if you have Hodgkin's disease? My mother has breast cancer; is she going to die? Why does my grandfather say such strange things? Will I be like that when I'm old? What will happen if I have V.D. and don't go to the doctor?

If a book on the physical body is to attract readers who aren't looking for specific answers, the book needs to have some distinctive quality. It might be an especially attractive format or it might be a specialized approach as in *The Sports Medicine Book* by Gave Mirkin, M.D., and Marshall Hoffman, which promises to present, "What every athlete, coach, trainer, and fitness buff needs to know about exercise, training, nutrition, drugs, injuries, environment, sex." Or it might be that the book is specifically aimed at teenagers as is *The Handbook of Adolescence* by Marvin J. Gersh and Iris F. Litt. This is a medical guide treating such topics as obesity, smoking, drugs, and suicide. The truly amazing photographs in the books of Lennart Nilsson, including *Behold Man* and *A Child Is Born,* make them appealing to both younger and older adults. A kind of health book that is read mostly by girls ties health in with physical appearance. *Look Good Feel Good Through Yoga, Grooming, Nutrition* by Joy Abrams, Ruth Richards, and Pam Gray is aimed at junior-high girls while Sara Gilbert's *Feeling Good: A Book About You and Your Body* and *Fat Free: Common Sense for Young Weight Worriers* are for high-school students. A much more specific book is *Between You and Me: A Sensible and Authoritative Guide to the Care and Treatment of Your Skin* by three doctors: John A. Parrish, Barbara A. Gilchrest, and Thomas B. Fitzpatrick.

Certainly many of the books mentioned in the next section, "Books About Sex," relate to both physical and mental health, but since sex is much more than a health problem, it is given a section of its own. However some sex-related books are primarily health manuals, for example *V.D.: Venereal Disease and What You Should Do About It* by Eric W. Johnson (with its cover message, "Don't Get Scared, Get Smart!"), *The Love Bugs: A Natural History of the VD's* by Richard Stiller, and *What About VD?* by Phyllis S.

People are rethinking their attitudes about death and dying.

Busch. Nearly all of the sex-related books given in the following section have chapters on birth control and pregnancy. Most books that are exclusively about pregnancy and parenthood are not aimed at teenagers. Instead they are written to the "typical" married couple somewhere in their mid-twenties. However Patricia Ashdown-Sharp has written *A Guide to Pregnancy and Parenthood for Women on Their Own.* Although not necessarily aimed at high-school girls, it does include sections on the legal rights and medical rights of mothers under eighteen and it gives information on state aid to single mothers; arrangements for adoption, abortion, and foster child care.

Another kind of book about the physical body is one in which an author treats various aspects of death. With factual books of this nature, the author expects more of an intellectual than an emotional involvement from the reader. Authors often illustrate the points they are making with anecdotes, but they do not usually focus on one person all the way through. This is the kind of book that John Langone's *Death Is a*

Noun: A View of the End of Life is, as is Buff Bradley's *Endings: A Book About Death* and David Hendin's *Death as a Fact of Life*. Several books about death are outgrowths of the work of Elisabeth Kubler-Ross, especially her *Death: The Final Stage of Growth* and *Questions and Answers on Death and Dying*.

There are several reasons that books of this type have recently proven to be of great interest to adolescents as well as to adults. Advanced medical technology has brought about many changes and with them have come moral and legal questions not yet answered. Newspapers, television, and magazines bring the controversies right into the family living room. For example, there is hardly anyone in the United States who can avoid thinking about whether or not abortions should be performed, and if so, to whom and at what cost?

The fact that it is now possible to predict with a fair amount of certainty when someone with a particular illness will die has also caused people to rethink attitudes about death and dying. In previous decades people may have suspected that they were going to die from a particular illness, but they did not have a mass of scientific data betting against their chances for survival.

Euthanasia is another controversial area. Who, if anyone, should pull the plug on hopeless cases? And when, if ever, is a person "a living vegetable"? When should a patient be allowed to opt for death rather than prolonged suffering? There is great interest in the Karen Quinlan case and the story as told by her parents in *Karen Ann: The Quinlans Tell Their Story* by Joseph and Julia Quinlan. When should someone be considered dead? People who have agreed to become organ donors do not want to be considered dead when there might still be hope for them. Modern medicine has made the old definitions of death obsolete. Many patients whose hearts stopped beating so that they were "clinically dead" are now alive and well. The book *Life After Life: The Investigation of a Phenomenon—Survival of Bodily Death* by Raymond A. Moody, Jr., is based on interviews with some of these survivors. The book, which gives the reader hope of an afterlife, was included on the American Library Association's 1976 list of "Best Books for Young Adults." A similar book by Jean-Baptiste Delacour *Glimpses of the Beyond* was listed as a favorite of sample readers in the University of Iowa Book Poll as published in the *English Journal* in 1975.

A much grimmer topic is that of suicide. The suicide rate for people between the ages of fifteen and twenty-four has doubled since 1970. Every year 400,000 young adults threaten or attempt suicide, and 4000 of them succeed. Francine Klagsbrun's *Youth and Suicide: Too Young to Die* is an informative book designed to help associates recognize the warning signals that precede suicide. Sylvia Plath's *The Bell Jar* and Hannah Green's *I Never Promised You a Rose Garden* are both powerful fictionalized accounts of attempted suicide.

Books about such once taboo subjects as death and suicide are an example of what Zena Sutherland has described as the tendency of books for young readers to follow in the patterns established for adult books. This is true not only for controversial topics but for others as well. For example, lists of best-selling adult books frequently include emotional self-help books. They are as wish fulfilling as any of the romances discussed in Chapter 7. They promise a slimmer, healthier, happier you, all accomplished quickly and easily. Young adults are almost as susceptible to such promises as are their elders, and many of them have read and enjoyed the same self-help books as their parents, for example, Thomas A. Harris' *I'm O.K., You're O.K.*

They have also appreciated books written specifically for young people such as Edward F. Dolan's *How to Leave Home—And Make Everybody Like it,* Jard DeVille's *Nice Guys Finish First: How to Get People to Do What You Want . . . And Thank You for It,* Dale Carlson's *Where's Your Head? Psychology for Teenagers* and Morton Hunt's *The Young Person's Guide to Love.* These books are more likely to be picked up and read because of general interest rather than to find an answer to a specific problem as with the books about physical health. In Hunt's book, he stresses that in his title, *love* is not a euphemism for *sex.* "*Love* deals, rather, with the emotional relationship known as love and all that is involved in it—including sex." Family relationships, especially if they have gone bad, are a primary concern of young readers. Seventh and eighth graders like *What Every Kid Should Know* by Jonah Kalb and David Viscott, M.D. *A Boys and Girls Book About Divorce* by Richard Gardner has good information in it, but one junior-high librarian reported that the size and the format made it seem too difficult for her readers, whereas the words *boys* and *girls* keep high-school students from approaching it. Probably the mental health book most appreciated by young adults is Robert M. Pirsig's *Zen and the Art of Motorcycle Maintenance: An Inquiry into Values.* In this the author writes a gently persuasive book about the Zen approach to working on "the motorcycle that is yourself." The narrative that holds it all together is an account of a cross-country motorcycle trip that Pirsig took with his eleven-year-old son.

Many of the self-help books are designed as preventive rather than curative medicine. They deal with such things as legal rights, as in Leland S. Englebardt's *You Have a Right: A Guide for Minors, You and the Law* by Jules Archer, and *The Rights of Young People* by Alan N. Sussman. These books include definitions of legal terms and general information about making purchases, suing and being sued, being the victim of a crime, being a witness to a crime, and being accused and/or convicted of a crime.

Books About Sex

It is interesting to note that in most subject areas, books are given plus marks if they succeed in getting the reader emotionally involved, but with books about sex, emotional involvement is thought to detract from their value. It is the same with movies. In some communities a sexually explicit film will be censored, not on the basis of the amount of vulgarity, violence, or dishonesty that is included, but rather on the basis of the degree to which viewers become emotionally involved. Since most movies have as their goal the emotional involvement of the audience it is ironic that the makers of the best movies, that is, the ones that succeed in reaching their goal, are the ones who are punished by having their films confiscated.

This is only one illustration of how materials dealing with sex are judged differently from materials on other, less explosive subjects. Another example more specifically related to young adults is the way that teachers, librarians, and critics ignore pornography as a reading interest of teenagers, especially boys. Most of us pretend not to know about pornography so that we won't have to analyze and evaluate it or talk with students about it. One of the few mentions of this kind of reading that has appeared in professional literature was a mid-1970s survey made by Julie Alm of the spare-time reading interests of high-school students in Hawaii. In this survey, fourteen students listed *The Sensuous Woman* by "J" as their favorite book. This was the same number as listed John Steinbeck's *The Pearl,* John Knowles' *A Separate Peace,* and the Bible.

The kind of sex book that we feel more comfortable with is the one that presents solid information, which gives it a "redeeming social value." But even these books are written with so many different approaches that opinions on them differ widely. One type is the book that attempts to give the whole matter a light and even humorous touch. The books by Peter Mayle are of this kind. The one for children is, because of its humor, still readable by adolescents: *Where Did I Come From?* Those specifically aimed at adolescents are *What's Happening to Me?* and *Will I Like it?* Some people applaud the refreshing forthright attitude, the combining of colloquial language and scientific terminology, and the truly funny cartoon illustrations, but others are offended.

Another controversial book dealing with the topic of sex is *Our Bodies, Ourselves: A Book by and for Women,* developed by a group of women called The Boston Women's Health Book Collective. It grew out of a 1969 conference and follow-up courses taught by members of the group. The chapters were originally research papers prepared for these courses. The 1976 revised and expanded edition is 383 pages long and came out as an oversized paperback. In what was probably their most controversial listing the American Library Association Young Adult Services Division chose it as one of the outstanding books of 1976.

What is distinctive about the book is its combining of discussions about the physical aspects of one's body with the mental and emotional aspects, and its depth of knowledge. The authors want women to be able to talk with their doctors on an equal footing. What is controversial about the book is its open acceptance of women's sexuality. It has a chapter on lesbianism and sections headed "Learning to Masturbate" and "There's More Than Intercourse." Rather than assuming that all women will become mothers, it has a chapter asking the question, "Shall I Become a Mother?" and another chapter advocating the repeal of laws banning abortions. In this chapter an explanation is given in a footnote:

> Because this is a chapter on abortion, it inevitably seems that we are
> advocating abortion as the "right" or the "best" or "most liberated" thing to
> do. We do not believe that everyone with an unplanned pregnancy "should"
> have an abortion. We give so much space to abortion information here
> because it has been so unavailable in the past and because it is an issue that
> so many are confronted with.

A much less controversial approach is the one taken in *From Woman to Woman: A Gynecologist Answers Questions About You and Your Body* by Lucienne Lanson. This is not a book simplified for teenagers, nor is it one that holds back or hides facts, so it is possible that censorship problems could result from its being on classroom or library shelves. The fact that it was written by a woman gynecologist lends believability and sincerity to it, as well as a different slant to such topics as intercourse and orgasm.

A well-received book specifically written for teenagers and now also available in Spanish is Andrea Boroff Eagan's *Why Am I So Miserable If These Are the Best Years of My Life?* The subtitle is "A Survival Guide for the Young Woman." It contains sections on sex, birth control, and relationships with parents. High-school students who read it as part of the University of Iowa's young adult book poll described it as "straightforward," "factual," and "not talking down to me." However, one critic noted that it contained the covert message that all teenagers are sexually active. She thought that readers who were not involved in a sexual relationship might get the impression that there was something wrong with them.

Sol Gordon has done several books on the topic of teenagers and sex. Some are aimed at adults while others, such as *Facts About Sex for Today's Youth* and *Facts About VD for Today's Youth* are specifically for young readers. The book that has gotten on best book lists is *You: The Teenage Survival Book*, which Gordon did with Roger Conant. Sections are done in comic-book style, and information on drugs as well as sex is included. Other informative titles that have made it to best book lists include Linda Bird Francke's *The Ambivalence of Abortion* and Gary F. Kelly's *Learning About Sex: The Contemporary Guide for Young Adults*. Among several titles recommended by the King County Library (Seattle, Washington) Young Adult Department are Gordon Jensen's *Youth and Sex: Pleasure and Responsibility*, Eric Johnson's *Love and Sex in Plain Language*, and Elaine Pierson's *Sex Is Never an Emergency*.

The sex-related topic that many young adults are hesitant even to read about is homosexuality. Morton Hunt who wrote that well-received *Young Person's Guide to Love* has also done *Gay: What You Should Know About Homosexuality*. (See Chapter 13, p. 410.) A less clinical approach is taken in *The David Kopay Story* in which a pro football player tells how he made his sexual preference public and the effect it had. Another book that has as its main attraction the exploration of someone's atypical sexual choice is *The Secret Life of Tyrone Power*. Its subtitle is "The Drama of a Bisexual in the Spotlight."

Dorothy Broderick points out that librarians give out sex information in exactly the opposite order from what teenagers want. Librarians first provide hardback scientific books, then paperbacks, then pamphlets, and finally comics. She thinks that the majority of young readers would want it the other way around.

These books on sex present one of the tougher issues librarians and teachers—indeed, all adults—face. Taste, family values, access, and *many* other thorny questions must be faced. We will talk more about this in Chapter 13.

Books About Drugs

Undoubtedly most teenagers think and know more about drugs than do most teachers and librarians, and this has resulted in a credibility gap. Few of us are able and/or willing to share drug-related experiences with students. To substitute for our own lack of experience, we need at least to provide realistic books. However this is not easy. Peter G. Hammond writing in *School Library Journal* said that after the National Coordinating Council on Drug Education, of which he was executive director, had studied some 1000 books and pamphlets and 300 drug abuse education films, they reached the conclusion that:

> You can trust most contemporary pieces of drug information to be valid and relevant about as much as you can trust the drug sold by your friendly street pusher to be potent, safe, and unadulterated. In both cases vested interests abound: scientists and drug educators can be just as irrational about the dangers and benefits of drugs as can those who promote these chemicals to the youth culture.[3]

In the late 1960s and early 1970s there was a blitz of information on drugs, but Hammond says that information and education are not the same thing. One of the problems has been that everyone wants a pat answer, a quick and easy solution to a very complex problem. Sociologists and anthropologists know it is a temptation when studying any new culture to want to simplify matters by lumping everything together in one clear-cut picture. Such a one-dimensional presentation would make the drug culture so much easier to comprehend, but in reality it isn't that simple.

One of the books that illustrates this variety is Harold Flender's *We Were Hooked*. It is based on interviews with thirteen relatively young ex-addicts. Flender cautions in his introduction that "It is easy to get hooked. It is much more difficult to get unhooked. Few actually make it." He explains that there is no one way to get off drugs. Some of his subjects were helped by psychiatry, "others are scornful of psychiatry. One ex-addict believes the only answer is Jesus, and another believes just as strongly in Yoga. These young people don't know what will help anyone else. They only know what helped them."

The tone of informational books dealing with drugs varies considerably. Henry Gregor Felsen who is well known for *Hot Rod*, tried for a light touch in *Can You Do It Until You Need Glasses? The Different Drug Book*. From beginning to end, the book is an argument against drugs. *Worlds Apart: Young People and Drug Programs*, edited by Dennis T. Jaffe and Ted Clark, has a more scholarly approach based on the results of a study done in 1971 and 1972 in which 150 young drug users were interviewed. Teenagers were asked how they first got involved with drugs, what drugs are most popular among the young, and what unexpected effects drug laws and their enforcement have had on users. Richard R. Lingeman tried to take an objective approach in his book *Drugs from A to Z: A Dictionary*. Definitions, some of them more like essays, are given on hundreds of drug-related terms and concepts.

One of the conclusions reached by drug educators in the 1970s was that any blanket condemnation of all drugs will automatically be rejected by most young readers. This has created a problem for writers who really do want to condemn all drugs. Some of them include alcohol and tobacco, calling them "legal drugs," then condemn them even more harshly than marijuana. By giving relative scores to different drugs,

they gain at least a measure of credibility. It was to improve credibility and communication between generations that anthropologist Margaret Mead testified to Congress
that marijuana should be legalized.

Most critics agree that what is missing from many of the informational books
about drugs is the human element, the feeling side of the story. This is corrected in the
best of the fiction, but still another problem arises, and that is the issue of language.
Realistic books written about the drug scene often use language that community standards define as inappropriate for school use. *A Hero Ain't Nothin' But a Sandwich* and *Go
Ask Alice* both come under censorship attacks even though they have strong and credible antidrug messages. Another difficulty in providing realistic books is that what one
person judges as realistic, another person may reject as contrived. A librarian whose
husband is a detective working with drug abuse swears by the authenticity of the
picture presented in *Go Ask Alice.* But university students who have dabbled in the
drug culture are just as certain that the book is a hoax. In their words, "It was probably
written by some Jesus freaks who wanted to make a case against drugs."

One realistic book that is based on a true story is *Richie* by Thomas Thompson.
The editors call this piece of new journalism "the ultimate tragedy between one decent
man and the son he loved." It is the story of the George Diener family and the son who
begins taking puffs of his friends' marijuana cigarettes and goes on to barbiturates.
When Richie is on drugs, he becomes very aggressive, quickly earning himself a police
record and his father's hatred. In the midst of one bitter quarrel after Richie had had
two automobile accidents in the same afternoon, George Diener shoots and kills his
son. At the trial he is acquitted. The concluding pages of the book make a vivid
statement about the generation gap. Other fictional stories in which drugs play a major
role are treated in Chapter 6.

How-To Books

Part of learning about the world is learning how to do things. How-to books
therefore fill an important need although very few of them ever find their way to best
book lists. This is not because there aren't good how-to books, but because how-to
books appeal to such specific interests, for example, how to invest, how to play soccer,
how to enamel jewelry, and how to get good marks on college entrance examinations.
The more specific such a book is the more it will appeal to a specialized—and therefore
limited—audience. For example, one year when books were being selected for an
honor listing, interviews were held with students concerning the book they liked best
from their past year's reading. One boy listed a book telling how to obtain survival
foods from nature. When he was asked if he thought it should be put on the honor list
recommending it for general library and school purchase around the country, he
looked incredulous and said, "Are you kidding? I'm a backpacker and I've been looking for a book like this for over a year, but I don't know a single other kid who would
want to read it."

Authors of how-to books need to be extremely good writers. Even one ambiguous
sentence can cause a project to fail. Directions that are hard to understand, failure to
list all the supplies and tools that will be needed, and come-on statements that make

projects look easier than they are set the stage for frustration. If there is no index to aid readers in finding what they need to know, or if the illustrations are inaccurate, then readers are apt to lose interest in the project and also to lose faith in books. But if the book outlines a project or a task that the reader really wants to accomplish, even reluctant readers are willing to struggle through pages and pages of big words and small type. The book does not have to be written specifically for young readers. Some libraries have given up stocking books in automobile and motorcycle repair because readers find them so useful that they never bring them back. *The Complete Motorcycle Book* by Lyle Kenyon Engel is one that is frequently stolen because it has easily read directions on repairing motorcycles and some appealing and sensible talk that counteracts the stereotype of motorcyclists as reckless speed-crazed menaces to society. A similarly appealing book is *All About Motorcycles: Selection, Care, Repair, and Safety* by Max Alth. Less technical how-to books such as Charles Coombs' series *Be a Winner in . . . (Tennis, Basketball,* and so forth) are more likely to be read and returned to the library

---

Readers find books on automobile and motorcycle repair so useful that they never bring them back to the library.

---

since the athlete doesn't usually feel the need to have a book nearby for handy reference in the same way that the mechanic does. One of the few how-to books to make it to several best book lists is Jean Young's *Woodstock Craftsman's Manual.* It comes in two volumes and includes directions for such crafts as quilting, wood carving and making stained glass windows. The topics for how-to books are almost unlimited. They range from something as simple as how to embroider your jeans to the moderately complex task of making your own shoes to the very complex task of building your own solar energy house. Some books that are not specifically designed as how-to books nevertheless may serve as inspirations and models for young readers. For example, Shirley Glubok's *The Art of Photography,* which contains forty-four prize-winning photos and a brief explanation of how each one was made, might well inspire amateur photographers. Amateur artists would probably get ideas from Elinor Lander Horwitz's *Contemporary American Folk Artists,* which presents the work of untrained sculptors, painters, and other artists. Among the most inspiring of the books of this type are *The Foxfire Books* edited by Eliot Wigginton, but written by teenagers. They were uninterested in school until an inspired teacher interested them in investigating and recording the everyday life around Rabun Gap, Georgia. The books show such varied skills as slaughtering hogs, reading weather signs, recording snake lore, and building log cabins.

In some cases how-to books open the door for high-school students who have never really gotten into books. They will come to the library seeking a book telling them how to accomplish a specific task. Their interest may be caught by a display or by a book someone else is checking out. Gradually they begin to feel at home in the library and to return for other how-to books as well as other informational books and perhaps an occasional fiction title.

Motivated students will read how-to books that are far beyond their school-tested reading levels. Perhaps one of the reasons is that how-to books incorporate the principles of programmed learning. Readers are punished for their inattention or poor reading by failing in their project, but on the other hand, they gain an immediate reward for their good reading by achieving success in their goal.

Books About Work

As an outgrowth of the 1960s when young adults in large numbers rejected the "American work ethic," federal and state governments have given a top priority to career education. This pressure has been increased by the shortage of jobs, especially for the young. Special career education programs in schools and communities have brought about a greatly expanded market, and greatly expanded the production of books about jobs. Many of these books come in sets under such titles as *Your Future in . . . , Jobs in . . . ,* or *Your Career in. . . .* Hundreds of different kinds of jobs are described in such books. The newer and better ones carefully include photographs of people from different races and groups and give realistic portrayals of a wide variety of jobs, not just the most prestigious ones. *Basic Training: A Portrait of Today's Army* by Burnham Holmes is a good example of the best of these books. It focuses on something in the immediate future, not twenty years off, and it includes many full-page photographs and quotes from people involved, especially trainees.

It is the human interest element that makes a career book stand out. As with many areas, modern readers show a preference for real people rather than the old-fashioned Nurse Cherry Ames kind of career book. Many of the popular new books feature several different individuals. For example, *Saturday's Child: 36 Women Talk About Their Jobs* by Suzanne Seed is an oversized book with appealing full-page photographs accompanying each of the two- or three-page interviews. A similar book appealing to older readers is Terry Wetherby's *Conversations: Working Women Talk About Doing a "Man's" Job.* A book for even more sophisticated readers is Ntozake Shange's *Nappy Edges.* Shange wrote the highly acclaimed play *For Colored Girls Who Have Considered Suicide, When the Rainbow Is Enuf* and in *Nappy Edges* she expounds on what it means to be a writer. These books are more-or-less feminist versions of Studs Terkel's best selling *Working.* Terkel's book is described in its subtitle: *People Talk About What They Do All Day and How They Feel About What They Do.* The success of *Working* is largely due to Terkel's skill in communicating the emotional side of people's jobs and how their work affects every aspect of their lives. This may be more important to Americans than to other people because of our frontier heritage and the value that was put on hard work. Folklorists point out that only frontier cultures such as those of the United States, Canada, and Australia have stories about work heroes like John Henry, Paul Bunyan, Pecos Bill, and Old Stormalong. In other cultures, it is common for the heroes of the folktales to be the tricky individuals, the ones who manage to get out of work. Anyway, in the United States more than in most other countries, people are accorded social standing in relation to the jobs they hold, rather than their ancestry, religion, or wealth. Even the children of very wealthy parents prepare for and usually pursue a career. Work is considered an essential part of a meaningful life.

The work heroes of today are individuals whose jobs may be quite ordinary but who have found personal fulfillment through what they do. Readers are interested first in the person as a whole and second in the job as it relates to the person. The best examples of this kind of book are James Herriot's books about his life as a country veterinarian in Yorkshire, *All Creatures Great and Small, All Things Bright and Beautiful,* and *All Things Wise and Wonderful.* The work that people do with animals seems especially suited to this kind of emotionally satisfying book judging from the success of Jane Van Lawick-Goodall's *In the Shadow of Man,* Joy Adamson's almost classic *Born Free,* David Taylor's *Zoo Vet,* and Margery Facklam's *Wild Animals, Gentle Women.* Presenting several individuals' stories that are in some way related is a common approach. In *Gifford on Courage* Frank Gifford put together ten short biographies of top athletes from various sports. Dozens of good books give the inside story of sports figures, and many of these are presented in Chapter 10 on heroes. One that isn't there is Ken Denlinger's and Len Shapiro's *Athletes for Sale,* an expose of the devious ways that colleges go about getting and keeping top high-school athletes.

Another successful presentation of a career as part of a total life story is Larry Ferazani's *Rescue Squad,* which shows the emotional and physical costs of being on a fire department rescue squad. We talked about *Serpico* by Peter Maas and *Report from Engine Co. 82* by Dennis Smith in our discussion of heroes in Chapter 10, but they are also good looks at careers. *Signal Zero* by George Kirkham shows a different side of public service. Kirkham, a criminology professor, took a year's sabbatical to work as a street cop on a tough beat. Young readers of *Deadline* by Kathleen Begley can easily identify with the author when she tells what it is like to be a newspaper reporter. Stephen Phillips, an assistant district attorney, reveals the pressures and satisfactions of his work by describing his most difficult case. He had to prosecute an accused cop killer who had retained the noted lawyer William Kunstler. The book is entitled *No Heroes, No Villains: The Story of a Murder Trial.* Wild animal trainer Pat Derby worked with Peter Beagle to write *The Lady and Her Tiger* in which she shows that love is stronger than force. Pat Toomay reveals in *The Crunch* that pro football isn't all glamourous and heroic, and neither is the world of dance according to Joan McConnell's *Ballet as Body Language.*

One more type of book that should be mentioned in relation to work is the general information book designed to provide knowledge but not about any one particular job. For example, *Thursday's Daughters: The Story of Women Working in America* by Janet Harris tells about agricultural work, factory work, and professional work. *People Who Make Things: How American Craftsmen Live and Work* by Carolyn Meyer provides detailed descriptions as well as photographs of eight different skills including bookbinding, silversmithing and quilting. *People and Spaces: A View of History Through Architecture* by Anita Abramovitz has only an indirect relationship to a career, but a young person may become interested in architecture as a result of reading it.

Career related books are extremely important to young adults. They are at a stage in their lives when they must make decisions that will strongly influence not only how they will earn their living, but because the two are so closely intertwined, what life-styles they will have. Teachers and librarians should make a special effort to bring books of this type to the attention of all students. The more knowledge students have, the better position they will be in to make the kinds of far-reaching decisions that society demands of its young adults.

Fun Facts

From the very beginning of life, babies are testing their limits. They want to know how much they can eat, how far they can reach, how loudly they can scream, and how much their parents will let them get away with. As the years go by and children grow into teenagers, they become more subtle and more sophisticated, but they are still interested in testing limits. The difference is that with young adults, their sphere of interest is now so much broader that it includes the whole world and even beyond. There is no way that they can personally test all the limits in which they are interested. Some would be too dangerous, some are mutually exclusive, some would take too long, and some cannot be entered into voluntarily. Because of these and other consider-ations, teenagers and adults turn to books that present the extremes of life's experi-ences.

Whatever is the biggest, the best, or the most bizarre is of interest. That is the basis of the *Ripley's Believe It or Not* series, as well as the *Guinness Book of World Records*. One librarian said that if she just had 100 copies of the latter title she could start a library by having students bring in books to trade for what she has found to be an all-time favorite. Part of the appeal of the Guinness book is that it is continually updated and many of the record setters are young. Of interest to less ambitious readers are the simplified versions, which have come out under such titles as the *Guinness Book of Amazing Achievements* and the *Guinness Illustrated Collection of World Records for Young People* by Norris and Ross McWhirter. These books are about 100 pages long and their appearance is similar to the original except that only one event is told about on each illustrated page. Because the nature of the subject matter makes this kind of book even more ephemeral than most, a large percentage of them come out only as inexpensive paperbacks, for example, Jeff Rovin's *Count Dracula's Vampire Quiz Book*, Al Jaffee's *The Ghoulish Book of Weird Records*, Bart Andrews *TV Picture Quiz Book*, and The World Almanac's *Book of the Strange*.

An almost opposite approach to the inexpensive paperback is that taken by some publishers who make a big investment in oversize and beautifully illustrated hardcover or trade paperback books. Wil Huygen and Rien Poorevliet's *Gnomes* and Peter Ho-garth and Val Clery's *Dragons* exemplify the most successful of these kinds of books. Reprintings of comic strips are also done this way as in Gary Trudeau's *Doonesbury's Greatest Hits* and in Michael Uslan and Bruce Solomon's *Pow! Zap! Wham! Comic Book Trivia Quiz*. An advantage to this kind of book is that it is instant entertainment. People who have only a minute or two can open the books anywhere and read a complete discourse. The same is true for David Wallechinsky and Irving Wallace's *The People's Almanac* and *The People's Almanac II. The Book of Lists* by David Wallechinsky,

Irving Wallace, and Amy Wallace is full of wonderful trivia such as the shoe sizes of twenty famous men, ten foods claimed to be aphrodisiacs, fifteen well-known love offerings, and fifteen famous events that happened in a bathtub.

Barbara Seuling is an author who has taken advantage of people's interest in real life extremes by putting together several short amusing books including *The Last Cow on the White House Lawn and Other Little-Known Facts About the Presidency, The Loudest Screen Kiss and Other Little-Known Facts About the Movies,* and *You Can't Eat Peanuts in Church and Other Little-Known Laws.* Alvin Schwartz has made collections of amusing jokes, beliefs, and superstitions in American folklore. They are more interesting than jokes created by an author because they have really been believed by at least some people. Some of the titles of Schwartz's well-illustrated books are *Kickle Snifters and Other Fearsome Critters Collected from American Folklore; Witcracks: Jokes and Jests from American Folklore; Tomfoolery: Trickery and Foolery with Words Collected from American Folklore;* and *Cross Your Fingers, Spit in Your Hat: Superstitions and Other Beliefs.* Contemporary folklore is just as interesting, which is why people like to read about the occult, the Loch Ness monster, Bigfoot, UFOs and other fantastic beings who may have visited the earth in prehistoric times. Melvin Berger's *The Supernatural: From ESP to UFOs* and R. Brasch's *Strange Customs: How Did They Begin? The Origins of Unusual and Occult Customs, Superstitions and Traditions* are only two of several books treating such topics.

THE NEW JOURNALISM

Many people believe that the most significant literary development of this century is the blending of fiction and nonfiction. Today it is very hard to make a clear-cut distinction between novels and some informational books that are based on real events. Writing styles and forms have changed from both directions. On one side are all the nonfiction writers who use the techniques of fiction including suspense, careful development of plot and characterization, and literary devices such as symbolism and metaphor. On the other side are the novelists who collect data as an investigative reporter would. For example, when Richard Peck wrote *Are You in the House Alone?* he gathered current statistics on rape and then fashioned his story around the most typical case, that is, a young girl in a familiar setting being raped by someone she knows who is not prosecuted for the crime. When Robin Brancato wrote *Winning,* she did a similar kind of investigation. She visited hospitals and rehabilitation centers and interviewed patients and their families and friends. And when she wrote *Blinded by the Light,* she not only gathered statistics and interviewed people whose lives had been affected by a religious cult, she temporarily joined a group in one of its weekend retreats. The books that resulted from these investigations are fiction in the sense that fictional names are used and also that they combine bits and pieces of many individual stories. Nevertheless, in another sense, these stories are more real and actually present a more honest portrayal than some pieces labeled nonfiction that are true accounts of bizarre or strange happenings.

SUGGESTIONS FOR EVALUATING JOURNALISTIC FICTION

A good piece of journalistic fiction usually has:	A poor piece of journalistic fiction may have:
An authentic story that is individual and unique but also representative of human experience as a whole.	A stacking of the evidence to prove a sensational idea. The author set out not to find the truth but to collect evidence on only one side of an issue.
Information that is accurate and carefully researched. This is extremely important because, with most of these stories, readers will have heard news accounts and will lose faith in the story if there are inconsistencies.	A trite or worn subject that is not worthy of book-length attention from either writer or reader.
A central thesis that has grown out of the author's research.	Evidence of sloppy research and little or no documentation of sources.
Enough development to show the relationship between the characters' actions and what happens. People's motives are explored, and cause and effect are tied together.	Conversations and other accessory literary devices that contradict straight news accounts.
	Inclusion of extraneous information that does not help the story build toward a central idea or thesis.
An author with all the writing skills of a good novelist so that, for example, the characters reveal themselves through their speech and actions, rather than through the author's descriptions.	A pedestrian style of writing that lacks drama.
A dramatic style of writing that draws readers into the story.	

In relation to these changing styles of writing, it is interesting to ponder just what we mean by "real." What is true (nonfiction) and what is untrue (fiction)? The question in this context might be compared to the one Margery Williams asked in her children's classic *The Velveteen Rabbit*. The answer in her book was that when something had lived a long time and was well loved and well worn through use, then it became real. According to this definition, Louisa May Alcott's *Little Women* is real. A mental image of the warm supportive family portrayed in the book is a real part of the psyches of literally millions of readers around the world who believe that the book is a true presentation of the Alcott family. In actuality, the genteel poverty that Alcott wrote about is a far cry from the facts. In real life it was not so much a question of the girls' not having matching gloves on their hands as it was a question of their not having food on the table. We can say, then, that the "reality" of *Little Women* exists quite apart from verifiable facts.

Similarly, the *Little House* books by Laura Ingalls Wilder, although based on her life, are not a totally factual account of the Ingalls family. For example, a baby was born and died who is never mentioned in the books. Laura's diaries, which she did not prepare for publication, were found and published after her death and show that there are distinct differences between the fiction and the facts. In her diaries she did not write down conversations or dialogues between people. It stands to reason that the diaries are more accurate than the fictionalized accounts, but it is hard to say which is more real, or at least which has the effect on the reader of being more real.

Literature—fiction and nonfiction—is more than a simple recounting or replaying of the life that surrounds the writer. It is a distillation and a crystallization. Only when an author skillfully chooses descriptive details and develops believable dialogue does the account of an actual event become "real" to the reader. Certainly Alex Haley's *Roots* became real to millions of television viewers as well as to millions of readers, yet the book contains many fictional elements in both subject matter and presentation. It is these elements that make the book stand out as "literature," whereas the histories of other families are nothing more than dreary records read on special occasions by dutiful family members. Although dozens of reasons could be given for the success of Haley's book, many of them would probably relate to the matter of choice. Alex Haley was a master at selecting the incidents and the details he wanted to include. A good writer of nonfiction does not simply record everything he or she knows or can uncover. For example, with Haley's book, people's imaginations were captured by the fact that on September 29, 1967 he "stood on the dock in Annapolis where his great-great-great-great-great grandfather was taken ashore on September 29, 1767," and sold as a slave to a Virginia plantation owner. From this point, Haley set out to trace backwards the six generations that connected him to a sixteen-year-old "prince" newly arrived from Africa.

What the public might not stop to consider as they read about this dramatic incident is that it is setting the stage for only a small portion of Haley's "roots." In 1767 there were people living all around the world in all kinds of situations whose blood lines are related to Haley's. It would be an impossible task of research to connect all of them. In the generation in which Haley started his story with the young couple Omoro and Binta Kinte and the birth of their first son, Kunta, there were 256 parents giving birth to 128 children each one of whom is also a great-great-great-great-great grandfather or grandmother to Alex Haley.

The point is that even though Haley was writing nonfiction he had an almost unlimited range of possibilities from which to choose. With the instincts of a good storyteller he chose to trace the family line that could be presented in the most dramatic fashion. At each stage of the writing, he made similar choices. Part of the reason that his book is literature, compared to other family records that are nothing more than family records, is that he made the choices as a storyteller rather than as a clerk.

Because of the mass media, today's readers are so accustomed to strange facts and hard-to-believe stories that they have begun consistently to ask such questions as "Is it true?" "Is that for real?" and "Honestly?" This emphasis on "truth" has put some writers of fiction in a peculiar situation. One of the most striking examples is the case of Clifford Irving, a successful novelist who early in the 1970s wrote a perfectly good piece of fiction about an eccentric billionaire. The book would have probably reached a modicum of success and then slipped unobtrusively into oblivion except that Irving said the story was true. He claimed that it was a biography of Howard Hughes and ended up serving a jail term for fraud.

A much less dramatic case was reported to the fourth annual conference of the Children's Literature Association. Alfred Slote, who writes sports stories, told how his publishers, in an attempt to make his fiction look more like true stories, which sell better, have begun to use photographs rather than drawings for illustrations. Slote is a photographer as well as a writer, so he offered to take the pictures. It was an interesting experience for him to discover that photographs are considered more "real" or persuasive than his own storytelling and that his writing was being influenced by whether or not he would be able to get an actual photograph. He wasn't sure that he liked what was happening, and he concluded his speech by questioning whether or not he could build castles in the sky if he had to produce a photograph of each one.

This emphasis on "truth" has put some writers of fiction in a peculiar situation.

There are probably several authors asking themselves similar questions. The public wants "true" stories, yet expects them to be as well crafted and as exciting as the best of fiction. The popularity of the anonymously written *Go Ask Alice* rests at least partially on its claim to authenticity. It was promoted as the diary of a middle-class teenage girl who became addicted to drugs. Supposedly there is a genuine diary locked in a safe at Prentice-Hall, but since it has never been shown to the book world, skeptics express doubts about how closely the published book follows the diary. They point out that the book is more of a collage of practically every drug-related incident that might happen to a girl such as Alice. They do not argue that all of these things could not have happened. They just point out that it is unlikely that they all happened to the same girl in such a short period of time. If the book were fiction, critics could accuse the author of crowding too much into a single story, but the fact that it was considered to be the diary of a deceased girl made the book more or less exempt from this kind of literary evaluation.

Several factors have contributed to the development of what Truman Capote calls, "the most avant-garde form of writing existent today." He is the one who coined the term "nonfiction novel" in reference to his book *In Cold Blood*, an in-depth account of an especially brutal murder and the subsequent trial. Tom Wolfe prefers the term "new journalism" and wrote a book by that name in which he proposes that it is the dominant form of writing in contemporary America. Other terms that are used include "creative nonfiction," "literary journalism," "journalistic fiction," and "advocacy journalism." Although its roots were growing right along with journalism in general, it did not really begin to flower until the 1950s and 1960s. Part of the reason for its development is the increased educational level of the American public. Newspaper readers, including young adults, are no longer satisfied with simplistic explanations in which people and issues are either all good or all bad. Readers recognize not just black and white but many shades of grey, which they are curious to read about.

Television has contributed in several ways. First, when television broadcasters give the basic facts of news stories, the print media is forced to do something more. The intriguing pictures that are shown on television whet the appetite for more information. Television builds up a market for in-depth reporting whether it appears in book form or as a television documentary or a nonfiction movie. And in what Marshall McLuhan calls the global village, all of us—writers included—find out about all kinds of interesting happenings that might be worthy of the effort required to write a good piece of creative journalism.

Our affluence, combined with modern technology, help make the new journalism possible. Compare similar incidents that happened 126 years apart. In 1846 a group of travelers who came to be known as the Donner party were trapped in the high Sierras by an early snow. They had to stay there all winter without food except for the flesh of their dead companions. After they were rescued, word of their ordeal gradually trickled back East so that for years afterwards sensationalized accounts were being made up by newspaper reporters who had no chance to actually come to the scene or interview the survivors.

Contrast that with what happened in 1972 when a planeload of Uruguayan travelers crashed in the Andes mountains. Just as in the Donner party, some of the people knew each other before the trip but others were strangers. During the terrible weeks of waiting they all got to know each other and to develop intense relationships revolving around leadership roles and roles of rebellion and/or giving up. They endured unspeakable hardships. Many suffered death. Those who lived did so because they ate the flesh of those who died. But in this situation, the people were rescued by helicopters after two of the men made their way out of the mountains. Word of their two-and-a-half month ordeal was flashed around the world and by the time the sixteen men, mostly members of a rugby team, had been flown back to Uruguay, reporters from many nations were there. A press conference was held, and the journalists were all told about the cannibalism at the same time.

This was the second big surprise in the story. The first had been their survival. The drama of the situation naturally fired imaginations all around the world. Lippincott suggested to writer Piers Paul Read that this was the kind of story that would make a good in-depth book. He went to Uruguay where he stayed for several months inteviewing survivors, rescuers, family and friends of both the deceased and the survivors and government officials who had been in charge of the search. More than a year later he came out with *Alive: The Story of the Andes Survivors*, which was on *The New York*

Times best seller list for seven months, and which will probably continue to be read by young adults for the next several years both in their English classes and in their free time.

The fact that the survivors were barely older than most young adult readers, undoubtedly helps teenagers to identify with the story, but so do the literary techniques that Read used. He focused on certain individuals, presenting minature character sketches of some and fully developed portraits of others. The setting was crucial to the story and he described it vividly. He was also careful to write in such a way that the natural suspense of the situation came through. His tone was consistent throughout the book. He respected and admired the survivors but he did not shy away from showing the negative aspects of human nature when it is sorely tried. In a foreword he says that the only liberty he allowed himself was the creation of dialogue between the characters, although, whenever possible, he relied on diaries and on remembered comments and quarrels as well as on his acquaintance with the speaking styles of the survivors.

The influence of the new journalism is seen in many aspects of books promoted for young readers. Theodore Taylor's *Battle in the Arctic Seas,* for example, is described as a "re-creation . . . drawn from naval records and a personal diary" and Colin Stuart's *Shoot an Arrow to Stop the Wind* is described as an "autobiographical novel."

Many professionals working with books no longer distinguish between fiction and nonfiction.

Such labeling makes classification difficult, and many professionals working with books no longer distinguish between fiction and nonfiction. When E. L. Doctorow made his acceptance speech for the best novel of 1975 before the National Book Critics Circle, he said, "There is no more fiction or nonfiction—only narrative." That the two types of books have blended together in the minds of teachers was shown by a survey in which 300 English teachers responded to a request to recommend ten adolescent novels and ten adult novels as worthy of young adult reading. All of the following nonfiction titles were recommended as novels by one or more teachers: Piers Paul Read's *Alive,* James Herriot's *All Creatures Great and Small,* Robin Graham's *Dove,* Peter Maas' *Serpico,* Doris Lund's *Eric,* Alvin Toffler's *Future Shock,* Maya Angelou's *I Know Why the Caged Bird Sings,* Dee Brown's *Bury My Heart at Wounded Knee,* Claude Brown's *Manchild in the Promised Land,* Eldridge Cleaver's *Soul on Ice,* John H. Griffin's *Black Like Me,* Carlos Castenada's *Journey to Ixtlan,* Vincent Bugliosi and Curt Gentry's *Helter Skelter,* Studs Terkel's *Working,* Pat Conroy's *The Water Is Wide,* Henry David Thoreau's *Walden,* Eliot Wigginton's *Foxfire* books, N. Scott Momaday's *The Way to Rainy Mountain,* Lorraine Hansberry's *A Raisin in the Sun,* and Annie Dillard's *Pilgrim at Tinker Creek.*

What most of these books have in common that probably caused the teachers to think of them as fiction is emotional appeal. Although they contain many facts, they are also the stories of people with whom readers can identify. Technically, they might be classified under many different genres: biography, history, drama, essay, and personal philosophy, but they all contain elements of the new journalism. The authors have gone behind the scenes and brought out fuller stories than can be told in concise news accounts. Shana Alexander's book *Anyone's Daughter: The Times and Trials of Patty Hearst* is a recent example of a journalist trying to put an exciting news event into focus. Irwin Shaw was quoted on the dust jacket as praising the book in a way that exemplifies just what the genre is all about. He wrote:

> It is in the tradition of the finest American journalism—personal, perceptive, meticulously researched, hard-headed and emotionally involved. It has a wide sweep to it that reaches far beyond the Patty Hearst case and tells us, with disturbing clarity, a great deal about the mores of our day, our system of justice, our notions of fame, our assumptions about American democracy.

Another piece of the new journalism that was well received by young adults was reporter Tom Wicker's *A Time to Die,* an account of the 1975 prison riot at Attica, New York. Three other reporters, Ninette Beaver, B. K. Ripley, and Patrick Trese covered a brutal killing spree in Nebraska in 1957. They were intrigued by one of the accomplices, fifteen-year-old Caril Fugate, who was given a life sentence. In the early 1970s, they returned to Nebraska and did a rewrite of the original story adding an account of the fifteen-year rehabilitation of Fugate. The book, which ends optimistically, came out under the title *Caril.*

Many other examples of the new journalism are discussed in other sections of this book, particularly in those dealing with biographical accounts and in Chapter 10 on heroes.

Since the information explosion of the last fifty years and the education explosion of the last twenty-five years, the number of informative books has increased tremendously. This chapter is far from complete, but we hope it gives at least an introduction to the wide range of books available and some idea of the classes into which they fall. However, our organization is purely arbitrary, and someone else might see things quite differently.

Informational books generally have shorter lifespans than fictional titles, and therefore many of the specific books that we mentioned will soon be out of date. But they will be replaced by other books on similar topics. Librarians and teachers have a heavy responsibility in this area. They must keep up with the selection and purchase of new titles, and weed out books that contain obsolete information. Evaluating informative books is difficult because of their widely varying purposes as well as the technical nature of many of them.

Informational books serve a broad range of individual tastes. When the subject is of interest to them, young adults will read books prepared for readers ranging all the way from middle-grade children to mature adults. Teachers and librarians truly face a challenging task as they try to keep up with this rapidly changing area and to match the right students to the right books.

ACTIVITIES

1. Select a subject that is of interest to young adults or that they might study in school such as: teenagers and the law, solar energy, consumerism, women's liberation, a recent controversy, or a particular profession. Prepare an annotated bibliography of relevant books. Ask teachers, librarians, and young adults for recommendations. Look through publishers' catalogues and read reviews and advertisements in *School Library Journal, English Journal, Booklist, ALAN Review, The Horn Book Magazine,* and *The New York Times.* Depending on your topic, you should probably also look at offerings for the general public since young adults read many informative books offered as adult titles. Browse through or skim as many of the books as you can find in libraries or bookstores.

2. Find and read (or skim) three informational books on the same subject, for example: gymnastics, UFOs, the supernatural, drugs, or sex education. Write a comparison of the three. How did tone differ? What about point-of-view? Reading level? Amount of information? Format and design? If you were a high school librarian and had only enough money to purchase one of them, which one would it be?

NOTES

[1]Personal correspondence, George A. Woods to Alleen Pace Nilsen, summer 1978.

[2]Milton Meltzer, "Where Do All the Prizes Go?: The Case for Nonfiction," *The Horn Book Magazine* (February 1976), pp. 17-23.

[3]Peter G. Hammond, "Turning Off: The Abuse of Drug Information," *School Library Journal* 19 (April 1973): 17-21.

TITLES MENTIONED IN CHAPTER ELEVEN

For information on the availability of paperback editions of these titles, please consult the most recent edition of *Paperbound Books in Print,* published annually by R. R. Bowker Company.

Books About the World Around Us

Amory, Cleveland. *Man Kind? Our Incredible War on Wildlife.* Harper & Row, 1974.

Batterberry, Ariane Ruskin. *The Pantheon Story of Art for Young People.* Pantheon, 1975.

Beck, Calvin Thomas. *Heroes of the Horrors*. Macmillan, 1975.

Behme, Robert L. *Shasta and Rogue: A Coyote Story*. Simon and Schuster, 1974.

Brown, Dee. *Bury My Heart at Wounded Knee: An Indian History of the American West*. Holt, Rinehart & Winston, 1971.

———. *Hear That Lonesome Whistle Blow: Railroads in the West*. Holt, Rinehart & Winston, 1977.

Brownmiller, Susan. *Against Our Will: Men, Women, and Rape*. Simon and Schuster, 1975.

Carlson, Dale. *Girls Are Equal Too: The Women's Movement for Teenagers*. Atheneum, 1973.

Collett, Rosemary. *My Orphans of the Wild*. J. B. Lippincott, 1974.

Conrat, Maisie and Richard. *Executive Order 9066: The Internment of 110,000 Japanese Americans*. California Historical Society, 1972.

Dekovic, Gene, ed. *Self Reliance: Ralph Waldo Emerson*. Funk & Wagnalls, 1975.

DePauw, Linda Grant. *Founding Mothers: Women of America in the Revolutionary Era*. Houghton Mifflin, 1975.

Faber, Doris. *The Perfect Life: The Shakers in America*. Farrar, Straus & Giroux, 1974.

Garrison, Webb. *Lost Pages from American History*. Stackpole, 1976.

Gerani, Gary and Paul Schulman. *Fantastic Television*. Harmony, 1977.

Greenfeld, Howard. *Gypsies*. Crown, 1977.

Gurko, Miriam. *The Ladies of Seneca Falls: The Birth of the Woman's Rights Movement*. Macmillan, 1974.

Habenstreit, Barbara. *"To My Brothers Who Did a Crime . . . " Former Prisoners Tell Their Stories in Their Own Words*. Doubleday, 1973.

Heyman, Abigail. *Growing up Female: A Personal Photo-Journal*. Holt, Rinehart & Winston, 1974.

Horwitz, Elinor Lander. *Capital Punishment*. J. B. Lippincott, 1973.

Janeway, Elizabeth. *Between Myth and Morning: Women Awakening*. William Morrow, 1974.

Jury, Mark and Dan. *Gramp*. Penguin, 1978.

Levitin, Sonia. *Reigning Cats and Dogs*. Atheneum, 1978.

Lopez, Barry H. *Of Wolves and Men*. Charles Scribner's Sons, 1978.

Macaulay, David. *Cathedral*. Houghton Mifflin, 1973.

———. *Pyramid*. Houghton Mifflin, 1975.

———. *Underground*. Houghton Mifflin, 1976.

McCartney, Linda. *Linda's Pictures*. Alfred A. Knopf, 1976.

Medea, Andrea and Kathleen Thompson. *Against Rape*. Farrar, Straus & Giroux, 1974.

Meltzer, Milton. *Bound for the Rio Grande: The Mexican Struggle 1845–1850*. Alfred A. Knopf, 1974.

———. *Never to Forget: The Jews of the Holocaust*. Harper & Row, 1976.

———. *Violins and Shovels: The WPA Arts Projects*. Delacorte, 1976.

Meyer, Carolyn. *Amish People: Plain Living in a Complex World.* Atheneum, 1976.

Mowat, Farley. *A Whale for the Killing.* Little, Brown, 1972.

Nelson, George. *How To See: Visual Adventures in a World God Never Made.* Little, Brown, 1977.

Palmer, Tony. *All You Need Is Love: The Story of Popular Music.* Viking, 1976.

Reynolds, Nancy. *Repertory in Review: 40 Years of the New York City Ballet.* Dial, 1977.

Robertson, Alden. *The Wildhorse Gatherers.* Sierra Club, 1978.

Rohe, Fred. *The Zen of Running.* Random House, 1975.

Rolling Stone Press. *The Rolling Stone Illustrated History of Rock and Roll.* Random House, 1976.

Ross, Frank. *Arabs and the Islamic World.* S. G. Phillips, 1978.

Ryden, Hope. *God's Dog.* Viking, 1979.

Saleh, Dennis, ed. *Rock Art: The Golden Age of Record Album Covers.* Ballantine, 1977.

Sandler, Martin W. *The Story of American Photography: An Illustrated History for Young People.* Little, Brown, 1979.

Schwartz, Alvin. *When I Grew Up Long Ago.* J. B. Lippincott, 1978.

Shanks, Ann Zane. *Old Is What You Get.* Viking, 1976.

Sharpe, Roger C. *Pinball.* E. P. Dutton, 1977.

Smith, Gary. *Windsinger.* Sierra Club, 1976.

Supree, Burton and Ann Ross. *Bear's Heart.* J. B. Lippincott, 1977.

Troyepolsky, Gavriil. *Beem.* Harper & Row, 1978.

Books About Physical and Mental Health

Abrams, Joy et. al. *Look Good Feel Good Through Yoga, Grooming, Nutrition.* Holt, Rinehart & Winston, 1978.

Archer, Jules. *You and the Law.* Harcourt Brace Jovanovich, 1978.

Ashdown-Sharp, Patricia. *A Guide to Pregnancy and Parenthood for Women on Their Own.* Random House, 1977.

Bradley, Buff. *Endings: A Book About Death.* Addison-Wesley, 1979.

Busch, Phyllis S. *What About VD.* Four Winds Press, 1976.

Carlson, Dale. *Where's Your Head? Psychology for Teenagers.* Atheneum, 1977.

Delacour, Jean-Baptiste. *Glimpses of the Beyond.* Delacorte, 1974.

DeVille, Jard. *Nice Guys Finish First: How to Get People to Do What You Want . . . And Thank You For It.* William Morrow, 1979.

Dolan, Edward F. *How to Leave Home—And Make Everybody Like It.* Dodd, Mead, 1977.

Englebardt, Leland S. *You Have a Right . . . A Guide for Minors.* Lothrop, Lee, & Shepard, 1979.

Gardner, Richard. *A Boys and Girls Book About Divorce.* Aronson, 1971.

Gersh, Marvin J. and Iris F. Litt. *The Handbook of Adolescence.* Dell, 1974.

Gilbert, Sara. *Fat Free: Common Sense for Young Weight Worriers.* Macmillan, 1975.

————. *Feeling Good: A Book About You and Your Body.* Four Winds, 1978.

Green, Hannah. *I Never Promised You a Rose Garden.* Holt, Rinehart & Winston, 1964.

Harris, Thomas A. *I'm O.K., You're O.K. A Practical Guide to Transactional Analysis.* Harper & Row, 1969.

Hendin, David. *Death As a Fact of Life.* Warner, 1974.

Hunt, Morton. *The Young Person's Guide to Love.* Farrar, Straus & Giroux, 1975.

Johnson, Eric W. *V.D.: Venereal Disease and What You Should Do About It.* Rev. ed. J. B. Lippincott, 1978. Spanish edition, 1979.

Kalb, Jonah and David Viscott. *What Every Kid Should Know.* Houghton Mifflin, 1976.

Klagsbrun, Francine. *Too Young to Die.* Houghton Mifflin, 1976.

Kubler-Ross, Elisabeth. *Death: The Final Stage of Growth.* Prentice-Hall, 1975.

————. *Questions and Answers on Death and Dying.* Macmillan, 1974.

Langone, John. *Death Is a Noun: A View of the End of Life.* Little, Brown, 1972.

Mirkin, Gave and Marshall Hoffman. *The Sports Medicine Book.* Little, Brown, 1978.

Moody, Raymond A. *Life After Life.* Stackpole, 1976.

Nilsson, Lennart. *Behold Man.* Little, Brown, 1974.

————. *A Child Is Born.* Rev. ed. Delacorte, 1977.

Parrish, John A., et al. *Between You and Me: A Sensible and Authoritative Guide for the Care and Treatment of Your Skin.* Little, Brown, 1978.

Pirsig, Robert M. *Zen and the Art of Motorcycle Maintenance: An Inquiry into Values.* William Morrow, 1974.

Plath, Sylvia. *The Bell Jar.* Harper & Row, 1971.

Quinlan, Joseph and Julia. *Karen Ann: The Quinlans Tell Their Story.* Doubleday, 1977.

Stiller, Richard. *The Love Bugs: A Natural History of the VD's.* Thomas Nelson, 1974.

Sussman, Alan N. *The Rights of Young People.* Avon, 1977.

Books About Sex

Arce, Hector. *The Secret Life of Tyrone Power.* William Morrow, 1979.

Boston Women's Health Book Collective. *Our Bodies Ourselves: A Book by and for Women.* Rev. ed. Simon and Schuster, 1976.

Eagan, Andrea Boroff. *Why Am I So Miserable If These Are the Best Years of My Life?* J. B. Lippincott, 1976. Spanish edition, 1979.

Francke, Linda Bird. *The Ambivalence of Abortion.* Random House, 1978.

Gordon, Sol. *Facts About Sex for Today's Youth.* Rev. ed. John Day, 1973.

————. *Facts About VD for Today's Youth.* John Day, 1973.

———— and Roger Conant. *You! The Teenage Survival Book.* Quadrangle/Times, 1975.

Hunt, Morton. *Gay: What You Should Know About Homosexuality.* Farrar, Straus & Giroux, 1977.

————. *Young Person's Guide to Love.* Farrar, Straus & Giroux, 1975.

"J." *The Sensuous Woman.* Lyle Stuart, 1970.

Jensen, Gordon. *Youth and Sex: Pleasure and Responsibility.* Nelson-Hall, 1973.

Johnson, Eric. *Sex: Telling It Straight.* J. B. Lippincott, 1970.

Lanson, Lucienne. *From Woman to Woman: A Gynecologist Answers Questions About You and Your Body.* Alfred A. Knopf, 1975.

Kelly, Gary F. *Learning About Sex: The Contemporary Guide for Young Adults.* Rev. ed. Barron, 1978.

Kopay, David and Perry D. Young. *The David Kopay Story.* Arbor House, 1977.

Mayle, Peter. *What's Happening to Me?* Lyle Stuart, 1975.

———. *Will I Like It?* Corwin, 1977.

———. *Where Did I Come From?* Lyle Stuart, 1973.

Pierson, Elaine. *Sex Is Never an Emergency: A Candid Guide for Young Adults.* J. B. Lippincott, 1973.

Books About Drugs

Felsen, Henry Gregor. *Can You Do It Until You Need Glasses? The Different Drug Book.* Dodd, Mead, 1977.

Flender, Harold. *We Were Hooked.* Random House, 1972.

Jaffe, Dennis T. and Ted Clark. *Worlds Apart: Young People and Drug Programs.* Random House, 1974.

Lingeman, Richard R. *Drugs from A to Z: A Dictionary.* 2d rev. ed. McGraw-Hill, 1974.

Thompson, Thomas. *Richie.* Saturday Review Press, 1973.

How-To Books

Alth, Max. *All About Motorcycles: Selection, Care, Repair, and Safety.* Hawthorne, 1975.

Coombs, Charles. *Be a Winner in Tennis* and other titles in this series. William Morrow, 1975.

Engle, Lyle Kenyon. *The Complete Motorcycle Book.* Four Winds Press, 1974.

Glubok, Shirley. *The Art of Photography.* Macmillan, 1977.

Horwitz, Elinor Lander. *Contemporary American Folk Artists.* J. B. Lippincott, 1975.

Wigginton, Eliot. *The Foxfire Book* and other titles in this series. Doubleday, 1972.

Young, Jean. *Woodstock Craftsman's Manual.* Praeger, 1972.

Books About Work

Abramovitz, Anita. *People and Spaces: A View of History Through Architecture.* Viking, 1979.

Adamson, Joy. *Born Free.* Random House, 1974.

Begley, Kathleen. *Deadline.* G. P. Putnam's Sons, 1977.

Denlinger, Ken and Len Shapiro. *Athletes for Sale.* Thomas Y. Crowell, 1975.

Derby, Pat and Peter Beagle. *The Lady and Her Tiger.* Dutton, 1976.

Facklam, Margery. *Wild Animals, Gentle Women.* Harcourt Brace Jovanovich, 1978.

Ferazani, Larry. *Rescue Squad.* William Morrow, 1974.

Gifford, Frank and Charles Mangel. *Gifford on Courage.* M. Evans, 1976.

Schwartz, Alvin. *Cross Your Fingers, Spit in Your Hat: Superstitions and Other Beliefs.* J. B. Lippincott, 1974.

————. *Kickle Snifters and Other Fearsome Critters Collected from American Folklore.* J. B. Lippincott, 1976.

————. *Tomfoolery: Trickery and Foolery with Words Collected from American Folklore.* J. B. Lippincott, 1973.

————. *Witcracks: Jokes and Jests from American Folklore.* J. B. Lippincott, 1973.

Trudeau, Gary. *Doonesbury's Greatest Hits.* Holt, Rinehart & Winston, 1978.

Uslan, Michael and Bruce Solomon. *Pow! Zap! Wham! Comic Book Trivia Quiz.* William Morrow, 1977.

Wallechinsky, David, Irving Wallace, and Amy Wallace. *The Book of Lists.* William Morrow, 1977.

Wallechinsky, David and Irving Wallace. *The People's Almanac.* Doubleday, 1975.

————. *The People's Almanac II.* William Morrow, 1978.

World Almanac. *The World Almanac: Book of the Strange.* New American Library, 1977.

The New Journalism

Alcott, Louisa May. *Little Women: Meg, Jo, Beth, and Amy. The Story of Their Lives. A Girl's Book.* Lee and Shepard, 1868.

Alexander, Shana. *Anyone's Daughter: The Times and Trials of Patty Hearst.* Viking, 1979.

Angelou, Maya. *I Know Why the Caged Bird Sings.* Random House, 1970.

Beaver, Ninette, et al. *Caril.* J. B. Lippincott, 1974.

Brancato, Robin. *Blinded by the Light.* Alfred A. Knopf, 1978.

————. *Winning.* Alfred A. Knopf, 1977.

Brown, Claude. *Manchild in the Promised Land.* Macmillan, 1965.

Brown, Dee. *Bury My Heart at Wounded Knee: An Indian History of the American West.* Holt, Rinehart, & Winston, 1971.

Bugliosi, Vincent and Curt Gentry. *Helter Skelter.* W. W. Norton, 1972.

Capote, Truman. *In Cold Blood.* Random House, 1966.

Castaneda, Carlos. *Journey to Ixtlan.* Simon & Schuster, 1973.

Cleaver, Eldridge. *Soul on Ice.* McGraw-Hill, 1968.

Conroy, Pat. *The Water Is Wide.* Houghton Mifflin, 1972.

Dillard, Annie. *Pilgrim at Tinker Creek.* Harper's Magazine Press, 1974

Go Ask Alice. Prentice-Hall, 1971.

Graham, Robin and Derek Gill. *Dove.* Harper & Row, 1972.

Griffin, John H. *Black Like Me.* 2d ed. Houghton Mifflin, 1977. First published in 1961.

Haley, Alex. *Roots.* Doubleday, 1976.

Hansberry, Lorraine. *A Raisin in the Sun.* Random House, 1959.

Herriot, James. *All Creatures Great and Small.* St. Martin's, 1972.

Lund, Doris. *Eric.* J. B. Lippincott, 1974.

Harris, Janet. *Thursday's Daughters: The Story of Women Working in America.* Harper & Row, 1977.

Herriot, James. *All Creatures Great and Small.* St. Martin's, 1972.

————. *All Things Bright and Beautiful.* St. Martin's, 1974.

————. *All Things Wise and Wonderful.* St. Martin's, 1977.

Holmes, Burham. *Basic Training: A Portrait of Today's Army.* Four Winds, 1979.

Kirkham, George. *Signal Zero.* Lippincott, 1976.

Maas, Peter. *Serpico.* Viking, 1973.

McConnell, Joan. *Ballet as Body Language.* Harper & Row, 1977.

Meyer, Carolyn. *People Who Make Things: How American Craftsmen Live and Work.* Atheneum, 1975.

Phillips, Steven. *No Heroes, No Villains: The Story of a Murder.* Random House, 1978.

Seed, Suzanne. *Saturday's Child: 36 Women Talk About Their Jobs.* O'Hara, 1973.

Shange, Ntozake. *Nappy Edges.* St. Martin's, 1978.

Smith, Dennis. *Report from Engine Co. 82.* E. P. Dutton, 1972.

Taylor, David. *Zoo Vet.* J. B. Lippincott, 1977.

Terkel, Studs. *Working: People Talk About What They Do All Day and How They Feel About What They Do.* Pantheon, 1974.

Toomay, Pat. *The Crunch.* W. W. Norton, 1975.

Van Lawick-Goodall, Jane. *In the Shadow of Man.* Houghton Mifflin, 1971.

Wetherby, Terry, ed. *Conversations: Working Women Talk About Doing a "Man's" Job.* Les Femmes, 1978.

Fun Facts

Andrews, Bart. *TV Picture Quiz Book.* New American Library, 1979.

Berger, Melvin. *The Supernatural: From ESP to UFO's.* John Day, 1977.

Brasch, R. *Strange Customs: How Did They Begin? The Origins of Unusual and Occult Customs, Superstitions and Traditions.* David McKay, 1976.

Hogarth, Peter and Val Clery. *Dragons.* Viking Press, 1979.

Huygen, Wil and Rien Poortvliet. *Gnomes.* Abrams, 1977.

Jaffee, Al. *The Ghoulish Book of Weird Records.* New American Library, 1979.

McWhirter, Norris. *The Guinness Book of World Records.* 17th ed. Bantam, 1979.

McWhirter, Norris and Ross. *The Guinness Book of Extraordinary Exploits.* Sterling, 1977.

Ripley's Believe It or Not—Of Stars, Space, and UFO's. Ripley's Pocket Books, 1978.

Ripley's Believe It or Not: Tombstones and Graveyards. Ripley's Pocket Books, 1977.

Rovin, Jeff. *Count Dracula's Vampire Quiz Book.* New American Library, 1979.

Seuling, Barbara. *The Last Cow on the White House Lawn and Other Little-Known Facts About the Presidency.* Doubleday, 1978.

————. *The Loudest Screen Kiss and Other Little-Known Facts About the Movies.* Doubleday, 1976.

————. *You Can't Eat Peanuts in Church and Other Little-Known Laws.* Doubleday, 1975.

Maas, Peter. *Serpico.* Viking Press, 1973.

Momaday, N. Scott. *The Way to Rainy Mountain.* University of New Mexico Press, 1976.

Peck, Richard. *Are You in the House Alone?* Viking, 1976.

Read, Piers Paul. *Alive: The Story of the Andes Survivors.* J. B. Lippincott 1974.

Stuart, Colin. *Shoot an Arrow to Stop the Wind.* Dial, 1969.

Taylor, Theodore. *Battle in the Arctic Seas.* Thomas Y. Crowell, 1976.

Terkel, Studs. *Working.* Pantheon, 1974.

Thoreau, Henry D. *Walden.* Ticknor and Fields, 1854.

Toffler, Alvin. *Future Shock.* Random House, 1970.

Wicker, Tom. *A Time to Die.* Quadrangle, 1975.

Wigginton, Eliot, ed. *Foxfire* books (4 vol.). Doubleday, 1972.

Wilder, Laura Ingalls. *Little House* books (9 vol.). Harper & Row, 1933.

Williams, Margery. *The Velveteen Rabbit.* Doubleday, 1958.

Wolfe, Tom. *The New Journalism.* Harper & Row, 1973.

PART FOUR

Adults and the Literature of Young Adults

12

Using and Promoting Books with Young Readers

Now it is time to look at the part you will play in relation to books and young people. Chances are that you are studying adolescent literature because you expect to work, or are already working, in some situation that calls for you to bring young adults in touch with books. This chapter is divided into five sections, each centered around a professional role for adults who work with books and young readers: the librarian, the reading teacher, the social studies teacher, the English teacher, and the counselor or youth worker. These areas were chosen for the sake of giving focus and organization to the information, but it should be realized that there is considerable overlap. Everyone working with young readers and books needs to be skilled in suggesting the right book for the right student or at least pointing someone in the right direction. When two people are talking honestly and openly about a book that they both enjoyed there is no way to divide the conversation into such discrete categories as literary analysis, personal feelings, sociological implications, and evaluation of potential popularity. Teachers and librarians will find themselves discussing books as if they were counselors and counselors will find themselves discussing books as if they were classroom teachers. Teachers can adopt some of the promotional techniques that librarians use, and librarians can use some of the book discussion tactics that teachers use. In short, the organization of this chapter may make it appear that the work that different professions do with young readers and books is quite separate. But in reality, nearly all adults who work with young readers and books have much the same goals and share many of the same approaches.

All of us will meet wide ranging differences in abilities and personalities, which implies great differences in interests. Those interests demand an alert and prepared adult who is aware of them, who can uncover them, and who knows an enormous number of titles to meet them. To an inexperienced person, the knowledge of books a librarian or teacher can call forth seems magical, but that repertoire of good books that students will like takes time, patience, and hard work to develop. Reading many young adult books comes with the territory for the professional, but then so does reading professional books, magazines of all sorts, several newspapers, adult books and much, much more. The professional likes to read (or would not be a librarian or teacher), so that makes the job easier and more fun, but the professional reads beyond the areas that are personally enjoyable. For example, whether a professional likes science fiction or not, he or she must know titles of new science fiction. When young adults ask a teacher or librarian for "another book like *The Martian Chronicles,* (or *Forever* or *Hot Rod* or *Ragtime* or *Gone with the Wind* or *Helter Skelter*)," they pay that person a sublime compliment. Woe unto the teacher or librarian who says, "I'm sorry, but I don't know anything about science fiction," or "Why don't you read something besides science fiction? Why not broaden your reading background just a bit?" Anything of that ilk kills interest and to do this to someone who is just beginning to try books is almost criminal and may very well turn someone away from reading.

In any given group, a teacher or librarian might find students like these and gradations between: Alice reads nothing at all (she did once but now that she has become a woman she has put away childish things); Brenda reads nothing because her reading skills are so poor she is virtually illiterate; Candy read a book once, her first book all the way through, and she hated it; Del reads magazines and an occasional sports biography if he's in an intellectual mood; Emily reads Harlequin romances; Fred reads all kinds of books as long as they're science fiction; George reads a few books but always classics ("He's going to college," his mother says proudly); Howie reads only religious books and has already warned the teacher about the Satanic powers in *Lord of the Flies* scheduled for class reading in two weeks; Imogene reads anything that is popular—Harold Robbins, best sellers, novelizations of movies and television specials; Jon reads classics, football stories, mysteries, and any and everything else and refuses to be pigeonholed; Jean reads from the Great Books list and anything else a college suggests for its prospective students; and Lynn reads all the time, perhaps too much—she's bright but socially immature.

Serving the needs of such a diverse group is far from easy, but when the job is well done, it's a valuable contribution.

IN THE LIBRARY

Most people working with books and young readers have come to accept the idea that there is no such thing as one sacred list of books that every student should read. The best that can be hoped for is agreeable matches between particular books and particular students. To do this adults have to be acquainted with a wide range of books and with individual students. A commonly used technique in getting to know students is to ask them what books they have previously enjoyed and then to suggest something similar or something by the same author. An alternative is to ask young readers to describe the book they would most like if an author were going to write a book just for them, and then to suggest three or four books that contain elements they have mentioned.

Other people use written forms as reader interest surveys in which students write down their hobbies, the kinds of classes they are taking, what they want to do for a career, what books they have read, and the kinds of stories they most enjoy. The problem with such forms is that they are usually filled out and then stored in a drawer. No one has time to interpret them. However, one creative librarian who had access to a computer terminal designed a reader interest survey that could be answered on a computer card to which she added the students' reading test scores. She programed the computer with one hundred of the best adolescent books that she had read. All of the students got individual computer print-outs suggesting six books that they would probably like and that would be within their reading level. Her students were intrigued with the idea of getting their own print-outs, but that wasn't what made the program successful; that was only the attention getter. What made it work was that the librarian had read and personally reacted to each of the books that she had programed into the machine and could talk knowledgeably to students about them. The print-out started conversations from which one-to-one relationships began to grow. She considered it well worth the effort because once the machinery was set in order, it could be done for hundreds of students almost as easily as for thirty.

The key to being able to recommend the right book to the right student is for the adult to have such a large and varied reading background that he or she can personally act as a computer. Skilled teachers and librarians program their minds to draw relationships between what students tell or ask and what they remember about particular books. Experience sharpens this skill, and those librarians who make an effort consistently to read a few new books every month increase their repertoire of books rapidly. As an aid to memory, many people keep a card file of the books they read. They glance through it every few weeks to remind themselves of all the books they know. They also use it as a handy reference when a title or an author slips their mind.

Book Talks

With all of their other responsibilities, few librarians have as much opportunity as they would like to guide individual reading on a one-to-one basis. The next best thing is giving presentations or book talks to groups. This establishes the groundwork for later interactions. Margaret Edwards has described the book talk as "a little piece of pie so good that it tempts one to consume the whole concoction." Another way to define the book talk is to compare it to a teaser or preview at a movie theater. It is a brief sampling, presenting the book in its most positive light, showing who's in it, what it's about, and why someone would want to read it. In *The Fair Garden and the Swarm of Beasts*, Edwards gives five reasons for giving book talks:

1. To sell the idea of reading for pleasure,
2. To introduce new ideas and new fields of reading,
3. To develop an appreciation of style and character portrayal,
4. To lift the level of reading by introducing the best books the audience can read with pleasure, and
5. To humanize books, the library, and the librarian.

TABLE ONE

Do	Don't
1. Do prepare well. Either memorize your talks or practice them so much that you can easily maintain eye contact.	1. Don't introduce books that you haven't read or books that you wouldn't personally recommend to a good friend as interesting.
2. Do organize your books so that you can show them as you talk. To keep from getting confused, you might clip a note card with your talk on it to the back of each book.	2. Don't "gush" over the books. If it's a good book and you have done an adequate job of selecting what to tell, then it will sell itself.
3. When presenting excerpts, do make sure they are representative of the tone and style of the book.	3. Don't tell the whole story. When listeners beg for the ending, hand them the book. Your purpose is to get them to read.
4. Even though you might sometimes like to focus on one or two themes, do be sure, over the months you meet with any group that you present a wide variety of books. Include informative books that young readers would probably like to know about but might be too embarrassed to ask for.	4. Don't categorize books as to who should read them, for example, "This is a book you girls will like"; or show by the books you have brought to a particular school, that you expect only Asian-Americans to read about Asian-Americans and only American Indians to read about American Indians, and so forth.

Mary K. Chelton has added her testimony:

> The best young adult librarians I have known, whether they see their book selection role as one of expanding horizons and literary tastes or of just giving kids what they want (and most of us usually fall somewhere in between) have a "hidden agenda" for promoting the love of reading for pleasure, and have found book talks a superb way of doing that.[1]

Chelton adds that giving book talks is one of the most valuable promotional devices around because:

> Once acquired, this skill can be adapted to floor work with individual readers, radio spots, booklist annotations, and class visits in the library or in the classroom. It can be combined with slide-tape, film, or musical presentations, and with outreach skills.

TABLE ONE (Continued)

Do	Don't
5. Do experiment with different formats, for example, a short movie, some poetry, or one longer presentation along with your regular book talks.	5. Don't give literary criticisms. You have already evaluated the books for your own purposes and if you did not think they were good, you would not be presenting them.
6. Do keep a record of which books you have introduced to which groups. This can be part of your evaluation when you compare before and after circulation figures on the titles you have talked about. Also, good record keeping will help you not to repeat yourself with a group.	
7. Do be assertive in letting teachers know what you will and will not do. Perhaps distribute a printed policy statement explaining such things as how much lead time you need, the fact that the teacher is to remain with the group, and how willing you are to make the necessary preparation to do book talks on requested themes or topics.	

The simplest kind of book talk may last only sixty seconds and consist of fewer than ten sentences. The book talker has the obligation to let listeners know what to expect. For example, it would be unfair to present only the funniest moments in a serious book—a reader might check it out expecting a comedy. If a book is a love story, then some clue to that effect should be given, but care needs to be taken because emotional scenes read out loud and out of context can sound silly. The cover of a book often reveals its tone, which is one of the reasons for holding up a book while it is being talked about. If a presentation is being given to a large audience, it might be worth the time to make slides that can be flashed on a screen while the book talk is being given.

Book talks need to be carefully prepared ahead of time. It takes both concentration and skill to select the "heart" of a story. People who try to ad lib have the advantage of sounding spontaneous, but they also run the risk of using up all their time telling about one or two books or of getting bogged down in telling the whole story, which would defeat the purpose. Most young readers do not want to hear a ten- or fifteen-minute talk on one book, unless it is dramatic and used as a change of pace along with several shorter book talks. This whole procedure works well if the librarian comes to a class with a cart full of books ready to be checked out. Most of the class period can be devoted to the book talks with the last fifteen minutes saved as question and answer, browsing, and check-out time.

This kind of group presentation has the advantage of introducing students to the librarian, which is especially important with public librarians. When students go to the library feeling already acquainted, they are more at ease in initiating a one-to-one relationship, a valuable part of reading guidance. It also has the advantage of giving students more freedom in choosing books that really appeal to them. For example, if a student asks a librarian to recommend a good book, the librarian will probably not have time to tell the student about more than two or three books. The student usually feels an obligation to take one of these books whether or not it really sounds appealing. But when the librarian presents twenty or thirty different titles, then students have the advantage of being able to choose from a much larger offering. This also enables students to learn about and to select books that might cause them embarrassment if they were recommended on a personal basis. For example, if a girl's parents are getting divorced, it may not help the situation for the librarian to hand her Judy Blume's *It's Not the End of the World.* But if this were included among several books introduced to the class and the student chose it herself, then it might fill a real need. And the fact that the librarian had talked about it, showing that she had read it, opens the door for the girl to initiate a conversation if she so desires.

Another advantage to group presentations is that they are obviously more efficient. For example, if a social studies class is beginning a unit on World War II in which everyone in the class is going to have to read a novel having something to do with the war and also write a small research paper, then it makes sense for the librarian to give the basic information in one group presentation. Being efficient in the beginning will enable the librarian to spend time with individual students who have specific questions rather than making an almost identical presentation to thirty individuals.

Table 1 gives some suggestions that should increase one's chances for success with book talks. Mary K. Chelton's article served as a basis for this table.

Displays

Making displays is another effective way to promote books. Most young adults have some common needs though they might not admit them or even be aware of them. The sensitive adult who knows books can quietly alert students to titles and authors that might prove worthwhile. It can be done simply, indeed the simpler and less obvious the better. Perhaps the librarian could do a simple bulletin display saying "If You Liked *Roots,* You'll Like These" or "Love John Wayne Films?—You'll Love These" (books on courage and facing death, though not identified in just that way) or "Did You Cry Over *Gone with the Wind?* So Did I" (books about love problems and divorce).

None of these simple gimmicks involves much work, but, more important, they do their job without the librarian seeming pushy or nosy. The point is to alert young adults to many titles on all kinds of themes. No book is required and no one will know whether John checks out Howard Fast's *April Morning* because his father recently died or because he likes American history.

When it comes to promoting books, librarians should not be ashamed to borrow ideas from the world of commerce. After all, we are in a competitive business. We are competing directly for students' time and interest and indirectly for a share of the library budget and the taxpayers' dollars. As part of this competition, we should not overlook the benefits of having attractive, professional looking displays and bulletin boards. They should give evidence that things are happening and they should help patrons develop positive attitudes towards books and reading.

Well-done displays draw attention to selected books and therefore make it more likely that they will be read. Even if there is no artwork connected with a display, it can still promote books simply by showing the front covers. Preparing displays can bring the same kind of personal satisfaction that comes from creatively decorating a room or painting a picture. People with negative feelings toward making displays have probably had bad experiences in which the results did not adequately compensate for the amount of time and effort expended. One way to correct this imbalance is to follow some general principles that help to increase the returns on a display while cutting down on the work. To help insure a good design, go window shopping in the best stores—the ones that appeal to the young adults that you are wooing—and when you see a display that you like, adapt its features to your own purposes. Promote more than one book and have multiple copies. Enthusiasm wanes if people have to put their names on a list and wait. Tie the displays into current happenings and take advantage of television and movie tie-ins with mini-displays including a poster and an advertisement supplemented by copies of whatever book is currently being featured.

Librarians should not be ashamed to borrow ideas from the world of commerce when promoting books.

Use displays to get people into the library. Offer free bibliographies and have announcements of their availability made through local media. A display can also be an announcement of, and a follow-up to, a program or special event. For example, if an author is coming to speak, include a photograph and articles about the author along with all of his or her books. The same type of display could work for a hang-gliding demonstration, a talk on the Bermuda triangle or on fashion modeling. Put your displays in high traffic areas where everyone, not just those who already use the young adult collection, will see them. For example, if a display is at the entrance to the young adult area rather than inside, then it can arouse interest and encourage respect for young adult books and concerns among both teenage and adult visitors.

Use interchangeable parts so that it isn't necessary to start from scratch each time. Coat hooks screwed into blocks of wood make good upright book holders as do drapery rod supports and the L-shaped metal doorstops available at hardware stores. These latter two are screwed into boards that either stand upright or lean against a wall. Standing boards are a good way to get some height into a display. Fruit baskets and crates from grocery stores can also be used as props. A wood stain is easy to apply and gives a finished effect. For making table displays, collect several sturdy cardboard cartons of various shapes and sizes. Tape them securely shut with strapping tape or plumber's tape and then sew cloth covers for them. Use the same cloth or coordinating colors so that they can be used together as mix and match stackable platforms. Books are much more attractive if they are put at different levels and at different distances from the viewers. Boxes that are not covered can still be used for this purpose if they are hidden beneath a tablecloth or drape.

Plain is better than figured cloth for table coverings and bulletin boards because books have their own designs. In displays featuring several books, the jackets are already competing with each other, and if they also have to compete with background patterns, then chances are that the display will look cluttered.

People lacking formal display areas and bulletin boards are fortunate in that they can make portable displays that can be set up in a variety of locations. The changing location is in itself an attention getter. A portable display can be as small as a foot square sandwich board set in the middle of a table or as large as a camper's tent set up in the middle of the room and surrounded by books about camping, hiking, backpacking, ecology, and nature foods. If space is a problem, small bulletin boards can be hung from the ceiling or stood against pillars or walls. They can be covered on both sides with cloth sewed like a snug pillow case, or stretchy tubular cloth can be slipped on them. This also works well for long narrow boxes that can be wedged between the floor or a table and the ceiling using the spring mechanism borrowed from a pole lamp. Such hanging or standing displays can do double duty, for example, dividing the children's section from the young adult section or separating a reading corner with its casual furniture from the desks and tables set aside for study.

It's a good idea to give students a sense of ownership over the displays by involving them as much as possible. Students in woodworking, plastics, and home economics classes will sometimes be glad to help in making display equipment. Occasionally students working as library interns or helpers will enjoy the challenge of doing displays all by themselves. Art teachers are usually happy to work with librarians in order to have a place where student work can be attractively displayed. Students enjoy lending such things as family portraits or baby pictures to add interest to a display of genealogy books. They will collect items from the city dump for a display on recycling or ecology or bring in an overstuffed chair and a footstool as the focal point of a display of leisure time books. Whatever is interesting and different is the key to tying books in with real life. A very ordinary object—a kitchen sink, a moped, or a torn and dirty football jersey—is out of the ordinary when it appears on a bulletin board or a display table.

Programs

Stores have special sales and events to get people into the marketplace where they will be tempted to buy something. In the same way ambitious librarians put on young adult programs to do something special for those who regularly use the library and, at the same time, to bring nonusers into the library. Opinions are divided on whether or not programs should necessarily be designed to promote the use of library materials, and on whether they should be educational rather than recreational.[2] Without getting into a discussion of both viewpoints or a complete description of how to set up young adult programs, we can offer some advice from people whose libraries have been especially active in arranging programs.

1. Take a survey, or better, talk with your teenage clientele to see what their interests and desires are.
2. Avoid duplicating the kinds of activities that students do in school and in conjunction with other community agencies.
3. Include young adults in planning and actually putting on programs. The library can be a showcase for young adult talent.
4. Work with existing youth service agencies to cosponsor events, or plan them in conjunction with school programs so as to have the beginning of an audience and the nucleus of a support group.
5. Do a good job of publicizing the event. The publicity may even influence people unable to come so that they will feel more inclined to visit the library at some other time.
6. Have a casual setting planned for a relatively small group with extra chairs available in case more people come than you expect. Bustling around at the last minute to set up extra chairs gives an aura of success to a program that is much more desirable than having row upon row of empty chairs with a few people sitting here and there.

Among the kinds of programs commonly held are film programs, outdoor music concerts featuring local teenage bands, talent shows in a coffee house setting, chess tournaments, and contests in such areas as filmmaking, decorating blue jeans, and the creation of posters or other kinds of art. Teenagers can meet with adult instructors for workshops in fields such as photography, creative writing, bicycle repair, and all sorts of crafts ranging from macrame and embroidery to T-shirt silk-screening. Another kind of program features a guest speaking or holding a workshop. In public libraries these are often on subjects that school librarians tend to shy away from such as self-defense and rape prevention, drug and birth control information, and an introduction to various hot lines and other agencies that help young adults. Large-scale workshops are sometimes held in libraries to which various schools bring their students. For example, in a town with three high schools, one big day on choosing careers may be planned at the community library. Guest speakers who could not give up three days of time are willing to make a single appearance; special exhibits and displays can be set up once rather than three times.

Regardless of the topic or format of a workshop or its main purpose, there are certain things that a librarian should do to reap full benefit from the extra effort that has gone into attracting extra visitors to the library. As librarians, our chief business is information and its retrieval, and today books are still the main carriers of information. Therefore it stands to reason that we will want to do whatever we can to encourage library visitors to become regular book users. The time of a program is the time to be sure that an attractive young adult display is out in full view of participants. If possible, hold the program so that it is in or very near the young adult books. If space precludes this, plan the traffic pattern so that visitors at least see the young adult area. Perhaps refreshments could be served there.

When there is a group audience, it is a good time to pass out miniature bibliographies, perhaps printed on a book mark. It's also a good time to sign up people for library cards. The program should be scheduled so that it ends at least a half-hour before the library closes. This way participants will have time to browse in the library

We want to do whatever we can to encourage library visitors to become regular book users.

rather than having to leave by the nearest exist because the building is being locked. Also, in the first ten or fifteen minutes, while the group is waiting for the latecomers to straggle in, the librarian could give a few book talks. Just as grocery and discount stores crowd the check-out areas with all kinds of tempting little items, it makes sense to place paperback book racks where they are equally tempting.

Some libraries have had success with book discussion groups in which teenagers serve as readers and critics. This usually works best if their evaluations can be publicized perhaps in a teen opinion magazine, through a display of books they recommend, on a bulletin board or in a set of file cards containing their reviews for others to look at, in a monthly column in a local newspaper, or through the periodic printing and distribution of annotated lists of favorites.

When an author is invited to speak, it is the host librarian's responsibility to begin several weeks in advance to be sure that people are reading the author's books. Several copies of each of them should be on display and available for check-out. English and reading teachers should be notified in advance so that they can devote some class time to the author's work. A panel of students who especially enjoyed the author's work might be set up to interact with the author at the end of the formal presentation. Another way to involve students, and perhaps teachers, would be to invite three or four to have lunch or dinner with the guest author. (Check this out first since some people prefer to be left alone before they are to speak.) If you are setting up an author's visit, it is usually best that you first write the publisher of the author's most recent book. State how much money, if any, you have available. Sometimes publishers will pay for the transportation of an author, but at your end you will usually need to pay at least for food and housing, and if possible, offer an honorarium. If you have no money, say so immediately, and then be patient, flexible, and grateful for whomever you get. What could happen is that an author will be scheduled to speak in or near your area and will come to you as an extra. If an author is being paid to come to a professional meeting, for example, you might write and ask if he or she will consider meeting with a group of young adults. Also, it is highly possible that there are young adult authors living in your own state. The Children's Book Council (67 Irving Place, New York, NY 10003) has a geographical listing of authors. However, it should be considered only a beginning as not all authors are listed with them.

Three Libraries

So far in this discussion we have assumed that most libraries have a young adult librarian and that there is a special section of the library serving young adults. We think that this is the ideal arrangement, but certainly there are many libraries where this is not the case. In such libraries, someone must still do the work of ordering young adult books and make a special effort to serve this age group. It is extremely important because this is the age at which many people become library dropouts. If a library is physically or financially too small to support a young adult section, then careful thought must be given to choosing the best alternatives.

In an attempt to get some specific information as to how library organization affects the acquisition and shelving of young adult books, we took the Honor Sampling of books listed in Appendix A and discussed in Chapter 1 and visited three public libraries. We chose, first, a big city library on the East coast (Washington, D. C.), second, a big city library on the West coast (San Diego, California), and, third, a rather typical middle-class suburban library (Tempe, Arizona). The card catalogues were checked to see where each of the sixty-three titles were shelved. In Washington, there is no separate young adult section. Instead, there is a "popular collection" that is set apart from the main library where patrons come to do research. This arrangement has the advantage of insuring that a young adult will not miss a book that in some other libraries might be in the adult section rather than young adult. However, not having anyone specifically looking out for young adults could be a disadvantage in that the acquisitions librarian may be less aware of, and therefore apt to miss, some of the popular juvenile titles. For example, the D. C. library was the only one that did not have *House of Stairs*, *The Friends*, *Teacup Full of Roses*, *Wild in the World*, *I'll Get There. It Better Be Worth the Trip*, and *Where the Lilies Bloom*. The majority of its patrons are black, so it seems especially strange that, in spite of a big emphasis on black studies, it did not have *The Friends* or *Teacup Full of Roses*. Another problem here is that young adults would be very hesitant to go to the separate children's room to get such titles as *Ludell and Willie*, *Trial Valley*, and *Never to Forget: The Jews of the Holocaust*, which were shelved as juvenile or children's books.

The San Diego library is the only one of the three that has a young adult division separate from the juvenile and adult divisions, so it is the most interesting to study. The library owns fifty-seven of the sixty-three books. Twenty-one of them are shelved only as young adult books, eleven are shelved only as adult books, and four are shelved only as juvenile books. Multiple copies of the others were purchased so that they could be shelved in two or more sections. Fourteen are shelved in both the adult and the young adult sections as compared to five shelved in both the young adult and the juvenile sections. The poetry collection *Reflections on a Gift of Watermelon Pickle* is the single title that is shelved in all three sections. This substantiates the feeling that poetry interests a much wider age span of readers than does either fiction or informative writing. The other poetry collection *Zero Makes Me Hungry* has the distinction of being in both the adult and juvenile, but not in the young adult section. Perhaps the library could afford only two copies and since teenage patrons are numerically outnumbered

---

It is probably preferable to link young adult services with the adult rather than with the children's section of a library.

---

by both children and adults, they were the ones to be left out. Nearly all of the books put only in the young adult section were published as juveniles whereas nearly all the books put only in the adult section were published as adult titles. We expect young readers to continuously work their way onward and upward out of juvenile books into the regular adult offerings, so of course we would expect a young adult collection to be partially made up of general adult titles, which the San Diego collection is. It is common to look at the adult titles that appeal to teenagers, but an interesting switch is to see which juvenile titles appeal to adults. One way to do this is to see which books are placed on the adult shelves in addition to the young adult shelves. In the San Diego library, the doubly shelved juvenile titles include *Z for Zachariah, A Day No Pigs Would Die, Go Ask Alice,* and the *Woodstock Craftsman's Manual.*

In the Tempe library we found a larger percentage of the juvenile titles shelved as adult books, but not necessarily because the books are of special interest to adult patrons. It appears that they were shelved that way to imply a restriction similar to that of the movie rating "PG," meaning "parental guidance advised." The youth section of the library is said to serve readers through twelfth grade, but many of the books with either language or subject matter that is "questionable" are to be found only in the adult section. These include *Trying Hard to Hear You, The Outsiders, Rumble Fish, Go Ask Alice,* and *His Own Where.* Obviously there is a relationship between this and the current issue in librarianship over whether or not young people should be issued restricted library cards or given access to the full range of library materials.

When a library does not have a special section for young adults, then for psychological reasons it is probably preferable to link the services more closely with the adult than with the children's section of a library. This is what the Washington library did with its "popular collection." The reasoning behind this is that, just like most people, young adults are looking to the future rather than the past. They would rather think of themselves as adults than as children. If young adult books must be shelved with children's books, then at the very least be sure that it is in a fairly sophisticated setting, somewhat removed from the easy-to-read books. Young adults will probably mind having to step over little chairs and toddlers who are meandering through the picture books section.

People working in libraries where there is no specific young adult section may tend to forget about this segment of their population. They should pay more attention, rather than less, to this group. In order to show young adults that the library has something for them, librarians must work twice as hard in setting up displays and programs, in giving book talks, and in making themselves available for reading guidance.

In all libraries, adult librarians should also have training and an interest in serving young adults because in successful library programs, there will be extensive crossing over. The young adult section of a library is first and foremost a bridge taking people from childhood to adult reading. What we want is for readers to move across—not park on it.

IN THE READING CLASS

In one sense this section is superfluous because this whole book is devoted to the teaching and promoting of reading, but there are some things about the interests and responsibilities of teachers of reading that differ from those of English teachers or of librarians. One difference is that, except for remedial programs, the teaching of reading as an academic discipline in the high schools is a fairly recent development. The assumption used to be that the normal student had received enough formal instruction in reading by the time he or she completed elementary school. The student was then turned over to English teachers who taught mostly literature, grammar, and composition. Certainly English teachers worked with reading skills, but they were not the primary focus. Today more and more states are passing laws setting minimal reading standards for high-school graduation, and this has meant that reading has become almost a regular part of the high-school curriculum. In some schools, all ninth graders now take a reading class, while in other schools, it is only for those students who test one or two years below grade level. Depending on how long it takes them to pass the test, students may take basic reading classes for several semesters.

In the teaching profession the reluctant reader is nearly always stereotyped as a boy from the wrong side of town. He is someone S. E. Hinton would describe as an outsider, a greaser. Actually reluctant readers come in both male and female varieties and from all social and I.Q. levels. Many of them have fairly good reading skills; they simply don't like to read. Others are poor readers partly because they get so little practice. What these students have in common is that they have been disappointed in their past reading. The rewards of reading, what they received either emotionally or intellectually, have not come up to their expectations, which were based on how hard they worked to read the material. They have therefore come away feeling cheated.

The reading profession has recognized this problem and has attempted to solve it by lowering the price the student has to pay. Publishing houses have worked very hard to devise reading materials that are easier, that demand less effort from the student. These are the controlled vocabulary books commonly known as high-low books, meaning high interest, low vocabulary. They are moderately successful. One problem is that there isn't enough variety to appeal to everyone. A disproportionate number of them have been written to the stereotyped target audience of the young male from a motorcycle gang. The authors are rarely creative artists; they are educators who have many priorities that come before telling a good story. An alternative approach to encourage reluctant readers is to make the rewards greater rather than to reduce the effort. This is where the best adolescent literature comes into the picture. The rewards are often high enough to fully recompense supposedly reluctant teenage readers. And once these readers enjoy the satisfaction of receiving what they consider full pay for their work, then they are happy to play the reading game.

In summary, adolescent literature has a good chance of succeeding with the reluctant reader for the following reasons:

1. It is written specifically to be interesting to teenagers. It is geared to their age level and their interests.
2. It is usually shorter and more simply written than adult material, yet it has no stigma attached to it. It isn't written down to anyone nor does it look like a reading textbook.
3. There is so much of it—almost 800 new books published every year—that individual readers have a good chance of finding books that appeal to them.
4. As would be expected since they are the creations of some of the best contemporary writers, the stories are more dramatic, better written, and easier to get involved in than are the controlled vocabulary books.
5. The language used in good adolescent literature is much more like the language that students are accustomed to hearing. In this day of mass media communication, a student who does not read widely may still have a fairly high degree of literary and language sophistication gained from watching television and movies.

Taking all of this into account, there are still some types of adolescent literature that will be enjoyed more than others by reluctant readers. In general, reluctant readers want the same things from the books they read that the rest of us want only they want them faster and in less space. If it's information they are looking for, they want it to be right there. If they are reading a book for thrills and chills, they really want it to be scary. And if it's for humor, they really want it to be funny. And if they're not sure about committing themselves for a large chunk of time, they want books in which they can get a feeling of accomplishment from reading short sections or even paragraphs. This helps explain the continuing popularity of the *Guinness Book of World Records.*

The push for higher reading scores has had the effect of opening the high-school curriculum to reading classes for all students, not just those with low reading scores. For example, study skills courses are commonly given in which students are taught principles of skimming, reading for the main idea, and speed reading.

Another class that has been taught since the 1930s, but which enjoyed a new surge of popularity in the 1970s, is individualized reading. In this class, students spend most of their time reading books of their choice. The thinking behind the organization of such classes is that one of the chief reasons that out-of-school reading drops off so dramatically when children leave elementary school is that the social structure of high-school students leaves them little time for it. Classes go under such titles as Paperback Power, Paperback Reading, Contemporary Reading, Individualized Reading, and Personalized Reading. The following guidelines have been gleaned from several successful programs, most notably that of the one at Cedar Falls High School in Cedar Falls, Iowa directed by Barbara Blow.[3]

1. Students can read any books they choose.
2. When students register for the course, a note goes home to parents explaining that the choice of books is up to the student and his or her parents. This is a friendly note, inviting parent participation, and quoting from parents of previous students who have enjoyed recommending books to their children and talking about reactions, and so on.
3. When students finish reading each book, they have a ten to fifteen minute individual conference in which they discuss the book with the teacher. The teacher makes suggestions for other books that the student will probably enjoy.
4. The teacher reads each book (or at least skims it) prior to the discussion. To enable teachers to build up a sufficiently large background of reading so that they can talk knowledgeably about the books, most programs have the same teacher handle several sections over an extended period of time. This contrasts with some unstructured (and usually unsuccessful) programs in which the course is seen more or less as a free reading study hall with little or no preparation required from the teacher.
5. The room is organized and students seated so as to minimize in-class visiting and to make it easy to take the roll and locate students for conferences.
6. Teachers' aides handle such clerical tasks as taking the roll, scheduling conferences, recording grades, and checking out books so that the teacher (or teachers if it is team-taught) can concentrate entirely on student conferences.
7. Conferences are held in nearby offices or screened-off areas so that they will not disturb the students who are reading and so that the teacher's attention will not be divided between the class and the individual student.

8. Nearly all class time is reserved for reading. The exceptions are three or four days in a semester when the librarian gives book talks.

9. Although students are allowed to select their own books from any source, a special individualized paperback collection is made available to them. This includes multiple copies of popular books so that when enthusiasm about a book spreads from one student to another, copies will be available.

10. Lists of the books most frequently read by class members are distributed at regular intervals to serve as idea sources for further reading.

11. Students sign up a week in advance for conferences so that the teacher has time to read the book and so that the student has time to plan an approach. Some schools give students suggestions for organizing their discussion so that the student takes the initiative. Others are teacher-directed.

12. Grading is handled in various ways including credit for promptness and good attendance, numbers of pages read, quality of preparation for conferences, selection of "challenging" books, and so forth. Some teachers reported that it was necessary to be fairly stringent so that students understood that the class was serious and not just a study hall.

13. Some programs emphasize the keeping of a record card marking down the number of pages read each day. Students get a feeling of achievement as their number of pages steadily increases.

The kind of individualized reading program that is described here is not for the dysfunctional or disabled reader. It is for the average or above-average student who simply needs a chance to read and discuss books. In effect, it is one last try on the part of the school to instill in young people the habit of reading for pleasure. The student who lacks the skills for this kind of reading class or for a more standard class in literature needs expert help from a professional reading teacher. Preparing teachers for that kind of role is beyond the scope of this book.

IN THE SOCIAL STUDIES CLASS

One of the great values and pleasures of literature is that it frees us to travel vicariously to other times and places. Movies, television, and photographs allow people to see other places, but literature has an added dimension. It allows the reader to share the thoughts of another person. It has been said that one never feels like a stranger in a country whose literature one has read. In today's jet age, distances are rapidly shrinking and it is more important than ever that people feel at home in other countries and with other cultures. People then begin to realize that members of the human race, regardless of where or how they live, have more similarities than differences.

Historical fiction, fiction set in other countries, fiction about members of ethnic groups in the United States, and well-written informative books should all be part of high-school social studies classes. When Lawrence Yep wrote *Dragonwings*, he fictionalized the true story of a Chinese immigrant in California who made a flying machine in 1909 that flew for twenty minutes. Yep explained in an afterword that very little was actually known about the man because, "Like the other Chinese who came to America, he remains a shadowy figure. Of the hundreds of thousands of Chinese who flocked to these shores we know next to nothing." What Yep wanted to do with his story was to change at least a few of these people from "statistical fodder" into real people with "fears and hopes, joys and sorrows like the rest of us."

This is what good literature can do for any mass of social facts, figures, and statistics. Esther Forbes' *Johnny Tremain* breathes life into a study of the American Revolution. Irene Hunt's *Across Five Aprils* does the same thing for the Civil War, and Anne Frank's *The Diary of a Young Girl*, Johanna Reiss' *The Upstairs Room*, and Nathaniel Benchley's *Bright Candles* do it for World War II. In thinking about history, these books

No one book can tell everything about what every person in a particular group thinks and feels.

come immediately to mind because it is the wars that have been covered in traditional history textbooks. But within recent years, critics have been vociferous in their objection to the glorification of violence and war in histories and the lack of information about the contributions of women and minorities. Such critics are asking for an enlarged view of history that will teach how everybody lived, not just soldiers and statesmen, not just the winners, but the ordinary people at home. What was happening in all the years when people were not fighting wars?

It may be in answering these questions that literature can make its biggest contribution to the social studies class. A book with the power of Robert Newton Peck's *A Day No Pigs Would Die* gives readers a feel for rural Vermont life in the 1920s; Anne Stallworth's *This Time Next Year* shows what the Depression really did to farm families; and Jessamyn West's *The Massacre at Fall Creek* makes readers think of what it meant in 1824 to have to change one's thinking on something so basic as whether or not it is murder to kill an Indian.

However, it is important for readers to realize that no one book can tell them everything about what every person in a particular group thinks and feels. Many different books need to be read, always keeping in mind the fact that each book presents only one perspective. Stereotypes exist in people's minds for two reasons. One is that the same attitudes are repeated over and over so that they become the predominant image in the reader's mind. Another is that an individual may have had only one exposure to a particular race, group, or country. For example, a young reader who knows nothing about Africa and then reads D. R. Sherman's *The Lion's Paw*, about a young Bushman caught in a conflict between white hunters and his and a lion's needs, can hardly be said to have developed an understanding of a whole continent and its people. Nevertheless, the reader will have caught a reflection from one facet of a multifaceted jewel and will perhaps have become intrigued enough to go on and look for other reflections. Similarly, a reader who finishes Chaim Potok's *The Chosen* doesn't know everything about Hasidic Jews, but he or she knows a lot more than before, including the fact that there are groups within groups.

By reading widely and sharing their findings, social studies class members can lead each other to go beyond stereotypes. They will begin to realize that every person is a unique blend of characteristics even though that person may be a member of a particular group.

IN THE ENGLISH CLASS

Hundreds of books are available telling English teachers how to teach literature. Rather than trying to condense all of that information into this small space, we have chosen to present some of the ideas that are specifically related to adolescent literature, that is, the junior novel.

Nearly everyone agrees that discussing books is valuable. It enables students to get feedback from others, to exchange ideas, and to practice their persuasive techniques by arguing about and discussing various interpretations. Another advantage of discussing a book is that, through verbalization, readers get a handle on their own thoughts. Their ideas and reactions intermingle with those of the author, which is one of the things that reading is all about.

Probably most adults who have worked with books and young readers remember having had some wonderful conversations about books, but they probably also remember having had some distinctly nondescript conversations in which students recited the plot of the story and then had nothing more to say. With a little planning and a modicum of skill, such negative experiences can be avoided or at least kept to a minimum.

Teachers know that one of their most valuable techniques is that of asking questions and responding carefully to student answers so that a genuine exchange of ideas occurs. The value of a discussion right after or during the reading of a piece of literature is that one is still shaping a response. In a good discussion, new information will be taken in, measured, evaluated, and integrated with the tentative conclusions already reached. This is the process called *expatiation* or "enlargement through talk."

To bring about the best kind of talk with young readers, adults have to walk a middle ground between accepting just any comment that a student makes and having a prepared list of examination-type questions with one and only one acceptable answer. The best discussions are the ones that resemble the kind of real-life conversations that good friends have when they've both read a new book and are anxious to share opinions and gain insights from each other.

The sense of equality necessary in this kind of discussion may be unsettling to teachers who are accustomed to arriving in class with either a lecture to be given or a set of dittos to be filled out. As Robert C. Small, Jr. wrote in "Teaching the Junior Novel,"[4] the generally accepted goal of a high-school literature program is to place the student in a position of incapacity while the teacher is elevated to that of translator. With most adult novels, students are at a tremendous disadvantage when they are asked to evaluate the accuracy with which an author has written about such concerns as marriage and divorce, ambition, greed, and hate. Even though these situations and feelings are related to teenage problems, they are not matters with which students have had experience. In contrast, when the subject of the book is a modern teenager, the balance of knowledge is changed. At least in the area of evaluating the characters, their problems, and the resolution of those problems, Small says "the students can justifiably be said to speak from a greater authority than their teacher." But of course the teacher still has greater knowledge than the students in such matters as the development of plot, setting, characterization, theme, dialogue, and point of view and can use this knowledge to lead the students to worthwhile analysis and evaluation.

The best discussions resemble real-life conversations between good friends.

Small thinks that the junior novel is the ideal material for starting students on their way to making worthy literary observations. He says that anyone wanting to teach a novice how a steam engine or an internal combustion engine works would be foolish to start with a TVA generating plant or the car that won the Indianapolis 500 because these would be too complex and have too many refinements that cover up the essential workings. The smart teacher would instead start with "a simple steam engine, a one-cylinder engine, a working model, where each part was one of its kind and its functions clear. The junior novel is, for all purposes, that simple but working model of the adult or classic novel."[5]

In his article on "The Adolescent Novel as a Working Model," he points out that well-written junior novels have plots, settings, characters, and themes. They also involve points of view and the use of dialogue and narrative. Small worked with librarian D. J. Kenney to draw up a list of adolescent novels that could be used with the kinds of activities he recommends as appropriate for high-school students who are at an early stage in their reading development.

For talking about plot, he recommends Edith Maxwell's *Just Dial a Number* and Finn Havrevold's *Undertow* as good examples of cause and effect relationships. A teaching suggestion is to develop with students a list of the traits of the main characters. Consider whether or not each trait affects the working of the plot. Choose some opposite traits and discuss what would have happened if these had been the characters' traits. Another idea is to have students keep notebooks for a period of time in which they list things that happen to them or to others that in turn cause still other things to happen.

After identifying the elements of plot, students trace the way these elements relate to setting. A book with a foreign or historical setting could be examined to see how the plot was influenced by that setting. The discussion could center on how the plot would have been changed if the story had been contemporary and set locally.

In relation to characterization, Small and Kenney recommend Mildred Lee's *The Skating Rink* and Katie Letcher Lyle's *The Golden Shores of Heaven* for major character development, M. E. Kerr's *Love Is a Missing Person* for minor character development, Reginald Maddock's *The Pit* for direct character description, and T. Degens' *Transport 7-41-R* and Margaret Craven's *I Heard the Owl Call My Name* for character analysis. Class activities could include a discussion of whether or not close friends are the same people they were a year ago. A follow-up writing exercise could make the transfer from third to first person and have students ponder whether or not they have changed over the past year, and if so, how? A related discussion could be on what students know about their friends and just how they know these things. How does the way they learn about their friends differ from the way they find out about characters on television, in movies, and in literature? The difference between the characterization in a biography such as Doris Lund's *Eric* might be compared with that in an autobiography such as Anne Frank's *Diary* and a novel such as Robert Lipsyte's *The Contender*.

When reading a book with several major characters, the class could be divided into groups with each group preparing a composite of everything they know about one of the main characters. The group builds on what the author has told them and writes a biography of the character filling in missing elements through speculation. An idea for a prereading activity is for the teacher to prepare a news story telling about one of the major events of the book that involves several characters. Students speculate on what might have led up to the event, what types of people were involved, and how the people probably felt about the event. Since newspaper accounts present so little information, it will be hard for the class to agree on the motives and characterizations. After reading the book, even though the specific information is not given, it will be fairly easy for the class to agree because the author will provide much fuller characterizations than did the news story.

Good books recommended to illustrate the importance of the physical setting to a story are Wilson Rawls' *Where the Red Fern Grows* and Frank Bonham's *Durango Street*. Recommended for their cultural settings are S. T. Tung's *One Small Dog*, Ivan Southall's *Ash Road*, and Jean George's *Julie of the Wolves*. Recommended for its period setting is Rosemary Sutcliff's *Warrior Scarlet*. John Christopher's *The White Mountains* and Mary Jo Stephen's *Witch of the Cumberland* are books in which the authors use direct descriptions whereas indirect descriptions are used in Robert Lipsyte's *The Contender*.

Activities related to setting could include having students watch one or more leading television series and make notes on the settings. Class discussion would revolve around how the series is affected by the setting and what would happen to two series if their settings were reversed. Another combination talking and writing assignment could be to pretend that a television show or a book is to be set locally. Students select a number of places that give the flavor of their town. After class discussion, they could select one to write about in such a way that readers would get a feel for the region.

Recommended as interesting because of the author's skill with dialogue are the conversations in Rosemary Wells' *The Fog Comes on Little Pig Feet* and Lila Perl's *Me and Fat Glenda*, the character monologues in Susan B. Pfeffer's *The Beauty Queen* and Mollie Hunter's *A Sound of Chariots*, and the presentations of the characters' thoughts in Paul Annixter's *Swiftwater* and Allan Eckert's *Incident at Hawk's Hill*. Books with good dialogue are especially suitable for readers' theatre and adaptation into radio scripts. Discussion might focus on what makes for interesting dialogue and how fictional conversations are much more interesting and to the point than real-life conversations.

To illustrate first person point of view, Paula Fox's *Blowfish Live in the Sea* and Judy Blume's *It's Not the End of the World* are recommended. Third person is shown in Betsy C. Byars' *The 18th Emergency* and Virginia Hamilton's *M. C. Higgins, The Great*, and contrasting viewpoints are shown in Alice Childress' *A Hero Ain't Nothin' But a Sandwich* and Paul Zindel's *The Pigman*.

All good pieces of adolescent literature have themes. One way to introduce the concept of theme is to read a paragraph that presents only facts and then a second paragraph or a poem that gives an opinion or a feeling about the same subject so that it contains a theme. A discussion of the difference illustrates the function of theme in literature. Another exercise on theme is to choose an emotion frequently felt by students such as loneliness or discouragement and develop a statement about the emotion that could be used as a theme. Develop a similar statement giving the opposite view. Divide the class in half. One group sketches a story that would illustrate the first theme and the second group sketches a story to illustrate the opposite theme. Comparing the two will show how theme guides all other aspects of the story.

In tying theme in with real life, students might be assigned to select a theme that has appeared in a book they have recently read and to observe and make notes on anything related to that theme in their daily lives. They might prepare a presentation using passages from any sources that illustrate the theme. A brief writing exercise would be for class members to prepare "Dear Abby" questions and answers that deal with aspects of a theme from a book being studied. A comparison of the letters would show how many facets there are to a theme and how it differs in that way from a plot.

When students are at a stage in their intellectual development in which their primary interest is in finding themselves and their peers in the books they read, it stands to reason that an appropriate approach to use in talking about books would be that of subjective response. Suzanne Howell uses the following questions as a "bridge" for those who are "just finding the way to affective response,"[6]

1. What was your immediate (first) response to the story? What was your immediate (first) feeling about the story? What were your immediate (first) associations? (What did the story remind you of?) What were your immediate (first) ideas? (What ideas came to your mind?)
2. Does the story remind you of anything you've seen on TV, anything you've read before, and so forth?
3. Can you relate the story to anything in your own experience?

4. Can you relate any characters in the story to anyone you know?
5. What questions does the story raise in your mind?

It is her experience that students do better in class discussion if they have first taken time to write down their responses. Otherwise, they tend to hide their feelings behind euphemisms or they resort to the objective kinds of analyses that they think most teachers really want. But as students become accustomed to the subjective response approach, they learn to trust their judgments and their feelings. Certainly some responses show more sensitivity than others, but no responses are "right" or "wrong," since each was triggered by something in the story. As classes work, there is a natural progression from subjective response to objective interpretation. As an example, Howell cites a discussion about Virginia Moriconi's short story "Simple Arithmetic," which is told through "letters to and from a boy whose parents give him everything but love." The subjective response of nearly everyone in the class was that they hated Stephen's father. These are the steps through which the class discussion went:

"I hated Stephen's father."

"Stephen's father is a cold person."

"Stephen's father is a cold, detached person, as shown by the fact that he corrects Stephen's spelling instead of dealing directly with his personal problems."

"The author reveals the character of Stephen's father indirectly through his tone and style of his letters to Stephen."

Larry Andrews is another teacher who recommends starting with the students' subjective responses and then working from there. He says:

Any critical approach to any text must be considered *in relation* to the adolescent reader. It would be much easier for us to consider only the texts themselves, but we can't do that because of our simultaneous responsibilities to our *students*, to the *texts* they read, and their *responses* to those texts.[7]

The disadvantage to be overcome, he feels, is that students typically have a superficial reaction consisting of little more than "I like it" or "I don't like it." These reactions may be based on only one aspect of the material, such as whether or not it had a happy ending or was about a subject that they like. Class discussions can encourage students to go beyond this initial response.

As one way to do this, he recommends the breakage technique in which the reading is broken into sections. At the end of a section, students express their response to a particular section and, based on these responses, they predict what will happen in the next section. By defending their predictions against others', students have to look more deeply at their responses, they have to see if their clues actually appear in the piece or whether they are so familiar with literary techniques and patterns that they are just making good guesses. As students try to agree on what will come next, they look carefully for the clues laid down by the author. Then as they read the rest of the piece to see how their ideas match the author's, they begin to see the difference between a quality piece of literature with its inevitable conclusion and the poorly written one in which an author cheated by relying on an unjustified coincidence or an unbelievable character to make the plot come out all right.

Another way to extend students' responses is to use semantic differentials. Prior to the discussion, students fill out a written form on which they rate different aspects of the piece. This encourages them to look beyond the one aspect they might have originally used to justify liking it or disliking it. It also enables them to speak in specifics rather than generalities. Thinking out their decisions and then explaining them forces students to take more than a cursory look at the text. The form should be

Transport 7-41-R

The setting in this story was:

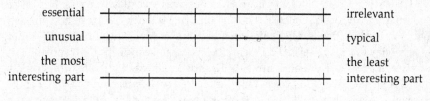

The plot was:

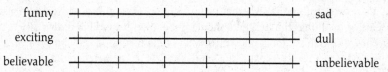

The feeling I was left with was:

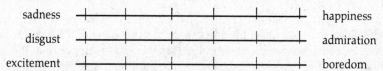

varied throughout the year with different aspects being examined as they apply to a particular book. Concentrating on only a few aspects at a time will keep from spreading thinking and discussion too thin on any one book. If the exercise is repeated with other titles and other aspects, then by the end of a semester or a year, students will understand the wide range of elements that determines the success of the author/reader communication. An example of how such a form might look for T. Degens' *Transport 7-41-R* is given here.

A practice that is becoming increasingly common in English classes is to concentrate on a theme rather than on a particular book. The teacher selects five to ten titles with a closely related theme and group members read one or more of them. When the group discussion is held, it centers on the common theme with readers of various books telling how the theme was developed in their particular books. Both small and large group discussions can be held.

The smaller the group doing the discussing, obviously the greater the number who get to talk. For example, when a class of thirty students spends a half-hour talking about a story, there will probably be time for a maximum of twenty well-developed comments. But if for half of the time the class were divided into five or six groups, then the number of comments offered by students could be increased to something like sixty or seventy. Worthwhile discussions do not happen automatically. Students must be trained and given guided practice. It's a good idea especially with inexperienced students for the teacher to get a discussion going in the class as a whole and then to offer suggestions or help in the continuation of the talk in the small groups. Students are apt to be more serious and to attend to the task at hand if they must come up with something to be shared with the group as a whole.

For a class to read different but related books has several advantages. It is easier to get four or five copies of a particular title than to get thirty. They can be borrowed from libraries and friends. Or if purchased with school funds, it seems to be a better use of money to acquire several different titles that will be available later for students to read individually. The books can also be at different reading levels with students self-selecting the one with which they feel most comfortable. And in this day of censorship, books that would perhaps cause public relations problems if they were assigned to a large group can be read and studied by a small number of students who make their own decision on whether or not they want to read a particular title.

One of the things that teachers should remember in any kind of discussion is that when they question students, they must allow time for thinking. When, for example, teachers ask students to explain the motivation of a character and then give them twelve seconds in which to do it, they force students to oversimplify.[8] Characters in literature are just as complex as those in real life and should be approached with equal respect.

The only questions that can be asked and answered in rapid fire order are those to which students already know the answers. At the beginning of a discussion these may serve to refresh memories and to insure that the class is starting from the same factual base, but even very simple-sounding questions may have very complex answers. It sometimes helps if during a discussion, the questioning begins at a concrete or factual basis and then moves progressively toward the abstract. One such schema has been developed and recommended by Edward J. Gordon and Dwight L. Burton. It is printed here as it appeared in an article by Burton based on an earlier one by Gordon.[9]

1. *Questions requiring the student to remember facts in a selection.* (What objects did the poet refer to? What happened in the story immediately after the storm?)

2. *Questions that require the student to prove or disprove a generalization someone else has made.* (One critic has said that _____. Can you cite any examples from the novel to substantiate this? Or, the teacher may pose an

hypothesis for the students to prove or disprove: This story is an attack upon _____.)

3. *Questions that require the student to derive his own generalizations.* (What relationship do the coffee drinking scenes in the novel have to the central theme? How does the poet make use of flower symbols? If there is little or no response to this question, the teacher needs to go back to simpler levels and build up to this level again: Where is a red rose referred to in the poem? Can you find any support for this interpretation: The rose symbolizes _____. Now what other flower symbols do you find?)

4. *Questions that require the student to generalize about the relation of the total work to human experience.* (What is the universal human problem dramatized in _____?)

5. *Questions that require the student to carry generalizations derived from the work into his own life.* (Is the kind of experience which this poem glorifies one that your friends value?)

In summary, adolescent literature can be the raw material from which a teacher fashions lessons to teach a great deal about literature. But we are certainly not recommending that all literature lessons be based on junior novels, nor are we recommending that whenever students read books a literary lesson should be attached. What we are saying is that English classes need to be filled with balance and variety and that including adolescent literature provides teachers with one more way to insure this.

IN CLARIFYING HUMAN RELATIONS AND VALUES

Workers with church and civic youth groups, teachers of classes in human relations, and professional counselors working with young adults have all found that adolescent literature can be a useful tool in the work they do. When talking about using books for the general purposes of helping students understand their own and other people's feelings and behavior, we sometimes use the term "bibliotherapy". But it is a word that goes in and out of fashion, at least in reference to the informal kind of work that most teachers and librarians do with young adults. Its technical meaning is the use of books by professionally trained psychologists and psychiatrists in working with people who are mentally ill. It is because of this association with illness that many "book" people reject the term. Their reasoning is that if a young adult is mentally ill and in need of some kind of therapy, then the therapy should be coming from someone trained in that field rather than from someone trained in the book business or in teaching and guiding normal and healthy young adults.

However, most people agree that normal and healthy young adults can benefit psychologically from reading and talking about the problems of fictional characters. They get the kinds of insights that are reflected in the following comments collected by Ina Ewing, a teacher at Maryvale High School in Arizona:

The book [Judy Blume's] *Forever* shows a girl making a hard decision. Every girl has to make that decision at one time or other and so Kathy is like a lot of girls I know. My friends don't talk about it though, so it's good to read about someone else's decision. I think it helps.

[In reference to John Neufeld's *Lisa, Bright and Dark*] I guess if you're going crazy you should try to get help from doctors yourself. Is that possible? Can you just walk into a hospital or someplace like that and ask for help? I'll have to check it out.

[Also in reference to *Lisa, Bright and Dark*] I never realized that even kids our age have big enough problems to go crazy. I always thought the ones who went nuts were the ones who were taking dope. I would sure try to help a friend of mine though who thought she was going crazy. It must be scary.

[In reference to Paul Zindel's *The Pigman*] When my grandma died my grandpa came to live with us. It was a big bother because I had to move into a room with my brother. Now I'm glad that he has a place to stay so he won't be so lonely.

[In reference to Paula Danziger's *The Cat Ate My Gym Suit*] I think that this book says that you should listen to your parents but I also think it says that you should stand up for what you believe in. This book made it seem so easy to stick to a cause. I would be so afraid like Marcy was. She was shy at first. That's me. Well then when she really believed in something it was easy not to be so shy. I could maybe find a cause.

[In reference to Ann Head's *Mr. and Mrs. Bo Jo Jones*] I liked the way the book told the side of a couple that makes it when they get married. Most books tell you that if a girl and guy have to get married, it won't last. Even though they had their share of problems, they made their marriage work in the end. It shows that sometimes pregnancy occurs because love is strong in spite of everything else.

All teenagers have problems of one type or another, and simply finding out that other people have them too provides some comfort. We are reassured to know that our fears and doubts have been experienced by others. We feel more confident when we read about people successfully coping with problems that we may have in the future. Notice that of the six student comments given here, only one refers to an actual event. The others are conjectures about things that might happen.

David A. Williams, a communications professor at the University of Arizona, said in a newspaper interview that he would die happy if he could "prove that a positive correlation exists between the rise in anxiety in the country and the decline of pleasure reading."[10] Research done during the 1950s and 1960s has shown that anxiety is directly related to a poor concept of oneself. "It seems to me," he says, "that the human being's major concern in life is to determine what it means to be a human being." The paradox is that before people can see themselves, they have to get outside of themselves and look at the whole spectrum of human experience to see where they fit in. He points out that, "When we are feeling anxious it is usually because we have a narrow perspective, a perspective which sees only what it wants to see." Someone who is anxiety-ridden, paranoiac, or resentful selects from life's experiences things to validate those feelings. For people like this, reading can put things back into perspective. "When we read about others who have suffered similar anxieties, we don't feel so cut off and, although the world doesn't change, we change the way we look at it."

Books put things back into perspective because they talk about the human experience in ways that everyday language cannot. Some of the human truths that most concern us are very difficult to talk about. We do not share our feelings with others because we think we are the only ones who feel this way. Reading brings us back to an awareness of our commonality with other human beings and opens up avenues of communication that successful discussion leaders tap into.

However, it is important for adults to be careful in guiding students to read and talk about personal problems. No one should be forced to participate in such a discussion nor should a special effort be made to relate stories to the exact problem that a group member is having. In fact, it would probably be best to avoid matching up particular problems with particular students. When someone is in the midst of a crisis, chances are good that he or she does not want to read and talk about someone else in a similar predicament. As a general rule, one will probably get the most from such a discussion before and/or after—rather than during—a time of actual crisis.

The kinds of groups in which such discussions are usually held are clubs, church groups, classes on marriage and human relations, counseling sessions, and "rap" sessions at crisis centers and various institutions to which young people are sent. Since these groups are often the kind where membership changes from meeting to meeting and there are no pressures for participants to do outside reading as "homework," a leader will probably be disappointed or frustrated if the discussion is planned around the expectation that everyone will have read the book. A more realistic plan is for the leader to give a summary of the book and a ten to twenty minute prepared reading of the part of the book that best delineates the problem or the topic for discussion.

Plan to use fairly well-known books so that the chances will be greater that someone in the group will have read the book or at least heard of it and therefore feel inclined to help get the discussion started, perhaps by filling in some of the background. Using popular books will also make it easier for students whose appetites have been whetted to find the book and read it on their own. In an adult group of professionals, the same purpose would be accomplished by reading a case study that would then be discussed. But case studies are written for trained adults who know how to fill in the missing details and how to interpret the symptoms. Teenagers are not psychologists, nor are they social workers or philosophers. Literature may be as close as they will ever come to discussing the kinds of problems dealt with in these fields. And the oral presentation of a well-written fictional account has the advantage of being entertaining and emotionally moving in ways that factual case studies could not be.

What follows the oral presentation can be extremely varied depending on the nature of the group, the leader's personality, and what the purpose or the goal of the discussion is. The literature provides the group—both teenagers and adults—with a common experience presented through the neutral (as far as the group is concerned) eyes of the author. This common experience can then serve as the focus for discussion. Pressures and tensions are relieved because everyone is talking in the third person about the characters in the book, although in reality many of the comments will be about first-person problems.

The theory developed by Lawrence Kohlberg and his associates about how moral problems are solved is relevant to this discussion. According to Kohlberg's theory, which was developed at Harvard University during the 1960s, moral judgment is not something that can be intellectually taught. Rather it develops with experience and age, and the interesting thing that Kohlberg's studies uncovered is that there is an invariant sequence in its development. Longitudinal studies conducted in many different cultures have shown that young people between the ages of ten and twenty-five go

---

TABLE TWO: Classification of Moral Judgment into Levels and Stages of Development

Levels	Stages of Development
Level I. Preconventional	Stage 1: Obedience and punishment orientation
	Stage 2: Naively egoistic orientation
Level II. Conventional	Stage 3: Good-boy orientation
	Stage 4: Authority and social-order maintaining orientation
Level III. Postconventional	Stage 5: Contractual legalistic orientation
	Stage 6: Conscience or principle orientation

Source: Adapted from Lawrence Kohlberg, "Stage and Sequence: the Cognitive Developmental Approach to Socialization," from Goslin, ed., *Handbook of Socialization Theory and Research,* copyright © 1969 by Rand McNally College Publishing Company.

through six stages of development in their attempts to solve moral problems. People sometimes become fixated at one of these stages, for example an adult operating at the second stage, that of immediate reciprocity, sort of a you-be-nice-to-me and I'll-be-nice-to-you approach. Typically, however, people continue to progress through the stages, which are grouped into three levels. Table 2 shows these levels and stages. It is taken from one of the few articles that has been written on the relationship between books and the behaviors involved in moral judgment, "Moral Development and Literature for Adolescents" by Peter Scharf.[11]

In Scharf's article he makes the point that the way a reader responds to a particular story will depend on the stage of moral judgment that he or she has reached. For example, at age thirteen a reader is apt to respond to Dostoevsky's *Crime and Punishment* as a mystery, but at age twenty the same reader would be more likely to look at it as a complex study of human morals. Great literature has an impact at almost any age, but naturally students will respond the most to that which fits the particular level at which they are struggling to make sense of the world. At the beginning levels (early teens), readers are reassured to read books in which there are definite rules and clear-cut examples of right and wrong. As readers move into the conventional or middle levels, they are interested in literature that focuses on social expectations. According to Scharf, this literature:

> stimulates a sense of moral conventionality by praising "appropriate" social attitudes. Often protagonists will represent heroic values which are reflected and emulated by young readers. Villains are often portrayed as "unfeeling" or "cruel" in often one-dimensional, somewhat stereotyped ways. Good literature of this type presents a coherent moral universe in which good and evil are polarized and defined. This provides a platform of social conventions upon which the early adolescent can differentiate his group's social ideology from other philosophies. While this type of literature may seem "corny" or "sentimental" to adults, it is a necessary stage toward the learning of more complex personal moral philosophies.

As students become confident at this level and feel that they understand the expectations of society, they begin tentatively to explore and question these expectations. It is at this stage that many young people reject the conventional moral order and seek to set up or to find a more satisfactory social order. Scharf wrote:

> Needless to say, this questioning is disturbing to many adults, including librarians. They fail to see that such a rejection of conventional societal truth is a critical step in the adolescent's defining for himself an autonomous value base.

Because many young adults are in the stage of rebellion and questioning, Holden Caulfield in Salinger's *The Catcher in the Rye* speaks forcefully to them. As people mature, they gradually pass through this stage of rebellion and are not so concerned with society and its expectations. Instead they develop their own internal system by which they make moral judgments. This final stage is distinct from both early adolescent conformity and the relativism and nihilism of middle adolescence. Scharf thinks that books and libraries have a unique role in providing readers with the range of material that they need to reflect upon in developing their own set of inner values.

In conclusion, literature can in no way solve someone's problems. But it can serve as a stimulus to thought, and it can open channels of communication. It can serve as a conversation topic while rapport and understanding grow between an adult and a teenager or among the members of a group. And reading widely about all kinds of problems and all kinds of solutions will help to keep young people involved in thinking about moral issues.

TABLE THREE

What Adolescent Literature Can Do:	What Adolescent Literature Cannot Do:
1. It can provide a common experience or a way in which a teenager and an adult can focus their attention on the same subject.	1. It cannot cure someone's emotional illness.
2. It can then serve as a discussion topic and a way to relieve embarrassment by enabling people to talk in the third person about problems with which they are concerned.	2. It cannot guarantee that its readers will behave in socially approved ways.
3. It can give young readers confidence that, should they meet particular problems, they will be able to solve them.	3. It cannot directly solve its readers' problems.
4. It can increase a young person's understanding of the world and the many ways that individuals find their places in it.	
5. It can comfort and reassure young adult readers by showing them that they are not the only ones who have fears and doubts.	
6. It can give adults as well as teenagers insights into adolescent psychology and values.	

Table 3 shows what adolescent literature can and cannot do when it is used as a tool to teach about human relations and values.

This chapter has shown that using and promoting books with young readers is a shared opportunity and responsibility. It belongs not only to librarians and English and reading teachers but to everyone who works closely with young people and wants to understand them better. It can serve as a medium through which to open communication with young adults about their concerns.

We specifically focused on librarians, teachers, and youth workers or counselors, but we could also have mentioned many others, including parents. Contrary to the impression given by the mass media (adolescent fiction included), many parents serve in the roles described here, that is, teacher, counselor, conversation partner, and reading friend.

ACTIVITIES

1. Write a lesson plan in which you use an adolescent novel to teach a literary concept.

2. Prepare a display of young adult books for a school or public library. Include a take-home bibliography, perhaps in the form of a bookmark or some other creative souvenir of the display. Most librarians would be pleased to have your volunteer services. If it is not practical for you to set up a real display, think up five different ideas. Write down the basic idea, a brief description, and list at least ten books that you would feature in each display.

3. Plan an informal discussion dealing with some affective area of young adult life, for example, social pressure, alienation, friendship, love, or discouragement. Prepare a reading from an adolescent novel that you will use to set the stage for the discussion. List several questions and ideas that you might use throughout the discussion.

4. Draw up a reader interest survey that you could have students fill out as part of getting acquainted with a class at the start of a semester. Design it so that it will take less than ten minutes for students to fill out and so that you could use it as the basis for an individual conference in which you would suggest books. You might have students list such things as their hobbies, the kind of books they like, the last book they read, a book they did not like, the television shows they watch, and the movies they have enjoyed most within the last year.

NOTES

[1]Mary K. Chelton, "Booktalking: You Can Do It," *School Library Journal* 22 (April 1976): 39–43.

[2]See the editorial, "Only Almost Anything," by Lillian N. Gerhardt, *School Library Journal* 25 (December 1978): 7.

[3]Barbara Blow, "Individualized Reading," *Arizona English Bulletin* 18 (April 1976): 151–53.

[4]Robert C. Small, "Teaching the Junior Novel," *English Journal* 61 (February 1972): 222–29.

[5]Robert C. Small, "The Adolescent Novel as a Working Model," *Alan Newsletter* 4 (Winter 1977).

[6]Suzanne Howell, "Unlocking the Box: An Experiment in Literary Response," *English Journal* 66 (February 1977): 37–42.

[7]Larry Andrews, "Responses to Literature: Enlarging the Range," *Ibid.*, pp. 60–62.

[8]This is what James Hoetker found in "better" schools with "better" staff. Teachers were asking five questions per minute. "Teacher Questioning Behavior in Nine Junior High School English Classes," *Research in the Teaching of English* (Fall 1968), p. 108.

[9]Edward J. Gordon, "Levels of Teaching and Testing," *English Journal* 44 (September 1955): 330–34, and Dwight L. Burton, "Well, Where Are We in Teaching Literature?" *English Journal* 63 (February 1974): 28–33.

[10]"Feeling Uptight, Anxious? Try Reading UA Prof Says," *Tempe Daily News*, December 15, 1977.

[11]Peter Scharf, "Moral Development and Literature for Adolescents," *Top of the News* 33 (Winter 1977): 131–36.

TITLES MENTIONED IN CHAPTER TWELVE

For information on the availability of paperback editions of these titles, please consult the most recent edition of *Paperbound Books in Print*, published annually by R. R. Bowker Company.

Annixter, Paul. *Swiftwater*. A. A. Wyn, 1950.

Benchley, Nathaniel. *Bright Candles*. Harper & Row, 1974.

Blume, Judy. *Forever*. Bradbury, 1976.

———. *It's Not the End of the World*. Bradbury, 1972.

Bonham, Frank. *Durango Street*. E. P. Dutton, 1965.

Bradbury, Ray. *The Martian Chronicles*. Doubleday, 1958.

Bugliosi, Vincent and Curt Gentry. *Helter Skelter: The True Story of the Manson Murders*. W. W. Norton, 1974.

Byars, Betsy C. *The Eighteenth Emergency*. Viking, 1973.

Childress, Alice. *A Hero Ain't Nothin' But a Sandwich*. Coward, McCann & Geoghegan, 1973.

Christopher, John. *The White Mountains*. Macmillan, 1967.

Cleaver, Vera and Bill. *Where the Lilies Bloom*. J. B. Lippincott, 1969.

Craven, Margaret. *I Heard the Owl Call My Name*. Doubleday, 1973.

Danziger, Paula. *The Cat Ate My Gym Suit*. Delacorte, 1974.

Degens, T. *Transport 7-41-R*. Viking, 1974.

Doctorow, E. L. *Ragtime*. Random House, 1975.

Donovan, John. *I'll Get There. It Better Be Worth the Trip*. Harper & Row, 1969.

———. *Wild in the World*. Harper & Row, 1971.

Dostoevsky, Fyodor. Translated by David Magarshack. *Crime and Punishment*. 1866.

Dunning, Stephen, et al., eds. *Reflections on a Gift of Watermelon Pickle*. Lothrop, Lee & Shepard, 1967.

Edwards, Margaret. *The Fair Garden and the Swarm of Beasts*. 2d. ed. Hawthorne, 1974.

Eckert, Allen. *Incident at Hawk's Hill.* Little, Brown, 1971.

Fast, Howard. *April Morning.* Crown, 1970.

Felsen, Henry Gregor. *Hot Rod.* E. P. Dutton, 1950.

Forbes, Esther. *Johnny Tremain.* Houghton Mifflin, 1943.

Fox, Paula. *Blowfish Live in the Sea.* Bradbury, 1975.

Frank, Anne. *Anne Frank: The Diary of a Young Girl.* Doubleday, 1952.

George, Jean. *Julie of the Wolves.* Harper & Row, 1972.

Go Ask Alice. Prentice-Hall, 1971.

Golding, William. *Lord of the Flies.* Coward, McCann & Geoghegan, 1955.

Guy, Rosa. *The Friends.* Holt, Rinehart & Winston, 1973.

Haley, Alex. *Roots.* Doubleday, 1976.

Hamilton, Virginia. *M. C. Higgins the Great.* Macmillan, 1974.

Havrevold, Finn. *Undertow.* Atheneum, 1968.

Hinton, S. E. *The Outsiders.* Viking, 1967.

———. *Rumble Fish.* Delacorte, 1975.

Hunt, Irene. *Across Five Aprils.* Grosset & Dunlap, 1965.

Hunter, Mollie. *A Sound of Chariots.* Harper & Row, 1972.

Jordan, June. *His Own Where.* Thomas Y. Crowell, 1971.

Kerr, M. E. *Love Is a Missing Person.* Harper & Row, 1975.

Lee, Mildred. *The Skating Rink.* Seabury, 1969.

Lipsyte, Robert. *The Contender.* Harper & Row, 1967.

Lueders, Ed and Primus St. John, eds. *Zero Makes Me Hungry: A Collection of Poems for Today.* Scott, Foresman, 1976.

Lund, Doris. *Eric.* J. B. Lippincott, 1974.

Lyle, Katie L. *The Golden Shores of Heaven.* J. B. Lippincott, 1976.

Maddock, Reginald. *The Pit.* Little, Brown, 1968.

Mathis, Sharon Bell. *Teacup Full of Roses.* Viking, 1972.

Maxwell, Edith. *Just Dial a Number.* Dodd, Mead, 1971.

Meltzer, Milton. *Never to Forget: The Jews of the Holocaust.* Harper & Row, 1976.

Mitchell, Margaret. *Gone with the Wind.* Macmillan, 1936.

Neufeld, John. *Lisa, Bright and Dark.* S. G. Phillips, 1969.

O'Brien, Robert C. *Z for Zachariah.* Atheneum, 1975.

Peck, Robert Newton. *A Day No Pigs Would Die.* Alfred A. Knopf, 1973.

Perl, Lila. *Me and Fat Glenda.* Seabury, 1972.

Pfeffer, Susan B. *The Beauty Queen.* Doubleday, 1974.

Rawls, Wilson. *Where the Red Fern Grows.* Doubleday, 1961.

Reiss, Johanna. *The Upstairs Room.* Thomas Y. Crowell, 1972.

Salinger, J. D. *The Catcher in the Rye.* Little, Brown, 1951.

Scoppettone, Sandra. *Trying Hard to Hear You.* Harper & Row, 1974.

Sleator, William. *House of Stairs.* E. P. Dutton, 1974.

Southall, Ivan. *Ash Road.* Greenwillow, 1978.

Stallworth, Anne Nall. *This Time Next Year.* Vanguard, 1971.

Stephens, Mary Jo. *Witch of the Cumberlands.* Houghton Mifflin, 1974.

Sutcliff, Rosemary. *Warrior Scarlet.* Henry Z. Walck, 1966.

Tung, S. T. *One Small Dog.* Dodd, Mead, 1975.

Wells, Rosemary. *The Fog Comes on Little Pig Feet.* Dial, 1972.

West, Jessamyn. *The Massacre at Fall Creek.* Harcourt Brace Jovanovich, 1975.

Wilkinson, Brenda. *Ludell and Willie.* Harper & Row, 1977.

Yep, Lawrence. *Dragonwings.* Harper & Row, 1975.

Young, Jean. *Woodstock Craftsman's Manual.* Praeger, 1972.

Zindel, Paul. *The Pigman.* Harper & Row, 1968.

13

Issues and Concerns for Adults

When there is a controversy over books or materials, the young adult librarian is right in the middle of it. There is an argument about the relative values of books and criticism. A question arises as to how to go about building a good collection of ethnically related books. There are problems in budgeting for and shelving audio-visual materials. Troubles develop from trying to touch every viewpoint in books that treat human sexuality. Or the class reading list provokes controversy among parents. Other issues will appear because of particular local conditions or changes in society.

Both teachers and librarians need to be alert to such matters and to be sensitive to the necessity of understanding many viewpoints. They must also realize that as professionals, it is part of their job to investigate and to develop their own personal philosophies. Some of the issues mentioned in this chapter are long-term problems that will be solved only gradually, if at all. Others are not really problems; they are simply signs of healthy growth. Other problems, however, demand that each of us take a stand. In the library or classroom, our daily activities will be affected by the decisions that we make whether or not we are aware of the underlying issues. We can't fully discuss all the opinions that are held on the issues that are mentioned in this chapter, much less all the other issues that might be talked about. But we hope this chapter will be enough to convince you that you are entering a dynamic field where thinking for oneself is not only desirable, it's a necessity.

EVALUATION, YES! BUT ACCORDING TO WHOSE STANDARDS AND FOR WHAT PURPOSES?

For all of us working with books and young people, skilled evaluation is a primary function. It is not always the same kind of evaluation, nor should it be. People select books for different purposes and evaluate them according to different criteria, but we should understand the reasoning and the value system behind the choices that are made, whether these choices are our own or those of a critic or reviewer.

Evaluation criteria fall into three general categories: literary quality, reader interest or popularity, and social or political philosophy. However, these criteria overlap somewhat and their purposes interweave. Nearly everyone wants to be able to predict which books will be successful, but each person's definition of success may be quite different.

Traditionally, most critics have been expected to review books on the basis of literary merit. But those who work with young adult books are growing dissatisfied with the evaluations they are getting because of confusion over the reviewer's objectives. Are recommendations being made on the basis of potential popularity, life expectancy of the piece and literary quality, or what it teaches and the example it sets?

Traditionally, most critics have been expected to review books on the basis of literary merit.

These three are closely related, yet they are not one and the same. There are subtle differences and it is hard for reviewers to communicate these. A critic may review a book positively because of its literary quality, which a librarian or teacher interprets as a prediction of popularity. The book is purchased and put on the shelf where it is ignored by teenagers. The purchaser feels cheated and loses confidence in the reviewing source.

Or the opposite happens. A reviewer makes positive comments about the high interest level of something like *Go Ask Alice* or *Bonnie Jo Go Home*. When the teacher or librarian reads it, he or she is disappointed in a lack of literary quality and style. This results in the kind of frustration that Lillian L. Shapiro expresses in an article for *School Library Journal*. She decries using popularity as a major evaluation criteria. "Who's in charge?" she asks and then goes on to caution:

> If the measuring stick for the selection of materials for children and young
> adults is simply "what they want," let us remember that under those
> conditions there is no need for a trained cadre of reading advisers. Let us
> remember also that what we want at any age is not always healthful;
> sometimes it may save one's life to listen to those whose expertise—doctors,
> parents, teachers—could make a difference in the road taken.[1]

In making a plea for selection based on "discriminating judgment" and "sensitivity" she proposes that young adult librarians consider the books from university presses that relate to young people's interests:

These are not easy reading but are all the materials libraries offer supposed to be? Is it not the very "raison d'être" of our profession to call to the attention of our young patrons those titles they would never find themselves?

As a concluding point, she says:

> Response to popular demand then turns libraries into what one librarian calls a drugstore collection. I would think the drugstore and the library serve different purposes. If this is not so, then why have professional personnel in one and not the other?

A different opinion on this subject holds that it takes a great deal of skill and training to pick out potentially popular books, and that the person who can do this is as necessary—or perhaps in young adult service more necessary—as the person who can analyze the literary qualities of a book. No matter how good a book is, it won't become popular unless young adults are given a chance to read it. In most cases this means that it must be brought to the attention of library and school personnel so that it will be purchased and made available. The University of Iowa's Books for Young Adults program, which started in 1972 and is under the direction of G. Robert Carlsen, is based on the goal of predicting popularity. Carlsen's graduate students take review copies of new books to individualized reading classes in the Iowa City area and get three or four students to read each new book and serve as critics. Individualized conferences are held with the sample readers whose opinions are then used to draw up an annual listing of the books that have proven themselves to be the most popular. Since 1973 this list has been published at the end of each year in *The English Journal.*

The disagreement over whether literary quality or popularity should be the yardstick of selection is reflected in how this listing has changed over the years. It was initially entitled the "Books for Young Adults Honor Listing," but by 1975 the title had changed to the "BYA Book Poll" because the students' selections didn't always qualify according to adult literary standards of "honorable." The new title was chosen to lessen the chances for confusion and to make clear the purpose of the program. However, that year three of the books were cited as "Honor Books," meeting the "criteria of literary quality, adolescent interest, and significant themes": *If Beale Street Could Talk* by James Baldwin, *A Cry of Angels* by Jeff Fields, and *House of Stairs* by William Sleator. By 1977, there was no mention of "Honor." Instead three books, *Ordinary People* by Judith Guest, *The Seeker* by William Alan Bales, and *The Shepherd* by Frederick Forsythe, were "Recommended for Teaching." In 1978 no books were given special designation. When Carlsen was questioned about this, he said that the adult staff who is responsible for drawing up the final list did not feel they could personally endorse any of the students' choices as "great literature."

Another example of the growing awareness that popularity and literary quality may not be the same thing is the evaluation code shown in Table 4 devised by Mary K. Chelton and Dorothy M. Broderick for their publication *Voice of Youth Advocates.* Each review of a teen or adult title is preceded by a Q number indicating quality and a P number indicating popularity.

TABLE FOUR

Quality	Popularity
5Q: Hard to imagine it being better written.	5P: Every young adult was dying to read it yesterday.
4Q: Better than most, marred only by occasional lapses.	4P: Broad general young adult interest.
3Q: Readable without serious defects.	3P: Will appeal with pushing.
2Q: A little better editing or work by the author would have made it 3Q.	2P: For the young adult reader with a special interest in the subject.
1Q: Hard to understand how it got published.	1P: No young adult will read unless forced to for assignments.

The editors suggest that one use for such a clearly outlined code is to help librarians analyze their buying patterns. Those who lean heavily toward either quality or popularity will see their biases and be able to strike a more appropriate balance. Patty Campbell reports in the Winter 1979 issue of *Top of the News* that:

> Not so long ago the YA librarians of Los Angeles Public Library engaged in a modest brouhaha about the phrase "literary quality." It had come time to revise the form used to evaluate young adult books, and there was a contingent that felt that LQ should be added to CV (current value), Pop (popular), RV (replacement value), etc., as one of the criteria for analyzing a book's appeal to YAs. "Not so!" cried the others. Literary quality, they argued, was not only not in it, it was completely out of it, the kiss of death. As the majority, of course, they prevailed. When the children's librarians heard about it they were horrified.[2]

She goes on to explain that although the decision was something of an overreaction since what the librarians probably had in mind was a self-conscious posturing kind of "literary quality," the story does point up a basic difference between the reviewing of children's and young adult books. Children are essentially passive and uncritical observers of society who are engaged in soaking up the data about the world around them. It is the role of the librarian to provide them with the very best of that data. But teenagers have passed through this stage. They are in the process of sorting out the data, deciding which of it they are going to reject, and which they are going to adopt as their own. Campbell comments:

This process is maddening to adults, but absolutely necessary if young adults are not going to end up puddings on legs. Remember always that the basic YA question is "Who am I, and what am I going to do about it?" In the turmoil of adolescence, the young adult no longer has much patience for new factual data, for the classics, for anything that doesn't bear on the answer to The Question.

It is her opinion that reviewers of books for young adults must first ask the question, "Will the kids think it's good?" then, only after "discussing relevance and format, may the question of literary value be considered."

That her ideas are shared by others is shown in the fact that one of the tasks of the 1979 Young Adult Services Division of the American Librarian Association was to devise a new name for their annual "Best Books for Young Adults" list. The majority of the committee members felt that the title was misleading since the list was not made up of the books with the highest literary quality.

A quite different set of criteria from either popularity or literary quality is that of social or political values, as exemplified in the publications of the Council on Interracial Books for Children whose goal is for books for young readers to "become a tool for the conscious promotion of human values that lead to greater human liberation."[3] To achieve this goal they have set up various sets of guidelines designed to evaluate books on whether or not they perpetuate or counterbalance old stereotypes either through omission or commission. Their checklist includes the following categories: racism, sexism, elitism, materialism, individualism, ageism, conformism, escapism, positive vs. negative images of females and minorities, cultural authenticity, and the level of inspiration toward positive action. At the bottom of the list comes literary quality and art quality.

Nat Hentoff said that when Ursula Nordstrom invited him to try his hand at writing a juvenile novel in the early 1960s, the thing that enticed him about it was her promise of complete freedom to write whatever he imagined. He commented that if she had handed him the CIBC checklist, he would have been appalled. Either he would not have written the story (which turned out to be the popular *Jazz Country*) or he would have ignored "these externally dictated 'standards' entirely because any writer who follows anyone else's guidelines ought to be in advertising."[4]

Other writers have expressed similar reactions to the CIBC guidelines. Judy Blume was criticized by the council in an article entitled, "Old Values Surface in Blume Country."[5] The author of the unsigned article took Blume to task for not having female characters who were actively involved in feminism, for picturing Tony's social-climbing family in *Then Again, Maybe I Won't* as Italian, and for having the mother get custody of the children in *It's Not the End of the World*. Audrey Eaglan, editor of *Top of the News*, interviewed Blume about her reactions to the accusations. Blume says that the article made her angry:

because they are giving outlines for what *they* want from *me*. They're telling me what I should have done and what I should do in the future. And books that are written to order are just not good. Fiction is about people, and when I am writing about people, if I have to think "Am I being sexist, am I being racist, am I dealing with this subject and that subject *properly*?" then *any* books I write will be terrible books. . . . When you write, you *can't* stop and think about all the possible sins you might be committing; what comes out comes out, and it has to be natural or it will be false.[6]

What Blume says about the freedom that writers must have is true, but nevertheless there are some reasonable bases for concern. The use of literary symbols—their figurative versus their literal interpretation—shows how complicated this can get. People are caused genuine distress by literary symbols that seem to refer to certain groups. Colors have symbolic meanings: white stands for goodness and innocence, but black stands for evil and wickedness. The symbolism may have grown out of primitive people's preference for the safety of daylight as compared to the danger of the night. Nevertheless, it is such an all-encompassing metaphor that people with dark skin are offended by such terms as "blacklist," "the black sheep of the family," and, for a dark cake, "devil's food cake." To combat the uses of black as a negative symbol, the slogan "Black is beautiful" was created.

A similar kind of symbolism is the use of male and female qualities to stand for such concepts as strength and weakness. But symbols are neither true nor false, they are operative or inoperative. That is, they either work or they don't work in making the receiver think of what the sender intended. The reason that literature is so full of symbols is that writers have to verbalize things that really happen deep within the subconscious. Making the transition from childhood to adulthood is one of those "inside" things that in literature is often shown through symbols. Jean McClure Kelty stirred up a controversy over symbols when she wrote "The Cult of Kill in Adolescent Fiction." She criticized Marjorie Kinnan Rawlings' *The Yearling,* Fred Gipson's *Old Yeller,* James Street's *Good-bye, My Lady,* Robert Newton Peck's *A Day No Pigs Would Die,* Paul Annixter's *Windigo* and *Swiftwater,* Ester Wier's *The Loner,* Armstrong Sperry's *Call It Courage,* Christopher Webb's *Quest of the Otter,* Maia Wojciechowska's *Shadow of a Bull,* Bryce Walton's *Harpoon Gunner,* and even Herman Melville's *Moby Dick* and Ernest Hemingway's *The Old Man and the Sea* for "the stereotype initiation of the male character who persistently becomes a man when he performs an act of violence against an animal and/or the natural world." In contrast she praised Hal Borland's *When the Legends Die* because the young Indian protagonist becomes a man, not when he rides the horses to death in the rodeo, but when he faces the giant bear and decides against shooting it because he realizes, "This bear did not make trouble. The trouble is in me."

Two different viewpoints are expressed in the quotes that follow. The disagreement between the two critics centers around the question of whether or not symbols directly communicate information about their sources as well as about their new referents:

I would contend that the books which condition boys to the cult of violence and killing as their initiation into the adult world are untrue to the very deepest meaning of the nature of life itself. It is up to us as teachers to make students aware of the fact—to show them that the true initiation is a recognition that violence and brutality and death, though sometimes necessary, are never praiseworthy, nor do they constitute a man's way. . . . So long as we condition young men to violence and killing as the initiation into manhood, so long as we teach them that the enemy is outside themselves, always there to be vanquished, so long as we continue to tell them that "that's the way it is to be a man"—we will go on fighting senseless wars in which everyone loses. Furthermore, we will continue to destroy what little is left of the natural world and to annihilate the myriad creatures with whom we share this fragile planet. It is absurd to preach ecology and reverence for life in the same breath with which we praise *The Yearling* and books like it. For these books are a contradiction of the very foundations of ecology. . . .[7]

Some recent critics of adolescent novels based on the archetypal pattern of initiation have questioned the propriety of presenting violence and inhumanity as identifying traits of manhood. This argument unfortunately ignores the rather long history of the use of myth and archetypes in literature. To dispense with this tradition would be to cut ourselves off from much of our religious and literary past. Furthermore, no serious piece of literature implies that an act of violence or inhumanity is what makes a boy a man. The acts of violence must be interpreted in the light of the changes they bring about in the boy's view of himself and his world. Typically, the initiating events in adolescent fiction introduce the protagonists to a particular pattern of loss that defines an adult's perception of the world. The killing of the pig in *A Day No Pigs Would Die* is not what makes Rob a man; it is rather his realization that being a man means "doing what's got to be done."[8]

Differences of opinion are natural. It is not possible or even desirable for all critics and reviewers to agree on the criteria they will use for evaluating books. But just as teachers and librarians explore their own reasoning, so must reviewers analyze their feelings and communicate the principles that underlie their personal reactions. With this kind of information and their own deductions about a writer's biases, people can interpret recommendations and make use of them in ways appropriate to their own needs.

WRITING ABOUT AND CRITIQUING YOUNG ADULT LITERATURE

The writing about and critiquing of young adult literature is not so much an issue as it is an area of concern. Three kinds of concerns will be discussed in this section. (1) What different types of writing meet specific needs, and how can they do it best? (2) Should reviews of young adult books be less promotional and more critical? (3) Is the current writing and scholarship in the field aimed too much at the uses of literature rather than at an analysis of the literature itself? Evaluation, which we have already discussed, underlies nearly all writing about books. Even when someone is simply making notes to serve as a reminder of the contents of a book, that person is making an evaluation and concluding that the book is one worth remembering.

It is important to understand that the kind of writing that is done will differ considerably depending on the purpose of the writer. The type of writing we will be doing most often is that of making note cards on our reading. College students in adolescent and children's literature classes sometimes look on this activity as little more than a teacher-imposed duty that they will be only too glad to leave behind once the class is finished. But in reality, making notes is probably going to be a lifelong activity for anyone who works professionally with books. Most librarians and teachers make note cards as a continuous record of the books about which they know. They use the cards to jog their memories when they compile book lists, when students ask for recommendations, and when they plan teaching units and promotional activities. A story is told about a library that caught fire. The librarian grabbed her card file, and only then did she run to warn the patrons.

The comments put on note cards vary according to the needs of the writer. Most people include the publisher and date, a short summary of the story, and perhaps an evaluative comment. It is usually wise to write down the characters' names and other details that make this book different from others. After this basic information, the writer might add a few comments suggesting future uses of the book. For example, if the book were Alice Childress' *A Hero Ain't Nothin' But a Sandwich*, a librarian who planned on introducing the book to patrons might make out the card in the form of a book talk and might also include information about the movie. An English teacher might note that it would be a good book for illustrating the literary principle of point of view. A reading teacher might note that it is short and easy reading, except that the use of black dialect could perhaps cause problems for less skilled readers. A youth worker might make a note about the potential of the book as a catalyst to get kids talking about what they think adults should do in situations like Benjie's, and whether or not the responsibility belongs to Benjie rather than to those around him. In a community where books are judged as appropriate for school study on the basis of their topic and such things as "perfect" grammar and happy endings, someone might note that it would be desirable to share the book with other professionals and adult friends of the library in order to develop community support for its use. Positive reviews and honors won might also be helpful information. The sample card on the next page was prepared by a student in an adolescent literature class who was planning to be an English teacher.

Annotations are similar to note cards but they are usually written for someone else to see rather than for the writer's own purpose. And since there are usually space limitations, most annotations are very short. They are not as easy to write as they might first appear. Four examples of annotations are given below. Notice how the second one includes a comment from a high-school student to show that the books on the list were chosen by young people themselves. On some of the lists, headings are used to communicate something about a number of books efficiently. Two annotations

```
A Hero Ain't Nothin' But a Sandwich by Alice Childress.
Coward, McCann & Geoghegan, 1973, Avon paperback.

    The best part of this drug-related book is that
it shows people really trying.  A family rallies
around thirteen-year-old Benjie.  The dad is just
living with the family, but he proves himself to be
a real father.  The story is told from several view-
points--one chapter at a time.  This makes it good
for showing that not all people who live in a ghetto
feel and act the same.  It's open-ended with the read-
er being left to wonder whether or not Benjie shows
up for drug counseling.  Realistic, black dialogue
adds to the authenticity.  I liked it.  Could be used
as a real-aloud introduction to a unit on drugs.
```

are from nationally published lists and two are from locally created and used lists. Bibliographical information was included on each annotation; to save space it has been deleted here.

Benjie, a thirteen-year-old in Harlem, cannot face the reality of his drug addiction nor the realization that someone cares for him.

"Best Books for Young Adults 1973," *Top of the News*, April 1974, p. 310.

Under the heading "Ethnic":
In fiction Childress depicts the tensions of ghetto life in *A Hero Ain't Nothin' But a Sandwich*. Benjie's mother, his stepfather, his friend Jimmy-Lee, his teachers, a local drug-pusher, and Benjie himself create a picture of individuals struggling against their environment. One senior remarked, "I like her style of giving each person part of the story to tell."

"Books for Young Adults 1974 Honor Listing," G. Robert Carlsen, Tony Manna, and Betty Lou Tucker, *English Journal*, January 1975, p. 113.

On a list of recommended books:
Plight of a 13-year-old drug addict related through vignettes of his thoughts and feelings and of those involved with him.

The Committee on Books for Young Adults, Cleveland Public Library, February 1974, mimeographed, unpaged.

On a list of recommended books:
Black, 13, and well on his way to being hooked on heroin, Benjie Johnson has lots of people who want to help him: his step-father, his mother, and his friends. JrH-Fiction

"Finding One's Identity: A Selected Booklist for Teenagers," compiled and annotated by young adult librarians of the Westchester Library System and the Ramapo-Catskill Library System in New York, and the Prince George's County Memorial Library System, Maryland, mimeographed, p. 12.

Another kind of writing about adolescent literature commonly done by librarians and teachers is the writing of reviews for local and national circulation newspapers, magazines, and journals. The practice of having books reviewed on a part-time and usually volunteer basis is more a part of the juvenile than the adult book world. Probably fewer than two dozen people in the United States are full-time reviewers of juvenile books, but hundreds of people do it on a part-time basis. One day you may be one of these reviewers.

A problem in the reviewing of juvenile books is that more books are published than there is room in the media for reviewing. When publishers send out their new books, the review editors glance through them and select the ones that they judge to be of the greatest potential interest to their readers. The company that sends books to the largest number of publications has the greatest chance of having them reviewed. And the authors who have already established names for themselves will probably have their books reviewed before newcomers will.

The fact that juvenile books are reviewed mostly by librarians and teachers working on a part-time basis is one of the reasons that the distribution of juvenile books is so different from that of adult books. Before an adult book is released, prepublication copies are distributed to the major reviewing sources, book clubs, and moviemakers. By the time the book actually arrives in bookstores, it is not unusual for excerpts to have been featured and for reviews to have appeared in national publications. It might also have been selected as a book-club offering and been sold to a movie maker and a paperback publisher.

Things do not work this fast with juvenile books. There are delays at each step. Quite often completed books, not prepublication galleys, are sent out to reviewing journals. Several weeks can pass before the editors decide whether or not to review a particular title, and if so, to whom it should be assigned. The reviewer is given between a month and six weeks in which to write the review, and it is fitted into the magazine as space permits. Sometimes it may appear within a month or two, but, in other cases, a much longer time elapses. If a reviewer takes the book to young adults and has them read and react to it, the whole process will be slowed down by many more months. The Books for Young Adults program at the University of Iowa is one of the few evaluation groups that attempts to do its work by using individualized reading classes in local high schools. Systematically incorporating feedback from young readers is something more reviewers probably should do, but the benefit has to be weighed against the time lost.

Because of these delays in the reviewing process, young adult books get off to a slower start than do adult books, but, once launched, they stay around longer. Teachers work them into classroom units, librarians promote them, and paperback book clubs keep selling them for years.

The fact that adolescent literature is a part of the massive business of public education undoubtedly contributes to its long life span. Children continue to grow older and to advance in their reading skill and taste so that every year there is a whole new set of students ready to read *A Separate Peace, The Catcher in the Rye,* and even *The Outsiders.* As a result, reviews, articles, and papers continue to treat particular titles years after their original publication date.

The field of juvenile reviewing is sometimes criticized for being too laudatory. When reviewers are writing for audiences who are not totally committed to the idea of buying books for children, the general public, for instance, a desire to "sell" literature may keep them from being as critical as they would be of adult books. Many editors feel that since they can bring only a limited number of books to the attention of their readers, it makes sense to write about the ones that they think are the best, so of course they are complimentary.

There are as many reviewing styles as there are journals and individual reviewers. But nearly all reviews contain complete bibliographical information including number of pages and price, the intended age level, a summary statement of the contents, and some hint of the quality of the book as evaluated by the reviewer.

The Winter 1979 issue of *Top of the News* had as its feature topic "Reviews, Reviewing, and the Review Media." Editor Audrey Eaglen solicited comments from people working in different roles with books and young readers. The question she asked them was, "What Makes a Good Review?" Author-illustrator Rosemary Wells said, "an *intelligent* review . . . is never obsequious, if it is favorable. It is never flip, if it is unfavorable. It *never* quotes from a front flap." School librarian, Katherine Heylman, wants reviewers to tell her of "any clever device or intriguing aspect of the book which could be used to pique the interest of a group and 'sell' the book." And she thinks reviewers should inform potential buyers "if there is a probable controversial issue in the book, be it strong language, explicit sex, violence, or whatever." She doesn't want to know this so she can avoid buying the book, but so that she can plan and prepare and thereby deal with a conflict should it arise.

Dorothy Broderick, an editor and educator, wants comments on the attractiveness of the cover illustration: "While we might feel that no one should judge a book by its cover," she says, "the truth is that everyone does." Author Walter Dean Myers wants every review to "contain a clear-cut commitment as to recommendation or nonrecommendation." He doesn't have the time to read every book published and he is hoping that some literate person will help him decide where he should invest his valuable reading hours.

Patty Campbell, a young adult librarian and review editor, wants to know first "if a book has magic for YAs." She wants "to be alerted to format faults: does the size and shape make it look like a baby book? . . . Is the word 'children' used anywhere on the dust jacket?" And if there is going to be a film or television tie-in, she wants to know who's starring in it and exactly when it's going to be released.

The reviewer must decide what information is most important for the particular book being reviewed and for the particular audience for which the review is being written. Writing reviews is a skill that improves with practice and effort. A good way to begin developing this skill is to study several reviews of the same book as they appear in different publications. Note the essentials that seem to be the same in each review and then compare the information that is different. See if you can explain the differences in light of the source's reading audience.

A fourth kind of writing about young adult books is made up of articles or papers that go into more depth than is possible in reviews. Since most reviewers of juvenile books have little hope of coming out with a "scoop" or of being the first one to pass judgment on a new book, they focus on deeper treatments or on tying several books together. Dorothy Matthews analyzed the writing about adolescent literature that appeared in professional journals between 1970 and 1975.[9] She categorized the writing into three types. First are those articles that focus on the subjective responses of readers to particular books, such as reader surveys, lists of popular titles, and reviews written from the point of view of how the book is likely to affect young readers. Articles of this kind are primarily descriptive.

The second type is also descriptive and consists of pedagogical articles giving teachers lists of books that fit together for teaching units, ideas for book promotion, and techniques for teaching reading, social studies, or English. They may include brief comments on the literary qualities of the novels, but, again, the writer's primary intention is to be informative.

The third kind of writing is that restricted to the books themselves. It is in this group that Matthews thinks hope lies for the development of a body of lasting scholarly knowledge that will be taken seriously by the academic community. These articles include discussions of adolescent literature as a genre, historical background of the field, relationships between authors and their work, patterns that appear in junior

---

The field as a whole will grow strong as a result of serious and competent criticism and analysis.

---

novels, and themes and underlying issues. More of this kind of literary analysis is being done as authors write books serious enough to support it. For example, in 1977, the English department at the University of Missouri accepted as a Ph.D. dissertation an in-depth analysis of a single adolescent novel: Kellie Corlew Jones' study of Madeleine L'Engle's *A Wrinkle in Time.* When we took a survey of adolescent literature courses in American colleges and universities, seven reported doctoral dissertations written during the 1970s dealing with adolescent literature. All were in English education or library science programs.

Another indication of a growing body of literary criticism dealing with books for young readers is the recent increase in the number of publishing markets for both pedagogical and literary articles about children's and adolescent literature; for example, *Children's Literature in Education: An International Quarterly, Phaedrus, Children's Literature, The ALAN Review,* and *The Lion and the Unicorn,* all developed in the 1970s and are promising to grow and add strength in the 1980s. They of course join other well-established journals.

In summary, writing about young adult books falls into four categories: notecards for personal use, annotations, reviews, and scholarly or pedagogical writing. Most of you will be involved in the first kind, that is, making notecards for your own use. But some of you will also be making annotations, writing reviews, and doing in-depth analyses. This latter kind of writing and critiquing can be especially intriguing because significant changes have occurred within recent years and relatively few scholars have worked with young adult literature. This means that there is ample opportunity for original and meaningful research and observation. The field as a whole will grow strong as a result of serious and competent criticism and analysis.

ETHNIC BOOKS: STRESSING DIFFERENCES OR COMMONALITIES?

Within the last decade many book lists have appeared with such titles as "The Black Experience," "The Mexican American," "Books About Asian Americans," "Women in American History," and "Books About Native Americans." These lists help teachers and librarians find supplementary materials and books about groups of people who may have been left out of history and social studies textbooks, anthologies of literature, and library collections. They are an intermediate step leading to a time when the stories of such groups are no longer excluded from these sources. There is a kind of racism and sexism inherent in having such lists and card catalogue entries such as "The Black Experience," or "American Indians," but they do prepare people for a fully integrated collection.

In the early 1960s, inspired by the civil rights movement, people began to look seriously at books for young readers. What they found was very disturbing. Rather than enriching and extending young readers' views of the world and the people around them, many of the books reinforced prejudices and relied heavily on negative stereotypes. This was more apparent in juvenile than in adult books because of two reasons. First, books for young people are often illustrated with either drawings or photographs, and, when nearly all of the people in the illustrations are white, it makes it more difficult for nonwhite readers to identify with the characters and to imagine that the books are about them and their friends. Second, juvenile books tend to be condensed. With less space in which to develop characters, authors are forced to develop background characters as efficiently as possible. One way to be efficient is to use stereotypes that people already recognize, for example, the stoic Indian, the happy black, the funny little woman, and so forth, down the line through many other demeaning and offensive stereotypes. When positive portrayals were made of blacks, Indians, Asians, and other minority group members, they were often historical or in a foreign setting. The characters were written about as "foreigners" not as Americans.

When the lopsidedness of all this was brought to the attention of authors, artists, publishers, and critics, considerable effort was expanded to make up for the inaccuracies and the unfairness. Part of the solution was simply to pay more attention to members of minority groups. In the cumulative list of the best books reviewed in the *Bulletin of the Center for Children's Books* between 1955 and 1965[10] there were twenty-five titles listed under the heading of "Negro," but in the next edition of the list, which covered only the seven years between 1966 and 1972,[11] there were seventy-six titles listed. Similar evidence can be noted through an examination of the winners of the Newbery Award. In all the years between 1922 and 1969, there were only two books—Elizabeth Yates' *Amos Fortune, Free Man* (1951) and Joseph Krumgold's . . . *And Now Miguel* (1954)—that featured nonwhite Americans, but in the 1970s four out of the ten winners were about black Americans: William Armstrong's *Sounder* (1970), Paula Fox's *The Slave Dancer* (1974), Virginia Hamilton's *M. C. Higgins The Great* (1975), and Mildred D. Taylor's *Roll of Thunder, Hear My Cry* (1977). As has already been mentioned, approximately forty percent of the young adult books on the Honor Sampling listed in Appendix A have main characters who are not white middle-class Americans.

But even with all of the efforts being made, there are still areas of disagreement and dissatisfaction about books featuring minorities. There are questions of authenticity, idealism versus realism, representative characteristics, and the degree to which differences should be stressed or minimized.

As a reaction against misinformation and writers who hurriedly seize on whatever ethnic interest seems to be selling at the moment, members of many ethnic groups have begun asking that only people in their group write about them. Although there are valid reasons for this, such a restriction might actually result in fewer books about minority groups. Fortunately not everyone feels this way. When people say that writers can only write about their own group, they are saying that it is impossible for us to understand one another. The developing relationships between and among groups makes for some of the most interesting stories. That is where the drama is.

If we analyze our reactions to what we read, we will see that there are many things that transcend ethnic or group identification. For example, Scott O'Dell's *Sing Down the Moon* is the story of the Navajo's forced march from Canyon de Chelly to Fort Sumner, New Mexico, in 1864. If sex or race is the most important thing in group identification, then Anglo readers should identify with Kit Carson and his "Long Knives," who are the soldiers driving the group on the tragic long walk. Students with Spanish surnames should identify with the Spanish slavers who steal Bright Morning and sell her as a slave. Male readers should identify with Bright Morning's young husband who gives up after the group arrives at its destination. But none of these things happen. Nearly everyone who reads the book identifies with Bright Morning, the young Navajo girl whose story is being told.

The negative light in which O'Dell places all the groups except the Navajos brings up another problem in ethnic literature. If each book is written strictly from the viewpoint of one group, then the tendency might be to build up that group at the expense of others. It is part of our literary heritage for there to be a "good guy" and a "bad guy." The result of being overly conscious of races or of other groups is that readers tend to classify the bad guys and the good guys according to their group rather than by their individual characteristics. To a large extent, this is what brings about stereotyping.

Sometimes when people think about groups other than their own, they expect everyone in the other group to be the same, to have the same attitudes and the same values. In John Patrick's play *The Teahouse of the August Moon,* one of the lines that gets a big laugh from the white middle-class American audience is about all Americans looking alike. The audience laughs because the tables are turned on an old joke, and they get a glimpse of how ridiculous it is to think of any group of individuals as carbon copies of one another.

Helping students to realize this and to apply it in their thoughts and their dealings with other people is not quite so simple. People may be grouped together on such bases as their sex, their age, their color, the origin of their last names, the neighborhood they live in, the language or dialect they speak, or the religion to which they subscribe. The problem with this kind of grouping is that not only can people be divided along many different lines, but there is constant shifting among people and the groups to which they belong. Sometimes authors, and in turn readers, falsely assume that people who belong to one group are like others in that group in every way. Naturally there are some relationships and carry-overs, but the correlation is far from perfect.

For example, Native Americans are often treated as one group, but when Europeans first landed on the American continent there were more than thirty distinct nations whose members spoke perhaps a thousand different languages. During the past 400 years these peoples have had certain common experiences—losing their lands, being forced to move to reservations, having to adapt their beliefs and life styles to a technological society. These experiences may have affected their attitudes in similar ways, but still it is a gross overgeneralization to write and to think about American Indians as though they were one people holding the same religious and cultural values. Perhaps

---

The "good guy" and "bad guy" are part of our literary heritage.

---

for the sake of efficiency, textbooks have to lump people together and talk about them according to the characteristics of the majority in the group. Good literature can counterbalance these generalizations and show the individual perspective. When students have read enough to go beyond the stereotypes with at least one group, then they will be more aware that the study of people as groups needs to be filled in with individual portrayals. Critics add to the enforced grouping of individuals when they use their own ethnicity as a basis for commenting on books—taking "the black point of view," "the Jewish point of view," "the Catholic point of view," and so forth. Again, they are generalizing if they assume that there is *one* black viewpoint or *one* Asian-American viewpoint.

At a recent National Council of Teachers of English convention, a panel made up of the library promotions directors of several paperback publishing houses reported that throughout the industry books about blacks were no longer selling nearly as well as they had a year or so earlier. One explanation for this was the shift in interest away from civil rights and into newer issues. After the convention, Al Muller added some other reasons for the decline that he had gathered from several adults who were in positions to use and recommend young adult novels. The extremely realistic depiction of ghetto existence in which "violence is common; sex is blatant . . . , language is characterized by the use of obscenities; and drug abuse is a way of life"[12] have caused school and library personnel to be more cautious with such books. But according to Muller, there is a larger problem than that of censorship—fears of racial unrest. He writes:

> The truth is that the depiction of the sordid and violent ghetto existence can enrage us regardless of race or political/social persuasion. For example, such a book as *Listen for the Fig Tree* can fuel a black adolescent's anger at the ghetto's existence, and the bigot can find in it "proof" for his attitudes.

Another reason for declining sales is that of stereotyping. Muller thinks that black novels today are stereotyped negatively to the same degree that young adult novels in general used to be stereotyped positively:

> The majority of black Americans are not pushers, pimps, or prostitutes. Not all black Americans are aspiring musicians, athletes, or welfare recipients. Not all black Americans live in ghettos. But, to a large extent, a composite of the above statements is the new "black image" presented (constructed?) by the popular media and, to an extent, adopted by the Y. A. novel.

Muller concludes that, "Perhaps our booklists, class-sets of novels, and library shelves are overstocked with novels about characters trying to survive in the ghetto or escape from the ghetto."

As an extension of the kind of stereotyping that Muller was writing about, many librarians and teachers color code books to match their own school population, buying many books about blacks if the school has black students but none if it doesn't. Professional adults also have a tendency to recommend books to young readers based on their sex or their ethnic group. But the ties that develop between characters, authors, and readers are the important things in reading. They sometimes are based on physical characteristics, but most often they are not. It is therefore inappropriate for professionals to match books with students on the basis of their sex, race, personal appearance, or some disability. Students are easily offended. Someone from a minority family that has struggled to rise may be either crushed or resentful if given a book about a ghetto family with the implication that "it's about people just like you and your family." Adults have no right to make such decisions for young readers. They do have an obligation to offer opportunities for readers to discover for themselves the similarities and differences between their lives and the lives they are reading about.

This means that a wide range of books about all ethnic groups needs to be available to all students. As writers dig deeper into cultural and ethnic backgrounds, they are producing some very good historical fiction exploring previously forgotten backgrounds. Lawrence Yep's *Dragonwings* is about Chinese immigrants in California during the early 1900s and Ann Nolan Clark's *Year Walk* tells about Basque sheepherders in Idaho, also during the early 1900s. In books like this, the difference in life-style between the characters and modern teenage readers is extreme. But while reading the books, students may find that deep down there is a great deal that they have in common. On the other hand, they may share very little with other characters even though they belong to the same cultural background. Either way, though, readers will develop a feeling of respect for the contributions of a particular group and they will have broadened their horizons at least a bit. They will also have come closer to the realization that every person is an individual.

Today, because of the tremendous variety of books available, this is an easier lesson to learn than it used to be. The best new books with ethnic group settings concentrate first on the individuals and then on their backgrounds. The setting is a part of the story, but it is not the whole story. There has been a swing away from the heavy-handed efforts that were made in the beginning years of consciousness-raising about minorities. In the early 1970s a writer could often be guaranteed library sales simply by featuring someone from a group about which there was a shortage of reading material. Today that is not enough. There are so many books about different ethnic groups that readers can pick and choose. The poorly written books are falling by the wayside because readers are demanding more sophistication and a better integration of ethnic stories with literary merit. But just because there are many ethnically related books does not mean that they no longer need to be written. There is always room for well-written stories about people who are interesting and this includes people from every group. Good literature is one of the few places left in modern life where the uniqueness of the individual is celebrated while at the same time the common threads that bind all people together are revealed.

YOUNG ADULT LITERATURE AND THE POPULAR MEDIA

In its finest moments, the modern mass media has brought to millions of people the best of our plays, poems, stories, and novels. Even at its worst, it has at least introduced people to literary traditions and certain symbols, and it has raised their expectations. But there are other far-reaching effects of the mass media that will probably never be completely measured or understood.

Television

Research is cloudy on most issues surrounding television, but certain problem areas have been identified and people have begun to investigate them. Here are some of the concerns that people feel in relation to television and the young adult reader:

1. Does television discourage reading by taking up too much of the time of young adults?
2. How is one's mental picture of life affected by the thousands of hours of viewing that most eighteen-year-olds have experienced?
3. Is television particularly damaging in the stereotypes that it presents, especially of women and minorities, and of male-female relationships?

4. If certain kinds of language and acts are commonplace on television, don't books have to offer similar sensationalism?

5. Does watching television promote passivity and laziness when it comes to reading?

We do not have answers to these questions, but we do think that they are worth asking. Television is a powerful tool of socialization and we know that people learn from models. Undoubtedly tastes and expectations are shaped by what is shown on television, and to a lesser extent in the other media. Serious research needs to be undertaken to answer these questions and to find solutions to the problems that are uncovered. Relationships between young adult books and other mass media need to be examined as well.

Movies

People love to discuss whether a book is better than the movie on which it is based. Judging the success of either presentation needs to be done within each genre's confines and traditions.

The typical pattern is for a book to be adapted into a play, a musical, a movie, or something for television as, for example, Judy Blume's *Forever* was adapted into a television special and Glendon Swarthout's *Bless the Beasts and Children* was adapted into a full-length movie. An adaptation has basically the same characters, plot, tone, and many of the words of the original piece. However, the printed story doesn't always come first. For example, Norma Klein's book *Sunshine* began as a tape-recorded diary made by a young mother dying of cancer as a legacy for her daughter. The diary was adapted for television where it appeared as a movie. Norma Klein used the television movie as a basis for a book, which she labelled "fiction." A brief television series also grew out of the story as did a full-length movie and a second book by Klein. At the point that Klein felt it appropriate to label her book "fiction," it probably became more appropriate to use the wording "inspired by" or "based on" rather than "adapted from."

Financial considerations have a greater influence on the production of television shows and movies than they do on books. A writer can create a story to appeal to a relatively small group of readers with particular interests and tastes, but a mass media piece must appeal to large numbers of people—the more, the better. That is why there are many more choices available in books than there are in visual entertainment. Because producing a movie is such a large task, it has to be done by a team of people rather than by one individual. Glendon Swarthout in talking about the movie version of his *Bless the Beasts and Children* spoke resignedly about the great part that luck plays in putting a film together. Writing the book was an individual artistic endeavor that he controlled with his own intellect, but once it got to the movie studios, literally hundreds of creative people had an input.

The topical nature of many young adult books makes them fairly short-lived, at least in comparison to children's books. But it is interesting that of the books that are approximately a decade old and still popular, a surprisingly large number were made into movies, for example, for television, *Mr. and Mrs. Bo Jo Jones, The Autobiography of Miss Jane Pittman,* and *Go Ask Alice,* and the full-length feature films *Red Sky at Morning, The Andromeda Strain, Sounder, Where the Lilies Bloom,* and *Bless the Beasts and Children.* It appears that a well-publicized mass media piece serves to keep a book before the public. Librarians report that every time *Go Ask Alice* or *Brian's Song* is shown, for example, there are many requests for the paperback book.

Brian's Song is an example of how intertwined different media presentations can be. It is the story of Brian Piccolo, a Chicago Bears football player who died of cancer. His teammate Gale Sayers included a chapter about Piccolo in his book *I Am Third.* This chapter inspired the making of a television drama, *Brian's Song,* which won five Emmy awards. It was such a well-liked production that the script was adapted into a Bantam paperback that has gone through many printings.

Paperback Books

It takes an unusual set of circumstances, such as that just discussed, for a paperback original to achieve success. Although nearly all teenagers would prefer to read paperbacks, the structure and traditions of the publishing world combined with school and library buying patterns makes it almost a necessity that to achieve respectability a book has to first come out as a hardback. Usually a book's future is determined in the first few months of its life as a hardback. It is during this time that it is reviewed in the media and considered for such best book lists as those drawn up by the Young Adult Services Division of the A.L.A., *School Library Journal,* and *The New York Times.* Paperbacks are not reviewed by these groups unless they are the oversize trade kind marketed through bookstores rather than through magazine outlets.

Paperback publishing companies often take advantage of the interest sparked by television and movies by publishing tie-in books. Of course it isn't necessary to have the official media tie-ins to take advantage of the enthusiasm generated by a mass media showing. The important thing is to find out about a presentation in time to have multiple copies on hand while interest is at its peak. There are several ways to keep up with this kind of news. Announcements of forthcoming television specials and movies are frequently made in newsletters and journals aimed at teachers and librarians. Book sellers who specialize in the school market provide newsletters and catalogues listing the tie-ins.[13] Teachers and librarians can ask to be put on a mailing list for promotional information from major paperback publishers.

Media Made for the Classroom

Although budgets are much smaller when media is being prepared specifically for schools, there are carry-overs from popular into school media. Sixteen millimeter films, sound recordings, filmstrips, and promotional posters are the items most commonly used in schools. The best of the recordings, such as those done by Caedmon (many of which feature the author as the reader), are also offered for sale outside of school markets, and some of the films are shortened versions of movies originally prepared for television.

It is not as easy to make filmstrips of young adult books as it is of children's books. Young adult literature uses words, not pictures. One solution is to make filmstrips from the frames of movies. Another possibility is for artists to paint pictures, but many stories don't have enough action to support the sixty or seventy illustrations needed for a filmstrip. A third kind of filmstrip is made from a combination of book illustrations and photographs relating the book or books to the author. It is a combination feature article on the author and television interview.

The length of visual presentations may be a problem because of expenses and because they must not be too long to be enjoyed in a single sitting. One philosophy is that it is better to present an uncut excerpt in the hope that the listener or viewer will be motivated to read the whole story. Another opinion is that it is better to present the whole story in shortened form so that seeing the filmstrip substitutes for reading the book. Some pieces of this kind have been so simplified that the heart of the story gets lost. Many teachers and librarians are appalled at what seems like misrepresentation, but others argue that a great service is being performed, especially for reluctant readers who are introduced in a pleasurable way to the books about which their friends are talking. They get at least some of the value of the piece, and many of them are motivated to begin reading once they get a taste of current young adult literature.

Teaching About Books and Media

The advent of mass media is proving to be a mixed blessing but there is much that teachers can do to make it more of a plus than a minus. Many of the paperback publishing houses expend considerable money and energy to help teachers succeed in the classroom. Dell is especially good at providing teaching guides for several of their most popular paperbacks, and others are following suit, in particular, Viking Penguin and Avon.[14]

In the classroom students can compare the techniques that authors and screenwriters use to establish such things as character, setting, and tone. The movie maker goes about establishing setting in an entirely different way from the storyteller. What makes it easier? What harder? The movie maker has an advantage over the writer when it comes to portraying action, but the writer has an advantage when it comes to revealing a character's inner thoughts. The storyteller writing from the omniscient viewpoint can simply tell what a character is thinking, but the screenwriter has to figure out some believable stage business to reveal the character's thoughts.

An especially important difference between characterization in a fully developed novel and in a shortened drama is that in the latter there is little or no room to show the relationship between the character's personality and the developments in the plot. Media critics have expressed concern over a generation that thinks people have no control over their destiny. Things seem to happen *to* the characters, but not in any way *because of* their actions, attitudes, or beliefs. Searching out cause and effect relationships can be a revealing exercise from both a literary and a personal development viewpoint.

For a discussion about the changes made in a book's plot, a class project may help students gain empathy for the group process which a film must undergo. Divide the class into task forces of three or four students. Each group draws up a proposal "to sell" a book that the class has just finished reading to a movie producer. Their proposal should include why they think it would be a good movie, what approach should be taken, an outline of the major events and characters, and suggestions for where it should be filmed and who should play the parts. A report from each group shared with the class will reveal some of the difficulties of getting total agreement on something as subjective as artistic creation.

SEX: BECAUSE IT'S THERE

The treatment of sex in young adult literature is an especially sensitive and controversial issue. There are several reasons for this:

1. Young adults are physically mature, but they probably have had little intellectual and emotional preparation for making sex-related decisions.
2. Parents are anxious to protect their children from making sex-related decisions that might prove harmful.
3. Old restraints and patterns of behavior and attitudes are being questioned so that there is no one clear-cut model to follow.
4. Sex is such an important part of American culture and the mass media that young people are forced to think about and take stands on such controversial issues as homosexuality, premarital sex, violence in relation to sex, and the role of sex in love and family relationships.

Many people would prefer to see young adult books ignore sex-related concerns. If it doesn't appear in a book, then there's no need to be concerned with it. Norma Klein points out how common this attitude is:

Some of the things we are writing about today are being written about in children's books for the first time. Therefore I think we sometimes make the mistake of thinking these things didn't happen before. In fact, for decades, even centuries, people have been getting divorced, men and women have been realizing that heterosexuality may not be suitable for them, little children and babies have been lying in their cribs exploring their bodies, girls have been getting their periods, boys have been having wet dreams. All these activities, and the thoughts and fears that accompany them, are not recent developments. They are part of the human condition.[15]

By ignoring something so basic, Klein feels that we end up stressing it and she has openly campaigned for more treatment of sexual matters in books for all ages of young readers. But among writers, critics, teachers, and librarians there are tremendous disagreements over what kinds of sexual matters should be treated, what the tone and attitudes should be, and whether factual or fictional treatments are best.

The opposing opinions given here, the first by Lillian L. Shapiro and the second by Jack Forman, are representative of the kind of disagreement that respected professionals engage in:

> Another phenomenon of our times is what Leona Nevier of Fawcett Books . . . calls the glut on the market of "lust in the dust" books. . . .
>
> The YA market is experiencing the same glut of books that find mayhem funny, as in Zindel's *Confessions of a Teenage Baboon* (Harper), and disgusting practices normal, as in Bredes' *Hard Feelings.* That it need not be so in order to be worthy of the young adult's attention is demonstrated by the difference between the televised version of Judy Blume's *Forever* and the book itself. This time the TV program was far better than the book. The production was tender, honest, tasteful, and beautifully done. The book, on the other hand, could have been entitled "I Was a Teenaged Lady Chatterley."[16]

> [Ms. Shapiro's] impreciseness leads not only to incomplete explanations, but also to literary and moral judgments that are not justified by the facts and reasoning presented. Ms. Shapiro disapproved of Paul Zindel's *Confessions of a Teenage Baboon* because the book "finds mayhem funny." Many readers will undoubtedly take issue with this unusual description of Zindel's latest novel. But even if one accepts this description, what basis is this for selecting or rejecting the story for young adult readership?
>
> Finally, Ms. Shapiro labels Judy Blume's *Forever* "I Was a Teenage Lady Chatterley," leading one to wonder whether she is trying to equate the seriousness, passion, and power of the Lawrence masterpiece to the humorous and relatively innocent experiences of two teenagers experiencing first sexual love in *Forever.* (Ms. Shapiro also believes that the TV film of *Forever* was better than the book—"tender, honest, tasteful, and beautifully done." My view is that the TV adaptation sugarcoated the teenage love affair, rendering it humorless and making it appear at the end that the two protagonists might eventually get together again, thereby negating a major value of the book: that teen love affairs are part of growing up and do not have to have lifelong consequences.)[17]

Shapiro concludes her article, "If Blume, Klein, and Zindel disappoint, there are still the Mazers, Holland, Bill and Vera Cleaver, and Cormier to set higher standards." The writers whom Shapiro does not like deal more explicitly with sex than do the writers of whom she approves. It is probably more than a coincidence that Shapiro is female and Forman is male. Mary K. Chelton in a *Voice of Youth Advocates* editorial suggests an interesting theory. She writes that, "While there have been many discussions in library literature about the problems of a feminized profession in terms of salary, status, and self-concept, there has been no discussion of the service 'blinders' imposed by this reality, especially in connection with male adolescent users."[18] In her editorial she states, "Adult women have been protected from the developmental realities of male adolescence by a combination of socialization, censorship, and ultimately, by the experience of different genital construction."

It is true that males and females have basically different attitudes towards sex, and it is also true that school and library materials and practices encourage this difference in attitude. In no other area, except perhaps athletics, is there such purposeful separation between boys and girls. Starting in the fourth grade, girls are taken off to see their first movie on menstruation and boys are left in the room to be given a talk by the coach. The ironic thing about this separation is that, in most cases, sex is something participated in by males and females together. But when children are given different instructions and exposed to different attitudes, then naturally there are communication problems that result.

In Chelton's editorial she observes that when this different socialization is combined with the fact that women's physical bodies are also different, the result is a bias against books that present honest portrayals of adolescent male sexuality. If a young man were able to smoothly integrate all of his physical, that is, sexual, feelings into satisfactory and socially approved personal relationships, then he would no longer be an adolescent. Chelton writes that, to males, achieving sexual maturity, "comes down to an overwhelming concern with performance—can I do it; how do I do it; how do I find somebody to do it with; what if she doesn't want to do it; what does "doing it" mean to me. . . ." Women look at sex quite differently. From their earliest years they have been taught that sex is not an act in and of itself. Rather it is the same as, or a part of, a loving relationship. This is why the emphasis that an author gives to the emotional or "spiritual" side of love as opposed to the purely physical side is proportional to the degree of acceptance that a book will receive in most libraries.

Chelton found it "interesting that most librarians who damn *Hard Feelings* and *The Terrible Love Life of Dudley Cornflower* adore *Very Far Away from Anywhere Else* for its espousal of abstinence within a meaningful relationship." Chelton thinks that librarians' concern for literary merit rises with the anxiety they feel over content. She says that librarians feel uncomfortable putting an "institutional seal of approval" on sexual depictions outside their personal experience. But she argues that this is a "restricted, adult, feminized, sanitized, elitist value system," and that "by damning fictional depictions of male adolescent sexuality, we also reinforce the stereotype that the penis is pornographic. Worst of all, though, we offer no way in which *vicarious* male sexual experimentation is presented to both sexes in the library setting, which leaves them to *actual* experimentation elsewhere."

It is interesting to ponder whether library collections would be very different if there were more male librarians. The sex-related materials that adolescent girls read come from libraries, but what adolescent boys read comes from the convenience food mart, the drugstore, or the porno shop. Related questions to think about are the following: Why do boys and girls read different sex-related materials when sex is something that is participated in by males and females together? Should libraries provide both types of material? Only one type? Or neither? Where does the school fit into the whole area of sex education? What are the purposes of reading sex-related material?

For many people, homosexuality is one of the subjects they have placed outside their circle of interest and acceptability. But in recent years the demands made by gay rights groups and the attendant publicity has forced many people to expand their circle to include at least an acknowledgment of homosexuality. A generation or so ago it was quite possible for sheltered individuals to grow up with little or no knowledge of homosexuality, but this isn't likely to happen today. However, it is still probable that many people have only the vaguest knowledge of homosexual practices and life-styles. For this reason, books treating the subject, especially for young readers, quickly come to the public's attention.

This whole area presents a difficult problem, made more so by the fact that there are not many books about homosexuality. Even if there were, students would shy away from reading many of them. Peer pressure is strong and young people seem to have an underlying fear that homosexuality is contagious. This means that each book that is read takes on a disproportionate level of importance. Even the nonfiction books which are supposed to present information in an objective manner are seldom free of bias. John Cunningham has criticized, for example, Morton Hunt's *Gay: What You Should Know About Homosexuality* because of its point of view. Cunningham points out that although it is common for sex education books to have a conversational style using the second person pronoun "you," in this book Hunt consistently uses the third person pronoun "them," which communicates that he does not intend "to put the gay reader at ease or to suggest that the book might be directed to gays."[19] Cunningham further criticizes Hunt's book because its tone is so different from his books about heterosexuality. Cunningham writes:

> Hunt clearly deplores what he terms "queer gays"—those that are obvious and refuse to blend into the heterosexual landscape. Anything from a flick of the wrist to a bitchy mood might be enough to qualify for this group. Flaming faggots, nellie queens, bull dikes, drags, leather numbers, hustlers and Saturday night cruisers all qualify. According to Hunt, "straight gays" find these people very objectionable; his implicit message is that the reader should also.

With fiction that treats sexuality it is important for adults to help young readers realize that only one person's story is being told. Sometimes these stories may be quite atypical, but young readers have very little real-life experience to use for background comparisons. It's not that we want everything to be as typical as possible. Surely that would be a deadly approach, but there is an obligation for adults who are providing books for young readers to provide a variety and to encourage the reading of accurate and well-balanced informative nonfiction. Again, the reader's purpose must be considered. If it is basic information that the reader wants, then nonfiction is far superior because it can present a wider range of information in a clear and unambiguous way. But if it is an understanding of the emotional and physical aspects of one particular relationship, then an honest piece of fiction does a better job. The important thing for adults to remember is that they should provide both kinds in conjunction with a listening ear and a willingness to discuss questions.

Because the area of sex is such a sensitive and personal one, this is probably the one area most in need of open discussion and exchanges of ideas. Schools and libraries need to seek community input in developing policies. Family values must be respected, but honest and accurate information must also be available for those who are seeking it. Charting a course along this delicate line is more than any one individual should be expected to do. People need to get together and work out the philosophy and policy that best fits their particular situation. But this cannot be done in ignorance. The general public may get away with objecting to or endorsing ideas and books that they have never really explored or read, but a professional working with books is obligated to find and study the latest, most authentic information and to bring that information to those who are helping to shape policies and practices. It is important to realize that such policies and practices will differ from group to group and from person to person. The more you understand about such differences the better able you will be to participate in book selection, discussion, and, sometimes, defense.

CENSORSHIP: IT'S HAPPENING ALL THE TIME

Some English teachers and librarians apparently believe that the censorship of young adult reading began only a few years back. As one teacher who had just been stung by a censor said, "It's all the fault of that damned *Catcher in the Rye.*" But it didn't begin with Salinger. It goes back much further.

Mark Twain's encounters with late nineteenth-century censors were described in Chapter 3, but he was hardly the only major writer to be attacked. *Huckleberry Finn* was criticized by a member of the Concord (Massachusetts) Public Library, so the *Boston Transcript* reported March 13, 1885, for being "coarse . . . trash . . . rough . . . inelegant . . . not elevating . . . more suited to the slums than to intelligent respectable people," and Stephen Crane's *The Red Badge of Courage* was attacked for lacking integrity and being inaccurate. At the sixth session of the American Library Association, meeting in 1896, a discussion of *The Red Badge of Courage* and whether it should be included in a list of A.L.A. recommended books brought forth comments that revealed more about the commentors than about the book:

> Mr. Larned: "What of Crane's *Red Badge of Courage?*"
>
> A. L. Peck: "It abounds in profanity. I never could see why it should be given into the hands of a boy." . . .
>
> G. M. Jones: "This *Red Badge of Courage* is a very good illustration of the weakness of the criticism in most of our literary papers. The critics in our literary papers are praising this book as being a true picture of war. The fact is, I imagine, that the criticisms are written by young men who know nothing about war, just as Mr. Crane himself knows nothing about war. Gen. McClurg, of Chicago, and Col. Nourse, of Massachusetts, both say that the story is not true to the life of the soldier. An article in the *Independent,* or perhaps the *Outlook,* says that no such profanity as given in the book was common in the army among the soldiers. Mr. Crane has since published two other books on New York life which are simply vulgar books. I consider the *Red Badge of Courage* a vulgar book, and nothing but vulgar."[20]

Censorship has changed little in quality over the years, but the number and intensity of attacks on English teachers and librarians has steadily risen. From 1972 through 1979, more episodes of censorship or attempted censorship were reported than in any comparable earlier period, and nationally reported attacks occurred in places as dissimilar as Randolph, New York; Anchorage, Alaska; Oakland, California; Warsaw, Indiana; Chelsea, Massachusetts; Island Trees, New York; and Kanawha County, West Virginia.[21] None of these were minor incidents, certainly not to teachers, librarians, administrators, parents, or—most important and sometimes forgotten—students. Too often, misunderstandings arose, tempers flared, values clashed, and demands and counterdemands sounded forth. In West Virginia bombs went off and a minister prayed publicly from his pulpit for the death of school board members who wanted to retain books the clergyman thought un-American and anti-Christian.[22]

Some assumptions can be drawn from censorship attacks over the years. First, anything is potentially censorable by someone, somewhere, some time, for some reason. If Anne Frank's *The Diary of a Young Girl,* James Agee's *A Death in the Family,* Harper Lee's *To Kill a Mockingbird,* S. E. Hinton's *The Outsiders,* William Shakespeare's *Macbeth,* and Thornton Wilder's *Our Town* can be attacked, and all have been, then nothing, absolutely nothing, is safe. Second, the newer the work the more likely the attack. Third, censorship is arbitrary and capricious, a book attacked in one school or library goes unnoticed and uncensored in another school or library only a few miles away. A teacher is criticized for using a book and another teacher two doors down the hall who has used the same book for several years hears not one peep of complaint. Fourth, censorship usually strikes without warning and causes ripples of fear in nearby schools and libraries, particularly when those schools and libraries have no formal policy to handle censorship when it comes. Fifth, censors are often people outside the schools—individuals or groups. However, administrators can become censors, just as teachers and librarians can turn against their professional training to do so too. Sixth, censors are usually decent and concerned parents who wish only the best for young people but who rarely understand that teachers and librarians feel precisely the same way. Unhappily, the basic similarities are often lost if censors argue that schools exist to indoctrinate students into the mores and morals of the community, and teachers and librarians argue that schools exist to allow young adults to pursue ideas wherever they may lead.

Jenkinson[23] believes that objectionable material usually falls within one of fourteen categories: (1) novels written specifically for young adults; (2) books using realistic language; (3) works of "questionable" authors, often labeled subversive; (4) literature written by homosexuals; (5) "trash," a common censorial label for J. D. Salinger's *The Catcher in the Rye,* Daniel Keyes' *Flowers for Algernon,* Judy Blume's *Forever,* or Eldridge Cleaver's *Soul on Ice,* among others; (6) ideas, teaching methods, or books exemplifying what censors often call "secular humanism"; (7) materials for units on ethnic studies and drug education; (8) items used in "role playing"; (9) English textbooks without sections on the rules of grammar; (10) materials that contain negative statements (or ideas) about parents; (11) electives taught by English teachers; (12) materials for sex education; (13) books that contain sexist stereotypes; and (14) writings that seem to make racist statements. Other reasons to censor books might be: (1) someone might interpret them as attacks on America or the American Dream; (2) someone might feel they were more properly the province of a sociology class than an English class, for example Eldridge Cleaver's *Soul on Ice* or Harper Lee's *To Kill a Mockingbird;* (3) someone might construe them as anti-Christian or even just neutral on religion; (4) they have "suggestive" or "explicit" portrayals of sexual behavior; and (5) they portray behavior someone might think inappropriate as a model for young adults.

This catalogue is so complete that it allows few books to be safe from potential attack. Carried to its logical conclusion, it would discourage teachers from using and librarians from stocking anything except the most innocuous and antiseptic. Basic to all the objections is a fear and distrust of points of view or ideas that differ from the censors'.

If anything can come under attack, some books are seemingly under perpetual siege,[24] especially significant and popular books such as Aldous Huxley's *Brave New World,* John Knowles' *A Separate Peace,* Ken Kesey's *One Flew Over the Cuckoo's Nest,* Claude Brown's *Manchild in the Promised Land,* Paul Zindel's *The Pigman* and *My Darling, My Hamburger,* George Orwell's *1984,* John Steinbeck's *The Grapes of Wrath* and *Of Mice and Men,* Joseph Heller's *Catch-22,* Kurt Vonnegut's *Slaughterhouse-Five,* William Golding's *Lord of the Flies,* Alexander Solzhenitsyn's *One Day in the Life of Ivan Denisovich,* Dalton Trumbo's *Johnny Got His Gun,* and J. D. Salinger's *The Catcher in the Rye.* So common are attacks on these books that any survey that did not report at least an example or two of attack on every book in the list would be thought superficial, incomplete, or severely limited in scope. *Catcher* leads the list in frequency (or persistence) of attacks, and although Holden Caulfield is nearing fifty, he is still the censor's favorite target. In May 1979, the *Newsletter on Intellectual Freedom* reported yet another attempt to smear *Catcher* because "exposure to any profane or vulgar language in books, no matter how good the story, will not help the students in their education."[25]

Anything is potentially censorable by someone, somewhere, some time, for some reason.

There is no single reason for the rise in number and fervor of censorship incidents, but several causes clearly move some censors to act. Contemporary realism in adult books, movies, and television has in turn led to increasing realism in books written specifically for young adults. A few years ago, parents might have objected to *The Catcher in the Rye* or *The Grapes of Wrath,* but young adult books were safe. Some people might have objected to the literary value of *A Horse for Emily, A Touchdown for Chester High,* or *Senior Class Prom Trouble,* but parents were unlikely to claim that the books corrupted anyone's morals. Today, young adult books may have incidents of sensuality, sexuality, homosexuality, lesbianism, rape, cruelty, alcoholism, and violence, just as those elements might intrude themselves into a young adult's life at school or at home. Robert Cormier's *The Chocolate War*, Judy Blume's *Forever*, and Isabelle Holland's *The Man Without a Face* deeply disturb many parents and other adults.

The new realism brought with it an emphasis on fairness and honesty in treating multiethnic themes, and more books about Chicanos, blacks, and Indians appeared in classrooms and libraries. Privately, and sometimes publicly, censors betray considerable antiethnic feeling, and dislike of another race (or several races) may lie only slightly below the surface of an attack. It is not, as one parent said, "like the old days," and of course today isn't, but then the old days weren't really like the old days either. We have taken some steps, not enough but some, toward making libraries and classrooms more honest and real, even a little like life. That will not necessarily please parents fearful of values, ideas, and attitudes that do not reflect those taught at home.

Inflation, depression, rising taxes, threat of war, and shortage of gas depress most of us, but there is so little that we can do about those things directly or indirectly that sometimes we turn to smaller things. So do censors. Believing that they cannot fight City Hall and get rid of adult bookstores, adult movie theatres, or even remove some supposedly immoral television shows from the networks, censors turn to the school as the one agency they can change. That has been especially noticeable in school bond elections, but attacking books is another way to hit back at what is seen as the establishment. Rising militancy among teachers and librarians has sometimes inadvertently advanced the cause of censorship as parents remind themselves of the old days "when teachers knew their place," another example of the fear that leads to attacks.

What can teachers or librarians do when censorship strikes or threatens? First, they should keep up to date on recent censorship incidents and on effective methods of fighting censorship. Perhaps, one person (or a committee) could be asked to serve as a censorship expert. Certainly, reading important journals such as *English Journal, Language Arts, School Library Journal, Wilson Library Bulletin, The Horn Book Magazine, Top of the News*, and *Media and Methods* helps (indeed, it would be an unprofessional teacher or librarian who did not read these magazines regularly), but the single best source of current information about censorship is the *Newsletter on Intellectual Freedom*.[26] For less recent incidents of censorship and articles on facing the censor, see two extensive and most helpful annotated bibliographies by Ralph E. McCoy.[27]

Second, both librarians and teachers should develop clear and succinct statements about the purposes of libraries and English classes. This might have salutary effects on librarians or teachers who have never clearly formulated the values and purposes of their own professions. These statements should be made available to the public so that it can determine whether the library or English classroom is what the professionals claim it should be. Writing such statements will probably not deter the censor, but it might convince other citizens and even the administration that the staff knows what it is doing.

Third, librarians and English teachers should work diligently to win community support for academic freedom and the right to read *before* censorship strikes. Any community has former teachers and librarians who may feel as strongly about censorship as the present ones, but wooing them is essential. Too often help is sought when trouble strikes, but by then it may be too late.

Fourth, librarians and teachers should attempt to communicate with parents and other interested citizens about the purposes of programs currently in progress. Parents have a right to know, and school personnel have a duty to communicate that information. Parents inevitably hear, though often inexactly, what is going on in classrooms and libraries. Some may argue that alerting parents to books or techniques will encourage censors to move more rapidly, but censors never need help to move. Informing parents assumes that librarians and teachers can explain to lay people why they are doing what they are doing.

Fifth, librarians and teachers should devise careful procedures for selecting books and for handling censorship when it comes.[28] Without a formal written policy, librarians and teachers are vulnerable. Censors should be asked to register complaints in written form, and a standard policy should be devised to handle these complaints. In any case, censors must be treated reasonably and courteously. The procedures teachers and librarians set up must be supported by their administration or controlling agency. Winning that support by establishing the need and the worth of the policies is the responsibility of librarians and teachers.

Sixth, English teachers should expect to prepare written rationales for any book to be used as common reading. To do that teachers should reread the work in question to discover the problems inherent in teaching the book, among them potential censorship problems. In writing the rationale, teachers should respond to five questions: (1) why will the teacher use this book for this particular class? (2) what objectives—literary, psychological, or pedagogical—does the teacher have in mind in using this book? (3) how will the teacher use this book to achieve those objectives? (4) what problems— stylistic, thematic, or censorial—exist in the book and how will the teacher face them? and (5) assuming the objectives are met, how will students using the book change? Such rationales are not easy to write[29]—and they should be written whether the book in question is *The Catcher in the Rye* or *Silas Marner*—but they can offer clear evidence that the teacher has thought through reasons for using a book and is prepared to talk about and defend the choice. Rationales certainly will not stop every censor, but they can help to win friends in high places who appreciate thinking and prepared teachers.

Seventh, librarians and teachers should know what organizations can offer support, moral or financial, when censorship strikes.[30] More important, they should know how to find local or national officials who can help. When censorship strikes, the first reaction is often fear and the feeling that no one cares or can help. Finding that help soon is essential, partly to overcome fear and develop confidence, partly to avoid the kind of advice that too many librarians, teachers, and administrators give: "Why don't you just give in this one time. It's not really worth fighting for this book, is it?" Yes, it is worth fighting for, for to give in on one book is to make every other book in the library or classroom vulnerable. But the fight is hard and help is essential.

Two court decisions about attempted censorship in classrooms and libraries have been favorable to teachers and librarians. The majority of legal decisions about censorship have little to do with librarians or teachers.[31] However, *Minarcini* v. *Strongsville City School District* in the U.S. District Court for the Northern District of Ohio (1976) and *Right to Read Defense Committee of Chelsea* v. *School Committee of Chelsea* in the U.S. District

Court of Massachusetts (1978) have gladdened the hearts of those who oppose censorship. *Minarcini* protested the removal of books from a school library at the request of the school board. After noting that "a library is a storehouse of knowledge," the court found for the opponents to censorship and concluded:

> We have no doubt that the School Board resolutions [removing books] would have a somewhat chilling effect upon classroom discussion. . . . [We] direct the members of the Strongsville School Board to replace in the library the books
> . . .

The Chelsea decision concerned a poem banned by school officials as "obscene" and "of no educational value." Finding for freedom to read in school, the presiding judge wrote:

> The Committee [officials] claims an absolute right to remove [the offending poem] from the shelves of the school library. It has no such right, and compelling policy considerations argue against any public authority having such an unreviewable power of censorship. . . . What is at stake here is the right to read and be exposed to controversial thoughts and language—a valuable right subject to First Amendment protection.

But an even more recent decision disheartened English teachers and librarians and confirmed that books are never safe from capricious censorship. Early in 1976, members of the Island Trees (New York) School Board received lists of "objectionable" books from a conservative group, Parents of New York United. Finding eleven books they deemed "anti-American, anti-Christian, anti-Semitic, and just plain filthy," the Board banned such books as Oliver LaFarge's *Laughing Boy,* Richard Wright's *Black Boy,* Alice Childress' *A Hero Ain't Nothin' But a Sandwich,* Eldridge Cleaver's *Soul on Ice,* Kurt Vonnegut's *Slaughterhouse-Five,* Bernard Malamud's *The Fixer,* and *Go Ask Alice,* though it later reinstated *Laughing Boy* and *Black Boy.* Later in 1976, the New York Civil Liberties Union filed a suit on behalf of several students (among them Steve Pico) asking the U.S. District Court for the Eastern District of New York to restrain the board and overturn the board's ban. On August 2, 1979, Judge George C. Pratt ruled in *Pico* v. *Board of Education, Island Trees Union Free School District* in favor of the school board, writing:

> While removal of such books from a school library may, indeed, in this Court's view does, reflect a misguided educational philosophy, it does not constitute a sharp and direct infringement of any First Amendment right. . . . [Removal of the books in question] fell within the broad range of discretion to educational officials who are elected by the community.[32]

Speaking of the decision, the attorney for the board said it was the board's "duty to reflect community values—to indoctrinate community values,"[33] a point many educators and librarians would dispute. An appeal to the U.S. Supreme Court seems likely.

Whether *Minarcini* or *Chelsea* or *Pico* will serve widely or successfully as precedents is conjectural. No appeal of film or book censorship in the schools has been heard by the U.S. Supreme Court—which can refuse to hear any appeal without explanation—and lower court findings are as significant as other judges choose to make them by citing them as precedents. Should *Pico* be heard by the Supreme Court, precedent might be established, but until *Pico* or some other decision is heard and precedent established, librarians and teachers—as well as parents, school officials, school boards, and students—will not know if books are safe from arbitrary censorship.

We believe that the school—classroom and library—must be a center of intellectual ferment in the community. This does not imply that schools should be radical, just that they should be one place where freedom to think and inquire is protected, where ideas of all sorts can be considered, analyzed, investigated, discussed, and their consequences thought through. We believe librarians and English teachers must protect these freedoms, not merely in the abstract but in the practical day-to-day world of the school and library. To protect those freedoms we must fight censorship, for without them no education worthy of the name is possible.

This chapter has asked more questions than it has answered, but perhaps you will be able to find some of the answers. As soon as you do, other questions will arise. This is the price—and the reward—for being in a dynamic field. New books, new issues, and new generations of young readers will keep you from becoming bored with the role you have chosen whether it is as teacher, librarian, writer, parent, or reader.

ACTIVITIES

1. Study three or four different reviewing sources (*English Journal, Council on Interracial Books for Children, The Horn Book Magazine,* or *Booklist*) and see if you can find evidence of the attitudes or the values of the editors. Is one more interested in the implied message, that is, the philosophical or social values; another in literary quality; still another in popularity? Report back to the class citing the evidence you found. Explain the different purposes of the publications as related to their reading audiences.

2. Select an issue—one that was treated in this chapter or another one that interests you. Talk to people about it and read what others have written. Perhaps some of the works listed in Appendix E will be helpful to you. After doing this research, write a statement of your own philosophy. Cite the sources that influenced you in developing this philosophy.

3. Do some research into the relationship between television and reading. You might try to uncover evidence about the interests of young adults in your community based on the television shows they prefer, explore possibilities for promoting television tie-ins, or compare the kind of material that is likely to be censored in young adult books with what is shown on television.

4. Report on an incident of censorship, perhaps a local or state one, perhaps one reported in a newspaper or journal. Include details about who (the school and teacher or librarian involved, the name of the censor), what (the title under attack), when, where, and why. The latter will be the most difficult to determine, but if reasons for the attack—whether it was successful or not—are given, attempt to analyze the underlying reasons. Assuming that you (or a friend) had been the teacher or librarian under scrutiny, what might you have done to lessen the force of the attack—without giving in to the censor's demands—and increase the likelihood of keeping the book (and your job)?

5. Select a book currently popular with young adults. Based on the section about rationales, develop one for the book that answers the questions listed. Avoid all terms (educational or literary) that would not be clear to intelligent laymen; the purpose of the rationale is to remove obstacles, not to create bigger ones.

NOTES

[1]Lillian L. Shapiro, "Quality or Popularity? Selection Criteria for YAs," *School Library Journal* 24 (May 1978): 23–27.

[2]Patty Campbell, "Only Puddings Like the Kiss of Death: Reviewing the YA Book," *Top of the News* 35 (Winter 1979): 161–62.

[3]Council on Interracial Books for Children, *Human and Anti-Human Values*, 1976, p. 4.

[4]Nat Hentoff, "Any Writer Who Follows Anyone Else's Guidelines Ought to Be in Advertising," *School Library Journal* 24 (November 1977): 27.

[5]"Old Values Surface in Blume Country," *Bulletin of the Council on Interracial Books for Children* 7 (1977): 8–10.

[6]Audrey Eaglen, "Answers from Blume Country: An Interview with Judy Blume," *Top of the News* 34 (Spring 1978): 233–43.

[7]Jean McClure Kelty, "The Cult of Kill in Adolescent Fiction," *English Journal* 64 (February 1975): 56–61.

[8]G. Melvin Hipps, "Male Initiation Rites in *A Day No Pigs Would Die*," *Arizona English Bulletin* 18 (April 1976): 161–63.

[9]Dorothy Matthews, "Writing About Adolescent Literature: Current Approaches and Future Directions," ibid., pp. 216–19.

[10]Mary K. Eakin, *Good Books for Children 1950–1965* (Chicago: University of Chicago Press, 1966).

[11]Zena Sutherland, *The Best in Children's Books 1966–1972* (Chicago: University of Chicago Press, 1973).

[12]Al Muller, "Some Thoughts on the Black Y.A. Novel," *ALAN Newsletter*, NCTE, vol. 5 (Winter 1978).

[13]Write for information to Sundance Paperback Distributors, Newton Road, Littleton, MA 91460 or to *Readers' Choice*, Scholastic Magazines, Inc., 50 W. 44 Street, New

York, NY 10036, and other similar companies. Bantam Books, Inc., 666 Fifth Avenue, New York, NY 10019 has many promotional materials which teachers find useful. One year, for example, they distributed a television calendar made especially for young adults listing four or five book-related movies for every month of the year.

[14]Information may be obtained from: Laurel-Leaf Library, Dell Publishing Co., Inc., 1 Dag Hammarskjold Place, New York, NY 10017; Viking Penguin, Inc., 625 Madison Avenue, New York, NY 10022; and Avon Books Education Department, 959 Eighth Avenue, New York, NY 10019.

[15]Norma Klein, "Growing up human: The case for sexuality in children's books," *Children's Literature in Education* 8 (Summer 1977): 80-84.

[16]Lillian L. Shapiro, "Quality or Popularity? Selection Criteria for YAs," *School Library Journal* 24 (May 1978): 27.

[17]Jack Forman, "YA Selection Criteria—A Second Opinion," *School Library Journal* 25 (September 1978): 51.

[18]Mary K. Chelton, untitled editorial, *Voice of Youth Advocates* 1 (June 1978): 5.

[19]John Cunningham, "Growing Up Gay Male," ibid., pp. 11-16.

[20]*Library Journal* 21 (December 1896): 144.

[21]See Ken Donelson, "Forty Iceberg Tips: The State of Censorship 1972-1978," *California Librarian* 39 (July 1978): 32-38; and L. B. Woods, "The Most Censored Materials in the U.S.," *Library Journal* 103 (November 1, 1978): 2170-73.

[22]For details on Kanawha County, see Lester Faigley, "What Happened in Kanawha County?" *English Journal* 64 (May 1975): 7-9; and "A Brief Chronology of the West Virginia Textbook Crisis," *Arizona English Bulletin* 17 (February 1975): 203-12.

[23]Edward B. Jenkinson, "Dirty Dictionaries, Obscene Nursery Rhymes, and Burned Books," in *Dealing with Censorship,* ed. James E. Davis (Urbana, Illinois: National Council of Teachers of English, 1979), pp. 7-11.

[24]See Woods, "Most Censored Materials"; Ken Donelson, "Censorship and Arizona English Teaching, 1971-1974," *Arizona English Bulletin* 17 (February 1975): 1-39; and the most recent censorship survey, Lee Burress, "A Brief Report of the 1977 NCTE Censorship Survey," in Davis, *Dealing with Censorship,* pp. 14-47.

[25]*Newsletter on Intellectual Freedom* 28 (May 1979): 59.

[26]*Newsletter on Intellectual Freedom,* American Library Association, 40 E. Huron Street, Chicago, IL 60611, published bimonthly.

[27]Ralph E. McCoy, *Freedom of the Press: An Annotated Bibliography* (Carbondale, Illinois: Southern Illinois University Press, 1968); and an excellent update, *Freedom of the Press: A Bibliocyclopedia. Ten Year Supplement* (Carbondale, Illinois: Southern Illinois University Press, 1979).

[28]Examples of policies can be found in two sources with which all librarians and English teachers should be familiar. *The Intellectual Freedom Manual,* published by the American Library Association, contains a wealth of information and help including the "Library Bill of Rights" and some interpretations and specific suggestions about what librarians can and should do before the censor comes. *The Students' Right to Read* is the official policy statement of the National Council of Teachers of English, and it too contains advice and specific help. (See Appendix C.) The last edition was published in 1972, and a new edition is expected by 1980 or 1981.

[29]See a rationale for writing rationales along with samples in Diane P. Shugert, "How to Write a Rationale in Defense of a Book," in Davis, *Dealing with Censorship,* pp. 187-201.

[30]Diane P. Shugert provides a handy list of helpful organizations in "A Body of Well-Instructed Men and Women: Organizations Active for Intellectual Freedom," in Davis, *Dealing with Censorship,* pp. 215-21.

[31]See Ken Donelson, "Obscenity and the Chill Factor: Court Decisions about Obscenity and Their Relationships to School Censorship," in Davis, *Dealing with Censorship,* pp. 63-75.

[32]"High Court Appeal Likely on Book Ban," *The New York Times,* August 5, 1979, p. 17.

[33]Ibid.

14

The People

Behind the Books

Having examined the past and the present states of young adult literature, we thought it appropriate in this final chapter to try for a glimpse into the future. To obtain that glimpse, we went to a representative sampling of those people whom we judge to be most likely to influence the future direction of young adult literature. We went first to an executive editor, then to a person in charge of sales and promotion, and finally to approximately thirty authors. The editor we chose to consult is Charlotte Zolotow. We went to a Harper & Row editor because almost one-fourth of the books on the Honor Sampling (Appendix A) were published by that company. For book promotion we consulted Doris Bass, Associate Sales Manager of Bantam Books, because she has had wide experience with both paperbacks and hardbacks. For several years she worked as the library promotion director for Random House/Knopf Pantheon. And the authors that we chose are those whose books we found ourselves coming back to time and again as we wrote the preceding chapters.

We asked all of these people two questions. First, we asked them to describe what they see as the future of their own work, and, second, to predict the future of the field of young adult literature as a whole. Some common themes run through their answers. Many of them avoid making predictions, especially about what other authors might do. They are more inclined to express their personal preferences and hopes. Several tell how they resent the boundaries that seem to segregate young adult books from a general readership. Others draw attention to the need for going deeper into and treating with more subtlety and sensitivity those areas that have only recently been opened up as possible book topics for young people. Still others speak out against writing books "to order."

Charlotte Zolotow focuses on the idea that books will be no better, no more honest, and no more interesting than the people who create them. Her statement serves as a good introduction to the comments of all the others, which are presented in alphabetical order. The titles listed for each author are representative of that person's work—the lists are by no means complete. The answers given by Charlotte Zolotow, Doris Bass, and thirty outstanding young adult authors present a composite picture that is both more accurate and complete than one that could be gotten in any other way. Additionally, they serve as introductions to some very interesting people.

CHARLOTTE ZOLOTOW

Vice-President, Associate Publisher
Harper Junior Books

Young people's books have come into a new era. They reflect new understanding, new insights, extended boundaries of mind and imagination. These books can change the shape of the world. For they reach young persons who are still searching for ways to reconcile their own emotions and life situations to a world that is whirling us all around too fast. The suicide rate among the young has increased alarmingly in the last decade. They are crying, "Stop the world. I want to get off." And books for them are important. If these books genuinely define the realities of life, if they are good enough to emotionally involve the young person, they can help slow things down a bit. Hope for a better world rests in the writers who are attempting to reach future adults with honesty, earnestness and compassion.

Mollie Hunter, one of our finer writers for young people, says in a book on writing, *Talent Is Not Enough:*

> A philosophy has to be hammered out, a mind shaped, a spirit tempered. This is true for all of the craft. It is the basic process which must happen before literature can be created. It is also the final situation in which the artist is fully fledged. And because of the responsibilities involved, these truths apply most sharply to the writer who aspires to create literature for children. TALENT IS NOT ENOUGH—no, by God it is not! Hear this, critics, editors, publishers, parents, teachers, librarians—all you who will shortly pick up a children's book. There *must* be a person behind that book.

This is because along with the wonderful fantasy and humor and imagination, a new realism has come into children's books. Even picture books for the very young deal now with loss and loneliness, with every possible emotion, with experience from birth to death. These changes have come about from our acknowledgement of the intensity of the child's and adolescent's emotions, and their ability and need to cope with the tragic and violent and hostile, as well as with the sweet and lovely and beautiful around us.

We can't shelter our youth in books from words and situations they will hear and see in their own lives and at school and on TV. There is no one answer to anything, sometimes there are no answers at all, but the books young people read should at least raise the problems they are living with, instead of pretending they don't exist. And if, as Mollie says, behind each book there is a thinking moral person, no matter what the subject being dealt with, the child will have new points of view rather than confusion to go forward with.

There are books now about broken homes, homes where parents are hypocritical or cruel or mistaken, books dealing with physical awakenings, not just between boys and girls, but between kids of the same sex, a boy's first homosexual encounter, a girl's love for another girl, unmarried sex, unwanted pregnancy. Children can't be helped by shielding them in books from what they face in life. The thing to remember is that these books, the good ones, are really good. They have in common beauty of language, dramatic dialogue, honest situations with no dishonest solutions, questions, tentative answers, possible hopes, sometimes despair but no morally dishonest endings that are untrue artistically as well as in human terms.

They are written by fine writers and published by courageous publishers not *because* of the controversial nature of the problems in which the young characters find themselves involved. We publish these books *despite* their controversial nature! For we have to face many adults who feel this material, the material of life itself, is not suitable for young people to read about. There is still a large group of parents who bring pressure on librarians to take off their shelves books that use language the children actually use themselves, or will hear at school from other kids; books in which the experience of young characters involves sex and nervous breakdowns, and class struggles and war and questions about obedience, blind obedience, which, in the light of Nazi Germany and other such phenomena of mankind, should indeed be examined early on.

It does take courage on the part of publishers to do these books, not only moral courage, but financial courage, because the risks are great. Anything new, any stylistic experiment, anything avant-garde of current taste and expectation can be misunderstood by well-meaning, but shortsighted, parents, reviewers, or librarians.

Before *The Effect of Gamma Rays on Man-in-the-Moon Marigolds* won either the Drama Critics' Award or the Pulitzer Prize, it was produced on TV. It was the portrait of two troubled teenagers and their struggle to cope with their excruciating home life that made Harper write Paul Zindel and ask if he would consider doing books for young people. But when his first book, *The Pigman,* was published it was met with storms of protest. It took courage to stand behind that book, which we were and are proud of, until it began to climb to an honored place in every library. And it then began a "trend" of other novels, books other publishers might not have been open to before Zindel broke ground for them.

We must take risks to break ground. We cannot predict what talented person may come our way, or what his or her concerns will be. We must be open to everything, the best of the old, and everything new, even if it seems at first bizarre or startling. If it is done with talent and if *by God* there is a person behind the book, we must be open. It is not the editor's job to suggest ideas, but to listen to what each author wants to say and see that it is said in the best way possible. I've had talented authors of adult writing come to me and ask what sort of books we need. But good books don't come without the author's compelling desire to write them. We editors must search out the gifted person who has that compelling need. In talking we judge the personality, the line to the person's childhood, we look for signs of insight, and, of course, talent. For few authors mail in, or come in, with a manuscript that is ready to be published. Certainly not on their first books. If there is enough in the manuscript to give us intimations of something fine, we will do everything editorially possible to help. We will do our best to create an atmosphere and climate of openness and interest in which authors can grow. We will listen and respond with all our senses to the ideas of these truly creative people and give our encouragement and support as they develop their work. We do so in the trust that in their intense and honest searching of themselves they will illuminate the world in a special way for us and for our young people.

DORIS BASS

Associate Sales Manager
Bantam Books, Inc.

Asking people in the book business to make predictions about this industry is terribly frustrating—there are as many variations as there are respondents. So herewith is an amalgam of opinions I've received.

1. Young Adult fiction continues to be an important genre, and no subject or treatment is taboo in itself. However, income from the sale of books to paperback houses is urgent, and since mass market houses are unwilling to pay a lot of money for YA books unless there is the possibility of classroom adoptions, a lot of YA publishing seems to be "safe" rather than daring.
2. Media tie-ins grow in strength, and decisions to publish may depend on whether or not there is the likelihood of a film or TV sales.
3. As blockbuster auctions continue to escalate, the "cross-over" trend will grow; hardcover houses will publish simultaneously in paper, and paperback houses will generate more originals.
4. The interrelationship between all markets (schools/libraries/book clubs/stores) and internal organizational factors seem to be leading toward "category" specialists rather than market specialists, so those who used to serve as library promotion personnel may become juvenile and YA product managers, responsible for these books in all markets.

What frightens me as I look at publishing in general is related to: problems of low-level literacy; a reactionary mentality among parents and teachers that continues to brand books as dangerous; the economics of inflation that make publishers less likely to seek out new talent. What I see that gives me confidence in the future is a lot of wonderful books that are, despite the odds, being published.

JAY BENNETT

The Dangling Witness
Deathman, Do Not Follow Me
The Long Black Coat
Say Hello to the Hit Man

What will happen in the field as a whole will definitely affect what I will be doing. I went into the field to try to reach the young with all the skill and thought I had learned in a lifetime of writing in many genres. I felt that the young were alive, questioning, and in the main were far more decent human beings than were their elders.

I still feel that way.

The future in the field will be decided by what happens upstairs in this country. Will we continue to divert billions for arms, for refurbishing Yankee Stadiums, and other such nonsense, at the same time closing schools, libraries, and museums, and beefing up television commercials and tinsel shows, or will we listen to that surplus generation—our young—and start giving them what is surely their right and privilege?

Instead of short-staffing the open libraries, give them full staffs. Instead of short-weeking the libraries, open them all week and give them more hours. Stock them with books. Have budgets so that competent and mature authors will be attracted into the field.

Well, a word about the future quality of the writing in the field of young adult literature. I fear it will go down and we will see the same destruction of standards that we find so sadly prevalent in the adult field. The first-novelist, the new author coming in with a new look and perspective on life, will probably be blocked out. The experimenter will be out. The writer who writes on more than one level will find it tough going unless he has the skills and art to tell a good story first. As for myself, I will stay in the field hoping that I am overstating the case and that things will turn out better. I have had offers to go back into television, but I have turned them down and will continue to do so. I started off by saying that the young are decent human beings, and I would like to stay with them and try to be decent too.

JUDY BLUME

Are You There God? It's Me, Margaret
Deenie
Forever
It's Not the End of the World
Then Again, Maybe I Won't

I need the freedom, the challenge, of dealing with all age groups. I expect to write novels about young people as well as adults. I expect to write about those subjects that are important to me. And what is especially important are human relationships. I hope to deal with the realities of life, to present characters and situations that will cause readers to think. I don't make moral judgments in my books. I would rather have my readers reach their own conclusions. I think our young people need to be better prepared for life. They need to learn to reason, they need to learn that there is more than one answer to most questions, they need to learn that they have choices and how to decide which ones will be best for them. Most of all they need to learn to think for themselves. To some people thinking for oneself is considered controversial. To me it is what life is all about!

SUE ELLEN BRIDGERS

All Together Now
Home Before Dark

The future of my work seems to reside in the past. The rural South is where I am comfortable and so writing about young people and families in small towns comes naturally to me. I have only to reach into my own experience and re-create an environment that is similar to the one in which I grew up in order to find my characters. In this setting, my characters reveal themselves and their stories.

Because my first novel appealed to young adults, I have been classified as a young adult author. However, I have never given much thought to what might or might not be appropriate for a particular group of readers. So far I have tried to write books that I like and I expect to continue to work to please myself, hoping to please other readers, both young and old, along the way.

Having come to young adult literature without scholarship or experience, I find I have ambivalent feelings about such a classification of books. I am not sure there needs to be a category of young adult literature at all, and I don't understand the criteria for its classification. If it means that, because of their style or subject matter, beautifully written, accomplished stories that stretch the reader's understanding of life are eliminated, then I hope young adult literature as a category dies quickly. If it means that young people are given access to good books that might otherwise go unpublished for lack of a market, then I have warm wishes for its future.

The placement of a book in libraries and book stores is not in the hands of the writer, and from where I sit, the dilemma of dual marketing looks like an insurmountable problem unless publishers, librarians and store managers engage in cooperative and creative thinking on the subject. One thing I know for certain. Young people deserve the best the community of writers has to offer. The quality of writing should carry the same weight as subject matter in the decision to classify a book. Young adult literature is transitional literature. By its nature, it should not only move the reader closer to maturity by its subject matter and philosophy, but also by its inventiveness of style, its characterization, sensitivity and discovery, and most of all, by the commitment of its writers to do their best work.

ALICE CHILDRESS

A Hero Ain't Nothin' But a Sandwich

I put aside any fear of writing on themes which seriously affect our lives. *A Hero Ain't Nothin' But a Sandwich* has created a fiery dialogue, pro and con, between librarians, teachers, parents and students, on the subject of drug abuse and the written word. The book is startling because I wanted the attention of the reader, without glossing over the subject matter to make it other than what it has proven to be . . . a tragic destruction, particularly of the young, by adults who profiteer from misery. The art of living cannot be taught or learned by rote, so I believe we should encourage our children to make inquiry and seek answers, directly, with honesty, through reading and open discussion in the home as well as at school. Young People send me admirable letters which show they have no difficulty in deciding *against* participation in the drug scene, expressing deep concern and regret for those who ruin their lives by using false bravado as a form of rebellion. Their letters let me know that "cinema verite," in writing, exposes the land mines and booby traps to be found on the contemporary scene. Now, and in the future, I hope we continue to enjoy great classics and the beautiful fairy tales of Grimm and Andersen, but with the full understanding that "Sleeping Beauty" no longer sleeps . . . and times grow "curiouser and curiouser."

VERA AND BILL CLEAVER

Dust of the Earth
Me Too
Trial Valley
Where the Lilies Bloom
The Whys and Wherefores of Littabelle Lee

From time to time we are told that we write literature. As opposed to what? Well, I suppose as opposed to the present boom-pah-pah, all the clangor for the sensational, all the occupation and preoccupation with the most intimate functions and the most basic responses of the human body set to paper by others whose views do not coincide with ours. We talk about the serious writer quite a bit. I guess the reason for this is because we tend to regard ourselves as being such.

Literature is the exploration of the human dilemma. It has always asked the questions: What are we? Why are we? What are we doing here? What may we expect of ourselves?

We, the Cleavers, have chosen to involve ourselves with all these investigations and shall continue to do so.

Comes now the question: Where do the Cleavers think the future of young adult literature in the United States is headed? Well, along with their owners, the appetites of people change, so who can predict anything which has to do with human expression and activity? Perhaps when writers and educators and others concerned with the future of young adult literature come around to the explorations of internal perceptions rather than those of mere conduct we shall have an answer to this question.

SUSAN COOPER

The Dark Is Rising
The Grey King
Silver on the Tree

I don't think I dare offer you any general predictions; we all work independently of each other, and only hindsight can show our similarities. Nor can I really chart my own future direction. I don't write "for" children, or young adults, or old adults; I simply write whatever my imagination happens at any given moment to offer me. To paraphrase C. S. Lewis: I write children's stories only when a children's story seems the best art form for something I have to say. And my imagination, always myth-haunted, turned to that form in the five-book fantasy sequence called *The Dark Is Rising*.

I write children's stories only when a children's story seems the best art form for something I have to say.

But haunting can take many forms. Since finishing that sequence I have written one fairy tale which will probably be published as a picture-book for younger children, and I hope to do one or two others. Most of my time, however, is now spent in writing for the theatre: itself an Other-World, which gives me a strong sense of having come home.

There is one insistent book taking shape at the back of my head which may, two or three years hence, end up on the "young adult" list. But the future is not neatly planned. Sometimes—but only sometimes—I wish it were. Life was so straightforward when I was writing the books of the *Dark Is Rising* sequence; the long idea stretched ahead, to be—with luck, and hard work—fulfilled. Now I am back at Square One: listening for the play, or book, or story that says, *"Write me."* In the long run, that's the erratic and exciting pattern to which every writer is doomed.

ROBERT CORMIER

After the First Death
The Chocolate War
I Am the Cheese

I have always been interested in the plight of the individual versus the system, whether the system is the family, the school, the government or society in general. I hope to pursue this theme on an increasingly broader and more penetrating level. However, I am really more interested in creating credible human beings in situations that provide shocks of recognition for the reader. And I'm willing to let these characters take me where they will, even if I have to abandon preconceived notions about a particular theme. What's beautiful about this is that I can deal with character and theme in a manner that satisfies me as an author and have my work accepted in the field of adolescent literature.

In the field as a whole, we may be approaching a time when, the old taboos having fallen, the themes pioneered in recent years—racial discrimination, drugs, homosexuality, among others—will be broadened and deepened by writers. While the novels dealing with these issues have been courageous and effective, they were, in a sense, door-openers. We now have to step inside, deeply inside, and explore the great and important issues of the day in all of their dazzling complexities.

JOHN DONOVAN

Family
I'll Get There. It Better Be Worth the Trip
Remove Protective Coating a Little at a Time
Wild in the World

There have been American books for adolescents for as long as we have recognized adolescence as a distinct time in a person's life. When, for only a year, I taught English—to eighth graders and in a junior college—I was, myself, younger than most of the junior college students in classes. Even so, I was astonished at how alike—emotionally, socially, and, in certain ways, intellectually—my fourteen-year-old and twenty-two-year-old students were. John Tunis' books saved my teaching year. I've read a couple of them again, years after I "used" them to rescue myself. The rereads were interesting because I knew straightaway that if I were teaching still I could talk with young people about John Tunis' books. On the surface he was writing sports stories. Anyone who knows his books understands that there's more to sports than meets a jock's eye. The thoughts, ideas, observations, etc., by eighth graders and junior college students were remarkably alike.

The books I write aren't at all like John Tunis' stories. A librarian has told me that she recommends my books to young readers "selectively." I'm not quite certain if it's the books or the readers she is selective about. And it doesn't matter. Her remark pigeonholes my work, however, and in a way I find rather appealing. A writer for young people who knows with certainty what his or her next book is "about" is in a lot of trouble. An affecting book is not "about" anything. It is, when it succeeds, an expression of a vision, or of a personal view of life. Life for me is a funny, sad, crazy, tragic, predictable, and ironic experience. I hope my view of life finds expression in any book that I write, if I should write another book.

LOIS DUNCAN

Down a Dark Hall
I Know What You Did Last Summer
Killing Mr. Griffin
Summer of Fear

The juvenile book field has changed tremendously since I was twenty and wrote my first teen novel which was returned to me for revisions because I had a nineteen-year-old drink a beer. The subject matter of today's youth novels has no boundaries. The only taboo seems to be sex discrimination. When I wrote *Down a Dark Hall*, a wild teenage gothic, my editor's concern was that the ghosts in the story were male and their victims female. When I changed the ghost of poet Alan Seeger to Emily Brontë, he felt much better.

I can only guess about where we're going, but I think we have come about as far as we can in the direction of "let-it-all-hang-out" realism. My reader-mail indicates that kids are beginning to feel bogged down with so much depressing slice-of-life. My

---

Kids are beginning to feel bogged down with so much depressing slice-of-life.

---

own most successful books have been those that were high in entertainment value, especially those touching on the supernatural. My most popular book, *Summer of Fear*, is about Ozark witchcraft, and *Killing Mr. Griffin*, also popular, is a tightly plotted suspense story.

My prediction is that the next few years will show an increase in the demand for such escape literature. There may even be a swing back toward fantasy, which to my way of thinking would be wonderful. The most valuable thing an author can do for today's teenagers is to help them to realize that it's as much fun to read a book as to turn on the television.

BETTE GREENE

Get on Out of Here, Philip Hall
Morning Is a Long Time Coming
Philip Hall Likes Me. I Reckon Maybe
Summer of My German Soldier

Becoming real is both my major personal problem and my major occupational problem. Being real, which would have to include a willingness to be intimate, is the problem and the challenge because I know of no way to be any more dimensional as an artist than I already am as a person.

If it is my job (and I believe that it is) to examine life, the only little grain of life that I know, then I should have no concerns with being either heroine or clown, but only with being real.

I only write about those things that make me burst out into song . . . or into tears because I believe that that's where all the good writing hides. But to strike at it, I must teach myself to have all the instincts of a kamikaze pilot. No more fears about seeing myself in print looking like so much exposed flesh.

Since intimacy is my greatest fear, I have discovered, quite by accident that confronting that fear has led to my most compelling writing: writing which I hope is populated with real breathing people who through painfully struggling towards new insights will offer vitality and truth to my work.

HOWARD GREENFELD

Books from Writer to Reader
Gertrude Stein: A Biography
Gypsies
They Came to Paris

I can't say with certainty what the direction of my work will be because my interests and enthusiasms are tremendously varied, and I can only write out of enthusiasm. The aim of my past work has been to stimulate and somehow broaden the horizons of young people and to encourage them to read beyond the introductory books I write for them. I certainly hope to continue to do this, especially in the fields of art, music, and literature.

Because I find that my curiosity is so great in so many areas of learning, I will depend to some extent on the advice of librarians and publishers as to specific subject matter—for it is the librarian above all who understands the needs and desires of young readers. I don't say that I write to order; I am not a machine, and I can't do that. But when my publisher suggests a subject to me—as was the case with my book on

Gypsies—and after some preliminary research I find that the topic fascinates me, then the writing of the book can be a most valuable educational experience for me as well as, I hope, for the reader.

VIRGINIA HAMILTON

The House of Dies Drear
Justice and Her Brothers
M. C. Higgins, the Great
The Planet of Junior Brown

Over the last decade I have come to feel less preoccupied with my own roots and heritage and more aware of survivors of all kinds. Questions of universal survival occur to me: Will the few who survive the cataclysm (and I assume the cataclysm) do so because they are genetically different from those who do not survive? Who are survivors? Are they our wit, our courage, our luck, or are they our genes? Perhaps our genes created us in body and mind just for themselves, with *their* preservation as the ultimate rationale for our existence, as some scientists now believe. Is it possible that telepathy, prophecy, genius are a mutation of genes? What a marvelous subject for speculation for the writer—that the fundamental unit of natural selection and therefore, self-preservation or self-interest, is not the species, nor the group or individual, but the unit of heredity, the gene.

I am at work on *The Justice Cycle*, fantasies about seemingly ordinary children who have tapped new gene information which is accessible after 30 million years of dormancy. Behind the *Cycle* fantasies is the assumption that the gifted among us, even the strange and the eccentric among us, might be nature's way of preserving special abilities which the human race may need in some future world. It is an idea for wonder. My work will continue exploring new ways to express my fiction.

JAMES HASKINS

James Van Derzee: The Picture Takin' Man
The Story of Stevie Wonder
Street Gangs: Yesterday and Today
Who Are the Handicapped?

The direction of my work will continue to follow what I feel is the course of adolescent literature in general. As young adults become more sophisticated and their awareness is increased by the other media, particularly the broadcast media, they will require more books addressed specifically to them on current political and social issues and on the personalities who have a significant bearing on those issues. I feel there will be a need for both fictional and nonfictional treatments of such subjects for young adults. However, my work will continue to be exclusively nonfiction.

SUSAN ELIZABETH HINTON

The Outsiders
Rumble Fish
That Was Then, This Is Now

It's hard to say what I'm writing now because I never really know what my books are about until two or three years after they come out and the kids write and tell me. I lucked out with *The Outsiders*. I didn't even know what it meant to try for "universality" or for something beyond the immediate topic, but today I get the same kinds of letters that I got ten years ago from readers who for one reason or another think of themselves as "outsiders." I'm a better writer now than I was when as a teenager I wrote my first book, but I'll never again have the emotional intensity. All I can do is try to remember how it felt.

The reason I wrote *The Outsiders* was that I had read all the horse stories and there wasn't anything else to read because I didn't want to read *Jeannie Goes to the Prom*. With the new trends in adolescent literature, I don't think kids will ever again have that experience. More and more good writers are realizing that teenagers make up a reading audience that in many ways is preferable to the adult audience. There's room in young adult books for all kinds of writing—nonfiction as well as fiction and fantasy.

Teenagers make up a reading audience that in many ways is preferable to the adult audience.

This probably sounds funny coming from me, but I think for a while the profession went out on a limb with stark realism. Writers were so relieved to be able to tackle any subject that they overdid it. To write a good book—a book that will last beyond its topic—an author has to start with people rather than problems. Of course there are problems, but the people own them, not the other way around. I was upset when *That Was Then, This Is Now* was advertised and written about as a drug book. I didn't intend it to be a drug book. I intended it to be a story about people growing out and away from each other.

ISABELLE HOLLAND

Heads You Win, Tails I Lose
Of Love and Death and Other Journeys
The Man Without a Face

My books have always dealt with the relationship between the child or adolescent and the adult or adults who live in and dominate the young person's portrait of self. In later years that child, become an adult, may be able to see that the first portrait was as much created by the prejudices, fears, anxieties and desires within the adult as within the child. But at the time the portrait was being painted—"You're lazy, you're stupid, you're untidy, you start well but you never finish, you're too . . ." (you can add anything to that)—they became the strong first strokes that created a self-image that the child will never wholly lose. He may use it intelligently, he may battle against it, he may suffer from self hatred, he may accept it and withdraw, he may reject it and fight the world—but it's there, like the monster over his shoulder, the shadow that follows him. And it is that struggle between the child and the adult in the creating of that self-portrait, that often preoccupies my writing. The lucky children are the ones who are taught to believe, as they go through life, that, whatever their faults may be, they themselves are lovable and estimable human beings. Most parents do not mean to convey a different message, but they often do. And if my books are about the wounds given in that message, they are also about the healing that can take place, given the right adult at the right time. And I suppose I will continue to write on this theme.

M. E. KERR

Dinky Hocker Shoots Smack
Gentlehands
If I Love You, Am I Trapped Forever?
I'll Love You When You're More Like Me

I cannot speak for my colleagues. For myself I *hope* I can woo young adults away from the boob tube, not just with entertaining stories, but also with subject matter which will provoke concern and a questioning about this complicated and often unfair world we live in. I would like my readers to laugh, but also to think; to be introspective, but also to reach out . . . and I hope I can give them characters and situations which will inspire these reactions. Now that the young adult field seems to have grown up, I hope it will grow out and touch, and that I'll be contributing.

MILDRED LEE

Fog
The Rock and the Willow
The Skating Rink
Sycamore Year

The categorization of libraries and book stores seems to me to have been too rigid—but so has everything else in our present age of specialization: the medical field for example and certain media of education. Young adults who are book lovers read whatever appeals to their taste and I wonder if having books labeled for them does not tend to turn them away rather than attract them. I do not know that anything can or should be done about this situation. I offer a personal opinion not intended to incite discussion, only consideration.

I believe labeling does affect an author and many editors' work; perhaps more than is desirable. Some of the latter tend to screen or have their authors "write down to" young readers, while others seem to feel that overly vivid bathroom and sex emphases are necessary in order to achieve realism—a description which seems to me to have been greatly overworked as well as misused for years. If fictional characters are alive and convincing I think the reader, whether a young or more mature adult will feel empathy or identification.

In our own main branch of the public library there is a sign conspicuously announcing that many of the young adult books are also in the adult section. This sign in our young people's department warms the cockles of my heart. Many young people's books too indicate that the partition between the two classifications is steadily thinning so that in the future it may dissolve completely. If it does it will almost certainly widen reader scope which will be a good thing for authors and—hopefully—for many readers also.

URSULA K. LE GUIN

The Dispossessed
The Farthest Shore
Very Far Away from Anywhere Else
A Wizard of Earthsea

To tell you the direction my own work is taking would be to tell you a great deal more than I know myself. Might I ask you to consider the fact that though we writers use words as our artistic medium, we are usually no more articulate, no more able to say what we are doing and why, than the most typically tongue-tied sculptor or composer. Words used by the intellect are a very different lot from words used by the daimon. And words used about daimons are generally inadequate if not downright lies. Particularly when people announce what they're going to do next. Your guess is absolutely as good as mine.

ROBERT LIPSYTE

The Contender
Free to Be Muhammad Ali
One Fat Summer
Sportsworld: An American Dreamland

Once, YA books could get by as superficial escapist mindwash, but now that television offers junkfood for the head, YA books have not only the responsibility (which they always had and often refused to assume) but the desperate need, if they wish to survive, to engage young people on a deeper level, on a searching, helpful, option-expanding level. For example, this current rage for "realistic sexuality"—Well, there's too much sexuality, unexplained, teasing sexuality in the culture as is. We don't need to know that boys and girls have sex. If YA literature is to be worthwhile, to be *necessary*, it must go beyond to expose more questions (young people often need the right questions more than answers) about relationships between girls and boys, about the possibility of relationships that don't put sexual pressure on boys and girls, about ways of diffusing the terrible pressures of "scoring" for boys, of losing or keeping virginity for girls, honest ways of looking at sex, through characters we can identify with and who entertain us, and perhaps coming to the radical conclusion that sex is at once *less important* than the deodorant makers would have us believe, yet more intrinsic a part of our lives than books up to now have told us. And abortion and birth control and loving and considerate sexual technique must eventually be dealt with, too, again in a way that is a part of the story being told—rather than the story being the candy-coating for a "problem" book that can move off the shelf. Gay sex must be treated as honestly as hetero-sex. Beyond sex, into sex roles, into job vs. family, into making money, into political involvement, YA books must also be ready to offer a view of the world that is uncompromising in realism, but also hopeful of improvement—and willing to leave unanswered, un-pat, major questions.

The world is going to get more complicated, not less, and young people are going to have more available information and more chances for physical and emotional encounters. If YA literature is going to be in their knapsack as they march up the electronic grid road then the entire community of interest here—writers, editors, publishers, teachers, and librarians—are going to have to be willing to admit we don't know the answers any better than the readers do, but we might have an idea what the most important questions are.

ANNE MC CAFFREY

Dragondrums
Dragonflight
Dragonsinger
Dragonsong
The Ship Who Sang

As to predictions about the field, or my part in it, I'm not good at such critical analysis. I'm a story teller, basically, and unconsciously reflect in my stories the pressures, the problems, and the ambiance which beset me and our world while I am writing a story. I can't predict what those pressures, problems, and vibrations will be: I haven't lived through and with them yet. I say I write love stories, and that is the truth. I also write xenophilic stories, rather than xenophobic since I do feel that we shall, one day or another, encounter other sentient beings. I can devoutly hope that our species will greet them with tolerance and an overwhelming desire to understand alien minds and mores. Alexander Pope said "Man must when he can,/Vindicate ways of God to man." I would paraphrase this . . ." Man must, when he can,/Vindicate the ways of Science to man." And, with that science, contact other sentient beings. I think educators are learning that the genre of science fiction is considerably more complex than has been thought: that *good* science fiction can be a teaching aid on many levels. This position and acceptance is bound to be strengthened since more top writers in the field are turning their attention to the young adult field as an audience, a vital and inspiring audience well worth cultivating.

PATRICIA A. MC KILLIP

The Forgotten Beasts of Eld
Heir of Sea and Fire
The Night Gift
The Riddle-Master of Hed

As far as my own future work is concerned, I haven't any definite ideas about what I might do in the realm of adolescent literature. I only know that adolescents are among the richest and most dramatically satisfying characters to invent. Their conflicts are legion, yet characters and readers alike demand one of the most persuasive elements of story-telling: hope. I will probably write more fantasy, since I like the colors and textures of it, and the unexpected things that chance out of my mind when I feel an urge to tell myself a story. But since I love, type, and pay taxes in the "real" world, I am also drawn to contemporary settings, and to writing about teenagers that I know. I think, in general, the boundary between adult and adolescent literature is becoming very tenuous. Nothing a teenager might worry about, from God to lesbianism, has remained unexplored, thanks to sensitive writers and publishers. Certainly, any teen-ager who takes reading seriously pays no attention to boundaries. But there is some basic integrity in the field of adolescent literature, that demands a discipline and honesty of its writers. Perhaps the crucial boundary lies there, and as the quality of adolescent literature seduces adolescent and adult readers alike, the flaccid realm of adult literature will begin to make more stringent demands upon itself. I hope so, anyway. That's something I would very much like to see.

HARRY MAZER

The Dollar Man
Guy Lenny
The Last Mission
Snow Bound
The Solid Gold Kid (with Norma Fox Mazer)

I sometimes think I'd like to do something historical, a book (a whole series, perhaps), rooted in an older period. Perhaps the trend has started in my work already with *The Last Mission* which is set in the Second World War. More and more, I find myself thinking back to those years, and the years earlier, to the years of my childhood. There is an aura, a glow to those years, a sense that those were better times: simpler, realer, families closer, friendships truer, the air purer, the world less complicated.

I'm probably kidding myself. Were things really better? Or only different? Still, I need to return to those years as to a well to connect to the child in myself.

As for the future, what I'd like to see in young adult literature is more direct contact between reader and writer. And the books of interest to young adults made widely and easily available. Paperbacks, of course, are the way. Libraries with the widest selection of what's available, paperback bookstores at the school's doorsteps, where the young congregate. I have a vision of an open market where the goods (the good books) are colorfully and abundantly displayed like fruit in season, and where pleasure (why else should anyone read?) is the first and foremost rule.

NORMA FOX MAZER

Dear Bill, Remember Me?
A Figure of Speech
Saturday, the Twelfth of October
Up in Seth's Room

I'm going to keep on writing books that are about and for the young, not just because the land of the young is the land of energy, enthusiasm, confusion, hope, despair, love, optimism, faith, and belief but also because I've never become completely convinced that my passport to that country has been stamped invalid. Every time I write a book about a young person, I sneak back in. What astounding good luck!

Books for the young are, I hope, getting tougher, realer, and truer. We're told the world is shrinking—yes and no. While it shrinks, it expands. Now we know not only what goes on in Syracuse, in New York, in the United States, in Canada, Mexico, England, France, and Hungary, but also in China, Ethiopia, and South Africa. The world is big, bigger, bigger than ever: hard, confusing, difficult, demanding. Lies won't do. The truth will help. I don't mean political truths, but the truth about people, human beings, how they live, what they feel, how they love, what they want—the truth about the human condition, if you will. It's the news of this truth which fiction has the power to bring us most accurately.

SHARON BELL MATHIS

Listen for the Fig Tree
Teacup Full of Roses

I do hope my writing nourishes young people, salutes them—portrays them in transition, examining their own adolescence, exploring their pursuit of independence. This pursuit—so natural for all of us—is often horrifying, but always triumphant. The field of adolescent literature is also in transition, as is any literature—constantly evolving, signaling and welcoming fresh insights—while continuing to be a storehouse filled with the treasures of wonder and enchantment.

MILTON MELTZER

Bound for the Rio Grande: The Mexican Struggle, 1845-1850
Langston Hughes: A Biography
Never to Forget: The Jews of the Holocaust
Violins and Shovels: The WPA Arts Projects

I will continue to write about the struggle for freedom and justice. Our need of them never disappears; it is only the form the struggle takes that changes. But that change offers the nonfiction writer an unlimited range of opportunity—not only in subject, but in the imaginative use of mind and heart to recreate the men and women and the times and trials which measure their humanity. I think critics, librarians, and teachers are coming to realize that nonfiction for children or adolescents, when it is honest and artful, can offer the reader as much reward in pleasure and expansion of the spirit as any other form of writing.

JOHN NEY

Ox Goes North: More Trouble for a Kid at the Top
Ox: The Story of a Kid at the Top
Ox Under Pressure

Obviously the future of young adult literature in the United States is tied to the readers rather than the writers. Modern writers have to be acceptable to young readers, whose interests and capabilities are not so broad and so extensive as they once were—i.e., see the statistics on the decline in reading ability. I have been fortunate in that

The young will read if it pleases them.

young readers from ghettoes to sheltered neighborhoods will read the *Ox* books. I did not design them as such—Ox, after all, is from a very special background—it was pure chance, and I am not sure I could duplicate it.

Ox, my rich boy from Palm Beach, views everything, including history, in a bemused sort of way which makes it easy for his readers to see him as one of them, however privileged. Reviewers have called them adult books in disguise, and have remarked on their pertinence vis-à-vis the state of the nation. All of which shows, I assume, that the young will read if it pleases them.

RICHARD PECK

Are You in the House Alone?
Father Figure
The Ghost Belonged to Me
Ghosts I Have Been

If we "YA" authors hang on and hang in, one of these days we'll find ourselves writing for the Second Generation—for the offspring of parents who grew up reading Judy Blume and Paul Zindel and S. E. Hinton. Is this bit of future shock sobering or heartening?

Heartening . . . I hope. The Word regarding YA books has not yet spread far. In the reviewing journals we speak mainly to each other. Parents are still about as unaware of our books as they are of what's going on in their children's schools. And those schools continue to be administered chiefly by people who don't value books of any sort.

Possibly the future of fiction and nonfiction addressed to adolescents will depend upon the nostalgia of parents who are presently passing through puberty. But what will life be like at the next turn-of-the-century when current writers are looked back upon as Betty Cavannas, Richard Halliburtons, and Booth Tarkingtons?

The themes that last will surely be rephrased in future volumes. I can only assume that the enduring ones will have nothing to do with the sexual revolution, the drug culture, and racial politics. The young now and in the future are not going to be able to solve these problems. It's a sickness from the '60s that we ever expected them to. They're going to continue to draw back from such problems in search of smaller, safer worlds. Possibly the writers' challenge will be to write adventurous books on "safe" subjects.

Books that explore friendship, which is a more potent preoccupation than sex to the young, and easier to contemplate. Books that continue to examine the family structure rather than celebrating collectivist alternatives. Books set in suburbs that still purvey a liberating hint of larger, more stimulating worlds.

A second generation of such books might do well to include a dimension now missing. We might continue plumbing the coming-of-age theme and then follow our young characters into adult life. That way we could depict not only actions, but their ultimate consequences. And I'm not talking about cautionary tales that warn young unwed mothers and fathers that they've blighted their entire lives. Such a message might not even be true.

But it would be pleasantly expansive to indicate to the young that all of life need not be as cruelly conformist and conservative as adolescence—unless you want it to be. That the most truly successful men and women were not high-school hotshots, beauty queens, super jocks, or manipulative gang leaders.

But maybe that's expecting too much. I imagine that the most acceptable new titles of the 1990s will be books about the sorrows of friendship and the painful necessity of growing up in a world new to no one but yourself. Books that include a little cautious nudge of optimism to offset what is blaring from a TV without an off knob. Books that invite the young to think for themselves instead of for each other.

ROBERT NEWTON PECK

A Day No Pigs Would Die
Fawn
Hang for Treason
Millie's Boy

As a farmer turned author, what I miss most of my Vermont boyhood is my work . . . haying, chores, helping Mama and Papa and strong, silent men do heavy labor. Tending the green and the growing. Teachers, librarians, farmers, are akin . . . custodians of growth, tenders and menders.

Boyhood wasn't all work. My best pal, Soup, and I really tore up the pea patch, as rascals. Yet our fervent respect of Miss Kelly (our teacher) always kept us straight as a fence. We believed in her. More importantly, she believed in us.

My future books will feature heroes with spunk and gumption, with the backbone to face a fury. Not really heroes, yet kids who can somehow muster enough bowels to perform one heroic act. Kids with a tough gut and a gentle heart.

And laughter . . . Soup and I had more fun and spent less money than any two kids in America. Maybe this was why, as I look back, we both grew up so rapturously rich.

KIN PLATT

The Boy Who Could Make Himself Disappear
Chloris and the Creeps
Chloris and the Freaks
Headman
Run for Your Life

The future I see for my own work is an ever widening and deepening spiral to get the most out of myself and my readers. Most of my books shake up current taboos and I hope to continue along that vein with occasional lighter work to keep me from being banned completely. I don't have those problems in my adult mysteries, the Max Roper series.

As for the future of the field, I think we're all making progress. I always make myself remember that we all came out of the primeval muck only a few billion years ago, and we have made some kind of step forward. There is always resistance to new ideas, enlightening concepts, or attacks on societal structures, but at times some will be permitted to filter through and reach and hopefully influence our growing audience.

My hopes are always for a higher human quality.

SANDRA SCOPPETTONE

Happy Endings Are All Alike
The Late Great Me
Trying Hard to Hear You

As you may know I write for adults as well and so I probably won't write more than one YA every two or three years. I plan to continue writing for young adults because I find it very rewarding. The mail I receive from kids tells me that I must be doing something right. I seem to write what are known as problem books. I don't know why exactly but I keep doing it. Anorexia, suicide, and learning disabilities interest me now. But who knows? I doubt if I will ever write something "beautiful" . . . it just isn't my style. You can count on me never to win the National Book Award!

Louise Fitzhugh opened the door for more realistic writing for teens and M. E. Kerr has kept that door open along with others. The only thing I can predict is that it . . . no, I won't say it . . . I was going to say we won't go back to the days of Nancy Drew but that's probably just what will happen. You see what I mean? Who knows?

BARBARA WERSBA

The Country of the Heart
The Dream Watcher
Run Softly, Go Fast
Tunes for a Small Harmonica

As an author of young adult books I may be prejudiced, but I feel that some of the finest talent in America is now writing for this audience. M. E. Kerr, John Donovan, and the late Louise Fitzhugh have made immeasurable contributions to the genre, and their works stand as literature. For myself, I can only say that I want to write about adolescents as they are—not as we would have them be—and that my own difficult journey is towards the truth. Adolescents today are not the adolescents *we* were, and to a writer such a fact can only be humbling.

BRENDA WILKINSON

Ludell
Ludell and Willie

Like my protagonist Ludell, I am a product of the last of the segregated school system in the South. What I've attempted in the trilogy I've written is to give a "factional" account of this period. I think my work will ultimately stand as a kind of continuation of the works that Wright, Killens, and other Southern black writers began. While they captured the 1930s and 40s, I have picked up at the 50s/60s. I felt it especially important that this period be recorded as it was the end of an era (segregation).

Presently I'm working on a novel of the "new South" drawn from the experiences of my younger sisters and brothers, who, unlike most of my generation and those before, view the north as "no promised land." The changes that have resulted from integration, both positive and negative, make for an interesting and important story.

While I don't want my work to become too political, preachy, or instructional—my overall objective in writing is to give young people a sense of where we've been in this country, and why. In giving them this history, I attempt to help them see that their experiences, fears, desires, and frustrations aren't that unique. Hopefully the writing will continue to come out in an entertaining and interesting manner, so that indeed my work will be a source of some direction in what I'm convinced is a difficult time to be young.

PAUL ZINDEL

The Effect of Gamma Rays on Man-in-the-Moon Marigolds
My Darling, My Hamburger
The Pigman
The Undertaker's Gone Bananas

Young adult books should be used to improve the lives of our youth. A book is created by a writer who observes life and then freezes it into words. I think here's where we really need the school experience and the inspired teacher and librarian. It's all very nice that kids can have good reading on their own. It's all very pleasant if a class, miraculously rare, can have their jollies at the same time, too. But what I find most exciting is when the words of the book are turned back into life. A book is a departure point from which kids can take a page, a written event, and turn it into an experience. The actual experience captured in the book is not half as important as kids themselves being able to speak out in a class and to say: 1) *Hey, I understand what these words say, that John Conlan sat across from his girlfriend and they had secrets to share over a candlelight dinner they concocted;* 2) *And Hey, I think I would have done something else if I was left alone in a house with a girl like that. I would have behaved differently here and the same as John at another point;* 3) *And Hey, this event reminds me of the time I was alone with a girl in a cemetery and we told each other we heard footsteps and thought we saw a hand reach out of a grave!*

What I'm trying to say is that a YA book in particular is a grand opportunity to take full advantage of word and phrase configuration as a take-off point from which a boy and girl can enter into *performance* of life. Jung knew a single alien letter from an unknown alphabet was enough to trigger endless thoughts in the human mind. Imagine the power of a whole book in the hands of a teacher and class. Right now in America we are just beginning to dream of turning away from fact bombardment and opening up our ears to listen to the kids. So many children in schools are denied expressing their experiences, and hearing of the experiences of others. So many never had a chance to think of goals, success paths, or, simply, opportunities to practice showing their emotions.

Our schools have been for open books and closed mouths. To hell with that. Let's let our kids lift their books *and* their voices. Maybe, just maybe, the young will no longer hate reading, school, and the world as much. Words should at every age mean a better life for the reader.

ACTIVITIES

1. Select one of the authors quoted in this chapter. Read several of that person's books and a write a paper in which you do an in-depth analysis and comparison of books.

2. One of the things that Doris Bass predicted was that media tie-ins would grow in strength and would have an influence on which books would be published. Do some research on current television specials and movies based on young adult literature. Prepare a listing that you might use to help promote the books from which these presentations were adapted. Jot down some ideas that you could use in this kind of book promotion.

3. Go back to books you have read during the semester and see if you can find relationships between the books and the philosophies of the respective authors as stated in this chapter.

Appendix A

Honor Sampling

Title and Author	Hardbound Publisher	Publishing Division	Paperback Publisher	ALA-YASD	SLJ	EJ*	NYT	A.L. Prof.	Genre	Sex	Age	Number of Pages	Filmed for T.V. or Movies	Ethnic Group
1977														
Hard Feelings Don Bredes	Atheneum	A	Bantam	•		•			Realistic Fiction	M	16	377		
I Am the Cheese Robert Cormier	Pantheon	J	Dell	•		•	•		Realistic Fiction	M	14	233		
Ludell and Willie Brenda Wilkinson	Harper & Row	J	Bantam	•		•	•		Realistic Fiction	F	16	181		Black
Trial Valley Vera and Bill Cleaver	Lippincott	J	Bantam	•	•	•	•		Realistic Fiction	F	17	158		Rural Isolated
1976														
Are You in the House Alone? Richard Peck	Viking	J	Dell	•	•	•	•	2	Realistic Fiction	F	16	156	•	
Dear Bill, Remember Me? Norma Fox Mazer	Delacorte	J	Dell	•			•		Short Stories	F	Teen	195		
The Distant Summer Sarah Patterson	Simon & Schuster	A	Pocket Books	•	•	•		2	Love-Romance	F	16	153		
Home Before Dark Sue Ellen Bridgers	Knopf	J	Bantam	•		•	•		Realistic Fiction	F	14	176		Migrant Workers

Title / Author	Publisher	J/A	Paper	●	●	●	●	No.	Genre	Sex	Age	Pages	Ethnicity
Never to Forget: The Jews of the Holocaust — Milton Meltzer	Harper & Row	J	Dell				●	4	Informative	—	—	217	Jewish
Ordinary People — Judith Guest	Viking	A	Ballantine		●	●	●		Realistic Fiction	M	17	263	
Singin' and Swingin' and Gettin' Merry Like Christmas — Maya Angelou	Random House	A	Bantam	●	●	●	●		Biography	F	Young Adult	269	Black
Tunes for a Small Harmonica — Barbara Wersba	Harper & Row	J	Dell	●		●	●		Realistic Fiction Humor	F	16	178	
Zero Makes Me Hungry: A Collection of Poems for Today — Ed. Edward Lueders and Primus St. John	Scott, Foresman	J			●	●	●		Poetry	—	—	139	
1975													
Circus — Alistair Maclean	Doubleday	A	Fawcett World		●	●	●		Realistic Fiction	M	Adult	192	
El Bronx Remembered — Nicholasa Mohr	Harper & Row	J	Bantam	●	●	●	●	1	Short Stories	Mixed	Mixed	149	Puerto Rican
How Democracy Failed — Ellen Switzer	Atheneum	J				●	●		New Journalism	M F	Teen	176	German
Is That You, Miss Blue? — M. E. Kerr	Harper & Row	J	Dell	●	●	●	●	1	Realistic Fiction	F	14	170	
The Lion's Paw — D. R. Sherman	Doubleday	A			●	●	●		Realistic Fiction	M	16	233	African
The Massacre at Fall Creek — Jessamyn West	Harcourt Brace	A	Fawcett World	●	●	●	●	2	Historical Fiction	M F	Adult Teen	373	Indian
Rumble Fish — S. E. Hinton	Delacorte	J	Dell		●	●	●	3	Realistic Fiction	M	14	122	

*The University of Iowa Book Poll has been printed in *English Journal* since 1972. Because this poll was not available before 1972, a list of popular books put out by the A.L.A. Young Adult Services Division called "Still Alive in '75" was used for books published in the years 1967 through 1971.

Title and Author	Hardbound Publisher	Publishing Division	Paperback Publisher	Listed by: ALA-YASD	SLJ	EJ*	NYT	A L Prof.	Genre	Protagonist Sex	Age	Number of Pages	Filmed for T.V. or Movies	Ethnic Group
Women of Wonder: Science Fiction by Women, About Women Ed. P. Sargent	—	A	Random House	•				1	Science Fiction Short Stories	F	Mixed	285		
You Can Get There from Here Shirley Maclaine	Norton	A	Bantam	•	•	•			New Journalism	F	40	249		
Z for Zachariah Robert C. O'Brien	Atheneum	J	Dell	•	•	•	•	1	Science Fiction	F	16	249		
1974														
Alive: The Story of the Andes Survivors Piers Paul Read	Lippincott	A	Avon	•	•	•	•	33	New Journalism	M	20s	352	•	
The Chocolate War Robert Cormier	Pantheon	J	Dell	•	•	•	•		Realistic Fiction	M	14	253		
Feral Berton Roueche	Harper & Row	A	Pocket Books	•	•	•			Suspense Fiction	M	Adult	137		
House of Stairs William Sleator	Dutton	J	Avon	•	•	•		4	Science Fiction	M / F	16	166		
M. C. Higgins the Great Virginia Hamilton	Macmillan	J	Dell	•	•	•	•	1	Realistic Fiction	M	13	278		Black
Trying Hard to Hear You Sandra Scoppettone	Harper & Row	J	Bantam	•	•	•		2	Realistic Fiction	F	16	264		
Watership Down Richard Adams	Macmillan	A	Avon	•	•	•	•	1	Fantasy	M	—	429	•	

1973

Title / Author	Publisher	J/A	Paperback				No.	Category	M/F	Age	Pages		Ethnicity
A Day No Pigs Would Die — Robert Newton Peck	Knopf	J	Dell	•	•	•	13	Historical Fiction	M	13	150		
The Friends — Rosa Guy	Holt, Rinehart	J		•	•	•	13	Realistic Fiction	F	14	203		W. Indian Black
A Hero Ain't Nothin' But a Sandwich — Alice Childress	Coward, McCann	J	Avon	•	•	•	10	Realistic Fiction	M	13	126	•	Black
If I Love You Am I Trapped Forever? — M. E. Kerr	Harper & Row	J	Dell	•	•		2	Humor Fiction	M	17	177		
Nilda — Nicholasa Mohr	Harper & Row	J	Bantam	•	•		1	Realistic Fiction	F	14	292		Puerto Rican

1972

Title / Author	Publisher	J/A	Paperback				No.	Category	M/F	Age	Pages		Ethnicity
Deathwatch — Robb White	Doubleday	J	Dell	•	•	•		Suspense Fiction	M	20s	228	•	
Dinky Hocker Shoots Smack — M. E. Kerr	Harper & Row	J	Dell	•	•		8	Realistic Fiction Humor	F	16	198	•	
Dove — Robin Graham	Harper & Row	A	Bantam	•	•	•	1	New Journalism	M	16	199		
Man Without a Face — Isabelle Holland	Lippincott	J	Bantam	•	•	•	6	Realistic Fiction	M	16	248		
My Name Is Asher Lev — Chaim Potok	Knopf	A	Fawcett World	•	•	•		Realistic Fiction	M	20s	369		Jewish
Sticks and Stones — Lynn Hall	Follett	J	Dell	•	•		2	Realistic Fiction	M	16	220		

Title and Author	Hardbound Publisher	Publishing Division	Paperback Publisher	ALA-YASD	SLJ	EJ*	NYT	A.L. Prof.	Genre	Protagonist Sex	Age	Number of Pages	Filmed for T.V. or Movies	Ethnic Group
Teacup Full of Roses — Sharon Bell Mathis	Viking	J	Avon	•				2	Realistic Fiction	M	17	125		Black
Woodstock Craftsman's Manual — Jean Young	Praeger	J	Praeger	•	•	•	•		Informative	—	—	253		
1971														
The Autobiography of Miss Jane Pittman — Ernest Gaines	Dial	A	Bantam	•	•	•			Historical Fiction	F	Life-time	245	•	Black
Go Ask Alice — anonymous	Prentice Hall	J	Avon	•	•	•	•	9	New Journalism	F	16	159	•	
His Own Where — June Jordan	Crowell	J	Dell	•	•	•	•	2	Realistic Fiction	M F	15	89		Black
That Was Then, This Is Now — S. E. Hinton	Viking	J	Dell	•	•	•		3	Realistic Fiction	M	16	159		
Wild in the World — John Donovan	Harper & Row	J	Avon	•	•	•	•	2	Realistic Fiction	M	17	94		Rural Isolated
1970														
Bless the Beasts and Children — Glendon Swarthout	Doubleday	A	Pocket Books	•	•	•		2	Realistic Fiction	M	Young Teens	205	•	
Daddy Was a Number Runner — Louise Meriwether	Prentice-Hall	A	Pyramid	•	•	•	•		Realistic Fiction	F	12	208		Black
I Know Why the Caged Bird Sings — Maya Angelou	Random House	A	Bantam	•	•	•	•	2	Biography	F	Child-hood-16	281		Black

1969

Title / Author	Hardcover	Level	Paperback				Number	Genre	Sex	Age	Pages		Setting
The Andromeda Strain Michael Crichton	Knopf	A	Dell	•				Science Fiction	Mixed	Mixed	295	•	
I'll Get There. It Better Be Worth the Trip. John Donovan	Harper & Row	J	Dell		•		4	Realistic Fiction	M	13	189		
Sounder William Armstrong	Harper & Row	J	Harper & Row			•	2	Historical Fiction	M	14	116	•	Rural Black
Where the Lilies Bloom Vera and Bill Cleaver	Lippincott	J	NAL			•	1	Realistic Fiction	F	14	174	•	Rural Isolated

1968

Title / Author	Hardcover	Level	Paperback				Number	Genre	Sex	Age	Pages		Setting
The Pigman Paul Zindel	Harper & Row	J	Dell		•		32	Realistic Fiction	M F	16	182		
Red Sky at Morning Richard Bradford	Lippincott	A	Pocket Books	•	•	•	3	Realistic Fiction	M	17	256	•	Mexican American
Soul on Ice Eldridge Cleaver	McGraw-Hill	A	Dell		•	•		New Journalism	M	20s	210		Black

1967

Title / Author	Hardcover	Level	Paperback				Number	Genre	Sex	Age	Pages		Setting
The Chosen Chaim Potok	Simon & Schuster	A	Fawcett Crest	•	•	•	2	Realistic Fiction	M	Teen	284		Jewish
House of Tomorrow Jean Thompson	Harper & Row	A			•	•		New Journalism	F	Teen	179		
Mr. and Mrs. Bo Jo Jones Ann Head	Putnam	A	Signet	•	•	•	5	Realistic Fiction	F	18	253	•	
The Outsiders S. E. Hinton	Viking	J	Dell		•	•	19	Realistic Fiction	M	18	156		
Reflections on a Gift of Watermelon Pickle Ed. Stephen Dunning	Lothrop	J		•	•		3	Poetry	—	—	160		

Appendix B

Book Selection Guides

The sources listed below are designed to aid professionals in the selection and evaluation of books and other materials for young adults. An attempt was made to include sources with widely varying emphases. However, in addition to these sources, most of which appear at regular intervals, there are many specialized lists prepared by committees and individuals in response to current and/or local needs. Readers are advised to check on the availability of such lists with librarians and teachers. For purposes of comparison the 1979 prices are included, but readers should expect that many of them will have risen because of inflation.

The ALAN Review. Assembly on Literature for Adolescents, National Council of Teachers of English, 1111 Kenyon Rd., Urbana, IL 61801. $5.00 for three issues. Order from Mary Sucher, ALAN Membership Chair, Dundalk Senior High, 1901 Delvale Avenue, Baltimore, MD 21222. (Subscribers do not need to belong to NCTE.)

> This publication has appeared three times a year since 1973. It is currently edited by W. Geiger Ellis of the University of Georgia and is unique in being devoted entirely to adolescent literature. Each issue contains "Clip and File" reviews of approximately twenty new hardbacks or paperbacks and includes two or three feature articles, news announcements, and occasional in-depth reviews of professional books.

Book Bait: Detailed Notes on Adult Books Popular with Young People. Ed. Elinor Walker. 3rd ed., 1979. American Library Association, 50 E. Huron Street, Chicago, IL 60611. $2.50.

> A useful bibliography for bridging the gap between young adult and adult novels, this listing contains one hundred books with extensive annotations that include plot summaries, discussions of appeal to teenagers, hints for book talks, and suggested titles for use as follow-ups. Arrangement is alphabetical by author; subject and title indexes are appended.

Booklist. The American Library Association, 50 E. Huron St., Chicago, IL 60601. $24.00 for twenty-three issues.

> The size of the reviews varies from twenty-word annotations to three-hundred-word essays. "Books for Young Adults" (ages fourteen through eighteen) is a regular feature. Occasionally books in both the children's and adult sections are also marked YA. A review constitutes a recommendation for library purchase. Stars are given to books of high literary quality. Multi-media materials are also reviewed and a special section highlights books that have both a high interest potential for teenagers and a lower-than-average reading level. An early spring issue includes the annual "Best Books for Young Adults" list drawn up by the ALA Young Adult Services Division.

Books for the Teen Age 1979. Ed. Marian E. White. New York Public Library, Fifth Ave. and 42nd St., Rm. 58, New York, NY 10018. $2.50.

This sixty-four-page guide with minimal annotations is updated yearly and is thus an outstanding source of current titles which have been "tested and tried with teen age readers." Grouping is by subject; title and author indexes are included.

Books for You: A Booklist for Senior High Students. Ed. Kenneth L. Donelson. Rev. ed., 1976. National Council of Teachers of English, 1111 Kenyon Rd., Urbana, IL 61801. $2.95.

A lengthy (440 pages) bibliography intended to help students find "pleasurable reading." Annotations consist of one or two sentence summaries. "Frank" or "Offensive" language is noted, as are additional titles of similar interest and appeal. Titles are grouped by subject or theme; title and author indexes are appended. The book is prepared by an ongoing committee in NCTE with a new edition appearing every six or seven years. Robert C. Small of Virginia Polytechnic Institute is editing the next edition.

Bulletin of the Center for Children's Books. Ed. Zena Sutherland. The University of Chicago Graduate Library School, University of Chicago Press, 5801 Ellis Avenue, Chicago, IL 60637. $10.00 yearly.

This monthly (except August) journal reviews approximately sixty new books for children and young adults each issue. Though there is a time lag between the publication date and the appearance of a review, the *Bulletin* includes both recommended and not recommended titles. Since it is under the editorship of a single individual, the consistency of the reviews can be depended upon. Listed on the back cover are books, articles, and bibliographies of current interest to teachers, parents, and librarians.

English Journal. National Council of Teachers of English, 1111 Kenyon Rd., Urbana, IL 61801. $25.00 for eight issues, which includes membership in NCTE.

Aimed at high-school English teachers, nearly every issue contains something about new books of interest to teenage readers. Reviews, articles about young adult literature in the classroom, interviews with successful authors, and a yearly "Young Adult Book Poll" are among the regular features.

High Interest-Easy Reading for Junior and Senior High School Students. Ed. Marian E. White. 3rd ed., 1979. National Council of Teachers of English, 1111 Kenyon Rd., Urbana, IL 61801, $2.75.

Grouped by subject, this listing is aimed at reluctant young adult readers rather than at parents or teachers. Criteria for inclusion is high interest, easy reading, and literary quality. The annotations are written in the form of miniature book talks; author and title indexes are appended.

The Horn Book Magazine. The Horn Book, Inc., Park Square Building, 31 St. James Avenue, Boston, MA 92116. $15.00 for six issues.

This magazine has been devoted to the critical analysis of children's literature since 1924. Reviews are approximately two hundred words long and in a typical issue seven or eight adolescent novels will be reviewed under the heading of "Stories for Older Readers." "Outlook Tower" highlights current adult books of interest to high-school readers. Popular appeal takes a back seat to literary quality in the selection of titles for review. Feature articles are frequently of interest to teachers and librarians working with young adults.

Interracial Books for Children Bulletin. Council on Interracial Books for Children, 1841 Broadway, New York, NY 10023. Institutions $15.00, Individuals $10.00 for eight issues.

Nearly all reviews and articles in this twenty-five-page bulletin are written for the purpose of examining the relationship between social issues and how these are treated or reflected in current fiction, nonfiction, and curriculum materials.

Journal of Reading. International Reading Association, 6 Tyre Avenue, Newark, DE 19711. $15.00 for nine issues, which includes membership in The International Reading Association.

The target audience for this journal is high-school reading teachers. Although most of the articles are reports on research in the teaching of reading, some articles do focus on reading interests and literature. Also included are reviews of new young adult books written by association members.

Junior High School Library Catalog. Ed. Ilene R. Schechter and Gary L. Bogart. 3rd ed., 1975. H. W. Wilson Company, 950 University Ave., Bronx, NY 10452. $42.00.

Designed as a suggested basic book collection for junior high school libraries, this volume is divided into two major parts. The first includes an annotated listing by Dewey Decimal Number for nonfiction, author's last name for fiction, and author's/editor's last name for story collections. The second part relists all books alphabetically by author, title, and subject. Cumulated every five years with yearly supplements, this is an outstanding reference tool for junior high school librarians.

Kirkus Reviews. Kirkus Service, Inc., 200 Park Avenue South, New York, NY 10003. $150.00 for 26 issues.

Although this is one of the most expensive sources, it is also one of the most complete and up to date. Reviews are approximately two hundred words long, and a section is devoted to young adult books.

Kliatt Paperback Book Guide. 425 Watertown St., Newton, MA 92158. $20.00 for three issues with five interim supplements.

Because it is paperbacks that teenagers prefer to read, this source serves a real need. It attempts to review all paperbacks (originals, reprints, and reissues) recommended for readers aged twelve through nineteen. A code identifies books as appropriate for advanced students, general young adult readers, junior-high students, students with low reading abilities, and emotionally mature readers who can handle "explicit sex, excessive violence and/or obscenity." Reviews are arranged by subject. A title index and a directory of cooperating publishers are included.

Media and Methods. North American Publishing Co., 401 N. American Building, 491 N. Broad St., Philadelphia, PA 19108. $11.00 for nine issues.

Aimed at high-school teachers and published nine times a year, the main value of this lively journal is the frequent articles featuring young adult books and ways of working with them in schools. A "Young Adult Reading" page gives extended annotations for approximately a dozen titles, and an annual listing appears each spring highlighting the best new paperbacks.

The New York Times Book Review. New York Times Co., Times Square, New York, NY 10036. 52 issues, $18.

The currency of the reviews makes this an especially valuable source. Most weeks there is a section featuring children's books, many of which are suitable for teenagers. Of special interest are the fall and spring issues which are devoted almost exclusively to children's books—the fall issue usually includes a round up of the "best books" of the year. Editor George A. Woods has a good record for predicting the popularity of books.

Reading Ladders for Human Relations. Ed. Virginia M. Reid. 5th ed., 1972. American Council on Education and National Council of Teachers of English, 1111 Kenyon Rd., Urbana, IL 61801. $4.95. (A new edition edited by Eileen Tway is scheduled to appear in 1981.)

This 312-page bibliography, spanning from picture books to mature novels, is of particular use to the young adult specialist because it focuses on four categories of interest to junior and senior high school readers: "Creating a Positive Self-Image," "Living with Others," "Appreciating Different Cultures," and "Coping with Change." Junior, senior, and mature books are listed separately within these categories. Annotations are written with an eye toward the human relations aspect of each book. Author and title indexes are appended; the introductory section addresses various topics relating to young people and books.

School Library Journal. R. R. Bowker Company, 1180 Avenue of the Americas, New York, NY 10036. $17.00 for nine issues.

The most comprehensive of the review media, SLJ reviews both recommended and not recommended books. Reviews are written by a panel of four hundred librarians who are sent books particularly appropriate to their interests and backgrounds. Starred reviews signify exceptionally good books. Books of interest to teenagers will appear in the children's listings identified by grade levels (5-up, 6-8, 9-12, etc.) if they come from the juvenile division of a publisher or in a special young adult listing if they come from the adult division of a publisher.

Senior High School Library Catalog. Ed. Gary L. Bogart and Karen R. Carlson. 11th ed., 1977. H. W. Wilson Company, 950 University Ave., Bronx, NY 10452. $50.00.

> Using the same format as the *Junior High School Library Catalog* (see above), this lists some books appropriate for both junior- and senior-high collections as well as those aimed specifically at readers in grades ten through twelve. Like its companion volume, it is cumulated every five years with yearly supplements and is an invaluable aid for anyone involved in the building of a high-school library collection.

Top of the News. Joint publication of the Association for Library Service to Children and the Young Adult Services Division of the American Library Association, 50 E. Huron St., Chicago, IL 60611. Included in the dues of ALSC and YASD members; nonmembers pay $15.00 for four issues.

> Although the journal does not have room to review juvenile books on a regular basis, feature articles are often of interest to young adult librarians. Also of interest is the "Added Entries" column in which professional publications are reviewed.

Voice of Youth Advocates (VOYA). Ed. Dorothy M. Broderick and Mary K. Chelton. 10 Landing Lane, Room 6M, New Brunswick, NJ 08901. $10.00 for six issues.

> One of the aims of this publication, founded in 1978, is "to change the traditional linking of young adult services with children's librarianship and shift the focus to its connection with adult services." Feature articles are especially good because they present viewpoints not commonly considered. About one-fourth of the journal is devoted to reviews in the following categories: pamphlets, mysteries, science fiction, audio-visual, adult and teenage fiction and nonfiction, and professional books.

Wilson Library Bulletin. H. W. Wilson Co., 1950 University Avenue, Bronx, NY 19452. $14.00 for ten issues.

> Although the focus of the *Wilson Library Bulletin* is much broader than young adult librarianship, "The Young Adult Perplex," edited by Patty Campbell, is a regular feature that reviews current books. "Cine-Opsis," edited by Jana Varlejs, is also helpful in reviewing media of interest to young adults.

Your Reading: A Booklist for Junior High Schools. Ed. Jerry Walker. 1975. National Council of Teachers of English, 1111 Kenyon Rd., Urbana, IL 61801. $1.95.

> In this companion volume to *Books for You*, over 1,600 titles are arranged under twenty-two major headings. Annotations are brief and, with the exception of the phrase "easy to read" and the listing of awards that particular books have received, critical comments are scrupulously avoided. Author and title indexes are appended and there is a short list of "standard books," i.e., classics. Jane Chris-

tensen heads an NCTE committee currently working to revise this list which appears approximately every five years.

Appendix C

The Students' Right to Read

The right to read, like all rights guaranteed or implied within our constitutional tradition, can be used wisely or foolishly. In many ways, education is an effort to improve the quality of choices open to man. But to deny the freedom of choice in fear that it may be unwisely used is to destroy the freedom itself. For this reason, we respect the right of individuals to be selective in their own reading. But for the same reason, we oppose efforts of individuals or groups to limit the freedom of choice of others or to impose their own standards or tastes upon the community at large.

The right of any individual not just to read but to read whatever he wants to read is basic to a democratic society. This right is based on an assumption that the educated and reading man possesses judgment and understanding and can be trusted with the determination of his own actions. In effect, the reading man is freed from the bonds of discovering all things and all facts and all truths through his own direct experiences, for his reading allows him to meet people, debate philosophies, and experience events far beyond the narrow confines of his own existence.

In selecting books for reading by young people, English teachers consider the contribution which each work may make to the education of the reader, its aesthetic value, its honesty, its readability for a particular group of students, and its appeal to adolescents. English teachers, however, may use different works for different purposes. The criteria for choosing a work to be read by an entire class are somewhat different from the criteria for choosing works to be read by small groups. For example, a teacher might select John Knowles' *A Separate Peace* for reading by an entire class, partly because the book has received wide critical recognition, partly because it is relatively short and will keep the attention of many slow readers, and partly because it has proved popular with many students of widely differing abilities. The same teacher, faced with the responsibility of choosing or recommending books for several small groups of students, might select or recommend books as different as Nathaniel Hawthorne's *The Scarlet Letter*, Jack Schaefer's *Shane*, Alexandr Solzhenitsyn's *One Day in the Life of Ivan Denisovitch*, Pierre Boulle's *The Bridge over the River Kwai*, Charles Dickens' *Great Expectations*, or Paul Zindel's *The Pigman*, depending upon the abilities and interests of the students in each group. And the criteria for suggesting books to individuals

This excerpt from the 1972 edition of *The Students' Right to Read* is an adaptation and updating of the original Council Statement, including "Citizen's Request for Reconsideration of a Work," prepared by the Committee on the Right to Read of the National Council of Teachers of English. The statement is currently being updated, and a new edition is planned for the near future.

or for recommending something worth reading for a student who casually stops by after class are different from selecting material for a class or group. But the teacher selects books; he does not censor them. Selection implies that a teacher is free to choose this or that work, depending upon the purpose to be achieved and the student or class in question, but a book selected this year may be ignored next year, and the reverse. Censorship implies that certain works are not open to selection, this year or any year.

Many works contain isolated elements to which some individuals or groups may object. The literary artist seeks truth, as he is able to see and feel it. As a seeker of truth, he must necessarily challenge at times the common beliefs or values of a society; he must analyze and comment on people's actions and values and the frequent discrepancy between what they purport to live by and what they do live by. In seeking to discover meaning behind reality, the artist strives to achieve a work which is honest. Moreover, the value and impact of any literary work must be examined as a whole and not in part—the impact of the entire work being more important than the words, phrases, or incidents out of which it is made.

Wallace Stevens once wrote, "Literature is the better part of life. To this it seems inevitably necessary to add, provided life is the better part of literature." Students and parents have the right to demand that education today keep students in touch with the reality of the world outside the classroom. Much of classic literature asks questions as valid and significant today as when the literature first appeared, questions like "What is the nature of humanity?" "Why do people praise individuality and practice conformity?" "What do people need for a good life?" and "What is the nature of the good person?" But youth is the age of revolt, and the times today show much of the world in revolt. To pretend otherwise is to ignore a reality made clear to young people and adults alike on television and radio, in newspapers and magazines. English teachers must be free to employ books, classic or contemporary, which do not lie to the young about the perilous but wondrous times we live in, books which talk of the fears, hopes, joys, and frustrations people experience, books about people not only as they are but as they can be. English teachers forced through the pressures of censorship to use only safe or antiseptic works are placed in the morally and intellectually untenable position of lying to their students about the nature and condition of mankind.

The teacher must exercise care to select or recommend works for class reading and group discussion which will not embarrass students in discussions with their peers. One of the most important responsibilities of the English teacher is developing rapport and respect among students. Respect for the uniqueness and potential of the individual, an important facet of the study of literature, should be emphasized in the English class. For students to develop a respect for each individual, no matter what his race or creed or values may be, multi-ethnic materials must become a part of the literature program in all schools, regardless of the ethnic composition of the school population. It is time that literature classes reflect the cultural contributions of many minority groups in the United States, just as they should acquaint students with contributions from the peoples of Asia, Africa, and Latin America.

What a young reader gets from any book depends both on the selection and on the reader himself. A teacher should choose books with an awareness of the student's interests, his reading ability, his mental and emotional maturity, and the values he may derive from the reading. A wide knowledge of many works, common sense, and professional dedication to students and to literature will guide the teacher in making his selections. The community that entrusts students to the care of an English teacher should also trust that teacher to exercise professional judgment in selecting or recommending books.

THE THREAT TO EDUCATION

Censorship leaves students with an inadequate and distorted picture of the ideals, values, and problems of their culture. Writers may often be the spokesmen of their culture, or they may stand to the side attempting to describe and evaluate that culture. Yet, partly because of censorship or the fear of censorship, many writers are ignored or inadequately represented in the public schools, and many are represented in anthologies not by their best work but by their "safest" or "least offensive" work.

The censorship pressures receiving the greatest publicity are those of small groups who protest the use of a limited number of books with some "objectionable" realistic elements, such as *Brave New World, Lord of the Flies, Catcher in the Rye, The Stranger, Johnny Got His Gun, The Assistant, Catch-22, Soul on Ice,* or *Stranger in a Strange Land.* The most obvious and immediate victims are often found among our best and most creative English teachers, those who have ventured outside the narrow boundaries of conventional texts. Ultimately, however, the real victims are the students, denied the freedom to explore ideas and pursue truth wherever and however they wish.

Great damage may be done by book committees appointed by national or local organizations to pore over anthologies, texts, library books, and paperbacks to find sentences which advocate, or seem to advocate, causes or concepts or practices these organizations condemn. As a result, some publishers, sensitive to possible objections, carefully exclude sentences or selections that might conceivably offend some group, somehow, sometime, somewhere.

Many well-meaning people wish to restrict reading materials in schools to books that do not mention certain aspects of life they find offensive: drugs, profanity, Black Power, anti-war marches, smoking, sex, racial unrest, rock music, politics, pregnancy, school dropouts, peace rallies, drinking, Chicano protests, or divorce. Although he may personally abhor one or more of these facets of modern life, the English teacher has the responsibility to encourage students to read about and reflect on many aspects, good and bad, of their own society and of other cultures.

THE ENGLISH TEACHER'S PURPOSES AND RESPONSIBILITIES

The purpose of education remains what it has always been in a free society: to develop a free and reasoning human being who can think for himself, who understands his own and, to some extent, other cultures, who lives compassionately and cooperatively with his fellow man, who respects both himself and others, who has developed self-discipline and self-motivation and exercises both, who can laugh at a world which often seems mad, and who can successfully develop survival strategies for existence in that world.

The English teacher knows that literature is a significant part of the education of man, for literature raises problems and questions and dilemmas that have perplexed and intrigued and frustrated man since the dawn of time. Literature presents some solutions to complex problems and some answers to abiding questions, perhaps incomplete but the best we have found. Even more important, literature continues to raise questions man can never wholly answer: What is the relationship between power and moral responsibility? Why does the good man sometimes suffer and the evil man sometimes go untouched by adversity? How can man reconcile the conflict of duty between what he owes society and what he owes his own conscience? The continued search for answers, tentative as they must prove, is a necessary part of the educated man's life, and the search for answers may in part be found through reading.

Aware of the vital role of literature in the education of mankind, the English teacher has unique responsibilities to his students and to adults in the community. To his students, he is responsible for knowing many books from many cultures, for demonstrating a personal commitment to the search for truth through wide reading and continual critical questioning of his own values and beliefs, for respecting the unique qualities and potential of each student, for studying many cultures and societies and their values, and for exhibiting the qualities of the educated man. To adults, he is responsible for communicating information about his literature program; for explaining, not defending, what books he uses with what students, for what reasons, and with what results; and for communicating the necessity of free inquiry and the search for truth in a democratic society and the dangers of censorship and repression.

THE COMMUNITY'S RESPONSIBILITY

American citizens who care about the improvement of education are urged to join students, teachers, librarians, administrators, boards of education, and professional and scholarly organizations in support of the students' right to read. Only widespread and informed support in every community can assure that

> enough citizens are interested in the development and maintenance of a superior school system to guarantee its achievement;
>
> malicious gossip, ignorant rumors, and deceptive letters to the editor will not be circulated without challenge and correction;
>
> newspapers will be convinced that the public sincerely desires objective school news reporting, free from slanting or editorial comment which destroys confidence in and support for schools;

the community will not permit its resources and energies to be dissipated in conflicts created by special interest groups striving to advance their ideologies or biases; and

faith in democratic traditions and processes will be maintained.

Appendix D
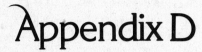

Sample Selection Policy

The following is an example of a policy regarding the selection of books and other instructional materials. This policy happens to be from Tempe Union High School in Tempe, Arizona. We include it here not as a model but simply as an example of the way one school chose to make a statement regarding its selection of books and other materials. In the event of a challenge to materials used in a school, a policy statement is an important part of the school's defense against censorship.

TEMPE UNION HIGH SCHOOL

Instructional Materials Policy*

The legal responsibility for instructional materials in the Tempe Union High School District rests with the Board of Education. Responsibility for selection shall be delegated to professionally trained personnel who know the course of study, the methods of teaching, and the individual differences of the students for whom the materials are provided.

The selection of instructional materials shall be in accordance with ARS 15-545 and the following objectives:

1. To implement the curriculum;
2. To enrich the curriculum;
3. To further intellectual, emotional, cultural, and ethical development of youth.

Instructional Materials Selection Guidelines

Three basic considerations are used in selecting instructional materials or in accepting gifts of such materials: the student, the subject, and the quality.

---

*In recent years this policy was changed from a "Book Selection Policy" that dealt mainly with library materials to an "Instructional Materials Policy" which covers classroom as well as library materials and personnel.

1. *Selection of instructional materials in relation to the student:* Materials shall be examined to select those in which theme and presentation of the subject matter are suitable for the ability and interest of the student.
2. *Selection of instructional materials in relation to appropriateness of subject:* Instructional materials shall be selected for their timeliness and timelessness. Timeliness is judged by the current interest or emphasis on an author or subject. Timelessness of instructional materials is judged according to its enduring quality, its uniqueness and significance, its historical value, and the eminence of the author or producer.

    The intent and honesty of the presentation are important criteria in selection. Instructional materials related to sex, morality, race or ethnicity, religion, sex roles, health and politics will be carefully chosen to insure fair and objective treatment of these significant areas.

    The presence of sexual incidents or profanity shall not automatically disqualify material. Rather, the decision shall be made on the basis of whether the material represents life in its true proportions, whether circumstances are realistically dealt with, or whether the material is of literary or artistic value.
3. Two basic factors, truth and art, will be considered in the selection of instructional materials. The first is factual accuracy, authoritativeness, balance and integrity. The second is a quality presentation—stimulating, imaginative and with style appropriate to the idea.

    Content is judged as to significance, responsibility of opinion, the authority and intent of the authors or producers, the reliability of the distributors, factual accuracy, and richness of ideas. A chief concern must be the values, strength, and virtues of the entire work, rather than minor weaknesses in any of its parts. Expression is judged as to clarity, artistry, originality, precision, choice of words, or readability. Format is judged as to durability and attractiveness.

Procedures for Reconsideration of Instructional Materials

1. Individuals or organizations, hereinafter referred to as the complainant, requesting reconsideration of instructional materials shall first complete a copy of "Citizen's Request for Reconsideration of Instructional Materials" which will be made available by the school principal. The completed "Request" must be submitted to the principal who will inform all school personnel involved of its receipt.
2. Within five (5) school days from receipt of a completed "Citizen's Request for Reconsideration of Instructional Materials" form, the principal will appoint a special review committee composed of a media specialist, teachers in the area(s) encompassing the questioned material, a building administrator, and a district administrator.
3. Within ten (10) school days from receipt of a completed "Citizen's Request

for Reconsideration of Instructional Materials" form, the principal will schedule a meeting of the review committee at a time acceptable to the complainant if the complainant wishes to appear before the review committee.

4. Within five (5) school days from the initial meeting stipulated in # 3 above, the review committee shall (a) complete its examination of the questioned material for suitability according to the criteria contained in Tempe Union High School District policy and guidelines governing selection of instructional materials and (b) submit a formal recommendation to the principal.

5. Within five (5) school days of receipt of the review committee's recommendation, the principal shall reach a decision and shall communicate his/her decision in writing to the complainant. Should the principal's decision be that the questioned materials continue in use, this written communication shall advise the complainant of his/her right to appeal through the channels established by Board of Education Policy GAE.

6. Use of the questioned material will not be discontinued during the period of reconsideration.

Appendix E

Some Outstanding Books and Articles about Young Adult Literature

The list below represents our personal choices. It is not at all an attempt at a complete listing of everything ever written about young adult literature. That might seem more difficult, but in some ways it would have been easier to pull together, for it would have avoided objections to what we included or ignored. We followed a few simple ground rules, and they may explain—if not justify—why some works were included or excluded.

1. Books or articles had to be primarily on young adult literature, not on the psychology of the young adult, the cultural milieu of the time, or literary history—not even general literary criticism. If we'd wanted to include the last, we'd have recommended Eudora Welty's *The Eye of the Story: Selected Essays and Reviews* and left it at that. But since we didn't, we won't.

2. Books or articles had to cover more than just one author. No matter how good articles may have been on Paul Zindel or M. E. Kerr or Virginia Hamilton (and many of them were very good), we ignored them in favor of works with greater and wider implications.

3. Books or articles had to excite us. Doubtless, some readers will find us culpable for our tastes in including this or ignoring that. So be it. We like the ones we list, and we believe others will, too.

4. No books or articles were included to fit some category otherwise ignored.

We did not try to balance our list so that we would have the proper number, or any particular number, of articles on censorship or sports or minority groups or anything else. We chose what we did because we believe in them.

5. No works by either Nilsen or Donelson were included. Readers may assume either that we believe none of our writings belong under the rubric "outstanding" or that we are modest to a fault—whichever pleases them or best fits their prejudices.

Brief annotations are provided for works where the titles were not already self-explanatory.

BOOKS

Histories of Young Adult Literature

Avery, Gillian. *Childhood's Pattern: A Study of the Heroes and Heroines of Children's Fiction 1770–1950.* London: Hodder and Stoughton, 1975.

Cadogan, Mary, and Patricia Craig. *You're a Brick, Angela! A New Look at Girls' Fiction from 1839 to 1975.* London: Victor Gollancz Ltd., 1976. A delightfully witty view of girls' books and social history.

Crouch, Marcus. *The Nesbit Tradition: The Children's Novel in England 1945–1970.* London: Ernest Benn Ltd., 1972.

————. *Treasure Seekers and Borrowers: Children's Books in Britain 1900–1960.* London: Library Association, 1962.

Darling, Richard. *The Rise of Children's Book Reviewing in America, 1865–1881.* New York: Bowker, 1968. Impressive and scholarly study of early children's and YA books, book reviewing, and reviewers.

Darton, F. J. Harvey. *Children's Books in England: Five Centuries of Social Use.* 2nd ed. Cambridge: Cambridge University Press, 1958. First published in 1932 and still worth reading.

Ellis, Alec. *A History of Children's Reading and Literature.* Oxford: Pergamon Press, 1968. Children's and YA literature from 1740 to 1965.

Eyre, Frank. *British Children's Books in the Twentieth Century.* New York: Dutton, 1973.

Girls' Series Books: A Checklist of Hardback Books Published 1900–1975. Minneapolis: Children's Literature Research Collections, University of Minnesota Library, 1978. Not quite as good as Hudson (below) but a helpful tool in working with series books.

Howarth, Patrick. *Play Up and Play the Game: The Heroes of Popular Fiction.* London: Eyre Methuen, 1973. On nineteenth century popular boys' books.

Hudson, Harry K. *A Bibliography of Hard-Cover Boys' Books.* Rev. ed. Tampa, Florida: Data Print, 1977. An outstanding checklist of boys' series books, mostly of this century.

Kiefer, Monica. *American Children Through Their Books, 1700–1835.* Philadelphia: University of Pennsylvania Press, 1948.

Kilgour, Raymond L. *Lee & Shepard: Publishers for the People.* Hamden, Connecticut: Shoe String Press, 1965. A history of a major publisher of boys' series books in the nineteenth and twentieth centuries.

MacLeod, Anna Scott. *A Moral Tale: Children's Fiction and American Culture, 1820–1860.* Hamden, Connecticut: Archon Books, 1975.

Mason, Bobbie Ann. *The Girl Sleuth: A Feminist Guide.* Old Westbury, New York: Feminist Press, 1975. Perceptive and witty comments about girls' series books, especially Nancy Drew.

Meigs, Cornelia, et al. *A Critical History of Children's Literature.* Rev. ed. New York: Macmillan, 1969. An encyclopedic study of children's literature, often including YA books, from ancient times onward.

Sloane, William. *Children's Books in England and America in the Seventeenth Century.* New York: Columbia University Press, 1955.

Thwaite, Mary F. *From Primer to Pleasure: An Introduction to the History of Children's Books in England from the Invention of Printing to 1914 with an Outline of Some Developments in Other Countries.* Boston: Horn Book, 1972. First published in England in 1963.

Townsend, John Rowe. *Written for Children: An Outline of English-Language Children's Literature.* Rev. ed. Philadelphia: Lippincott, 1975. Perhaps the most readable history, albeit more English than American, and also available in a handy Penguin paperback.

Criticism of Young Adult Literature

Broderick, Dorothy M. *Image of the Black in Children's Fiction.* New York: Bowker, 1973. Racism and YA literature.

Chambers, Aidan. *The Reluctant Reader.* London: Pergamon Press, 1969. One of the great books about YA literature, sympathetic and helpful ideas about bringing books to the hard-to-get-to reader.

Hazard, Paul. *Books, Children and Men.* Trans. Marguerite Mitchell. Boston: Horn Book, 1944. Nominally about children and literature but really about readers of any kind with clear implications for young adults.

Lukens, Rebecca. *A Critical Handbook of Children's Literature.* Glenview, Illinois: Scott, Foresman, 1976. Criteria and aspects of children's literature easily applicable to YA literature.

Salmon, Edward. *Juvenile Literature as It Is.* London: Henry J. Drane, 1888. Sympathetic and forward-looking views on the values of children's and YA literature. Neglected but deserves close reading.

Sloan, Glenna Davis. *The Child as Critic.* New York: Teachers College Press, 1975. Application of Northrop Frye's critical theories to children's and YA literature.

Libraries and Young Adult Literature

Carrier, Esther Jane. *Fiction in Public Libraries, 1876–1900.* New York: Scarecrow Press, 1965. The "fiction question" and YA literature.

Edwards, Margaret A. *The Fair Garden and the Swarm of Beasts: The Library and the Young Adult.* Rev. ed. New York: Hawthorn Books, 1974. The problems and joys of being a young adult librarian, from the author's own experiences.

English Classrooms and Young Adult Literature

Burton, Dwight L. *Literature Study in the High Schools.* 3rd ed. New York: Holt, 1970. For many English teachers, *the* book that introduced them to YA literature.

Carlsen, G. Robert. *Books and the Teen-Age Reader.* Rev. ed. New York: Harper and Row, 1971. A new edition is promised in 1979 or 1980.

Fader, Daniel. *The New Hooked on Books.* New York: Berkley, 1976. First published in 1966 as *Hooked on Books* and revised in 1968 as *Hooked on Books: Program and Proof,* Fader's book probably influenced more English teachers to consider YA literature than any other single source. Still highly readable and contagious in its enthusiasm.

Authors of Young Adult Literature

Commire, Anne, ed. *Something About the Author.* Detroit: Gale Research, 1971. A continuing series about many authors, their lives and their books. An indispensable source of help.

———. *Yesterday's Authors of Books for Children.* Detroit: Gale Research, 1977. A continuing series of authors who died prior to 1961. Some entries run to many pages. An extremely useful guide.

Jones, Cornelia, and Olivia R. Way. *British Children's Authors: Interviews at Home.* Chicago: American Library Association, 1976. Interviews with authors Nina Bawden, Alan Garner, Allan Campbell McLean, Kathleen Peyton, Rosemary Sutcliff, Barbara Willard, and others.

Kirkpatrick, D. L., ed. *Twentieth-Century Children's Writers.* N.Y.: St. Martin's Press, 1978. A mammoth (1507 pages) index of authors listing biographical and bibliographical details along with a brief to fairly lengthy critical assessment.

Sarkissian, Adele, ed. *Children's Authors and Illustrators: An Index to Biographical Dictionaries.* 2nd ed. Detroit: Gale Research, 1978. A handy help for locating information about past or present YA authors (Jonathan Swift to Robert Cormier) in more than thirty biographical dictionaries from many-volumed works to single-volume dictionaries.

Townsend, John Rowe. *A Sense of Story: Essays on Contemporary Writers for Children.* Philadelphia: Lippincott, 1971. Essays on authors H. F. Brinsmead, John Christopher, Paula Fox, Leon Garfield, Alan Garner, Scott O'Dell, K. M. Peyton, Ivan Southall, Patricia Wrightson, and others.

Weiss, M. Jerry, ed. *From Writers to Students: The Pleasures and Pains of Writing.* Newark, Delaware: International Reading Association, 1979. Interviews with authors Judy Blume, Vera and Bill Cleaver, Mollie Hunter, M. E. Kerr, Norma and Harry Mazer, Laurence Yep, and others.

Wintle, Justin, and Emma Fisher, eds. *The Pied Pipers: Interviews with the Influential Creators of Children's Literature.* New York: Paddington Press, 1974. Interviews with authors Scott O'Dell, Leon Garfield, Alan Garner, Lloyd Alexander, K. M. Peyton, and Judy Blume, and others.

Books of Readings About Young Adult Literature

Egoff, Sheila, G. T. Stubbs, and L. F. Ashley, eds. *Only Connect: Readings in Children's Literature.* New York: Oxford University Press, 1969. Significant articles by

Edward W. Rosenheim, John Rowe Townsend, Donnarae MacCann, C. S. Lewis, Rosemary Sutcliff, and others.

Fox, Geoff, et al., eds. *Writers, Critics, and Children: Articles from Children's Literature in Education.* New York: Agathon Press, 1976. Articles from an important journal by authors Nina Bawden, Peter Dickinson, Myles McDowell, John Foster, Edward Blishen, and others.

Haviland, Virginia, ed. *Children and Literature: Views and Reviews.* Glenview, Illinois: Scott, Foresman, 1973. Articles by Hester Burton, Frank Eyre, Peter Dickinson, Sylvia Engdahl, and others.

Meade, Richard A., and Robert C. Small, Jr., eds. *Literature for Adolescents: Selection and Use.* Columbus, Ohio: Charles E. Merrill, 1973. Important articles (the majority from *English Journal*) by Dorothy Petitt, Dwight L. Burton, Hugh Agee, Stephen Dunning, Richard S. Alm, and others.

Salway, Lance, ed. *A Peculiar Gift: Nineteenth Century Writings on Books for Children.* London: Kestrel, 1976. Articles and excerpts from books about children's and YA British literature from such authors as Edward Salmon, Arthur Conan Doyle, and Joseph Conrad.

Varlejs, Jana, ed. *Young Adult Literature in the Seventies: A Selection of Readings.* Metuchen, New Jersey: Scarecrow Press, 1978. Articles by G. Robert Carlsen, Dorothy Matthews, Linda Lapides, Richard Peck, Al Muller, Lou Willett Stanek, Dorothy Broderick, Mary Chelton, and others.

PERIODICALS

History and Young Adult Literature

Cantwell, Robert. "A Sneering Laugh with the Bases Loaded." *Sports Illustrated* 16 (April 23, 1962): 67-70, 73-76. Baseball novels for boys—especially novels by Barbour and Heyliger.

Carlsen, G. Robert. "Forty Years with Books and Teen-Age Readers." *Arizona English Bulletin* 18 (April 1976): 1-5. From 1939 to 1976 in YA literature.

Crandall, John C. "Patriotism and Humanitarian Reform in Children's Literature, 1825-1860." *American Quarterly* 21 (Spring 1969): 3-22. An excellent overview of children's and YA books and periodicals before Alcott.

Edwards, Margaret A. "The Rise of Teen-Age Reading." *Saturday Review of Literature* 37 (November 13, 1954): 88-89, 95. The state of YA literature in the 1930s and 1940s and what it led to.

Evans, Walter. "The All-American Boys: A Study of Boys' Sports Fiction." *Journal of Popular Culture* 6 (Summer 1972): 104-121. Formulas underlying boys' school sports books, notably Barbour and series books.

"For It Was Indeed He." *Fortune* 9 (April 1934): 86-89, 193-94, 204, 206, 208-9. An important and influential article about Stratemeyer and his Literary Syndicate but biased against him. Readers should look at another article to balance the scales: John T. Dizer, Jr., "Fortune and the Syndicate," *Boys' Book Collector* 2 (Fall 1970): 146-53 and 2 (Winter 1971): 176-86.

Geller, Evelyn. "The Librarian as Censor." *Library Journal* 101 (June 1, 1976): 1255–58. Social control as censorship in library selection in the late nineteenth century.

———. "Tom Sawyer, Tom Bailey, and the Bad-Boy Genre." *Wilson Library Bulletin* 51 (November 1976): 245–50.

Hutchinson, Margaret. "Fifty Years of Young Adult Reading, 1921–1971." *Top of the News* 29 (November 1973): 24–53. An attempt "to survey the field of young adult reading for the last fifty years by examining articles indexed in *Library Literature* from its inception in 1921." Successful and admirable.

Lapides, Linda F. "A Decade of Teen-Age Reading in Baltimore, 1960–1970." *Top of the News* 27 (April 1971): 278–91. YA favorites over a ten-year span.

Kelly, R. Gordon. "American Children's Literature: An Historiographical Review." *American Literary Realism, 1870–1910* 6 (Spring 1973): 89–107. A bibliographical overview of children's and YA literature.

Radner, Rebecca. "You're Being Paged Loudly in the Kitchen: Teen-Age Literature of the Forties and Fifties." *Journal of Popular Culture* 11 (Spring 1978): 789–99. The ways in which Maureen Daly and other popular writers of 1940s girls' books influenced young women, not always for the best.

Trensky, Anne. "The Bad Boy in Nineteenth-Century American Fiction." *Georgia Review* 27 (Winter 1973): 503–17.

Vostrovsky, Clara. "A Study of Children's Reading Tastes." *Pedagogical Seminary* 6 (December 1899): 523–35. The first attempt at a statistical account of the kinds of books children and young adults read.

Criticism and Young Adult Literature

Abrahamson, Jane. "Still Playing It Safe: Restricted Realism in Teen Novels." *School Library Journal* 22 (May 1976): 38–39.

Burton, Hester. "The Writing of Historical Novels." *Horn Book* 45 (June 1969): 271–77. Responsibilities of the writer and difficulties in writing historical novels.

Carlsen, G. Robert. "For Everything There Is a Season." *Top of the News* 21 (January 1965): 103–10. Stages in reading growth and reading tastes.

———. "The Interest Rate Is Rising." *English Journal* 59 (May 1970): 655–59. YA literature, the nature of literature, and the reality of YA readers.

Davis, James E. "Recent Trends in Fiction for Adolescents." *English Journal* 56 (May 1967): 720–24.

Early, Margaret J. "Stages of Growth in Literary Appreciation." *English Journal* 49 (March 1960): 161–67. A seminal article.

Edwards, Margaret A. "A Time When It's Best to Read and Let Read." *Wilson Library Bulletin* 35 (September 1960): 43–47. Some myths of buying books for young adults demolished.

Engdahl, Sylvia. "Do Teenage Novels Fill a Need?" *English Journal* 64 (February 1975): 48–52. Justification and criteria for the best YA novels.

Green, Samuel S. "Sensational Fiction in Public Libraries." *Library Journal* 4 (September–October 1879): 345–55. All the usual warnings about dime novels and other sensational literature coupled with some extraordinarily forward-looking and intelligent comments about young adults and books. The entire issue for September–October is worth reading, especially for T. W. Higginson, "Address," pp. 357–59, William P. Atkinson, "Address," pp. 359–62, and Mellen Chamberlain, "Address," pp. 362–66.

Hanckel, Frances, and John Cunningham. "Can Young Gays Find Happiness in YA Books?" *Wilson Library Bulletin* 50 (March 1976): 528–34. An argument for more authenticity and less preachiness in YA books about gays.

Hentoff, Nat. "Fiction for Teen-Agers." *Wilson Library Bulletin* 43 (November 1968): 261–64. Worries about the shortcomings and superficialities of YA books.

———. "Tell It as It Is." *New York Times Book Review,* May 7, 1967, p. 3, 51. On writing for young adults.

Hinton, Susan. "Teen-Agers Are for Real." *New York Times Book Review,* August 27, 1967, p. 26–29. A plea for integrity and honesty and reality in writing for young adults. Brief but worth several readings.

Hipps, G. Melvin. "Adolescent Literature: Once More to the Defense." *Virginia English Bulletin* 23 (Spring 1973): 44–50. One of the most intelligent arguments for YA books.

Janeczko, Paul B. "Seven Myths About Adolescent Literature." *Arizona English Bulletin* 18 (April 1976): 11–12.

Kraus, W. Keith. "Cinderella in Trouble: Still Dreaming and Losing." *School Library Journal* 21 (January 1975): 18–22. Pregnancy and YA novels from Felsen's *Two and the Town* (1952) to Neufeld's *For All the Wrong Reasons* (1973).

———. "From Steppin Stebbin's to Soul Brothers: Racial Strife in Adolescent Literature." *Arizona English Bulletin* 18 (April 1976): 154–60.

McDowell, Myles. "Fiction for Children and Adults: Some Essential Differences." *Children's Literature in Education* 4 (March 1973): 48–63.

Martinec, Barbara. "Popular—But Not Just a Part of the Crowd: Implications of Formula Fiction for Teenagers." *English Journal* 60 (March 1971): 339–44. Formulaic elements in six YA novelists. Provocative.

Matthews, Dorothy. "An Adolescent's Glimpse of the Faces of Eve: A Study of the Image of Women in Selected Popular Junior Novels." *Illinois English Bulletin* 60 (May 1973): 1–14.

———. "Writing about Adolescent Literature: Current Approaches and Future Directions." *Arizona English Bulletin* 18 (April 1976): 216–19. Discusses the different kinds of current writings about YA literature and the needs for the future.

Meltzer, Milton. "Where Do All the Prizes Go? The Case for Nonfiction." *Horn Book* 52 (February 1976): 17–23. An argument for more recognition for outstanding YA nonfiction.

Merla, Patrick. " 'What Is Real?' Asked the Rabbit One Day." *Saturday Review* 55 (November 4, 1972): 43–49. Comments on the rise of YA realism and adult fantasy.

Neufeld, John. "The Thought, Not Necessarily the Deed: Sex in Some of Today's Juvenile Novels." *Wilson Library Bulletin* 46 (October 1971): 147–52. Urges that the YA novel needs the "whole kid," sex, warts and dirty jokes as well as naiveté and freedom.

Peck, Richard. "In the Country of Teenage Fiction." *American Libraries* 4 (April 1973): 204-7. Concerns about young adults' needs and the books being written for them.

———. "Some Thoughts on Adolescent Literature." *News from ALAN* 3 (September-October 1975): 4-7. The "discernible traits" of YA novels.

Popkin, Zelda F. "The Finer Things in Life." *Harpers* 164 (April 1932): 602-11. The contrast between what young adults like to read and what parents and other adults want them to read.

Repplier, Agnes. "Little Pharisees in Fiction." *Scribner's Magazine* 20 (December 1896): 718-24. Assessment of the didactic and often embarrassingly joyless tone of the "goody-goody" school of writing for girls.

Root, Shelton L. "The New Realism—Some Personal Reflections." *Language Arts* 54 (January 1977): 19-24. What the new realism brought to children's and YA literature and the criteria by which it should be evaluated.

Silver, Linda R. "Criticism, Reviewing, and the Library Review Media." *Top of the News* 35 (Winter 1979): 123-30. On reviewing YA books. The entire Winter 1979 issue is worth any librarian's or teacher's time, especially for Rosemary Weber, "The Reviewing of Children's and Young Adult Books in 1977," pp. 131-37, Melvin H. Rosenberg, "Thinking Poor: The Nonlibrary Review Media," pp. 138-42, "What Makes a Good Review? Ten Experts Speak," pp. 146-52, and especially Patty Campbell, "Only Puddings Like the Kiss of Death: Reviewing the YA Book," pp. 161-62.

Stanek, Lou Willett. "Adults and Adolescents: Ambivalence and Ambiguity." *School Library Journal* 20 (February 1974): 21-25. Comments on the "innocent youth" myth and analyzes several YA novels.

———. "The Junior Novel: A Stylistic Study." *Elementary English* 51 (October 1974): 947-53. A pioneer study of YA novels.

———. "The Maturation of the Junior Novel: From Gestation to the Pill." *School Library Journal* 19 (December 1972): 34-39. Fiction formulas and the YA novel about pregnancy.

Stein, Ruth. "From Happiness to Hopelessness: A Decade of Adolescent Girls." *Arizona English Bulletin* 18 (April 1976): 144-50.

Townsend, John Rowe. "Didacticism in Modern Dress." *Horn Book* 43 (April 1967): 159-64. Argues that nineteenth century didacticism is remarkably similar to the didacticism in modern YA novels.

———. "Standards of Criticism for Children's Literature." *Top of the News* 27 (June 1971): 373-87.

Unsworth, Robert. "Holden Caulfield, Where Are You?" *School Library Journal* 23 (January 1977): 40-41. A plea for more books on the male experience by male writers.

Using Young Adult Literature in Classrooms and Libraries

Chelton, Mary K. "Booktalking: You Can Do It." *School Library Journal* 22 (April 1976): 39-43. A rationale for book talks for young adults and some ways of giving book talks.

Hipps, G. Melvin. "Adolescent Literature and Values Clarification: A Warning." *Wisconsin English Journal* 20 (January 1978): 5–9.

Mearns, Hughes. "Bo Peep, Old Woman, and Slow Mandy: Being Three Theories of Reading." *New Republic* 48 (November 10, 1926): 344–46. Witty, profound, and deserving of reading every year.

Nelms, Ben F. "Reading for Pleasure in Junior High School." *English Journal* 55 (September 1966): 676–81.

Peck, Richard. "Ten Questions to Ask About a Novel." *ALAN Newsletter* 5 (Spring 1978): 1, 7.

Scharf, Peter. "Moral Development and Literature for Adolescents." *Top of the News* 33 (Winter 1977): 131–36. Application of Lawrence Kohlberg's six stages of moral judgment to YA books.

Scoggin, Margaret C. "Do Young People Want Books?" *Wilson Bulletin for Librarians* 11 (September 1936): 17–20, 24.

Small, Robert C., Jr. "The Junior Novel and the Art of Literature." *English Journal* 66 (October 1977): 56–59. Using YA novels to teach aspects of the novel.

———. "Teaching the Junior Novel." *English Journal* 61 (February 1972): 222–29. Using YA novels in the classroom.

Thurber, Samuel. "Voluntary Reading in the Classical High School from the Pupil's Point of View." *School Review* 13 (February 1905): 168–79. An extraordinarily modern point of view from the best writer and thinker of the time on teaching English. Thurber's articles are always worthwhile.

Acknowledgments

"Some thoughts on the Black Y.A. Novel," by Al Muller from ALAN Newsletter, Assembly on Literature for Adolescents—NCTE, Vol. 5, No. 2, Winter, 1978. Reprinted by permission. Excerpt from "Only Puddings Like the Kiss of Death: Reviewing the YA Book" by Patty Campbell from Top of the News, Winter 1979, vol. 35, no. 2. Reprinted by permission of the American Library Association. Excerpt from "Some 'Isms' Revisited: An Interview with Judy Blume" by Audrey Eaglen from Top of the News, Spring 1978, vol. 34, no. 3. Reprinted by permission of the American Library Association. Excerpt reprinted by permission of the American Library Association from the "May Hill Arbuthnot Honor Lecture: Beyond the Garden Wall" by Sheila Egoff, from Top of the News, Spring 1979, p. 264. Copyright © 1979 by the American Library Association. Excerpt reprinted by permission of the American Library Association from "Moral Development and Literature for Adolescents," by Peter Scharf, Top of the News, Winter 1977, p. 134 and table 1. Excerpt adapted from "Individualized Reading" by Barbara Blow, from Arizona English Bulletin, Vol. 18, No. 3, April, 1976. Reprinted by permission of the author and the Arizona English Teachers Association. Excerpt from "Male Initiation Rites in A Day No Pigs Would Die" by G. Melvin Hipps, from Arizona English Bulletin, April, 1976. Reprinted by permission of the author and the Arizona English Teachers Association. "Ghost ship sailed world for 24 years" from The Arizona Republic, January 28, 1979. Copyright © 1979 by The Associated Press. Reprinted by permission of The Associated Press. Front covers from Crash Club, Hot Rod and Road Rocket by Henry Gregor Felsen. Used by permission of Bantam Books, Inc. All rights reserved. Excerpt from "Sentimental Education" by Harold Brodkey. Reprinted by permission of International Creative Management. First published in The New Yorker. Copyright © 1958 by Harold Brodkey. Excerpt adapted from "Booktalking: You Can Do It" by Mary K. Chelton. Reprinted with permission of Mary K. Chelton from School Library Journal, April, 1976. R. R. Bowker Co./A Xerox Corporation. From "Paperbacks in the Classroom" by S. Alan Cohen from Journal of Reading, Vol. 12, No. 4, January, 1969. Reprinted with permission of S. Alan Cohen and the International Reading Association. Excerpt from an introduction to Lord of the Flies by E. M. Forster. Copyright © 1962 by Coward-McCann, Inc. Reprinted by permission. Excerpt from "An Open Letter to American Women About Men" by Dr. Jessie Potter. Copyright © 1975 Forum: The International Journal of Human Relations. Reprinted by permission of the copyright owner and Dr. Jessie E. Potter. Title and frontispiece from The Khaki Girls of the Motor Corps by Edna Brooks, and the title page and frontispiece from Ruth Fielding and Her Greatest Triumph by Alice B. Emerson. Reprinted by permission of Grosset & Dunlap, Inc. Illustration: "Oh, do help Sammy!" begged Tess, with clasped hands. As appeared on page 214 of book entitled The Corner House Girls On A Tour, by Grace Brooks Hill. Reprinted by permission of Grosset & Dunlap, Inc. Excerpt from a review by Irwin Shaw of Anyone's Daughter: The Times and Trials of Patty Hearst by Shana Alexander. Reprinted by permission of Hope Leresche & Sayle. "A Gallery of Girls" by Alice M. Jordan. Reprinted from The Horn Book Magazine (September-October, 1937). Copyright 1937 by The Horn Book, Inc. "Best Sellers And Modern Youth" by Louise Dinwiddie. Reprinted, with permission, from The Library Journal, November 15, 1940, Vol. 65. R. R. Bowker Co./A Xerox Corporation. "Bibliotherapy and The School Librarian" by Willard A. Heaps. Reprinted, with permission, from The Library Journal, October 1, 1940, R. R. Bowker Co./A Xerox Corporation. "Ray Guns and Rocket Ships" by Robert A. Heinlein. Reprinted, with permission, from The Library Journal, July, 1953, Vol. 78, No. 13. R. R. Bowker Co./A Xerox Corporation. Jacket from Jamie by Jack Bennett, 1963. Reprinted by permission of Little, Brown and Co. Illustration from The Moved-Outers by Florence Crannell Means. Copyright 1947 and © renewed 1972 by Florence Crannell Means. Reprinted by permission of Houghton Mifflin Company. Excerpt from "Bibliotherapy" by Frank Ross from Media & Methods, January, 1969, vol. 5, no. 5. Copyright © 1969 Media and Methods Institute, Inc. Reprinted by permission. Excerpt from "Responses to Literature: Enlarging the Range" by Larry Andrews, from English Journal, February 1977, vol. 66, no. 2. Copyright © 1977 by the National Council of Teachers of English. Reprinted by permission of the publisher and the author. Excerpt from "Well, Where are We in Teaching Literature?" by Dwight L. Burton, from English Journal, February 1974, vol. 63, no. 2. Copyright © 1974 by the National Council of Teachers of English. Reprinted by permission of the publisher and the author. Excerpt from "Behind Reading Interests" by G. R. Carlsen from English Journal, January 1954, vol. 43, no. 1. Copyright © 1954 by the National Council of Teachers of English. Reprinted by permission of the publisher and the author. The Students Right to Read by Ken Donelson. Reproduced with the permission of the National Council of Teachers of English, Urbana, Illinois. Copies of this policy statement are available from NCTE, 1111 Kenyon Road, Urbana, Illinois, 61801 for $.70 each, or 3 for $1.50, or $.35 each for ten or more copies./Order No. 48174. Excerpt from "Junior Book Roundup" by Stephen Dunning, from English Journal, December 1964, vol. 53, no. 9. Copyright © 1964 by the National Council of Teachers of English. Reprinted by permission of the publisher and the author. Excerpt from "Unlocking the Box: An Experiment in Literary Response" by Suzanne Howell, from English Journal, February 1977, vol. 66, no. 2. Copyright © 1977 by the National Council of Teachers of English. Reprinted by permission of the publisher and the author. Excerpt from "Junior Book Roundup" by Stanley B. Kegler and Stephen Dunning from English Journal, May 1964, vol. 53, no. 5. Copyright © 1964 by the National Council of Teachers of English. Reprinted by permission of the publisher and the author. Excerpt from "The Cult of Kill in Adolescent Fiction" by Jean Kelty from English Journal, February 1975, vol. 64, no. 2. Copyright © 1975 by the National Council of Teachers of English. Reprinted by permission of the publisher and the author. Excerpt from "Diversifying the Matter" by Lou La Brant from The English Journal, March 1951, vol. 40, no. 3. Copyright © 1951 by the National Council of Teachers of English. Reprinted by permission of the publisher and the author. Excerpt from "The Virtues of the Second-Rate" by William Lyon Phelps, from English Journal, January 1927, vol. 16, no. 1. Copyright 1927 by the National Council of Teachers of English. Reprinted by permission of the publisher and the author. Excerpt from "Speaking of Books" by J. Donald Adams, from The New York Times Book Review, May 14, 1961. © 1961 by The New York Times Company. Reprinted by permission. Excerpt from "Pele's Farewell: What Soccer Has Meant" by Pele, from The New York Times, August 25, 1977. © 1977 by The New York Times Company. Reprinted by permission. Excerpt from "Paperback Talk," by Ray Waiters, from The New York Times Book Review, November 13, 1977. © 1977 by The New York Times Company. Reprinted by permission. Illustration reproduced with the permission of Farrar, Straus and Giroux, Inc. from Pollyanna by Eleanor H. Porter. Copyright 1913 by L. C. Page & Co., copyright renewed 1941 by L. C. Page & Company, now a division of Farrar, Straus and Giroux, Inc. Front cover from Bertie Makes a Break. Cover courtesy of Scholastic Magazines, Inc. "YA Selection Criteria—a Second Opinion" by Jack Forman. Reprinted, with permission, from School Library Journal, September, 1978, Vol. 25, No. 1. R. R. Bowker Co./A Xerox Corporation. "Turning off: The Abuse of Drug Information" by Peter G. Hammond. Reprinted with permission from: School Library Journal, April, 1973. R. R. Bowker Co./A Xerox Corporation. "Quality or Popularity? Selection Criteria for YAs" by Lillian L. Shapiro. Reprinted, with permission, from School Library Journal, May, 1978, Vol. 24, No. 9. R. R. Bowker Co./A Xerox Corporation. "Holden Caulfield, where are you?" by Robert Unsworth. Reprinted with permission from: School Library Journal, January, 1977. R. R. Bowker Co./A Xerox Corporation. Excerpts from When I Grew Up Long Ago collected and edited by Alvin Schwartz. Copyright © 1978 by Alvin Schwartz. By permission of J. B. Lippincott, Publishers and Curtis Brown, Ltd. Excerpt from Old Is What You Get: Dialogues on Aging by the Old and the Young by Ann Zane Shanks. Copyright © 1976 by Ann Zane Shanks. Reprinted by permission of Viking Penguin Inc. Excerpt from Policy IFA "Instructional Materials Policy" and Policy IFA-G "Instructional Materials Selection Guidelines" of Tempe Union High School District.

Reprinted by permission.   Illustration by Hans Walleen from *All-American*, copyright 1942 by John R. Tunis; renewed 1970 by Lucy R. Tunis. Reproduced by permission of Harcourt Brace Jovanovich, Inc.   Excerpt from an editorial by Mary K. Chelton from *Voice of Youth Advocates* Vol. 1, No. 2, June 1978. Reprinted by permission.   Excerpt from an interview with Leon Garfield by Justin Wintle from *The Pied Pipers: Interviews with the Influential Creators of Children's Literature* by Justin Wintle and Emma Fisher. Copyright © 1973 and 1974 by Justin Wintle. Reprinted by permission of Paddington Press Ltd.   Excerpt from a letter from George A. Woods to Aleen Pace Nilsen, August 8, 1977. Reprinted by permission of George A. Woods.

Subject Index

Author, Title Index